MW00676797

Client/Server
Survival Guide

with OS/2

Robert Orfali • Dan Harkey

VAN NOSTRAND REINHOLD
An International Thomson Publishing Company

New York • London • Bonn • Boston • Detroit • Madrid • Melbourne • Mexico City
Paris • Singapore • Tokyo • Albany NY • Belmont CA • Cincinnati OH

Copyright © 1994 by Van Nostrand Reinhold

Library of Congress Catalog Card Number QA76.9.C55075
ISBN 0-442-01798-7

All rights reserved. No part of this work covered by the copyright hereon may be reproduced or used in any form or by any means—graphic, electronic, or mechanical including photography, recording, taping, or information storage and retrieval systems — without written permission of the publisher.

I(T)P Van Nostrand Reinhold, an International Thompson Publishing Company. ITP logo is a trademark under license.

Printed in the United States of America

Van Nostrand Reinhold
115 Fifth Avenue
New York, N.Y. 10003

International Thompson Publishing GmbH
Königswinterer Strasse 418
53227 Bonn
Germany

International Thompson Publishing
Berkshire House, 168-173
168-173 High Holborn
London WC1V 7AA
England

International Thompson Publishing Asia
221 Henderson Road
#05 10 Henerson Building
Singapore 0315

Thomas Nelson Australia
102 Dodds Street
South Melborne, Victoria 3205
Australia

International Thompson Publishing Japan
Hirakawacho Kyowa Building, 3F
2-2-1 Hirakawa-cho, Chiyoda-Ku
Tokyo 102
Japan

Nelson Canada
1120 Birchmount Road
Scarborough, Ontario
M1K 5G4, Canada

RRDHB 16 15 14 13 12 11 10 9 8 7 6 5 4 3

Library of Congress Cataloging in Publication Data

Orfali, Robert.
    Client server survival guide with OS/2   / Robert Orfali, Dan Harkey
        p.   cm.
    Includes index.
    ISBN 0-442-01798-7
    1. Client/server computing   2. OS/2 (Computer file)   I. Harkey,
Dan. II. Title.
QA76.9.C55075   1994
004'.36--dc20

                                     94-1825
                                       CIP

VNR's OS/2 SERIES

Writing OS/2 2.1 Device Drivers in C, Second Edition
by Steven Mastrianni

The OS/2 2.1 Corporate Programmer's Handbook
by Nora Scholin, Marty Sullivan, and Robin Scragg

OS/2 2.1 REXX HANDBOOK: Basics, Applications, and Tips
by Hallet German

OS/2 2.1 Application Programmer's Guide
by Jody Kelly, Craig Swearingen, Dawn Bezviner, and Theodore Shrader

OS/2 and Netware Programming: Using the Netware Client API for C
by Lori Gauthier

OS/2 Remote Communications: Asynchronous to Synchronous — Tips and Techniques
by Ken Stonecipher

Objects for OS/2 2.1
by Bruce Tate, Scott Danforth, and Paul Koenen

Developing C and C++ Software in the OS/2 Environment
by Mitra Gopaul

OS/2 Functions Quick Reference Library, Vol 1. WIN Functions
by Nora Scholin

Dedication

This book is dedicated to my wife and daughter, Michiko and Tomomi, and to my parents, Howard and Barbara. Their support and encouragement were invaluable.

— *Dan Harkey*

This book is dedicated with love to my wife Jeri and my mother Mimi.

— *Robert Orfali*

Foreword

by Zog the Martian

Captain Zog

Hello! My name is Zog and I'm captain of a Martian team who visited earth to understand what client/server computing is all about and what it can do for us today. We found **Client/Server Survival Guide with OS/2**, by Orfali and Harkey, to be an invaluable tour guide in helping us understand this new technology. It was written in a very Martian-friendly style. The cartoon characters even look like Martians.

So what did I like about this book? It felt like it was talking directly to me and to my crew in a friendly voice. We were initially apprehensive about visiting a foreign planet, but the book made it painless and fun. We covered a lot of territory—including OSs, NOSs, middleware, database, TP monitors, groupware, distributed objects, and system management. It was a comprehensive tour; we got our money's worth many times over. We now have a good feeling for where the opportunities are in client/server technology. Martians plan to make a big investment in distributed objects. This book has the most detailed treatment on the subject—more than 120 pages.

The product sections helped us understand what's real today. We even took some client/server products back to Mars to show the folks how these things really worked; they were impressed. Looking at actual products gave us all a warm, fuzzy feeling about the technology. I even discovered OS/2 and learned to like it; we Martians hadn't even heard about it before we landed on earth. (No, we don't watch the Fiesta Bowl.) OS/2 has some cool technology that can be very useful to us on both the client and server. Dan and Bob admit they're biased toward OS/2, but they use soapboxes to express any strong opinions. By the way, these soapboxes are a lot of fun to read. We like to hear *real* earthling debates—not just the sterilized material we read in most books.

In summary, this book helped me understand client/server technology and how to use it in practical Martian situations. The personal touch was great; it felt like we had our own private tour guide. The artwork, cartoons, and soapboxes were wonderful. I can't recommend this book enough to my fellow Martians. Through this foreword, I highly recommend this book to earthlings. If I can understand it, so can you.

Preface

We Live in Uncertain Times

For better or for worse, our industry is going through a deep paradigmatic shift. The old paradigm—centralized mainframe computing—is being replaced by a new paradigm—open client/server computing. A paradigm shift is akin to a revolution: Dominant structures crumble, vacuums are created, and the world is in turmoil. The transition period is marked by confusion, deep uncertainty, and exhilaration. Confusion is the result of seeing familiar bedrock structures disappear. Uncertainty comes from not knowing what the next day will bring. And the exhilaration comes from realizing the new possibilities that are being created by the new paradigm. The **Client/Server Survival Guide with OS/2** is our attempt to understand this revolution. The new client/server paradigm is fielding a lineup of competing technologies, each vying to become the new emperor. We hope the new emperor will have clothes.

And We Can't Turn Back the Clock

Before we tell you all about this book, let's answer some questions that we've been wrestling with: Is client/server just a passing fad? Can mainframes make a comeback? Can things go back to the way they were? We're the first to admit that client/server has become the industry's most overhyped and overloaded term; but it's not a passing fad. This is because the world is populated with 120 million PCs (and growing) that need to be served in the style they expect. The *client is the application*; servers are just an extension of the client's universe. Client/server computing is unabashedly client-centric, and there's no turning back of the clock to mainframe-centric computing. This is not to say that mainframes will disappear—there's room for them to thrive as long as they can transform themselves into humble servants of the client. It's an open world where only the most competitive servers can survive. However, the deployment of intergalactic client/server technology will not be a picnic either. So mainframes will survive until they can be replaced by a technology that's got the same built-in robustness. The revolutionary chaos of the open systems world may make many MIS managers yearn for the good old days, but the time machine only marches forward.

Why the Focus on OS/2?

We needed a reality check. With all the hype, it is important to get a good feel for what products are really available. OS/2 offers a great selection of products on both the client and server sides of the equation. In addition, we know OS/2 like the back of our hand; we've written tons of code to test what can really be done. If you don't like OS/2, just skip over the product chapters. All the concepts we discuss are operating system independent, and most of the products we cover run on multiple platforms. But, for heaven sakes, don't miss the soapboxes—they're a lot of fun, even if you disagree with us.

What the Survival Guide Covers

This survival guide explores client/server computing from the ground up. It consists of nine parts, each one can almost be read independently. (One of our reviewers even read the book backwards and found that it made sense.) We'll give you a short description of what the parts cover. If you find the terminology too foreign, then by all means read the book to find out what it all means.

- **Part 1** starts with an overview of what client/server is and what the fuss is all about. We develop a client/server model that will serve as a map for the rest of the book. Finally, we go over the state of the client/server infrastructure to get a feel for how much of it is already here and what remains to be built.

- **Part 2** examines the client/server capabilities of our current crop of operating systems—including OS/2, Windows NT, Windows 3.X, Unix, and NetWare. We feel like war correspondents covering the battlefield of the operating system wars.

- **Part 3** explores the NOS and transport middleware substrate. We take a closer look at communication stacks such as TCP/IP, SNA, and NetBIOS. Then we look at the distributed computing environments created by NetWare, LAN Server, and DCE. We also look at messaging middleware from Covia, PeerLogic, and Systems Strategies.

- **Part 4** explores the currently very popular database server model of client/server. We cover SQL-92, SQL3, ODBC, IDAPI, SAG, DRDA, RDA, stored procedures, and triggers. We spend some time looking at new database opportunities such as information warehouses and middleware for federated databases. The product chapters cover DB2/2, Oracle7 for OS/2, SQL Server, Information Warehouse, and database gateways such as DDCS/2 and EDA/SQL.

■ **Part 5** explores the TP Monitor model of client/server. We cover the different transaction types—including flat transactions, sagas, nested transactions, chained transactions, and long-lived transactions. We bring you up-to-date on what's happening with the X/Open Distributed Transaction Model standard. Then we dive into the great debate that's pitting the *TP Lite* model offered by the database servers against the *TP Heavy* model offered by TP Monitors. We explain why TP Monitors are needed in a world dominated by database servers. We then look at transactional middleware and products—including CICS OS/2 V2 and Encina.

■ **Part 6** explores the groupware model of client/server. We look at the world of Lotus Notes, workflow, and interpersonal applications. Groupware shows us what client/server can really do—its paradigm goes much further than just recreating mainframe-like applications on PCs.

■ **Part 7** explores the distributed object model of client/server. We look at DOMs, CORBA, Object Databases, OpenDoc, OLE-2, and Taligent frameworks. We explore how object technology can be used to create a new generation of client/server information systems. The product chapters cover DSOM and Object Design's ObjectStore.

■ **Part 8** is about how to manage client/server applications. The biggest obstacle to the deployment of client/sever technology is the lack of integrated system management platforms. Fortunately, the situation is changing. We will look at some exciting frameworks that will semi-automate the management of client/server systems. We also cover system management standards—including SNMP2, RMON, CMIP, DMI, UI-Atlas, and DME.

■ **Part 9** is about how to design, build, and deploy client/server applications. We look at what tools can and cannot do for you. This part ends the survival journey and ties all the pieces together.

Don't Let the Size of This Book Turn You Off

Client/Server is recreating all of computing technology; we wanted this book to describe it all in-depth. To do that took over 900 pages. The best way to read this book is to ask your boss for a one-week, paid sabbatical to go sit on a beach and read it. Tell him or her it's the cheapest way to revitalize yourself technically and find out where this industry is going. The good news is that you'll only have one book to pack for the trip; the bad news is that it weighs a ton. But once you sink into that comfortable chair overlooking the ocean, keep in mind that even though this book is fat, you don't have to read it all. We recommend, however, that you carefully go over the cartoons so that you have something to tell the boss back at the office. You can jump into any part of the book and start reading it. You won't get bored; but if you do, simply jump to the next part until you find something you like. Those of you who don't care about real-life products or OS/2 can easily skip over one-third of the book. And don't forget that with over 400 illustrations, it's not all heavy-duty reading.

What if you have friends (or a manager) that can't imagine carrying, much less reading, a 900-page book? They can read our shorter book, the **Essential Client/Server Survival Guide**. The book you are reading is a much expanded version of that book with a focus on OS/2 client/server products. We personally like the current level of depth. We like the luxury of being able to cover almost 100 products and being able to delve into some of the issues. It's this broad coverage that makes the current book unique. However, just keep in mind that we do have that shorter version.

What the Boxes Are For

We use shaded boxes as a way to introduce concurrent threads in the presentation material. It's the bookform version of multitasking. The *soapboxes* introduce strong opinions or biases on some of the more "controversial" topics of client/server computing. Because the discipline is so new and fuzzy, there's lots of room for interpretation and debate—so you'll get lots of soapboxes that are just another opinion (ours). The *briefing* boxes give you background or tutorial type information. You can safely skip over them if you're already familiar with a topic. The *detail* boxes cover some esoteric area of technology that may not be of interest to the general readership. Typically the same readers that skip over the briefings will find the details interesting (so you'll still get your money's worth). Lastly, we use *warning* boxes to let you know where danger lies—this is, after all, a survival guide.

Who Is This Book For?

The answer is—we hope—anybody who's associated with the computer industry and needs to understand where it's heading. We know we enjoyed reading it over three times (but we're biased). We're relying on word-of-mouth to let people know about the book, so if you enjoy it please spread the word. It was a big effort with long hours of "labor of love" on our part; we hope you'll find it valuable and helpful. So who should know about this book? Here's our short list:

■ The person sitting on that beach chair next to you. They may have run out of reading material.

- The people you work with. Use this book to get the people around you to join the postmodern bandwagon. We found that people are easier to work with if they share a common mindset. We could have sure used this book to educate the people that were doing the business forecasts and the marketing of our client/server product.

- Anybody involved with computers—including system analysts, programmers, managers, pundits, marketing people, instructors, computer science students, and those of us that are between jobs, contemplating a career change, or working on resumes.

We hope you enjoy the reading, the cartoons, and the soapboxes. Drop us a line if you have something you want to "flame" about. We'll take compliments too. We also want to thank you, as well as our Martian friends, for trusting us to be your guides.

Acknowledgments

- To Jeri Edwards, who created *all* the illustrations. She brought life and humor to this thick book with her incredible gift for making the most complicated system concepts "obvious" through images and icons. Jeri is an expert in client/server computing and has taught us a lot.

- To our reviewers: Lisa Haut, Claus Mikkelsen, Lynda Hansen, Bobby Sujishi, Theo Mandel, and Phil Garett. They helped us catch all the first pass of "nasty errors" and gave us some valuable feedback. If you're lucky, they left some errors for you to discover.

- To Dave Coffman and David Pacheco. They lent us a hand when we really needed it.

- We thank our tireless copy editor, Larry Mackin, for keeping us honest.

- To Dianne Littwin, Executive Editor at Van Nostrand Reinhold. She is a pleasure to work with. We also thank the members of Dianne's staff.

- To the grassroots movement that is known as *Team OS/2*. This movement of free spirits decided it was time to "do the right thing," then *did it*.

- To Lee Reiswig, John Soyring, Jim Cannavino, Art Olbert, Larry Loucks, Cliff Reeves, and Tom Furey. They helped create the OS/2 client/server vision.

The authors and publishers of this book have used their best efforts in preparing this book. The authors and publisher make no warranty of any kind, expressed or implied, with regard to the documentation contained in this book. The authors and publishers shall not be liable in any event for incidental or consequential damages in connection with, or arising out of the use of the information in this book.

The product descriptions are based on the best information available at the time of publication. Product prices are subject to change without notice. Contact the product suppliers for the latest pricing and product information.

Some illustrations incorporate clip art from Corel Systems Corporation's Corel Draw 4.0 clip art library.

All the views expressed in this book are solely the Authors' and should not be attributed to IBM or any other IBM employee. The two authors contributed equally to the production of this book and are still alive to see it published.

Contents at a Glance

Contents

Part 3. Base Middleware: Stacks and NOSs 213

Chapter 21. DCE: The Postmodern NOS. 379

Chapter 22. MQSeries: The MOM Middleware. 401

Part 5. Client/Server Transaction Processing 551

Chapter 27. The Magic of Transactions 555

Chapter 28. TP Monitors: Managing Client/Server Transactions 575

Chapter 29. TP-Lite or TP-Heavy? 593

Part 8. Distributed System Management 823

Chapter 40. Client/Server Distributed System Management . . . 827

Chapter 41. Distributed System Management Standards. 843

Chapter 42. LAN NetView: The OS/2 DSM Platform. 871

Part 1
The Big Picture

An Introduction to Part 1

Welcome to our client/server planet. We hope you will like it here because there's no going back. You've long passed the point of no return. Don't panic: you're in good hands. We'll somehow find our way through the swamps, deserts, and roaring waters. We will show you how to avoid the dangerous paths infested with rattle-snakes and scorpions. Our adventure will be challenging—and exciting. In the course of the journey, we may even help you find the fabled land of client/server "milk and honey."

Part 1 of any good survival guide always starts with mapping the "treacherous" terrain. This is where you get the birds-eye view of things—continents, oceans, forests, and Manhattan traffic jams. We create such a map for the world of client/server.

We start with an overview of what client/server is and what the fuss is all about. We explain what client/server computing can do and what makes a product client/serv-er. Then we develop a game using client/server building-blocks that will help you navigate through the treacherous terrain. Finally, we go over the state of the client/server infrastructure—the equivalent of roads, bridges, and airports for client/server.

Chapter 1

Your Guide to the New World

Don't stand in the doorway
Don't block the hall
For he that gets hurt
Will be he who has stalled...
    For the times they are
    a-changin

— Bob Dylan, 1963

THE GOOD OLD DAYS

Back in the days when mainframes roamed the earth, life was simple. The big choice of the day was how to pick the "right" computer vendor. And there were only a few to choose from. Once that choice was behind you everything else fell into place. A staff of superbly trained analysts supervised the powering up of a great big box with a matching operating system. Data communications specialists could fine-tune, in a matter of hours, the octopus-like front-end network that brought hundreds of remote terminals into the fold. They were followed by storage specialists who would hookup "farms" of disk and tape drives. Maintenance and system management were built into every component. If anything went wrong, you knew exactly who to call—your on-site systems engineer.

If you had to write applications, your vendor would provide the "right" set of top-down methodologies, case tools, and run-time subsystems. There were, of course, five-year plans and grand architectures to help you design your future growth and budget for it. Most importantly, there was job security, a career path, and a bright future for everybody in the computer industry. And revenues were good for mainstream computer vendors and the niche players that marketed within their orbits. These were the good old days before the client/server and "open" systems revolution.

LIFE AFTER THE REVOLUTION

Life is not as simple in the new world of client/server and open systems. Client/server computing is the ultimate "open platform." Client/server gives you the freedom to mix-and-match components at almost any level. You can put together an incredible variety of networked client and server combinations. Everything in the client/server world is sold *a la carte*.

At every turn, you will be presented with a Chinese restaurant menu of choices: Which server platform? Which client platform? Which network protocols? Which distributed computing infrastructure? Which database server? Which set of middleware? Which system management base? If you get past the first set of choices, you will face even tougher new choices in the area of client/server application development and tools. There are at least four major technologies that can be used to create client/server applications: Database Servers, TP Monitors, Groupware, and Distributed Object Managers. Which one is best?

You're the one who makes the tough decisions in this new world order. To succeed, you'll need to pick the right client/server platform, tools, vendors, and architecture base. You must identify and ride the *right* client/server technology wave. If the winning wave is distributed objects, it doesn't make sense to invest time and energy in database servers. But if you pick the object wave too soon, it may shipwreck your business. So it's important that you know exactly what the technology can do for you at a given point in time. To figure this out, you must be able to sort your way through the marketing slogans and architectural promises. Most importantly, you need to know exactly what existing products can do for you *today*.

The good news in all of this is that client/server technology is liberating, low-cost, and allows you to do the great things we will describe later in this book. The bad news is that you're on your own. The vendors will sell you their products at near-commodity prices, but you'll have to figure out how to make the pieces work together. If they don't work, it's your problem. No promises were made when the

goods were sold. Yes, system integrators can help, but they don't come cheap. So what happened to the good old days? They're gone. Vendors now sell piecemeal components. Everything is unbundled. Even service is priced separately. In this new *a la carte* world, you are the system integrator.

THE SURVIVAL PLAN

We, the authors, have been roaming in the wilderness for quite some time, and the result is this client/server survival guide. It will help you survive, but it won't be easy. Nobody, unfortunately, has that magic map with all the correct paths. We will share with you our insights which, when combined with yours, may help you take the least treacherous path. A survival guide is more than just a map. It contains instructions for how to find food, build shelter, navigate in strange terrain, and protect yourself from snakes and scorpions. We'll provide the same.

We will first go over the client and server sides of the equation. We will then work on the slash (/) in client/server—that's the glue that ties the client with the server. We will go over the four leading technologies for developing client/server applications: database servers, TP Monitors, groupware, and distributed objects. We will conclude by covering system management platforms and tools. Wherever possible, we will present industry standards ("de facto" and "de jure") and existing products that implement them. We picked product examples that run on the OS/2 platform.

CAN YOU SURVIVE WITHOUT OS/2?

We chose to base our survival guide examples on OS/2 for the following reasons:

■ OS/2 plays very well on both the client and server sides of the equation. On the client side, OS/2's Workplace Shell seamlessly integrates Windows, DOS, and OS/2 applications; it also provides some very advanced multimedia facilities. On the server side, OS/2 is being ported onto the industry's most advanced microkernel, and it will be able to share device drivers and services with many flavors of Unix, Apple's System 7, and Taligent.

■ OS/2 has incubated some of the most *avant-garde* server products in the industry—including Lotus Notes, a groupware server; DSOM, a distributed object manager; CICS OS/2 V2, a TP Monitor; and Oracle, Sybase, Gupta, XDB, Ingres, and DB2/2, some of the leading SQL database servers.

■ OS/2 supports more middleware, communication stacks, and network operating systems than any other platform. OS/2 supports NetWare, LAN Server, LAN Manager, DCE, VIM, Message-Oriented Middleware (MOM), and multivendor communications stacks.

■ OS/2 is emerging as one of the industry's best managed client/server platforms. The LAN NetView family of products from IBM allows an OS/2 PC to manage any device on the network that talks SNMP or CMIP (both open standards). LAN NetView uses the Workplace Shell to visually display the managed devices. It's open, so vendors can easily plug their management products into the managing platform. And, last but not least, it's low-cost.

■ OS/2 is a PC-based platform that runs on commodity hardware. You can easily acquire OS/2 and use it to experiment with the software described in this book.

Most importantly, we (the authors) have accumulated years of *practical* experience developing client/server code on the OS/2 platform.[1] We've done a lot of tire-kicking, and we now feel comfortable with the products and architectures we describe in this book. Running code is the ultimate reality check. And you'll need those constant reality checks to sort out fact from fiction in the hype-filled client/server marketplace.

---

[1] See our 1100-page book **Client/Server Programming with OS/2 2.1, Third Edition** (Van Nostrand Reinhold, 1993). This is a shameless advertisement.

Can you use this book to survive without using OS/2? Yes—this is primarily a client/server book. And client/server is very *secular* when it comes to operating systems: it must make them all work together. The purpose of this book is to create a model that will help you navigate through the client/server offerings and make some informed choices. The OS/2 examples will help clarify what you can do today with client/server technology. By the time you finish reading this book, you'll know what client/server technology is available, how the pieces work together, and you'll be exposed to many of our biases in the Soapboxes. But you'll still have to make those difficult choices yourself. This survival guide will just make it easier.

OK, So We're OS/2 Bigots!

Soapbox

We will admit it up front—we're OS/2 bigots. So what does that do for readers who don't like OS/2 or have chosen another platform? You can always get a refund (Sorry Dianne—that's our editor)! However, you should know that over 80% of the material in this book also applies to other major client/server platforms. We will be covering standards, middleware, server products, system management, and tools that run on all major platforms. Many of the OS/2-exclusive products will eventually be ported to other platforms. The early exposure you'll be getting in this book can't hurt. In general, client/server is client/server and operating systems are just a sideshow. We will, however, be giving OS/2 the praise it deserves as a client/server platform. If you don't like our biases, you can always skip over the soapbox sections. But you'll miss out on all the good stuff! ❏

Chapter 2

Welcome to Client/Server Computing

Downsizing and client/server computing have become the hottest topics in the computer industry...IS managers need to learn how to retool IS to take advantage of this new technology.

— James Martin (1993) [1]

I'm not sure if I'm downsizing, upsizing, rightsizing, or capsizing.

— Anonymous

At times, it seems as if everyone associated with computing has something to say about the client/server relationship. In this chapter, you get one more "definitive" viewpoint of what this all means. We will first look at the market forces that are driving the client/server industry today. We then peek through our crystal ball at the computer industry in the advanced stages of the client/server era. After coming this far, we feel we can handle even more danger in our lives, so we tackle the big

---

[1] This is from the foreword by James Martin to Dawna Dewire's excellent book **Client/Server Computing**, (McGraw-Hill, 1993).

issue of trying to answer the question: *Just what is client/server anyway?* We end this chapter with a lively diatribe on fat clients versus fat servers.

THE MARKET FORCES DRIVING CLIENT/SERVER

Client/Server computing is an irresistible movement that is reshaping the way computers are being used. Although this computing movement is relatively young, it is already in full force and is not leaving any facet of the computer industry untouched. Big transformations in the computer industry are usually driven by a combination of new technologies and needs. The technologies and needs pushing client/server computing come from three directions: *downsizing, upsizing,* and *rightsizing* (Figure 2-1).

Downsizing

Downsizing is the downward migration of business applications from superminis and mainframes to PCs, PS/2s, Macintoshes, and Unix workstations. The downsizing process breaks up large supermini and mainframe-type applications into program modules that run on one or more network servers. User-interface functions move to the client workstations and replace the "green screen uglies" with state-of-the-art graphical user interfaces. The centralized processors with time-shared terminals are replaced by networked client/server machines.

Client/Server software solutions on low-cost standard hardware are the driving force behind downsizing. Today's low-cost desktop machines are as powerful as last decade's top-of-the-line mainframes. Client/Server software solutions allow us to create coherent environments out of these autonomous desktop machines. By doing this, client/server computing combines the best of two worlds: the cost-effective and almost addictive power of desktop computers with multiuser access to shared resources and data.

Upsizing

Upsizing is the bottom-up trend of networking standalone PCs at the departmental or workgroup level. The majority of PCs are no longer living in isolation. The early PCs were originally attached to LANs to share expensive peripheral devices such as laser printers and scanners. The LANs are now used primarily for electronic mail and for sharing databases and files (including repositories of images and documents). In addition, a new generation of client/server groupware software promises to introduce finely tuned levels of interaction in the workgroup.

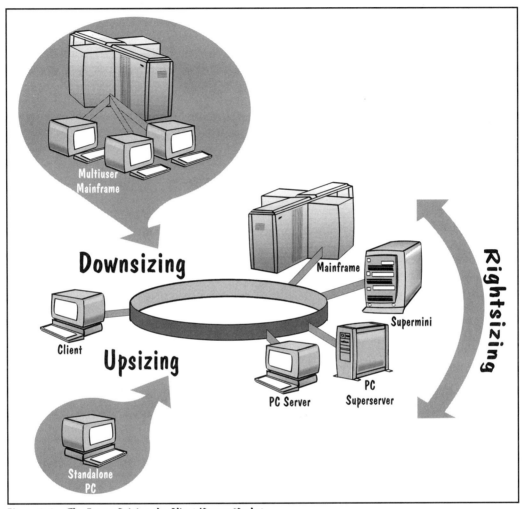

Figure 2-1. The Forces Driving the Client/Server Market.

PC LAN connections are growing equally among all types of environments. Growth is particularly strong in small (PC only) business environments: "the forgotten one million." Intel-based PCs account for over 95% of all servers. According to Forrester, roughly 411,000 Intel-based servers shipped in 1992—a 20-22% growth over 1991.[2]

---

[2] Source: **Update on the Server Market**, Forrester Research (January 27, 1993).

Rightsizing

Rightsizing moves applications to the most appropriate server platform. Clients request services over the network and the server best suited for the job provides it. In this "open" model, a server can be a PC, a supermini, or a mainframe. Servers from different vendors can happily coexist: *the network is the system.* This is especially important for large companies, where this *enterprise network* articulates the business. Rightsizing moves information and server power to the points of impact. It matches the job to the server without having to resort to "islands of automation."

Personal computers and LANs are now equipped with the technology to support enterprise networking. Mainframes and superminis are learning how to compete on the enterprise network. Open standards for enterprise client/server interoperability are now in place that define exactly what it takes to become "just another server." Computer system vendors—such as IBM, DEC, HP, and Tandem—are embracing client/server open standards as the strategic platform that ties together their disparate product lines (workstations, superminis, and mainframes). For their customers, client/server standards finally enable cost-effective, multi-vendor integration at the enterprise level.

According to the Gartner Group, the *Enterprise Server Platform (ESP)* will allow large corporations to leverage the benefits of personal, workgroup, and mainframe resources. Instead of centralized enterprise megaservers, Gartner envisions "a collection of services, which will typically be distributed across a variety of computers for price/performance, high availability, and platform specialization advantages." The critical services provided will include mail routing, file and print sharing, OLTP and decision support, network and systems management, resource brokering, software distribution and license management, security, and inter-enterprise gateways.[3]

THE CLIENT/SERVER COMPUTING ERA

What will the brave new world of client/server computing look like? What effect will it have on MIS shops? What does it mean to compete in an open client/server computing market? What new opportunities does it create for software developers? Let's try to answer these questions now.

---

[3] Source: "Client/Server Computing: Exploiting the Inevitable", Gartner Group (February 12, 1992).

Which Client/Server Vision?

Client/Server computing has the unique distinction of having strong champions across the entire spectrum of the computer industry. For the "PC can do it all" crowd, client/server computing means scrapping every mainframe that can't fit on the desktop and the demise of host-centric computing. For mainframe diehards, client/server computing means unleashing a new breed of "born-again" networked mainframes that will bring every PC in the enterprise back to the fold. For the middle of the roaders, client/server is "computer glasnost," which really means a new era of coexistence and openness in which all can play.

There is some truth in all these visions. Client/Server computing provides an open and flexible environment where mix and match is the rule. The client applications will run predominantly on PCs and other desktop machines that are at home on LANs. The successful servers will also feel at home on LANs and know exactly how to communicate with their PC clients. Beefy PCs make natural superservers. For mainframes to succeed as servers, however, they will have to learn how to meet PCs as equals on the LAN. In this world of equals, mainframe servers cannot treat PCs as dumb terminals. They need to support peer-to-peer protocols, interpret PC messages, service their PC clients' files in their native formats, and provide data and services to PCs in the most direct manner. Ultimately, the server platform with the best cost/performance and services wins.

Client/Server and the "New MIS"

Client/Server application development requires hybrid skills that include transaction processing, database design, communications experience, and graphical user interface savvy. The more advanced applications require a knowledge of distributed objects and object DBMSs. Mastering these skills will require renaissance programmers who can combine the best of "big-iron" reliability-driven thinking with the PC LAN traditions. Where will these renaissance programmers come from? Will MIS shops be able to provide solutions and services in this new computing environment? Or will that service be provided by consultants and system integrators who have taken the time to learn these new skills?

Most client/server solutions today are PC LAN implementations that are personalized for the group that uses them. Everything from LAN directories to security requirements must be properly configured, often by the users themselves. MIS departments have the skills to not only manage and deploy large networks but also to provide interoperability standards. They also know how to fine-tune applications, distribute fixes, and ensure data integrity. MIS traditionally caters to the large data centers and not the line departments that own the PCs and LANs. The key is for them to do what they do well in a distributed client/server environment where they share the power, responsibility, computing know-how, and financial budgets with the line business managers (the end users). Consequently, distributing the MIS function is essential.

Client/Server computing may be best served by two-tiered MIS organizations: a line MIS for managing and deploying departmental systems, and an enterprise MIS for managing the internet and setting interoperability standards. This type of organization will not only preserve departmental autonomy but also allow the local LANs to be part of the multiserver, multivendor enterprise internet.

Competition in the Client/Server Market

Client/Server, the *great equalizer* of the computer business, encourages openness and provides a level playing field in which a wide variety of client and server platforms can participate. The open client/server environment serves as the catalyst for "commoditizing" hardware and system software. The PC is a good example of a computer commodity; it can be obtained from multiple suppliers and is sold in very price-competitive market situations. LAN adapters, LAN protocol stacks, network routers, and bridges are also becoming commodities. On the software side, workstation operating systems, SQL Database Management Systems (DBMSs), and imaging software are approaching commodity status. The Distributed Computing Environment (DCE) will make instant commodities out of remote procedures, network directory software, security services, and system management. These trends are good news for computer users.

But, where are the *great differentiators* that will set vendors apart in this highly competitive commodity environment? What will happen to the computer vendors when commodity-priced client/server computing power satisfies the needs for computerization as we know it today?

Computer vendors will in the short run differentiate themselves by the power of the superservers they provide. This will last until commodity operating systems start to routinely support multiprocessor hardware platforms. We anticipate that the most sustained differentiation will be in the area of new client/server software and not hardware platforms. Low-cost, easy to deploy client/server solutions will unleash a massive new wave of computerization. For example, image and multimedia enhanced client/server solutions have ravenous appetites for storage, network bandwidth, and processing power. These solutions will easily consume the new supply of low-cost client/server systems as long as software providers can create enough applications.

We foresee a brave new era of ubiquitous client/server computing. Clients will be everywhere. They will come in all shapes and forms including desktops, palmtops, pen tablets, intelligent appliances, mobile personal communicators, electronic clipboards, TV sets, intelligent books, robots, automobile dashboards, and myriads of yet-to-be-invented information hungry devices. These clients, wherever they are, will be able to obtain the services of millions of other servers. This bullish view of the industry puts us in the camp of those who believe that *the supply of low-cost MIPs creates its own demand.*[4]

WHAT IS CLIENT/SERVER?

Even though client/server is the leading industry buzzword, there is no agreed upon definition of what that term means. So, we have a fine opportunity to create our own definition. As the name implies, clients and servers are separate logical entities that work together over a network to accomplish a task. So what makes client/server different from other forms of distributed software? We propose that all client/server systems have the following distinguishing characteristics:

■ *Service:* Client/Server is primarily a relationship between processes running on separate machines. The server process is a provider of services. The client is a consumer of services. In essence, client/server provides a clean separation of function based on the idea of service.

■ *Shared resources:* A server can service many clients at the same time and regulate their access to shared resources.

■ *Asymmetrical protocols:* There is a many-to-one relationship between clients and server. Clients always *initiate* the dialog by requesting a service. Servers are passively waiting on requests from the clients.

---

[4] The Forrester report, **The Third Act** (January 27, 1993), is in the same bullish camp. Forrester predicts that the next phase of client/server is social computing, "a type of computing that will be embedded in the way people work, live, and play by permeating, but not intruding on, all facets of human interaction and life."

■ **Transparency of location:** The server is a process which can reside on the same machine as the client or on a different machine across a network. Client/Server software usually masks the location of the server from the clients by redirecting the service calls when needed. A program can be a client, a server, or both.

■ **Mix and match:** The ideal client/server software is independent of hardware or operating system software platforms. You should be able to mix and match client and server platforms.

■ **Message-based exchanges:** Clients and servers are loosely coupled systems which interact through a message-passing mechanism. The message is the delivery mechanism for the service requests and replies.

■ **Encapsulation of services:** The server is a "specialist." A message tells a server what service is requested; it is then up to the server to determine how to get the job done. Servers can be upgraded without affecting the clients as long as the published message interface is not changed.

■ **Scalability:** Client/Server systems can be scaled horizontally or vertically. Horizontal scaling means adding or removing client workstations with only a slight performance impact. Vertical scaling means migrating to a larger and faster server machine or multiservers.

■ **Integrity:** The server code and server data is centrally maintained, which results in cheaper maintenance and the guarding of shared data integrity. At the same time, the clients remain personal and independent.

The client/server characteristics described here allow intelligence to be easily distributed across a network. These features also provide a framework for the design of loosely coupled network-based applications.

WILL THE REAL CLIENT/SERVER PLEASE STAND UP?

Many systems with very different architectures have been called "client/server." System vendors often use client/server as if the term can only be applied to their specific packages. For example, file server vendors swear they first invented the term, and database server vendors are known in some circles solely as *the* client/server vendors. To add to the confusion, this book adds distributed objects, TP Monitors, and Groupware to the list of client/server technologies. So who is right? Which of these technologies is the real client/server? The answer is all of the above.

The idea of splitting an application along client/server lines has been used over the last ten years to create various forms of Local Area Network software solutions.

Typically these solutions sell as shrink-wrapped software packages, and many are sold by more than one vendor. Each of these solutions, however, is distinguished by the nature of the service it provides to its clients as shown in the following examples.

File Servers

With a file server, the client (typically a PC) passes requests for file records over a network to the file server (Figure 2-2). This is a very primitive form of data service that necessitates many message exchanges over the network to find the requested data. File servers are useful for sharing files across a network. They are indispensable for creating shared repositories of documents, images, engineering drawings, and other large data objects.

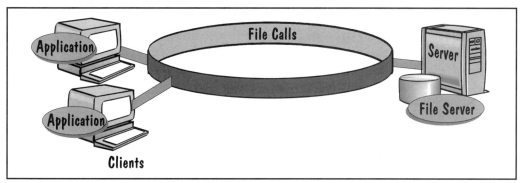

Figure 2-2. Client/Server with File Servers.

Database Servers

With a database server, the client passes SQL requests as messages to the database server (Figure 2-3). The results of each SQL command are returned over the network. The code that processes the SQL request and the data reside on the same machine. The server uses its own processing power to find the requested data instead of passing all the records back to a client and let it find its own data as was the case for the file server. The result is a much more efficient use of distributed processing power. With this approach, the server code is shrink-wrapped by the vendor. But you often need to write code for the client application (or you can buy shrink-wrapped clients like Enfin/3, Quest, or Paradox). Database servers provide the foundation for decision-support systems that require ad hoc queries and flexible reports.

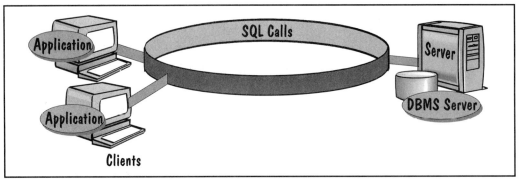

Figure 2-3. Client/Server with Database Servers.

Transaction Servers

With a transaction server, the client invokes *remote procedures* that reside on the server with an SQL database engine (Figure 2-4). These remote procedures on the server execute a group of SQL statements. The network exchange consists of a single request/reply message (as opposed to the database server's approach of one request/reply message for each SQL statement in a transaction). The SQL statements either all succeed or fail as a unit. These grouped SQL statements are called *transactions*.

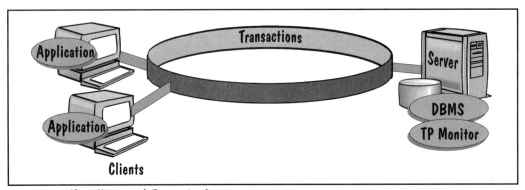

Figure 2-4. Client/Server with Transaction Servers.

With a transaction server, you create the client/server application by writing the code for both the client and server components. The client component usually includes a Graphical User Interface (GUI). The server component usually consists of SQL transactions against a database. These applications have a name: "Online Transaction Processing," or *OLTP.* They tend to be mission-critical applications that require a 1-3 second response time 100% of the time. OLTP applications also require tight controls over the security and integrity of the database. Two forms of

OLTP will be discussed in this book: *TP Lite*—based on the stored procedures provided by database vendors, and *TP Heavy*—based on the TP Monitors provided by OLTP vendors.

Groupware Servers

A new class of systems is emerging today to address the management of semi-structured information such as text, image, mail, bulletin-boards, and the flow of work. These new client/server systems place people in direct contact with other people. Lotus Notes is the leading example of such a system, although a number of other applications—including document management, imaging, multiparty applications, and workflow—are addressing some of the same needs. Specialized groupware software can be built on top of a vendor's canned set of client/server APIs. In most cases applications are created using a scripting language and form-based interfaces provided by the vendor. The communication middleware between the client and the server is vendor-specific (Figure 2-5).

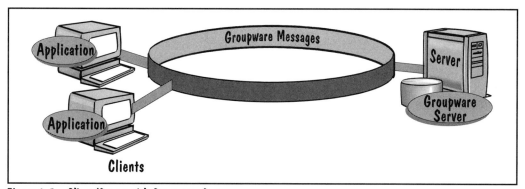

Figure 2-5. Client/Server with Groupware Servers.

Object Servers

With an object server, the client/server application is written as a set of communicating objects (Figure 2-6). Client objects communicate with server objects using an *Object Request Broker (ORB)*. The client invokes a method supported by an object server class. The ORB locates an instance of that object server class, invokes the requested method, and returns the results to the client object. Server objects must provide support for concurrency and sharing. The ORB brings it all together. After years of incubation, some "real life" commercial ORBs have shipped. Examples include **DSOM** from IBM, **DOMS** from HyperDesk, **DOMF** from HP, and **DOE** from Sun.

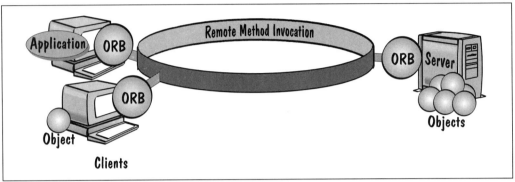

Figure 2-6. Client/Server with Distributed Objects.

FYI

So What is "Middleware"?

Briefing

Mid.dle.ware: 1) A hodgepodge of software technologies; 2) a buzzword; 3) a key to developing client/server applications.

— *Information Week (November 1, 1993)*

Middleware is a vague term that covers all the distributed software needed to support interactions between clients and servers. Think of it as the software that's in the middle of the client/server system. In this book we refer to middleware as the slash (/) component of client/server. It's the glue that lets a client obtain a service from a server. Where does the middleware start and where does it end? It starts with the API set on the client side that is used to invoke a service, and it covers the transmission of the request over the network and the resulting response. Middleware does not include the software that provides the actual service—that's in the server's domain. Nor does it include the user interface or the application's logic—that's in the client's domain.

We divide middleware into two broad classes:

■ **General Middleware** is the substrate for most client/server interactions. It includes the communication stacks, distributed directories, authentication services, network time, remote procedure calls, and queuing services. This category also includes the network operating system extensions such as distributed file and print services. Products that fall into the general middleware category include OSF's DCE, NetWare, Named Pipes, LAN Server, LAN Manager, Vines, TCP/IP, APPC, and NetBIOS. We also include the Message-Oriented Middleware (also known as MOM) products from Peerlogic, Covia, Message Express, and System Strategies.

■ *Service-specific Middleware* is needed to accomplish a particular client/server type of service. This includes:

◆ Database-specific middleware such as ODBC, IDAPI, DRDA, EDA/SQL, SAG/CLI, and Oracle Glue.

◆ OLTP-specific middleware such as Tuxedo's ATMI and /WS, Encina's Transactional RPC, and X/Open's TxRPC and XATMI.

◆ Groupware-specific middleware such as MAPI, VIM, VIC, and Lotus Notes calls.

◆ Object-specific middleware such as OMG's ORB and Object Services and ODMG-93.

◆ System Management-specific middleware such as SNMP, CMIP, and ORBs.

You can probably tell by now that middleware was created by people who love acronyms. To the best of our knowledge, few technologies have as many buzzwords and acronyms as client/server middleware. We will cover, in gruesome detail, the middleware standards that apply to the different client/server application types. By the time you finish reading this book, you'll know exactly what all these middleware acronyms mean. In the meantime, please bear with us as we gradually pull together the pieces of this story. ❑

FAT SERVERS OR FAT CLIENTS?

So far, we've shown you that client/server models can be distinguished by the service they provide. Client/Server applications can also be differentiated by how the distributed application is split between the client and the server (see Figure 2-7). The *fat server model* places more function on the server. The *fat client model* does the reverse. Groupware, transaction, and object servers are examples of fat servers; database and file servers are examples of fat clients.

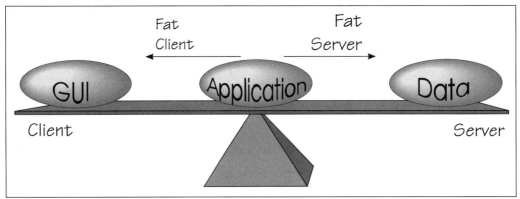

Figure 2-7. Fat Clients or Fat Servers?

Fat clients are the more traditional form of client/server. The bulk of the application runs on the client side of the equation. In both the file server and database server models, the clients know how the data is organized and stored on the server side. Fat clients are used for decision support and personal software. They provide flexibility and opportunities for creating front-end tools that let end users create their own applications.

Fat server applications are easier to manage and deploy on the network because most of the code runs on the servers. Fat servers try to minimize network interchanges by creating more abstract levels of service. Transaction and object servers, for example, encapsulate the database. Instead of exporting raw data, they export the procedures (or methods in object-oriented terminology) that operate on that data. The client in the fat server model provides the GUI and interacts with the server through remote procedure calls (or method invocations).

Each client/server model has its uses. In many cases, the models complement each other, and it is not unusual to have them coexist in one application. For example, a groupware imaging application could require an "all-in-one" server that combines file, database, transaction, and object services. Fat servers represent the new growth area for PC-based client/server computing. They require people like us creating *custom* applications that use the client/server model and build on top of shrink-wrapped system components. The idea is to create vertical, mission-critical application packages that provide total business solutions using low-cost commodity hardware and LANs.

Chapter 3

Client/Server
Building Blocks

---

*W*hat are you able to build with your blocks? Castles and palaces, temples and docks.

— *Robert L. Stevenson,*
A Child's Garden of Verses

We are all familiar with the concept of *architecture* as applied in the construction of buildings. Architectures help us identify structural elements that may be used as building blocks in the construction of ever more complex systems. Just like we buy homes, not plans, users in the computer industry buy solutions to business problems, not grand client/server architectures. But architecture determines the structure of the houses, high-rises, office buildings, and cities we live and work in. In the computer analogy, architecture helps us determine the structure and shape of the client/server systems we can build to meet various needs.

The "million dollar" architectural questions we will cover here are: How is the application split between the client and the server? What function goes in the client and what function goes in the server? Can the client/server model accommodate businesses of all sizes? How are the new tribes of nomadic laptop users brought into the client/server fold? Can client/server play in the home? Where do peer networks fit in this picture? Will client/server disappear in a post-scarcity computing world?

We start this chapter with a quick discussion of how business demographics are changing. We then present a model of client/server topologies that can accommodate the new demographic patterns. We end this chapter with a discussion of peer networks. In future chapters we will go over the extensive software, middleware, and communications infrastructure that is needed to transform these topologies into real systems.

NEW AGE BUSINESS DEMOGRAPHICS

A few years ago, we came across an IDC study of business demographics that changed our perspective of the client/server market (to put it mildly—we were never the same after that). Table 3-1 is a top-level summary of this report. Please take a minute to digest the implications. Yes, there are an overwhelming number of small establishments. They are called the *forgotten one million*. They're forgotten in the sense that the major computer vendors don't cater to their needs—they are too busy selling to the Fortune 500.

Table 3-1. IDC US Business Demographics (1991).

Business Sector	Small Businesses	Medium Business	Large Business
Retail	1,055,000 (under $50M)	773	236
Discrete Manufacturing	256,000 (under $100M)	930	345
Process Manufacturing	26,500 (under $100M)	230	170
Travel	25,000 (under $10M)	900	100
Wholesale	324,000 (under $50M)	1,900	286
Insurance	30,000 (under $100M)	1,600	400
Banking	12,000 small banks	2,200	600
Higher Education	2,250 (under 2,500 students)	850	362

Big Business, Nomads, and the Forgotten Millions

A huge transformation of the workforce has taken place since IDC published its 1991 report. Large companies are going through a massive restructuring that includes scaling back staff, outsourcing work, and using more outside contractors.

The parts of the business establishment that survived the restructuring are becoming more decentralized, autonomous, and loosely coupled. This restructuring is also creating millions of new one-person "establishments" in homes—in 1992, more than 23 million people in the US worked out of their home. The drop in prices of basic office equipment such as computers, printers, modems, and fax machines is making it possible to operate almost any type of enterprise from the home. Client/server technology allows home offices to connect to the world-at-large as either clients, servers, or both.

For many of us, the office of the future will increasingly mean *no office at all*, especially in occupations with high levels of customer contact: sales positions, telemarketers, insurance adjusters, and so on. These folks will likely be given a laptop, a cellular telephone, and a way to hook into the client/server network from the road—we call this the *portable office*. By the end of the century, more than 13 million PCs may be using wireless networks, which will result in a $4 billion new market. Nomadic users hardly existed when IDC published its demographic findings.

Home and portable offices have made the number of small establishments larger than ever before. They should now, more appropriately, be called the *forgotten multiple millions*.

So What Do the Numbers Say?

Over 80% of LAN-based client/server solutions are deployed on PC LANs. They run in departmental-sized establishments consisting of twenty (or fewer) clients talking to a single PC server that provides database, file, and mail services. The other 20% run on mixed LANs, involve one or more servers (PCs, workstations, superminis, and mainframes), support thirty or more clients, and are more likely to be attached to an enterprise backbone. There is also a growing population of mobile users that are part of "nomadic" client/server establishments. Finally, we're seeing many more home users that run businesses from the home—these are really one-person establishments.

CLIENT/SERVER: A ONE SIZE FITS ALL MODEL?

Can a single client/server model accommodate all these types of users? We think we have such a model. It is deceptively simple, and it works well with today's technologies. It is ideally suited for dealing with the needs of a *post-scarcity computing* world, where client/server becomes the ultimate medium for sharing and collaborating.

The model we present in this section is really a game of putting together things with building blocks. We will show you how we can meet a wide spectrum of client/server needs—from the tiny to the intergalactic—with just three basic building blocks: a client, a server, and the slash (/) that ties the client to the server (see Figure 3-1). Kids of all ages will love this game. It should help you identify some durable structures in the design of client/server systems.

Figure 3-1.   The Three Basic Building Blocks of Client/Server.

The Building Blocks of Client/Server

We make the claim that the three basic building blocks can be used to create client/server configurations that range from the tiny to the intergalactic. To prove it, after a few days of deep thinking and heavy meditation, we created four basic Client/Server *arrangements*. We propose that these four arrangements can handle all of today's (and tomorrow's) client/server needs. Yes, you read that right. We claim these four arrangements cover the entire spectrum: from the nomadic user to the largest corporate establishments. Yes, they're also ideal for introducing new post-scarcity software technologies. Yes, they can take care of the needs of the new one-person establishments that are sprouting from homes everywhere. Yes, they make the world look simple and things will never be the same after that. Have we got your attention?

In the next few sections, we explain (and illustrate) how the four building block *arrangements* are used to do all these wonderful things. But it will help if we first give them some meaningful names:

■ *Client/Server for tiny shops and nomadic tribes* is a building block implementation that runs the client, the middleware software, and most of the business services on the same machine. It is the suggested implementation for the one-person shops, home offices, and mobile users with well-endowed laptops. This is a new opportunity area for client/server technology.

■ ***Client/Server for small shops and departments*** is the classic client/single-server building block implementation. It is used in small shops, departments, and branch offices. This is the predominant form of client/server today.

■ ***Client/Server for intergalactic enterprises*** is the multiserver building block implementation of client/server. The servers present a single system image to the client. They can be spread out throughout the enterprise, but they can be made to look like they're part of the local desktop. We will be discussing two variations of this model: one that we like, and one that we don't like.

■ ***Client/Server for a post-scarcity world*** transforms every machine in the world into both a client and a server. Personal agents on every machine will handle all the negotiations with their peer agents anywhere in the universe. This dream is almost within reach.

You will discover many similarities in the four arrangements. This is because they all use the same type of software, middleware, and communications infrastructure. Different arrangements handle the different topologies, business sizes, and budget sizes. You pick the level of service and complexity that satisfy your business needs. It's your choice.

Client/Server for Tiny Shops and Nomadic Tribes

The nice thing about client/server is that it's infinitely malleable. It is easy to run the client and server portion of an application on the same machine. Vendors can easily package single-user versions of a client/server application (Figure 3-2). For example, a client/server application for a dentist office can be sold in a single user package for offices consisting of a single dentist and in a multiuser package for offices with many dentists. The same client/server application covers both cases. The only caveat is that you need to use an operating system that is robust enough to run both the client and server sides of the application.

Figure 3-2. Client/Server for Tiny Shops and Nomadic Users.

The example of the tiny dentist office also works for the tiny in-home business office and the mobile user on the road. In all cases, the business-critical client/server application runs on one machine and does some occasional communications with outside servers to exchange data, refresh a database, and send or receive mail and faxes. For example, the one-person dentist office may need to communicate with outside servers such as insurance company billing computers.

Can that one person computer also act as a server for the outside world? Yes, but it's not very easy to do today. In order for this to become a reality, we need ubiquitous ISDN-like digital telephones in every home and office; we need higher-bandwidth (lower-cost) cellular networks that integrate the nomadic road warriors. In other words, we're waiting for the portions of the information highway—the pieces promised by the Clinton/Gore administration—to materialize! We'll have more to say about that in the post-scarcity section.

So, we've used a client, server, and middleware (/) block to create a very workable client/server environment for tiny offices and people on the road. Let's move on and see what other magic can be performed with these three blocks.

Client/Server for Small Shops and Departments

The client/server architecture is particularly well-suited for the LAN-based single server establishments. So, it's no wonder that they account for around 80% of today's client/server installations. This is the "archetypical" model of client/server. It consists of multiple clients talking to a single "local" server (Figure 3-3). This is the model used in small businesses—for example, a multiuser dentist office—and by the departments of large corporations—for example, the branch offices of a bank.

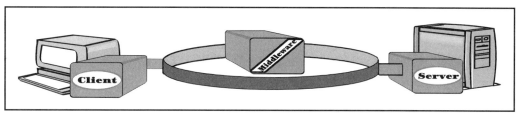

Figure 3-3.   Client/Server for Small Shops and Departments.

The single-server nature of the model tends to keep the middleware simple. The client only needs to look into a configuration file to find its server's name. Security is implemented at the machine level and kept quite simple. The network is usually relatively easy to administer; it's a part-time job for a member of the group. There are no complex interactions between servers, so it is easy to identify failures—they're either on the client or on the local server.

Braver souls may be using their server to interact in a very loosely-coupled way with some enterprise server. For example, data (such as a price list) may be downloaded once a day to refresh the local server. Or inventory data may be uploaded to an enterprise server. Fax and mail can be sent or received any time through the mail server gateway. Typically, the software that interacts with remote servers will reside on the departmental server.

Departmental servers will continue to be popular, especially in large enterprises, because they provide a tremendous amount of user autonomy and controls. Users feel that it is *their* server and they can do anything they want with it. A departmental server's applications typically address the specific needs of the local clients first, which make users very happy. With fiber optic and high-speed ATM connections, it will be hard to detect a performance difference between a "local" departmental server and an enterprise server a continent away. However, the psychology (and politics) of "ownership" will always provide a powerful motivator for holding on to that "local" server.

In summary, this classical implementation of client/server uses our three building blocks to create the "classical" single-server model of client/server that is so predominant. This model works very well in small businesses and departments that depend on single servers or on very loosely-coupled server arrangements. In its marketing literature, Oracle calls this model the "first generation" of client/server. This implies that there is already a "second generation" of client/server, which is the topic of our next section.

Client/Server for Intergalactic Enterprises

The client/server intergalactic model addresses the needs of establishments with a mix of heterogeneous servers (about 20% of the current client/server market). This is an area that's getting a lot of industry attention as solutions move from a few large computers to LAN-based servers. Multiple servers are used in environments that require more processing power than that provided by a single server (see Figure 3-4). One of the great things about the client/server model is that it is upwardly scalable. When more processing power is needed for various intergalactic functions, more servers can be added (thus creating a pool of servers), or the existing server machine can be traded up for the latest generation of superserver machine.

We can partition servers based on the function they provide, the resource they control, or the database they own. In addition, we may choose to replicate servers for fault tolerance or to boost an application's performance. There can be as many server combinations as your budget will tolerate. Multiserver capability, when properly used, can provide an awesome amount of compute power and flexibility, in many cases rivaling that of mainframes.

To exploit the full power of multiservers, we need low-cost, high-speed bandwidth and an awesome amount of middleware features—including network directory services, network security, remote procedure calls, and network time services (see next Soapbox). Middleware creates a common view of all the services on the network called a "single system image."

Good software architecture for intergalactic enterprise client/server implementations is all about creating system "ensembles" out of modular building blocks. With some practice, you may develop creative skills akin to those of a symphony composer in the articulation of servers. You will need to find creative ways to *partition work among the servers*. For example, you may partition the work using

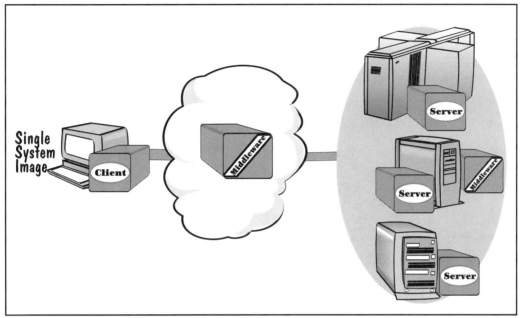

Figure 3-4. Client/Server for Intergalactic Enterprises.

the concept of object managers.   An object manager accepts message-based requests to perform actions against the objects it controls.

You will also need to design your servers so that they can *delegate work* to their fellow servers. A complex request may involve a *task force* of servers working together on the request. Preferably, the client should not be made aware of this *behind-the-scenes* collaboration. The server that the client first contacted should be in charge of orchestrating the task force and returning its findings to the client.

Intergalactic client/server is the driving force behind middleware standards and distributed objects. We're all looking for that magic bullet that will make the distributed multivendor world as integrated as single-vendor mainframes. Tools for creating, deploying, and managing scalable client/server applications are getting a lot of attention. There are fortunes to be made in intergalactic client/server because nobody has yet put all of the pieces back together.

Middleware Servers to the Rescue?

Soapbox

Middleware is an exploding area. Vendors keep adding layer upon layer of software, promising that the last layer is the ultimate "glue" that will finally tie all clients to all servers. We don't believe the ultimate glue will materialize in our lifetimes. In the meantime, it's important to create a "single system image" of all the services a client workstation can use. This is really a Houdini-sized illusion that makes all servers of the world—we're talking about a multiserver, multiservice, multivendor, and multinetwork world—appear to the client as one big happy family. So the "million dollar" question is: What middleware software (or "glue") should reside on each *client* machine to create such an illusion?

There are two evolving approaches for solving this problem:

■ The ***brute force approach*** adds new middleware software on each client machine as fast as vendors roll-out the new pieces. The problem with this approach is that your client machines and applications are always in a state of flux, playing catch-up with all the new and exciting middleware that's constantly being introduced. The clients will grow very fat over time. The complexity of the client environment greatly increases with each new added piece of middleware. Who works out the coexistence issues? How is the mixed environment managed? Nobody knows.

■ The ***middleware gateway approach*** introduces a middleware service that handles all communications with the servers of the universe on behalf of its clients. The gateway server is just a piece of software that typically runs on the "local" server. The client only needs to run the minimum amount of middleware (a "skinny" layer) that allows it to communicate with the server where the middleware gateway software resides. This approach buffers the client from the middleware flux and makes it easier to introduce new server functions without involving every client machine. Of course, if you can afford the fat, you can always run the middleware gateway server on every client machine. This is precisely how the tiny shop and post-scarcity world arrangements are packaged.

We obviously prefer the gateway approach. It provides maximum flexibility using the client/server model. Because the gateway software is itself a server package, it can be moved to any machine on the network to fit your needs. If you run the gateway software on every client machine, you're back to the first option. We like this flexibility. ❏

Client/Server for a Post-Scarcity World

In this section, we up the ante. We will investigate what new systems can be created on a client/server platform when memory and hardware become *incredibly afford-able*. Every machine is both a client and a full-function server (see Figure 3-5). We call this plentiful environment *the post-scarcity world*. We imagine the typical post-scarcity machine as a $1000 cellular notebook powered by a 200 MHz Pentium and loaded with a gigabyte of non-volatile RAM and 100 GBytes or more of disk space. And, of course, this machine runs all the middleware that vendors will be able to dream of over the next few years.

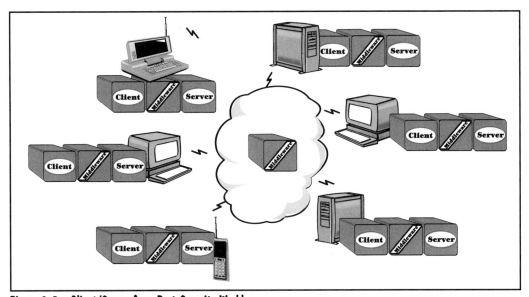

Figure 3-5. Client/Server for a Post-Scarcity World.

What do we do with all this power other than run middleware? What happens when every machine in the world becomes a universal server and client? Because every machine is a full-function server, we should assume it will run, at a minimum, a file server, database server, mail server, TP Monitor, and Distributed Object Manager (DOM). This is in addition to all the client software and middleware.

What we're saying is that in the next few years, say by 1997, a hundred million machines or more may be running *almost all* the forms of client/server software described in this book. This should be good news to TP Monitor, DOM, groupware, and database vendors—it's a huge opportunity. Are they thinking about it? Do they have the proper packaging and marketing channels to go after it? After you read this book, you'll have a better appreciation for how complex, powerful, and essential this software is.

So who will manage and run all that software on behalf of the user? *Personal agents*, of course. The best way to understand the capabilities of agent technology is to read the next Briefing box that describes an agent-controlled automated travel agency.

The Automated Travel Agent is an example of a new type of cooperative application that makes full use of the advanced software features of PCs. From an architectural viewpoint, we've gone past the concept of client/server where every event is generated by the client. We've augmented this architectural paradigm with the concept of *autonomous agents* that reside in the network machines and perform background tasks. The agents can analyze data and perform actions based on a set of rules. And the agents are always on *fact-finding* missions on the network working on your behalf.

It is easy to imagine that the next step is to have a personal version of the Automated Agent run on your own PC. You will have your own personal agent to take care of your vacations. Your agent knows your vacation schedule and preferences. It has also kept a history of your previous vacations in the database and has learned your likes and dislikes from it. Your personal agent knows you like to take your vacations in March, so it started a search sometime in December to find you the best bargains. Your agent is of course always negotiating with other agents all over the world, always "wheeling and dealing" on your behalf. Your agent and you communicate using multimedia, continuous speech recognition facilities, and e-mail. It communicates with the world at large using the intergalactic services of an Object Request Broker (ORB). The best part is that you do not have to babysit your agent while it's out there doing all this work on your behalf. Wouldn't you love to have one of those agents? The post-scarcity age of client/server computing is sure to be amazing, at least to those of us who are trying to make today's technology work.

How far in the future is this post-scarcity vision? In November 1993 at Comdex, IBM demonstrated an intelligent rules-based agent technology that allows an OS/2 or Windows user to delegate all kinds of everyday work to an agent. The agent can intercept input from many devices—including phones, fax machines, e-mail, and server applications—make decisions based on inputs, and act on the decisions. The agents can be programmed using instruction "rule books" created with a graphical instruction editor. The agent-managed objects can be expanded to include IBM and customer objects.

In January 1994, General Magic unveiled Telescript, a communication language that will provide the foundation of AT&T's Personal Link on-line service, scheduled to begin later this year. With Telescript, a computer user has no idea of "connecting" to a remote service at all. Instead, an agent travels from the user's computer through the network, looking for information or even making purchases based on commands given by the user.

FYI   **A View of Post-Scarcity Paradise**

Briefing

You walk into the *Paradise Travel Agency* to discuss your vacation plans. Its name is definitely enticing. You are greeted by the Automated Travel Agent, a PC with an Object-Oriented User Interface (OOUI). You start a friendly conversation with the Automated Agent. A few interactions later (this machine does advanced continuous speech recognition), the Automated Agent knows that you have ten days of vacation coming in March, you want to spend them on a nice beach, and you have at most $2000 to spend on your vacation.

The Automated Agent searches its local database for a vacation strategy that fits your needs, and offers you a set of alternative choices in the form of icons placed on a map. The best choices for this time of the year are Tahiti, Hawaii, Cancun, and other "paradises." You pick Tahiti, and the Automated Travel Agent displays a set of resort choices that include the Club Meds at Bora Bora and Morea. You choose to explore the Club Med alternative, and then ask for more information about the Club Med Villages in Tahiti. You are now placed in a Hypermedia-like environment that allows you to explore the sports offered, the beaches, the room accommodations, and so on. Embedded in the Hypermedia displays are *links* that allow you to view and zoom in on pictures and videos of beaches, lagoons, huts on the water, and romantic restaurants with views of the sunset. After spending a delightful 30 minutes or so browsing through screens of dreamland and imagining what your vacation will be like, you decide to book your vacation now!

The Automated Agent presents you with more choices, and by the time you are finished you've decided you want to spend six days in Bora Bora and four in Morea. You want a hut on the lagoon, of course, with a double bed, and you opt for low-cholesterol dinners. You may even decide to make table reservations for your first night in the romantic restaurant with the view of the sunset.

The Automated Agent now has all the information it needs from you to carry out the transaction, so it starts a background process that places a call to Club Med's computer using its Object Request Broker (ORB). It also starts another background ORB process that deals with your credit card company's computer. While all this activity is happening, the Automated Agent keeps you occupied by listing information in a window that may be relevant to your trip, like what kind of clothes to bring, passport requirements, and so on. It can even sell you the clothes while you're waiting!

A few seconds elapse. Now all the parties are ready to carry out the transaction. We have established an inter-ORB rendezvous between the Club Med computer, the credit card company's computer, and the Automated Agent who is your broker. The transaction is electronically prepared. You have your reservation, Club Med has your money, the Automated Agent has the commission, and you are set for a wonderful vacation. You are asked one last time if you want to confirm the transaction. Click OK and you will be in Morea next March. Life is sweet!

Now, here's what was happening behind the scene. The Automated Travel Agent application maintains, in its private database cache, the list of multimedia files (viewing objects) and a reference to the network drives on which they reside. The application may maintain a local copy of some of the files using its own hard disk as a cache. The Automated Travel Agent can talk to remote service providers such as the airlines, Club Med, and the credit card services. The service may range from a simple file download or upload to a series of requests and replies that lead to the commitment of a transaction. Authentication and network security are essential in this environment.

The Automated Travel Agent and the service providers cooperate to perform business transactions. During non-peak hours, the Automated Travel Agent (with a ravenous appetite for information) downloads price lists and other related information from the service providers and caches it on its local database server. This downloading allows the Automated Travel Agent to provide extensive searches against local data to find the best rates for a given function. ❑

Sharing Data in the Post-Scarcity Age

What does "post-scarcity" mean to database servers? With disk prices being reduced every day and with the database software running on every PC, we can now enjoy the luxury of storing large amounts of data in our personal databases. This luxury will make life very pleasant for personal software providers; however, the question which we must ask is: How is shared data handled in a post-scarcity data storage world? There are two strategies to shared data:

■ Keep all shared data on servers using the technology developed for servers and multiservers. This is the straight client/server model we previously discussed.

■ Allow outsiders to access the public parts of your shared data and obtain, when you require it, access to other people's data. This is, of course, done using a *network of information agents* that use the client/server model to exchange services and data.

We will now look into the information agent approach to shared data.

Each machine on the network contains an *information agent* that runs in the background and performs useful tasks, such as dealing with requests for remote information, both outgoing and incoming. Your machine's information agent—think of it as a specialized personal agent—is always operating on your behalf in the background accumulating and sorting information on topics that interest you. It does this by conducting constant transactions with fellow information agents on remote machines. The information agents communicate with one another using the client/server remote procedure call (RPC) exchanges. More sophisticated agents may incorporate a TP Monitor that can handle X/Open's transactional RPC (TxRPC) and participate in a two-phase commit. The most sophisticated agents will implement the OMG's ORB 2 with object-oriented transactional services.

The local information agent acts as a client to a remote agent server when it needs data from the server's database and vice versa. The agent client/server paradigm provides excellent local autonomy. A node can change its database designs without affecting clients. The database design and structure does not have to be known to the outside world. The only things that cannot easily change are the RPC service interfaces (or the request and reply message formats for applications that issue their own messages).

We're creating a brave new world of *agents* that are programmed to have a ravenous appetite for information on a list of topics. Data agents are more than just background tasks; they know how to cooperate with other agents on the network through the client/server interface to get their work done. They are also programmed to understand their user's personal information needs. The background

agent is always ready to immediately service any request for information from either a foreground process on your machine or from a *cooperative* network agent.

ARE PEER SERVICES A VIABLE ALTERNATIVE?

If you're coming from the low-end of the networking business, you may already be familiar with products such as Artisoft's LANtastic, Novell's NetWare Lite, IBM's LAN Server 3.0 Peer Services, AppleTalk, and Microsoft's Windows for Workgroups and Windows NT. These products provide file and print sharing and some kind of electronic mail without requiring a dedicated server. Everybody is equal on the peer network. Each computer on the network is both a client and a server. Further, each computer is responsible for controlling access to its own resources and has equal access to resources that are on any other computer.

Peer services usually sell for a fraction of the cost of equivalent client/server software. So is it time to toss away the local server? Has post-scarcity client/server already arrived? No! No! (see the following Soapbox). Peer servers are usually very limited in function and they typically will only let one client connect at a time to access a shared resource. So peer networks support multiuser sharing as long as only one user gets in at a time. Is that a problem? Not if you have a small office environment and you don't mind waiting.

But how do peer networks handle distributed security, audit trails, fault tolerance, and all the good things you expect to get on a shared server? Peer services are too limited to give you all that function. And don't even think about running a shared database server, TP Monitor, or Distributed Object Manager in that environment.

Remember, in the post-scarcity model of client/server, every machine is a client and a *full-function* server. Without these features you're liable to get into a lot of trouble. Peer services are *not* full-function servers, and they're notoriously hard to manage and control. You need the sophisticated agent software we described in the previous section to create *true* peer services. Without this function you have a network of crippled peers.

To Peer or not to Peer?

Soapbox

Peer-to-peer networks are still not ready for prime time for many reasons. A single peer can kill an entire network by limiting access to a key shared file (for example, if the owner of that machine calls in sick). And everybody must keep their shared machines powered up over the weekend to let workaholics access the information they need at all hours. In addition, a single peer can break the security of the entire network by providing shared access to sensitive files. And, with today's peer technology, it is almost impossible for an administrator to fully control every machine on a peer network: When are resources backed up? When can a system shut down safely? Who gets to run *Popeye* on their machines (or any other program that chews up system resources)?

But let's face it, peer services are very attractive because they're an embryonic microcosm of our final destination—post-scarcity client/server computing. Should you deploy peer services today? Yes, as long as you have at least one machine that's a full-function server on the network. This is the machine with the redundant disk drives, uninterruptable power supply (UPS), full-function server software, and network security. It's the machine that always stays up— after hours and on weekends. In other words, it's a *super peer* also known as the local server. So much for equality and freedom for all! ❏

Chapter 4

The State of the Client/Server Infrastructure

If something inert is set in motion, it will gradually come to life.

— *Lao Tzu*

We hope to have convinced you, by now, that our planet will soon be covered with ubiquitous client/server webs. Using these webs, we will be able to communicate more effectively with other humans—customers, suppliers, the boss, coworkers, family, and friends—and with the everyday machines that serve us—cars, gas pumps, TV sets, and even intelligent homes.

This chapter provides an overview of the extensive infrastructure that supports these client/server webs. An *infrastructure* provides the components that make it easy to create, deliver, and manage client/server applications. We will identify the components of this infrastructure and use them to create the roadmap that ties together the pieces of the puzzle. We will briefly explain the different components and where they fit. But our emphasis will be on the lower level middleware and base components of the infrastructure—the bedrock elements on top of which everything else is built. We've got to start somewhere.

WHAT'S AN INFRASTRUCTURE?

Every epoch-making technology requires an infrastructure. For example, where would airplanes be today without the vast commercial airway infrastructure that provides airports, traffic controllers, air corridors, flights, booking agents, customs, security gates, ground transport, and luggage handling systems? This infrastructure has grown over the years and now has the bandwidth to comfortably move hundreds of millions of passengers across the globe (except around Christmas, it seems). Entire industries were created around this infrastructure—car rentals, air cargo, shuttle services, travel agents, mass tourism, long-term parking, hotels, and airport shops and restaurants.

Client/server, of course, has its own infrastructure. The industry has recently delivered many of the key software technologies needed to create ubiquitous client/server webs. But the technology to help deliver, deploy, and manage the client/server applications that reside on the web is still in its infancy. To use the airway analogy, the client/server infrastructure is at the stage that the airline industry found itself right after World War II. We have many airplane builders, some great battle-tested airplanes (from the OS wars), a few semi-isolated airports, and great radar technology. But we still haven't found the Howard Hughes of client/server (young Howard created TWA and started the modern airline industry).

The horizontal diversification and commoditization of the computer industry may have come a tad too early for the client/server mass market. Nothing is better than horizontal competition within an established vertical infrastructure. Unfortunately, the vertical infrastructure that will create the client/server playing field still needs to be deployed. The next soapbox speculates on who may pull the pieces together for the client/server industry to take off big time.

The telephone and cable companies are doing a phenomenal job renewing the physical infrastructure and paving the country with 1) high bandwidth transport media—the fiber backbones already strung across the US by AT&T, MCI, and Sprint; 2) the coax connections installed in millions of homes by cable TV companies; and 3) the twisted pair connections brought to nearly every home by local telephone companies. In addition, they are developing the new generation of switching systems that will transfer the voice, video, and data around the network using several technologies, including ATM, FDDI, and Frame Relay.

The challenge for the computer industry is how to add on top of this physical infrastructure the client/server structures that bring all the pieces together. We must provide:

■ The transport protocols that support networked exchanges and allow information to be moved reliably.

- The network operating systems that guarantee security and privacy and help users and programs find the services they need on the internet.
- The databases for storing, retrieving, and organizing massive amounts of multimedia information.
- The groupware systems that enable networked person-to-person exchanges and group conferencing.
- The intelligent agents that help humans organize their activities in cyberspace.
- The distributed system management platforms that keep the whole thing running on a day-to-day basis.

So what's the state of our infrastructure?

Who Can Bring the Pieces Together?

Soapbox

Networks will get faster, possibly offering hundreds of times more bandwidth for data links than is possible today through the telephone switching system.

— *Nick Lippis, Data Communications*
(October, 1993)

Everywhere you turn these days, someone is talking about the "digital highway." For now, the network providers are the big spenders in the digital highway convergence. The spate of alliances involving cable TV, Telcos, and entertainment companies are creating physical transmission backbones that are faster, cheaper, more widespread, and have more capacity than anything the phone companies could have created on their own. The merger of the US West Telco with Time Warner's fiber optic networks can result in the offering of transparent LAN services on a nationwide basis. AT&T spent $12.6 billion to acquire McCaw Cellular Communications to consolidate its end-to-end offerings. .

These companies are renewing the existing voice network and augmenting it with the bandwidth to support highly interactive multimedia transmissions. But the infrastructure they're creating is not being neatly planned and then built. Instead, a large "multifaceted communications web" is being spun that is already expanding in fits and starts, across the globe.

In the midst of this chaotic growth, who in the computer industry will provide the *client/server nervous system* that articulates this physical infrastructure? Our short list of potential candidates includes Bill Clinton, Bill Gates, system integrators (like Arthur Anderson or EDS), a "born-again" client/server IBM, a Novell/Oracle alliance, and a super-consortium that includes everyone but Microsoft. Here's how each of them might do it:

■ **Bill Clinton** wants an information highway that will bring together the worlds of CATV and data networks. His *National Information Infrastructure (NII)* will use existing transports and concentrate on smoothing the path for developing the "on-ramps" and "off-ramps" to this highway. The "NII Testbed" is also helping explore several switching technologies, including ATM, FDDI, and Frame Relay. Could the airline infrastructure have succeeded without government intervention? It's doubtful. Bill Clinton proposes to build the client/server equivalents of airports.

■ **Bill Gates** is cooking up his *At Work* and *At Home* strategies based on "Windows everywhere." His *Windows Open Systems Architecture (WOSA)* is an ambitious plan to bring every gadget, appliance, workstation, and server into the Windows fold. Windows APIs are being proposed for every known activity. WOSA may succeed on the client, but it will go nowhere without the server side of the equation. This is where Windows NT comes into the picture. Microsoft now spends more than $100 million a year and employs more than 200 people to research and develop software for interactive TV and other technologies to connect homes to the data highway. Microsoft, like everybody else in the industry, is going after the strategic "set-top box" that sits on the TV—it's working on MIMOSA, an operating system for interactive TV.

■ **The System Integrators**—like Arthur Andersen and EDS—are some of the main beneficiaries of the fragmentation of the computer industry. They're getting paid to bring the pieces back together using "vendor-neutral solutions." Can they pull enough of the pieces together to create a vendor-neutral cohesive infrastructure?

■ **The new IBM** is leapfrogging the competition by combining client/server and distributed object technologies. Its goal is to create a client/server infrastructure around a "sea of objects." This time IBM is leading the push for "open" standards based on objects and the OSF DCE technology. DSOM and Taligent object frameworks are making IBM the technology leader in distributed objects. In spite of all the layoffs, IBM still has the industry's largest channel for distributing, deploying, and supporting client/server applications. Finally, IBM has a lot of in-house experience in the area of mission-critical distributed systems. As Jim Cannavino puts it, "IBM has had a decade of experience making heterogeneous systems work together—mostly our own."

■ *The Novell/Oracle alliance* created around *OracleWare*. The packaging of the Oracle DBMS with NetWare brings together two very potent technologies and, even more importantly, two major distribution channels. Novell wants to embed NetWare, or some mutation of it, everywhere—including in our refrigerators and toasters. And Oracle is working with US West to build a worldwide digital network to be managed by massively parallel versions of the Oracle7 database. This network is also intended to support interactive wireless and cable services. What we're seeing here is a marriage of LANs, WANs, and massively parallel database technology—all the pieces needed to move, distribute, and store massive numbers of multimedia objects.

■ *The "Everybody but Microsoft" alliance*, called COSE, is intended to shake the balance in the industry and accelerate the introduction of de facto standards. The stability of the COSE alliance is directly proportional to how well Microsoft does with Windows NT. If NT falters, so will the COSE alliance. Can a consortium built for defensive purposes create the infrastructure that brings the industry together?

Finally, there are those who dream that the invisible hand of the market coupled with open standards will create this infrastructure from the bottom up—no divine intervention required.

Which are you betting on? ❑

CLIENT/SERVER INFRASTRUCTURE: THE COMPONENTS

Last chapter we introduced the three *building blocks* of client/server: the client, the server, and the middleware slash (/) that ties them together. Figure 4-1 peels the next layer off the onion and provides more detail about what goes into each of the building blocks. What you see in this figure is, in a nutshell, the entire client/server software infrastructure. Let's go over the pieces:

■ *The client building block* runs the client side of the application. It runs on an operating system (OS) that provides a graphical user interface (GUI) or an Object Oriented User Interface (OOUI) and that can access distributed services, wherever they may be. The operating system most often passes the buck to the middleware building block and lets it handle the non-local services. The client also runs a component of the *Distributed System Management (DSM)* element. This could be anything from a simple agent on a managed PC to the entire front end of the DSM application on a managing station.

■ *The server building block* runs the server side of the application. The server application typically runs on top of some shrink-wrapped server software package. The four contending server platforms for creating applications are SQL Database Servers, TP Monitors, Groupware Servers, and Object Servers. The server side depends on the operating system to interface with the middleware building block that brings in the requests for service. The server also runs a DSM component. This could be anything from a simple agent on a managed PC to the entire back end of the DSM application (for example it could provide a shared object database for storing system management information).

■ *The middleware building block* runs on both the client and server sides of an application. We broke this building block into three categories: transport stacks, network operating systems (NOSs), and service-specific middleware. Middleware is the nervous system of the client/server infrastructure. We will explain the division in the middleware building block in the next section. Like the other two building blocks, the middleware also has DSM software components.

The Distributed System Management application runs on every node in a client/server network. A *managing* workstation collects information from all its *agents* on the network and displays it graphically. The managing workstation can also instruct its agents to perform actions on its behalf. Think of management as running an autonomous "network within a network." It is the "Big Brother" of the client/server world, but life is impossible without it.

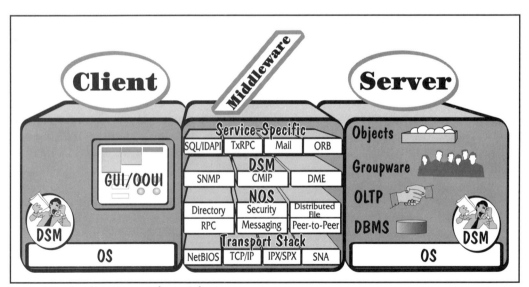

Figure 4-1. The Client/Server Software Infrastructure.

THE MIDDLEWARE BUILDING BLOCK: A CLOSER LOOK

Middleware is a very convenient term, which, unfortunately, also creates a lot of confusion. This is not surprising because middleware refers to the software that's in the *middle* of the client/server system. In this book, we use middleware to refer to the software component that starts with the API set on the client side to invoke a service and covers the transmission of the request over the network and the resulting response. We're using middleware as a general "catch-all" term that refers to three layers of glue: the transport stacks, the network operating system (NOS), and service-specific middleware. This division should make it easier to understand all those strange interactions that take place between the clients and the servers on the network.

The Transport Stacks Middleware

The transport stacks middleware consists of transport protocols—including TCP/IP, NetBIOS, IPX/SPX, DECnet, AppleTalk, OSI, and SNA/APPN—that provide reliable end-to-end communications across Wide Area Networks (WANs) and Local Area Networks (LANs). How do all these protocols seamlessly work together? They use the magic of LAN/WAN/LAN interconnect technology—such as routers, bridges, and gateways—that transport multiprotocol traffic across a campus or wide area network in an integrated fashion (see the following Briefing box). Groups can decide for themselves what protocols to run on their local networks and leave it up to the backbone providers to collect these protocols and route them across networks.

Figure 4-2 shows how bridges, routers, and gateways are used in a modern backbone network. As you can see, today's enterprise networks are made up of a combination of LANs, including Token Rings and Ethernets; WANs, including public and private packet switched networks that run X.25 and Frame Relay; and the bridge, routers, and gateways that provide the internetworking, multiprotocol "glue" that ties the LANs and WANs together.

The Bridge/Router phenomenon is not the only area that experienced great progress. Modern operating systems—like OS/2, NetWare, Windows NT, and Unix SVR4—are becoming much more network friendly. They've introduced features that allow multivendor communication stacks and network adapters to easily plug into them. And they also make life easier for programmers by providing APIs that are stack independent.

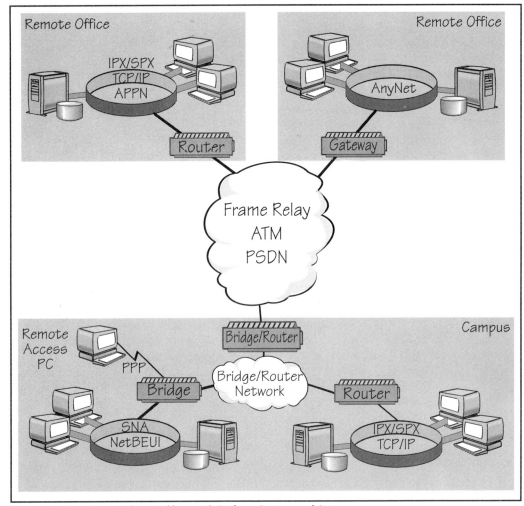

Figure 4-2. Creating a Modern Backbone with Bridges, Routers, and Gateways.

Here's a summary of some of the new operating system features that make that possible:

■ *The stack sandwich* provides the hooks for snapping multivendor protocol stacks into an operating system. To accommodate multivendor networks, modern operating systems must support multiple protocols, redirectors, and APIs. To do that effectively, the operating system must provide well defined interfaces between components. A modern operating system usually "sandwiches" the transport stacks between a transport-independent interface at the top of the stacks and a logical interface to the network device drivers at the bottom of the stacks (see Figure 4-3).

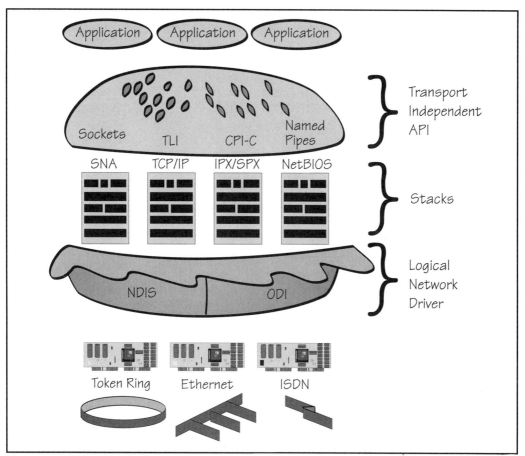

Figure 4-3. The Stack Sandwich.

- ***The logical network driver*** provides a single interface to all the network adapters. This interface between the network adapter and the transport stacks is particularly important. The last thing vendors who provide transport stacks want is to write a driver for every possible network adapter. And, of course, network adapter vendors want to avoid having to interface to every possible stack. Microsoft/3Com's NDIS and Novell's ODI are the two most widely supported de facto standards for interfacing protocol stacks to network adapter device drivers. They do so by providing a logical network board that makes it easy to interface different network adapters with multiple protocol stacks (see Figure 4-3). Transport stack providers can use NDIS or ODI as the common interface to all network adapters. And network adapter vendors can use NDIS or ODI as the top layer for their network drivers. NDIS and ODI take care of sending and receiving data and managing the adapter card.

■ *The transport-independent APIs* sit on top of the transport stacks and allow developers to plug their programs into a single interface that supports multiple protocols. The Berkeley socket interface is becoming the premier choice on most operating system platforms for interfacing to multivendor multiprotocol stacks. Other choices include the *Transport Layer Interface (TLI)* used in NetWare and many Unix implementations; *CPI-C*, the modern SNA peer-to-peer API that can now run over both SNA and TCP/IP stacks; and *Named Pipes* that runs on top of NetBIOS, IPX/SPX, and TCP/IP stacks.

■ *The protocol matchmakers,* which allow applications written for a specific transport—such as SNA—to run across other networks—such as TCP/IP or IPX/SPX (see Figure 4-4). This strategy eliminates the need for gateways and works well with existing applications. For example, a Lotus Notes application written for NetBIOS could be made to run over SNA networks without changing a line of code. IBM's *AnyNet* product line currently offers protocol matchmakers for TCP/IP and SNA on the OS/2 and MVS platforms. IBM intends to add matchmakers for NetBIOS, IPX/SPX, and OSI. The formal IBM name for this matchmaker strategy is the *The Multiprotocol Transport Network (or MPTN)*. Several companies are in discussion with IBM about using MPTN, including Apple, HP, Oracle, and Ki Research.

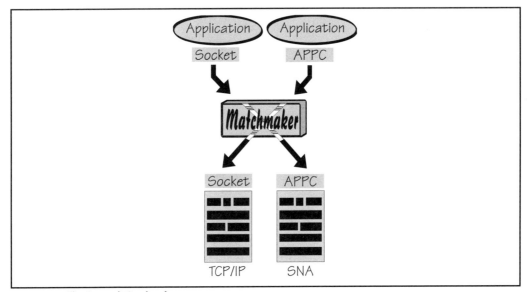

Figure 4-4. The Protocol Matchmaker.

In summary, today's network environment is a truly heterogeneous hodgepodge of protocols and media options. Network routers, gateways, and bridges insulate the application developer from having to worry about cabling, network adapters, or protocol transport choices. Multiprotocol API sets make it easier for service providers to develop client/server applications that run over multiple protocol stacks. And we're getting closer to the day when client/server programs can be plugged into any protocol stack (on any machine) almost as easily as appliances plug into electrical outlets.

Bridges, Routers, and Gateways

Briefing

Bridges are computers or devices that interconnect LANs using link layer routing information and physical addresses; protocols that do not support internetworking, like NetBIOS, are bridged. *Routers* interconnect LANs using protocol-dependent routing information. Routers create and maintain dynamic routing tables of the destinations they know. They are typically used with protocols such as TCP/IP, IPX/SPX, APPN, XNS, AppleTalk, and OSI. *Multiprotocol Routers* support different combinations of network layer protocols. *Bridge/Routers* are single devices that combine the functions of bridges and routers; they are quite popular today. *Gateways* are devices that perform brute force translations between protocols. They are used in situations where the backbone can only support one protocol, and all other protocols get translated to it.

Bridge/Routers started as a bottom-up phenomenon—they solved practical problems and were not part of a grand architecture. The Router products from Cayman Systems, Cisco, Wellfleet, IBM, DEC, and Novell can now encapsulate NetBIOS, AppleTalk, SNA, and IPX/SPX to allow only a single protocol to run on the backbone (usually IPX/SPX, APPN, or TCP/IP). The industry is still learning how to make these products work in environments that require the load balancing of traffic between links and the handling of high-priority traffic. Bridges use fixed path, one-route only schemes; only a few know how to re-route traffic to alternate paths when a link fails. While they can handle any LAN-based protocols, they do not perform very well when large amounts of broadcast packets are propagated throughout the network. But, the Bridge/Router industry is extremely competitive and it will undoubtedly solve these problems. The industry is continously introducing newer features and more robust models. For example, the newest routers use specialized protocols to determine the best paths for network traffic and can even perform load-balancing across multiple parallel paths.

Despite their popularity, bridges and routers are no panacea. Segmenting LANs with bridge and routers is a bandaid, not a long-term cure. When the widespread use of multimedia starts to dramatically increase our traffic loads, routers will become *incredibly expensive* bandaids. Routers will become much harder to manage and will introduce delays that are unacceptable for real-time data flows, like motion pictures. We anticipate that routers will eventually get replaced by ATM-based backbones, which we discuss later in this chapter. Of course, if you're in the router business, you may call these high-speed ATM switches the new routers of the mid-1990s. ❏

What's Missing?

The vision is nomadic, ubiquitous, client/server computing everywhere.

— *Tom Furey, 1993*

In order for the "ubiquitous network socket" to see the light of day, and for Figure 4-5 to become a reality, the following hurdles still have to be overcome:

Bringing the digital highway to the home: To do so requires a solution to the impedance mismatch (or bottleneck) created by the "last mile" of telephone cable that connects homes and offices to the long-distance service providers. In the US alone, telephone companies still own more than 100 million pairs of copper wire local loops. But, over the past decade, the long-distance carriers replaced their copper wire backbones with a network of superfast, high-bandwidth, low-tariff, fiber-optic cables. However, bringing these advantages into the home requires the upgrading of that last mile of local cable to fiber—a mind boggling expense.

But there's good news on the horizon in the form of two related technologies that promise to speed up the local loops without replacing the existing wiring: ISDN (see next Briefing box) and the ISDN-based T1 over copper connection (also known as HDSL). And if these don't work out, there's always the cable TV alternative.[1] Cable companies are already exploring the use of their coaxial cabling to include telephone services and connections to computer data networks such as the Internet. AT&T is also working on an adapter, called Sage, that may provide "universal access" into the home by plugging into both the existing telephone and cable networks. In addition, some cable operators (such as Time Warner) are installing fiber as a replacement for coax. And some local telephone companies are also expanding fiber beyond switching offices to the curbs of residential customers.

---

[1] In the US, the Telecommunications Infrastructure Act of 1993 (S 1086) proposes to free up regional telephone companies and cable companies to play into each other's territories, allowing them to offer "on ramp" connections to the information highway.

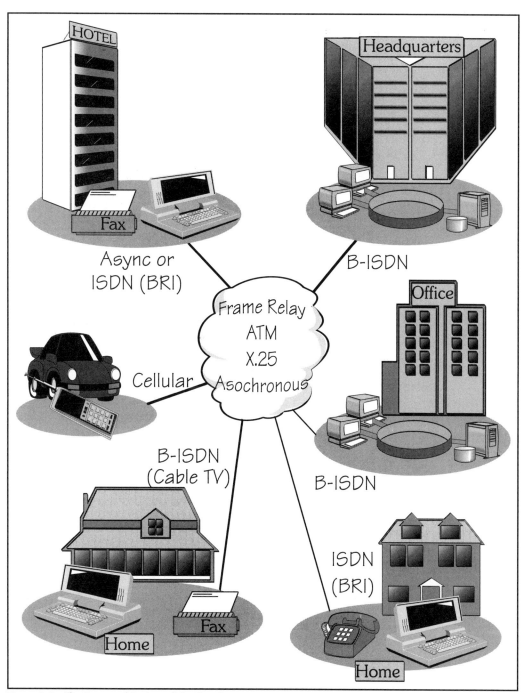

Figure 4-5. The Connected Society of the Near Future.

ISDN, B-ISDN, and ATM

Briefing

Integrated Services Digital Network (ISDN) is a digital telephony technology that supports the high-speed transfer of voice and data over telephone lines. The most prevalent ISDN service is the *Basic Rate Interface (BRI)*, also known as *2B + D*. This service works over regular telephone lines by creating two independent 64 Kb/s "B channels" for information (data or voice) and one 16 Kb/s "D channel" for signaling and placing calls. The Basic Rate telephone line is clocked at 192 Kb/s and uses time division multiplexing to allocate the two B and D channels; the extra 48 Kb/s is reserved. Basic Rate uses the standard 4-wire telephone jack that is used in homes and offices. A higher-capacity version of ISDN is also available; it is called the *Primary Rate Interface (PRI)*, or *23B + D*. PRI can deliver 1.544 Mb/s, but it is rarely used.

ISDN BRI is the digitization of the telephone line. It's an order of magnitude faster than anything you can do with a modem today. In addition, ISDN provides a lower-cost form of communication because it charges by connect time (like normal voice calls) rather than by the packet (like some PSDNs). Its higher speeds can reduce the connect time and save you some money. So why isn't everybody using ISDN? ISDN's acceptance depends on being able to "call out and reach anyone." To do that, all the central office switches involved in an ISDN connection must be digital. Today over 65% of US Centrex switches are ISDN-capable; Europe and Japan are further along. Forrester predicts that ISDN will become prevalent in 1995. According to Forrester, Pacific Bell, Bell Atlantic, Ameritech, US West, and Nynex will provide over 70% ISDN coverage at low cost by 1995. Southwestern Bell is the laggard, with less than 25% coverage. Mobile users with laptops should be able to use ISDN from their hotel rooms much before 1995. Forrester calls ISDN the LAN Outer Network (LON) because it extends the LAN's remote coverage, it provides decent bandwidth, it's reliable, it provides fast remote dial-up (1 second or less), and it's inexpensive (remote lines can be installed at a cost of $10 to $20 per month).

The proponents of ISDN feel it provides the ideal end-user entry point to the "data highway" because the telephone is ubiquitous. Another camp argues that 128 Kb/s does not provide enough bandwidth for multimedia and would rather go with coax (cable TV) and bypass ISDN (PRI or BRI). However, this is where an exciting technology called *Broadband ISDN or B-ISDN* comes into the picture. B-ISDN supports a bandwidth of 150 Mbit/s and above. It's an excellent candidate technology for the data highway because it can bring interactive voice, data, and video into the home using Cable TV's broadband channels. B-ISDN uses *Asynchronous Transfer Mode (ATM)* in both its connection-oriented and connectionless (also known as SMDS) modes. The B-ISDN standard defines an ATM adaptation layer (AAL) that is responsible for mapping data, voice, and video information to and from ATM-defined cell formats.

So what is ATM? It is the current darling of the network industry. ATM has the potential of revolutionizing networking at the LAN, WAN, campus Router, and home connection levels. ATM's high-speed, cell-based switching protocols permit the mixing of different traffic including data, voice, and video. Its system of transmitting small cells of information is flexible enough to work at capacities ranging from megabits to gigabits. ATM bandwidth is demand-based and scalable, meaning that each node can access the network at the speeds required by an application. ATM is the favorite building block technology for the construction of the digital highway. ATM can provide seamless networking and remove the current distinctions between LANs and WANs. Several telephone and cable TV companies, such as Time Warner, are installing ATM switching systems. However, many standards are still needed to make implementations of ATM interoperate.

Any of these approaches is better than what we have today: POTS (Plain Old Telephone Service). We wouldn't mind BRI using one B channel for data (or voice) while the other B channel is transmitting an image, fax, or movie, in the background. And it beats installing two telephone lines and dial modems. BRI will do fine until we get B-ISDN on ATM and live happily ever after in bandwidth heaven. ❑

Bringing the digital highway to the mobile user: Many alliances are being formed to create the ultimate network that will let users "communicate anywhere, anytime." The alliances are between various computer and telephone companies. Their aim is to glue together wired and wireless networks so that they can shoot high-speed data through the air to mobile users. RAM Mobile Data claims that it already can provide two-way wireless services to 90% of the U.S. urban population. RAM is expected to announce the availability of AT&T Mail and Lotus cc:Mail on RAM networks. ARDIS, the IBM/Motorola digital wireless network, is another contender. In 1994, Cellular-Vision plans to cover the New York city area with a 1 Gbit/s wireless network that supports multimedia and interactive television. AT&T spent $12.6 billion to acquire McCaw Cellular Communications to "round-out" its end-to-end wireless suite of offerings.

McCaw is testing an evolutionary technology called *Cellular Digital Packet Data (CDPD)* that allows data to be transmitted over the existing analog cellular network. CDPD can dynamically pick the open voice channels and use them for data traffic. Two warring digital alternatives to CDPD are also being proposed: *Time-Division Multiple Access (TDMA)* and *Code-Division Multiple Access (CDMA)*. Regardless of which technology is chosen, we expect cellular data networks to really start catching on.

In September 1993, the US Federal regulators (FCC) cleared the way for a dramatic expansion of wireless services by allowing 200 MHz of government-held radio frequency to be auctioned to private developers. This is five times the spectrum originally allocated to the cellular phone industry. This action could conceivably lead to a day when wired phones are seldom used and are replaced by small mobile phones carried by nearly everyone at all times. Phone numbers will be individually assigned to individuals, not locations.

The FCC action includes the allocation of 40 MHz of spectrum bandwidth for LAN-based wireless office applications at frequencies between 1.85 GHz and 2.2 GHz, which can be supported by low-cost, low-power, small-cell, one-chip transceivers. This dedicated spectrum, called the *Personal Communication Services (PCS)*, will eliminate interference from other radio sources, including cellular phones, garage door openers, and security devices. PCS will help create private networks that incorporate different data-transmission methods and easily provide links at 32 kbit/s (or more). PCS will open up entire new industries based on low-cost and ubiquitous wireless technology for data transmissions.

But who will maintain order in the friendly skies? Currently, each wireless network provider is building its own "skyway." To bring order out of that chaos, the IEEE 802.11 committee was given the thankless task of creating standards for wireless networks. The standards are intended to cover the following areas: wireless modems, APIs, PCMCIA devices, data security in the sky, bridges from wired-to-wireless LANs, guidelines to prevent broadcast interference, and a media-access protocol for radio and infrared transmissions.

Bringing "isochronous" multimedia support to the digital highway: What is an isochronous network? It's a network that provides very low and predictable node-to-node delays (or latencies). Isochronous networks are capable of dealing with the steady, immediate delivery, and high-bandwidth requirements of multimedia technology. For example, networks that support desktop training videos or videoconferencing need to supply, on demand, 1.5 Mbits/s (or more) to each PC. We can accommodate some of that demand by exploiting the prioritized traffic services of existing Token Ring and Ethernet networks. Higher priority frames are assigned to the delay-sensitive traffic. But what we really need are high-speed networks with separate voice/video and data traffic channels (also called virtual circuits) that can guarantee a fixed delivery time for multimedia traffic (see next Briefing box).

Near completion is the *Fiber Distributed Data Interface* II (*FDDI II)*, a virtual circuit standard that divides *FDDI's* 100 Mbit/s bandwidth into 16 separate circuits, each of which can be allocated to either data or isochronous traffic (see next Briefing box). ANSI is also working on a gigabit-speed version of FDDI called FFOL (for FDDI Follow On LAN). Two competing 100 Mbit/s Ethernet proposals were ratified by IEEE in July of 1993 in addition to a 16 Mbit/s isochronous Ethernet. Further on the horizon are Asynchronous Transfer Mode (ATM) networks that are being built from the ground up to handle voice, video, and data. Currently, FDDI products (over copper) sell for one-fifth the price of equivalent ATM offerings. The first $1000 per node FDDI offerings are expected in 1994. Table 4-1 compares the contending high-speed network technologies.

Table 4-1. Comparing High-Speed Network Technologies.

Networks	Isochronous support	Bandwidth	Access Scheme	When
FDDI	No	100 MBit/s	Contention	Now
Synchronous FDDI	Yes	100 MBit/s	Contention (with Priority)	Now
FDDI II	Yes	100 MBit/s	Contention and Virtual Circuits	1994-5
FFOL	Yes	2.40 GBit/s	Contention and Virtual Circuits	1995
Ethernet II	No	100 MBit/s	Contention	1994-5
ATM	Yes	2.48 GBit/s	Pure Circuit Switch	1994-5

In conclusion, the transport elements of the middleware infrastructure are coming together at a fast pace. We have a pretty good idea of how everything will eventually interconnect with everything else. But interconnectivity is only a first step in the long road to ubiquitous client/server computing. In the next few sections, we explain how the NOS and service-specific middleware conspire to create a single system view on top of these raw transports. In other words, *the network is the computer.*

What's a Virtual Circuit?

Briefing

Virtual circuits are like the phone system. They get established when two nodes need to communicate, and relinquished after they're not needed. Because video and voice are carried over the network in streams within virtual circuits, delays are low and constant. For example, the Frame Relay Wide Area Network (WAN) packet switching technology uses virtual circuits to allocate bandwidth on demand and optimize the use of the existing bandwidth.

In contrast, today's LAN technology allocates bandwidth by *contention*. Everybody is bidding with everybody else to obtain the use of the broadcast medium. To get on the LAN, you must either wait for a token (Token Ring) or start broadcasting; you must be prepared to back off if you detect a collision (Ethernet). Contention methods cannot guarantee deterministic response times (or delays). It's a matter of luck, and things get worse around rush-hour. The situation can be improved by assigning priorities, but there's still contention within the same priority levels.

Some of the new isochronous LAN technologies propose a *hybrid* environment that allocates a certain amount of bandwidth to contention traffic and gives the rest to virtual circuits. For example, isochronous FDDI, FDDI II, FFOL, and Ethernet allocate a certain percentage of the network bandwidth to multiple 64 kbit/s virtual circuits and give the remainder to normal contention-based data.

However, *purist* technologies, like ATM, only provide virtual circuits. ATM uses high-speed, hardware-based, circuit-switching technology that is potentially capable of unleashing an awesome amount of isochronous bandwidth at very low cost (every node is given its own dedicated LAN segment into the switch). ❑

The Network Operating System Middleware

The Network Operating System (NOS) Middleware:

■ ***Extends the local operating system's reach to include networked devices such as printers, file directories, and modem pools.*** These are the classical functions provided by network operating systems such as NetWare 3.1 and LAN Server 3.0.

■ ***Provides a distributed computing foundation that helps create a "single system" out of all the diverse resources distributed on the network.*** This includes directory services that provide a way to find things on the network, "federated" naming services that allow things to be uniquely named, distributed security and authentication services, a single logon, network time, and many others. These global services provide the distributed software infrastructure required for creating "intergalactic" client/server applications that span across multiple organizations within a company or across companies. The trick is for that infrastructure to attain this level of cohesion and trust *without sacrificing the autonomy of local administrative units*. This infrastructure is starting to appear in products like NetWare 4.0, Banyan Vines, and the OSF Distributed Computing Environment (DCE).

■ ***Supports the coordination of applications that are split across client/server lines***. Two types of client/server exchanges are supported: tightly-coupled request/reply interactions and loosely-coupled queue-based interactions. *Remote Procedure Calls (RPCs)* provide tightly-coupled interactions. They can invoke remote services using synchronous request/reply exchanges without having to worry about which transport protocol is used, how messages are exchanged, or how different machines represent their data (such as Little-Endian Intels and Big-Endian RISC). The OSF *Distributed Computing Environment (DCE)* and the Sun/USL *Open Network Computing (ONC)* provide two different RPC infrastructures. *Message-Oriented Middleware (or MOM)* is used for loosely-coupled exchanges of work packets across multiple operating systems. These queues can be very important to laptop users who are not always connected to the client/server network.

The basic NOS infrastructure is currently in place. The challenge is for organizations and programmers to absorb this new paradigm. They will need to relook at the world in distributed, cooperative, client/server terms. This is a difficult transition for people who come from a centralized-mainframe or single-user PC environment. How do you create and administer federations of peers? How are systems managed in intergalactic environments? The technology is here, but are our current organizations ready for it?

The Service-Specific Middleware

This is the most exciting area of client/server middleware. It deals with the avant-garde technologies that are not yet ripe for integration into the NOS. This is an area where the standards are still fluid and new structures are being discovered. It is also the area where all the new client/server applications are being created. Unfortunately, we can't discuss middleware without introducing a ton of acronyms. We will explain what they all mean later. The good news is that these acronyms show that some kind of multivendor infrastructure is in place.

We will look at five service-specific middleware standards:

- ■ **Database middleware** allows clients to invoke SQL-based services across multivendor databases. The database middleware is defined by "de facto" standards such as ODBC, IDAPI, DRDA, RDA, Oracle Glue, and SAG's CLI. These standards define a call level interface for SQL and address some of the issues of multivendor SQL interoperability "on the wire."

- ■ **Transactional RPC middleware** allows clients to invoke services across multiple transaction servers. TP Monitors allow the different servers to control their local resources and to cooperate with other TP Monitors when they need access to resources that are not local. The TP Monitors guarantee the integrity of all the activities within and across servers. The TP Monitor middleware consists of the transactional RPCs that allow clients to specify transactional boundaries and the interserver calls necessary to coordinate the multisite transaction. The "standards" in this area include Tuxedo's ATMI and /WS, Encina's Transactional RPC, and X/Open's TxRPC and XATMI.

- ■ **Groupware middleware** allows clients to invoke services on a groupware server. This is a new area where middleware standards are being created almost every day. The middleware "du jour" is MAPI and VIM in the area of electronic mail, VIC for group calendaring, and the Lotus Notes APIs for almost everything else.

- ■ **Object middleware** allows clients to invoke methods that reside on remote servers. The key middleware is the OMG's CORBA specification for interfacing to object request brokers (ORBs), the OMG's Object Services, and the ODMG-93 API set for interfacing to Object DBMSs.

- ■ **Distributed System management middleware** allows managing stations to talk to managed services. The current standards in this area are SNMP and CMIP.

In summary, it is becoming almost feasible to place data where it is needed, regardless of vendor platform. TP Monitors are making it easier to distribute function across network servers. Groupware is extending the frontiers of client/server to include people-to-people activities. And distributed objects today allow us to split applications at the object boundary level. As you will find out by reading this book, there is a rudimentary infrastructure in place for all these leading edge client/server technologies.

Server-to-Server Middleware

Middleware does not include the software that provides the actual service. It *does*, however, include the software that is used to coordinate inter-server interactions (see Figure 4-6). Server-to-server interactions are usually client/server in nature—servers are clients to other servers. However, some server-to-server interactions require specialized server middleware. For example, a two-phase commit protocol may be used to coordinate a transaction that executes on multiple servers. Servers on a mail backbone will use special server-to-server middleware for doing store-and-forward type messaging. But most modern software (even on operating system kernels) follows the client/server paradigm. And at least one TP Monitor (CSI/Bachman's Ellipse) goes as far as protecting the client's GUI state using the two-phase commit transactional discipline.

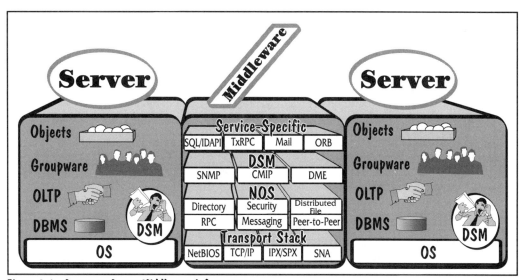

Figure 4-6. Server-to-Server Middleware Infrastructure.

CLIENT AND SERVER BUILDING BLOCKS REVISITED

The client and server building blocks are, of course, the other two major components in the client/server infrastructure. It takes all three to tango. Both the client and server sides require robust operating systems that are network savvy. And they both need distributed system management elements.

The client side of the application typically requires an operating system that provides a GUI. The client must be low cost and able to run personal applications. The client's middleware must also be able to make remote resources appear to be local.

The server side must be able to run generic server platforms such as SQL Database Servers, TP Monitors, Groupware, and Object Servers. It must also run the NOS services such as shared printers, files, modem pools, authentication services, and network directories. The server operating system must also be able to scale upwards in a manner that's transparent to the software.

It would be ideal if a single operating system could run both the client and server sides of the equation. It would simplify the infrastructure and allow us to concentrate on building function. But this is like saying that the airline industry would be in better shape if they didn't have to deal with airports in 200 or more countries. Airlines created their industry in a multinational world, and we have to create ours in a multivendor, multiorganizational world where the diversity of hardware and operating systems is a fact of life.

THE STATE OF THE CLIENT/SERVER INFRASTRUCTURE

> *MIS is the only group who can understand the implications of extending communications and strategic systems to customers and employees.*
>
> — *George Colony,*
> *President of Forrester Research Inc.*
> *(November, 1993)*

So what can we say about the state of the client/server infrastructure? The transport network is in place (with more coming). A vast physical "info-zone" is starting to connect the separate worlds of computers, telephones, and cable TV. As George Colony observes, "smart companies will take advantage of the connections to their customers, suppliers, and workers." This means that corporate enterprise networks will expand their coverage as the high-speed services reach out to smaller offices, homes, and mobile users.

The NOS distributed computing environment is more than adequate for creating applications that can span across multiple organizations and companies. We have a rudimentary infrastructure for managing client/server systems (based on the classical OSF DME model). The completed system management platform requires distributed object technology, which will not be available until late 1994 at the earliest.

The current crop of 32-bit commodity operating systems is quite capable of running the client and server sides of the equation. Our application server technology—including Database Servers, TP Monitors, Groupware, and Object Brokers—allows us to create very imaginative, high-quality client/server applications. And this is only the beginning; there is an awesome amount of application server technology on the horizon.

The most difficult question is: How to pick the client, server, and middleware building blocks that give you the biggest bang for the buck within the constraints of your budget? You're confronted with a wide variety of choices: the operating system, the GUI, the network protocol, the RPC, the NOS, the tools, and the database. And these are the easy choices. The more difficult choices are: Which competing technology is best: database servers, TP Monitors, groupware, or objects? When you get past these choices, you'll need to develop a mind-set that will help you seize the opportunities created by the client/server infrastructure. Using the airline analogy, now that we have the airports, planes, and control towers, where's the opportunity? For users the opportunity is cheap transcontinental travel and for entrepreneurs, the sky is the limit!

THE ROAD MAP FOR WHAT'S COMING

Figure 4-1 on page 50 is the road map we will follow in our client/server guide. You will need this map to navigate through the guide and see where we're going. You can't leave home without it. By now, you should be able to see the client/server picture at the "building block" level. Here's a preview of the coming attractions:

■ **Part 2** examines what our current crop of operating systems—including OS/2, Windows NT, Windows 3.X, Unix, and NetWare 4.X—can do can do for each side of the client/server equation.

■ **Part 3** explores the NOS and transport middleware substrate. We take a closer look at communication stacks such as TCP/IP, SNA, and NetBIOS. Then we look at the distributed computing environments created by NetWare, LAN Server, and DCE. We also look at message queuing middleware from Covia, PeerLogic, and Systems Strategies.

■ **Part 4** explores the database server model of client/server. In addition to middleware, we look at products such as DB2/2, Oracle7 for OS/2, and SQL Server. We also look at database gateways such as DDCS/2 and EDA/SQL.

■ **Part 5** explores the TP Monitor model of client/server. We dive into the great debate that's pitting the *TP Lite* model offered by the database servers against the *TP Heavy* model offered by TP Monitors. We explain why TP Monitors are needed in a world dominated by database servers. We then look at transactional middleware and products—CICS OS/2 V2 and Encina.

■ **Part 6** explores the groupware model of client/server. We look at the world of Lotus Notes and interpersonal applications. The groupware model shows us what client/server can really do—its paradigm goes much further than just recreating mainframe-like applications on PCs.

■ **Part 7** explores the distributed object model of client/server. We look at DOMs, CORBA, and Object Databases. We explore how object technology can be used to create a new generation of client/server information systems.

■ **Part 8** is about how to manage client/server applications. The biggest obstacle to the deployment of client/sever technology is the lack of integrated system management platforms. Fortunately, the situation is changing. We will look at some exciting frameworks that will "semi-automate" the management of client/server systems.

■ **Part 9** is about how to design, build, and deploy client/server applications. This part ends the survival journey and ties all the pieces together.

Part 2
Clients, Servers, and Operating Systems

An Introduction to Part 2

Now that you've got the bird's eye view of our planet, are you ready for some action? We've got a dangerous outing coming—did you bring your bullet-proof vests? Don't panic, you're in good hands. We're only going to cross an active war zone. No, it's not Yugoslavia. It's the client/server operating system wars and they're just as dangerous. But don't panic—we will do a lot of preparations for this journey. You'll live.

We start Part 2 with an overview of what clients and servers do in life and what they require from their operating systems. Then we pick an operating system—now *that's* dangerous living! As you may have guessed from the title of this book, we chose OS/2. We're not innocent onlookers any more. We've taken sides in the operating system war. To protect ourselves from the angry competition, we will do our homework and give you an overview of what OS/2—as a client and server platform—can do for you today. We then peek into the near future and look at all the heavy artillery that OS/2 is bringing into the battle: object frameworks and a heavy-duty microkernel.

All this preparation will serve as our bullet-proof vest. We're now ready to walk into the OS war zone waving our OS/2 flags. Oh boy! You'll feel the bullets coming right out of the book. On the client side, we'll face the Windows and DOS crowds. Then we'll hear from Macintosh, Windows NT, and the new breed of desktop Unix variants. On the server side, we'll face NetWare, the mighty NT, and a mob of Unix variants. You'll wish you never left Mars. But eventually we'll get through it, and you'll have a very good feel for the passion that surrounds the OS issues.

There's no right or wrong when it comes to OSs—it's one big balancing act with hundreds of shades of gray. Everything is fuzzy and constantly in flux. If you make the wrong decision or ride the wrong client/server wave, you simply go broke (or take the next spaceship back to Mars). This guide takes you through a simulated surf ride—like the ones in Paramount Studios—of what it's like to ride a wave all the way to the end. But you first have to pick the wave in order to ride it, which is why OS choices are important.

Some of the big players in client/server can afford to take a more secular view of OSs. They put out enough surf boards to ride all the waves at once and hedge their bets. We call that the "secular" school of client/server—or the "port to every platform" school. If you can afford to be secular, do it. Otherwise, read every page in Part 2 carefully. But be careful: we're only giving you a snapshot of what the market looks like as we go to press. You'll need to extrapolate the thinking to the new market conditions you'll face when you're ready to ride your wave. Happy surfing.

Chapter 5

Clients, Servers, and Operating Systems

---

*L*ook at every path closely and deliberately. Try it as many times as you think necessary. Then ask yourself, and yourself alone, one question...Does this path have a heart? If it does, the path is good; if it doesn't, it is of no use.

— *Carlos Castaneda,*
The Teachings of Don Juan

This chapter starts with a brief description of what typical clients and servers do in life. We then examine what each side of the client/server equation needs from an operating system. By the time you reach the end of this chapter, you should be better prepared to know what to look for in a client/server platform.

THE ANATOMY OF A SERVER PROGRAM

The role of a server program is to *serve* multiple clients who have an interest in a shared resource owned by the server. This section describes a day in the life of a typical server. Here's what a typical server program does:

■ *Waits for client-initiated requests*. The server program spends most of its time passively waiting on client requests, in the form of messages, to arrive over a communication session. Some servers assign a dedicated session to every client. Others create a dynamic pool of reusable sessions. Some also provide a mix of the two environments. Of course, to be successful, the server must always be responsive to its clients and be prepared for *rush hour traffic* when many clients will request services at the same time.

■ *Executes many requests at the same time*. The server program must do the work requested by the client promptly. Clearly a client should not have to depend on a single-threaded server process. A server program that does will run the risk of having a client hog all the system's resources and starve out its fellow clients. The server must be able to concurrently service multiple clients while protecting the integrity of shared resources.

■ *Takes care of VIP clients first*. The server program must be able to provide different levels of service priority to its clients. For example, a server can service a request for a report or batch job in low priority while maintaining OLTP-type responsiveness for high-priority clients.

■ *Initiates and runs background task activity*. The server program must be able to run background tasks triggered to perform chores unrelated to the main program's thrust. For example, it can trigger a task to download records from a host database during non-peak hours.

■ *Keeps running*. The server program is typically a mission-critical application. If the server goes down, it impacts all the clients that depend on its services. The server program and the environment on which it runs must be very robust.

■ *Grows bigger and fatter*. Server programs seem to have an insatiable appetite for memory and processing power. The server environment must be upwardly scalable and modular.

WHAT DOES A SERVER NEED FROM AN OS?

In distributed computing environments, operating system functions are either *base* or *extended* services. The base services are part of the standard operating system, while the extended services are add-on modular software components that are layered on top of the base services. Functionally equivalent extended services are usually provided by more than one vendor. There is no hard rule that determines what gets bundled in the base operating system and what goes into the extensions. Today's extensions are usually good candidates for tomorrow's base system services.

Base Services

It should be apparent from the previous description that server programs exhibit a high level of concurrency. Ideally, a separate task will be assigned to each of the clients the server is designed to concurrently support. Task management is best done by a multitasking operating system. Multitasking is the natural way to simplify the coding of complex applications that can be divided into a collection of discrete and logically distinct, concurrent tasks. It improves the performance, throughput, modularity, and responsiveness of server programs. Multitasking also implies the existence of mechanisms for intertask coordination and information exchanges.

Servers also require a high level of concurrency within a single program. Server code will run more efficiently if tasks are allocated to parts of the same program rather than to separate programs (these tasks are called coroutines or threads). Tasks within the same program are faster to create, faster to context switch, and have easier access to shared information. Figure 5-1 shows the type of support that servers require from their operating system. Let's go over these server requirements starting with the bottom layer and working our way up.

■ *Task Preemption*. An operating system with preemptive multitasking must allot fixed time slots of execution to each task. Without preemptive multitasking, a task must voluntarily agree to give up the processor before another task can run. It is much safer and easier to write multitasking server programs in environments where the operating system automatically handles all the task switching.

■ *Task Priority*. An operating system must dispatch tasks based on their priority. This feature allows servers to differentiate the level of service based on their client's priority.

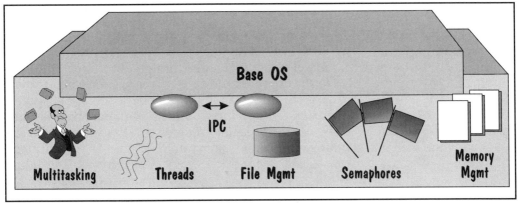

Figure 5-1. What Server Programs Expect From Their Operating System.

■ **Semaphores**. An operating system must provide simple synchronization mechanisms for keeping concurrent tasks from bumping into one another when accessing shared resources. These mechanisms, known as semaphores, are used to synchronize the actions of independent server tasks and alert them when some significant event occurs.

■ **Interprocess Communications (IPC)**. An operating system must provide the mechanisms that allow independent processes to exchange and share data.

■ **Local/Remote Interprocess Communications**. An operating system must allow the transparent redirection of interprocess calls to a remote process over a network without the application being aware of it. The extension of the interprocess communications across machine boundaries is key to the development of applications where resources and processes can be easily moved across machines (i.e., they allow servers to grow bigger and fatter).

■ **Threads**. These are units of concurrency provided within the program itself. Threads are used to create very concurrent, event-driven server programs. Each waiting event can be assigned to a thread that blocks until the event occurs. In the meantime, other threads can use the CPU's cycles productively to perform useful work.

■ **Intertask Protection**. The operating system must protect tasks from interfering with each other's resources. A single task must not be able to bring down the entire system. Protection also extends to the file system and calls to the operating system.

■ **Multiuser High Performance File System**. The file system must support multiple tasks and provide the locks that protect the integrity of the data. Server programs typically work on many files at the same time. The file system must support large number of open files without too much deterioration in performance.

■ **Efficient Memory Management**. The memory system must efficiently support very large programs and very large data objects. These programs and data objects must be easily swapped to and from disk preferably in small granular blocks.

■ **Dynamically Linked Runtime Extensions**. The operating system services should be extendable. A mechanism must be provided to allow services to grow at run time without recompiling the operating system.

Extended Services

The extended services must provide the advanced system software that will exploit the distributed potential of networks, provide flexible access to shared information, and make the system easier to manage and maintain. It should also make it easier for independent software vendors (ISVs) and system integrators to create new server applications. Figure 5-2 shows some of the extended services server programs expect from their operating system. We will go over these expectations, starting from the bottom layer and working our way up. Some of these expectations read more like wish lists. They will eventually find their way into most operating systems.

■ **_Ubiquitous Communications_**. The operating system extensions must provide a rich set of communications protocol stacks that allow the server to communicate with the greatest number of client platforms. In addition, the server should be able to communicate with other server platforms in case it needs assistance in providing services.

■ **_Network Operating System Extensions_**. The operating system extensions must provide facilities for extending the file and print services over the network. Ideally, the applications should be able to transparently access any remote device (such as printers and files) as if they were local.

■ **_Binary Large Objects (BLOBs)_**. Images, video, graphics, intelligent documents, and database snapshots are about to test the capabilities of our operating systems, databases, and networks. These large objects (affectionately called BLOBs) require operating system extensions such as intelligent message streams and object representation formats. Networks must be prepared to move and transport these large BLOBs at astronomic speeds. Databases and file systems must be prepared to store those BLOBs and provide access to them. Protocols are needed for the exchange of BLOBs across systems and for associating BLOBs with programs that know what to do when they see one.

■ **_Global Directories and Network Yellow Pages_**. The operating system extensions must provide a way for clients to locate servers and their services on the network using a network directory yellow page type of service. Network resources must be found by name. Servers must be able to dynamically register their services with the directory provider.

■ **_Authentication and Authorization Services_**. The operating system extensions must provide a way for clients to prove to the server that they are who they claim to be. The authorization system determines if the authenticated client has the permission to obtain a remote service.

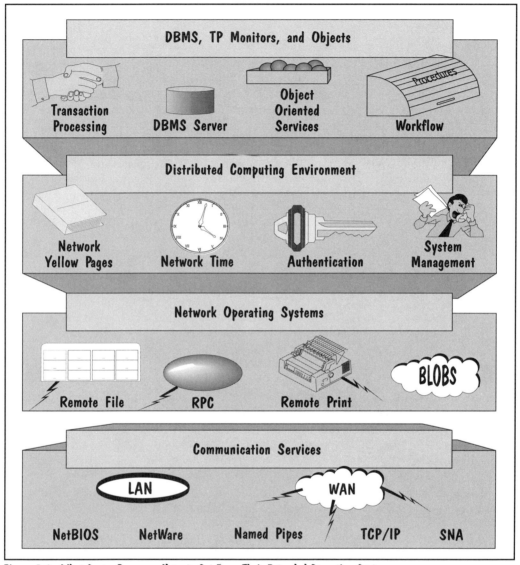

Figure 5-2. What Server Programs Hope to Get From Their Extended Operating Systems.

■ *System Management*. The operating system extensions must provide an integrated network and system management platform. The system should be managed as a single server or as multiple servers assigned to domains. An enterprise view that covers multiple domains must be provided for servers that play in the big leagues. System management includes services for configuring a system, facilities for monitoring the performance of all elements, generating alerts when things break, distributing and managing software packages on client workstations, checking for viruses and intruders, and metering capabilities for pay-as-you-use server resources.

■ *Network Time*. The operating system extensions must provide a mechanism for clients and servers to synchronize their clocks. This time should be coordinated with some universal time authority.

■ *Database and Transaction Services*. The operating system extensions must provide a robust Multiuser Database Management System (DBMS). This DBMS should ideally support SQL for decision support and server-stored procedures for transaction services. The server-stored procedures are created outside the operating system by programmers. More advanced functions include a *Transaction Processing Monitor (TP Monitor)* for managing stored procedures (or transactions) as atomic units of work that execute on one or more servers.

■ *Object-Oriented Services*. This is an area where extended services will flourish for a long time to come. Services are becoming more object-oriented. The operating system will be required to provide "object broker" services that allow any object to interact with any other object across the network. The operating system will also have to provide object interchange services and object repositories. Client/Server applications of the future will be between communicating objects (in addition to communicating processes). Object groups will come together in loose associations to provide a service. The Object Management Group (OMG) is working on an architecture that allows objects to communicate across networks, hardware platforms, and operating systems.

As you can see extended does mean "extended." It covers the universe of current and future services needed to create distributed client/server environments. No current operating system bundles all the extended functions. Most can be purchased *a la carte* from more than one vendor.

THE ANATOMY OF A CLIENT PROGRAM

Client/Server applications are *client-centric*. The client side provides the "look and feel" for the services a system provides. All client applications have this in common: they request the services of a server. What makes client applications different is what triggers the requests and what Graphical User Interface (GUI), if any, is needed. Based on these differences, we can classify clients into three categories: *Non-GUI Clients*, *GUI Clients*, and *OOUI Clients* (see Figure 5-3).

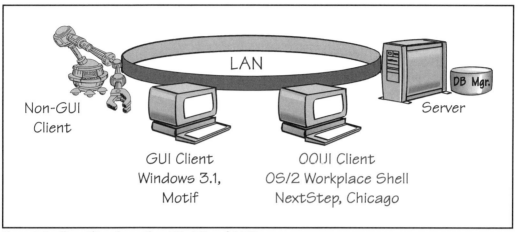

Figure 5-3. Three Client Types: Non-GUI, GUI, and OOUI.

Non-GUI Clients

Non-GUI client applications generate server requests with a minimal amount of human interaction (see Figure 5-4). Non-GUI clients fall into two sub-categories:

■ ***Non-GUI clients that do not need multitasking.*** Examples include automatic teller machines (ATMs), barcode readers, cellular phones, fax machines, smart gas pumps, and intelligent clipboards (future). These clients may provide a simple human interface in the request generation loop.

■ ***Non-GUI clients that need multitasking.*** Examples include robots, testers, and daemon programs. These clients often require very granular, real-time, event-driven multitasking services.

GUI Clients

Simple GUI Clients are applications where occasional requests to the server result from a human interacting with a GUI. The simple GUI interface is a good fit for mainstream, OLTP-type business applications with repetitive tasks and high volumes. They also make good front-end clients to database servers. Simple GUI client applications are graphical renditions of the dialogs that previously ran on dumb terminals. GUIs replace the "green screen uglies" with graphic dialogs, color, menu bars, scroll boxes, and pull-down and pop-up windows (see Figure 5-5). Simple GUI dialogs use the object/action model where users can select objects and then select the actions to be performed on the chosen objects. Most dialogs are serial in nature.

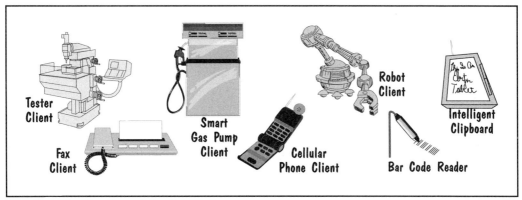

Figure 5-4. The Many Faces of Non-Gui Clients.

This model of user interaction is predominantly used in Windows 3.X and OSF Motif applications. It is also known as the CUA 89 graphical model.

Object Oriented User Interface (OOUI) Clients

The *Object Oriented User Interface (OOUI)* metaphor is used to provide what Microsoft Chairman Bill Gates calls *information at your fingertips*. This "universal client" interface is a highly-iconic, object-oriented user interface that provides seamless access to information in very visual formats.[1] OOUIs are used by information workers doing multiple, variable tasks whose sequence cannot be predicted. Examples include executive and decision-support applications, multimedia based training systems, system management consoles, and stockbroker workstations. OOUIs have an insatiable appetite for communications. OOUI desktop objects need to communicate among themselves and with external servers. The communications are, by necessity, real time, interactive, and highly concurrent.

Examples of OOUIs are the OS/2 Workplace Shell, NextStep, and Macintosh. Current OOUIs provide a visual desktop metaphor (think of it as an arcade game) where related objects and programs can be brought together to perform a task. The desktop can contain multiple workplaces running concurrently (see Figure 5-6). Each workplace may be running parallel dialogs, also called *modeless dialogs*, over parallel sessions with the server. With advanced multimedia-type applications, these parallel dialogs may be used to display images, video, multiobject folders, and

---

[1] The term "Universal Client" was coined by Gartner Group. They define it as "a personal information appliance that helps people get and understand information they need, wherever it may be, and to communicate it with other people." Source: **Client/Server Computing: Exploiting the Inevitable**, Gartner Group (February 12, 1992).

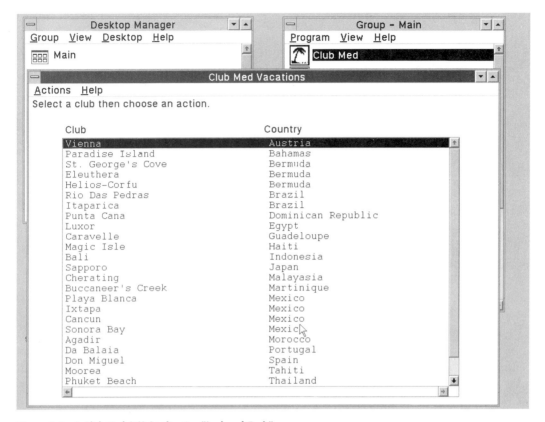

Figure 5-5. A Club Med GUI Application "Look and Feel."

voice annotated mail. Information is displayed to the user in the foreground windows, while background tasks are constantly moving information to and from servers. For example, the first page from a multimedia document is displayed in a window while a background task is busy prefetching the rest of the document from the server.

OS/2's Workplace Shell OOUI, for example, supports the following features:

■ The direct manipulation of iconic objects through mouse *drag and drop* techniques
■ Advanced interobject communications using Named Pipes, DDE, and SOM
■ Parallel dialogs over concurrent information channels

OOUIs focus on the objects required to accomplish a task. OOUIs provide folders, workareas, shadows, and associations that allow users to personalize their desktops and manage their objects. OOUIs provide a common metaphor for creating,

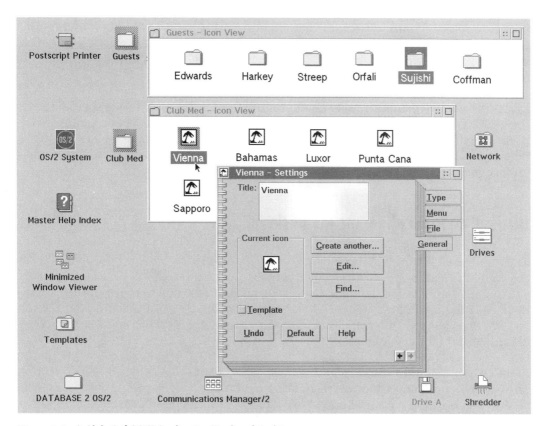

Figure 5-6. A Club Med OOUI Application "Look and Feel."

copying, moving, connecting, and deleting any object on the desktop. One of the major features of OOUIs is the concept of multiple views of objects.

GUI VERSUS OOUI: A CLOSER LOOK

OOUIs allow users to work with objects that are representative of the environment they work in, rather than objects the computer understands.

> — *Theo Mandel*
> *The GUI-OOUI War:*
> *Windows vs. OS/2 (VNR, 1994)*

The style of the user interface is an important issue for the client desktop. It defines the paradigm by which many applications can share a screen in a multitasking networked environment. Currently, the OS/2 Workplace Shell and NextStep are the best examples of "pure" OOUIs. The Macintosh is a hybrid—its "look and feel" is OOUI, but its underlying structure is mostly GUI. But Apple, with its OpenDoc strategy, is rapidly moving toward a document-centered OOUI approach. And, the future Taligent and Chicago Interfaces will be OOUIs.

In this section we examine, in some depth, the features of OOUIs as represented by the OS/2 Workplace Shell. We compare the OOUIs with the more familiar GUI paradigm of Microsoft Windows 3.X. Much of the look and feel of GUIs and OOUIs may seem the same on the surface, but the main difference lie in the models underlying the interface.

OOUI: A New Paradigm for the Desktop?

The familiar GUI paradigm defines an *application-centered* user interface. This is the familiar Windows 3.X desktop in which a user interacts with a computer by starting an application from a list of programs (or icons representing them) displayed in a window. The OOUI paradigm, on the other hand, defines an *object-centered* user interface that lets users interact with the computer by manipulating visual business objects.

In an OOUI, the application is transparent to the user. The desktop is a collection of objects (icons) and windows associated with those objects, as opposed to GUIs, where the desktop is a collection of windows or icons representing windows associated with applications. In OOUI environments, the user interacts with objects rather than with the operating system or with separate programs. The interaction has the same look and feel across all tasks.

In a GUI, the icons on the screen represent operating system constructs like programs and files. In an OOUI, the icons represent business objects that have a relationship with other objects on the desktop. The OOUI is a simulation of how users interact with objects in real life. It is a computer visual of the real life situation. OOUIs are closer to arcade games.

OOUI: Object Types

An object is a visual component with which a user can work, independently of other items, to perform a task. An object can be represented by one or more graphic images, called icons. The user can interact with an object (or its icon) just as the user can interact with objects in the real world. The OS/2 Workplace Shell supports three types of visual objects:

The Future Is OOUI

Soapbox

An OOUI utilizes a GUI for its set of componentry but adds to it significant semantic content on the meaning of objects and user gestures.

— *John Tibbets*
Keynote Address, OOPSLA 1991

OOUIs are the up-and-coming trend in user interfaces. The next generation of Windows from Microsoft—Chicago and Cairo—is rumored to be "pure" OOUI. Why is Microsoft going OOUI when it has the world's most popular GUI product? Can the answer have something to do with "information at your fingertips" or is it related to multimedia data types? Taligent's interface is also rumored to be pure OOUI. And a future version of COSE will move the "unified" Unix desktop to OOUI (but not in the first release). So why is everybody moving to OOUI?

OOUIs provide a more natural front end for client/server applications. They provide the *framework* for integrating objects from different vendors at the visual level. OOUIs are the visual part of the object paradigm. Visual objects will replace application suites as the way to integrate the desktop. Applications, as we currently know them, will no longer be built. Instead, software will be provided as object *components* that plug-and-play into an OOUI *framework*.

OOUIs offer many benefits to end users and to object component vendors. If you want to get the inside scoop on the "GUI versus OOUI," we recommend Theo Mandel's excellent book, **The GUI-OOUI War: Windows Versus OS/2** (VNR, 1994). You'll get a cognitive psychologist's viewpoint of how humans interact with computer user interfaces, and you'll also learn the relative "psychological" merits of OOUI versus GUI. Our opinion (we're on the soapbox, remember) is that once you start using an OOUI, there's no going back to GUIs.

So why aren't OOUIs everywhere? This is Theo Mandel's answer: "Probably the biggest drawback to the OS/2 Workplace Shell and the OOUI is that it really requires a paradigm shift from many of today's GUI products. It is a strange situation, but because the popular GUIs don't mirror the real world very well, it takes time for users of these systems to get used to something that more closely matches the way they work in the real world. Strange but true!" ❏

■ **Container Objects** are used to organize your "working objects." A container can store any other object including containers. The Workplace Shell provides a standard container called the *folder* whose icon looks like a manila folder. Folders are used as desktop organizers. The folder is "passive" in nature; it simply stores objects and allows them to be opened (or started) from within it.

■ **Data Objects** contain text, graphics, audio, video, or tabular information. Data objects can contain other objects. For example, a folder can contain database objects.

■ **Device Objects** often represent a physical device in the real world such as telephones, mailboxes, and printers. Some devices represent logical objects. For example, a shredder object can represent a logical object that disposes of other objects. Device objects can also contain other objects. For example, a printer object can contain a queue of objects to be printed.

OOUIs: Views of Objects

A view is simply a way of looking at what's inside an object (i.e., its information). The user opens the object, usually by double-clicking on the icon, to get to the different views that lurk beneath its iconic surface. An object can have more than one view type. The OS/2 Workplace Shell supports four types of views:

■ **Composed Views** arrange the object's data in a structure that conveys the data's meaning. Examples include a directory tree structure or a city map with blinking red squares that denote the five-star restaurants.

■ **Contents Views** display the components of an object in lists or tabular formats. OS/2 provides three kinds of contents views: 1) *Icon Views*, which display each object as an icon that can be directly manipulated by the user; 2) *Details Views*, which combine small icons with text to provide additional information about objects; and 3) *Tree Views*, which display icons and text in a hierarchical format.

■ **Settings Views** display information about the characteristics, attributes, or properties of an object, and provide a way for the user to change the settings of some characteristics or properties. A settings view is typically provided for each type of object in the form of a notebook.

■ **Help Views** display information that can assist the user in working with an object.

OOUIs: Object Templates

In the OOUI environment, the users do not load programs. In fact, they're not even supposed to know what a program is. So how does anybody get any work done without programs running on a desktop? You work with objects, of course. OK, but how are these objects created? Where do they come from? The Workplace Shell provides some predefined system objects like clocks, games, shredders, and so on. The user supplements these objects with "user objects" that they create by cloning a template of an existing object. A *template* is object terminology for a cookie cutter. Instead of creating cookies, it creates identical objects. Where does the user get these templates from? The Workplace Shell provides a special folder called the *templates folder*. This folder is your "object factory." Users "tear off" templates from the templates folder and drag them to the folder or desktop area where they want to work (see Figure 5-7). *Who creates these object templates?* The software component providers who create specialized *objectware* for a living.

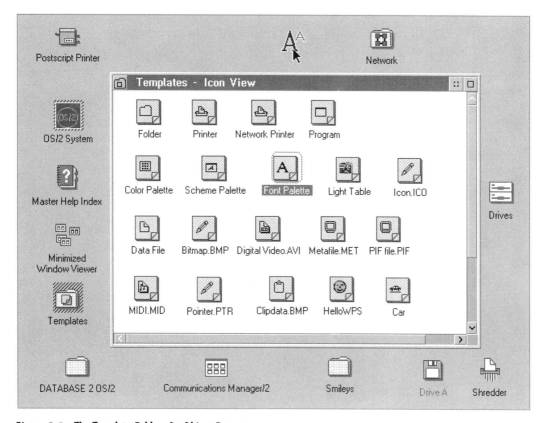

Figure 5-7. The Template Folder: An Object Factory.

So how does this objectware plug into the Workplace Shell? It is supplied to users in the form of a Dynamic Link Library (DLL) that gets placed in a subdirectory. After that is done, the new object class will automagically appear in the *templates folder* the next time it is opened. For the users, it's all fun and games from then on: *cookie cutting and cloning objects.*

OOUIs: Interacting With Objects

Most objects on the Workplace Shell have pop-up menus (also called context menus) that appear next to an object when the user presses the appropriate mouse button (see Figure 5-8). The pop-up menu tells shows the user the set of actions an object is capable of performing in its current state. The interaction with an object through menus is called *indirect manipulation.*

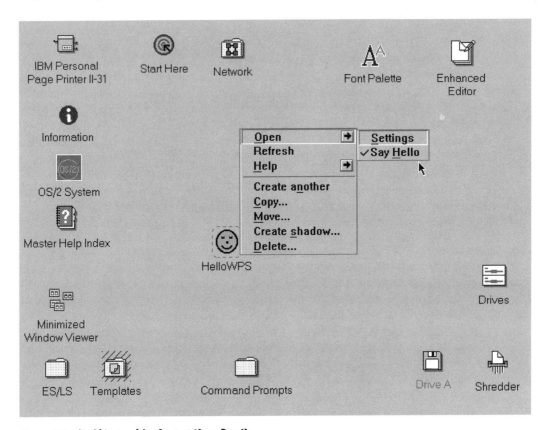

Figure 5-8. An Object and Its Context Menu Pop-Up.

The other way to interact with objects is by *direct object manipulation*, a technique that allows objects to have actions directly performed on them. This technique gives the user the freedom to carry out some functions without a menu. A mouse is used to *drag* an object and *drop* it on its target. For example, the user can pick up an object and put it into a folder or FAX it to the next continent. This computer simulation of the way users interact with real world objects is known as "drag and drop." Direct manipulation frees the user from language and makes applications more graphic. It provides a good fit with object-orientation and the OOUI paradigm, but there are some pitfalls (see Warning box that follows).

OOUIs will encourage applications to become less monolithic and evolve into sets of objects or the tools that manipulate existing objects. For example, the OS/2 version of Lotus *cc:Mail* does not feel like a single application. It acts more like a seamless extension of the Workplace Shell. Lotus cc:Mail provides in-box and out-box icons for receiving and sending mail. The mail containers are ordinary Workplace Shell folders. Any object in the Workplace Shell can be mail-enabled by adding the mail action to its pop-pup menu. Or the object can be simply dragged and dropped onto the out-box icon. Junk mail can be disposed of by a simple drag and drop onto the OS/2 Workplace Shell shredder. So where does cc:Mail start and the Workplace Shell end? They've merged!

The Pitfalls of Direct Manipulation

Warning

Currently, some of the pitfalls associated with direct manipulation are:

- Some actions are impossible to specify with any precision.
- Actions with more than two objects are difficult.
- Some of the graphic metaphors are *overly stretched* and may end up confusing the user.
- Icons drawn by amateurs may not be recognizable to the user.
- Highly iconic interfaces make inflexible database front ends. The current relational paradigm for database is centered around alphanumeric data tables. The most flexible front end to such a database is a tabular view of rows and columns of alphanumeric information. Custom graphics, however, can be hand-tailored to create very visual database front ends that are application-specific. ❑

OOUI: Primary and Pop-Up Windows

The Workplace Shell recognizes only two types of windows: Primary and Pop-Up. In OOUIs, windows are just a way to look inside objects; they provide views. Here's what the two window types do:

- **Primary Windows** present the user with object choices, a menu bar, and pull-down menus. OOUIs treat primary windows as mere windows into objects. The heart of the application is the collection of user objects. In GUIs, on the other hand, every application must have a primary window that serves as the main focal point of the user's activity. Primary windows in GUI applications persist throughout the life of an application.

- **Pop-Up Windows** present the user with choices that are supportive of the primary window or the object. In GUIs, secondary windows were used to conduct parallel dialogs with users. This is not needed in OOUIs because the dialog is conducted with the object, and parallel dialogs are simply dialogs that involve more than one object.

Application Features: GUI Versus OOUI

The best way to compare GUIs and OOUIs is to put the two side-by-side and contrast some of their features. Let's go back to Figures 5-5 and 5-6, the GUI and OOUI vintages of our Club Med application.[2] By just looking at these two pictures, can you tell what the OOUI fuss is all about?

■ The OOUI Club Med is an extension of the Workplace Shell. You can't tell where the application starts and OS/2 ends. They appear to be seamlessly integrated. The clubs on the Workplace Shell look like any other object.

■ The OOUI Club Med invites the user to manipulate the visual Club Med objects through drag-and-drop. For example, a transaction may be triggered by dragging a guest object to the shredder to delete it. Or, if we want to be kind, we'll drop it on the FAX machine icon to send a confirmation of the reservation.

■ The OOUI Club Med icon can be opened at any time to reveal a notebook view of the information inside it. The notebook control makes it possible to visually staple together many dialog windows and let the user find the information needed. This is a giant step forward for OLTP-type of applications.

■ The OOUI Club Med setup will reappear the way the user left it when the machine is turned on again. The desktop configuration is persistent.

■ The OOUI Club Med is very familiar, especially to kids. It feels like a video game. Kids feel quite at home with drag and drop, icons, and direct manipulation. The OOUI is a simulation of reality that they can easily recognize. Can we say the same about adults?

■ The OOUI Club Med can be extended to seamlessly work with any other OOUI object and with very little new code. We could easily think of mail-enabling it or allowing scanned pages to be dragged into the notebook view. The OLTP transaction is starting to look more like its real-world counterpart.

■ The GUI Club Med, on the other hand, is your typical WIMP (Windows, Icons, Mouse, and Pointer) interface. The icon is just there to represent the application to the desktop. You're not invited to play with it. You start the application by clicking on the icon. From then on, you're in menu land. The user is quite aware that there is a running Club Med application.

Table 5-1 provides a quick summary of the features that distinguish OOUIs from GUIs.

---

[2] The GUI Club Med was developed in the first edition of our book **Client/Server Programming with OS/2**. The OOUI Club Med was developed for the second and third editions of the same book. It's a true Workplace Shell application.

Table 5-1. GUI Versus OOUI.

Feature	Graphical User Interface (GUI)	Object-Oriented User Interface (OOUI)
Application structure	A graphic application consists of an icon, a primary window with a menu bar, and one or more secondary windows. The focus is on the main task. Ancillary tasks are supported by secondary windows and pop-ups. Users must follow the rigid task structure (and may get trapped in a task). An application represents a task.	A graphic application consists of a collection of cooperating user objects. Everything that you see is an object. Each object is represented by an icon and has at least one view. Objects can be reused in many tasks. The application's boundaries are fuzzy. The user defines what's an application by assembling a collection of objects. These objects may come from one or more programs and are integrated with the desktop objects the system provides (like printers and shredders). The users can innovate and create their own "lego-like" object collections.
Icons	Icons represent a running application.	Icons represent objects that may be directly manipulated.
Starting an application	Users start applications before selecting an object to work with.	Users open the object on the desktop, which causes a window view of the object to be displayed.
Windows	Users open a primary window and then specify the objects they want to interact with. The same window can be used to display other objects.	A window is a view of what's inside an object. There is a one-to-one relationship between a window and an object.
Menus	Menus provide the primary method for navigating within an application.	Each object has a context menu. You navigate within an application or across applications by directly manipulating objects. The desktop functions as one big menu; icons represent the objects that you can manipulate.
Dialogs	The application leads the user through a series of dialog windows.	In addition to dialog windows, new CUA'91 controls like the notebook may contain a collection of dialogs. The user controls the dialog by flipping pages.
Active application visual	Icons represent minimized windows of active applications.	Icons are augmented with the *in-use* emphasis to represent an active object.
Direct manipulation	An application may provide direct manipulation on an ad hoc basis.	Objects are created, communicated with, moved, and manipulated through drag-and-drop manipulation.

Table 5-1. GUI Versus OOUI. (Continued)

Feature	Graphical User Interface (GUI)	Object-Oriented User Interface (OOUI)
Creating new objects	Objects are created in an application-specific manner, usually through some form of copy mechanism or using the menu choices: new or open.	A templates folder contains a template for every object type. To create a new instance of an object, drag its template to where you want the new object to reside.
Actions	Choose object; then choose action from menu bar.	In addition to choosing actions from menus, a user can drag objects to icons to perform operations, for example, drag a file to a printer icon.
Containers	Text-based list boxes provides the primary form of containment.	In addition to list boxes, CUA'91 defines new container objects, including folders and notebooks. These in turn can contain other objects. Actions performed on container objects affect all the objects inside them.
Focus	Focus is on the main task.	Focus is on active objects and tasks.
Related tasks	Related tasks are supported by other applications or product suites using DDE, OLE, and OpenDoc.	Related tasks are supported by communicating objects using DDE, OLE, OpenDoc, Direct Manipulation, and Object Request Brokers (ORBs).
Closing an application	No desktop information is retained.	The visual state and settings of an application are saved. The application will restart where you left off.
Who is in Control?	Control alternates between the user and the application.	All the applications behave the same and the user acts as the conductor. Think of the user as the visual programmer of the desktop.
Product Examples	Windows and Motif	OS/2 Workplace Shell, NextStep, Macintosh and the future Chicago and Taligent.

WHAT DOES A CLIENT NEED FROM AN OS?

Each of the three types of clients described here place a different set of requirements on the operating system. These requirements are listed in Table 5-2. As you can see, all client applications need some mechanism to communicate service requests and files to a server. All three client categories will function best in a robust, multitasking environment. It is particularly important for the client environment to be robust because it is impossible for system providers to test the client software on all possible hardware/software combinations (you can't dictate what people run on their PCs). It is important to use an operating system that can protect programs from clashing and crashing. No client program should cause the system to hang (requiring a reboot).

Table 5-2. What Does a Client Need From an OS?

Requirement from an OS	Non-GUI Client		Simple GUI Client	OOUI Client
	Without Multitasking	**With Multitasking**		
Request/reply mechanism (preferably with local/remote transparency)	Yes	Yes	Yes	Yes
File transfer mechanism to move pictures, text, database snapshots	Yes	Yes	Yes	Yes
Preemptive multitasking	No	Yes	Desirable	Yes
Task Priorities	No	Yes	Desirable	Yes
Interprocess communications	No	Yes	Desirable	Yes
Threads for background communications with server and receiving callbacks from servers	No	Yes	Yes (unless you like the hourglass icon)	Yes
OS robustness including intertask protection and reentrant OS calls	No	Yes	Desirable	Yes
Window 3.X GUI (CUA '89 vintage) with menus, scroll bars, and so on	No	No	Yes	Yes
OOUI framework, object-based interactions, drag and drop, multimedia support, OS/2 Workplace Shell, or NextStep vintage	No	No	No	Yes

GUI and OOUI clients work best with a thread-like mechanism for handling the background requests. By using separate threads for the user interface and background processing, the program can respond to user input while a separate thread handles the interaction with the server. This is how GUIs avoid the notorious "hourglass" icon, a sure sign that the computing environment is not keeping up with the human. Threads also help clients respond to asynchronous calls from a server (callback). Priority-based preemptive multitasking is also required to respond to multimedia devices and to create client applications where multiple dialogs are displayed in parallel.

CLIENT/SERVER HYBRIDS

Another point to consider is that the industry is moving beyond the pure client/server model. This is because more intelligence (and data) is moving onto the client. Database clients keep snapshots of tables locally. TP Monitor clients coordinate multiserver transactions. Groupware clients maintain queues. Multimedia clients check-in and check-out folders. And distributed object clients accept requests from objects anywhere. These "new age" clients must provide a "server lite" function—an interim step toward fulfilling the post-scarcity vision of a full client and server function on every machine.

A "server lite" function is a thread, queue, or background process on the client machine that can accept *unsolicited* network requests—usually from a server. For example, a server may call its clients to synchronize locks on a long duration transaction, refresh a database snapshot, or recall a checked-out multimedia document. A "server lite" (as opposed to a full-blown server) does not need to support concurrent access to shared resources, load balancing, or multithreaded communications. We call clients that provide a "server lite" function *hybrids* (as opposed to pure).

Chapter 6

What OS/2 Brings to Client/Server

You will rarely find an unconnected OS/2 system.

— **Art Olbert, IBM Director of LAN Systems**

This chapter examines what OS/2 offers each side of the client/server equation. A client/server platform on PCs must meet most of the requirements we listed in the last chapter. The PC platform must provide a robust operating system that supports multitasking, a multiuser database engine, and LAN communications. The server should be able to handle concurrent requests from clients with minimal performance degradations. The client must be robust, must be capable of running concurrent tasks, and must provide a highly graphical user interface. The bottom line is that client/server solutions on PCs must provide the same level of service as multiuser superminis while maintaining the autonomy of the client PCs.

OS/2 AS A CLIENT PLATFORM

OS/2 provides the almost *ideal client platform for the PC world*. Compared to other advanced client platforms, OS/2's resource requirements fall into the "modest" category. OS/2 can run comfortably on the very large installed base of Intel 386 and 486 PCs. Here are some of the highlights of what OS/2 has to offer on the client side of the equation:

■ OS/2 lets multiple applications run concurrently while providing the necessary protection so that they don't bump into each other. It helps insulate the providers of client software from the vagaries of the desktop. Remember, you can't dictate what people run on their PCs. So you need all the protection an operating system can provide to keep client workstations up and running and to identify the errant culprits.

■ OS/2 provides an integrated environment for running DOS, Windows, and OS/2 applications. The Workplace Shell makes the desktop appear seamless to the end user; it even supports cut and paste between MS-DOS, MS-Windows, and OS/2 applications. The 32-bit Presentation Manager engine provides state-of-the-art GUI services (see Figure 6-1).

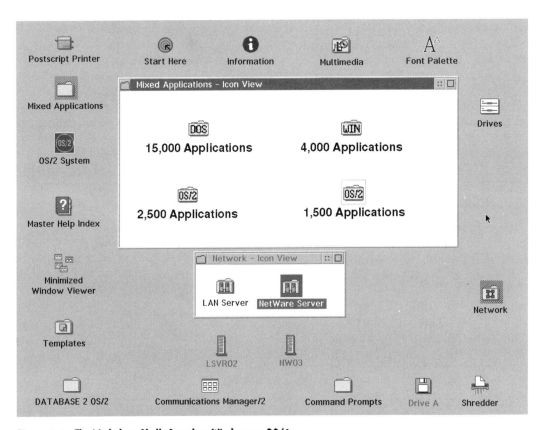

Figure 6-1. The Workplace Shell: Seamless Windows on OS/2.

■ OS/2 supports more shrink-wrapped applications than any other operating system. It does that by running MS-DOS, MS-Windows, 16-bit OS/2, and 32-bit OS/2 applications right out of the box (see Figure 6-1).

■ OS/2 creates a seamless client desktop (see Figure 6-1) environment where all the network services—including Printers, e-mail, File Server Directories, and Decision Support Tools—appear as groups of *smart icons*. Network services on LAN Server, LAN Manager, NetWare, and Vines servers are obtained by clicking on icons. Users can move business objects across networks by simply grabbing an icon and dropping it on the appropriate destination icon.

■ OS/2 provides superb built-in multimedia player facilities for video, sound, and animation. OS/2's preemptive multitasking supports the deterministic throughput requirements for synchronizing digital video and sound. Your PC should also be able to grab off the network a voice message or a movie clip in real time (in the background) while you're using it in the foreground. OS/2's paged memory supports very large data objects in memory, which is an important requirement for multimedia applications.

■ OS/2 provides the hooks for managing client applications. You can never get enough system management in networked client applications; they can fail in the most sadistic ways. OS/2's background tasks are ideal for running system management agents on the client PCs. These agents report failures, react to events, and provide service to network management stations using protocols such as SNMP, CMIP, and MIBs.

■ OS/2 provides LAN-based, unattended installation support. OS/2 can be remotely installed from a LAN-based code server. OS/2 provides the hooks to allow software (including OS/2 itself) to be automatically installed and distributed to client machines. The installation can be done in either a lightly attended or unattended mode. Most OS/2 system software is enabled for automated LAN-based installation using OS/2's NTS/2 services.

■ OS/2 provides a "laptop-friendly" environment. Mobile clients enhance the reach of client/server applications by making it easier to capture transactions wherever they occur. OS/2 provides power-saving support for notebook and laptop computers that implement the Advanced Power Management (APM) specifications. OS/2 also supports the credit-card size adapters that use the new PCMCIA bus standard. In addition, OS/2's Remote Access Services products (for example LAN Distance) allow mobile clients to remotely access LAN-based servers.

It is hard (if not impossible) for any operating system platform to beat OS/2's robust and seamless integration of all DOS, MS-Windows, and OS/2 environments in its Workplace Shell. OS/2's preemptive multitasking is exactly what's needed for networked client applications. When multimedia finally gets on the network, these advanced preemptive facilities will become even more essential. The bulk of PC LAN clients may initially be DOS and Windows machines. As LAN-based applications grow more sophisticated, many of these machines will be replaced with OS/2's all-in-one client environment. The more adventurous are already there.

OS/2 AS A SERVER PLATFORM

OS/2 servers provide minicomputer power at PC prices. The 32-bit OS/2 on a Pentium processor has the power of a minicomputer, both in terms of brute processor speed and system software sophistication through features like preemptive multitasking, multithreading, and built-in memory protection. OS/2 is in many ways a modern variant of Unix; however, it is not encumbered by a debt to history. OS/2 combines the best of Unix, Windows 3.X, and DOS and brings it to the market as a shrink-wrapped operating system package. OS/2's communications and database offerings are very similar to their Unix counterparts. They are almost always easier to install, use, and manage. And, as a rule, they are much less expensive.

OS/2 itself only provides the base server functions. IBM, in its new spirit of openness, is encouraging the development of *a la carte* extended server offerings (from IBM and other vendors). This unbundled philosophy has generated *avant-garde* server software packages on OS/2 (for example, Lotus Notes and DSOM). Customers pick and choose the server software and middleware that works best for their environments. Figure 6-2 provides a sampling of the types of extended services that run on the OS/2 platform. Some of these services are mature and battle tested. Others are at the cutting edge of server technology. We will start with the more mundane services at the bottom and work our way up towards the more esoteric ones. This section gives you a gestalt view. Many of the products and acronyms are covered in great detail later in the book.

■ OS/2 supports a rich multivendor set of communications stacks that allow OS/2 servers to talk to almost any client or server on any type of network. These stacks include TCP/IP, NetBIOS, IPX/SPX, Named Pipes, and APPC/APPN (see Figure 6-2). IBM's NTS/2 product provides an open substrate for protocol stacks to share NDIS compliant network device drivers. The Remote Access Services (RAS) allow dial-in clients to access servers on the LAN. Because of its ubiquitous communications, OS/2 is widely used as a gateway server.

■ OS/2 provides the most complete set of distributed computing services in the industry. An OS/2 machine can simultaneously act as a NetWare 4.0 and LAN Server 3.0 file, print, and directory server. OS/2 provides a very complete implementation of the OSF Distributed Computing Environment (DCE). OS/2 also supports the Sun, NCS, and DCE RPC environments. For those who don't like RPCs, OS/2 supports Messaging, Queuing, and Event notification middleware from PeerLogic, Covia, and System Strategies.

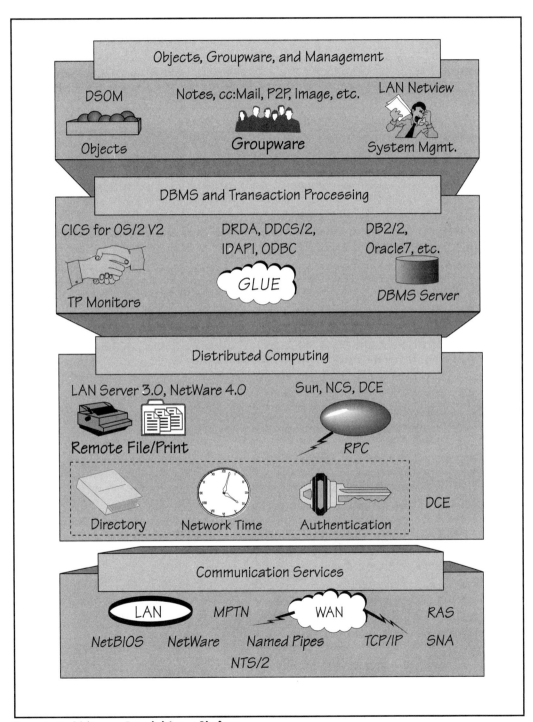

Figure 6-2. OS/2 as an Extended Server Platform.

- OS/2 supports multivendor database server platforms including Oracle, Sybase, DB2/2, XDB, and Gupta. OS/2 supports "glue" standards (such as DRDA and IDAPI) that allow multivendor databases to interoperate and work with different front-end tools. CICS V2 is a solid client/server implementation of a TP Monitor on OS/2. The thin client for DOS, OS/2, Windows, and Mac clients was first introduced on the CICS OS/2 server platform. Encina for OS/2 is another TP Monitor that will soon be available on the OS/2 platform (on top of DCE). TP Monitors make it possible to create "mission-critical" systems using personal computers.

- OS/2 supports multivendor groupware offerings that facilitate person-to-person communications and collaborative work. A cottage industry has developed around the Lotus Notes groupware server. OS/2 provides top-of-the-line multivendor offerings for document imaging and workflow (such as IMARA and ImagePlus). Products like Person-to-Person provide real-time multimedia interactions.

- OS/2 is currently at the leading edge of distributed object technology. DSOM was the first ORB to fully implement the CORBA object broker specification. OS/2 supports Object Database Management Systems (ODBMSs) from companies such as Versant and ODI. OS/2 will be one of the first platforms to host the Taligent object frameworks. IBM is also creating object frameworks that encapsulate client/server middleware—including the network operating system, service-specific middleware, and distributed system management. Taligent is creating application-level frameworks.

- OS/2 is emerging as one of the industry's best managed client/server platforms. The LAN NetView family of products from IBM allows an OS/2 PC to manage any device on the network that talks SNMP or CMIP (both open standards). LAN NetView uses the Workplace Shell to visually display the managed devices. Vendors can easily plug their management products into this open (and low-cost) management platform. LAN NetView intends to implement, in its second release (late 1994), the object version of OSF's DME, the DMTF desktop management interface, and SNMP2.

In summary, OS/2 provides an "open" PC-based server platform. Open means that there is a wide choice of vendor products and services at competitive prices. These translate into enormous savings in hardware and software system costs, especially when compared to an equivalent supermini solution.

OS/2 AS A CLIENT AND SERVER PLATFORM

PC Magazine columnist John Dvorak's first law of client/server says: "If you can run the same OS on both clients and servers—do it!"[1] Yes, it is true that client/server allows us to "mix and match," but it's simpler to avoid this. Running the same OS on both clients and servers makes LANs simpler to administer, and you can easily move programs (and functions) between clients and servers. In addition, the installation procedures, the file systems, and the interfaces to the operating system are the same on both the clients and the server. This familiar setting makes it easy for departments and small organizations to introduce client/server solutions.

OS/2 is one of the few operating systems that performs very well on either side of the client and server equation. This "Janus-like" role of OS/2 makes it a natural contender in the hybrid client market. OS/2 servers, unlike minicomputers, were designed from the ground up to communicate seamlessly with PC clients. This means the clients and servers use the same file types, commands, and internal data representations. Operating system calls can be transparently redirected to the server via a network operating system.

---

[1] Source: **Dvorak's Guide to OS/2** (Random House, 1993).

BETTING YOUR BUSINESS ON AN OS PLATFORM

Picking a client/server platform is not an easy task. New operating systems for the desktop seem to be sprouting like weeds, while older operating systems are fragmenting into mutant "sibling" variants. This is not necessarily bad news for the client/server architecture model, which thrives on diversity. However, it can be bad news if you're trying to develop a software product and you end up picking the wrong client/server platform. This section gives you a synopsis of the client/server platform choices.

Which Mass Market Will You Choose?

To choose an operating system platform, you must first decide which mass computer market (or culture) you're going to play in. A computer mass market provides distribution channels, a support infrastructure, user groups, mass publications, trade shows, complementary products, and large installed bases of users that are potential customers for your product. Here are the leading contenders:

■ **The PC world**, includes all types of Intel-based machines that run DOS (and its variants), Windows 3.X, OS/2, Windows NT, and NetWare. PCs are ubiquitous in the business world.

■ **The Macintosh world**, is strongly entrenched in certain sectors of the business world (among writers, illustrators, and marketing departments).

■ **The Unix world**, in all its variants and hardware platforms, is the world of engineering workstations and power users.

■ **The supermini world** is dominated by DEC hardware and VMS-based solutions.

■ **The mainframe world** is dominated by IBM's mainframes and its SAA standards. Parts of SAA have been adopted by many non-IBM system vendors. OS/2, OS/400, and AIX/6000 are non-mainframe members of the SAA family.

Like the cartoon character, we decided to focus on the *PC world*, which provides by far the largest market, with an installed base of 120 million machines and growing at twenty million a year. This is a world of highly commoditized software that boasts thousands of high-quality, low-cost, shrink-wrapped applications that users can buy off a retailer's shelf and easily install and run on millions of PCs.

Going through the motions of picking a client/server platform is a good mental exercise. It helps sharpen our understanding of the issues and platform trade-offs. In the "real world," things are not black and white. There are no hermetically sealed computer worlds at the intergalactic client/server level. And very few machines started life as green-field client/server systems—most of the world's computers, even the PCs, are "legacy systems" (see the following Soapbox). You'll typically be dealing with heavy doses of platform mixing. Luckily, client/server middleware is starting to become the *cross-platform unifier*. So once you're fully proficient with one platform you'll be able to pick the next one without too much sweat. In the meantime, diversity is what makes client/server so much fun.

OS/2 Made Good Business Sense

Soapbox

As you can see from the title of this book, we decided that OS/2 was our client/server platform of choice. In retrospect this was a good business decision. Our 1100 page programming book, *Client/Server Programming with OS/2 2.1*, (VNR, 1993), is now in its third edition. The second edition of this book made it to the number three spot on the *Barnes and Noble* Computer Book Bestseller list after *DOS For Dummies* and *PCs For Dummies*. We had the number one book for "non-dummies."

Aside from making good business sense, we find that OS/2 embodies some of the best technology in the PC World on both the client and server sides of the equation. With OS/2, we are in the doubly fortunate position of being able to create solutions for the PC mass market that build on top of a state-of-the-art platform. OS/2 and its extensions come close to providing the industry's most complete platform for handling both the client and server needs, as defined in this chapter. OS/2 has the advantage of playing well with mainframes, as well as interoperating with the Unix world. OS/2 also provides the best platform for understanding the up-and-coming client/server technologies like groupware (Lotus Notes) and distributed objects (DSOM and Taligent Frameworks).

Our choice of a platform may not suit your needs if you're dealing with customers who have exclusive Macintosh or Unix shops, or if you're writing a client/server application that works with an existing piece of software that does not run on PCs (a rare occurrence given the huge number of DOS, Windows 3.X, and OS/2 applications that are on the market). ❑

Chapter 7

Servers: Reaching for the Limits

All things...are aggregations of atoms that dance and by their movements create sounds.
When the rhythm of the dance changes, the sound it produces also changes...Each atom
perpetually sings its song, and the sound, at every moment, creates dense and subtle forms."

— A Tibetan Lama,
From Alexandra David-Neel's
Tibetan Journey

In this chapter, we continue our exploration of OS/2 as a client/server platform by looking at the question of server upward scalability. Most LANs in operation today have less than 50 clients. A normal PC server can handle these situations without too much effort. The trend, however, is to put more PCs on the LAN. At some point, we will have to answer the question: When does an OS/2 server run out of steam?

SERVER SCALABILITY

OS/2's support for multiple LAN adapters, in theory, allows 1000 clients to be in session with a single server machine. If datagrams or non-persistent sessions are used, a single server machine could, again in theory, talk to hundreds of thousands of clients. What are the upper limits of PC servers running OS/2? The limits depend on the type of service required by these clients. If they require simple services such as "give me the time," then a single server could probably handle thousands of clients. On the other hand, if they're each asking the server to perform a complicated weather report, then there will only be a small number of satisfied clients. We will look at some of the factors affecting the scalability of the PC running OS/2 as a server platform. Figure 7-1 shows the different levels of escalation in server power. It starts with a single PC server that reaches its limits with the top-of-the-line processor and I/O power. The next level of server power is provided by superservers populated with multiprocessors. If that is not enough power, the client/server model allows you to divide the work among different servers. These multiservers know no upper limits to power. But they must know how to work together.

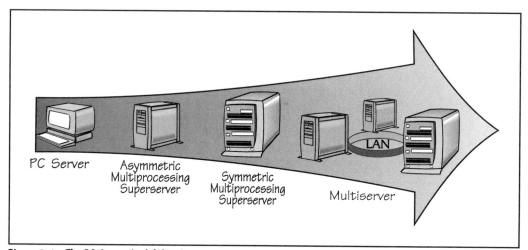

Figure 7-1. The PC Server Scalability Story.

RISC VERSUS INTEL

At the heart of each PC is at least one Intel microprocessor that is a key factor in determining how fast that machine will run. Will Intel deliver enough power to fuel servers? Or, is it time to move on to *RISC* (Reduced Instruction Set Computer) technology? RISC has traditionally been available only in the Unix workstation market such as Sun's SPARC and IBM's RS/6000 series. Microsoft's Windows NT operating system supports Intel as well as the RISC R4000 and Alpha. The IBM Microkernel will allow Taligent and the Workplace OS (with the OS/2 personality and others) to run on Intel and a variety of RISC engines. RISC provides a very steep price/performance improvement curve. RISC architectures place only the most used instructions in hardware. This results in smaller chips that allow the introduction of a new generation of processors with double the performance every sixteen months, on average. Vendors of RISC microprocessors believe that they have an insurmountable advantage over Intel's Complex Instruction Set Computer (CISC) 80X86 family.

Intel, however, claims that it is working on three generations of microprocessors at the same time. Its Pentium processor uses a *superscalar RISC* technology that comes close to matching the performance of the best of today's RISC processors.[1] Intel, which is outshipping all competitive microprocessors at a ratio of one hundred to one, is known for its continuous breakthroughs in process technology. The numbers in Table 7-1 show that the firm is accelerating the rate of its performance upgrades and should be able to keep up with most of its RISC competitors.

Table 7-1. Intel Processor Speeds.

Intel Micro Name	Introduction Date	Clock Speed	Processor Speed	Comments
8086	1978	10 MHz	0.7 Mips	First IBM PCs
80286	1982	12 MHz	2.6 Mips	AT class machine
386SX	1988	20 MHz	4.2 Mips	Entry level 386
386DX	1987	20 MHz	7 Mips	Top-of-the-line 386
486DX	1989	25 MHz	20 Mips	Single clock technology.
	1990	33 MHz	27 Mips	
	1991	50 MHz	40 Mips	
486DX (double)	1992	50 MHz	40 Mips	Double clock technology
	1992	66 MHz	54 Mips	
Pentium	1993	66 MHz	100 Mips	More than two instruc-
	1994 (early)	100 MHz	135 Mips	tions per clock cycle
	1994 (late)	166 MHz	200 Mips	
786	2000	250 MHz	2000 Mips	Compatible with 80386

Intel's promise to deliver RISC performance on the 80X86 gives PC servers the best of all worlds. They get the benefits of RISC performance, and at the same time they maintain backward compatibility with the large base of existing PC software. Most

---

[1] The results of a Spec92 benchmark of integer performance conducted by Intel and published by **Spec Newsletter** (December, 1992) show Pentium performing almost twice as fast as an 80486. It is faster than all other RISC chips except DEC's 133 MHz Alpha 21064. Gartner (March, 1993) and InfoCorp (May, 1993) agree with the Intel numbers, but they both add the HP PA7100 to the list of RISC processors that are faster than a 66 MHz Pentium. The MIPs R4400 and the latest PowerPCs were not included in the comparison.

importantly, they avoid the pitfalls associated with multihardware (portable) OS platforms.

PC servers have indeed come a long way. The power of a Pentium today is equivalent to that of a top-of-the-line mainframe circa 1990. The Pentium will help create even more formidable PC-based server platforms. But this is not the entire story. We can do better than wait for future speed improvements in processor technology by exploiting multiprocessing and parallel architectures, which are the topics of the next section.

MULTIPROCESSING SUPERSERVERS

If you need more server power, you'll be looking at a new generation of PC-based *superservers*. These are fully-loaded Intel PCs equipped with multiprocessors, high-speed disk arrays for intensive I/O, and fault-tolerant features. Machines that run OS/2 with different levels of asymmetric multiprocessing support include the IBM PS/2 Models 195 and 295, Compaq SystemPro, NetFrame NF400, Parallan 290, and Tricord PowerFrames. These machines are rapidly coming down in price. They provide a growth path for OS/2 servers without moving to multiservers.

Operating systems can enhance the server hardware by providing support for multiprocessors in a single machine. With the proper division of labor, multiprocessors should improve job throughput and server application speeds. A multiprocessor server is upwardly scalable. Users can get more performance out of their servers by simply adding more processors instead of additional servers. Multiprocessing comes in two flavors: asymmetric and fully symmetric (Figure 7-2).

Asymmetric Multiprocessing

Asymmetric multiprocessing imposes hierarchy and a division of labor among processors. Only one designated processor, the master, can run the operating system at any one time. The master controls (in a tightly-coupled arrangement) slave processors dedicated to specific functions such as disk I/O or network I/O. For example, the OS/2 LAN Server allows a master Pentium to run OS/2 and all the application tasks in parallel with a peripheral Pentium that executes OS/2's HPFS file system.[2]

---

[2] A coprocessor is an extreme form of codependency where one processor completely controls a slave processor through interlocked special-purpose instructions. The coprocessor has unique special-purpose hardware that is not identical to the main processor. An example is a graphic coprocessor.

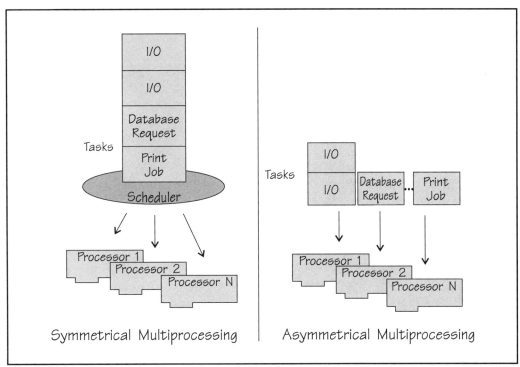

Figure 7-2. Symmetric and Asymmetric Multiprocessing.

Symmetric Multiprocessing

Symmetric multiprocessing treats all processors as equals. Any processor can do the work of any other processor. Applications are divided into threads that can run concurrently on any available processor. Any processor in the pool can run the operating system kernel and execute user-written threads. Symmetric multiprocessing improves the performance of the application itself as well as the total throughput of the server system. Ideally, the operating system supports symmetric multiprocessing by supplying three basic functions: a reentrant OS kernel, a global scheduler that assigns threads to available processors, and shared I/O structures. Symmetric multiprocessing requires multiprocessor hardware with some form of shared memory and local instruction caches. Most importantly, symmetric multiprocessing requires new applications that can exploit multithreaded parallelism. There are very few of these applications on the market, with the exception of some SQL database managers such as Oracle7 and Sybase.

OS/2 Multiprocessing

By the end of 1994, all the major 32-bit operating systems—including Unix, OS/2, and NT—will support symmetric multiprocessing (SMP).[3] These operating systems will run on commodity superserver platforms; the hardware vendors have been gearing up for these OSs for quite some time. Microsoft's Windows NT Advanced Server supports up to 4 processors in SMP mode (vendor-specific drivers can support more). USL's UNIX System V Release 4 with multiprocessing extensions (SVR4MP) provides threads for parallel processing in SMP-based configurations. OSF, the other major Unix standard provider, is working on a Mach-based multiprocessor Unix microkernel. Many proprietary or hardware-specific Unix multiprocessor offerings are currently available including Sun's Sparcserver 600MP series, Banyan's VINES SMP, SCO's Unix MPX, Sequent Computers, and Pyramid Technology. In December 1993, IBM shipped the beta version of OS/2 SMP, which supports 16-processor SMP configurations on Intel.[4] IBM also demonstrated its Workplace OS running in SMP mode at Fall Comdex, 1993. We discuss the Workplace OS in the next chapter.

MULTISERVERS: UNLIMITED SERVER POWER

Multiservers are used in environments that require more processing power than that provided by a single OS/2 server. The client/server model is upwardly scalable. When more processing power is needed, more servers can be added (thus creating a pool of servers). Or, the existing server machine can be traded up to the latest generation of PC superserver machine. Multiservers remove any upward limits to the growth of server power. This power can be provided by ordinary PC servers working in all kinds of ensembles. As we explain in later chapters, network operating system extensions like the *Distributed Computing Environment (DCE)* and TP Monitors like CICS and Encina provide the plumbing needed to create cooperating server ensembles.

---

[3] A good discussion of the issues involved in creating a multiprocessor version of OS/2 is provided by Deitel and Kogan, **The Design of OS/2**, (Addison Wesley, 1992).

[4] A future version of OS/2 SMP will support Intel's APIC chip. Intel will announce an SMP standard in 1994 based on APIC. Currently each SMP port must be hand crafted for a PC superserver platform. An OS-independent standard for SMP interfaces to the hardware will help commoditize SMP-based superservers (at least on Intel hardware).

Is the Move to RISC Inevitable?

Soapbox

Commodity Intel-based servers supplemented with SMP are powerful enough to handle more than 90% of client/server application needs. These servers can run ordinary PC software and have a strong affinity with clients. The current breed of 32-bit OSs are finally taking advantage of the Intel hardware. It's not clear that there's a pressing need to move to RISC. The next step in servers and OSs will be support for megaclusters. Servers can also take advantage of loosely coupled multiservers using TP Monitor technology.

So where does RISC fit in this scenario? It will mostly be used for non-Intel applications that run natively on RISC. For example, Apple is in the midst of a huge software conversion to PowerPC exploitive applications. What is gained by going to RISC? Smaller chip footprints, lower power, and perhaps lower prices. If nothing else, it spurs some competition with Intel, which should help push prices down. IBM is reportedly developing a version of its PowerPC RISC chip that interprets X86 instructions and can run Intel Software at the same performance as a 66 MHz Pentium (Source: PC Week, February 14, 1994). If IBM succeeds, Intel may face some tough competition from the PowerPC. But according to PC Week, that won't happen till mid-1995; so don't hold your breath waiting. ❑

Chapter 8

Coming Soon: Workplace OS

To predict the future, you'll have to create it.

— Tom Peters

Investing in a client/server platform is a long-term commitment, so it's important to understand future directions. In the near future, OS/2's destiny is intertwined with the Workplace OS, the IBM Microkernel, and "object frameworks everywhere." Further on the horizon there is Taligent. How does this all come together? How does OS/2 2.X evolve to get there? What are the implications for developing client/server solutions on an OS/2 2.X platform?

THE FUTURE OF OS/2

Where are OS/2's advanced server features such as portable Symmetric Multiprocessing (SMP) and RISC support? These features allow Unix and Windows NT—when they run on clustered servers—to provide power that rivals mainframes. OS/2 will get all these advanced features. In addition, OS/2 will play a leading role in introducing distributed object frameworks that will form the basis for new advances in client/server technology. Objects are a natural way to build distributed client/server applications that span multiple machines. This section gives some details on how this technology will come to life.[1]

OS/2 2.X and Workplace OS

In Figure 8-1, we offer a "fearless forecast" of how the desktop operating systems from IBM and Taligent come into the picture over the next few years. In all cases, the future lies in operating systems that embrace object-oriented technology. OS/2 2.X is optimized for Intel processors and will continue to evolve throughout the '90s. The Workplace OS is a portable environment designed to run on top of Intel and RISC hardware from a variety of vendors, with the portability layer provided by a common microkernel. The 32-bit OS/2 applications you create should run on all platforms. Taligent will start by producing frameworks and technology that can be added to existing OSs, and its full object-oriented OS will come in 1995 (or later).

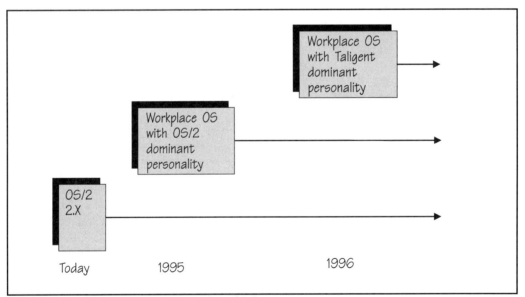

Figure 8-1. How IBM Operating Systems Evolve and Relate.

---

[1] Also see Orfali and Harkey, "Spotlight On Taligent," **OS/2 Developer** (July/August, 1993). What we present here is an updated version of that article. The original article included an in-depth interview with Joe Guglielmi, Taligent's CEO, and Mike Potel, Taligent's Vice President of Technology. We feel confident that the views presented here are accurate. The original article was extensively reviewed by the top decision makers and architects at IBM Personal System Products (PSP) and Taligent. Subsequent events demonstrate that we were on the right track.

IBM plans to begin implementing the first Taligent frameworks for system-level services, including two-dimensional graphics in OS/2 starting in 1994 (a limited beta shipped in December 1993). IBM intends to keep introducing Taligent technology on top of its existing operating systems and evolve them to the full Taligent environment.

In our scenario, objects become very important. Distributed object services based on the System Object Model (SOM) become a vehicle to share objects across operating systems such as OS/2, DOS, Windows, Unix, AS/400, and MVS. In addition, object-oriented application frameworks containing both IBM and Taligent technology will be offered for OS/2 2.X, Unix, and Workplace OS.

Figures 8-2 and 8-3 show that both OS/2 2.X and the Workplace OS support system frameworks (DSOM and object services), and OO application frameworks. OS/2 2.X continues to evolve, providing optimal performance on the large installed base of Intel machines. The Workplace OS is a portable operating system that exploits a multiplicity of hardware architectures.

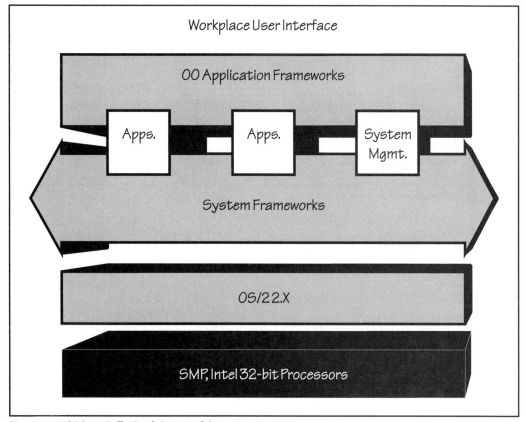

Figure 8-2. OS/2 2.X: The Intel-Optimized Operating System.

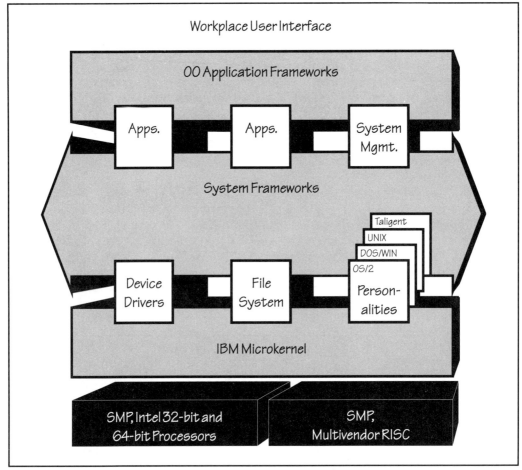

Figure 8-3. The Workplace OS.

Your Guide to Microkernels, Personalities, and Frameworks

We will use Figure 8-3 to explain all the "new age" terminology. You'll need it to understand how Taligent and OS/2 are coming together. As you can see from the figure, there are several pieces in the Workplace OS that play together: the IBM Microkernel, the OS personalities, the system frameworks, the OO application frameworks containing Taligent technology, and the Workplace user interface. We will briefly introduce these pieces.

■ ***The IBM Microkernel*** utilizes technology from Mach 3.0 research. Mach 3.0 is a portable microkernel developed by Carnegie-Mellon University. The IBM microkernel and Mach 3.0 remove the Unix-specific elements and provide a few well-defined services—including interprocess communications, virtual memory, ports, task dispatching, and threads—used to build all system services. The rest of the operating system functions—file I/O, user interface services, device drivers, and communications—are implemented outside the microkernel. As a result, the microkernel can be smaller, faster, and more scalable while providing a higher level of robustness, security, and integrity. Elements outside the microkernel, such as the device drivers and file systems, can be shared by the operating systems that run on top of it. IBM's multithreaded microkernel supports Symmetric Multiprocessing (SMP), a technique that allows programs to run concurrently on multiple processors in tightly-coupled configurations. The microkernel is intended to support both Intel and a variety of RISC processors.

■ *The personality modules* provide the operating system-specific API services. IBM intends to support DOS, Windows 3.X, OS/2 2.X, and Unix personalities. The microkernel will concurrently execute multiple OS personalities on one machine. One personality is designated as *dominant*, which means that it controls the appearance of the desktop. The personalities will preserve investments in code and application packages. The microkernel also provides the means to build specialized servers (such as object DBMSs) and OS replacements.

What Are Frameworks?

Briefing

A framework is a working subsystem consisting of a set of tightly-coupled class libraries that give you a jump-start for writing applications. You begin with complete working subsystems that you can customize to create your own applications. Taligent calls these subsystems "prefabricated templates." Taligent believes that frameworks, which are central to its new operating environment, are "the most important advancement in object-oriented technology." ❑

■ *The system frameworks* provide an object-based infrastructure for client/server middleware—including NOS, transports, service-specific middleware, and distributed system management. The system frameworks also include some key operating system functions such as installation and configuration, file systems, and Taligent-based operating system extensions. The system frameworks build on top of IBM's OMG-compliant Distributed System Object Model (DSOM) technology that allows objects to interoperate across networks. The frameworks also include OMG-compliant services for storing, replicating, shadowing, creating, destroying, and specifying objects. IBM also intends to provide SOM-wrappers for the most popular forms of client/server middleware—including NOS functions, DCE, messaging, transactions, database, groupware, telephony, and sockets. The bottom line is that object frameworks will be created to encapsulate most of the client/server middleware discussed in this book. This is really wonderful news!

■ ***The application frameworks*** provide a portable distributed set of object services to help you create end-user applications. The applications will be created by wiring together subsystems using visual application assembly tools. Taligent shipped the first beta of its application frameworks in December 1993.

■ ***The user interface*** for IBM's "Workplace" line is (you may have guessed from the name) based on OS/2's Workplace Shell and the Taligent OOUI. This is an Object-Oriented User Interface (OOUI) that will be adapted for DOS, Unix, and OS/2. Users think in terms of directly manipulating objects on the desktop rather than dealing with programs and other computer-based metaphors. IBM and Taligent are working on making the user interface even easier to use by adding powerful new visual metaphors and 3-D widgets. According to Cliff Reeves, IBM's Director of Objects, "the idea of the Workplace OS now is to have this superset OOUI that could have different appearances."

The pieces all seem to be coming together. The Workplace OS lets various operating system personalities share a common microkernel that runs on a variety of hardware platforms, from laptop PCs to multiprocessor clusters. For example, OS/2 applications will be able to run on the small mobile palmtops, desktops, and superserver clusters—one size fits all (see Figure 8-4). So, from an application viewpoint, we're talking about a single OS solution for hardware that spans from a $300 oven—OS/2 for microwave ovens—to a $3 million megacluster—OS/2 for massively parallel computers.[2]

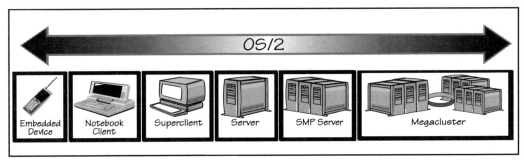

Figure 8-4. OS/2 Spread: From Laptops to Superservers.

---

[2] We are indebted to Larry Louckes, the visionary who is leading the Workplace OS effort, for some of these metaphors. Larry also joked about an OS/2 for refrigerators that could be asked to "pour the beer."

Even more exciting is the pervasive use of object technology at the application, system, and client/server levels. SOM and DSOM provide the standards-based glue that allow applications on all personalities to communicate using distributed object technology. We will spend the remaining of this chapter taking a closer look at the Workplace OS and the IBM Microkernel. In Part 7, we look at object frameworks, a technology that has the potential of changing the way we build client/server systems.

THE WORKPLACE OS: A CLOSER LOOK

Let's take a closer peek at the Workplace OS family and the IBM Microkernel. You can think of the Workplace OS family as a set of components that can be packaged into a series of products. It is the next generation integrating platform. The magic is accomplished by a set of modular OS Legos that plug into a portable *microkernel*. Think of the microkernel as an operating system whose inner guts were removed, and thus leaving a raw skinny "kernel."

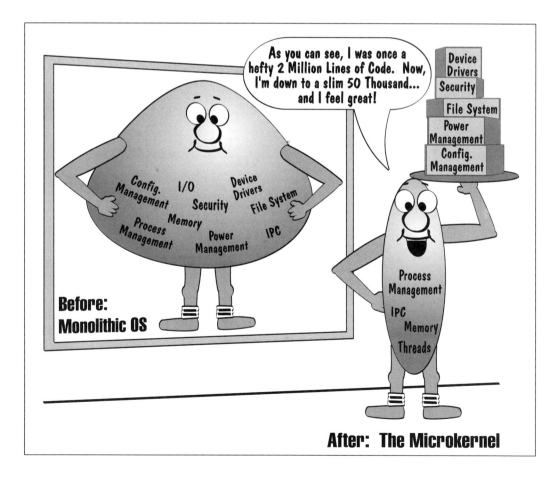

But where did the "inner guts" end up? They were repackaged as modular components that can plug-and-play on top of the microkernel.[3] These repackaged, inner-gut components include personality-neutral servers—such as device drivers, security services, file systems, memory managers, and network stacks—and personality servers that create an environment for running applications (see Figure 8-5).

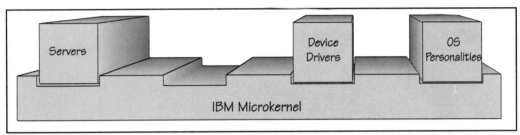

Figure 8-5. The IBM Microkernel Components.

The components work together by using a microkernel-based client/server messaging system. Clients request operating system services by invoking the services of a server (see Figure 8-6). The microkernel doesn't need to know whether the message comes from a local or remote process. Everything is kept loosely coupled, and the microkernel becomes the message-switch. The beauty is that all the clients and servers run as applications on top of the microkernel. Only the microkernel—about 50K lines of code—runs in the protected space. This makes all these services very portable.

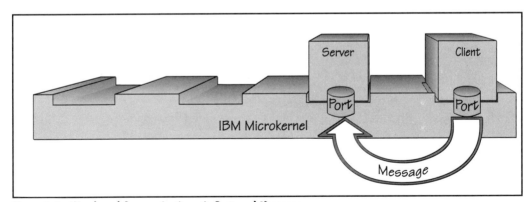

Figure 8-6. Microkernel Communications via Ports and Messages.

---

[3] The Mach microkernel was originally developed as an alternative to the bloated Unix kernel, which grew over the years to include more functions at the expense of size and performance.

123

What Does the IBM Microkernel Do?

The IBM Microkernel isolates the critical machine-dependent services from the OS components above it. IBM based its microkernel on Mach's proven foundation for portability and parallel processing, enhanced it, and turned it into an industrial-strength product.[4] The IBM microkernel adds the following enhancements to Mach: 1) support for objects, 2) support for real-time applications, 3) improved storage efficiency, 4) out-of-kernel device driver support, and 5) industry-approved enhanced microkernel external interfaces.

The major functions of the IBM microkernel include:

- *Intertask communications using ports and messages.* Messages are self-describing data structures that are passed between ports. The microkernel takes care of queueing messages and can treat a *set of ports* as a single unit when receiving a message. Messages are unidirectional, but reliable delivery is supported as an option. The microkernel appends to each message the identity of the sending task and its security rights. Each message can be validated by the server receiving the message with the help of an optional security server. The rights to access a port (local or remote) may be passed in a message. To enhance performance, large blocks of data can be referenced into the receiver's address space instead of copied. The microkernel will detect any attempt to change the data in the sender's space before the message is processed. It will then create a private copy of the unchanged message for the server. This allows processing to continue in parallel between the OS client and server.

- *Task and thread management.* Threads are the basic unit of execution and scheduling. A task consists of one or more threads. A task is allocated resources such as memory and ports. Threads can execute in parallel either by time-slicing a single processor or on separate processors. The scheduling policy is dictated by the personality.

- *Basic memory management.* The microkernel interfaces to the paging hardware and provides a set of virtual address spaces that is owned by a task. The microkernel depends on a personality-specific memory pager (outside of the microkernel) to implement policies such as when to swap pages from memory disk. It is very unlikely, for example, that the Unix and OS/2 personalities will have the same paging policies.

- *Scalable multiprocessor support.* The microkernel allocates a pool of threads to a pool of processors. Processors that have the same hardware

---

[4] As described by Paul Giangara and Viktors Berstis, both senior staff members of IBM's Personal Software Products (PSP) division.

attributes (for example, a math coprocessor) can be grouped in *sets*. The *host* is the multiprocessor system as a whole. And a *node* is an individual multiprocessor within a multicomputer system (see Figure 8-7).

- **Miscellaneous system functions.** The microkernel also supports kernel devices, clocks, and system events.

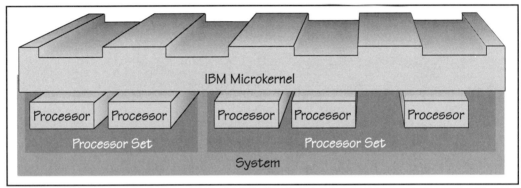

Figure 8-7. Multiprocessor Combinations Using the IBM Microkernel.

As you can see, the microkernel only handles the most essential and critical hardware and operating system functions. It also enforces security at the message level between all the components of the system (OS clients and servers). The microkernel does not implement operating system policies or services. It leaves this function to the components that operate above the kernel. This is how the system is kept modular, robust, and under 50K lines of code.

What Do Personality-Neutral Servers Do?

As the name implies, personality-neutral servers can be shared by different operating system personalities (for example OS/2 and Unix). This capability is one of the Workplace OS's greatest strengths and allows very flexible systems to be created on a single hardware platform. Examples of personality-neutral servers include network servers, file systems, device drivers, security servers, boot and configuration services, memory managers, database servers, the Workplace Shell, and object stores. The clients for these services are typically the OS personalities, but they can also be other servers. For example, the memory manager may require the services of the file server. Leverage will be obtained by creating servers that can be reused across personalities (see Figure 8-8).

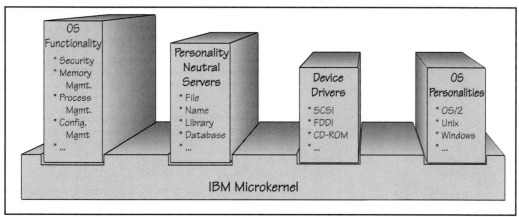

Figure 8-8. The IBM Microkernel: Personality-Neutral and OS Dependent Servers.

What Do Personality Servers Do?

The Workplace OS will run OS/2, DOS, Windows, Unix, OS/400, and Taligent applications. This miracle is achieved by creating for each of these applications an operating system environment that executes the services required by each operating system. This environment is the operating system *personality server*. The personality servers map the OS calls to personality-neutral servers. They must also take care of any additional services required by an operating system environment.

The *dominant* personality server establishes the GUI (or OOUI) look for the entire machine. For example, an OS/2 personality will run PM applications on the desktop (PM itself is an application). *Alternate* personalities can run their applications from the dominant personality. An alternate personality must be able to accept requests from the dominant personalities. For example, an OS/2 dominant personality will depend on Windows and Unix alternate personalities for running their respective applications. The trick is to make the alternate personalities fit seamlessly into the dominant personality's desktop. This is similar to how OS/2 runs seamless Windows from the OS/2 Workplace Shell today. The Workplace OS intends to run the Workplace Shell—a personality-neutral server—as the seamless integrator of the desktop. Taligent will be offered as a dominant personality only. DOS and DOS/Windows will only be offered as alternate personalities. OS/2 and Unix will support both roles.

Why Is the Microkernel Important?

The microkernel offers the following architectural advantages:

■ *Support for real-time tasks.* The tight microkernel code offers more control over key resources and shorter path lengths (less latency) in critical sections of the code. This will make the microkernel an operating system of choice for embedded controllers and smart devices. For example, we can start thinking of a tight, superfast, customized *OS/2 for Cars*, an *OS/2 for TV Sets*, or an *OS/2 for Robots*.

■ *Leaner multiprocessor implementations.* Shared-memory multiprocessor configurations will only need to run a small microkernel on each processor instead of the entire OS/2.

■ *Support for multiprocessor clusters.* The microkernel's message passing structure makes it transparent whether resources are on the same multiprocessor (local) or on a remote multiprocessor.

■ *Room to add more personalities.* The IBM microkernel is based on the OSF Mach standard. It provides an open substrate on top of which vendors can add their own OS personalities (see Figure 8-9). IBM is talking with a number of OS vendors—including Apple, Novell, SunSoft, and HP—about porting their OSs to the Workplace OS microkernel as personalities (Source: **PC Week** February 14, 1994). IBM is also working on a Workplace OS Personal Digital Assistant (PDA) personality. And there is room for more. The microkernel as a substrate for operating systems gives users more freedom to choose. The microkernel that can seamlessly run the most applications will win!

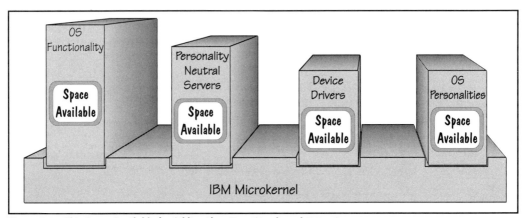

Figure 8-9. This Space Available for Adding Your Own Microkernel Extensions.

■ **Support for pluggable OS parts**. The microkernel's open architecture—and the volume market provided by the multiple personalities and the portable hardware—will help spawn an entire cottage industry of personality-neutral servers. The microkernel provides a level playing field for new file systems, security services, naming services, device drivers, memory paging systems, real-time services, and database engines. New file systems include transactional file systems with journalling support, object databases, memory-mapped file systems, fault-tolerant file systems, and file systems that support the real-time streaming requirements of multimedia. Each component can reside in its own separate address space. The microkernel provides the glue for the entire system.

In summary, the IBM microkernel is creating new opportunities for component vendors. Everything in the system is open and modular. And the system can be repackaged in thousands of ways. If you like building blocks, you'll love this microkernel.

The Future Looks Good

Soapbox

OS/2, as we know it today, provides a solid platform for both clients and servers on Intel hardware. The future of OS/2 is based on an open industry microkernel that will form the basis for IBM, Taligent, and Apple desktop operating systems (as well as many other vendors). OS/2 2.X will continue to directly support Intel for maximum performance at the desktop. The OS personalities provide a way to accommodate existing OSs and user interfaces while leaving the door open for Taligent-type advances that will bring objects all the way down to the metal.

OS/2's SMP strategy provides the best of two worlds: 1) OS/2 2.X will run natively on ubiquitous Intel multiprocessors without being slowed down by a portability layer; and 2) The Workplace OS will provide a choice of multiprocessor platforms—Intel or RISC—using the most advanced microkernel technology in the industry. This means that the same OS/2 applications will be able to run on notebooks as well as clusters of superservers. And you get all this scalability using the *existing* OS/2 32-bit API set and object frameworks as they become available.

When will all this be available? How will it be packaged? According to various IBM statements that appeared in the Computer Press, OS/2 will be packaged in the following flavors:

- **Slim OS/2** is a version of the current OS/2 (with some added features) that runs comfortably in 4 MBytes of memory; it will ship in 1994.

- **OS/2 for Clients** is a souped-up version of OS/2 that is bundled with peer networking and a variety of client middleware including DSOM and a slim DCE RPC; it will ship in 1994.

- **OS/2 for Servers** is a souped-up version of OS/2 that is bundled with DCE services, LAN Server, LAN NetView, C2 Security, and 16-processor symmetric multiprocessing on Intel; it will also ship in 1994.

A bit further on the horizon is the OS/2 personality for the Workplace OS; it is scheduled to go to beta in mid-1994. All told, about 90 new OS/2 features will ship in 1994—it will be a busy year for OS/2. ❏

Chapter 9

OS/2 2.1:
A Grand Tour

I believe OS/2 is destined to be the most important operating system, and possibly program, of all time.

— *Bill Gates, 1988* [1]

This chapter introduces OS/2 2.1 and gives you the bird's eye view of the software components provided by a modern desktop operating system. The shrink-wrapped OS/2 2.1 package consists of two major components: the base OS services and the presentation services—including multimedia, the Workplace Shell, and Presentation Manager. This chapter reads like a feature, function, and benefit list of what OS/2 2.1 offers *client* applications. The server and middleware components— provided by IBM and hundreds of vendors—are sold as add-ons to OS/2 2.1. We will cover these add-ons in the remaining parts of this book.

---

[1] Foreword to Iacobucci's **OS/2 Programmer's Guide** (McGraw Hill, 1988).

To Bundle or Not to Bundle

Soapbox

IBM went out of its way to unbundle the system software from the base OS/2, while Microsoft is going in exactly the opposite direction. IBM's 1990 version of OS/2, the **Extended Edition**, included a multiuser SQL database engine, a multiprotocol communications engine, and the LAN Requester. Today, OS/2 2.X is totally unbundled. It does not include any middleware or server software. IBM claims that its customers prefer it that way. They want to pick and choose the middleware and system software that runs on the base operating system.

Microsoft's **Windows NT Advanced Server**, on the other hand, seems to be loaded with everything but the kitchen sink (and perhaps they'll throw that in next year). Which approach is better? It depends on whether you like *a la carte* or *prix fixe*. It also depends on how much fat you can afford on every PC. ❑

THE OS/2 2.1 BASE SERVICES

OS/2 2.1 is the first major single-user, multitasking operating system developed specifically for personal computers. Unix, for example, runs on personal computers and provides multitasking. It does this, however, by creating a time-share multiuser environment that is not optimized for single-user situations. The OS/2 2.1 base services provide multitasking, interprocess communications, memory management, device I/O, and support for running DOS and Windows applications. Large portions of the OS/2 2.1 base services were written in C for portability. This section presents the major features and functions provided by the OS/2 2.1 base services.

Multitasking

Multitasking, or the ability to run multiple programs concurrently, is one of OS/2's most powerful features. OS/2 provides a very granular level of multitasking that is optimized for concurrency on a single-user machine. The architecture builds on a three-tiered tasking model: the thread, the process, and the session (or screen group). Threads run within processes that in turn run within screen groups. Figure 9-1 shows the relationships in the hierarchy. The *thread* is the basic unit of concurrency and CPU allocation in OS/2. The *process* provides a level of multitasking that roughly corresponds to a running program. A process consists of one or more threads. So, in addition to having multiple programs execute at the same time, a single program may have multiple threads that are executing concurrently. OS/2 controls multitasking by using a preemptive priority-based scheduler. A thread can be assigned to one of four priority classes, and within each class the scheduler recognizes 32 priority levels. The *priority classes* are:

- *Time-critical* for threads that require immediate attention; these threads are used in communications and real-time applications.
- *Fixed-high* for threads that require good responsiveness without being critical.
- *Regular* for normally executing threads.
- *Idle-time* for very low priority threads.

OS/2 uses time-slicing to ensure that threads of equal priority are given equal chances to execute. OS/2 can preempt a thread when its time slice expires if a thread with a higher or equal priority is ready to execute. If not defined otherwise, the default minimum time-slice is 32 milliseconds (for non-kernel applications). You can configure the timeslice from 32 to 65,536 milliseconds. The elaborate OS/2 scheduling capabilities make it possible to create real-time applications that have almost deterministic response times. The system guarantees that time-critical threads are dispatched within 6 milliseconds of becoming ready to run. The maximum interrupt disable time is 400 milliseconds.

In addition, OS/2 makes available an even higher level of multitasking: the *session* or *screen-group*. The session represents a logically separate unit of screen, keyboard, and mouse, and the group of processes associated with those resources. You can think of the session as providing a virtual personal computer. OS/2 also provides the capability to start a process in the background. A *background process* will not have its own screen. It will continue executing in the background even if you exit from your OS/2 screen group (background processes should be self-terminating). You can start a background process using the DETACH command.

This three-level hierarchy of multitasking control—sessions, processes, and threads—addresses the user's need to control concurrent execution and the developer's need to design applications whose activities can be controlled at a very granular level.

OS/2 treats all applications in the system as protected mode processes that are provided full preemptive multitasking and memory protection. This includes DOS and MS-Windows applications. OS/2 supports a total of 4096 threads and processes.

Virtual Resources

The basis for multitasking is to manage the physical resources of the computer in such a way that multiple programs can run at the same time without bumping into each other as they use the PC's resources. This is where the OS/2 kernel comes in;

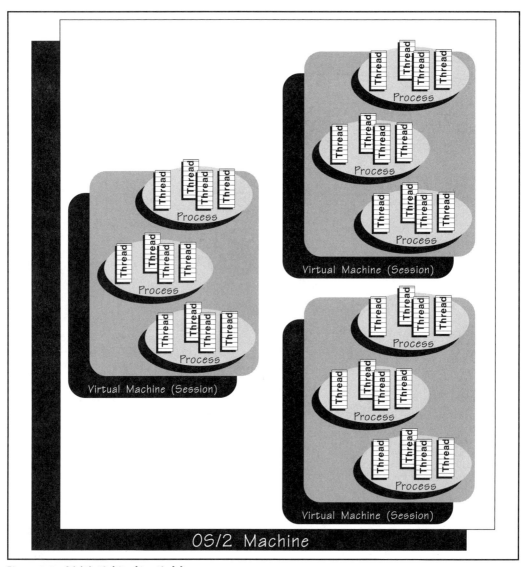

Figure 9-1. OS/2's Multitasking Model.

it sits between the programs and the hardware, and it regulates the access to memory, disks, printers, screens, and modems. Applications interact with virtual memory and devices that OS/2 then maps to real devices. OS/2 maintains order when many programs go after the same resource. It also serializes access from the virtual device to the actual physical device automatically without user intervention. This ability of OS/2 to *redirect* output (without the application knowing it) is essential for networked environments. Resources can be mapped across a LAN to remote machines, thus extending OS/2's *virtual* reach.

Interprocess Communication

Interprocess communication is a corollary of multitasking. Now that PCs can have more than one program running at the same time, there will most likely be a need for those programs to exchange information and commands. OS/2 provides the facilities for separate programs, each running in their own address space, to communicate information through system supported interprocess communication protocols (*IPCs*). Some of the IPCs can operate across machine boundaries and are key to the development of LAN-based client/server applications. OS/2 provides a rich set of IPCs. These include Anonymous Pipes, Named Pipes, Queues, and Shared Memory.

An **Anonymous Pipe** is a fixed length circular buffer in memory that can be accessed like a file of serial characters through a write handle and a read handle (handles are pointers into the file). Anonymous pipes are used mostly by a parent process to communicate with its descendants by passing the pipe handles through inheritance.

Named Pipes provide two-way communications among unrelated processes either locally or remotely. The server side of an OS/2 process creates the pipe and waits for the clients to access it. Clients use the standard OS/2 file services to gain access to the Named Pipe. Multiple clients can be serviced concurrently over the same pipe. The elegance of Named Pipes and their support for *remote* interprocess communication makes them the IPC of choice for client/server software development.

A **Queue** allows byte stream packets written by multiple processes to be read by a single process. The exchange does not have to be synchronized. The receiving process can order the access to the packets or messages in one of three modes: first-in/first-out (FIFO), last-in/first-out (LIFO), or priority. Items can be retrieved from the queue either sequentially or by random access. The OS/2 queues contain pointers to messages, as opposed to a copy of the data itself.

Shared Memory is another interprocess communication protocol. OS/2 provides facilities for creating named objects in shared memory. Any process that knows the memory object's name has automatic shared access to it. Processes must coordinate their access to shared memory objects through the use of semaphores.

Interprocess Synchronization

Interprocess synchronization is another corollary of multitasking. It consists of the mechanisms for keeping concurrent processes or threads from interfering with one another when accessing shared resources. The idea is to serialize the access to the shared resource by using a protocol that all parties agree to follow. OS/2, like most operating systems, provides an atomic service called the *semaphore*, which applications may use to synchronize their actions.

OS/2's semaphores reside in the OS's protected address space and can only be manipulated through API calls. OS/2 provides two classes of semaphores: private and shared. *Private semaphores* are used to synchronize threads within a process. A process may have up to 64K private semaphores. *Shared semaphores* are available to all processes in the system. OS/2 supports up to 64K shared semaphores.

Dynamic Linking

Dynamic linking allows a program to gain access at run time to functions that are not part of its executable code. These functions are packaged in *Dynamic Link Libraries (DLLs)* that contain executable code but cannot be run as applications. Instead, your application can load the appropriate DLLs and execute the functions in the libraries by linking to them dynamically. Your applications are linked with library routines at load time (or at run time) instead of at compile time. Dynamic linking solves two problems:

- It allows functions to be added to a program without having to relink the entire program, which makes it easier to add new extensions to a system. OS/2 uses Dynamic Linking to provide its system extensions.

- It removes the need to store on disk and load in memory multiple copies of the same code, which is especially important in a multiprogram environment where each application may require the same code library. Without dynamic linking, each program would have to load its own copy of the system library in memory, even if some other executable program has already loaded a copy of the library in memory. Dynamic linking allows an application to load a DLL only when it needs to execute a function in the library. Once a DLL is loaded, it can be shared with other applications. Only one copy of the DLL is in memory at any one time.

You should be aware of the benefits of DLLs and how they are used to extend system code. You may want to consider the benefits of packaging your programs as DLLs for commercial distribution.

The File Systems

OS/2 has two file systems: the **File Allocation Table (FAT)** and the **High Performance File System (HPFS)**. The FAT system is the default file system and does not need to be installed. HPFS can be installed during system initialization. OS/2 manages its disk files and devices in the same way. For example, an application uses the same API calls to open and read from a disk file as it uses to open and read from a serial port.

The OS/2 file system is compatible with that of MS-DOS. Both file systems represent a hierarchy of files on physical disk. The disk can also be subdivided into logical disks or partitions; each has its own hierarchy. Using the CONFIG.SYS file, OS/2 allows you to specify the number of KBytes allocated to a cache in RAM. The system then uses a Least Recently Used (LRU) algorithm to manage the cache. The file system can accommodate 64,000 file handles, with a maximum of 32,000 handles per process.

OS/2 provides *locking and sharing* facilities to support concurrent file access in a multitasking environment. A process can open a file in exclusive mode (not allowing other processes access); or it can provide read access while denying write; or it can share the file for read/write access with other processes. A process can lock any contiguous range of bytes within a shared file. These services allow multiple processes to share information at the byte level on a single file. This sharing also applies to devices that a process might open.

The **High Performance File System (HPFS)** is optimized for the management of large disk media in a fast and consistent manner. The HPFS supports disk partitions with capacities of up to 512 Gigabytes. The maximum file size supported is 2 Gigabytes. HPFS maintains compatibility with FAT at the API level. However, it is less performance sensitive as file sizes or directories get very large. The HPFS also supports long file names, but it can still work with the traditional eleven-character file names (the infamous 8.3 format). Fully qualified path names can be up to 260 characters.

OS/2 provides an HPFS device driver that is designed to optimally exploit the power of SCSI devices. The file system and the device driver communicate through *command chains* that contain lists of prioritized commands. The device driver may choose to reorder the execution of commands to optimize disk access. After the completion of the I/O, the device driver calls the notification procedure specified in the command chain. A feature called *scatter/gather* allows data to be transferred to and from discontiguous memory buffers in a single operation. This allows multiple page-in and page-out requests to be supported in a single logical operation. The cache system allows the HPFS driver to recognize devices that have outboard caches and incorporate them into the total caching scheme (for example, it may send them data prefetch requests). The SCSI drivers in OS/2 are generic and designed to work with all SCSI drives.

The **FAT** system under OS/2 is also greatly improved. The maximum size of a FAT disk partition is 2 Gigabytes, which is also the maximum file size. The caching is now moved from the device driver to the FAT, where more intelligence resides. FAT is also optimized to exploit the capabilities of the newer SCSI adapters and disks. The FAT driver, like its HPFS counterpart, supports command chaining and scatter/gather. FAT provides faster allocation of free space on the logical drive, using a bitmap to track free clusters. It also automatically bypasses bad sectors on reads.

OS/2 introduces an important feature in both of its file systems: the *Extended Attributes*. This feature allows each file to have up to 64 KBytes of file-related descriptive information, which can be used to create object-oriented file systems.

Memory Management

With OS/2 2.X, PCs finally have a world-class memory management facility that fully supports DOS, Windows, and OS/2 applications. All applications, regardless of their OS origin, run as OS/2 processes. OS/2 processes really get to enjoy the good life when it comes to superabundant memory. Perhaps this is to compensate for the many years of starvation under DOS's 640 KByte limitation. Here's a list of memory management features that each of OS/2's 4095 processes get to enjoy:

■ OS/2 provides each process with its own *virtual address space*, which is up to 512 MBytes for application processes and 4 GBytes for privileged system processes.[2] OS/2 provides protection against memory violations by misbehaved programs, and will prevent concurrently executing programs from clobbering each other's memory. If a program attempts to access memory outside its address space, a general protection fault is generated by the hardware. OS/2 is notified of the fault and terminates the process that caused it.

■ OS/2 uses the paging feature of the Intel 80386 (and above) machines to provide a *demand-paged virtual memory* environment. The 512 MByte per/process virtual memory system allows you to run programs that are much larger than the available physical memory on your machine. Memory is allocated in 4 KByte blocks called *pages*. OS/2 creates a virtual memory environment by giving each process its own set of page tables. A process can *overcommit* the memory of the system. If a page is not in memory, OS/2 will automatically swap to the disk some of the least-used pages to make room for the newly requested page.[3] The overflow memory goes to a swap file on disk. The sum of the space required by

---

[2] OS/2 supports a variety of DOS memory expanders without added hardware. In addition to Windows, it supports the Expanded Memory Specification (EMS), with up to 32 MBytes of memory per DOS process; the Lotus-Intel-Microsoft (LIM) and Expanded Memory Specifications (XMS), with up to 16 MBytes of memory; and the DOS Protected Mode Interface (DPMI), with up to 512 MBytes of memory. OS/2 2.1 has been upgraded to provide a subset of DPMI 1.0 support, which enables WIN-OS/2 3.1 to provide both standard and enhanced compatibility modes.

all your active applications must not exceed the available RAM plus the disk space available for the swap file (SWAPPER.DAT). OS/2's swap file is *elastic*; it grows and shrinks as needed. In previous versions it only grew. The fixed size pages help simplify and speed up the swapping algorithms.

- OS/2 provides APIs that let you create *memory objects* whose size can vary up to 512 MBytes. Memory objects consist of one or more pages. When you allocate your memory objects you can tag them with attributes such as read, read/write, execute, etc. These tagged objects are protected by the hardware at the page level. OS/2 also lets you share memory objects with other processes. *Shared objects* reside in a reserved address range that starts at the top of every process's address space and grows downward. Figure 9-2 shows the OS/2 process address space. Notice that the system sits on top of the process address space. Shared memory allocations grow down from the top and private memory grows up from the bottom.

- OS/2, in conjunction with the 80386 hardware, ensures that less privileged code stays within its address boundaries and uses a carefully restricted *call gate* to police access to more privileged code. Likewise, the 80386 controls access to input/output and interrupt instructions using a program's I/O privilege level (IOPL for short). The privilege level mechanisms prevent a program from accessing any part of OS/2 in an uncontrolled manner. The 80386 supports four privilege levels (or rings), which are arranged hierarchically from level 0 (maximum protection) to level 3 (minimum protection). The OS/2 core runs in level 0, level 1 is not used by OS/2, level 2 is used by programs that directly manipulate I/O devices (have IOPL privilege level), and level 3 is where your normal OS/2 programs run.

In summary, OS/2's flat memory model makes life easier for programmers writing new 32-bit applications. Gone are the calls that manipulate segment selectors. Large objects are easier to create and manipulate, and performance is better because all calls are near. The near and far keywords are not needed. The complications associated with the different memory models and their corresponding function libraries are gone. Programs that use the 32-bit model are also easier to port to non-Intel platforms. The OS/2 memory management also makes life easier for DOS and MS-Windows programs. It allows multiple DOS and Windows applications to run simultaneously; each has more virtual memory (512 MBytes) and more protection than was ever available through DOS memory extenders such as Window 3.X.

---

[3] The 80386 architecture, which OS/2 2.X fully exploits, provides a total virtual address space of 64 Terabytes. In comparison, the 80286 is limited to 1 Gigabyte.

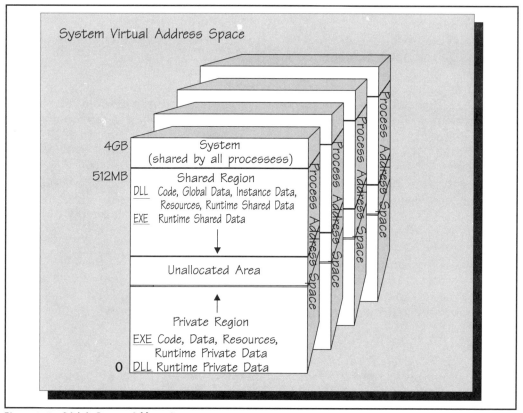

Figure 9-2. OS/2's Process Address Spaces.

Exception Handling

In a multitasking environment, a serious error occurring in one application must not be allowed to damage other applications that are running in the system. Unexpected errors, such as memory violations, are called *exceptions*. When OS/2 detects an exception, it will usually end the application unless the application has registered its own exception-handler function. This function allows an application to correct the error and continue. Four API calls have been defined for creating exception handlers on a "per-thread" basis. Unlike previous versions of OS/2, these exception handlers can be written in a high-level language like C.

What's New in OS/2 2.1?

Briefing

OS/2 2.1, introduced by IBM in June 1993, provides major enhancements in the following areas:

- *Windows 3.1 support*. OS/2 now supports Windows 3.1 applications (including Windows multimedia) running in both seamless and full-screen modes (seamless Windows applications run alongside DOS and OS/2 applications on the Workplace Shell desktop). The performance of Windows applications has been substantially improved and is now comparable to native Windows 3.1. The WinBench benchmark shows that WIN-OS/2 3.1 is 82% faster than WIN-OS/2 3.0 in full-screen mode and 77% faster in seamless mode. Depending on the configuration, WIN-OS/2 is within 5-10% of the performance of native Windows on the same hardware (in some cases it is faster). WIN-OS/2 is IBM's version of Windows. OS/2 2.1 includes TrueType font support, the Windows File Manager, and the Windows 3.1 applets. It is now possible to start (in other words, shell) DOS and OS/2 applications from within a Windows application. OS/2 2.1 now supports enhanced-mode applications such as Mathematica for Windows and Omnipage Professional.

- *Built-in Multimedia support*. The Multimedia Presentation Manager/2 product is now included with OS/2 2.1 (see Figure 9-3). Now that OS/2 is multimedia-enabled, application providers and users can depend on the native operating system to play and record software motion video, audio, CD, and image. OS/2 also enhances DOS and Windows multimedia applications by providing thread support that will make them run smoother. For example, threads allow them to simultaneously read from disk, paint the screen, and play sounds.

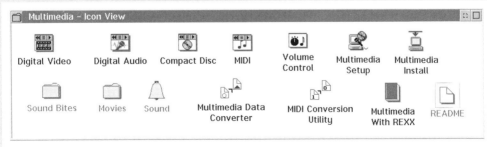

Figure 9-3. OS/2's Multimedia Presentation Manager.

■ *Better DDE, clipboard, and OLE support*. The clipboard and DDE functions were rewritten to run faster. They can be used to exchange data between DOS, OS/2, and Windows (WIN-OS/2) applications. The Windows applications can run in different address spaces (VDMs) or in the same address space. OLE allows the information in one or more documents to be linked to different applications (usually the ones that created the information in the first place). OS/2 2.1 supports Windows applications with OLE capabilities within the same WIN-OS/2 session.

■ *More hardware support*. This includes support for additional SCSI adapters, CD-ROM drives, 32-bit seamless display drivers (XGA, 8514, VGA, and SVGA), and printer drivers for both PM and WIN-OS/2. OS/2 2.1 is now preloaded by many PC manufacturers (including AST, Toshiba, Dell, Compaq, Everex, Northgate, and IBM).

■ *Superserver support*. OS/2 2.1 supports asymmetric multiprocessing (along with LAN Server 3.0) and can take advantage of the multiprocessing capabilities of superservers (such as the PS/2 Server 295). OS/2 also includes changes to support fault-tolerant RAID disk drives at the firmware level (such as those used in the PS/2 Server 295). In addition, changes have been made in OS/2 2.1 to exploit the Pentium chip.

■ *Enhancements for Laptops and Notebooks*. OS/2 2.1 supports the Advanced Power Management (APM) standard to extend the battery life of portable computers (see Figure 9-4).

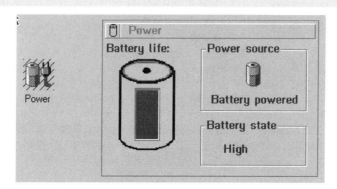

Figure 9-4. OS/2's Advanced Power Management for Laptops.

■ *Easier installation*. OS/2 2.1 can now be installed from CD-ROM. Two installation diskettes are provided to start the CD-ROM installation process. In addition, OS/2 2.1 enhanced the Selective Install feature which makes it easier to add new display drivers, SCSI adapters, CD-ROM drives, and printers.

■ **Additional security.** The Workplace Shell can now be configured to lockup automatically on system startup and require that the user enter a password before using OS/2. Previously, it was possible to software-lock the system, but you could get around that by rebooting. This loophole is now closed. Be careful, if you forget your password you'll need to reinstall OS/2 2.1. Security is a double-edged sword.

OS/2 2.1, is finally, the "better Windows than Windows" that IBM promised. Its multimedia platform makes it a very attractive desktop client. ❑

THE OS/2 2.1 PRESENTATION SERVICES

OS/2's presentation services consist of Presentation Manager (PM) 32-bit graphics engine, the Workplace Shell OOUI interface, and the multimedia facilities. The OS/2 presentation services are state-of-the-art. Everything on the Workplace Shell is a visual object that can be directly manipulated using drag and drop. But the Workplace Shell is not just object "smoke and mirrors." It is built on top of a true object framework: the SOM Workplace Shell class libraries. Programmers can build on top of these class libraries and extend the system. The Presentation Manager provides two powerful controls for creating compound objects (objects that visually contain other controls): the *Container* and *Notebook*. The 32-bit graphic engine makes it easy to manipulate very large data structures. OS/2 provides the most advanced multimedia platform in the industry. The following sections give you the details.

PM's Origins

The core Presentation Manager (PM) window services are similar to the Microsoft Windows environment under DOS. This similarity is not surprising because much of PM's windowing technology, user interface, raster graphics, and bitmap support comes directly from Microsoft Windows. IBM's contribution to PM is the powerful vector-graphics draw commands called the Graphic Programming Interface (GPI).

New Graphic Engine (GRE)

The PM Graphics Engine (the GRE) was almost completely rewritten in portable C code by a joint team from Micrografx and IBM. The new code takes full advantage of the 32-bit flat memory model, resulting in noticeably improved performance. Some of PM's more sluggish features, such as area fills and polygons, are performing much better. A new **GpiPolygon** API improves high-speed drawing of polygons.

Compressed bitmaps can now be displayed more quickly, and it is much easier to overlay images on top of each other.

Another feature is a *palette manager* that lets applications change the color set "on the fly" with eight new API calls. For example, you can use this feature to change the palette when focus is switched from one window to another. The palette manager provides a way to share the color tables and give each application the color sets it needs.

The GRE now supports 32-bit drivers in addition to 16-bit drivers. 32-bit drivers are faster than their 16-bit equivalents because the flat memory structure doesn't limit them to 64 KByte segments. The removal of these limits will make life easier for application programmers. Many of the PM limits have been greatly increased in OS/2 2.1.

OS/2 2.X Controls

With OS/2 2.X, PM added considerable support for new graphical features, including two standard dialogs (see Figure 9-5) for opening files and selecting fonts (these are features most applications had to constantly reinvent), and six nifty new controls (see Figure 9-6). The *Notebook* control allows an application to create hypercard-like pages organized in a notebook. The *Container* control can display objects in various formats and views. This super-powerful control supports direct manipulation and allows users to move objects between containers. The *Value Set*, another powerful control, allows a user to select from a group of icons or images. A *slider* enables a user to change or view a value by moving a slider arm.

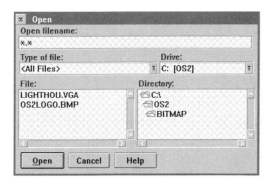 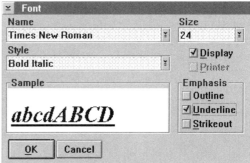

Figure 9-5. OS/2's Standard File and Font Dialogs.

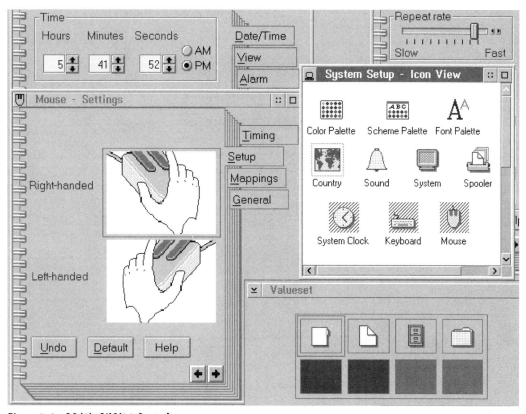

Figure 9-6. OS/2's CUA'91 Controls.

Messages and Object Orientation

PM enforces an *object-oriented*, message-based style of programming. The core of a Presentation Manager program is a set of window procedures that you write to process outside events such as the mouse or keyboard input associated with a particular window. Presentation Manager will call the appropriate window procedure and pass it parameters in the form of a message (see Figure 9-7).

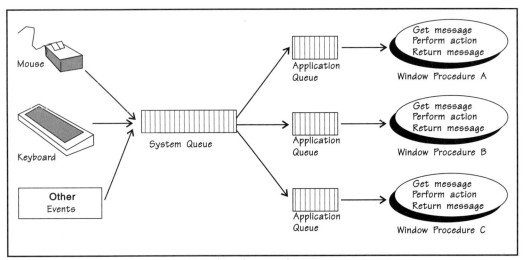

Figure 9-7. Presentation Manager's System and Window Procedures Queues.

PM's Programming Services

The following is a list of PM's most important API services:

■ *Managing windows*: PM provides a large set of API calls for controlling windows. This includes calls to allow an application to create, size, move, and control windows and their contents.

■ *Graphic primitives*: The PM GPI primitives allow you to create lines, markers, areas, arcs, and character fonts. Using these primitives, you can construct complete graphic objects that can then be displayed, printed, or stored. You can invoke the primitive set with specific attributes such as color, type of line, shape to fill, or shading levels.

■ *Graphic object management*: PM provides a set of API calls to manage graphic objects. The PM API allows you to place the graphic objects you construct (known as graphic segments) in libraries. It allows you to reuse your stored segments by drawing the same segment repeatedly into a single picture or on many graphic devices.

■ *Graphic object manipulation*: PM provides a set of API calls through which you can transform a graphic object by scaling it in size, rotating it, translating its position, or changing its slant. PM will also clip the parts of an object that lie outside a specified boundary.

■ **Presentation spaces**: PM provides a set of API calls to manage the presentation space while assembling an object from "world coordinates" to the coordinates of your display device or printer. PM allows you to draw in a virtual space and then associate your drawing with a device context. You can then switch your associations to a different device context. For example, you assemble your drawing in a virtual space; then you can choose to associate that space with a printer, display, or plotter. Consequently, PM provides a device-independent graphic system. The presentation drivers virtualize the display environment (screen, printer, and plotter). Your API calls interact with the virtual driver (a device independent interface), which then translates the request into commands for a specific device driver when you request an association.

■ **Metafiles**: PM provides a set of API calls to import or export an image object. Pictures created with the PM API can be packaged in a metafile that conforms to IBM's Mixed Object Document Content Architecture (MODCA) interchange standard. This allows another application to run the metafile and recreate the picture. The metafile contains all the PM API instructions to create the final version of the picture.

■ **Bitmaps**: PM provides a set of API calls for bitmap manipulation. Bitmap operations are very useful for animation and when areas of a screen need to be filled, moved, or restored. The PM API supports high-speed operations on bitmap representations of a screen.

■ **Clipboard**: PM provides a set of API calls that enable user-initiated exchanges of data between applications using the clipboard. A user first copies selected data into the clipboard, deletes (cuts) it from the source application, and then inserts (pastes) it into the target application from the clipboard. The cut, copy, and paste commands must be supported by an application. They are implemented as a set of PM API calls.

■ **Dynamic Data Exchange (DDE)**: PM provides a set of API calls that support the DDE protocol for message-based exchanges of data among applications. DDE can be used to construct *hot links* between applications where data can be fed from window to window without operator intervention. For example, the changes in an inventory table in a database window can be fed directly into another window where a spreadsheet is dynamically displaying inventory in graphical bar-chart format. As the inventory changes in the database, the changes get automatically reflected on the bar charts. Hot links provide a level of integration between PM applications that goes beyond the Clipboard's "cut and paste." The hot link ties the data in an application to its source. When the source data changes, the pasted data is updated automatically via the hot link. DDE defines the data format and control sequences of the message exchange. The data is exchanged using OS/2's shared memory services. Through a DDE API call, an application can automatically be advised by way of a message when

some data of interest has changed. Two DDE compliant applications having no prior knowledge of each other can negotiate (in theory) an interchange format and exchange details such as the length of each message.

■ *Drag and Drop*: PM provides a set of API functions that support protocols for the direct manipulation of objects. These protocols allow a user to visually drag a *source object* and drop it on a *target object*. The drag causes a message exchange, which may be accompanied by a data exchange, to take place between the two objects.

System Object Model (SOM)

The OS/2 2.1 Toolkit includes an object-oriented programming facility called the *System Object Model*, or SOM. SOM includes a precompiler that lets you create class libraries with any language you choose (although in the current release only C and C++ are supported). SOM is not a language; it is a system for defining, manipulating, and releasing class libraries. You use SOM to define object-oriented classes and their interrelationships (including inheritance, encapsulation, and method overrides). The methods themselves are written in C or C++.

You can think of SOM as a language-neutral object-oriented environment. You create an application by defining your classes using the SOM *Interface Definition Language (IDL)*. The IDL is then processed by a SOM precompiler to create a set of language-specific binding files (currently C and C++ only). SOM, of course, provides functions that help you debug and work with your object. SOM first became famous by providing a set of canned classes that allow you to inherit the Workplace Shell's capabilities in your own applications.

The Workplace Shell was created using SOM classes. In fact, every object in the Workplace Shell is an instance of a SOM class. Your applications can use the Workplace Shell class library "as is" to create containers, context menus, folders, and notebooks. You can also create new classes that inherit characteristics from existing Workplace Shell classes. If this is not enough, you can extend and modify the functions of any SOM class by substituting (overriding) the class-provided methods with your own.

Is DSOM the OS/2 "Killer App"?

SOM first grabbed attention when programmers discovered that it provided the *magic* for inheriting the Workplace Shell's graphical capabilities. With the release of the DSOM ORB, SOM is going into prime time and may become the "killer app" that OS/2 has been craving. The new DSOM extends SOM communications across address spaces and machines. In fact, it is emerging as the industry's premier implementation of the OMG's CORBA specification for an Object Request Broker (ORB). With the release of the C++ class bindings, SOM could set in motion a whole new objectware industry—object providers can now sell language independent object components. We cover SOM and DSOM in Part 7.

Where Does OpenDoc Fit?

Briefing

OpenDoc is a technology that enables end users to express their information in active document formats. We saw the beginning of this trend with business analysts exchanging spreadsheets loaded with data and macros over networks. Technologies, like OpenDoc, allow us to create active links between documents (and programs) scattered across the network. OpenDoc uses a distributed object infrastructure to create logical links between active documents. You won't have to ship that spreadsheet over the network, instead the data it needs will be automatically obtained and kept up-to-date by an embedded database query that resides within the document itself. Live documents will provide another communication medium. We will cover OpenDoc in Part 7.☐

Multimedia

In June of 1992, IBM introduced Multimedia Presentation Manager/2 (MMPM/2), the first multimedia extensions for OS/2. The MMPM/2 product was too late to be part of OS/2 2.0. A more advanced version of this leading-edge product was incorporated into OS/2 2.1, where it really belongs. The OS/2 2.1 multimedia supports software motion video, audio, CDs, and image. Every copy of OS/2 2.1 ships with the best multimedia engine for PCs. What does that do for programmers? It gives us a way to create some more "killer apps." Multimedia can turn a boring user interface into a one that sizzles. And this applies to any product that needs to present information and communicate with people. With OS/2, it only takes a few lines of easy REXX code to create very sophisticated multimedia effects. So may the best multimedia-enabled application win!

OS/2 2.1's multimedia facilities consist of a set of APIs, a run-time environment, and CUA '91 controls for multimedia. The API is based on the *Multimedia Programming Interface and Data Specifications* that was developed jointly by IBM and Microsoft in August of 1991. These extensions allow you to use common multimedia APIs and file formats across OS/2 and Windows. OS/2's multitasking and support for large memory objects makes PM the better platform for the development of advanced multimedia applications.

Multimedia APIs can be noisy: *they talk, sing, and play movies.* Luckily, a set of visual knobs allow you to control the volume. The new multimedia controls (see Figure 9-8) include a volume knob (also called a circular slider), an animated push button, and a two-state push button. With these standardized controls, you should

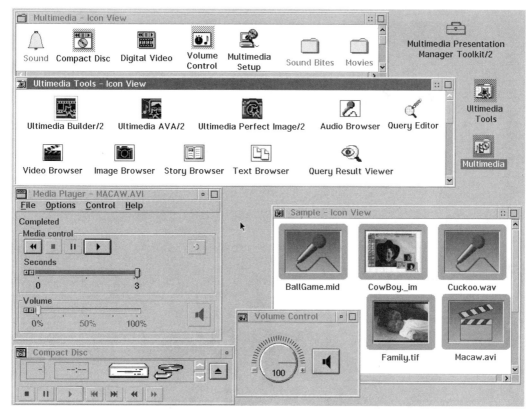

Figure 9-8. OS/2's CUA'91 Controls for Multimedia.

be able to provide consistent interfaces to any multimedia device no matter which product is being used.

Multimedia provides some very exciting architecture extensions to OS/2. Some of these extensions can be very useful to programs that have nothing to do with multimedia. A quick overview of the multimedia architecture will provide you some insight into what this feature can do for you. The multimedia subsystem (see Figure 9-9) consists of three components: the Media Control Interface (MCI), the Synchronization/Streaming Programming Interface (SPI), and the Multimedia I/O Programming Interface (MMIO). What a mouthful! The explanation follows.

The Media Control Interface (MCI)

The IBM/Microsoft MCI interface provides the heart of multimedia programming support. MCI provides a well thought-out, consistent, and device-independent

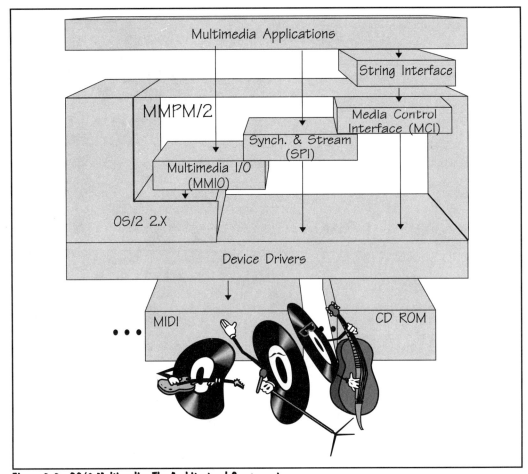

Figure 9-9. OS/2 Multimedia: The Architectural Components.

interface to different media devices. It masks the complexity and variety of multimedia devices—including video, CD audio, waveform audio, MIDI, audio amp/mixer, and videodisc—by creating a "logical device" patterned after an Audio/Video home entertainment metaphor. Commands supported by most devices include open, play, pause, stop, record, seek, and close. The first two are all that's required to get most multimedia devices to play (or display) their output.

The interface consists of two API calls: *MCISendCommand* and *MCISendString*. *MCISendCommand* is a procedural interface, while *MCISendString* allows the application to send a textual string representing the command. Here's an example of a three-command string that plays a CD: *open cdaudio alias bob; play bob; close bob.* Playing any other media is just as easy. These command strings can also be executed using the REXX interpreter.

The MCI interface allows two or more applications to share the same device, either serially or in parallel, depending on the capabilities of the device. This is an area where OS/2's preemptive multitasking provides more granular levels of device sharing than the Windows alternative.

The Synchronization Programming Interface (SPI)

The SPI component controls the synchronization of multimedia data streams such as audio and video. It ensures that video and audio playback is smooth. SPI provides a low-level interface that can be used by applications or subsystems within MMPM/2 to stream (move) data from a source device to a target device—for example, from memory to an audio adapter—without interruptions. SPI also allows applications to synchronize multiple data streams and receive notifications of real-time events. This is done by defining synchronization groups consisting of collections of streams with one data stream acting as the master. The master sends synchronization pulses to the slave streams at predefined intervals.

The SPI service really takes advantage of the preemptive multitasking capabilities of OS/2. For example, with the synchronization services you can be playing music in the background while a voice is narrating in the foreground. Or you can mix different audio tracks and create sound tracks for digital video streams. The SPI service uses OS/2's threads to provide a fine degree of real-time control over the flow of data streams to media devices. The flat memory of OS/2 is essential for handling very large data streams.

The Multimedia I/O Programming Interface (MMIO)

The MMIO is an extension of the OS/2 file services. It provides a powerful mechanism for accessing and manipulating multimedia data files. These files may contain a variety of media elements, including digital audio, digital video, images, graphics, and others. MMIO provides standard methods for applications to manipulate—open, read and write data, query the contents, and close—multimedia files.

The MMIO manager provides the following services:

- Buffered file I/O

- Functions that locate, create, enter, exit, and access RIFF data chunks (RIFF is the IBM/Microsoft Resource Interchange File Format for multimedia)

- Memory File I/O that makes a block of memory look like a file to an application

- Installable I/O procedures that allow you to supply your own functions, such as open, read, write, seek, and close on non-RIFF multimedia files (such as TIFFs)

- User-written data handlers through which you can provide additional MMIO controls for data format translations

Software Motion Video

Software Motion Video is another great OS/2 technology. You can play video synchronized with audio *without the need for special video hardware* (you need an audio card for the sound). Please take a moment to digest the implications of what this means. Are you done? Yes, you can add silent movies to your programs with a few lines of REXX code, and they will play on any OS/2 machine at no additional cost. If you don't like silent movies, add a Sound Blaster card.[4] OS/2 can play movies at 15 frames per second with a size of 320 x 240 pixels (that's 25% of a VGA or SVGA screen). This is *four* times better than the competition (which we will not name).

Movies can be created with up to 30 frames per second and in full screen. If the playback system does not support the frame rate, OS/2 will automatically scale down the video to match the processor speed. The audio will play back at the speed it was originally created, and the video will stay synchronized with it. You can also scale the movie during playback by changing the window size. OS/2's movie decompressor will scale the colors to match the video adapter during playback. *One movie covers all target playback systems.*

Be sure to play with the video applet that comes with OS/2. It will play movies recorded in Ultimotion or Indeo formats. OS/2 also supports hardware-assisted video in analog (M-Motion) or digital (ActionMedia II) form.

Sound and Music

To take advantage of the audio multimedia capabilities, you will need some additional hardware, depending on your tastes:

- A digital audio board that can be used to play (.WAV) files. These files can store representations of any sound, and they tend to be very large (compared to MIDI files). Many public bulletin boards have (.WAV) files containing everything from the sound of jets taking off to Clint Eastwood's "Go ahead...make my day!"

---

4 In addition to *Sound Blaster* from Creative Labs, OS/2 supports IBM's *M-Audio Capture and Playback* adapter and Media Vision's *ProAudio Spectrum 16*.

■ A digital audio board that supports the Musical Instrument Device Interface (MIDI) will let you record and play (.MID) files. These files contain music scores such as the sounds of guitars, drums, horns, and thundering applause.

■ Boards for other supported media types, including audio CD, videodisc, audio amp/mixer, and video overlay. Each of these types requires additional hardware and drivers from vendors.

Be sure to play with the MIDI, Compact Disk, and Digital Audio applets that come with OS/2. The *Sound Bites* folder contains a set of short digital audio and MIDI sequences. You can also associate sound bytes with 13 system events: startup/shutdown, window open/close, drag/drop, shred, desktop lockup, information, error, warning, alarm, and printer error (see Figure 9-10).

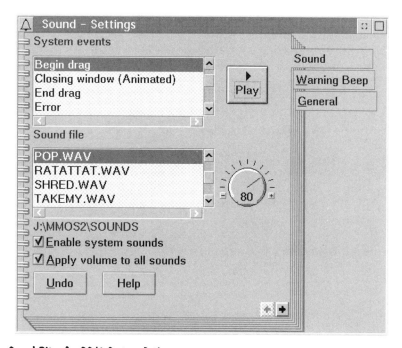

Figure 9-10. Sound Bites for OS/2 System Actions.

OS/2 2.1 DEVELOPMENT TOOLS

This section covers some of the core tools that are available to create OS/2 applications. We will have more to say about OS/2 client/server tools in Part 9.

Programming Tools

If you're getting ready to program some OS/2 applications, you'll be happy to know that there are more than 300 products that can help you develop your applications. This long list includes compilers for all the 3 GL and OO languages, class libraries, application generators, code management tools, testing tools, code analysis tools, GUI generators, multimedia tools, image document management tools, and all types of utilities. There are tools from familiar vendors—such as Borland, WATCOM, SAS, Norton, Zortech, IBM, and Bachman—and from new startups such as HockWare and Gpf. IBM publishes the **OS/2 Development Tools Guide** (G326-0326) on a quarterly basis. It should help you find the tools you need. CompuServe's OS2DF1 and OS2DF2 forums are also a good place to get information on the latest tools.

Multimedia Tools: The Ultimedia Series

You'll find your OS/2 multimedia programming support in the OS/2 2.1 Developer's Toolkit. In addition, IBM shipped in July 1993 three new OS/2 2.1 power tools for creating multimedia presentations, modifying or enhancing images, and organizing multimedia objects. These new products are:

■ **Ultimedia Builder/2**, an authoring tool that allows you to quickly and easily create multimedia presentations that can be shown as is, or embedded into everyday business letters, reports, spreadsheets, and training materials. It provides a filmstrip-like work area where users can simply drag and drop audio, video, graphics, and animation files to create their "story" or presentation. You can invoke REXX MCI string commands from the filmstrip and create sophisticated multimedia applications such as interactive kiosks, training materials, or sound and image-rich marketing demos.

■ **Ultimedia Perfect Image/2**, a tool that lets you capture images from a variety of sources, then modify and enhance them. You can resize, copy, paste, crop, or rotate digitized images. This tool can also be used to convert images between various file formats—including Audio Visual Connection (AVC), TIFF/Fax compressed, OS/2 bitmap, Windows 3.x bitmap, PCX, and TARGA. With a Video Capture Adapter card installed, you can capture still image frames from a variety of video sources, including videotape and laser disc. Images can be printed on any OS/2-supported printer.

- **Ultimedia Workplace/2**, a database for multimedia objects. A special OS/2 folder lets you see and work with miniature pictures (called *thumbnails)* of the contents of multimedia files. A media browsing facility lets you view or play the multimedia files. The tool provides an SQL query capability that allows you to join information with tables in dBase IV, Oracle, and DB2/2.

- **Video In/2** is a tool that lets you create movies on OS/2 in a few easy steps from a camcorder or VCR. The product does compression, video recording, video editing, and still image capture. So you should soon be able to create your own version of Jurassic Park on OS/2. George Lucas watch out!

The bundled Ultimedia Builder and Ultimedia Perfect Image sell for $345 (with an introductory price of $99). The Ultimedia Workplace/2 sells for $345 (with an introductory price of $99).

In addition, IBM hopes to offer the first commercial video search-and-retrieve product in the first months of 1994. Currently in beta test, the **Ultimedia Manager/2** provides the ability to search and retrieve images based on their color, texture, shape, and layout. It also lets you analyze, annotate, classify, identify, and sort images by their content. And this is not all—the tool can recognize such simple shapes as triangles, circles, and squares, as well as complex forms such as a fish or a tree. You can use this tool to query by image content or by the database records that describe your images.

GUI Tools

There is a wide selection of PM application development tools on the market. Most of these tools allow your applications to also run on Windows 3.X. Here's a sample of what tools are available:

- **EASEL** and **Enfin/3** from Easel Corp.
- **VisPro/REXX** from HockWare, Inc. (formerly UCANDU).
- **VX REXX** from WATCOM Corp.
- **Micro Focus Client/Server Solutions** from Micro Focus Corp.
- **KASE:VIP** from KASEWORKS, Inc. (formerly Caseworks).
- **Object/1** from mdbs, Inc.
- **Parts** from Digitalk, Inc.
- **ParcPlace** from ParcPlace, Inc.
- **Extensible Virtual Toolkit** from XVT Software, Inc.
- **Open Interface** from Neuron Data, Inc.
- **Applications Manager** from Intelligent Environments, Inc.
- **VZ Programmer** from VZCorp, Inc.
- **Gpf** from Gpf Systems, Inc.

- **Borland C++ with Application FrameWorks** from Borland International, Inc.
- **ObjectVision** from Borland International, Inc.
- **UI C++ Class Library** from IBM.
- **VisualAge** from IBM.

To program directly to the PM interface, you will need IBM's **OS/2 Developer's Toolkit**, which provides language-independent build tools, PM tools, multimedia header files, productivity tools, sample programs, IPF tools, SOM tools, online reference information, and a kernel debugger.

SOMobjects Developer Toolkit

SOMobjects are professional programming tools for OS/2's System Object Model (SOM) and Distributed System Object Model (DSOM) technologies. This is the toolkit for creating objects for that famous CORBA-compliant Object Request Broker (ORB). It's the "killer app" we described earlier. Here's what you get with this toolkit:

- The *DSOM ORB Services* let objects communicate across processes in a single workstation or across multiple machines on a TCP/IP or NetBIOS LAN.

- *Language Bindings for C and C++* let programmers in those languages use SOM objects and create new SOM object classes.

- The *SOM/IDL Compiler* provides language neutrality using OMG's Interface Definition Language (IDL). IDL is how objects tell potential clients what operations are available, and how they should be invoked.

- A *Replication Framework* lets you create copies of objects and synchronize changes made by multiple clients. Updates are automatically propagated to all the copies. This is great for creating groupware-like applications.

- A *Persistence Framework* lets you save and restore SOM objects to and from a repository that can be a file system, database, or object database.

- A *Framework of Collection Classes* lets you create compound objects (that is, objects that point to other objects) and navigate through the elements. SOM provides the following object container types: lists, sets, queues, and dictionaries. You can inherit from and use these SOM classes in your applications.

In Part 7, we cover SOM, DSOM, and the SOM frameworks in detail.

OS/2 2.1 was certified by IBM to run on over 1000 personal computers from 150 manufacturers. OS/2 supports just about any printer or plotter you can attach to your PC. Drivers are provided for over 260 of them in the OS/2 2.1 box; you can selectively add new ones when they become available. Drivers are provided for almost every CD-ROM and disk drive. At last count, 67 SCSI and 87 network adapters are supported. OS/2 2.1 provides 30 display drivers for VGA, SVGA, XGA, 8514, with many types of chipset combinations. OS/2 supports notebooks with Advanced Power Management (APM), PCMCIA drivers, and visual controls for battery status. So it looks like OS/2 2.1 was able to solve the "lack of driver" support issues that plagued OS/2 2.0 in its early days.

New drivers can easily be created with the support provided by a new Device Driver Kit (DDK) for writing device drivers (16-bit and 32-bit), mostly in C. The toolkit includes source code for every possible device driver type. A special Boca swat team (under the legendary Steve Mastrianni) was put in place to help you write your device drivers in record time.

In Summary

This concludes our "short" introduction to the base OS/2 system platform, which provides most of the ingredients needed to create a new generation of super-client applications. In the next chapters, we will discuss the commodity operating systems that are in direct competition with OS/2: Windows, Windows NT, NetWare 4.0, and Unix.

Soapbox or Reality?

Soapbox

I'm just a Microsoft Salesman. I tell Customers to stay away from OS/2. It's dead.

> — *Steve Ballmer, Microsoft Executive VP*
> *(October, 1993)*

IBM has a 2-year lead with OS/2 2.1.

> — *Forrester Report on Super Clients*
> *(October 1993)*

Yes, this was a long list of features, functions, and benefits. Should we count this whole chapter as one long soapbox? No, we simply presented the technical facts. Ever since OS/2 2.1 shipped in June 1993, it got nothing but rave reviews from the technical press. Independent benchmarks by that same press seem to agree that IBM has finally delivered a "better Windows than Windows 3.X" and a "better DOS than DOS." Even the predecessor, OS/2 2.0, received "best software product" awards from the major industry rags, including *PC Week*, *Datamation*, *PC Magazine*, *InfoWorld*, *PC Computing*, *PC World*, and *Computer Language*.

So what do the detractors have to say? They say, "OS/2 is OK, but..." Then take your pick on one of the following:

- "Windows owns the desktop."
- "Unix owns the server."
- "Novell owns the network, the server, and Unix."
- "NT will own the world."
- "Wait till you see Chicago."
- "Wait till you see Cairo."
- "IBM is not serious about OS/2."

Have we got them all? We will cover all these *buts* in the next chapter (get ready for some strong soapbox material). But let's answer the last one now. *Is IBM not serious about OS/2?* How can it be serious when it's got its hands in at least seven operating systems: OS/2, DOS, Taligent, AIX, OS/400, VM, and MVS?

Based on the information we presented in the last few chapters, it appears that IBM is investing heavily into OS/2's future. The Workplace OS may bring some convergence in at least five of IBM's operating systems. Since 1989, IBM has never wavered in its support of OS/2. *That's a fact*. Now that OS/2 is gaining market share, why should IBM abandon it? What alternatives does IBM have to OS/2 and the Workplace OS? The answer is not mainframes.

OK, but you may say that OS/2 is not making much money. Lee Reiswig, the President of Personal Systems Products (PSP), has publicly stated that "his business is in the black." And Jim Cannavino, a senior IBM VP, claims that IBM's PSP group is one of the largest and fastest-growing PC software companies. Despite huge cutbacks in IBM, the company says more than 1000 people were recently hired to sell OS/2 (Source: Information Week, September 6, 1993).

As you will discover in this book, IBM sells hundreds of OS/2 based products; many are very profitable. If IBM abandons OS/2, the Workplace OS, and the object frameworks, it might as well get out of the computer business. But all indications are that IBM is dead serious about these products and about staying in the computer business. It considers these products to be the basis for its future software business: ubiquitous client/server computing, distributed objects, and system integration services. Lou Gerstner, the new IBM CEO, has stated repeatedly that OS/2 and AIX are key to IBM's future. In fact, Gerstner always cites OS/2 as an example of an IBM success story.

The next question you may ask is: Will IBM survive? The answer to this question is beyond the scope of this soapbox! We don't think you'll find the answer in Paul Carroll's **Big Blues** book either. The world is moving to client/server in a big way. IBM is as well positioned as anybody else in the computer business to win the client/server sweepstakes. All we're saying (from this soapbox) is that IBM is betting its future computer business on OS/2, the Workplace OS, and object frameworks. Paul Carroll may eat his words someday if *Jim Cannavino, not Bill Gates,* ends up delivering the ubiquitous client/server computing platform. ❏

Chapter 10

OS/2 vs. DOS, Windows, and Chicago

The dominant MS-DOS environment at the desktop is technologically impoverished. Building a client/server architecture on MS-DOS is like building a house on sand. Microsoft Windows 3.X does not solve the problem because it relies upon the MS-DOS foundation.

— Gartner Group[1]

OS/2 faces some stiff competition on both the client and server sides of the platform. On the client side, the main competition comes from DOS and Windows. On the server side, the main competition comes from Unix, NT, and NetWare. We will discuss OS/2's competitors in broad terms and base our comparisons on market realities as well as the technical criteria introduced in Chapter 5, "Clients, Servers, and Operating Systems". The comparisons will help you situate OS/2 in the context of other client/server operating systems. It will also give us a chance to get on the soapbox and present some opinions and biases. "Yes, Virginia, there is an operating system war."

---

[1] Source: **Client/Server Computing: Exploiting the Inevitable**, Gartner Group (February 12, 1992).

DOS AND WINDOWS 3.X

The large installed base of PCs creates a high-quality, shrink-wrapped, software commodity market for DOS, Windows, and OS/2 application software. Bad products cannot survive for long in the mass market because they will face a costly maintenance nightmare; it takes a lot of resource to support thousands of irate customers. The software that survives on the open market is usually of very high quality, and it sells at rock-bottom commodity prices. The PC software base is the prize any OS platform must shoot for. Can we salvage that software base without the limitations of DOS and Windows?

The bad news is that in spite of Gartner's warnings, DOS and Windows clients will be with us for a long time to come. The good news is that MS-DOS, PC-DOS, DR-DOS, Windows 3.X, Windows NT, and OS/2 are all part of the same family of operating systems. This means that there is a smooth migration path from DOS and Windows to OS/2 and NT. We anticipate that the bulk of clients may initially be DOS and Windows machines and that these will be replaced with OS/2 2.1, or Chicago.

What's Wrong With DOS and Windows?

While DOS and Windows are great desktop platforms, they turn into instruments of torture when placed on a network. DOS was built as a single-tasking operating system and offers no protection between applications. Windows provides a *cooperative* form of multitasking that relies on the good will of applications to share the processor. Neither DOS nor Windows provide the typical built-in facilities for interprocess communications and synchronization.[2] Of course, neither DOS nor Windows support threads. And, finally, both DOS and Windows are 16-bit OSs with limited virtual memory facilities, which make it difficult to handle large data objects.

The lack of protection makes it difficult to manage a DOS/Windows client machine across a network. When an application crashes, it brings down the whole system and it is hard for network administrators to isolate the culprit. The lack of preemptive multitasking makes it difficult to run agents that manage the client machine on the server's behalf. DOS terminate-stay-resident programs are a crude and conflict-prone attempt to allow for server callbacks. The lack of interprocess communications makes it difficult to pass information to a particular task. The lack of support for threads causes the infamous hourglass icon to appear every time a long-winded client/server exchange takes place. Finally, the lack of preemptive

---

[2] Windows allows a user to pass data between applications using the clipboard. DDE provides a crude (and slow) form of interprocess communications. OLE 1 is really a document-centered application launcher that allows multiple applications to work on the same files. OLE 2 provides RPC-like facilities that could be useful.

Chapter 10. OS/2 vs. DOS, Windows, and Chicago

multitasking and support for large memory objects makes both DOS and Windows very limited client platforms for networked multimedia.

DOS: The OS That Won't Go Away

It will take a long time before OS/2 (or any other 32-bit OS) completely supplants DOS in the business environment for the following reasons:

■ DOS machines, when not running Windows 3.X, are significantly less expensive than OS/2 (and, of course, NT) machines. They require a lot less memory, a lot less disk, and may run on low-cost 8086-type machines.

■ DOS is an acceptable operating system for many applications that do not require multitasking or large amounts of memory.

■ There is a large inventory of 8086 type machines that cannot run Windows 3.X, OS/2, or NT.

■ There is a huge investment in DOS application software. OS/2 2.1 (and to a lesser extent NT) allows users to salvage this software investment while providing a migration path for those who can afford the hardware upgrades.

■ DOS is familiar to large numbers of users, and there may be a reluctance to migrate away from a familiar base. Again, OS/2 2.X (and to a lesser extent NT) helps alleviate that problem.

Paradoxically, these reservations do not carry over to OS/2 and NT as servers for DOS machines in a networked environment. In such an environment, OS/2 machines can cost-effectively provide shared services to DOS client machines on a network. Networks give DOS clients access to the advantages of 32-bit servers without requiring an all-at-once switch from DOS. Both OS/2 and NT seamlessly support the DOS file system and are natural servers for MS-DOS machines. The same organizations that find it too costly to put OS/2—and certainly NT—on every workstation will find that servers running these operating systems can help them leverage their existing MS-DOS machine base.

Does Windows 3.X Lead to OS/2?

Microsoft's May 1990 introduction of Windows 3.0 sparked a debate that pitted Windows against OS/2. The phenomenal acceptance of Windows and the continued popularity of MS-DOS was seen by some as a rebuff of OS/2. However, we see

Windows 3.X as providing the foundation for the mass acceptance of OS/2. Here's why:

- Windows 3.X running on DOS helped introduce a sizeable portion of the 120-million plus DOS community to the wonders of a graphical user interface and multitasking. These applications can now run unchanged on OS/2 2.1 with better multitasking, better performance, better memory management and protection, better integration with DOS applications, and better file services.

- OS/2 runs Windows and DOS applications unchanged. These applications run directly on top of the OS/2 kernel, not in emulation mode. Unlike Windows and other DOS extenders, OS/2 is not just a GUI running on top of DOS real-mode; it is a protected-mode operating system that provides exceptional stability. OS/2 provides an almost bullet-proof environment for running ordinary DOS and Windows PC applications.

- Windows 3.X applications can easily be migrated into OS/2 2.1's PM using tools such as the Micrografx Mirrors Toolkit and the new *Source Migration and Reporting Tool (SMART)* from One Up Corp. SMART, which is also marketed by IBM, includes an expert system that takes care of many of the migration chores between Windows and OS/2. The porting can be done by programmers without much PM experience. Ported applications will typically run as fast under the 32-bit PM engine. A toolkit is also provided for porting Windows 3.X drivers to OS/2.

- Millions of PCs were upgraded to run Windows 3.X. These PCs usually have enough memory, disk space, and processing power to run OS/2. This large installed base of well-endowed PCs makes the transition to OS/2 easier.

- Presentation Manager versions of Windows programs can be made more reactive by using OS/2's powerful multithreaded capabilities. A PM application designer can schedule computational or I/O bound activities as separate threads to ensure crisp user interaction at all times. The multithread PM versions of Windows applications may entice power users to migrate to OS/2.

- We need an environment to protect us from Windows crashes, especially in client/server situations where we can't tolerate unpredictable crashes that can damage work in progress. OS/2 provides such an environment.

- OS/2 provides preemptive multitasking, while Windows 3.X provides cooperative multitasking (a form of task switching). Peter Lewis of the **New York Times** explains the difference: "OS/2 can walk and chew gum at the same time. Windows takes a step, chews, takes another step, chews some more." Preemptive multitasking (some call it "true" multitasking) is needed for multimedia and networked applications.

165

Chapter 10. OS/2 vs. DOS, Windows, and Chicago

- Windows 3.X made GUI "addicts" out of masses of PC users. Once hooked on GUIs, users will always want more and more graphical sizzle. The object-oriented Workplace Shell provides the next level of sizzle. It transforms the GUI into the OOUI (pronounced "oooey")—or Object Oriented User Interface.

- Windows 3.X is introducing multimedia to thousands of PC users. OS/2 2.1— with its advanced multithreading, interprocess communications, and support for very large memory objects—provides a superior platform for multimedia. Both OS/2 2.1 and Windows 3.X support the same multimedia API extensions. This makes it easy to convert a Windows 3.X multimedia application to OS/2.

We see Windows as a low-end version of the OS/2 operating system. It's still "all in the family." OS/2 2.1 embraces DOS and Windows 3.1 and provides a smooth upgrade path. You only need to install and purchase OS/2 2.1 to get support for OS/2, Windows, and DOS applications. If you have any doubts, take a look at the OS/2 2.1 workplace shell and get a first-hand look at how it integrates *all* flavors of DOS, MS-Windows, and OS/2 applications, including device drivers (see Figure 10-1).

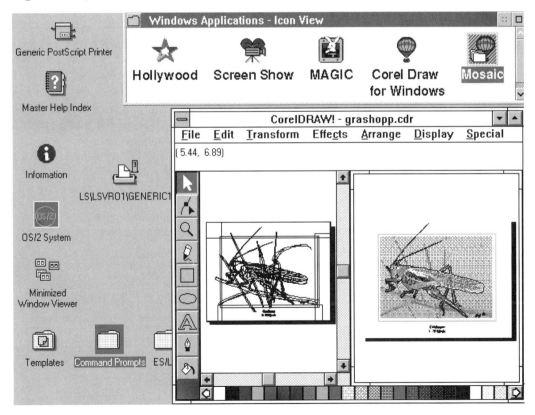

Figure 10-1. The Workplace Shell: Seamless Windows on OS/2.

In summary, OS/2 allows PC users to leverage their investment in DOS and Windows 3.X software. The potent 32-bit OS/2 platform allows PC users to take full advantage of multimedia and client/server technologies. OS/2 is currently the top 32-bit OS contender for the replacement of DOS and Windows on personal computers. We're talking about a huge market opportunity.

What About Chicago?

OS/2 delivers on the promise of Chicago today.

— Mike Kogan (January, 1994)

OS/2's first real 32-bit competition for the desktop will come from Microsoft's **Chicago**—also known as Windows 4.0—in late 1994.[3] Chicago is a 32-bit Intel-based OS that incorporates some of the OS/2 fundamentals. An early beta of Chicago reveals some OOUI elements in the still evolving user interface. Chicago also implements long file names with the FAT file system.

---

[3] Chicago hasn't even been announced and was already delayed several times.

In terms of networking support, Chicago incorporates a NetWare compatible redirector and the peer services that resemble those in Windows for Workgroups. Chicago implements the *Win32c* variant of the Windows API—a subset of the NT API that does not implement security and event-logging. Win32c also introduces additional APIs that handle the new features in the user interface. Chicago promises to support the *Plug and Play* initiative—a standard that will allow OSs (including OS/2) to automatically discover and configure hardware adapters. There is some talk of Chicago supporting replicated file synchronization.

Microsoft promises to run Chicago comfortably on 80386-based PCs with 4 MBytes of memory. IBM is also talking about a slimmer OS/2 that will fit within Chicago-like constraints. OS/2 2.1 currently requires 6 MBytes to run comfortably.

According to columnist Will Zachmann, Chicago is Microsoft's attempt to regain the 32-bit OS momentum that slipped from it when it became obvious that NT was not going to be a smashing success. *Daytona* (the 3Q 1994 NT upgrade) does too little to turn the tide. Microsoft could have cut corners by shipping a new 16-bit version of Windows but it chose not to do so; scaling down NT also proved unfeasible. So Microsoft is creating a new OS from scratch. Most Microsoft observers are skeptical that Chicago will ship in 1994. It typically takes at least two years to wring the bugs out of a new *monolithic* operating system; microkernels have better track records.

At the end of the long wait for Chicago, we'll be getting an OS that looks like OS/2 today, provides the same functionality, and may weigh two MBytes less. The industry will then spend some time getting out applications that work on Chicago and exploit its snazzy new OOUI-look. In the meantime, Chicago will run 16-bit DOS and Windows applications and will be judged by how well it does that. If this all seems like *deja vu*, it's because we're replaying the OS/2 2.X story a few years later. Of course, OS/2 won't sit still in 1994—it too will shed a few MBytes (and add more than 90 new features).

However, in this business the winners are not determined through features and functions alone; if that were the case NextStep would have carried the day. Let's face it, Chicago—whatever year it ships—will be an instant success. This is because Microsoft will preload it on most new PCs that ship that year—that's instant success! Of course, the PC software houses know that, so they're probably going to spend the bulk of their 32-bit development dollars on Chicago applications. IBM is rumored to have a kit that converts 32-bit OS/2 applications to Chicago. The idea is: "Develop for OS/2 today and then instantly port your applications to Chicago when it ships."

Of course, IBM hopes to create a critical mass market for OS/2 *before* Chicago ships and then run a Chicago personality from within OS/2 *after* it ships (see Soapbox). This will allow OS/2 to maintain its lead as the integrating platform for the desktop. *OS/2 For Windows*, or as Jerry Pournelle prefers to call it "OS/2 for

Windows Users," provides a wonderful role model for how to seamlessly integrate future Microsoft OSs without paying royalties. Can IBM repeat that trick? Can it ship *OS/2 for Chicago Users* on time? Find out by reading the Soapbox.

Can OS/2 Do Chicago?

Soapbox

I think IBM is quite capable of providing Windows capability, at least in the short term.

— Paul Grayson,
Chairman of Micrografx Inc.
(September 13, 1993).

OS/2 has a tremendous headstart over Chicago in running DOS and Windows applications in a 32-bit environment. Objects, Multimedia, and the Workplace Shell OOUI may create a huge installed base of OS/2-centered applications. Can OS/2, in addition, continue to provide a "better Windows than Windows" that includes Chicago?

The critics claim that OS/2 will not be able to keep up with Windows because IBM stopped getting source code from Microsoft in September of 1993. Even when it had access to the code, the critics claim, it took IBM one year to provide support for Windows 3.1 on OS/2. Can IBM meet the challenge of providing seamless Windows support in OS/2 within 3 months (or less) of a new Windows release? Can it incorporate Chicago seamlessly into OS/2? IBM appears not to be worried. Here's some soapbox speculation why that's so:

■ IBM has the full rights to clone the Windows API, either with or without the use of source code, in perpetuity.

■ **OS/2 2.1 for Windows 3.1** uses the real Windows from within the OS/2 environment. OS/2 locates windows files on the user's machine then incorporates the subdirectory as the Windows subsystem used to run Windows from within OS/2. IBM has a huge financial incentive not to use Windows source code licensed from Microsoft. According to **ComputerWorld** (September 13, 1993), "IBM won't have to pay Microsoft $20 for every copy of OS/2 it ships" if it does not incorporate Windows 3.X code.

Chapter 10. OS/2 vs. DOS, Windows, and Chicago

169

- OS/2 2.1 includes some breakthrough technology that allows a Windows application to literally appear in a "hole" carved into the Workplace Shell. This technology potentially allows any GUI to seamlessly integrate into the Workplace Shell. One reason it took IBM so long to incorporate Windows 3.1 was to create that "seamless hole." This is one key piece of code that won't need to be recreated the next time around. This hole makes it possible to create **OS/2 for Windows** within OS/2. And in the future it may be used to create **OS/2 for Chicago Users**.

- IBM was given the September preliminary release of the Chicago code. The *Win32c* API was published and given to developers. IBM has more than a year to reverse engineer this API set.

- It is much easier to port a 32-bit API, like Chicago, to OS/2 than a 16-bit Windows API. You don't have to deal with thunking layers, incompatible memory models, and 16-bit device drivers. And since OS/2 2.X is a superset of Chicago, the port should be easy. We wouldn't be surprised if IBM's Chicago on OS/2 isn't more stable than Microsoft's Chicago 1.0—the first release of a new OS.

- The Windows market is too large for Microsoft to introduce undocumented APIs without creating an industry uproar (and the lawsuits that come with it).

- IBM simply has to stay ahead of the thousands of Windows apps. The major apps are much harder to change (or develop) than any emulation code IBM creates.

In summary, OS/2 2.1 provides the most advanced technology in the industry for the seamless integration of multiple GUIs on a single desktop. This technology will be used in the Workplace OS to support multiple personalities. We speculate that IBM has the technology to easily create a Chicago personality within OS/2. ❑

What About Macintosh

Soapbox

The Macintosh is a powerful desktop client machine, but the size of its installed base and market is dwarfed by that of the PC. Macintosh has its own obvious "niche" in the client market. The Macintosh provides a nice user interface but it is limited by the System 7.1's inability to provide preemptive multitasking. Instead, System 7.1 provides a form of cooperative multitasking that leaves it up to the applications to determine how the processor is shared. Cooperative multitasking is not well-suited for handling desktops with highly concurrent activities. System 7.1 provides a limited mount of intertask protection, and its virtual memory support is limited (Apple recommends you not go over twice the amount of physical memory). System 7.1 provides built-in support for peer networking by allowing users to share folders (directories) and printers on the network.

Apple's strategy is to turn the Macintosh into a modern client/server platform. It plans to do that by providing a microkernel version of System 7.X that runs on PowerPC RISC processors as well as on Motorolla 680X0 CISC processors. The PowerPC version of System 7.X—some call it System 8—will probably run on the IBM Microkernel (or OSF/1) and emulate the 680X0 instruction set. In addition, Apple may provide a microkernel for the 680X0 to support its existing installed base. The new Apple operating system will support preemptive multi-tasking, symmetric multiprocessing, threads, OpenDoc, object frameworks, and all the good stuff that's expected in a modern operating system. We speculate that the Macintosh will become another personality on the Workplace OS that runs existing System 7.X programs. The future Macintosh, like OS/2, will be a heavy user of Taligent technology. In fact, it will be hard to draw the lines between these three operating systems (other than by their support of legacy applications). ❑

Chapter 11

OS/2 vs.
Windows NT

We love them all equally and we hate them all equally. Our strategy is operating system agnosticism.

> — *Jim Manzi, Chairman of Lotus Corp.*
> *(New York Times, April 25, 1993).*

What is a 32-bit OS that runs on Intel and RISC, ends the war in Bosnia, and provides a cure for cancer? NT, of course! Yes, Microsoft Windows NT (New Technology) poses the greatest challenge to OS/2 2.1 as the premier server platform for PCs. This is not surprising since NT started out as the portable OS/2. It was designed to be the portable OS/2 kernel that would run on multiple hardware platforms (Intel and RISC) and support symmetric multiprocessing. It was to be a "better OS/2 than OS/2" by supporting Windows, DOS, OS/2, and POSIX-compatible applications. Building such a full featured operating system is enormously complex. Today, both IBM and Microsoft are creating their own versions of portable OS/2. **Byte** magazine's editor, Michael Nadeau, finds it worth cheering about that "two strong companies competing fiercely to develop a 32-bit OS ensures that OS/2 and NT will evolve rapidly in response to one another and that end-user concerns will be quickly addressed." Nadeau feels that this contest will energize the PC market and create

operating systems that support features such as multimedia and object-based technologies.

WINDOWS NT'S FEATURES

Windows NT, like OS/2, is a thread-based preemptive multitasking operating system. NT supports symmetric multiprocessing with a microkernel-like executive that runs on Intel 80386 (and above) as well as the MIPS and Alpha RISC platforms. NT runs DOS, 16-bit Windows, 32-bit Windows (Win32), POSIX, and 16-bit OS/2 (without PM) applications. NT, like OS/2, uses the flat memory model and can support up to 4 GBytes of RAM. NT supports lots of storage—up to 24 volumes of 17 billion GBytes each. NT supports three file systems: NTFS, DOS and OS/2's FAT, and OS/2's HPFS. NTFS, which stands for *NT File System*, maintains a transaction log of all file accesses. This helps in the recovery of data lost due to power failures. The NTFS file system is C2 certifiable (the actual certification process takes more than a year to complete from the time an OS ships). C2 is a government security standard for operating systems; it requires that users and applications get authenticated before gaining access to any operating system resource. NT supports memory-mapped files that allow disk-based files to be assigned a range of virtual memory addresses.

NT's Distributed Services

In addition to the typical operating system functions described previously, NT bundles the following distributed services:

- **Built-in networking.** NT provides built-in support for the following protocols: TCP/IP, IPX/SPX, NetBIOS, Named Pipes, Mailslots, and a DCE-like RPC.

- **Resource sharing.** NT clients can share resources such as printers and files (this is like Windows for Workgroups). *Windows NT Advanced Server* provides a full function implementation of LAN Manager.

- **Groupware.** This includes a limited version of MS-Mail, MS-Schedule, and TCP/IP utilities such as Telnet and FTP.

- **System management.** This includes an SNMP agent, built-in statistics gathering, and an automated network configurator called the Registry. The Registry contains all the information found in INI files, and you're not supposed to mess around with it.

- **Windows NT Advanced Server.** This server version of NT includes all the NT client functions, LAN Manager, Remote Access Services for dial-in clients, and Macintosh client support. NT Advanced Server uses a trusted server domain type of administration, similar to the one used in IBM's LAN Server for OS/2. NT Advanced, like LAN Server for OS/2, supports Uninterrupted Power Supplies (UPS), disk mirroring, and RAID disk drives.

In summary, NT packs an impressive list of features that makes it easy to understand what the fuss is all about. But there's more to the story.

NT and NT Advanced Server

NT comes in two flavors—the desktop operating system, called simply Windows NT; and Windows NT Advanced Server, which is positioned as an enterprise-wide network operating system. Table 11-1 compares the features of NT and NT Advanced Server.

Table 11-1. Windows NT Base and Extended Features.

Feature	Microsoft Windows NT	Microsoft Windows NT Advanced Server
Retail Price	$500	$3000
Minimum Memory	12-16 MBytes	16+ MBytes
Disk Space	70 MBytes	100 MBytes
SMP Processors	2	4 (see note)
Network Support	TCP/IP, IPX/SPX, NetBIOS, Named Pipes, Mailslots DCE RPC	Same as NT, plus Remote Access, Macintosh clients, single logon for all clients.
Network Services	File and Print sharing	Same as NT, plus LAN Manager support (including remote administration using domains, UPS, and RAID support).
File Systems	FAT, HPFS, NTFS	FAT, HPFS, NTFS
Multimedia	MCI, MIDI, Sound	MCI, MIDI, Sound
User Interface	Windows 3.1	Windows 3.1

Note: More processors can be added by creating special drivers that plug into NT's Hardware Abstraction Layer (HAL). This is what vendors like Sequent and Net-Frame are doing.

NT AS A CLIENT

Microsoft is positioning NT as an advanced server platform. NT is certainly not the migration platform for your average MS-Windows client workstation. NT's resource requirements—over 12 MBytes of RAM and 100 Mbytes of disk—is more than what most Notebooks can handle today. NT's other major drawback as a client platform is that it does not run all existing Windows applications out-of-the box. The problem is that all Windows applications need to be tested for compliance with NT, and there are thousands of such applications. NT runs all 16-bit Windows applications in the same address space and only supports them in cooperative multitasking mode (like Windows 3.X does today). NT does not support PM (or OS/2 2.X) or GUI-based POSIX applications in its first release, which limits NT's effectiveness as an integrating client desktop.

NT's strongest features as a client platform is its support for multitasking and its familiar Windows GUI environment. Techies like NT's multiple input queues because now each application can do its own thing without causing the entire system to lock (the hourglass pointer). NT is also relatively easy to install and configure.

Soapbox

Client Wars: NT Versus OS/2

One look at Table 11-1 should convince you that NT is too bulky (twice the size of OS/2) and too bloated for a client platform. That's why Microsoft is working so diligently on Chicago. In the meantime, OS/2 is getting better every day as millions of users stress its existing 32-bit client features.

If you were to pick NT for a client, what type of applications could you run on it? Mostly Windows and DOS. There are very few native NT applications—even Microsoft won't come out with an NT application spread any time soon. So how well does NT run Windows and DOS? Not very well, at least when compared with OS/2, which provides a much better environment for running DOS and Windows applications. For starters, OS/2 runs these applications faster than NT. Independent tests published in **PC Magazine** (September 28, 1993) show that OS/2 runs DOS and Windows applications faster than NT. Going to an Alpha or MIPS machines only makes NT run DOS and Windows much slower (it now needs to translate the processor calls). Can you imagine buying Alpha and MIPS machines that can only run Intel software slower than a 386? Oh boy!

OS/2 runs most DOS and Windows 3.1 programs out of the box, while NT's security system limits its backward compatibility with some DOS and Windows 3.1 applications. NT runs all 16-bit Windows applications in the same address space and only supports them in cooperative multitasking mode. OS/2, on the other hand, can protect the client environment from misbehaved Windows applications by providing each 16-bit Windows application with its own separate address space. OS/2 also provides preemptive multitasking support for Windows 3.1 applications. NT supports Win32s applications. IBM has indicated OS/2 will do the same. NT supports multiple queues. IBM has indicated OS/2 will do the same. Both NT and OS/2 are easy to install from a CD-ROM. Otherwise, you'll get elbow fatigue inserting 18 floppies for OS/2 and 22 for NT. OS/2 has better multimedia than NT (it supports full motion video). OS/2 provides better desktop integration by letting DOS, Windows, and OS/2 applications share the same clipboard.

Finally, the OS/2 Workplace Shell provides the basis for an object-oriented user interface (OOUI). OOUIs will transform the way we interact with computers for the better. With NT, you're still faced with the dreadful Windows File and Program Managers. NT even uses the old Windows help engine. If you're into nostalgia and old Frank Sinatra songs, you'll love NT. However, this industry needs to keep moving. We can't freeze the user interface with a 1988 vintage Windows-look forever. PCs are progressive desktop machines. If we wanted to freeze the user interface forever, we should have stuck to terminals and the "green screen uglies". Where's Steve Jobs? We need to overthrow the totalitarian Windows interface. The Workplace Shell and NextStep are trying to do just that. So, whose got the better client? ❏

NT AS A SERVER

NT Advanced Server is an attractively priced package that sets a new bar for PC servers. On paper, NT is the ideal server system for PCs—it removes most of the system limits, supports symmetric multiprocessing, and provides a familiar user interface. The Win32 programming environment and tools are familiar to programmers versed in Microsoft tools. So we can expect to see some great server applications appear some day on the NT. All this sounds idyllic, so where's the catch?

There really is a catch: NT is great until you start comparing it with rival server platforms like NetWare, Unix, and OS/2 (with Workplace OS). Here are some examples of reality intruding on the dream:

■ *NT Advanced Server is slow and bulky as a file server.* NT Advanced server is slower than both NetWare and IBM's LAN Server, it also eats up a lot more resources. **PC Week** (August 16, 1993) published benchmark results that show NT Advanced Server to be considerably slower than NetWare 3.11 as a file server, and it needed 4-8 MBytes more memory. According to *LANQuest LABs*, an independent test lab, IBM's OS/2 LAN Server 3.0 is 45% faster than the NT Advanced Server. "Overall, OS/2's LAN Server 3.0 supported up to 4 times the number of users and 2.4 times the peak throughput of Microsoft Windows NT Advanced Server."[1]

---

[1] Source: **LANQuest** (October, 1993). According to the LANQuest report, "NT's performance fell off significantly after more than 100 users. Above this load, too few clients completed the test to produce valid results. Microsoft's LAN Man 2.2 on OS/2 was able to do 200 equivalent users, but fell apart at 300." OS/2's LAN Server was tested successfully at 300 and 400 users.

■ ***NT's SMP does not scale well.*** NT's version of SQL Server got some good reviews as a high performance database. However, when it came to Symmetric Multiprocessing (SMP) scalability, *ZD Labs* discovered that NT running SQL Server can only deliver an 85% increase in throughput using a 4-CPU machine.[2] In this case Microsoft makes both the operating system and the database server, so the two are optimally integrated. The 4-CPU results show that NT's SMP is far from delivering linear scalability, even with a thread-intensive application like SQL Server.

■ ***NT does not support a command language.*** System administrators found NT's lack of support for a batch command language (like REXX) to be a major nuisance.

We will introduce more of these comparisons later in this chapter. You'll discover that NT does not support NetWare well and a few other nasty little details.

As more applications go into production, the NT dream will be replaced by the even harsher reality of everyday server life. *Rome wasn't built in one day, and neither is a server platform.* Server platforms get seasoned with mission-critical usage. Most importantly, server middleware such as communication protocols, network operating systems, DBMSs, TP Monitors, Distributed Object Managers, and System Management software have to go through long gestation periods in production environments that catch the bulk of the bugs. NT and everything else on top of it is starting at ground zero. In contrast, Unix, NetWare, and OS/2 are seasoned server platforms.

It's Rough Out There

NT as a server is competing in a marketplace where training, installation, support, system integration, and client/server skills are critical for the success of the product. An advanced server platform requires a long sales cycle and a lot of customer hand-holding. NT must learn how to coexist with every form of legacy system if it is to play a role in the enterprise. Who will provide all this system integration and support? This is an area where Microsoft is very weak. It has had practically no success with client/server or multiuser products. Microsoft's forte is shrink-wrapped products. In contrast, OS/2 is supported by thousands of IBM system engineers who have some of the industry's best system integration skills. NetWare is supported by Novell's vast army of certified resellers who are very experienced at installing and supporting networks. Unix can count on vast pools of client/server specialists. There are more trained client/server consultants on SCO Unix alone than in all of Microsoft.

---

[2] Source: **PC Week** (September 13, 1993).

In addition to NT, Microsoft has many other irons in the fire—Cairo, Chicago, DOS, and its application software. Can Microsoft stay focused on NT? Can it dominate the client/server market? Unfortunately, we don't know the answers. It is foolish, of course, to underestimate Microsoft and the vast financial, technical, and marketing resources it controls.

Server Wars: NT versus OS/2

Soapbox

NT as a server platform appears overwhelming at first glance. It's a modern 32-bit operating system that seems to be preloaded at the factory with everything it takes to create server applications. How can OS/2 compete against such a monster? The answer is very well. Now let's look at why OS/2 2.X (and Workplace OS) make a *better* server platform:

■ *OS/2 2.X is optimized for Intel*. OS/2 2.X exploits Intel. There are no portability layers. It is a very suitable platform for 90% of the server applications that do not require C2 security, SMP, and a portable kernel. OS/2 2.X should provide SMP support by the end of 1994.

■ *Workplace OS provides a better microkernel architecture*. Workplace OS is based on the IBM Microkernel, which combines the proven Mach 3 technology with innovation from IBM and four years of object-oriented microkernel research at Taligent (the details are in Chapter 8, "Coming Soon: Workplace OS"). The IBM Microkernel is a real screamer that can handle very large numbers of objects (of all sizes) at very high levels of performance. Like NT, it will provide C2 security. A nice feature of the IBM Microkernel is that it allows different personalities to share device drivers and server subsystems because they run in the microkernel user space. In contrast, NT's device drivers and the file system reside in the microkernel itself, which makes it more difficult to port existing personalities. IBM was able to port DOS, Windows, OS/2, and AIX personalities to the Workplace OS in record time because of that clean separation. Some of this work is documented in the "USENIX Mach Symposium Proceedings" (April, 1993).

Another shortcoming is the overhead NT introduces by using Win32 as the intermediary between the different personalities (NT subsystems) and the microkernel (the NT executive). The IBM Microkernel treats all personalities as equals (the user chooses the dominant personality for the desktop). Finally, IBM is making its microkernel more open by licensing it to other vendors and universities.

You may recall that NT was initially co-developed by IBM and Microsoft when both companies were working together on portable OS/2 in the fall of 1988. And for many years after that, IBM continued to fund the development of NT. In July of 1992, IBM decided not to exercise its right to the NT technology and chose instead to go with the Mach 3.0 derived microkernel (a parallel effort it was working on). IBM must believe its microkernel is superior to NT.

■ ***Workplace OS provides better personality support***. Workplace OS will surface each personality's user interface (Workplace Shell, Motif/COSE, Taligent, or Windows). NT takes a more totalitarian approach and assumes the only GUI for all times is Windows; other personalities are relegated to the character I/O penalty box. NT does not support a Unix personality (it just runs the POSIX APIs and does not deliver all the functions specified by POSIX, including a Unix shell and utilities). Workplace OS will run multiple variants of Unix. In addition, Workplace OS will support DOS, Windows, OS/2, and Taligent personalities. You can remove a personality when it is no longer needed (for example, 16-bit Windows).

■ ***NT's C2 security is overplayed***. NT won't have C2 certification until 1995. In any case, C2 may be useful for marketing purposes (and government contracts), but it doesn't make much sense in heterogeneous client/server environments with DOS and Windows clients. C2 requires that all clients and servers be secure. You can never get that with DOS and Windows clients. These clients can copy files from a C2 server to anywhere else. C2 security is not provided for the FAT or HPFS file systems on NT. So much for certification. In the meantime, setting up security on NT is a pain. You must add your ID to every PC you need to access on the network. Interestingly, Microsoft is making such a big play on C2 security and yet is not providing a minimal network authentication service.

■ ***NT does not run NetWare Server***. As we explain later in the next chapter, the NetWare 4.0 server code runs on OS/2. This is a great advantage for small shops and departments that cannot afford a proliferation of servers. Novell holds the keys to the LAN. OS/2 learned how to coexist with NetWare servers (even on the same machine). OS/2's system management supports Novell's NetWare Management System (NMS) offering. NT doesn't.

■ ***OS/2's "a la carte" middleware is superior to what NT bundles***. Microsoft is not known for its great networking software. NT's TCP/IP offering is incomplete and is no match against OS/2's best-of-breed TCP/IP offering. NT's DCE RPC APIs and stub compiler are not fully OSF/DCE-compliant. Microsoft does not offer DCE directory services or DCE Kerberos-based authentication. The OSF DCE works with these two services (RPC clients use the directory to locate servers and Kerberos to authenticate themselves). OS/2's DCE is complete and OSF-compliant. Microsoft's system management offering in NT is minimal compared to OS/2's LAN NetView. Even *Hermes* will not come near what OS/2 has to offer. It's relying on NetView/6000 to fill the holes. The mail and calendaring products included with NT are inferior to products such as *cc:Mail* or *Time And Place/2*. Finally, NT's Remote Access Service is inferior to OS/2's superb LAN Distance Product.

- ■ *OS/2 has a single 32-bit API base for both the client and server.* OS/2, unlike Windows and NT, has one 32-bit API base for OS/2 2.X, Workplace OS, and object frameworks. Windows and NT have five different API bases to support: Win16, Win32, Win32s, Win32c, and Cairo. This proliferation of APIs makes it difficult and expensive for programmers to write (and maintain) client/server applications in the Windows and NT environments. Microsoft recently reorganized its API variants into a "single" Win32 API. However, this doesn't change the fact that there are different Windows products, each requiring a different API subset.

- ■ *NT does not do distributed objects.* This is a technology where OS/2 has a one-year headstart. Organizations that learn how to tap the power of distributed objects will develop better client/server applications sooner. With OS/2's DSOM, you can start doing real work with objects now.

- ■ *OS/2 supports a large base of server products.* OS/2 currently supports products like Lotus Notes, Person-to-Person, CICS, Oracle, and DB2/2. With NT, you'll have to wait for the "seasoned" ports. This puts you behind. However, Microsoft's SQL Server on NT is a nice piece of work (hat's off on that one).

In summary, we like NT's advanced architecture, but we're convinced the Workplace OS is better. We also like the "lean and mean" OS/2 2.X optimized for Intel (it will remain our favorite server for 90% of the jobs). And OS/2, unlike Windows and NT, has one 32-bit API base to support. We like Microsoft's idea of bundling together a client/server platform. Unfortunately, what they put together was not too thrilling. OS/2's *a la carte* client/server offerings are superior. IBM is rebundling some of that software to offer an NT-like packaging scheme. As you'll see throughout this book, IBM's *a la carte* offerings are very tightly integrated. For example, LAN Server 3.0 and NetWare 4.0 for OS/2 (the server) are integrated down to Ring 0 (the privileged kernel area). ❑

Chapter 12

OS/2 vs.
NetWare 4.0

NetWare NLMs do crash unpredictably and without resolution.

— Richard Finkelstein (October, 1993)

NetWare 4.0, released in the early part of 1993, offers an attractive 32-bit server platform for Intel machines. In addition to Novell's very popular file server, communications protocols, messaging, and LAN administration services, NetWare 4.0 introduces a new security service and a distributed directory patterned after the X.500 international standard. The main weakness of NetWare 4.0's enterprise server strategy is that it is not DCE-compliant. This means that NetWare does not interoperate with DCE's directory services, security services, or RPC. This may be a significant problem in an enterprise setting. Another problem is that NetWare's messaging directory and the NetWare Directory Services are different. This separates mail from the rest of the distributed services.

Novell built its reputation as the superfast file server vendor. To become a general purpose application server vendor, Novell needs to find a way to open its server platform. With NetWare 3.1, Novell introduced *NetWare Loadable Modules (NLMs)*, which are special name spaces set aside on the server that allow programmers to provide new system services. The NLM server modules you create get loaded by NetWare to manage these name spaces. Your NLMs, in effect, become part of the NetWare operating system kernel. Novell provides tools and a programming environment for the development of NLMs.

THE NLM PROBLEM

NLMs are the Achilles' heel of NetWare and have been slow to catch on with third-party developers used to writing applications for conventional operating systems such as Unix and OS/2.[1] Here's some of the problems with NLMs that make it very difficult (if not impossible) to use NetWare as a general-purpose application server platform:

- *Lack of memory protection.* NLM applications in NetWare 3.1 are not memory protected. They operate in Ring 0, which is reserved for the operating system. A bug in an application can bring the whole system down. The applications and the NetWare OS can conflict. NLMs crash unpredictably and without resolution. NetWare 4.0 partially alleviates the problem by providing optional memory protection. Novell gives users the option of running NLMs outside of Ring 0 (with 20% performance degradation). The tradeoff is one of speed versus a slightly higher level of memory protection—if an application crashes in the "protected domain," it still brings down the Ring 3 apps but not NetWare itself. OS/2, NT, and all Unix variants provide bullet-proof memory protection.

- *Lack of memory management.* NetWare treats all memory as one flat segment. It does not support virtual memory services, a standard service in conventional operating systems such as OS/2, NT, and Unix. The lack of virtual memory (that is, no support for paging code in and out of memory) limits the number of NetWare applications that can run on a server. Developers must worry about memory conflicts, which are always a real danger in NetWare.

- *Lack of preemptive multitasking.* NetWare will not interrupt a running application to allow one with higher priority to run. A misbehaved application

---

1 The exception is the database vendors who broke their teeth porting their DBMSs to the NetWare platform. Nine popular database servers were ported to NetWare 3.1. Oracle reported in 1991 that its 32-bit NetWare product was significantly faster than its 16-bit OS/2 version. Database benchmarks tend to cache in memory the bulk of the database (NetWare 3.11 supports 4 GBytes of RAM address space to 16-bit OS/2's 16 MBytes). Of course, OS/2 2.1 does not have the 16-bit limitation and supports very large memory objects (up to 512 MBytes in size). Here's what **PC Magazine** (October, 1993) had to say about its annual SQL shootout, "The big news this year is that for the first time OS/2 databases can keep up with NetWare NLMs." What made that possible is the new crop of 32-bit OS/2 database engines from Oracle, Ingres, IBM, XDB, Raima, and Gupta.

that runs for a long time (such as a batch job) can cause problems for everybody else. Developers are responsible for structuring and managing the priority of running tasks within the NLMs they create. OS/2, NT, and most Unix variants support preemptive multitasking.

- **Limited programming tools**. With NLMs, you are dependent on a Novell-specific programming environment. OS/2 and Unix support a very rich general-purpose programming environment with compilers available from all major vendors.

- **NetWare lock in.** NLMs will run only on NetWare networks. OS/2 and Unix server applications will run on anyone's network, including Novell.

WHAT DOES NOVELL DO FOR AN ENCORE?

In summary, NLMs grew as ad hoc tools to allow non-Novell vendors to extend the NetWare platform. They do not provide the robustness you expect from general-purpose operating systems such as OS/2 or Unix. According to Richard Finkelstein, NetWare's non-preemptive status puts too much of the burden on the application developer because it requires applications to be bug free, "a virtual impossibility with the complexity of software we are talking about."[2] To ease some of the NLM problems, Novell established an NLM certification program. In general, it's not a good idea to run application NLMs on the same machine that provides the file or database servers. Some people even recommend that you only run one NLM on each server, but it's untenable.

Novell's acquisition of USL may be an admission that it needs a general-purpose programming platform such as Unix to become a major player in the application server market. With Novell as the proud owner of USL, NetWare is sure to become an integral part of Unix (or vice versa). But in the meantime, how will Novell position NetWare as an application development platform? They can't just openly say, "NLMs are bad for apps...move on to UnixWare."

---

[2] Richard Finkelstein is president of *Performance Computing, Inc.*, a Chicago-based database consulting firm.

NetWare and OS/2: Friend or Foe?

Soapbox

OS/2, unlike NT, is in the fortunate position of being able to run the NetWare 4.0 server platform on top of native OS/2 2.X. NetWare on OS/2 runs at 92% of the performance of native NetWare. You should be able to run your favorite NetWare server software and any OS/2 programs on the same machine. This feature is very attractive (in terms of maintenance and costs) to small shops and departments. They can economically run a NetWare file server and an OS/2 application server on the same physical machine. With NT (and most Unix variants), they will need two separate server machines. Even UnixWare, Novell's own Unix product based on System V Release 4.2 (SVR4.2), currently only supports the NetWare client feature. Novell is planning to integrate its NetWare server software with a future version of UnixWare.

NetWare servers compete head-on with OS/2 servers in installations that only require a file server or database server. However, installations that use OS/2 as their application server can pick either the OS/2 LAN Server or NetWare on OS/2 as their file server. OS/2 is also a good choice for installations that need to run a NetWare file server and an OS/2 transaction server on the same machine.

OS/2 and NetWare will compete in the area of distributed objects—NetWare intends to provide a built-in NLM version of HyperDesk's Distributed Object Manager (DOM), while OS/2 supports DSOM. However, an OS/2 server running the DOM NLM and the OS/2 version of DSOM can provide the perfect gateway between these two ORBs.

OS/2 complements NetWare by providing Symmetric Multiprocessing (SMP) for NLMs. NetWare does not support SMP, but OS/2 will do so in 1994. NetWare on OS/2 is the first Intel platform that provides SMP support for NetWare servers. This means that NetWare NLMs—including database and file servers—may get some of the scalability benefits of SMP on an OS/2 platform.

In summary, OS/2 and NetWare complement each other when they both run on the same machine and compete in single service types of situations. On the other hand, NT and NetWare are in the middle of a "winner take all" competition. NT and NetWare servers can only coexist if they're on separate machines (and even then it is not very smooth). ❑

Chapter 13

OS/2 vs. UNIX

Unix is kind of like a cookie—it looks tempting, but you shouldn't succomb...While the technical prowess of Unix is more than adequate...the continued "version warfare" makes Unix a problem in real life.

— *Aaron Goldberg, President of InfoCorp, (March 22, 1993)*

Which Unix? At last count, there were over 40 variants of Unix on the market. Which of these variants will compete against OS/2 and NT? All of them, of course. Our immediate dilemma is how to introduce Unix as a competitive platform without covering all 40 variants, each of which has something a bit different to offer. We will first go cover the tumultuous evolution of Unix—these folks make the Windows versus OS/2 wars look tame—and then try to do some technical comparisons with OS/2.

UNIX: THE IDEALISTIC DAYS

In 1969, Ken Thomson of Bell Labs wrote in C a tiny time-shared OS kernel for the DEC PDP-7 minicomputer; they called it Unix. In 1970, Thomson and his partner Dennis Ritchie moved Unix to the more popular PDP-11 and made history. Unix quickly grew popular because several generations of OS developers were able to add new layers of functions, device support, and other extensions on top of the original Thomson/Ritchie kernel—the system is highly extensible.

In 1975, AT&T made the critical decision of making the Unix code available to universities at virtually no charge. Several generations of computer scientists learned how to program on Unix systems. More importantly, they learned how to port Unix to different computers and extend its basic facilities. Every computer science department seemed to have invented the "perfect set" of Unix extensions. The most popular of these extensions—known as *Berkeley Software Distribution (BSD) Unix*, created at the University of California, Berkeley—added built-in networking support (TCP/IP and sockets). BSD Unix was widely redistributed and quickly became the most popular version of Unix.

 FYI

POSIX and X/OPEN

Briefing

In 1981, the POSIX (Portable Operating System Interface) committee was charted to create a Unix-like, ANSI-standard OS—back then the US government wanted a specification for Unix that didn't belong to a single vendor. It was the first attempt to control the chaos in the Unix marketplace. The POSIX specification, which finally appeared in 1984, was too watered down and weak to constrain the chaos and creativity in the Unix industry. In 1984, X/Open was founded by European systems vendors to establish open software systems. In 1987, X/Open endorsed POSIX. X/Open still has a say in Unix standards.

Today, POSIX is a set of ISO and IEEE standards for "open" operating systems. The POSIX 1003.1 standard is a watered down subset of AT&T's Unix SVR4 operating system interface. POSIX, for example, does not specify any system calls for memory management. Because it is so watered down, POSIX compliance can easily be provided on non-Unix operating systems such as DEC VMS, OS/2, MVS, NT, and OS/400. In September 1992, the IEEE approved POSIX 1003.2, which includes the base shell programming language required for shell-script portability. It also defined POSIX 1003.2a, which defines a set of portable utilities. ❑

The 1980s were the golden days of Unix innovation. BSD Unix became the basis for Sun Microsystems' Solaris (originally known as SunOS). Of course, Sun added its own extensions such as the *Network File System (NFS)* and the *Remote Procedure Call (RPC)*. Apollo (later acquired by HP) added a rival set of distributed services called the *Network Computing Services (NCS)*. And Carnegie-Mellon University created a bare-bones Mach microkernel that was a reincarnation of the old spirit of a "portable Unix." Unix was getting too fat with all its extensions and Mach provided the ideal way to keep Unix portable while not sacrificing its extendibility.

THE COMMERCIALIZATION OF UNIX

In 1984, AT&T went commercial with Unix System III, which was not well received. The company replaced it a year later with System V—the great "Trivial Pursuit" question is whatever happened to System IV? AT&T licensed Unix System V source code to computer manufacturers and OS providers such as DEC, HP, IBM, Sun, and Microsoft. And as expected, vendors added their own extensions to the AT&T source code, which led, at last count, to over forty variants of Unix. The big players are IBM's AIX, HP's HP-UX, Sun's Solaris, Siemens' Sinix, Silicon Graphics' Irix, Apple's A/UX, and DEC's ULTRIX. Microsoft developed Xenix, which it later sold to Santa Cruz Operation (SCO). Today, SCO Unix is by far the most prevalent variant of Unix on Intel PCs.

THE UNIX WARS HEAT UP

Early in 1988, AT&T, the godfather of Unix, acquired a 20% equity in Sun Microsystems. In May 1988, a broad industry coalition (including DEC, HP, and IBM) set aside their differences and created the **Open Software Foundation (OSF)**, a consortium whose purpose was to coordinate the development of "open systems" software. OSF's initial goal was to wrest control of Unix from AT&T (and Sun) and provide a vendor-neutral, hardware-independent Unix. OSF members were afraid that Sun would have a disproportionate influence in determining the future of Unix System V. In the view of Scott McNealy, Sun Microsystem's CEO, "OSF" stands for "Oppose Sun Forever." The OSF group developed an alternative Unix, OSF/1—based on the Mach kernel technology from Carnegie-Mellon University and IBM's AIX—that vendors could create products around without paying licensing fees to AT&T. Over the next few years, OSF spent over $80 million developing OSF/1, which now runs on 300,000 systems (see the next Briefing box).

Soon after, vendors who supported System V formed a new consortium called the *Friends of AT&T*, which in December of 1988 became **Unix International (UI)**. UI, which included Sun and AT&T, was to set the course of Unix System V development. In 1990, AT&T spun off Unix development from Bell Labs into a separate subsidiary, **Unix System Lab (USL)** that was to develop the code and control the licensing of Unix. And the Unix war only got hotter.

UNIX SVR4.2: THE GREAT UNIFIER

Don't hold your breath. You'll see a unified Yugoslavia before you'll see a truly unified Unix.

— **Bill Laberis, Editor in Chief,**
ComputerWorld, (October 4, 1993)

In 1989 AT&T introduced Unix System V Release 3.2 (SVR3.2), a version of Unix that unified AT&T's Unix System V with SCO's Xenix. Then in 1990, USL and Sun introduced System V Release 4 (SVR4), which made System V compatible with SunOS and BSD—meaning that legacy Xenix, SunOS, and BSD applications can be recompiled to work on SVR4. USL then released SVR4 MP, a version of SVR4 that supports a multithreaded kernel and allows up to 16 processors to operate in SMP mode. And finally, the current version SVR4.2 adds B2-level security and a dual-GUI desktop manager that runs USL's OpenLook GUI and a simulation of the more popular OSF/1 Motif GUI. A reduced client version of SVR4.2—also known as Destiny—is available. Over 20 Unix variants today are based on some level of SVR4 compatibility.

Where Does OSF/1 Stand?

Briefing

We feel our operating system [OSF/1] is a couple of years ahead of the equivalent offering from USL.

— *Chuck Reilly, OSF VP*
(March 2, 1993)

OSF/1 is based on the Mach 2.5 kernel. Mach was the first Unix version to support the concurrent use of threads. The threaded Mach kernel makes it easy to implement symmetrical multiprocessing (SMP); kernel threads can simply execute on multiple processors simultaneously. The newest OSF/1-MK release, based on the Mach 3.0 microkernel, leaves the tasking control in the kernel while running most of the operating system as user tasks.

Aside from dissimilar kernels, the two Unix standards—OSF and the ex-USL—are promoting dissimilar GUIs, multiprocessor standards, microkernels, and distributed computing standards. The situation improved after the COSE "summit meeting." The most tangible outcome was Sun's agreement to drop OpenLook in favor of a new Motif-based user interface. But with Novell pushing NetWare as the distributed computing standard, we're back to more fragmentation.

So who is using OSF/1? OSF received payments for over 300,000 systems shipped with OSF/1-related technology. DEC is running OSF/1 in its entirety—including Mach. IBM is running the full OSF/1 on the ES/9000 mainframes. The IBM RS/6000 is shipping commands, libraries, and other OSF/1 technologies but not the kernel. HP uses OSF/1 libraries in its server systems and may soon support OSF/1 in its workstations. The Workplace OS and NextStep are based on the Mach microkernel. One of the Unix personalities in the Workplace OS is expected to run OSF/1. The future Macintosh System 8 may be based on OSF/1.

❑

IS NOVELL KILLING UNIX OR SAVING IT?

When Novell acquired Unix we had this romantic notion that somehow Novell, with its noble nature, would come in and put an end to the Unix wars.

> — *Kanwal Rekhi, Novell VP,*
> *General Manager of Unix*
> *(October 3, 1993)*

In early 1992, Novell formed a joint venture with USL, called Univel, and co-developed its own variant of SVR4.2 called UnixWare. Then in June of 1993, Novell acquired USL (and sole rights to UnixWare) from AT&T in a stock swap valued at $320 million. A few months later Novell dissolved USL and merged it with its Unix Systems Group—the developers of UnixWare. Does this mean that Unix SVR4 is dead? Yes and No.

In September of 1993, in a bizarre twist, Novell decided that instead of developing SVR4, it would make its own variant, UnixWare (the Unix standard), and resell it to other Unix system vendors, such as Sun, Silicon Graphics, IBM, HP, and SCO. In addition, Novell will sell UnixWare directly to Intel PC and RISC workstation makers in an attempt to bundle it and make it a volume desktop and server OS rivaling OS/2 or Windows NT. For users, it would mean that any Unix application could run on all Unix platforms and they'd get the portability PC users have always enjoyed.

Novell wants to make UnixWare 1.0 "as is" the Unix standard. In late 1994, UnixWare 2.0 with multiprocessing extensions will become the new source code for Unix. At that time, NetWare and UnixWare will be a matched pair. Novell wants to integrate NetWare's Server, Global Directory, Messaging System, and Common Network Management into the new UnixWare source code.

What Novell is proposing is the Unix-equivalent of a Yeltsin coup. To sweeten the deal and preserve some fig leaf of "openess," Novell, in a mainly symbolic gesture, gave X/Open the right to "license and brand" the Unix name—the one it acquired for $320 million. In return, Novell wanted all vendors to adopt UnixWare as the sole Unix.

UNIX VENDORS RESPOND TO NOVELL

We don't need source code from them [Novell] ever again.

> — *Scott McNeally, Sun's President*
> *(Sept. 27, 1993)*

Novell hasn't unified Unix. It has just caused more divisiveness.

> — *Scott McGregor, SCO's Senior VP*
> *(Sept. 27, 1993)*

Of course, the rest of the Unix industry cried foul play. Novell's plan drew anger from vendors that use Unix source code such as SCO and Sun. Neither company expressed interest in the UnixWare source code, saying they would instead continue to develop separate versions of Unix using previous source code. Many Unix long-time vendors—including Sun, HP, SCO, Tandem, Stratus, IBM, NextStep, and OSF—can easily claim to have a "better Unix than UnixWare." Going to shrink-wrapped UnixWare is a setback for those vendors who have collectively spent billions of dollars adding extensions to Unix and making it robust.

There is also the question of survival and self-interest. The combined shipments of the ex-USL's Unix SVR4.2 and UnixWare gives Novell fifth place in Unix market share (behind Sun, HP, IBM, and DEC). Only 30,000 copies of UnixWare shipped in 1993. In contrast, IBM's AIX is selling at a rate of 100,000 units a year.[1] Why should SCO, the dominant player in the desktop Unix market, endorse UnixWare, a bit player? Dominant players never willingly invite their competitors to take away their market share. And Novell, of course, is not *that* altruistic (or "noble") that it will hand over its $320 million investment without getting something in return. In addition, Novell doesn't have AT&T's deep pockets; it can't just keep on enhancing Unix forever for the common good. For its investment to make sense, Novell must become the Unix market leader.

In November of 1993, Novell gave up some ground and agreed that compliance with Unix will be measured by adherence to *Spec 1170*, adopted by more than 75 computer makers in early September. X/Open pledged to make full test suites available by late 1994. Novell did not relinquish to X/Open the Unix System V source code or licensing rights.

---

[1] Source for the AIX numbers: Jim Cannavino as quoted in **PC Week**, November 8, 1993.

UNIX: WHERE ARE WE?

Novell giving up intellectual property rights to Unix is 100% public relations. It doesn't further the unification of Unix in any way.

— *Scott Winkler,*
Gartner Group (October, 1993)

So where does this leave Unix industry? In December 1993, the UI consortium formally disbanded (with USL gone, there was no UNIX standard to guide). Novell will most likely forge ahead with its plan to create a volume market based on UnixWare. It will continue to sell its System V operating system source code under the name UnixWare, which is a Novell-specific implementation of the Spec 1170 APIs. The rest of the Unix vendors may create alliances to develop common Unix elements. Examples of such alliances are:

- **_The Common Software Environment (or COSE)_**, which was founded in March 1993 to unify the Unix desktop environment, graphics, multimedia, object technology, and systems management; backers include HP, IBM, SCO, Sun, and Novell.

- **_The September 1993 API unification treaty_** by more than 75 Unix vendors to create the _Spec 1170_ draft specification, which supports over 1,170 kernel APIs selected from the top 50 Unix applications. But don't hold your breath, you won't see total vendor compliance until mid-1995. But the good news is that X/Open will use Spec 1170 for its branding of Unix.

The problem with all these alliances is that they only provide the "least common denominator" for Unix. All the good stuff (like multimedia and objects) will first appear in vendor-specific proprietary extensions. The bottom line is that to get anything interesting (and useful) out of Unix, you'll have lock yourself into a vendor-specific proprietary "Unix" implementation.

So who said that the Unix wild west days were over? The Unix world never sits still. By the time you read this book, there'll be even more surprises on the various Unix fronts. However, 1993 will go down in history as one of the great vintage years of the Unix "war and peace" saga.

Novell Should Have Bought OS/2 Instead

Soapbox

I believe [Unix] is a horizontal technology and should be part of many products. Novell believes it's a vertical product—a value by itself.

— Roel Pieper, CEO of ex-USL
(Sept. 13, 1993)

When Novell bought USL, it thought it was buying a product—Unix SVR4.2. Instead, it was really buying an entire industry. For Novell, Unix was a way to buy an application server platform that would make NetWare competitive with NT and OS/2. Perhaps Novell would have been better off going into partnership with IBM in the development of OS/2. NetWare on OS/2 already provides much of what is promised in UnixWare 2.0 (late 1994 or later). OS/2 and NetWare are both aimed at the shrink-wrapped mass market. Combining the OS/2 and NetWare client/server marketing and support channels could have created an unbeatable combination.

As it stands, Novell's UnixWare strategy has bombed, with dismal sales of 30,000. Novell failed to unify the Unix camps; it let go of some key Unix marketing talent, including Roel Pieper, the president of the ex-USL. According to Scott Winkler, a **Gartner Group** strategist, the NetWare channel isn't right for selling high-volume Unix solutions. The resellers don't have the expertise to support Unix or get UnixWare into the enterprise. And Novell is having a tough time moving from its traditional turf—departmental LANs—to the new territory of the enterprise network.

The thorny question for Novell and IBM was probably: What do we do about OS/2's LAN Server and DCE? DCE (and ONC) are also very popular in the Unix world, so Novell will still run into that problem. Of course, this is all 20/20 hind-sight and wishful thinking. The decision was already made. And nobody asked for our advice. But it will be interesting to see how long Novell remains "noble" in the fragmented Unix world. It's a bit like the UN troops going into Somalia. ❑

UNIX AS A SERVER

Can a Unix server platform beat OS/2 or NT on their own turf? What can Unix servers offer PC clients running DOS, Windows, and OS/2 beyond what OS/2 or NT can? Unix proponents claim three advantages for their platform: it is open, it provides a function-rich operating system, and it is scalable from the desktop to the supercomputer.[2] We will briefly look at each of these issues form the viewpoint of how Unix compares to OS/2 as a server platform.

How Open Is Unix?

Unix is not really open. Most Unix vendors currently ship what we have dubbed a closed Unix system strategy with an open rhetoric disguise. Caveat Emptor.

— Gartner Group (June, 1991)

Open can mean different things to different people. The PC industry has its own cult of openness. In the PC world, open means a market with hundreds of PC vendors, shrink-wrapped commodity software selling at highly competitive prices, and a cut-throat competition for every conceivable type service. Open means designing a new operating system with the help of 20,000 beta testers, a Blue Ninja, and daily headlines in the computer press and occasionally in the mass tabloids. If OS/2 2.1 is not the better system that the market expects, there is NT. If NT cannot do it, there is Taligent. This is an open, fiercely competitive environment where innovation and the "market" rules.

For all its talk of "openness," the Unix world is different from the PC world where software comes in low-cost, shrink-wrapped floppy packages that can run on any PC clone that runs MS-DOS or OS/2 2.1. There is still no single Unix standard. There are about forty Unix variants converging on two Unix standards: OSF and the ex-USL's System V Release 4 (SVR4). At best, Unix variants may someday achieve the elusive goal of *conditional portability.* There is no inexpensive, easy to install, run-time Unix version that can be used as an application platform.

Interoperability is another form of "openness." It means that various operating systems can continue doing what they each do best, as long as they can "plug and play" together like the components of a stereo system (also see Soapbox). OS/2 is very well equipped to interoperate with the Unix world (and almost everything else). Its advanced TCP/IP services include most of BSD Unix's network extensions, Sun's RPC and NFS, and the Apollo NCS distributed environment. OS/2 supports OSF's

---

[2] The case for Unix is very well presented by Ed Dunphy in **The Unix Industry**, (QED, 1991).

Distributed Computing Environment (DCE), the ultimate standard for interoperability. DSOM, OS/2's distributed object broker, is based on CORBA, an industry standard for object interoperability and portability. Sorry for this burst of acronyms, we're just trying to make a point. We will fully explain what they mean in future chapters.

What Is an Open System?

Soapbox

Given all the hype about "open systems", it may come as a surprise that there is no consensus in the industry about the definition of an *open system*. Everyone agrees that open is desirable. Users seem to equate open with interoperability, freedom of choice, integrated multivendor solutions, and the disintegration of the Soviet Union. Vendors equate open with standards and focus on portability. Users do not trust the vendors or standards groups. There is obviously a mismatch in perceptions. Let's work our way through some of the open mythology:

- *Myth #1: Open systems mean Unix.* Open systems are not about any single technology. Unix-derived systems were first to use the open systems code-phrase in advertising their products. But Forrester Research discovered in an extensive user survey that Unix got a 71% open rating, AIX got 29%, and SunOS only got 17%. The conclusion is that users see Unix as open, but perceive its commercial implementations as being proprietary. (The users are right. Unix SVR4 is a technology, not a standard or a product. Each company that sells SVR4 does something different with it. Sun added a thousand person years of value-added effort to its SVR4 product). In contrast, MS-DOS got a 42% rating and OS/2 got 32%. Forrester concluded that users accept the reality that multiple operating systems will forever be the norm. A consensus seems to be emerging that "open" has to encompass more than just Unix, or else 90% of the computer industry will be left out. (Source: **Open Systems Agony**, Forrester Research, Inc., July, 1991).

- *Myth #2: Open means application portability.* Portability seems to be the primary issue for vendor-dominated "standards" groups. Forrester discovered that portability ranked low on users' agenda. X/Open's **Xtra** 1991 Open System Directive came to the same conclusion. The **Xtra** survey lists the five top strategic priorities as: 1) interoperability across heterogeneous systems, 2) an overall architecture for enterprise open systems computing, 3) heterogeneous networked database access, 4) integrated open and proprietary network management, and 5) open access to proprietary mainframe applications.

■ *Myth #3: Open means the arrival of standards.* The Forrester survey detects a deep user mistrust of standards. Users perceive standards bodies as just vendors in disguise. They think that vendors actively resist the shift to openness and create confusion by subsidizing competing standards, consortia, and technology frameworks. In the "open wars," there are as many standards as consortia attempting to define them.

So what does "open" really mean? For the purposes of this book, "open" means standards that facilitate the creation of flexible distributed solutions between dissimilar platforms. We subscribe to the *open is choice* and *open is interoperability* viewpoints. Interoperability, of course, has several dimensions: network connectivity, data sharing, multiclient support, and integrated system management. These are all areas where standards, both de facto and de jure, are essential.

In areas such as portability, we feel standards should be used only when they are already available (one of the authors got badly burned waiting for MAP standards to materialize many years ago). Be warned, standards are literally designed by committees. The process tends to produce mediocrity and does not easily keep up with new technology. The various consortia try to speed up the process by offering working technologies. But, they also end up creating a proliferation of competing "standards." This multiplicity of standards leads to more bodies (and consortia) that form to pick out groups of "correct" standards. ❑

Is Unix More Advanced Than OS/2 2.1?

Unix is the melting pot of the computer industry. Its close connection with universities makes it a great incubator of new ideas. Most of these ideas first appear on the commercial market as Unix extensions and variants. The Unix mainstream, on the other hand, moves a lot more cautiously. Because of debt to history, multiple platform portability issues, and getting many vendors to agree on the least common denominator, it takes much longer to bring extensions into the commercial offerings of Unix standards. Unix's continuing usability problems stem from its debt to history (that is, backward-compatibility issues). Revamping Unix completely is out of the question; too much Unix software relies on the old text-mode environment and utilities. Motif and OpenLook sit on top of X Windows, which run on top of the Unix kernel. This layering may help mask some of the ugliness, but it introduces more overhead and bulk. And, there is still no standard Unix GUI (see Soapbox).

OS/2 is in many ways a modern variant of Unix; however, it is not encumbered by a debt to history. OS/2 combines the best of Unix, Windows 3.X, and DOS, and also brings it to the market as a shrink-wrapped operating system package. It incorpo-

What About COSE's Unix "Dashboard"?

Soapbox

COSE is working on a unified Unix desktop—the Unix "dashboard." This effort is still in its proof-of-concept stage. The idea is to create a Common Development-ment Environment (CDE) toolkit that different Unix vendors can adapt to their specific platforms (mid-1994 or later). Don't count on seeing applications that exploit the Unix dashboard before 1995 at the earliest.

So what will go into that Unix dashboard? As usual, a bit of everything—remember, it is being developed by a Unix coalition. COSE will create the "mother of all desktops" by grafting together at least three existing desktop managers: HP's VUE, SVR4.2 Desktop Manager, and elements of the Workplace Shell (see Figure 13-1). The GUI engine will be provided by OSF/Motif running on top of X Windows. Finally, Sun Solaris' ToolTalk will provide the desktop messaging facility—including data format negotiations. Think of ToolTalk as the DDE/OLE of Unix. Will all these pieces work together? How well will the dashboard work? Will Steve Jobs convert his superb NextStep OOUI to this new common environment? We don't have all the answers. ❑

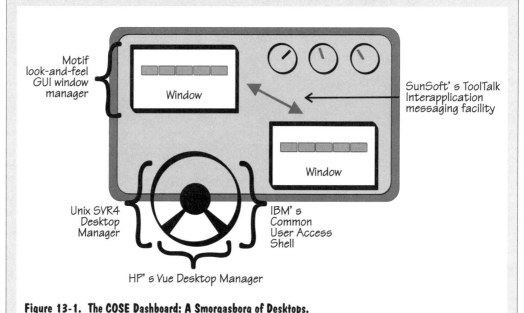

Figure 13-1. The COSE Dashboard: A Smorgasborg of Desktops.

rates many of the most advanced features in SVR4 and OSF/1, including dynamic link libraries, demand-paged virtual memory, multitasking, interprocess communications, and an installable file system. Advanced OS/2 features, such as threads, are now slowly making their way into the Unix mainstream. With OS/2 2.X, Unix loses its 32-bit advantage. OS/2 programming APIs are better architected, more consistent, and less cumbersome (they carry less luggage) than their Unix counterparts. OS/2 is not burdened with thousands of cryptic commands from the era of text-based computing.

OS/2's communications and database offerings are very similar to their Unix counterparts. They are almost always easier to install, use, and manage. And, as a rule, they are much less expensive.

Arguments are frequently made that OS/2 is multitasking but not multiuser. Unix is both. Is this a problem for OS/2? The multiuser feature is a remnant of the old timeshare, terminal-based paradigm of Unix. It was only a few years ago that Unix systems with dumb terminals were positioned as the alternative to PC LANs. Because of these origins, Unix comes standard with a security system that lets systems administrators restrict access to files, directories, and other system resources. Unix's multiuser administrative features are cumbersome and complex for single user client machines. In multiuser client/server environments, Unix's administrative features compete with the server software's own multiuser facilities.

The client/server architecture is *multiclient rather than multiuser*. The client is usually on a remote machine. The server does not manage the client's workstation; it simply provides concurrent services to multiple clients using its multitasking facilities. Different OS/2 services, like the database manager and the file server, provide their own very sophisticated multiuser paradigm on top of the base operating system. Other services, like remote procedure calls, may not even require the notion of a user or a session (authentication and security may be provided at the call level by a trusted third-party node like a Kerberos authentication server).

In general, OS/2 provides operating system functions that are at least as good as those of Unix while remaining within the PC paradigm. OS/2 servers use the same file system, device drivers, and presentation services as their MS-DOS and Windows clients.

HOW SCALABLE IS UNIX?

Because Unix is a hardware independent operating system, an application should, in theory, be able to run on any machine that supports Unix, from a PC to a Cray supercomputer. This server scalability story is very attractive, but it is not realistic. In real-world situations, what keeps that from happening are three factors: binary

---

Some Things Unix SVR4.2 Does Well

Soapbox

There's a few things we like in the "generic" (meaning they're not necessarily implemented in all the Unix variants) SVR4.2 that are *still* lacking in OS/2. Here's the list:

- **The Veritas file system that is included with the latest version of SVR4.2.** This journalling file system supports disk mirroring and striping with parity—just like OS/2's LAN Server 3.0's HPFS386. However, Veritas can also recover (rollback) from power failures that corrupt the file system. This feature is similar to NT's NTFS file system. OS/2 should get similar capabilities soon.

- **The memory-mapped files that SVR4.2 borrowed from SunOS.** This is a single level store concept that treats all memory (disk and RAM) as one address space. The file I/O becomes an extension of the paging system. Programmers like this feature because they can access their files directly without having to issue explicit seeks. It makes programming more "orthogonal," but it's also more error-prone.

In addition, we like the fault-tolerant hardware support for Unix created by vendors such as Tandem (the S2 series) and Stratus. These proprietary hardware-based, fault-tolerant platforms are very useful in mission-critical environments. Their boxes, however, don't come cheap. ❑

---

incompatibility, Unix variants, and applications that are optimized for a particular operating system platform.

We already discussed the Unix variants and the binary incompatibilities between the various machines. The third factor is probably the Achilles' heel of scalability: operating systems are usually optimized for the hardware they manage. Portable Unix applications rarely outperform applications that are optimized for a native operating system. For example, it is very hard for a database application ported to IBM's S/370 Unix (AIX) to outperform a DB2 or CICS application running on MVS, the S/370's native operating system.

Unix applications are at a price/performance disadvantage against applications that were designed to take advantage of an optimized solutions-oriented operating system with a supporting hardware platform. For example, Unix OLTP applications on RISC cannot provide the overall price/performance of OLTP applications running on Tandem Computers' Guardian, an operating system that is designed to exploit a loosely-coupled RISC multiprocessor network optimized for OLTP, parallelism, and high availability (no shared memory anywhere).

Likewise, the AS/400, a recent vintage non-Unix IBM midrange computer, generated sales of about $13 billion in 1992, which is about 70% of the worldwide Unix market, including operating systems and hardware.[3] The OS/400 operating system was designed specifically to exploit the AS/400. It offers a turn-key solutions environment with excellent price/performance.

Unix's niche is in technical workstations where it provides unchallenged leadership and price/performance. The new generation of workstations from HP/Apollo, Sun, and IBM were designed for Unix as their primary operating system. The networking requirements of these workstations were fed into Unix and became part of the operating system. Today, as these workstations start to exploit symmetrical multi-processing, they feed their advanced new requirements into Unix. Workstations are a Unix stronghold.

Scalability Alternatives

We're comparing OS/2 and Unix in terms of scalability, so we will take a short detour and explain some of the alternative scalability options (see Figure 13-2). Here are the different ways to scale server applications:

- *Use a single scalable operating system that runs on multiple hardware platforms*. This is the Unix call to arms—it runs on PCs, RISC workstations, and mainframes. Of course NT (and very soon OS/2) can claim scalability via the power of symmetric multiprocessing. NT and OS/2 will not run on main-frames. However, a dozen (or so) Pentiums in an SMP superserver, loaded with fast DASD, can match the power of a contemporary mainframe. But you have to buy that superserver, while the mainframe may already be there. And there are many skeptics who do not believe in the "one size fits all strategy."

- *Build on a portable programming environment based on formal indus-try standards*. This means you develop applications that run on top of suites of standards such as Motif, POSIX, SQL, and the X/Open Portability Guide (XPG4). The problem with these portability standards is that they can't keep up with leading edge technology such as objects and multimedia. They also tend to provide the least common denominator approach.

- *Build on a portable programming environment based on a single vendor's portable architecture*. IBM's SAA, for example, provides scalability

---

[3] In spite of all the hype Unix accounts for only 11% of the total systems market.

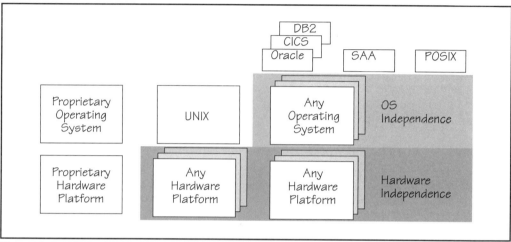

Figure 13-2. Different Approaches to Scalability and Portability.

by publishing a set of APIs that can be ported to different operating systems.[4] One of the benefits of this membership is upward (and downward) scalability. The SAA model represents an alternative to "single operating system" scalability. In the SAA model, each operating system is optimized for its respective platform.

- ■ *Build on a single vendor product family that runs on multiple operating system platforms*. Examples of such product families include Oracle, Sybase, DB2, and CICS. The price is that they lock you into a single vendor programming environment.

As you can see, the scalability story is not that very pretty. All the options, with the possible exception of SMP, at the minimum require a recompile. This recompile can easily turn into a sizeable porting effort. Neither OS/2, Unix, or NT can currently claim total transparent portability from the smallest laptop to a supercomputer.[5]

---

[4] SAA is similar in spirit to POSIX, except that it provides a much wider range of specifications. SAA applications running on OS/2 PCs could, in theory, be scaled upwards by a source-level recompile to either an AS/400 running OS/400 or a S/370 running MVS or VM.

[5] An example of a computer operating system that scales very gracefully is Tandem Computer's Guardian. Because of its loosely coupled message-based multiprocessing, distributed database, and TP monitor, Tandem can provide smooth upward scalability (with fault-tolerance and very few limits, it seems). However, Tandem starts at $20,000, which is not exactly the low end of the scale.

UNIX AS A CLIENT

The ex-USL (now Novell) is aggressively trying to promote its new UNIX System V Release 4.2 (named Destiny) as a contender for the client desktop. Destiny somewhat improves the packaging and installation of Unix, provides a choice of two GUIs on the desktop, a DOS emulator, and has Novell's backing. However, even Destiny is not doing too well as a client platform.[6] One shortcoming is that the DOS/Windows emulation is still abysmally slow and consumes some serious processing power when overlaid on top of Unix. Windows emulation running on top of X Windows is resource hungry—it requires about 12 MBytes of RAM. On the Intel architecture, Unix appears to run slower than Windows or OS/2. Unix on non-Intel architectures introduces an extra layer of instruction set emulation when it runs 16-bit programs. As a result, the fastest Unix RISC workstation may be slower than a 386SX when running DOS and Windows applications (this is also true for NT).

Unix is still too fragmented to be a strong contender as a desktop client. You still can't call an 800 number or walk into the local Egghead store and buy standard Unix. DOS, Windows, and OS/2 2.1 are much more available, applications-rich, and entrenched on the desktop. Installing Unix is still a chore. Unix SVR4.2 requires 93 diskettes (versus 18 for OS/2). Expect several hours of tedious disk swapping unless you have a CD-ROM. Unix is also tough to administer and can easily intimidate your average desktop user.

UNIX ON INTEL VARIANTS

The Unix on Intel variants probably have the best chance of penetrating the mass client market. Future Apple (and IBM) PowerPC versions of Unix may also have popular mass appeal, but today most of the client hardware runs with "Intel inside." The Unix on Intel vendors understood the PC market dynamics and introduced low-cost client versions of their Unix offerings throughout 1993—the server prices are much higher.

Table 13-1 compares the features of the four most popular versions of Unix on Intel. The first thing to notice is that these platforms are very different. They run different Unix kernels each with their own extensions and peculiarities. Each platform requires its own device drivers, which can be a problem. Unix products come with a certain number of standard device drivers, such as low-resolution VGA, SCSI, and Logitech mouse drivers. If the device driver is not supported by the Unix variant,

---

[6] Source: **A Cold Shower for UNIX**, (Forrester, April 1993). This extensive study by Forrester shows that UNIX is not viewed as having a role on the desktop. Only 8% of the respondents would consider Unix on Intel. 78% reported that the Novell buyout of USL would not change that view.

then it becomes your problem. Each platform has its own desktop manager; they all look pretty, but they're very different. In addition, each platform runs DOS and Windows differently—in most cases, you will need an add-on emulation package (see the following Soapbox).

Wabi or Insignia?

Soapbox

Unix proper does not run either DOS or Windows. Instead, the industry relies on third-party emulation tools like Insignia's SoftPC and SoftWindows, Locus's Merge, and Phoenix Technologies' VP/ix. Most of these emulators run 16-bit Windows applications in standard mode. (OS/2 runs Windows in both standard and enhanced modes). The third-party emulation tools pay licensing fees to Microsoft and tend to be expensive. Insignia Solutions' SoftWindows (the replacement of SoftPC) is priced at $549. Insignia emulates a 286 chip as a subtask that lets you run your DOS or Windows applications from within a Unix OS. The drawback is that it takes a lot longer to execute instructions in software than in hardware.

Sun's Windows Application Binary Interface (Wabi) takes a different approach. Instead of emulating the Intel instruction set or requiring Windows, Wabi intercepts Windows calls and converts them to the equivalent X Window and Unix calls. In other words, Wabi provides *translation technology, not emulation*. With Wabi, you are not required to purchase a copy of Windows. Many Unix vendors are lined up to license Wabi—including IBM, HP, Novell, and SCO. IBM is even contributing its PC-SIM (AIX PC emulator) technology to make Wabi run faster. Why all this Wabi excitement? Because it means not having to pay Microsoft for DOS and Windows.

Sun, the new Robin Hood of the computer industry, is even going one step further in its crusade: It is promoting Wabi's Public Windows Interface (PWI) as an official industry standard. The idea is to put the Windows API under the control of a standards body rather than leave it in Microsoft's hands. PWI is a long shot, but Wabi is almost a sure thing barring a lawsuit by Microsoft. However, be warned that Wabi 1.0 is buggy and doesn't support some key Windows 3.X features (such as help). Sun's Wabi 2.0 is reportedly much more stable and complete. ❑

Table 13-1. Comparing the UNIX Intel Desktop Variants.

Feature	SCO Open Desktop	UnixWare 1.1	NextStep 3.2 for Intel	Solaris 2.1 for Intel
Unix Kernel	SVR3.2	SVR4.2	BSD/Mach	SVR4
Unix Extensions	SCO Unix	UnixWare	NeXT	Solaris
X Window Base	Yes	Yes	No	Yes
Motif GUI	Yes	Yes	No	No
OpenLook GUI	No	Yes	No	Yes
Desktop Manager	Open Desktop	USL Desktop	Workspace Manager	OpenWindows
CD-ROM Install	Yes	Yes	Yes	Yes
DOS Emulator	Optional	DR DOS 6.0 Locus' DOS	Optional (Insignia)	Optional (Wabi)
Windows Emulator	Optional	Optional (Merge)	Optional (Insignia)	Optional (Wabi)
Retail Price	$695	$249	$795	$795

The good news is that all the Unix variants shown in the table can be installed from CD-ROM (this will save you hours of diskette swapping). More good news is that they can all act as NFS or NetWare clients. SCO can also act as a client to OS/2's LAN Server and NT. Now here's the hard question: Which of these variants is the best Unix client? There's no easy answer because each of these variants has its strong points and weak points. They're also as different from each other as night and day. But here's some points to consider:

- **SCO** boasts the largest installed base of Unix on the Intel platform. SCO, based on Unix SVR3.2 (the engine of the late-80s), has gone its own way and not followed USL's lead. Programmers and administrators used to the newer SVR4 systems will feel the difference. SCO Unix uses an OOUI-like desktop on top of Motif and X Windows. The SCO Unix (and Xenix) platforms boast 3000 applications (mostly vertical packages). An SCO strength is that it treats DOS files (resident on a DOS partition) as Unix files. You can run multiple DOS sessions (but each session costs you 2.5 MBytes of RAM).

- **UnixWare** will appeal to Novell shops. Its kernel runs the latest Unix SVR4.2 engine, which supports the Intel *Binary Compatibility Standard 2 (iBCS2)*. This means that you can run not only System V binaries but also SCO Unix and SCO Xenix programs. UnixWare bundles a NetWare client that uses IPX/SPX out-of-the box. Support is planned for Windows emulation using the Locus Merge package (standard-mode Windows).

■ **Solaris** will appeal to shops that already own Sun Workstations. Many of the 4,000 software packages that run on Sun's RISC platform may *eventually* be ported to Solaris on Intel (very few have so far). The Solaris desktop provides powerful graphics capabilities and supports multimedia mail using an underlying information exchange engine known as ToolTalk. Wabi is available on Solaris as an add-on.

■ **NextStep** runs on Mach and provides an object-oriented user interface (OOUI) on top of an object-oriented environment (with some old BSD Unix 4.3 underneath). NextStep does not run Unix V (or Xenix) programs so it needs to rely on its own 32-bit applications. The OOUI is very much like the Workplace Shell: file manipulation and program launching is all done by drag-and-drop direct manipulation. The OOUI also provides its own form of OLE-like object links so that changes made in one document element are reflected wherever that element appears. NextStep is also a great multimedia platform—it includes video-in-a-window, full audio, and multimedia e-mail enclosures. The visual effects that can be generated on NextStep are first class. For example, it provides an image transparency that lets you see images through other images. NextStep bundles NetWare and Apple clients. NextStep 3.2 bundles Insignia's SoftPC Windows' emulator and provides a 30-day license with option to buy. With NextStep 3.2, the GUI can be networked to an object server (or engine)—the two pieces are now separate.

As you can see, it's not choices that are lacking in the Unix world. You're always faced with great diversity. Can we really call NextStep Unix when it doesn't even run Unix programs? But this is Unix: an explosion of choices and technologies.

Client Wars: Unix Versus OS/2

Soapbox

Unix may yet hit it big as a server operating system, but it's time to let the desktop versions fade gracefully away.

> — Mark L Van Name and Bill Catchings,
> PC Week columnists
> (December 20, 1993)

OS/2 2.1, except for UnixWare, is about 30% the cost of a comparable Unix client platform. OS/2 also requires less than half the disk and memory. OS/2's threads provide more responsive user interfaces than the various Unix GUIs. Of course, OS/2's seamless integration of DOS and Windows on the Workplace Shell is a tough act for most Unix machines to follow. OS/2 runs comfortably on 386 class machines, while some of the Unix platforms—such as Solaris and NextStep—require a 486 (or above).

Several of the Unix desktops—such as SCO's Open Desktop, NextStep's Workspace Manager, Solaris' OpenWindows, and NetWare's Desktop Manager—are much more OOUI-like and advanced than Windows 3.X. The NextStep user interface is even more OOUI-like than the Workplace Shell and has superb graphics to boot. However, NextStep's advanced capabilities do not come cheap. NextStep requires a 486 (or above), 24 MBytes of RAM (for 16-bit color), 120 MBytes of disk space, and it retails for $795 (versus $225 for OS/2). So NextStep is not your average client platform, but it's nice!

The problem with desktop Unix as PC Week columnists Van Name and Catchings point out is poor sales. In an industry that numbers desktop systems in tens of millions, desktop Unix sales are in the noise level. At the end of 1993 the Solaris install base stood at 15,000 copies; UnixWare stood at 30,000 (Source: PC Week, February 14, 1994). Most of these sales went to Sun and NetWare accounts. These numbers are not enough to attract vendors of desktop applications. Let's face it Unix was never a hit on PCs and the new desktop Unixes are not doing any better. ❑

THE OS/2 CHALLENGE

If you think about it, the client/server market really has three key players—Novell, Microsoft, and IBM—and hundreds of niche players. The three key players are each trying to enlist the largest number of niche players to join their camp. Novell is a key player because it controls Unix, NetWare, and a huge army of certified NetWare distributors. Microsoft controls the desktop and volume distribution channels. IBM controls the largest sales and systems integration channel in the computer business, and its products cover every facet of client/server computing. Niche players include server vendors of all stripes, database vendors, middleware providers, horizontal application houses, system integrators, consultants, etc.

To net it out, servers are needed, but there are hundreds of those to choose from and they all work with everything else. Software and middleware is important, but the vendors that provide those services are totally secular and, for the right price, will port them to any platform. So what does that leave us with? The *systems integration and distribution channels* and the *client*.

The systems integration and distribution channels are very important to the success of client/server computing. This industry knows how to sell and support shrink-wrapped packages (commodities) and mainframes (the long sales cycle). We're having a very hard time selling client/server solutions that need some handholding and at the same time consist of commodity-like components. IBM controls the high end of the client/server channel and is strengthening it with its client/server toolkits and frameworks. Novell controls the low-end of the client/server channel. Microsoft controls Windows.

The client is probably the single most important component in client/server. Whomever controls the client is, at least, halfway there. We showed in Chapter 10 that the ubiquitous DOS and Windows do not make very good client platforms. Their poor little computer brains are too weak to give us what it takes to build universal clients and fulfill the vision of post-scarcity client/server computing where each machine is both a client and a server. For client/server computing to unleash its potential, we must move to 32-bit client platforms. Microsoft understands that and is working on Chicago. Novell understands that and is proposing the shrink-wrapped UnixWare—a heroic first try. And there is OS/2, which is uniquely positioned *today* to fulfill the role of the universal client.

As you can see in Figure 13-3, OS/2 as a 32-bit client platform starts out at the very low-end of the spectrum. OS/2's main competition as a client platform comes from the extreme low end of the PC spectrum: DOS machines that cannot afford the upward migration, and from Windows 3.X. DOS and Windows will continue to rule supreme on low-end machines (80286 and below). OS/2 2.X's market potential is as large as the population of installed 80386, 80486, and Pentiums systems, which is about 50 million PCs (and growing at a very fast rate).

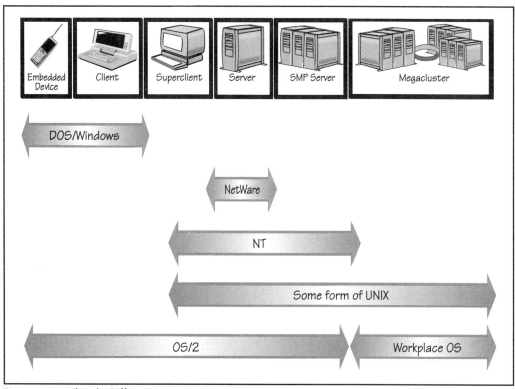

Figure 13-3. What the Different Operating Systems Cover.

Figure 13-3 illustrates that the competition is fierce on the server front. OS/2 2.X makes a good LAN server; OS/2 2.X with symmetrical multiprocessing on Intel makes a good advanced server; and OS/2 on the IBM microkernel, with its support of multiclustered superservers, is a good candidate for replacing mainframes as a corporate backbone server. Of course, you'll have to wait until late 1994 to get the high-end server features. But it may be worth the wait because the IBM Microkernel (based on Mach 3) has some very powerful parallel processing features.

OS/2 2.1's most serious competitor in the low-end server range comes from NetWare 4.0, NT Advanced Server, and the Unix on Intel variants. In the mid-range server front the competition is from Unix and NT (NetWare drops out because it does not provide SMP support). Finally, in the high-end server range, NT drops out; but any mainframe or supermini worth its salt that can act as a server to PCs is a potential competitor. The most serious competitors are the RISC mainframe vendors that can provide massively parallel computing to PCs. The fault-tolerant vendors such as Tandem and Stratus also have a lot to offer as scalable server platforms. The MVS-based IBM mainframes with their transaction engines, enterprise-based system management, and large databases are also formidable competitors. Taligent's impact as a server platform is still unclear.

If we extend OS/2 to include the microkernel-based Workplace OS, then it appears, from a hardware viewpoint, that OS/2 has the potential to run any type of client or server application (from a laptop to clusters of superservers). OS/2 will be able to run its distributed object client/server frameworks on top of this hardware. This will take some of the pain out of developing and maintaining client/server applications. Can OS/2 (with Workplace OS) emerge as the winner of both the client and server wars? The technology and timing is perfect. But wars are not won on technology alone.

Remember Dvorak's Law

Soapbox

If you can run the same OS on both clients and servers—do it!

— *John Dvorak*

Servers that are not members of the PC family of operating systems will have a hard time beating OS/2 on its home turf. OS/2 as a server platform makes it possible to create homogeneous LANs where clients and servers run the same operating system family (OS/2, DOS, and Windows). Homogenous LANs are simple to administer, and you can easily move programs (and function) between clients and servers. In addition, the installation procedures, the file systems, and the interfaces to the operating system are the same on both the clients and the server. This familiar setting makes it easy for departments and small organizations to introduce client/server solutions. Remember, the majority of client/server installations are in single locations consisting of less than twenty clients. These are predominantly PC LAN installations.

Unix and mainframe servers for PCs result in heterogeneous client/server solutions, which is not good for the small shops. NetWare does not own the client, but it more than compensates for that by owning the network operating system on more than fifty percent of PC LAN installations. NT is part of the PC family and will fiercely compete with OS/2 as a server platform. ❏

Does OS/2 Own the 32-Bit OS Market?

Soapbox

Users will not convert to another operating system in large numbers, no matter how attractive it is, unless they can take with them the application software and ways of doing things they're used to. The failure of NeXT's heroic efforts shows that clearly.

— **William Zachmann,
President of Canopus Research
(January, 1994)**

OS/2 2.1 is the *ideal client platform for the PC world.* It is hard (if not impossible) for any operating system platform to beat OS/2 2.1's robust and seamless integration of all DOS, MS-Windows, and OS/2 environments in its Workplace Shell. OS/2 creates a client desktop environment where all the network services—including Printers, e-mail, File Server Directories, and Decision Support Tools—appear as groups of *smart icons.* Network services are obtained by simply clicking on icons. Users can move business objects across networks by simply grabbing an icon and dropping it on the appropriate destination icon. The network essentially becomes an arcade game. Users are encouraged to directly interact with objects. How much friendlier can it be?

In addition, OS/2 2.1's advanced 32-bit features and page-based virtual memory are ideal for multimedia applications. OS/2 2.1 packs a formidable amount of power, yet it is easy to use and install. It provides that "friendly feel" associated with PCs. All this helps make OS/2 2.1 an irresistible client platform.

By year-end 1993, OS/2 *sold* over four million copies; this is more than the combined shipments of NT and all the Unix variants. OS/2 provides the largest 32-bit OS install base—it may be the right critical mass to justify writing 32-bit applications directly for that platform (instead of some of the poorly implemented Window ports it's been getting). But doesn't the Windows install base dwarf that of OS/2? Yes, it's true that Windows has an install base that's ten times that of OS/2. However, almost every copy of OS/2 is directly purchased; in contrast, most copies of Windows are preloaded on PCs.

The new **OS/2 For Windows** may help OS/2 achieve a critical mass in the Windows market. But, in any case, we shouldn't be comparing OS/2 to DOS and Windows—that's looking backwards. OS/2 should be compared with other modern 32-bit OSs. There it emerges as the clear winner. Can OS/2 2.1 sustain this momentum? Proper marketing is essential to get the masses of Windows users to move on to OS/2. They need to understand the advantages of OS/2 2.1 as a multimedia, client/server, and laptop platform.

OS/2 2.1 will continue to face stiff marketplace competition from Windows on the client side. On the server side, the competition will be from Windows NT and many of the Unix variants, including NextStep, Solaris, SCO, UnixWare, DEC's OSF/1, and IBM's own AIX. So far, the desktop has been almost a *Unix-free* zone. The divisions in the Unix camp may keep it that way for a long time. Yes, it appears we are "condemned" to live in fascinating, and fiercely competitive, times. ❑

Part 3
Base Middleware:
Stacks and NOSs

An Introduction to Part 3

Congratulations, you're still alive after going through the OS wars. Wasn't that exciting? Yes, the Earth people are always fighting over one thing or another. That seems to be in their nature. But we're going to change the pace now and take you through some more secular terrain. Instead of fighting each other, the client/server vendors will now try to hide their differences behind a facade called the "single system image."

Now don't get us wrong. The folks you met in Part 2 are far from burying the hatchet. Instead, they're all trying to make everybody else's system look like their own. If they can't get rid of the other systems, the next best thing is to make them disappear (the politically correct term is to "make them transparent"). So how do they do that disappearing trick? By throwing layer upon layer of middleware until everything becomes one. Now that's magic!

Part 3 is about the base middleware that is used to create the "single system illusion." We will start with a brief tutorial on *Network Operating System (NOS)* middleware. You'll discover the "bag of tricks" NOSs use to create illusions that would put to shame the great Houdini himself—that's one of our better magicians who lived on Earth not too long ago. There were no NOSs in Houdini's time.

After exploring the NOSs, we go into the *stacks* middleware, which introduce their own repertoire of tricks. Eventually, nothing is what it appears to be. Everything gets deconstructed, reconstructed, and then repackaged so that it "appears to work" with everything else. But you'll know better, of course.

You'll soon discover that each vendor will be glad to sell you a different set of middleware products. Unfortunately, middleware does not extend its disappearing act to make the products themselves transparent. This is because middleware is a lucrative business in its own right. And when there's money to be made, nothing disappears. And we pay for the pleasure of seeing the heterogeneous world look like it's one happily integrated system. Yes, we pay for illusions on Earth. Look at our movie industry.

Finally, we will introduce you to the products you'll need to create the type of illusions that meet your fancy (or real needs). You can create almost any type of facade as long as you have the money to pay for it. Another important reason to look at products is to get a reality check of what's really there. The middleware vendors are practitioners of magic who, like all magicians, sometimes forget what's real. So it's essential to go behind the stage and see what's really there, at least in terms of product. We hope you'll enjoy the show.

Chapter 14

NOS: Creating the Single System Image

Single system image creates an illusion in the minds of users that all the servers on the network are part of the same system or behave like a single computer.

— **Andrew Tanenbaum (1992)** [1]

This chapter goes over the functions that the Network Operating System (NOS) middleware must provide to create a "single system image" of all the services on the network. As we explained earlier, this is really a Houdini-sized illusion that makes all servers of the world—we're talking about a multiserver, multiservice, multivendor, and multinetwork world—appear to the client as one big happy family. In a sense, the NOS middleware provides the glue that recreates the single system out of the disparate elements. It's a thankless job, but without it there can be no client/server computing. By the end of this chapter, you'll get a better appreciation of the "bag of tricks" that are used by clients and servers to create the *grand illusion*.

---

[1] Source: Andrew S. Tanenbaum, **Modern Operating Systems** (Prentice Hall, 1992).

NOS MIDDLEWARE: THE TRANSPARENT ILLUSION

NOSs are evolving from being a collection of independent workstations, able to communicate via a shared file system, to becoming real distributed computing environments that make the network *transparent* to users.

What Does Transparency Really Mean?

Transparency means fooling everyone into thinking the client/server system is totally seamless. It really means hiding the network and its servers from the users and even the application programmers. Here are some of the types of transparencies the NOS middleware is expected to provide as part of its "network disappearing act":

- **Location transparency**—You should not have to be aware of the location of a resource. Users should not have to include the location information in the resource's name. For example, *Machine**directory**file* surfaces the name of the server machine. This is a transparency violation.

- **Namespace Transparency**—You should be able to use the same naming conventions (and namespace) to locate any resource on the network. The whole universe is one big tree (see Figure 14-1). This includes every type of resource on any vendor's product.

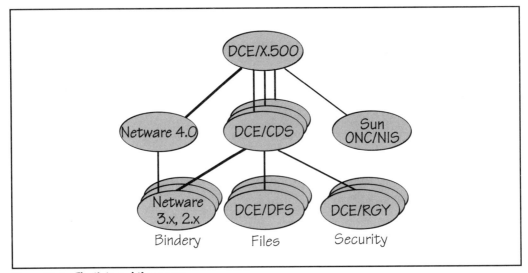

Figure 14-1. The Universal Namespace.

■ *Containment transparency*—You should be able to move resources on the servers without requiring any changes on the client. For example, you should be able to move a file from one subdirectory to another on the server and make it totally transparent to the client machines.

■ *Logon transparency*—You should be able to provide a single password (or authentication) that works on all servers and for all services on the network.

■ *Replication transparency*—You should not be able to tell how many copies of a resource exist. For example, if a naming directory is shadowed on many machines, it is up to the NOS to synchronize updates and take care of any locking issues.

■ *Distributed access transparency*—You should be able to work with any resource on the network as if it were on the local machine. The NOS must handle access controls and provide directory services.

■ *Distributed time transparency*—You should not see any time differences across servers. The NOS must synchronize the clocks on all servers.

■ *Failure transparency*—You must be shielded from network failures. The NOS must handle retries and session reconnects. It must also provide some levels of service redundancy for fault-tolerance.

■ *Administration transparency*—You should only have to deal with a single system management interface. The NOS must be integrated with the local management services.

The challenge for the NOS middleware is how to provide this high level of transparency *without sacrificing the autonomy of the local OS*.

NOS Middleware: A Bird's Eye View

The NOS middleware provides all the basic software components needed by clients and servers to seamlessly communicate at a very basic level (i.e., not service-specific). Think of this middleware as the base system components all client/server providers would have to reinvent over and over again if they did not already exist.

At a minimum, today's NOS middleware is expected to:

■ *Extend the local operating system's reach to include networked devices such as printers, file directories, and modem pools.* These are the classical functions provided by network operating systems.

■ *Provide a distributed computing foundation that creates a "single system" out of all the diverse resources distributed on the network.* This includes directory services that provide a way to find anything that's on the network, federated naming services that allow things to be uniquely named, distributed security and authentication services, a single logon, network time, and many others.

■ *Support the coordination of applications that are split across client/server lines.* At least three types of client/server exchanges must be supported: general purpose peer-to-peer communications, tightly-coupled RPC-like request/reply interactions, and loosely-coupled message queued interactions.

As client/server computing evolves, more services will move into the NOS "common middleware" category. For example, electronic mail will eventually move from the specialized service category into the NOS.

What's in a Name?

Briefing

In client/server systems, names must be unique within the context in which they are resolved (and used). You can think of a context as an autonomous naming authority. It's like the area code in the telephone system. A federated naming scheme (or *namespace*) is a conglomeration of independent naming authorities. In a federated namespace, each name must include its naming authority. For example, if you're within the US telephone naming authority, you can only call somebody in Switzerland by including the country code for Switzerland along with the person's telephone number. It's a tree-like (or hierarchical) naming scheme. If you create enough layers of hierarchy, you'll end up with a namespace that includes every communicating entity in the universe. ❏

NOS MIDDLEWARE: THE LAN IS THE SYSTEM

In a nutshell, the NOS middleware must make the network disappear. All remote resources must behave as if they were part of a single system. This section explores the mechanisms that a modern NOS provides to make that happen.

NOS: Extending the Local OS's Reach

One of the functions of a NOS is to make the physical location of resources (over a network) transparent to an application. The early NOSs were in the business of virtualizing the file and printer resources and redirecting them to LAN-based file and print servers. These NOSs provided agents on the local machines—the *requesters*—that intercepted calls for devices and *redirected* them to servers on the LAN. The only way an application (or user) could tell the difference between a local or remote resource was from a pathname, which includes its machine name. But aliases could be used to even hide the pathnames from the users.

The NOS thus extends the local OSs device support transparently across the network. Practically anything that can be done on a local OS can be done remotely and transparently. Basic file sharing is done using logical drives. Users map their own virtual drives to drives and directories on various file servers. Printer sharing is done with virtual printer ports. Users can redirect their serial or parallel printer ports to logical ports on various servers. Named pipes can be moved at will, and so can applications. The NOS allows applications written for the local OS to become networked without changing a line of code. NOSs allow clients that run on different OSs (such as DOS, Mac, and Unix) to share files and other devices. A Mac client sees DOS files in the Mac format and so on.

A new generation of network file servers promises to introduce even more transparency into the file systems. For example, the DCE *Distributed File Service (DFS)* provides a single image file system that can be distributed across a group of file servers (see Figure 14-2). The DFS file naming scheme is location-independent. Each file has a unique identifier that is consistent across the network. Files use the DCE global namespace just like the rest of the network resources. And the file system is integrated with the DCE security mechanisms.

DFS provides a *Local File System (LFS)* with many advanced features, including replication facilities that make the file system highly available. Fast response is achieved with a distributed cache. A snapshot of the file system can reside on the client, which can operate on files even if the server is down. Backups and file relocations can take place without making LFS unavailable. LFS also provides transactional log support. In case of a system crash, file records can be replayed to bring the system to a consistent state. LFS still has a few problems that need to be ironed out; but when it is ready, it will raise the bar for distributed file systems. DFS can work with other local file systems, such as NFS, or the Unix file system.

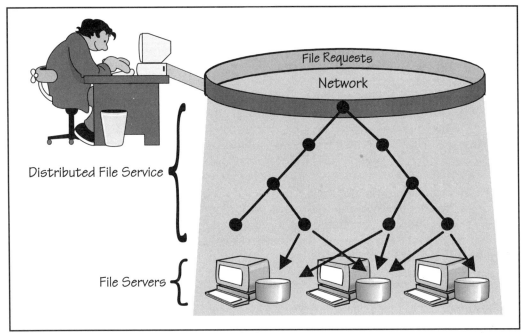

Figure 14-2. The New Generation: DCE's Distributed File Server.

A Tale of NOSs and OSs

Soapbox

Is a NOS an extension of the local OS? Or, is it a new type of distributed OS that simply grafts itself onto an existing OS? Or, is it simply middleware glue, which lives in a *no man's land* until it finds the right home? Or, is it "glue" that's working its way toward replacing the local OS? The answer is a bit of all of the above.

The early NOSs, like NetWare 2.X and LAN Manager, were mainly in the business of providing shared file and printer access to DOS machines. LAN Manager went one step further and created network extensions of Named Pipes, OS/2's local interprocess communication mechanism. With Windows NT, Microsoft went *all the way* and bundled the entire NOS (LAN Manager) with the OS. As far as Microsoft is concerned, the NOS is dead. Of course, Novell's fortunes depend on keeping the NOS separate from the OS. But when it comes to UnixWare, Novell does quite a bit of bundling itself—it currently incorporates both the Network File Server (NFS) and the NetWare client (two NOS functions) with the Operating System.

Sun Microsystems, the pioneer of the modern NOS, placed NFS in the public domain along with "pure glue" including the Sun RPC and the *Network Information Service (NIS)*—formerly known as the yellow pages. NIS provides a secured network directory service that maps user names to encrypted passwords, as well as machine names to network addresses and other items. The NISs are replicated using a master/slave arrangement.

DCE goes even further than Sun by providing an OS-independent layer of glue that includes distributed directory services, network security, RPC, threads, and distributed time. DCE is the epitome of *pure middleware*. But even DCE went beyond the pure middleware business and is offering a distributed file system.

Eventually every resource will be virtualized. We won't be able to tell where anything resides. Clients can hide the location of the servers and make all resources appear to exist on the desktop. After all, the goal is to provide a fully transparent single system image of the universe. However, there are at least two ways to get to that goal: by introducing super NOSs (the DCE model), or by making the OSs do it all themselves (the NT model). In the meantime, until we find a smart OS that can really do *everything* for us, it is better to live with the NOSs—they provide us with more choices. ❏

Global Directory Services

Distributed applications will move information between people. To do that, they'll need a way to find people—a directory. And when applications and services—like messaging—all start using a single directory, then user management will be centralized, making your life easier.

— *Jamie Lewis, Burton Group*
(December 20, 1993)

The state of a client/server system is always in flux. Users join and leave the network. Services can be added and moved around at will. Data is always being created and moved around. So who keeps track of all this activity? How do clients find their servers in a constantly changing universe? Where is the single system image kept? It's kept in the NOS's directory service, of course (see Figure 14-3). This essential component tracks all the NOS's resources and knows where everything is. Without it, we would be lost. Ideally, a distributed directory should provide a single image that can be used by all network applications—including e-mail, system management, network inventory, file services, RPCs, distributed objects, databases, authentication, and security.

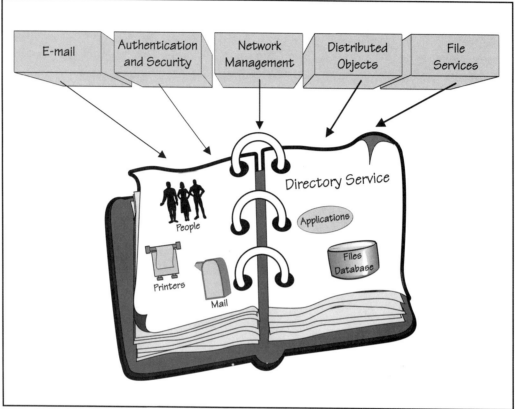

Figure 14-3. Global Directories: Keeping Track of NOS Resources.

In a modern NOS, the directory service is implemented as a distributed, replicated, object database. It is *distributed* to allow different administration domains to control their environment. It is *replicated* to provide high availability and performance where needed. Remember, if the directory is down, all the network activity comes to a grinding halt. Nothing can be found anymore. It's an *object database* in the sense that everything that is tracked is an instance of an object class. Inheritance can be used to derive new object types.

A typical directory is implemented as a set of named entries and their associated attributes. For example, "MyServer" may be an instance of an application server type (or class). Its attributes can be: room number = 54, status = up, and CPU utilization = 54 percent. MyServer may also contain a list of the functions it exports and their interface definitions.

Modern NOS directories have APIs and user interfaces that allow programs (or humans) to locate entities on the network by querying on the name or attributes. For example, a program can issue a query to locate all the 1200-dpi printers that are not busy. If you know the name of an entity, you can always obtain its attributes. The directory service itself is a well-known address known to all the trusted users on the network (and sometimes even intruders).

How do directories maintain their autonomy in a global network environment? How do they let us create unique names on the network without bumping into each other? How do we accommodate legacy naming services? This is usually accomplished by introducing hierarchical namespaces like in a file system (see Figure 14-4). In each name, there is a *global component* and a *local component*. The global component is the name by which the local directory is known at the intergalactic level. The global component manages a federation of loosely-coupled local directories. The local component can then be named according to local conventions. In addition, a

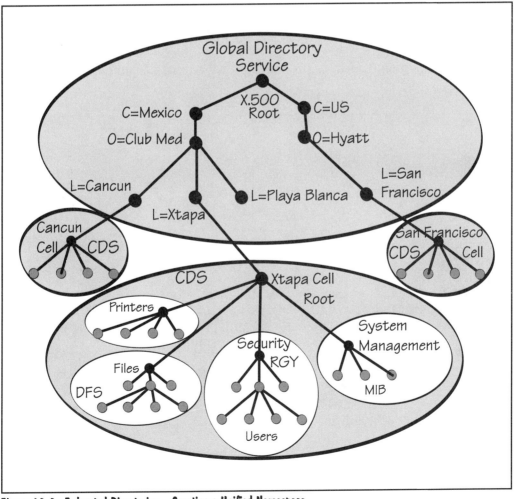

Figure 14-4. Federated Directories—Creating a Unified Namespace.

gateway agent can reside on each local directory and can forward queries for non-local names to a global directory (or naming service).

How are directories replicated? Typically, a directory maintains a master copy and read-only shadow replicas. Two types of synchronization schemes are used to refresh the replicas:

■ ***Immediate Replication*** causes any update to the master to be immediately shadowed on all replicas.

■ ***Skulking*** causes a periodic propagation (for example, once a day) to all the replicas of all changes made on the master.

In summary, the new generation of NOS directory services uses some of the most advanced distributed database and object technology to keep track of distributed system resources. The technology is flexible enough to manage and track today's coarser network entities—such as printers, users, programs, and servers—and the more fine-grained entities that are beginning to appear—such as distributed objects.

The X.500 Global Directory Standard

Briefing

Warning: This box is filled with TLAs (Three-Letter Acronyms).

The industry standard for global directories, X.500, is based on a replicated distributed database (see Figure 14-5). Programs can access the directory services using the X/Open Directory Service (XDS) API. The XDS APIs allow programs to read, compare, update, add, and remove directory entries; list directories; and search for entries based on attributes. The X/Open Management (XOM) API is used for defining and navigating through the information objects that comprise the directory. Think of XOM as an object metalanguage. Each object in an X.500 directory belongs to a class. A class can be derived from other classes. XOM provides an API for defining object classes and their attributes. XOM APIs also define basic data types such as string.

The X.500 client component—the Directory User Agent (DUA)—and server component—the Directory System Agent (DSA)—communicate using the Directory Access Protocol (DAP). Servers talk to each other using the Directory System Protocol (DSP). The DAP and DSP formats and protocols are defined in the X.500 standard and provide worldwide interoperability among directory services.

The X.500 standard was written to run on top of the OSI communication protocol. OSI is not very popular, so many implementations of X.500 cheat and use alternatives like TCP/IP or IPX/SPX. Regardless, X.500 is a standards success story. It is our best hope for finding things on intergalactic networks. Sorry for all the acronyms! ❑

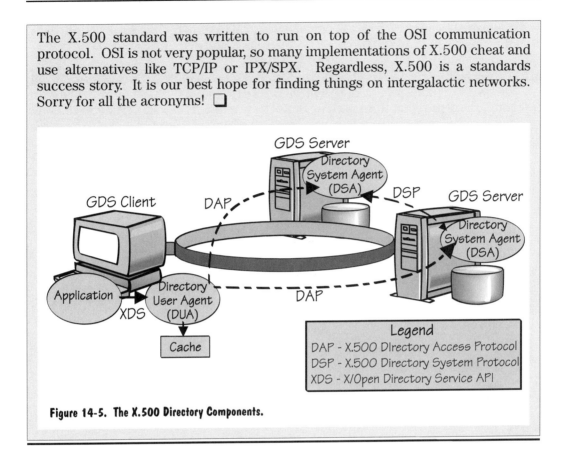

Figure 14-5. The X.500 Directory Components.

Distributed Time Services

Maintaining a single notion of time is important for ordering events that occur on distributed clients and servers. So how does a client/server system keep the clocks on different machines synchronized? How does it compensate for the unequal drift rates between synchronizations? How does it create a single system illusion that makes all the different machine clocks tick to the same time? With the NOS's distributed time services, of course.

Typically, the NOS addresses the problem of distributed time using two complementary techniques:

■ ***It periodically synchronizes the clocks on every machine in the network.***
The NOS typically has an agent on each machine—DCE calls it a *Time Clerk*—that asks *Time Servers* for the correct time and adjusts the local time accordingly. The agents may consult more than one Time Server, and then calculate

the probable correct time and its inaccuracy based on the responses it receives. The agent can upgrade the local time either gradually or abruptly.

■ *It introduces an inaccuracy component to compensate for unequal clock drifts that occur between synchronizations.* The local time agents are configured to know the limits of their local hardware clock. They maintain a count of the inaccuracy factor and return it to an API call that asks for the time. The time agent requests a synchronization after the local clock drifts past an inaccuracy threshold.

As you can see, today's NOSs may have even surpassed the Swiss in their attention to intricate timing details.

FYI

What Does a Time Server Do?

Briefing

The Time Server is a node that is designated to answer queries about the time. A DCE LAN provides at least three Time Servers; one (or more) must be connected to an *External Time Provider.* The Time Servers query one another to adjust their clocks. The External Time Provider may be a hardware device that receives time from a radio or a telephone source. If no such source is available, the system administrator's watch may do. The commonly used time format in the industry is the UTC standard, which keeps track of time elapsed since the beginning of the Gregorian calendar—October 15, 1582. This time is adjusted using the Greenwich time zone differential factor (for example, -5 hours in New York City). ❑

Distributed Security Services

The client/server environment introduces new security threats beyond those found in traditional time-shared systems. In a client/server system, you can't trust any of the operating systems on the network (our apologies to NT's C2-certifiability) to protect the server's resources from unauthorized access. And even if the client machines were totally secure, the network itself is highly accessible. Sniffer devices can easily record traffic between machines and introduce forgeries and Trojan Horses into the system. This means the servers must find new ways to protect themselves without creating a fortress mentality that upsets users.

To maintain the single system illusion, every trusted user must be given transparent access to all resources. How is that done when every PC poses a potential threat to network security? Will system administrators be condemned to spend their working lives granting access level rights to users, one at a time, for each individual application on each server across the enterprise? Let's find out what the NOSs have to offer.

Can We Obtain C2-Level Security on the LAN?

To date, no NOS has yet achieved C2 level security (but DCE may be coming close). You may recall from the NT discussion that C2 is a government security standard for operating systems which requires that users and applications be authenticated before gaining access to any operating system resource. To obtain C2 certification on a network, all clients must provide an authenticated user ID, all resources must be protected by access control lists, audit trails must be provided, and access rights must not be passed to other users that reuse the same items. Let's go over the security mechanisms a modern NOS can provide to meet (and even beat) C2 level security on the network.

■ *Authentication: Are you who you claim to be?* In time-shared systems, the authentication is done by the OS using passwords. NOSs have to do better than that. Any hacker with a PC and network sniffer knows how to capture a password and reuse it. OK, so let's encrypt the password. Oh boy! Who is going to manage the secret keys and all that good stuff? Luckily, NOSs have an answer: *Kerberos*. You'll get all the gory details in the DCE chapter. But for now, think of Kerberos as the trusted third party that allows two processes to prove to each other that they are who they claim to be. It's a bit like two spies meeting on a street corner and whispering the magical code words that establish the "trust" relationship.

Kerberos: "You Can't Trust Anyone"

Briefing

MIT's project Athena adopted the position that it is next to *impossible* to make sure each workstation on the network is secure. Instead, the MIT folks took it as a given that some "impersonation" would take place on the LAN and decided to protect themselves against it. The result was a software fortress called Kerberos that delivers a higher level of security than traditional passwords and access control lists. Kerberos automatically authenticates every user for every application. The Kerberos protocol, especially with the add-ons introduced by the OSF DCE, fulfills the authentication requirement of C2. It allows servers to trust their clients (mostly PCs) and vice versa. You must remember that we could always put a Trojan Horse on the server side, so the servers also need to prove their identity. ❑

■ *Authorization: Are you allowed to use this resource?* Once clients are authenticated, the server applications are responsible for verifying which operations the clients are permitted to perform on the information they try to access (for example, a payroll server may control access to salary data on a per-individual basis). Servers use *Access Control Lists (ACLs)* to control user access. ACLs can be associated with any computer resource. They contain the list of names (and group names) and the type of operations they are permitted to perform on each resource. NetWare's administration services, for example, make it easy for network managers to add new users to groups without having to specify access rights from scratch. NOSs can easily meet C2's ACL requirements.

■ *Audit Trails: Where have you been?* Audit services allow network managers to monitor user activities, including attempted logons and which servers or files are used. Audit services are a piece of the arsenal needed by network managers to detect intruders in their own organizations. For example, they can monitor all the network activity associated with a suspect client workstation (or user). Knowing an audit trail exists usually discourages insiders from tampering with servers using their own logon, but they can do it under somebody else's logon.

Most NOSs support audit trails, and that should make the C2 accreditation people happy.

Also, many add-on tools are available to help secure a particular PC. For example, Mergent International's **PC/DACS** product (for DOS and OS/2) offers audit trails to monitor user activity and prevent system files (such as CONFIG.SYS and AUTOEX-EC.BAT) from being altered—these are the files that start the security program. PC/DACS also offers some security against users who boot their PCs from the A: drive. In summary, it looks like "C2 security on a LAN" is well within the reach of a modern NOS, like OSF's DCE.

DCE and Access Control Lists

Briefing

Modern NOSs, like the OSF DCE, provide a set of APIs that allow servers to create and manage their ACLs. The DCE NOS also provides hooks that help the clients present their authorization credentials to the server applications. DCE calls it the *Privilege Attribute Certificate (PAC)*—a security-server issued ticket the client must present to the server. PACs contain authorization information specific to the client, such as the groups it belongs to. DCE provides a set of server APIs that can read the information contained in the PACs and match them with the information in the ACLs. ❏

Can We Do "Better Than C2" on the LAN?

We need "better than C2" security when traffic moves over unsecured wide area networks. How can we guarantee that vital messages are not tampered with? You don't want the data in an electronic fund transfer to be intercepted and rerouted from your account to somebody else's. Modern NOSs, like the OSF DCE, provide at least two mechanisms for dealing with these type of situations:

■ *Encryption* allows two principals to hold a secure communication. Each principal must obtain a copy of a "session key" from a trusted third party (for example, a Kerberos server). This "session key" can then be used for encoding and decoding messages. Another approach is to use a public key encryption technique. But encryption may be an overkill in some situations: It introduces performance overheads and may be subject to governmental restrictions.

■ *Cryptographic checksums*, a less extreme solution, ensure that data is not modified as it passes through the network. The sender calculates a checksum on the data, using a "session key" to encrypt it, and appends the result to the message. The receiver recalculates the checksum, decrypts the one received in the message using the "session key," and then compares the two. If they don't match, the message is suspect. Without the "session key," intruders will not be able to alter the data and update the checksum.

In summary, new NOS technologies like Kerberos, provide a versatile mechanism for establishing the right level of security in a distributed environment.

Single Logon Makes it Easier for the User

Users are already complaining about having to do multiple logons to different servers and resource managers. Modern NOSs provide the technology that allows a user to access any server resource from anywhere—including hotel rooms, offices, homes, and cellular phones—using a single signon. How's that done? With Kerberos-like security, of course.

You simply logon once (see Figure 14-6) get authenticated, and then obtain a set of security tickets (also called tokens) for each server with which you want to communicate. All this activity is conducted under-the-cover by the NOSs security agents. No password is stored in the login script on the client, and no telephone callbacks are required. It doesn't get any easier, as long as you can remember your password.

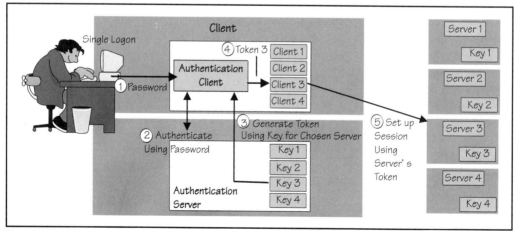

Figure 14-6. Logon to One and Get to Everything You Need.

How About the Poor Administrator?

Soapbox

The good news is that modern NOSs like DCE provide most of the features it takes to beat almost any intruder. And within a single NOS environment, the security administration is very consistent. A single namespace is used for tracking and registering all resources; the new NOSs hide the details of location. Access control lists use the same namespaces as everything else and are easier to maintain. However, to make all that work, the NOS requires a certain level of cohesion and uniformity. The bad news is that the world is already populated with existing NOSs that have their own ways of doing things. Even Novell is having a very hard time migrating its installed base from NetWare 3.X to the postmodern NetWare 4.X.

So how do network administrators deal with security in mixed NOS environments (for example, networks that run both NetWare and DCE)? It can be done, but it's a major headache. It seems the single system image today is mostly benefiting the users. Security administrators in mixed NOS environments have been overlooked. To make everything work together, the NOS vendors must agree on a single namespace standard, a single registry database structure, interoperable authentication mechanisms, and a common format for representing and manipulating access control lists. Don't hold your breath waiting. The good news, however, is that IBM is working with Novell on making NetWare and the OSF DCE more consistent at every level. ❑

Chapter 15

RPC, Messaging, and Peer-to-Peer

---

*G*ood middleware protects the application from the different networking layers and even from the different sets of hardware.

— Leslie Yeamans,
VP System Strategies, Inc.
November, 1993

Client/server applications are split across address spaces, physical machines, networks, and operating systems. How do clients and servers talk to each other? How are the requests and responses synchronized? How are the dissimilar data representations on different computers handled? What happens if one of the parties is unavailable? How is error-recovery managed? You guessed it: The modern NOS is taking on a lot of these responsibilities. It comes with the territory. The purpose of the NOS is to make distributed computing transparent. This means it must create an environment that hides the nastiness of dealing with communication protocols, networks, and stacks.

All NOSs offer *peer-to-peer* interfaces that let applications communicate using "close to the wire" send/receive semantics. Most NOSs provide some form of

Remote Procedure Call (RPC) middleware that hides "the wire" and makes any server on the network appear to be one function call away. An alternative type of model—message queuing or simply, *Message-Oriented Middleware (MOM)*—is gaining new converts. It turns out that messaging is incredibly helpful in situations where you do not want the clients and servers to be tightly synchronized. The current NOSs don't include MOM in their offerings. However, some very powerful product offerings are available from companies that specialize in this field. Let's take a closer look at what each type of interface has to offer.

PEER-TO-PEER COMMUNICATIONS

The peer-to-peer communication model is used to create both cooperative and client/server applications. The term "peer-to-peer" indicates that the two sides of a communication link use the same protocol interface to conduct a networked conversation. Any computer can initiate a conversation with any other computer. The protocol tends to be symmetric, and it is sometimes called "program-to-program." The peer-to-peer interface tends to be "close to the wire" in the sense that it does not fully mask the underlying network from the programmer. For example, the interface will surface transmission timeouts, race conditions, and network errors, and then leave it to the programmer to handle.

A NOS will typically support the peer-to-peer APIs that work with its native stack (NetWare, for example, supports IPX/SPX) and emulate some of the other popular APIs—NetWare, for example, supports NetBIOS, Named Pipes, and Sockets on top of IPX/SPX. The modern thinking is that the NOS should provide a stack-independent protocol that works on any transport, as well as stack-specific APIs that are made to work on top of other stacks.

A stack-independent API leads to a least common denominator solution. This can be very limiting. Over the years, each peer-to-peer API set introduced its own unique flavors of communication semantics. For example, NetBIOS is very good with broadcast (one-to-all) and multicast (one-to-some) communications. APPC is a master of robust conversations. Named Pipes makes it very easy to write client/server (many-to-one) applications. A least common denominator approach ends up supporting simple session-based conversations between two parties (one-to-one). We will have more to say about the peer-to-peer API offerings when we discuss stacks in the next chapter.

REMOTE PROCEDURE CALL (RPC)

RPCs hide the intricacies of the network by using the ordinary procedure call mechanism familiar to every programmer. A client process calls a function on a remote server and suspends itself until it gets back the results. Parameters are passed like in any ordinary procedure. The RPC, like an ordinary procedure, is synchronous. The process (or thread) that issues the call waits until it gets the results. Under the covers, the RPC run-time software collects values for the parameters, forms a message, and sends it to the remote server. The server receives the request, unpacks the parameters, calls the procedure, and sends the reply back to the client.

While RPCs make life easier for the programmer, they pose a challenge for the NOS designers who supply the development tools and run-time environments. Here's some of the issues they face:

■ *How are the server functions located and started?* At a minimum, somebody's got to provide a run-time environment that starts a server process when a remote invocation is received, passes it the parameters, and returns the response. But what happens when multiple clients go after the same function? Is each function packaged as a process? Pretty soon you discover that an entire environment is needed to start and stop servers, prioritize requests, perform security checks, and provide some form of load balancing. It also becomes quickly obvious that threads are much better at handling these incoming requests than full-blown processes. And it is better to create a server loop that manages a pool of threads waiting for work rather than create a thread for each incoming request. What is really needed on the server side is a full-blown *TP Monitor*. This is, of course, a lot more function than what the current NOSs provide.

■ *How are parameters defined and passed between the client and the server?* This is something NOSs do quite well. The better NOSs provide a *Network Interface Definition Language (NIDL)* for describing the functions and parameters that a server exports to its clients. A *NIDL compiler* takes these descriptions and produces source code stubs (and header files) for both the client and server (Figure 15-1). These stubs can then be linked with the client and server code. The client stub packages the parameters in an RPC packet, converts the data, calls the *RPC run-time library*, and waits for the server's reply. On the server side, the server stub unpacks the parameters, calls the remote procedure, packages the results, and sends the reply to the client.

■ *How are failures handled?* Because both sides of the RPC can fail separately, it is important for the software to be able to handle all the possible failure combinations. If the server does not respond, the client side will normally block, time out, and retry the call. The server side must guarantee *only once semantics* to make sure that a duplicate request is not re-executed. If the client unexpectedly dies after issuing a request, the server must be able to undo the effects of that transaction. Most NOSs provide connection-oriented and connectionless versions of their RPCs. If you need a more robust environment, use the connection-oriented RPC.

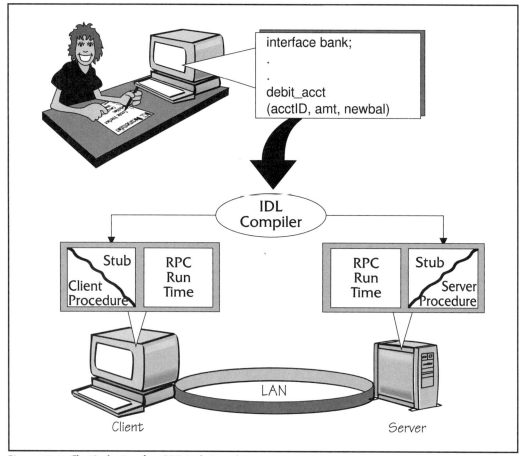

Figure 15-1. The Mechanics of an RPC Stub Compiler.

■ *How is security handled by the RPC?* Modern NOSs make it easy to automatically incorporate their security features into the RPC. All you need to specify is the level of security required (authentication, encryption, etc.) and the RPC and security feature will cooperate to make it happen.

■ *How does the client find its server?* The association of a client with a server is called *binding*. The binding information may be hardcoded in the client (for example, some services are performed by servers with *well-known* addresses). Or a client can find its server by consulting a configuration file or an environment parameter. A client can also find its server at run time through the network directory services. The servers must, of course, advertise their services in the directory. The process of using the directory to find a server at run time is called *dynamic binding*. The easiest way to find a server is let the RPC do it for you. This is called *automatic binding*, meaning that the RPC client stub will locate a server from a list of servers that support the interface. Finally, clients may use a broadcast method to indicate that they want a particular service done. The servers then respond by bidding for the job. While bidding sounds like a great idea, it is rarely used in practice.

■ ***How is data representation across systems handled?*** The problem here is that different CPUs represent data structures differently (for example, *big-endian* versus *little-endian*). So how is data transparency achieved at the RPC level? To maintain machine-independence, the RPC must provide some level of data format translation across systems. For example, the Sun RPC requires that clients convert their data to a neutral canonical format using the *External Data Representation (XDR)* APIs. In contrast, DCE's *Network Data Representation (NDR)* service is multicanonical, meaning that it supports multiple data format representations. The client chooses one of these formats (in most cases, its own native data representation); tags the data with the chosen format; and then leaves it up to the server to transform the data into a format it understands. In other words, the *server makes it right*. DCE assumes that in most cases the client and server will be using the same data representation, so why go through the translation overhead? Sun assumes that client MIPs are cheap, so it lets the client do the translation, which makes life easy for the server. With Sun, all clients look the same to the server: The *client makes it right*.

Figure 15-2 shows how the RPC mechanism all comes together. The scenario shows a simple seat reservation application. We didn't show the RPC reply in the figure because it's just more of the same in the reverse direction.

As you can see in Figure 15-2, the seating server first starts up, advertises its location and service in the network directory, and begins its continuous cycle of receiving and servicing requests. A ticketing client keeps in its cache the location of the server. When a customer is ready to buy a ticket for a Madonna concert, an RPC is issued to reserve a seat. Notice how the client and server stubs cooperate to make that happen. In short, it takes a lot of work to make that reservation for the Madonna concert. RPCs take away some of that drudgery.

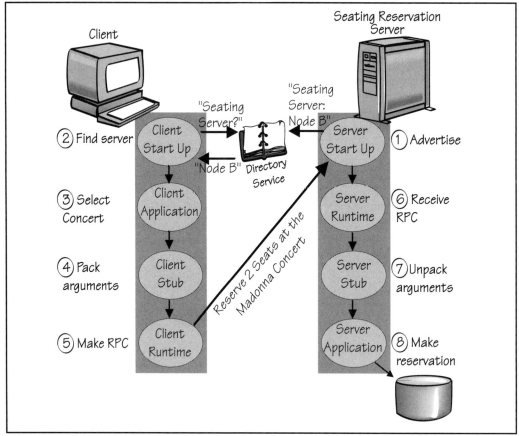

Figure 15-2. Getting a Seat for a Madonna Concert Using RPCs.

MESSAGING AND QUEUING: THE MOM MIDDLEWARE

Message-Oriented Middleware (MOM) allows general-purpose messages to be exchanged in a client/server system using message queues. Applications communicate over networks by simply putting messages in queues and getting messages from queues. MOM hides all the nasty communications from applications and typically provides a very simple high-level API to its services. A MOM Consortium was formed in mid-1993 with the goal of creating standards for messaging middleware. Members include DEC, IBM, Covia, Peerlogic, Horizon Strategies, and System Strategies. So what can you do with MOM?

MOM's messaging and queuing allow clients and servers to communicate across a network without being linked by a private, dedicated, logical connection. The clients and servers can run at different times. Everybody communicates by putting messages on queues and by taking messages from queues (see Figure 15-3). Notice that the server sends back the reply via a message queue. Messaging does not impose any constraints on an application's structure: If no response is required, none is sent.

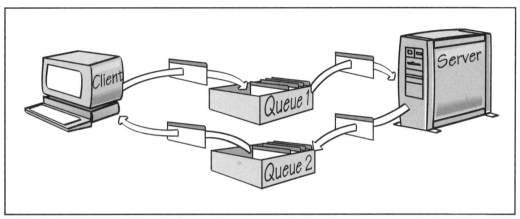

Figure 15-3. MOM: Two-way Message Queuing.

Programs do not talk to each other directly, so either program can be busy, unavailable, or simply not running at the same time. A program can decide when it wants to retrieve a message off its queue—there are no time constraints. The target program can even be started several hours later. Or, if you're using a laptop on the road, you can collect outgoing requests in a queue and submit them to the server when you get to a phone or to an office LAN. Messaging allows either the client or the server to be unavailable (see Figure 15-4).

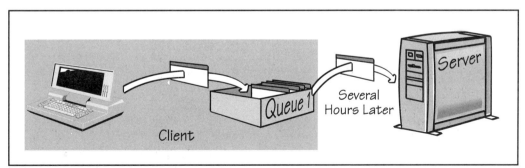

Figure 15-4. MOM: Save Your Messages Until You Get to a Server.

Messaging queues are very versatile. You can use them to create one-to-many or many-to-one relationships (see Figure 15-5). In the figure, many clients are sending requests to one server queue. The messages are picked off the queue by multiple instances of the server program that are concurrently servicing the clients. The server instances can take messages off the queue either on a first-in/first-out basis or according to some priority or load-balancing scheme. In all cases, a message queue can be concurrently accessed. The servers can also use the messaging filters to throw away the messages they don't want to process, or they can pass them on to other servers.

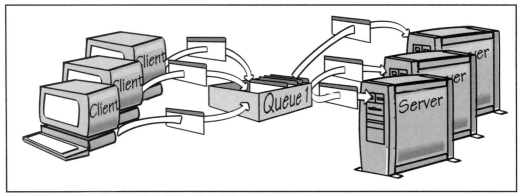

Figure 15-5. MOM: Many-to-Many Messaging via Queues.

Most MOM messaging products make available a single API set that runs on multiple operating system platforms. Most messaging products provide *persistent* (logged on disk) and *non-persistent* (in memory) message queues. Persistent messages are slower, but they can be recovered in case of power failures after a system restart. In both cases, messages can be either copied or removed from a queue. A message queue can be *local* to the machine or *remote*. System administrators can usually specify the number of messages a queue can hold and the maximum message size.

MOM products provide their own NOS services—including hierarchical naming, security, and a layer that isolates applications from the network. They use virtual memory on the local OS to create their queues. Most messaging products allow the sender to specify the name of the reply queue. The products also include some type of *format field* that tells the recipient how to interpret the message data.

Most messaging products provide a minimum level of fault-tolerance in the form of persistent queues. Some of the products provide some form of *transactional protection*, allowing the queue to participate in a two-phase commit synchronization protocol. And some may even reroute messages to alternate queues in case of a network failure.

MOM VERSUS RPC

Comparing the Messaging and RPC paradigms is like doing business via a telephone call versus exchanging letters or faxes (see Figure 15-6). An interaction using a

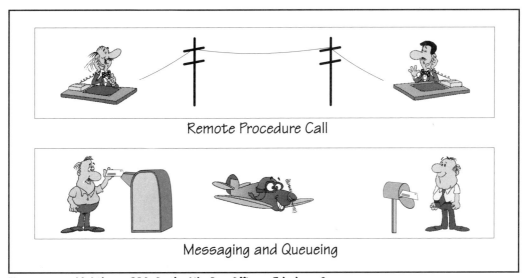

Remote Procedure Call

Messaging and Queueing

Figure 15-6. MOM Versus RPC: Do You Like Post Office or Telephones?

telephone call is immediate—both parties talk to each other directly to conduct their business. At the end of the phone conversation, a unit of work is concluded. Conducting business via mail allows you to stage work, prioritize it, and do it when you're ready for it. You're in control of the workflow, not that ringing phone. On the other hand, it may be frustrating on the client side not to receive immediate feedback.

Table 15-1 compares the messaging and RPC architectures. Messaging is, of course, more flexible and time-tolerant than RPC. However, messaging only skews things in time and may create its own level of complications. In the telephone analogy (i.e., RPC), you complete the work as it arrives; you don't have to manage stacks of incoming letters (or faxes). Your clients are happy they get immediate service. When you close shop at the end of the day, you're all done with your work. In the mail analogy, letters may start to pile up and clients may be polling their incoming mailboxes continuously, waiting for a response. We may have made life easier for the server at the expense of the client. On the other hand, messaging does free clients from being synchronized to their servers; this can be very liberating for mobile and home users.

In summary, there's plenty of room for messaging, RPCs, and peer-to-peer styles of communication on the modern NOS. Each distinctive style presents its own paradigm for conducting business. You'll end up choosing the style that provides the best fit for your particular needs.

Table 15-1. Comparing MOM and RPC.

Feature	MOM: Messaging and Queuing	Remote Procedure Call (RPC)
Metaphor	Post office-like	Telephone-like.
Client/Server time relationship	Asynchronous. Clients and servers may operate at different times and speeds.	Synchronous. Clients and servers must run concurrently. Servers must keep up with clients.
Client/Server sequencing	No fixed sequence	Servers must first come up before clients can talk to them.
Style	Queued	Call-Return
Persistent Data	Yes	No
Partner needs to be available	No	Yes
Who maintains the communications session?	The queue manager	The RPC run time. The client and server communicate directly with each other.
Load balancing	Single queue can be used to implement FIFO or priority-based policy.	Requires a separate TP Monitor.
Transactional support	Yes (some products). Message queue can participate in the commit synchronization.	No. Requires a transactional RPC.
Message filtering	Yes	No
Performance	Slow. An intermediate hop is required.	Fast
Asynchronous processing	Yes. Queues and triggers are required.	Limited. Requires threads and tricky code for managing threads.

CONCLUSION

As you may have surmised from this chapter, the NOS middleware pieces are of interest to all client/server apps. If you don't acquire the pieces "off-the-shelf," you'll have to recreate them in some shape or form. After all, a network is almost unusable without security, directory, and naming services. And everybody needs a MOM, RPC, or peer-to-peer communications. The NOS creates a "gentle and civilized environment" on raw networks that lets you focus on your client/server business. The next chapter, on stacks, takes you closer to the network wire. After reading it, you'll get a better appreciation for the value-added provided by the NOS middleware.

Chapter 16

Stacks:
Ubiquitous
Communications

---

*T*herefore, ye soft pipes, play on.

— *Keats*

This chapter provides a brief overview of the transport stacks middleware. We cover the "big five" of networking: TCP/IP (with sockets), IPX/SPX (with TLI), NetBEUI (with NetBIOS), APPC/SNA (with CPI-C), and Named Pipes. Obviously, there's no way we can do justice to the communication stacks and their interface protocols in one "very long" chapter. Instead, we will give you a feeling for what the big five have to offer in terms of features and what makes them important.

WHAT'S A STACK ANYWAY?

The stacks middleware must provide "any-to-any" ubiquitous communications—including the communications stacks proper and the interface to the network adapters that drive local, wide-area, and wireless networks. In Part 1, we provided a brief glimpse of the communications infrastructure that's covering most of our planet. The transport stacks are the nervous system that make the physical pieces come together.

Communications software vendors have tackled the problem of network complexity by breaking down complex protocols into layers (see the following Briefing box). Each layer builds on top of the services provided by the layers below it. Eventually, you get a *stack* of layers that looks like a birthday cake. Vendors sell their communication products as stack offerings that are architected to work together. In theory, each stack layer has a well-defined set of APIs and protocols so that it should be possible to mix-and-match different vendor offerings within the same stack. In practice, this is not the case. You buy an entire stack from a single vendor and pray that it works with the hardware.

The lowest layer of communication software belongs to the device drivers that provide an interface to several types of communication hardware adapters. The bottom of the stacks sits on top of the device drivers. The top of the stacks sits right below the NOS.

The stacks and NOS are simply divisions that help us create a Survival Map. The layers we just described are part of the *OSI Reference Model*. To help you navigate through this chapter, we couldn't resist coming up with our own interpretation of where the different pieces fit in the OSI reference model (see Figure 16-1). Remember, it's just a reference model. So take it in with a grain of salt. As you will discover in the next few chapters, *real* products don't have any notion of architectural boundaries or reference models—they just get a job done.

So what do stacks provide? At the lower layers, they interface to the hardware using the physical *Media Access Control (MAC)* protocols defined by the IEEE. The *Logical Link Control (LLC)* provides a common interface to the MACs and a reliable link service for transmitting communication packets between two nodes. The link layer combines the LLC and MAC functions. On top of this layer is the *network* layer that allows packets to be routed across multiple networks. The *transport* layer sits on top of the network layer and provides some form of reliable end-to-end delivery service. The *session* layer deals with network etiquette—who goes first, who reconnects in case of failure, and synchronization points. On top of the session layer is a *presentation* layer that deals with data representation. Finally, the *application layer* provides network services and interfaces to an application.

The boundary between the stacks and NOS gets fuzzy at the upper layers. For example, is the peer-to-peer interface an application, presentation, or session layer service? Does it belong to the NOS or the stacks? But, then, everything in client/server is a bit fuzzy.

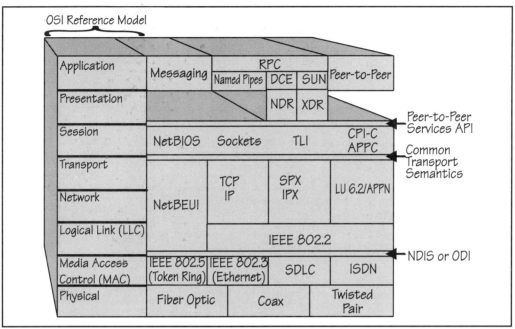

Figure 16-1. Where the Most Popular Stacks Fit in the OSI Reference Model.

FYI

Layering: Breaking Down Complexity

Briefing

Layering is a software design technique used to break down complex programs into a hierarchy of services. Powerful new services can be provided by adding new layers on top of more primitive service layers. A service interface defines the services provided by an underlying layer to the layers above it.

Layering also provides an ideal framework for explaining and organizing the communications between two independent programs. Program-to-program communications is broken down into exchanges between the corresponding peer layers in each program. The following three concepts form the basis for the layered approach:

■ At each layer, client and server peers cooperate jointly to provide a service. Of course, one peer can end up doing all of the work, but the service is still considered to be a joint effort by the peers for that layer. The *protocol* is the contract the peers abide by. It specifies how the work is divided among the peers, the semantics of the message exchanges for that layer, and the handshake sequences.

■ Each layer builds on top of the services provided by the layers beneath it. A *service interface* specifies how a layer can obtain access to the services of the layer directly below it. The interface should hide all the nasty details of the workings of the underlying layer while providing a complete set of services.

■ Services become more abstract the higher the layer. For example, the lower layers may be concerned with the interfaces to the hardware or the operating system, while the higher layers may provide a more application-specific type of service, such as a file transfer.

Layering is quite popular in the area of data communications. There are several examples of layered protocol stacks in this chapter. ❏

STACK MIDDLEWARE

Some of the stacks we cover in this chapter are more complete than others. For example, SNA and IPX/SPX cover all the traditional layers. TCP/IP does not support a link layer and depends on sockets for its session and presentation services. NetBIOS does not provide a network layer. Named Pipes is a client/server protocol with RPC-like functions. However, all the Named Pipes implementations now include both the client and server sides—this means that it is also a peer-to-peer protocol. Named Pipes is just an interface layer that sits on top of other protocols (such as NetBEUI and IPX/SPX). In this section, we look at the services provided by each stack. We also try and give you some flavor of how they work.[1]

TCP/IP and Sockets

TCP/IP—originally the network of choice for the government, the Internet, and the universities—is now increasingly finding its way into commercial environments. TCP/IP is particularly strong in enterprises that require internetworking between different LAN environments. The TCP/IP protocol runs on virtually every operating system platform. Over 300 vendors sell TCP/IP communications products, and that market is rapidly growing.

Internet Protocol (IP)

The network layer of the TCP/IP stack is provided by the **Internet Protocol (IP)**. It provides the basic mechanism for routing packets in the internet. IP is not a reliable communication protocol. It does not understand the relationships between packets and does not perform retransmissions. IP requires higher-level protocols such as TCP or UDP, to provide a reliable class of service (see the following Briefing box).

---

[1] You can get more of the gory details—including programming examples for NetBIOS, APPC, Named Pipes, TCP/IP, and NetWare—in our book, **Client/Server Programming with OS/2 2.1** (VNR, 1993).

Datagrams Versus Sessions

Briefing

Connection-oriented protocols—also known as *session-based protocols, virtual circuits*, or *sequenced packet exchanges*—provide a reliable two-way connection service over a session. Each packet of information that gets exchanged over a session is given a unique sequence number through which it gets tracked and individually acknowledged. Duplicate packets are detected and discarded by the session services.

The price you pay for this reliable class of service is the overhead associated with creating and managing the session. If a session is lost, one of the parties must reestablish it. This can be a problem for fault-tolerant servers that require automatic switchovers to a backup server if the primary server fails. The backup server needs to reestablish all the outstanding sessions with clients. In addition, sessions are inherently a two-party affair and don't lend themselves well to broadcasting (one-to-many exchanges).

Datagrams—also known as *connectionless protocols* or *transmit and pray* protocols—provide a simple but unreliable form of exchange. The more powerful datagram protocols such as NetBIOS provide broadcast capabilities. NetBIOS allows you to send datagrams to a named entity, to a select group of entities (multicast), or to all entities on a network (broadcast). Datagrams are unreliable in the sense that they are not acknowledged or tracked through a sequence number. You "transmit and pray" that your datagram gets received. The recipient may not be there or may not be expecting a datagram (you will never know). Novell literature estimates that about 5% of datagrams don't make it. You may, of course, design your own acknowledgement schemes on top of the datagram service. Some stacks (for example, LAN Server's Mailslots) provide an acknowledged datagram service.

Datagrams are very useful to have in "discovery" types of situations. These are situations where you discover things about your network environment by broadcasting queries and learning who is out there from the responses. Broadcast can be used to obtain bids for services or to advertise the availability of new services. Broadcast datagrams provide the capability of creating electronic "bazaars." They support the creation of very dynamic types of environments where things can happen spontaneously. In situations where the name of the recipient is not known, broadcast datagrams are the only way to get the message out. The cost of broadcast datagrams is that, in some cases, recipients may get overloaded with "junk mail." The multicast facility helps alleviate this problem because broadcast mail can then be sent only to "special interest" groups. The alternative to broadcast is the network directory services.

Datagrams are also very useful in situations where there is a need to send a quick message without the world coming to an end if the message is not received. The typical situation is sending control-like information, such as telling a network manager "I'm alive." It doesn't make sense to go through all the overhead of creating a session with the network manager just to say "I'm alive," and what if there are 500 nodes on the network? The manager will need 500 permanent sessions, an exorbitant cost in resources. This is where the datagram alternative comes in. With datagrams you can send your "I'm alive" message. And if the manager misses your message once, it will get another one when you send your next heartbeat (provided you're still alive). ❑

TCP and UDP

The transport layer of TCP/IP consists of two protocols that provide end-to-end transport services:

■ *Transmission Control Protocol (TCP)* provides a reliable, session-based service for the delivery of sequenced packets across an internet.

■ *User Datagram Protocol (UDP)* provides a datagram service. Datagrams are unreliable but fast.

The TCP/IP protocol does not specify an application interface layer. However, sockets have emerged as TCP/IP's premier peer-to-peer API.

Sockets

Sockets were introduced in 1981 as the Unix BSD 4.2 generic interface that would provide Unix-to-Unix communications over networks. In 1985, SunOS introduced NFS and RPC over sockets. In 1986, AT&T introduced the *Transport Layer Interface (TLI)* that provides functionality similar to sockets but in a more network-independent fashion. Unix SVR4 incorporates both sockets and TLI. As it stands, sockets are far more prevalent than TLI in the Unix world. The good news is that sockets and TLI are very similar from a programmer's perspective. TLI is just a cleaner version of sockets. We cover TLI in the IPX/SPX stack section.

Support for sockets exists on a multiplicity of operating system environments, including MS-DOS, Windows, OS/2, UNIX, Mac OS, and most mainframe environments. The Windows socket API, known colloquially as *WinSock*, is a multivendor specification that standardizes the use of TCP/IP under Windows. The WinSock API is based on the Berkeley sockets interface. In the BSD Unix system, sockets are part of the kernel and provide both a standalone and networked IPC service. Non-BSD Unix systems, MS-DOS, Windows, Mac OS, and OS/2 provide sockets in the form of libraries. In Unix SVR4, sockets are implemented in terms of streams. Streams in SVR4 provide the mechanism for hooking external drivers to the kernel. It is safe to say that sockets provide the current "de facto" portable standard for network application providers on TCP/IP networks.

The three most popular socket types are *stream*, *datagram*, and *raw*. Stream and datagram sockets interface to the TCP and UDP protocols, and raw sockets interface to the IP protocol. The type of socket is specified at creation time. In theory, the socket interface can be extended, and you can define new socket types to provide additional services. The following describes the characteristics of the three socket types:

■ **Datagram Sockets** provide an interface to the UDP datagram service. UDP handles network transmissions as independent packets and provides no guarantees. UDP does include a checksum, but it makes no attempt to detect duplicate packets or to maintain any form of sequencing on multipacket transmissions. You're on your own—data can be lost, duplicated, or received in the wrong order. You're in charge of retransmissions when an error occurs (UDP does not save your message either). No acknowledgement of receipt is built into the protocol. The size of a datagram is limited to the size that can be sent in a single message (the maximum length is usually 32,768 bytes).

■ **Stream Sockets** provide an interface to the reliable TCP transport protocol. The stream socket guarantees that packets are sent without errors or duplication, and that they are received in the same order as they are sent. No boundaries are imposed on the data; it is considered to be a stream of bytes. On the plus side, TCP provides a reliable peer-to-peer mechanism. On the negative side, TCP is slower than UDP and requires more programming overhead. Be warned: *TCP knows nothing about the preservation of message boundaries*. This is to be expected because the Unix file system, whose semantics TCP models, knows nothing about record boundaries.

■ **Raw Sockets** provide an interface to the lower-layer protocols such as IP and *Internet Control Message Protocol (ICMP)*. This interface does not provide traditional peer-to-peer services. It is used to test new protocols or to gain access to some of the more advanced facilities of an existing protocol.

A socket address on the TCP/IP internet consists of two parts: an internet address (IP_address) and a port number (see Figure 16-2). So what's an internet address? And what's a port number?

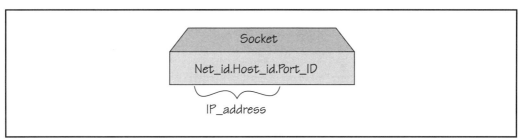

Figure 16-2. SOCKET = Internet Address (IP) + Port Address.

An *internet address* is a 32-bit number, usually represented by four decimal numbers separated by dots, that must be unique for each TCP/IP network interface card within an administered AF_INET domain. A TCP/IP *host* (i.e., networked machine) may have as many internet addresses as it has network interfaces.

A *port* is an entry point to an application that resides on a host. It is represented by a 16-bit integer. Ports are commonly used to define the entry points for services provided by server applications. Important commercial server programs—such as Oracle and Sybase DBMSs—have their own *well-known* ports.

The TCP/IP socket API consists of about 60 API calls; 21 of these are *socket core* commands (see Table 16-1). These are the original socket API calls included with all the major implementations of sockets (usually at the kernel level). These calls allow you to create sockets, manage sessions, transfer data using datagram or session-based exchanges, and provide miscellaneous functions that help you with socket dynamics. The core socket calls use familiar file-like semantics and are easily understood.

The Portmapper Network Service

Briefing

How do applications discover their ports at run time? Most socket implementations support the *portmapper network service* developed by Sun Microsystems. The portmapper is a directory service for ports (think of it as the network yellow pages). At startup, server applications—the non-famous ones—request an available port from the system and then register their services and port numbers with the portmapper. The client processes can query the portmapper (using qualifiers) to obtain the port number associated with a particular server application. So how do you find the portmapper? It's the well-known port number 111. ❑

Table 16-1. Main Socket Calls.

Socket Endpoint Setup	Connection Management	Connected Data Exchanges	Unconnected Data Exchanges	Miscellaneous Socket Functions
sock_init	connect	send	sendto	gethostid
socket	listen	recv	recvfrom	getpeername
bind	accept	writev		getsockname
soclose	shutdown	readv		getsockopt
				setsockopt
				select
				ioctl

The Anatomy of a Sockets Exchange

Figure 16-3 describes a client/server interaction using sockets:

1. ***Create the socket endpoints***. Every process that uses sockets must first initialize the sockets run-time environment using the **sock_init** call. Next, each process must create a socket using the **socket** call.

2. ***Establish a well-known service port***. Server processes must **bind** their sockets to a unique port name to become known on the network.

3. ***Listen for connection requests to arrive***. Server processes using stream sockets must issue a **listen** call to indicate their readiness to accept connections from clients. The server is now open for business on this socket. The call defines the size of the queue for incoming requests. Additional requests are ignored by the server.

4. ***Connect to server***. The client issues a **connect** call on a stream socket to initiate a connection to the port with the well-known service. The client process must first locate the internet address of the server from either a name server or from a local configuration file. The client may optionally block until the connection is accepted by the server. On a successful return, the client socket is associated with the connection to the server.

5. ***Accept the connection***. The server side accepts a connection request on a stream socket with the **accept** call. The call will optionally block if no connections are pending. If many requests are pending, it will pop the first one off the queue. When the call returns, it will have created a *new* socket that has its destination connected to the requesting client. This is the socket that will be used for all subsequent communication with the connected client. This leaves the original well-known server socket free to receive requests from new clients. The server process can choose to handle the communication with the connected client on the current thread, or it can start a new thread and hand it the new

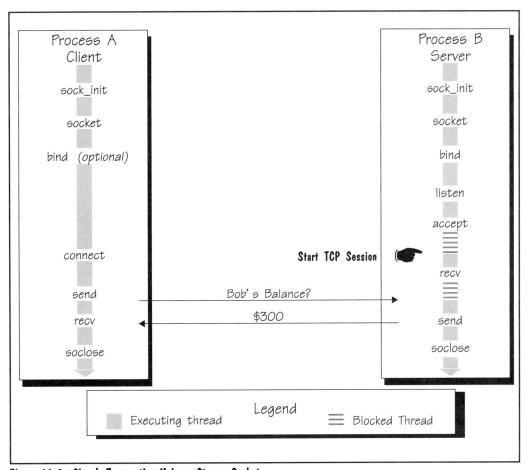

Figure 16-3. Simple Transaction Using a Stream Socket.

socket. The original thread will continue looking for new clients on the well-known socket.

6. **Conduct network business**. Clients and servers have many calls from which to choose for their data exchanges. The **readv, writev, send** and **recv** calls can be used only on sockets that are in the connected state. The **sendto** and **recvfrom** calls can be used at any time, but they require additional address information.

7. **Close the socket**. The client and server must both issue **soclose** to terminate their end of the TCP session. The well-known socket on the server side is still open and ready for new business. If the server executes on a separate service thread, it terminates the thread.

8. ***Accept new business or close for the day.*** The server can accept new connections from clients or issue **soclose** to close the original well-known socket.

The client/server interaction described here was conducted on a stream socket.

FYI

Blocking Is Dangerous Under Windows

Briefing

The Windows client platform introduces the following problem for network programmers: How do you handle calls that block waiting for something to happen? With DOS, this is not a problem because a single program owns the entire machine; it can simply block the CPU and wait. This is not a problem for Unix and OS/2 because they support preemptive multitasking and threads. A blocking operation can be handled in OS/2 by a thread that relinquishes the use of the CPU until an event causes it to unblock. In the meantime, the thread that handles the user interface can keep up with user inputs. Under Windows, we have a difficult environment: a GUI interface that belongs to more than one program (and needs to remain interactive) without the benefit of preemptive multitasking or threads. So, in contrast to Unix and OS/2, a call that blocks under Windows is literally *blocking* the CPU. Every program on the machine—including the GUI—hangs until the call completes.

So how do programs under Windows work with protocols—such as sockets—that originated on preemptive multitasking OSs? How do they handle functions that block until they complete? They simply issue nonblocking calls and perform some form of cooperative polling around a **PeekMessage** loop waiting for the function to complete. For example, *WinSock* specifies that under Windows, a socket function that blocks must include a PeekMessage loop, which periodically yields the CPU. In addition, the specification forbids *any* network command (blocking or non-blocking) to be issued while a blocking command is in progress. So it's a bit of a mess. ❑

NetWare: IPX/SPX and TLI

Because Novell owns—depending on whose numbers you quote—between 50% and 75% of the network market, it follows that IPX/SPX, NetWare's native stack, must be the most widespread stack in the industry. IPX/SPX is also popular with network managers in large enterprises who are delighted with its internetworking capabilities. This means that IPX/SPX covers the entire spectrum, from PC LANs to enterprise LANs. IPX/SPX is an implementation of the *Xerox Network Services (XNS)* transport and network protocol. Banyan Vines is also an adaptation of XNS, but it uses a TCP/IP-like addressing scheme. XNS, developed by the Xerox PARC research institute, is a much cleaner architecture than the older TCP/IP protocol. It's ironic that XNS (in the form of IPX/SPX) is the world's most predominant stack. This is another example of a PARC technology that Xerox was not able to exploit.[2]

Internal Packet Exchange (IPX)

The IPX/SPX network layer is provided by the *Internet Packet Exchange (IPX)* protocol. This is a "send and pray" datagram type of protocol with no guarantees. It is used as a foundation protocol by sophisticated network applications for sending and receiving low-overhead datagram packets over the internet. Novell's SPX builds a reliable protocol service on top of IPX. NetWare provides 12 API calls that can be used to obtain datagram services using IPX.

Sequence Packet Exchange (SPX)

The transport layer of IPX/SPX is provided by the *Sequenced Packet Exchange (SPX)* protocol, which provides a reliable connection-oriented service over IPX. The service consists of 16 API calls that provide a reliable, guaranteed delivery service over IPX.

Transport Layer Interface (TLI)

NetWare provides four peer-to-peer protocols on top of the IPX/SPX stack: NetBIOS, Named Pipes, TLI, and the IPX/SPX APIs. These protocols are supported in

---

[2] Xerox also missed similar opportunities in such areas as mice, GUIs, workstations, Ethernet, PostScript, Smalltalk, agents, global directories, etc. These technologies were all developed at PARC, but they helped make the fortunes of companies like Apple and Microsoft (the Mac and Windows), Sun (workstations), 3Com (Ethernet), Adobe (PostScript), ParcPlace (Smalltalk), and Banyan Vines (global directories). Many companies are now working on the commercial exploitation of agents.

the DOS, Windows, OS/2, and NLM environments. After its acquisition of USL, Novell now owns TLI—remember, that's the *Transport Layer Interface* designed by AT&T as the sockets replacement. The Novell **Programmer's Guide for C** (June, 1993), states that "Novell has adopted TLI as a standard for applications that need a transport layer." We cover NetBIOS and Named Pipes later in this chapter, so let's use this opportunity to go over TLI.

An application written to TLI is, in theory, stack independent. It should run on IPX/SPX or TCP/IP with very few modifications. TLI is a modern implementation of Berkeley sockets, so it should be familiar to Unix programmers. Like sockets, TLI hides many of the time-consuming details associated with lower-level protocols (such as IPX/SPX). The TLI API consists of about 25 API calls (see Table 16-2).

Table 16-2. The TLI Commands.

Endpoint Setup	Connection Management	Connection-Oriented Exchanges	Datagram Exchanges	Miscellaneous functions
t_bind	t_connect	t-snd	t_sndudata	t-alloc
t_unbind	t_listen	t-rcv	t_rcvudata	t-free
t_open	t_accept		t_rcvuderr	t-error
t_close	t_rcvconect			t-getinfo
	t_rcvdis			t-getstate
	t_rcvrel			t-look
	t_snddis			t-optmgmt
	t_sndrel			t-sync

The Anatomy of a TLI Exchange

Figure 16-4 describes a client/server interaction using TLI:

1. ***Open the endpoints***. Every process that uses TLI must first open an endpoint using the **t_open** call. You specify the transport stack (for example, TCP/IP or IPX/SPX) and configuration information. The function returns a handle.

2. ***Bind the endpoint to an address.*** After opening an endpoint, you must assign (or let TLI do it for you) an address to the endpoint by issuing a **t_bind** call. The characteristics of the address depend on the underlying transport.

3. ***Listen for connection requests to arrive***. Server processes must issue a **t_listen** call to indicate their readiness to accept connections from clients. The call only receives connection requests; it doesn't respond to requests.

4. ***Connect to server***. The client issues a **t_connect** call to request a connection. If IPX/SPX provides the underlying transport stack, the call must pass the IPX address of the destination server. The client must first locate the IPX address

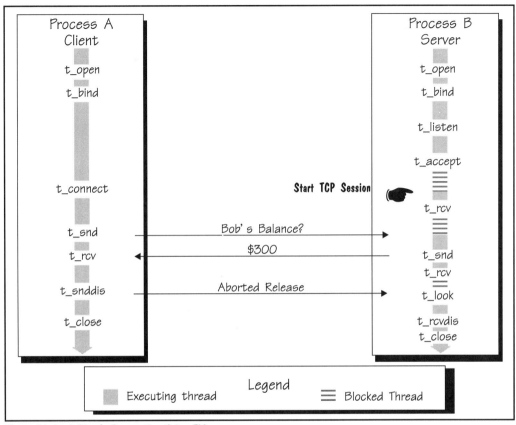

Figure 16-4. A Simple Transaction Using TLI.

of the server from either a name server or from a local configuration file. The client may optionally block until the connection is accepted by the server. On a successful return, the client endpoint is associated with the connection to the server.

5. *Accept the connection*. The server side accepts a connection request with the **t_accept** call. The call will optionally block if no connections are pending. If many requests are pending, it will pop the first one off the queue. When the call returns, it will have transferred the connection from the endpoint that received the request to another endpoint that handles the connection. The *new* endpoint is connected to the requesting client's endpoint. This leaves the original well-known server endpoint free to receive requests from new clients. The server process can choose to handle the communication with the connected client on the current thread, or it can start a new thread. The original thread will continue looking for new client connections on the well-known endpoint.

6. ***Conduct network business***. Once the client and server have established the connection, they can send and receive data with the **t_snd** and **t_rcv** calls. Both functions can be executed in blocking or nonblocking modes, depending on how the endpoint was configured. If the data to be received is fragmented or exceeds the receiving buffer size, a *more* flag is set. You should continue issuing **t_rcv** until the flag is cleared.

7. ***Release the connection***. TLI provides two connection release mechanisms: an *abortive release* that does not prepare the partner for the release; or an *orderly release*, with both sides signaling to each other that they are ready to release the connection. The orderly release ensures that all outstanding data is processed before the connection is released. Figure 16-4 shows an abortive release using **t_snddis**. Because the IPX/SPX stack does *not* support the orderly release, the server side gets an error indication on the next read. The server can issue a **t_look** to obtain an explanation of why it was aborted. It then issues **t_rcvdis** to release the connection. In an orderly release—not supported by IPX/SPX—the client issues **t_sndrel** to indicate a request for a connection release and waits for the partner to respond. The server issues a **t_rcvrel**, followed by a **t_sndrel**, that tells the client the release was accepted.

8. ***Accept new business or close for the day***. The server can accept new connections from clients or issue **t_close** to release the endpoint.

In summary, TLI improves on sockets in two areas: the endpoint registration is more stack independent, and the session release mechanism is more orderly. In addition, the API calls and data structures are more consistent.

NetBIOS and NetBEUI

NetBIOS is the premier protocol for LAN-based, program-to-program communications. Introduced by IBM and Sytek in 1984 for the IBM PC Network, NetBIOS now runs with almost no changes on Ethernets, Token Rings, ARCnets, StarLANs, and even low-cost serial-port LANs. NetBIOS is used as an interface to a variety of stacks—including IBM/Microsoft LANs (NetBEUI), TCP/IP, XNS, Vines, OSI, and IPX/SPX protocol stacks. Support for a NetBIOS platform exists on a multiplicity of operating system environments, including MS-DOS, Windows, OS/2, Windows NT, Unix, and some mainframe environments. NetBIOS is currently the de facto portable standard for network application providers. One of the many reasons for NetBIOS's success is its intuitive simplicity.

What Is NetBEUI?

NetBEUI is the protocol stack that comes with IBM and Microsoft LAN products—including Windows for Workgroups, NT, LAN Manager, LAN Server, DB2/2, and SQL Server. It came to life as the original transport for NetBIOS commands. The literature often uses the term NetBIOS to refer to the combination of the NetBIOS interface and the NetBEUI stack.[3] This can be misleading. NetWare, for example, has nothing to do with NetBEUI, yet it uses NetBIOS as an interface to both IPX/SPX and TCP/IP. IBM and Microsoft use NetBIOS as an interface to both TCP/IP and NetBEUI. So be careful, especially when you read our books; we've been known to use NetBIOS and NetBEUI interchangeably.

NetBEUI offers powerful datagram and connection-oriented services. It also offers a dynamic naming service based on discovery protocols. NetBEUI's main weakness is the lack of a network layer. Its other weakness is the lack of security. The broadcast mechanism, used to dynamically "discover" names, can be a liability on a unsecured internet where it's not a good idea to expose names. Broadcasting names also causes unwanted traffic on the internet. Luckily, most bridges and routers have ways to filter the discovery packets and block them from propagating to other networks.

NetBIOS Commands

The NetBIOS services are provided through a set of commands, specified in a structure called the *Network Control Block (NCB)*. The structure also contains the parameters associated with the command and the fields in which NetBIOS will return information to the program. A command can be issued in either wait or no-wait mode. In the *wait* mode, the requesting thread is blocked until the command completes. In the *no-wait* mode, control is returned to the calling thread at the earliest time possible, usually before the command completes. When the command completes, the NetBIOS DLL places a return code in the NCB.

---

[3] The confusion may have started with Microsoft's naming of NetBEUI. It stands for *NetBIOS Extended User Interface* (NetBEUI).

Table 16-3. NetBIOS: Command Categories.

General Services	Name Services	Session Services	Datagram Services
Reset	Add Name	Call	Send Datagram
Status	Add Group Name	Listen	Send-Broadcast Datagram
Cancel	Delete Name	Send	Receive Datagram
Alert	Find Name	Chain Send	Receive-Broadcast Datagram
Unlink		Send No-Ack	
		Chain Send	
		No-Ack	
		Receive	
		Receive Any	
		Hang Up	
		Session Status	

The NetBIOS commands (see Table 16-3) fall into the following four categories:

■ *General services commands* provide miscellaneous types of networking services.

■ *Name support commands* support both unique names and group names. If a name is unique, NetBIOS will make sure no such name already exists on the network before it gets added to the name table. Group names are used for sending messages to a group of workstations. NetBIOS returns a name handle that identifies successfully registered names, and it allows you to deregister a name when it is no longer needed.

FYI

Why Logical Naming?

Briefing

With NetBIOS's name services, a LAN adapter card can have multiple logical names, each consisting of 16 bytes. Logical naming makes your programs independent from burned-in adapter numbers. Not having to rely on a stream of digits makes communications programs clearer and less error-prone. It is much more convenient (and more personal) to call a remote adapter by a logical nickname, such as "Bob," instead of a burned-in address like X'444221113355'.

■ *Session support commands* provide a reliable connection-oriented service over which a pair of network applications can exchange information. Applications create sessions between two adapter names. You tell NetBIOS through a listen command who you want to talk to, and NetBIOS will inform you when you've been called. Using an asterisk (*), you can specify that you will accept a connection from *any* adapter that calls you. Once a session is in place, applications can send messages, up to 64 KBytes (contiguous in memory), with a single send command. If this is not enough, the Chain Send command can be used to send two buffers of user data for up to 128 KBytes. Applications can find out the status of a session and determine if it is still active or if it got cancelled.

■ *Datagram support commands* allow you to send a datagram to a recipient name; this may either be a unique name or a group name (multicast). You can also send datagrams to all the adapters (broadcast) on a network, including the sending machine's adapter. The default size of a datagram is 512 bytes; the maximum size of the datagram is based on the size of the LAN adapter's transmit buffer. Datagrams cannot be received and filtered based on specific sender names.

The Anatomy of a NetBIOS Exchange

Figure 16-5 describes a client/server interaction using a NetBIOS connection-oriented exchange:

1. *Reset the adapters*. The **Reset** command is used to allocate resources for the process's exclusive use from the NetBIOS environment. The three important resources you need to allocate on a per-process basis are sessions, names, and commands.

2. *Add the adapter names*. The next thing a process does is issue **Add Name** and **Add Group Name** commands to create the unique and group logical names that identify an adapter to the network.

3. *Start the persistent sessions*. The Server process issues a **Listen** command for each session that will be initiated by an incoming **Call**. The server can accept a **Call** from a particular name; or by specifying (*), it can accept calls from any name on the network. The client issues a **Call** for each session it needs to initiate. The session will persist for the duration of an application or until it is explicitly terminated with a **Hang Up** command.

4. *Conduct network business*. The client and server exchange messages over the session using NetBIOS's session-based **Send** and **Receive** commands. Notice that the client issued a **Receive** command before sending its data. Why? NetBIOS allows us to issue multiple outstanding commands in no-wait mode.

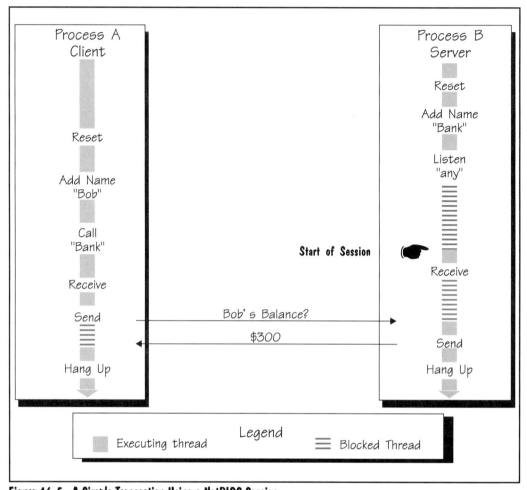

Figure 16-5. A Simple Transaction Using a NetBIOS Session.

Issuing a receive before the send is a way to make sure that the reply will not get lost. This may happen, for example, if the server code runs on a very fast machine and the client runs on a very slow machine.

5. **Disconnect the session.** When the client and server are through conducting their business, each party issues a *Hang Up* command.

6. **Log off the Network.** A well-behaved network citizen "logs off the network" by issuing a NetBIOS *Reset* with the deallocate option. This returns all the process's resources to the NetBIOS pool—including deleting all current NetBIOS names, aborting all sessions, and canceling all pending commands.

Named Pipes

Remote Named Pipes extend the OS/2 Interprocess Communication (IPC) mechanism across the network. Most LAN vendors now support Named Pipes on MS-DOS, Windows, and OS/2. This includes Novell's NetWare, Banyan's Vines, and the LAN Manager/LAN Server family of products from IBM and Microsoft. Named Pipes are built-in networking features in both Windows NT and Windows for Workgroups. Unix support for Named Pipes is provided by LAN Manager/X (or Advanced Server for Unix). Named Pipes run on NetBIOS, IPX/SPX, and TCP/IP stacks.

Named Pipes provide highly reliable, two-way communications between clients and a server. They provide a file-like programming API that abstracts a session-based two-way exchange of data (see Table 16-4). Using Named Pipes, processes can exchange data as if they were writing to, or reading from, a sequential file. Named Pipes are especially suitable for implementing server programs that require many-to-one pipelines. A server application can set up a pipeline where the receiving end of the pipe can exchange data with several client processes. Then Named Pipes can handle all the scheduling and synchronization issues. A very important benefit of Named Pipes, at least for OS/2 client/server programmers, is that they're part of the base OS/2 interprocess communications service. The Named Pipes interface is identical, whether the processes are running on an individual machine or distributed across the network.

Table 16-4. Named Pipe Commands.

Pipe Creation	Pipe Connection	Pipe Data Exchange	Pipe Close
DosCreateNPipe	DosConnectNPipe DosOpen DosWaitNPipe	DosTransactNPipe DosCallNPipe DosRead DosWrite	DosClose DosDisconnectNPipe

Creating a Named Pipe

To establish a Named Pipe, a server process must first create the pipe by issuing a **DosCreateNPipe** call, which returns a handle that identifies the pipe. A Named Pipe is identified by a unique name that conforms to the file naming convention. Remote pipes are referenced using the DOS/Windows and OS/2 *Universal Naming Convention (UNC)* for file names. Using UNC conventions, a networked pipe is named as *server**PIPE**name*, where "server" is the network name of a server machine.

When a server process first creates a Named Pipe, it specifies several parameters that will determine the nature of that Named Pipe and how it can be used. For example, you can specify the direction of a pipe as either *in-bound*, *out-bound*, or *duplex*. You also specify whether the pipe can be used in byte-stream or message-stream mode. In byte stream mode, the processes read and write bytes; in message-stream mode, they read and write messages with Named Pipes providing a system-supplied length header.

What happens when many clients want to open the same Named Pipe? You can specify through an *instance count* the number of times a Named Pipe can be opened by clients at the same time. Pipe instances are actually separate pipes that share the same name. Each instance of the pipe has its own handle and file buffer. Pipe instances allow a server to communicate with multiple clients at the same time. When clients connect to the same pipe, each connection is assigned its own instance (handle) of the pipe.

You can also specify for remote pipes whether the data is to be sent over the remote pipe immediately (flushed) as it is written, or whether it gets blocked and then sent when an internal buffer fills up. Blocking reduces the message traffic over a network and improves performance. The cost, however, is the loss of the immediate acknowledgement that the data arrived at its destination.

Making the Named Pipe Connection

Once the pipe is created on the server, it must be in a listening state before a client can connect to it. The server does that by issuing **DosConnectNPipe**. At this point, any client process that knows the fully qualified path name of a Named Pipe can open the pipe by issuing a **DosOpen**. This is the same OS/2 call that is used for opening a regular file.

If the call fails and returns a busy error code, the client issues **DosWaitNPipe**, which will block the process until the first pipe instance becomes available. What happens when many clients are waiting on the same pipe? Named Pipes will wake up the process that has waited the longest when an instance of the pipe becomes available. The *unblocked* process must then reissue **DosOpen** to connect to the pipe.

Exchanging Information on the Named Pipe

Once a pipe is in the connected state, server and client processes can use the regular OS/2 file-subsystem calls to communicate over it. In addition, Named Pipes provides two API calls that are ideally suited for transaction processing: **DosTransactNPipe** and **DosCallNPipe**. These two calls can only be issued on a duplex message pipe that is setup for the message-stream mode.

- *DosTransactNPipe* writes a message and receives a reply in one single operation. The request/reply pair can be used to trigger a transaction or a Remote Procedure Call. If the pipe contains unread data or is not a message pipe, the call fails. The call will not return until a complete message is read. **DosTransactNPipe** is typically issued over "persistent" connections. In this type of connection, several transactions are usually issued over an open pipe before the connection is terminated. The persistent connection is appropriate for remote pipes because their overhead for establishing connections is high.

- *DosCallNPipe* combines a **DosOpen**, **DosTransactNPipe**, and a **DosClose** in a single operation. It is used in "non-persistent" connections that get established and terminated just to issue a single Remote Procedure Call. Non-persistent connections are ideal for simple request/reply transactions.

Terminating a Named Pipe Dialog

When a client process is done using a Named Pipe, it closes the pipe by issuing a **DosClose**. This is the same OS/2 call that is used for closing regular files. The server process can then issue a **DosDisConnectNPipe** followed by a **DosConnectNPipe**, and then wait for the next client. This allows the server to create the Named Pipe and reuse it to communicate with many clients without having to recreate the pipe each time. The server can always close the Named Pipe for good by issuing a **DosClose**. A server may also issue a **DosClose** without a preceding **DosDisConnectNPipe**. This will free the pipe handle and still enable the client to read any data remaining in the buffer. However, a closed pipe cannot be reused again without reissuing **DosCreateNPipe**.

The Anatomy of a Named Pipes Exchange

Figure 16-6 describes a client/server interaction using a Named Pipes **DosCallNPipe** RPC-like call:

1. *Create the Named Pipe*. The server side of an application creates a Named Pipe by issuing **DosCreateNPipe**. The instances parameter specifies how many clients can use this pipe concurrently.

2. *Wait for the clients to connect*. The server application creates as many threads as the number of simultaneous clients it wants to service. Each "server" thread issues a **DosConnectNPipe** and blocks waiting for a client to connect to the other end of the pipe instance.

3. *Establish the connection with the clients*. The client connects to its end of the pipe by issuing a **DosCallNPipe** (which performs the DosOpen automati-

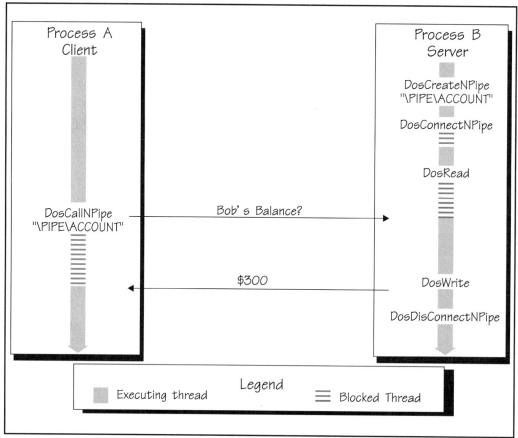

Figure 16-6. A Simple Transaction Using Named Pipes.

cally). On the server side, the **DosConnectNPipe** succeeds.

4. ***Conduct your business***. The client's **DosCallNPipe** automatically sends the request and waits for the reply. The server issues a **DosRead** followed by a **DosWrite** to service the client's request.

5. ***Disconnect and take the next call***. When the business is completed, the server side of the pipe issues a **DosDisconnectNPipe**. The client side does not issue a **DosClose** because DosCallNpipe does that automatically. The server can then execute another DosConnectNPipe and wait on the next client to call.

6. ***Terminate the pipe***. When the server thread wants to stop accepting calls from clients, it issues a **DosClose** to delete that instance of the Named Pipe. When the last instance is closed, the pipe no longer exists.

In summary, the Named Pipes **DosCallNPipe** is very suitable for a single request/reply exchange over a non-persistent connection.

The New SNA: APPC, APPN, and CPI-C

The *new SNA* is a network of peers where PC programs can talk to the host programs at a program-to-program level through the use of well-defined *verb* commands (this type of session is called an LU 6.2 type in SNA terminology). Physically, the PCs are endowed with local intelligence to provide parallel session initiation services without VTAM host involvement. A node with those attributes is an SNA PU 2.1 node.

APPN

IBM is evolving SNA into a true distributed operating system that supports cross network directory services, transparent network access to resources (such as servers, applications, displays, printers, and data), common data streams, and integrated network management. *Advanced Peer-to-Peer Network* (or *APPN)* is the network infrastructure responsible for this "true distribution." APPN creates an SNA internet without the mainframe-centric hierarchy of traditional SNA configurations. The mainframe is just another node on the internet. APPN allows LU 6.2 SNA applications, using APPC or CPI-C APIs, to take full advantage of peer networks. It also greatly simplifies SNA configuration, provides better availability through dynamic routing, makes it easier to maintain SNA networks, and meets the flexibility requirements of modern networks.

APPN is becoming *another* de facto routing protocol standard. In September 1993, Cisco buried the hatchet with IBM and chose to support the APPN standard for routing SNA packets. Previously Cisco, the market leader in IP routers, was proposing a scheme for "tunneling" SNA traffic over IP backbones called *Advanced Peer-to-Peer Internetworking (APPI)*. Other major router vendors—including Wellfleet, Ungermann-Bass, 3Com, N.E.T, Crosscom, and IBM's 6611—are also going with APPN. The result is that router vendors are standardizing on APPN to route SNA traffic.

APPC

Using APPC or CPI-C, an OS/2 program can converse through one of SNA's 50,000 installed networks with peers located anywhere in the world. These peers can run on PCs, RS/6000s, AS/400s, S/38s, and S/370s, as well as on many non-IBM host platforms. *Advanced Program to Program Communication (APPC)* is IBM's architected solution for program-to-program communication, distributed transaction processing, and remote database access across the entire IBM product line. An application program, called a *Transaction Program (TP)*, uses the APPC or CPI-C APIs to communicate with other TPs on systems that support APPC/SNA. This includes MS-DOS/APPC, OS/400s, and System/370 (MVS/XA, TSO-E, VM/APPC, and CICS/MVS environments). APPC is also supported by many non-IBM host vendors. APPC supplies a variety of advanced communication functions, including password validation, starting a remote program and sending it Program Initialization Parameters (PIP), and distributed checkpoints. The checkpoint function can be used to synchronize distributed applications; it will eventually be used to synchronize distributed databases using a two-phase commit protocol.

APPC's weaknesses include the lack of support for datagrams, broadcast, and multicast services. The APPC model is inherently conversational. APPC's other weakness is the lack of a consistent API across all platforms (see next section).

CPI-C

CPI-C, SAA's official *Common Programming Interface for Communications*, builds on top of APPC and masks its complexities and irregularities. Every product that supports APPC has a slightly different API. CPI-C fixes that problem. Writing to the CPI-C API allows you to port your programs to other SAA platforms, such as S/370 and AS/400. Networking Services/DOS (NS/DOS) provides CPI-C/APPC for DOS and Windows using less than 140 KBytes of memory. From a programmer's perspective, APPC provides a *verb with control-block* API, while CPI-C provides a consistent *call-based* API on top of APPC (see Figure 16-7).

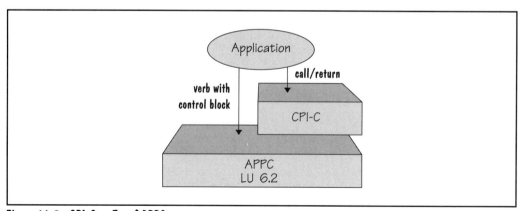

Figure 16-7. CPI-C on Top of APPC.

The CPI-C API is common across different operating systems and programming languages. IBM provides CPI-C language bindings for all its SAA compilers. APPC offers interoperability and platform-specific optimizations. CPI-C offers *both* portability and interoperability, but it gives up some of the platform-specific features of APPC. And, of course, CPI-C programs can talk to APPC partners.

The X/Open consortium has licensed the CPI-C interface from IBM; so have several other companies (including Novell and Apple). In addition to *all* the IBM platforms, CPI-C APIs are provided by Insession Inc. (for Tandem Computers), Systems Strategies (for Unix), Rabbit Software (for DOS), and DCA Inc. (for DOS and OS/2). Apple has announced planned support for CPI-C on Macintosh. Bull, Brixton, and HP are working on Unix versions. Microsoft is working on a Windows version— CPI-C is one of the four SNA APIs supported by the *WinSNA* standard.

In summary, it looks like CPI-C is becoming *another* important "de facto" (and possibly "de jure") API standard for peer-to-peer communications. With the Any-Net/2 multiprotocol common transport (also known as MPTN), CPI-C applications are to run unchanged on a broad selection of transport stacks—including TCP/IP, and SNA today—and OSI, IPX/SPX, and NetBIOS in the near future (see Figure 16-8).

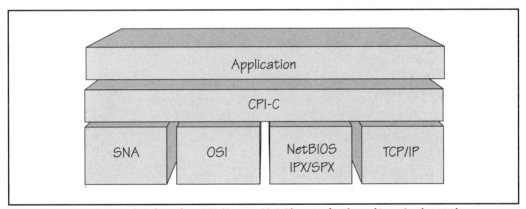

Figure 16-8. CPI-C: A Stack-Independent API (Source: IBM Blueprint for Networking, March 1992).

The CPI-C API consists of about 40 calls; APPC consists of over 60 calls. Most of these calls deal with configuration and services. The *core conversational APIs* for both CPI-C and APPC are shown in Table 16-5. As you can see, the CPI-C calls are functionally equivalent to their APPC counterparts.

Table 16-5. A Comparison of CPI-C Calls and APPC Conversational Verbs.

CPI-C Call	Pseudonym	Corresponding APPC Calls
CMACCP	Accept_Conversation	CONVERT followed by RECEIVE_ALLOCATE
CMALLC	Allocate	ALLOCATE
CMCFM	Confirm	CONFIRM
CMCFMD	Confirmed	CONFIRMED
CMDEAL	Deallocate	DEALLOCATE followed by TP_ENDED
CMFLUS	Flush	FLUSH
CMINIT	Initialize_Conversation	CONVERT followed by TP_STARTED
CMPTR	Prepare_To_Receive	PREPARE_TO_RECEIVE
----	----	RECEIVE_AND_POST
CMRCV	Receive	RECEIVE_AND_WAIT RECEIVE_IMMEDIATE
CMRTS	Request_To_Send	REQUEST_TO_SEND
CMSEND	Send_Data	SEND_DATA
CMSERR	Send_Error	SEND_ERROR
CMTRTS	Test_Request_to_Send_Received	TEST_RTS

Demystifying the SNA Jargon

Briefing

One of the barriers to understanding SNA is the nearly unintelligible jargon that surrounds it. Programmers need to understand this jargon to configure an APPC node and understand the mechanics of starting an SNA session. If you want to take advantage of the "intergalactic" connectivity that APPC offers, you'll have to learn how to configure an SNA node. In practice, what this means is figuring out how to answer a score of arcane questions about your application and all of its partners. These questions ask you to specify things like the SNA base profile, the PU name, the LU profiles, session limits, the TP profiles, the conversation type, security, and the synchronization level. Worse yet, you will almost inevitably need to interface to system programmers from the host MIS group, and you will need to tell them what you need from VTAM and CICS on the host side of the interface. The purpose of this section is to give you a very quick guide to SNA terminology.

- ■ *What is a Transaction Program (TP)?* It's the logical network name that an application uses to communicate over the network. An application can define itself to APPC/CPI-C as multiple transaction programs (TPs). A single OS/2 process can contain many TPs. The primary goal of APPC/CPI-C is to provide the ability for transaction programs to communicate via conversations across the SNA network.

- ■ *What is a Logical Unit (LU)?* This is the "logical port" used by a Transaction Program to obtain access to an SNA network. The LU is the SNA software that accepts and executes the verbs from your programs. An LU manages the network on behalf of TPs and is responsible for the routing of data packets. A TP gains access to SNA via an LU. Multiple TPs can use the services provided by one LU. The LU to which the transaction program issues APPC API calls is the local LU. The local LU communicates with partner LUs on other nodes. The new SNA uses a particular type of LU known as LU 6.2, which is SNA's version of a peer-to-peer protocol. The APPC stack is an implementation of the LU 6.2 architecture.

■ **What is an SNA Session?** This is an SNA logical connection between two LUs across the network. Before TPs can talk to each other, their LUs must be connected through a session. Sessions can be seen as providing the LU-to-LU links over which conversations can flow. In network protocol terms, sessions provide a reliable sequenced packet protocol service. Parallel sessions denote situations where more than one session is active between an LU pair. These sessions are used to allow multiple conversations to take place concurrently between the same LU pair. Typically, sessions remain active even when there are no active conversations. This ensures that a session is available when a conversation requests it.

■ **What is an APPC Conversation?** The actual exchange of information between two TPs is done over a conversation. Conversations are TP-to-TP links that are carried out over a session. Preferably, a conversation lasts only a short time, typically the time it takes to process a simple transaction. The idea is to have a series of conversations use the same session, one after the other. You can look at conversations as the mechanism to serially share sessions. However, only one conversation can be carried over a session at any one time. Conversations provide a way to avoid the overhead of establishing an SNA session for each network transaction (for our readers who are SNA experts, it's the cost of an SNA bracket versus that of an SNA Bind). Two TPs involved in a conversation are referred to as partners.

■ **What is a Physical Unit (PU)?** This is a program on an SNA node that manages certain network resources on behalf of all the LUs on that node. A PU, for example, manages the connections of the node to adjacent nodes. The PU manages the physical data links on behalf of LUs that manage the sessions or logical needs between nodes. There needs to be one PU on each SNA node. PUs have types that distinguish a node's connection and routing capabilities. Your PU needs to be defined only once for each machine. The PU 2.1 was designed to serve as the platform for LU 6.2's symmetrical form of peer-to-peer communications. It provides support for multiple links, multiple sessions, and parallel sessions between directly attached nodes (for example, nodes on the same LAN). The more restrictive PU type 2.0 may also be used for communication with host subarea nodes. A PU 2 node can only support a single active session, and its partner can only be a host LU (i.e., a subarea node).

■ *What are the synchronization services?* Client/server transactions may require the update of resources that reside on multiple nodes. Synchronization capabilities are very important for such occasions. The APPC architecture specifies three levels of synchronization services: None—no synchronization is required; Confirm—this allows TPs to agree that processing has been completed without errors; Syncpoint—this is an even more stringent level of synchronization, which requires the LU to participate (on behalf of its protected resources) in a full implementation of a two-phase commit protocol with rollback and resynchronization capabilities.

The relationship between TPs, LUs, PUs, conversations, and sessions is depicted in Figure 16-9. The example shows a local workstation where TP C is involved in active conversations with the remote TPs: A and D. Remote TP B is also waiting for TP A to finish so that it can start its own conversation with TP C. Notice that the LU in the local workstation can handle more than one session; it is in active session with its partner LUs on workstations X and Y, simultaneously. Notice also that the session with the partner LU (in workstation X) is used to support multiple conversations in serial fashion.

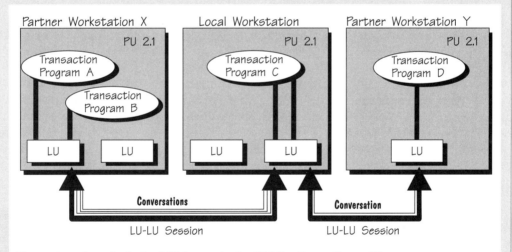

Figure 16-9. Example of a Local LU Communicating With Two Remote Partner LUs.

In summary, an APPC network is made up of SNA nodes and links. A node has a PU, one or more LUs, and one or more TPs. LUs communicate through sessions, and TPs communicate through conversations over those sessions. Finally, your user program will consist of a series of verbs that are organized into conversations. The conversations are carried out with partner TPs over the network in accordance with the rules of the APPC protocol. ❑

The Anatomy of a CPI-C Exchange

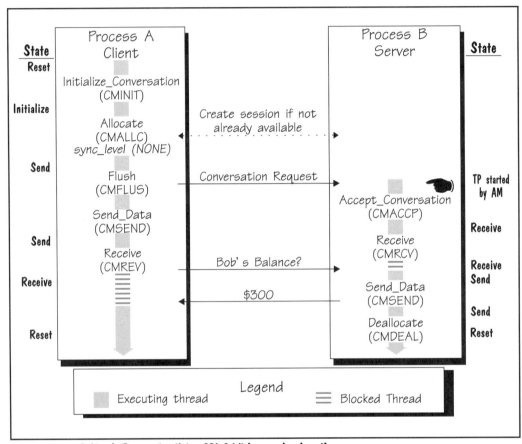

Figure 16-10. A Simple Transaction Using CPI-C With sync_level = None.

Figure 16-10 describes a client/server interaction using CPI-C:

1. ***Create the TPs***. The server program is either already launched waiting for work, or it can be launched by the CPI-C *Attach Manager* when a conversation request arrives. The client issues an **Initialize_Conversation** verb to start a Transaction Program (TP). CPI-C will return a TP ID, which all subsequent verbs must use with this TP.

2. ***Request the conversation***. The client then requests a conversation by issuing an **Allocate** verb. Note that the sync_level parameter is set to NONE (the CPI-C default), meaning that no confirmation services are required. CPI-C returns a conversation ID and starts an LU-to-LU session if none is available. The actual request for a conversation is not yet sent because CPI-C blocks records into a

logical record. This means that, so far, no information was passed between the client and server TPs. The client issues a **Flush** verb to force the conversation request to flow to the partner. Otherwise, the control data may not be sent until CPI-C has a full buffer.

3. *Accept the conversation*. The server issues a **Accept_Conversation** verb, which returns both a TP ID and Conversation ID. Now both sides have established their end of the conversation. Note that the server is immediately placed in the **Receive** state after a conversation is created.

4. *Conduct network business*. The server issues a **Receive** call (the CPI-C default is RECEIVE_AND_WAIT) to find out what the client wants. Meanwhile, the client has issued a **Send_Data** requesting Bob's balance, followed by a **Receive,** which flushes the message and changes the state to **Receive**. The client is now blocked, waiting for the reply to arrive. The server has received the right to transmit. All business can be conducted in an orderly, logical, half-duplex fashion. The server sends back the reply.

5. *Deallocate the conversation*. The server still hasn't relinquished its turn to send, so it issues a **Deallocate** to close the conversation and release the TP. The client receives the reply and issues a **Deallocate** to release its side of the conversation.

YOUR GUIDE TO NOS AND STACKS PRODUCTS

This concludes our *brief* overview of the underlying principles behind NOS and Stacks middleware. The next step is to look at some representative OS/2 products that provide NOS and Stack solutions. We must warn you that OS/2 supports an overwhelming number of products, from dozens of vendors, that fall into that category. We will only cover a few selected products to give you a feel for what type of solutions are available. A **Client/Server Survival Guide** without pointers to real products is almost meaningless. Please note, however, that making it on our list is not an endorsement for a product or an implication that it's best-of-breed.

Chapter 17

NTS/2, LAN Distance, RouteXpander/2, AnyNet/2

IBM has had a decade of experience making heterogeneous systems work together—mostly our own.

> — Jim Cannavino,
> IBM Senior Vice President

The four products from IBM covered in this chapter provide a powerful and very flexible communications foundation on OS/2. **NTS/2** provides a base substrate that allows you to mix-and-match mulivendor hardware adapters and mulivendor communications stacks. **LAN Distance** transparently extends the LAN to include remote sites. **RouteXpander/2** transforms a PC running OS/2 into a high-speed bridge/router. **AnyNet/2** allows existing programs to work with different communications stacks and provides a transport level gateway service between stacks.

Each product introduces unique communication features by providing some form of "wedge" whose job is to sit between stack layers and perform magic. The products complement each other nicely and allow you to create very flexible networking solutions. While it is unlikely that you will use all four products in one installation, you should still be aware of what they can each do for you. Even if you do not plan to use OS/2, you should still review these products to understand some of the new and unique data communications features they introduce.

NTS/2: THE COMMUNICATIONS SUBSTRATE

NTS/2 is an important product that provides three essential functions to OS/2 client/server products (Figure 17-1):

■ The **NDIS** standard interface for network adapters. NDIS creates a "logical network board" that lets multiple protocol stacks coexist and interface with multiple LAN adapters. NTS/2 also provides an ODI to NDIS converter that lets the NetWare stacks use NDIS drivers.

■ The LAN **Configuration Installation Distribution (CID)** utilities. CID is an IBM standard for automating the installation and configuration of OS/2-based products on LANs.

■ Two protocol stacks: **NetBIOS** and **IEEE 802.2**. These stacks are used by many LAN-based products.

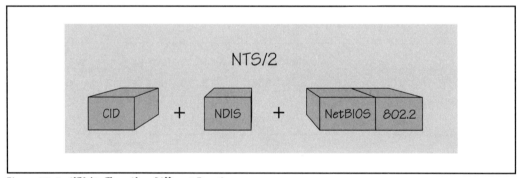

Figure 17-1. NTS/2: Three Very Different Functions.

We'll now give you a quick tour of NTS/2's four functions. The NetBIOS interface is definitely of interest to programmers. CID is something you'll want to know about if you plan to automate the installation and distribution of your OS/2 products. By the way, most OS/2 client/server products are now CID-enabled. You'll need to know something about NDIS to pick the right LAN adapter and to avoid potential stack coexistence problems.

NDIS: The Logical Network Board

To accommodate multivendor networks, modern operating systems must support multiple protocols, redirectors, and APIs. To do that effectively, the operating system must provide well-defined interfaces between components. The interface between the LAN adapter and the transport stacks is particularly important. The last thing vendors who provide transport stacks (like TCP/IP and SNA) want is to write a driver for every possible network adapter. And, of course, network adapter vendors want to avoid having to interface to every possible stack.

NTS/2 solves that problem by supporting the *Network Driver Interface Specification (NDIS)*. This is the Microsoft/3Com standard for interfacing protocol stacks to network adapter device drivers. NDIS creates a "logical network board" that makes it easy to interface different LAN adapters with multiple protocol stacks (see Figure 17-2). Transport stack providers can use NDIS as the common interface to all network adapters. And network adapter vendors can use NDIS as the top layer for their network drivers. NDIS allows several transport layers to share a single adapter card. NDIS takes care of sending and receiving data and managing the adapter card. It handles the I/O on the card and notifies the stack software when transfers are complete or when incoming messages are received. NTS/2 supports the NDIS 1.02 spec and the NDIS 2.01 extensions for network management.

NDIS is a standard interface, so fewer drivers need to be installed and maintained. All the OS/2 LAN adapters and protocol stacks, including NetWare and Vines, now

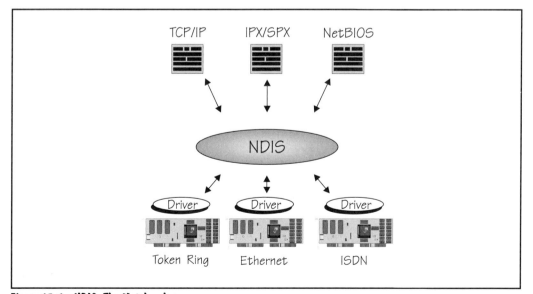

Figure 17-2. NDIS: The Matchmaker.

support NDIS. NetWare runs on NDIS using NTS/2's very efficient ODI to NDIS converter (we explain it in the NetWare chapter). NDIS network adapters are readily obtainable from vendors such as Ungermann-Bass, 3Com, and Western Digital. An OS/2 workstation can support a maximum of four NDIS LAN adapters.

NTS/2 ships with a suite of NDIS-compliant network drivers that are certified by an independent test organization—the National Software Testing Labs (NSTL). You can download the latest certified drivers from CompuServe and IBM's National Support Center BBS. NTS/2 supports over 100 LAN drivers from IBM and all the major LAN vendors. You can find drivers for IEEE 802.5 (Token Ring), Ethernet V2.0 (also known as Ethernet DIX for DEC, Intel, and Xerox), IEEE 802.3 (the new Ethernet), and the IBM PC Network.

The various LAN adapters provide a wide choice of physical layer cabling options. Token Ring LAN adapters support low-cost telephone twisted-pair cable at 4 Mbit/s bandwidth. The more reliable shielded twisted-pair cable supports 16 Mbit/s bandwidth, and the fiber-optic cable can be used for wiring long segments (up to 2 KM). The PC Network Broadband LAN adapter works with cable TV technology and in theory can support multiple (2 Mbit/s) LAN channels over the same cable. The PC Network Baseband LAN adapter, also from IBM, provides low-cost, low-bandwidth communication over ordinary telephone cables. The various Ethernet adapters usually work with baseband coax cable that comes in a variety of cable thickness and prices.

In summary, NDIS provides a "wedge" that sits between the protocol stacks—starting at the Logical Link Control (LLC) layer and above—and the device drivers—at the Media Access Control (MAC) layer and below. The magic provided by the NDIS wedge is to make the device drivers transparent to the stacks and vice versa.

Let CID Do the Install

Probably the least glamorous area in client/server computing is installing, configuring, and updating software on network machines. If you get *elbow fatigue* with a 20-diskette installation on your machine, it only worsens when you do it for an entire department. How do you handle the new software updates? More elbow fatigue. How do you deal with the uniqueness of each client workstation? More Aspirin. Finally, how do you keep track of who's got what? No, even Aspirin won't do it; *you'll need CID* (see Figure 17-3).

Integrated with NTS/2 is this magical CID utility that can store, distribute, and maintain software on a NetBIOS-based LAN. CID-enabled products can be installed from a code server with a minimum level of interaction on the client workstations. Yes, you have to turn on the power and "seed" the installation (two diskettes), but

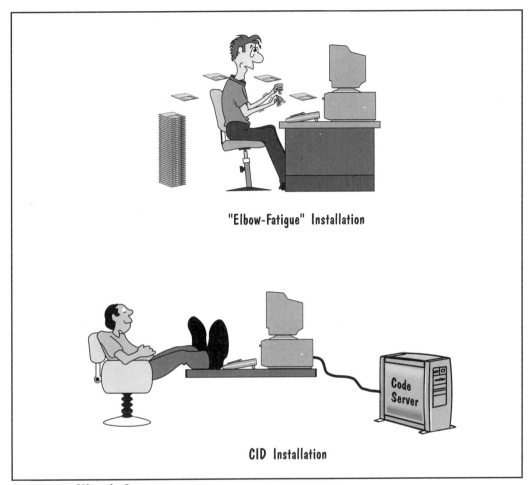

"Elbow-Fatigue" Installation

CID Installation

Figure 17-3. CID to the Rescue.

the installation is automatic from then on. You don't have to be at the client workstation feeding diskettes or responding to the software's questions. You can install OS/2 and many of the software packages described in this book on a pristine machine this way.

NTS/2 does all that by providing two pieces of software:

■ A very small, NetBIOS-based requester (not to be confused with the OS/2 LAN Requester) that allows a pristine machine—that is, with no software on it—to access files on a code server. The OS/2 kernel plus the ultra-lite requester fit on the two "seed" diskettes.

■ The code server, which acts as a simple file server for installation.

OK, so NTS/2 gets the code from the code server to the pristine machine, but how does it deal with each machine's particular configuration needs? It does that by using *response* files. The answers to each product's installation questions are kept in response files that can be customized for each client workstation. The response files are unique to each product. Software vendors must provide either a utility or a model of a response file for their CID-enabled products.

An administrator can initiate a multiple-product installation by writing a REXX procedure and executing it from the code server. This procedure file can contain a series of chained commands that initiate the installation of different software packages—each machine can be customized.

NTS/2 is a "poor man's" solution to installation and configuration. IBM supplies a *deluxe* product—called NetView Distribution Manager/2 (NetView DM/2)—that uses CID to fully automate the installation process. DM/2 *pushes* the code from the server to the workstation rather than *pull* it from the workstation as NTS/2 does. On the other hand, NTS/2 is very inexpensive, and it does part of the job relatively well. And anyway, you need it for NDIS. We'll have much more to say about installation and software distribution in Part 8.

NetBIOS and 802.2 Stacks

NetBIOS and the IEEE 802.2 logical link layer are two protocols that get used by many client/server products. These two stacks ended up in NTS/2. Most OS/2 client/server products need NTS/2 because it provides NDIS support; therefore, they get NetBIOS and 802.2 for free. NTS/2 provides a superfast implementation of the NetBEUI stack called JetBEUI.

NetBIOS

NetBIOS is currently the premier protocol for LAN-based program-to-program communications. One of the many reasons for NetBIOS's success is its intuitive simplicity, which makes it easy to master. NetBIOS provides a naming service that allows a LAN adapter card to have multiple logical names. Through NetBIOS, you can write LAN applications that can exchange information between named entities on the network. NetBIOS provides two classes of network transmission services: sessions and datagrams. NTS/2 implements the NetBIOS peer-to-peer API set on top of JetBEUI (a faster version of NetBEUI).

Two NetBIOS APIs?

Details

The NetBIOS API consists of about 20 commands grouped into four categories: general-purpose (such as reset, cancel, adapter status), name support (such as add name, add group name), datagram support (such as send datagram, send broadcast datagram), and session support (such as call, listen, hang up, send, receive). While the NetBIOS commands perform the same standard functions, there are two ways to invoke them:

■ Using the **IBM NetBIOS API** (also known as NB30). This API is shipped with Extended Services, LAN Server 3.0, and NTS/2. It has a superfast kernel application interface component and is documented in the **IBM LAN Technical Reference** (SC30-3383-03). The files that implement this interface are NETBIOS.OS2 and ACSNETB.DLL.

■ Using the **NetBIOS Submit API**. This API is shipped with LAN Server 3.0, Microsoft LAN Manager, and NetWare. No application-level kernel component is available. The NetBIOS Submit API is documented in the **IBM LAN Server 3.0 API Reference** (S96F-8440) and in Novell's **NetWare Client Transport Protocol API for C**. The file that implements this interface is NETAPI.DLL.

These are the little hurdles of life. However, once you get past them, NetBIOS is NetBIOS. ❑

IEEE 802.2

IEEE 802.2 API provides a low-level interface to the 802.2 Local Area Network Logical Link Control (LLC) layer. 802.2 is the ISO standard that defines the protocol for accessing LAN link layer services in a media-access independent manner. The LLC interfaces to the Media Access Control (MAC) link protocols such as Token Ring (IEEE 802.5) and CSMA/CD (IEEE 802.3).

The 802.2 API provides a set of commands for directly controlling the LAN adapters, such as Open and Close. The API supports two types of service: *Connectionless* and *Connection-oriented*. The Connectionless service provides datagram-like "unreliable" frame transmissions between Service Access Points (SAPs). The Connection-oriented service provides reliable sequenced packet exchanges over a session between link station interfaces. The number of link stations that can be supported is adapter dependent. For example, an IBM Token Ring Adapter/A supports 64 link stations.

You should program to the IEEE 802.2 API only if you have serious memory constraints and cannot afford NetBIOS or TCP/IP, or if you need to provide special network utilities that require an intimate control of the communication facilities (it's like programming in assembler versus a high-level language).

NTS/2: What's Coming Next?

IBM has stated that it is working on NDIS-compliant drivers for wireless, FDDI II, multimedia, and PCMCIA devices. A future release of NTS/2 may include the TCP/IP protocol stack and sockets—these two functions are currently provided by the **TCP/IP for OS/2** product.

NTS/2 Packaging

NTS/2 retails for $85. Some products, like the IBM LAN Requester, Communications Manager/2 V1.1, and TCP/IP bundle NTS/2. You only need one copy of NTS/2 per machine. You can either use the bundled NTS/2 or buy the $85 package. In either case, it's the same NTS/2.

LAN DISTANCE: BRINGING THE LAN HOME

LAN Distance, shipped by IBM in November 1993, lets you connect into the "office LAN" from anywhere. LAN Distance also lets you set-up "makeshift" LANs using the telephone system. The product offers a highly-iconic, object-oriented user interface that makes it easy to dial in, control the local/remote environment, and take care of things like security. A "shuttle mode" allows you to attach your PC directly into your LAN (when you're in the office) or to dial in from a telephone. As a personal testimonial, we find this product extremely liberating—we can now work in our client/server lab from our favorite coffee house by the sea, which is now part of our office LAN.

With LAN Distance, you can use any dial-in connection—including asynchronous, synchronous, ISDN or X.25—to access LAN resources transparently. It's as if you were physically connected to the LAN. Because LAN Distance provides transparency at the NDIS level (device driver), most of your LAN applications should run remotely with no changes required. From a remote location, you can access multiple LAN servers physically attached to a LAN without redialing. LAN Distance supports both Ethernet and Token Ring LANs (and provides transparent bridging for both of them).

LAN Distance: Client and Server

LAN Distance consists of two separately packaged client and server components (see Figure 17-4):

■ *LAN Distance Connection Server* is the server component that accepts incoming connections from remote PCs and allows them to access LAN resources on any station. The Connection Server bridges the local and remote networks and takes care of routing and security. All the PCs attached to the LAN become part of the LAN Distance Wide Area Network (WAN), even if the LAN Distance product is not installed on them. A Connection Server program does not require a dedicated PC.

■ *LAN Distance Remote* allows a remote PC to dial either the Connection Server or another remote PC and establish a LAN session.

The LAN Distance Remote does not require a Connection Server (or LAN) in WAN-only situations, where it acts as a WAN-based peer network.

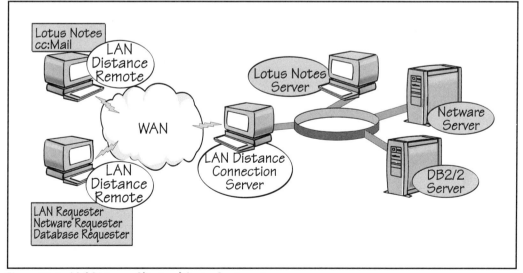

Figure 17-4. LAN Distance: Client and Server Components.

Setting Up Inexpensive Virtual LANs

A PC running Remote LAN Distance can accept calls and create a virtual LAN (see Figure 17-5). You don't need a Connection Server or physical LAN. The "virtual" LAN is created using existing telephone wires. This is a very inexpensive peer networking WAN solution.

Nomadic and home users will appreciate the possibilities this "virtual LAN" offers. For example, it can be used with LAN conferencing applications (such as Person-to-Person/2) to establish desktop conferences across multiple remote locations. You can even setup a Database Server on the makeshift LAN to take orders or provide information. Or, you can create an application server that becomes the common access point for all other remote workstations to dial into so that they can share the information collected at the application server.

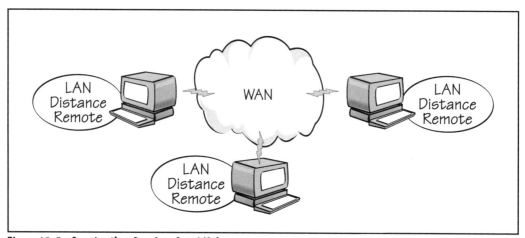

Figure 17-5. Creating Your Own Low-Cost WAN.

How Does the LAN/WAN Connection Work?

LAN Distance creates a virtual WAN/LAN network by redirecting traffic at the NDIS device driver level (see Figure 17-6). Here's how it works:

■ **At the remote client site**, the LAN Distance Remote component intercepts LAN-based application calls (for example, a NetWare Requester call) by providing a LAN Distance Logical Adapter (or "wedge") on top of NDIS. The intercepted call gets redirected to a WAN adapter. Technically speaking, the LAN Media Access Control (MAC) drivers are replaced with LAN Distance MAC drivers to transport the LAN protocol over the link.

- ■ *At the LAN site*, the LAN Distance Server receives the call on its WAN adapter and completes the virtual LAN by routing the call (at the NDIS level) to its LAN adapter that sends it to the destination PC on the LAN.

- ■ *At the destination PC*, the call is handled like any ordinary LAN message and passed on to the application (for example, NetWare on OS/2). The LAN-based PC knows nothing about LAN Distance. A possible exception is time outs. They may have to be made longer if the WAN is too slow.

In summary, LAN Distance provides a "wedge" that sits between NDIS and the device drivers. The magic of the LAN Distance wedge is to provide transparent WAN access to every protocol stack (and application) that supports NDIS drivers. This is powerful magic.

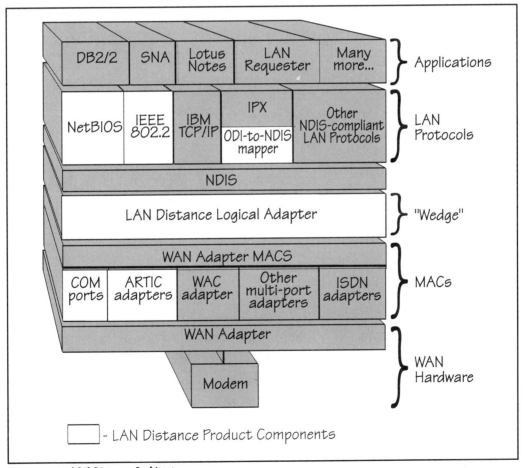

Figure 17-6. LAN Distance Architecture.

LAN Distance: The User Interface

LAN Distance provides a phonebook/dialer that makes it easy to establish connections by simply selecting a Connection Server's WAN number. The phonebook uses an OS/2 Notebook to help you organize the information (see Figure 17-7).

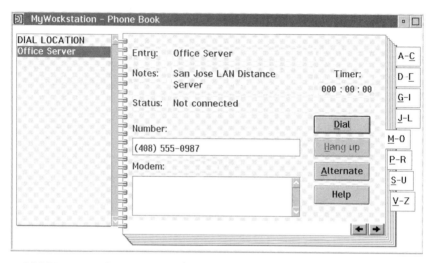

Figure 17-7. LAN Distance: Exploiting the OS/2 Workplace Shell.

The *LAN/WAN shuttle* feature makes it easy to "dock" your laptop directly to the office LAN when you're not on the road. The user interface allows you to specify, when terminating a session, if your connection will be through the LAN or WAN. This vastly simplifies the use of a single PC for home, office, or travel.

LAN Distance Security Features

Security is a touchy subject when dealing with remote PCs. LAN Distance meets the challenge by providing several unique security features while not compromising ease of use. Security is a configuration option for the LAN Distance Remote product for OS/2 and the LAN Distance Connection Server products. The LAN Distance product security is intended to be independent of any LAN network security or LAN-based application security mechanism currently in use; it will not interfere with those operations. LAN Distance product security is offered as an additional layer of security that can compensate for the inherent reduction in physical security that is associated with using remote LAN access products (see next Details box).

LAN Distance Security: The Nasty Details

Details

If you're an intruding hacker, take a deep breath and three aspirins. Here's a detailed list of the security features LAN Distance provides:

- ■ *Multiple user permission types.* These include user, administrator, and security administrator. A specific, fixed set of privileges can be associated with each type of user.

- ■ *Two-party, two-way entity authentication protocol.* A secret session key may be used for message authentication between the remote workstation and server. As a configuration option, LAN Distance security at the server provides functions to ensure that the request to logon has not been modified in transit and that the current message is not a copy of a prior message sent by someone masquerading as the previously authorized user.

- ■ *Passphrases.* Instead of standard passwords, LAN Distance passphrases consist of 4 to 32 case-sensitive characters (including blanks). Passphrases have proven to be easier for users to remember and make offline dictionary attacks impractical.

- ■ *Encryption.* Passphrases can be encrypted using DES (a private key encryption standard) to form a password key. The password key is used to develop message authentication codes using the X9.9 standard. These codes are exchanged across the WAN link using a three-round, two-party, two-way LAN Distance entity authentication protocol. A secret session key, a by-product of the protocol, is used to authenticate all LAN Distance "request for service" messages used during the ensuing session. Like the passphrase, the session key is also never transmitted across the link between the two parties.

- ■ *Policy options.* These can be set by administrators; options include maximum and minimum passphrase age, minimum passphrase length, passphrase history, maximum unsuccessful logon attempts, and valid logon intervals.

- ■ *Single logon among LAN Distance workstations.*

- ■ *Callback support.* Any user can be specified as a callback user. Two different types of callback are supported—fixed and variable. *Fixed* callback disconnects and calls back the user at a preconfigured telephone number defined within the user's account. *Variable* callback allows the user to submit a telephone number as part of the logon process. The user is called back at the number submitted.

■ *Calling workstation restrictions*. Users can be restricted to call only from workstations configured with specific network addresses. The set of network addresses allowed for each user is defined within the user's account. Users can also be restricted to call only during specified hours of the day and days of the week.

■ *Security audit trail*. LAN Distance can record the following in an audit file located at each secure LAN Distance workstation: the identity of each user attempting to log on and the duration of each logon session; any unexpected event that occurs during the logon protocol; all attempts to modify the security user account database (whether successful or not); and any attempt to change the security status from enabled to disabled.

In summary, LAN Distance will make sure that any "request for service" message received at a secure LAN Distance workstation has been sent by an authorized user, has not been modified in transit, and is not a duplicate or "fabricated" message. ❏

LAN System Administration Functions

LAN Distance provides a nice graphic user interface that helps administrators monitor, manage, and configure many simultaneous connections from multiple remote workstations.

The IBM LAN Distance Connection Server product is available with support for either eight ports or greater than eight ports depending on the customer's requirements. During configuration, ports and channels can either be assigned to specific phone numbers for dialing, assigned for call answering, or dynamically assigned on a first-come, first-serve basis.

LAN Distance allows administrators to set message filtering criteria. Ethernet and NetBIOS environments will require some form of bridge-filtering criteria to make sure unwanted data traffic doesn't flow over the WAN. This will help your performance. You don't need to set filters in environments where LAN data traffic is consistently light. The product also collects statistics that may help systems administrators with their capacity planning. For example, it provides statistics on a per-port usage.

LAN Distance helps administrators monitor the network. It shows which resources are currently in use. A server port status may be monitored locally or remotely. In case of security violations, the port may be disconnected. Administrators can view the name and ID of a workstation using a particular port. They can also view the names of all users dialing into a selected server. LAN Distance helps in problem determination by providing alerts, audit trails, error logs, error messages, problem determination information, and trace information. SNMP-based Bridge management is provided by Connection Server workstations running IBM's OS/2 version of TCP/IP.

LAN Distance: What's Coming Next?

Future versions of LAN Distance will allow workstations physically connected to a LAN to dial out and establish logical connections with workstations that are not physically connected to that LAN (see Figure 17-8).

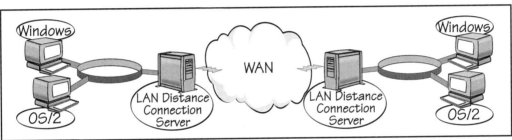

Figure 17-8. LAN Distance Futures: Dial-Out LAN-WAN-LAN.

Packaging

The **LAN Distance Remote for OS/2** product sells for $59. It requires about 700 KBytes of RAM and 8 MBytes of disk space. A version of LAN Distance Remote is available for Windows 3.X.

The LAN Distance Connection Server only runs on OS/2 2.X; it comes in two flavors:

■ **LAN Distance Connection Server (8-ports)** sells for $595 and is limited to eight concurrent users.

■ **LAN Distance Connection Server** sells for $1,995 and supports more than eight concurrent users depending on the capabilities of the WAN adapter. For example, if your PC is installed with four IBM Realtime Interface Co-Processor (ARTIC) adapters, you can configure up to 32 LAN Distance ports.

Both server products require about 700 KBytes of RAM and 8 MBytes of disk space. All the LAN Distance products are CID enabled.

ROUTEXPANDER/2: AN OS/2 BRIDGE/ROUTER

RouteXpander/2, introduced by IBM in January 1993, is an OS/2 2.X program that allows an ordinary PC to provide WAN-based routing and bridging functions. The RouteXpander/2 source-route bridge and multiprotocol routing facilities transport multiple protocols—including TCP/IP, SNA/APPN, and NetBIOS—over a single physical link, using either a Frame Relay or point-to-point connection. The RouteXpander/2 is the first PC product from any vendor to perform both bridging and routing for Token Ring LANs. It was also the first product to provide peripheral SNA routing over Frame Relay. To grasp the benefits of RouteXpander/2, you'll need to understand a hot new WAN technology called *Frame Relay* (see next Details box).

RouteXpander/2 Backbones

RouteXpander/2 can be used to create a bridge/router backbone that interconnects LANs over high-speed WANs (see Figure 17-9). Because it does not require a dedicated PC, RouteXpander provides a low-cost alternative to dedicated (non-PC) bridge/routers that typically sell for more than $10k. It is ideal for departments or locations with small LANs running multiple protocols that require LAN-WAN-LAN (or LAN-WAN) connectivity. When used with the IBM *Wide Area Connector (WAC)* adapter, RouteXpander/2 provides high-speed wide area network communications up to 2.048 Mbit/s (E1 line speeds). RouteXpander/2 can bridge traffic to a maximum of 200 destinations over Frame Relay logical link connections (over one physical network). In this configuration, the OS/2 workstations form a bridge/router backbone WAN that transports multiple communications protocols between remote LANs.

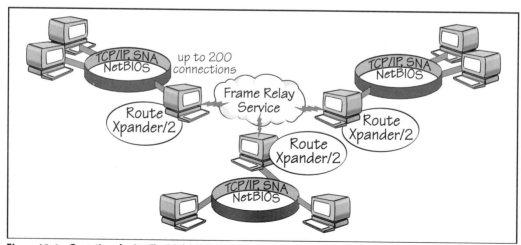

Figure 17-9. RouteXpander/2: The LAN-WAN-LAN Backbone Using Frame Relay.

What Is Frame Relay?

Details

Frame Relay is a packet-switching, link-layer technology that routes variable length packets over Wide Area Networks (WANs). Frame Relay, originally developed for ISDN, is a streamlined version of the X.25 packet switch technology. Frame Relay delivers 10 times more throughput than X.25 by moving the virtual circuits into the *link layer*. Frame Relay departs from X.25 by checking for errors at the endpoints of a network of leased lines instead of at the midpoints. It assumes that today's network segments are more reliable than the ones in the days when X.25 was designed.

Frame Relay is attractive because it increases network speeds by providing a simple software upgrade on top of existing packet-switching equipment. Router vendors use Frame Relay as an inter-router protocol that provides LAN-WAN-LAN connectivity. Using Frame Relay, the WAN segments can operate up to T1 (1.54 Mbit/s) or E1 (2.05 Mbit/s) line speeds. Frame Relay and a competing WAN technology called *Switched Multimegabit Data Services (SMDS)* support the allocation of bandwith on demand. In contrast, ISDN allocates fixed amounts of bandwidth. Why is that important? Because LAN-to-LAN communication tends to be very bursty by nature. Large amounts of bandwidth can be allocated "on demand" to handle the bursts when they occur, and there is much less bandwidth in between. Frame Relay helps optimize the use of data links by allowing the bandwidth to be shared among a large number of bursty users.

Frame Relay is the "hottest" WAN packet switching technology to appear since X.25 was introduced in the mid-70s. However, Frame Relay is an *interim* WAN technology that supports T1/E1 speeds on today's packet-switched networks. The more advanced WAN technologies—including B-ISDN, ATM, and SMDS—require both hardware and software upgrades. These advanced technologies are needed to transport full motion video and multimedia on WANs. In the meantime, we have Frame Relay. ❑

In addition, RouteXpander/2 can provide wide area attachment over non-switched Point-to-Point Protocol (PPP) lines between two OS/2 workstations; each can be attached to a LAN. PPP is one of the few standardized (see RFC 1171, 1172, and 1331) WAN protocols that ensures compatibility among vendors' products. Vendors that don't support PPP end up using proprietary versions of HDLC or SDLC. This configuration offers direct LAN-to-LAN multiprotocol communications in situations where a network is not required or not available (see Figure 17-10).

Figure 17-10. RouteXpander/2: The Point-to-Point Wide Area Connection.

RouteXpander/2 can also be used as a low-cost feeder node—of SNA and/or NetBIOS LAN Traffic—to dedicated bridge/routers. It offers applications access to Frame Relay and router networks without requiring a dedicated processor for the connection. For example, a single non-switched line from an OS/2 workstation running RouteXpander/2 can be attached to a 6611 Router, allowing multiple protocols to be routed and bridged to the multiple destinations that can be reached through the router's network (see Figure 17-11).

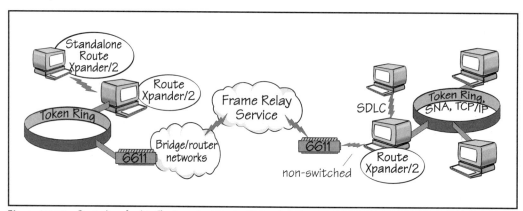

Figure 17-11. RouteXpander/2: The Low-Cost Feeder Network.

RouteXpander/2 conforms to international standards for Frame Relay and the emerging standards for multiprotocol routing over Frame Relay—including RFC 1294, which defines how to encapsulate various protocols in frame relay packets. This is done using a header, which assigns a unique protocol identifier to each of the industry's standard protocol suites. RFC 1294 supports both routed TCP/IP traffic and source-routed bridge frames. This means that RouteXpander/2 can interoperate with multivendor products that conform with the Frame Relay standards (see Figure 17-12). IBM tested RouteXpander's RFC 1294 implementation with its own 6611 high-end router and with the Wellfleet Backbone Node router (Wellfleet supports RFC 1294 in all its routers).

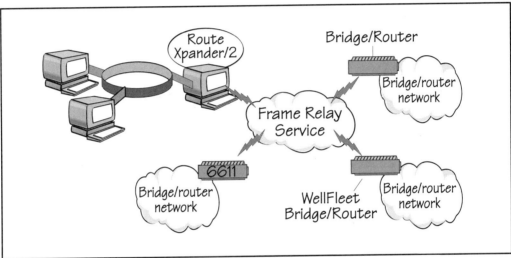

Figure 17-12. RouteXpander/2: Playing in a Heterogenous Bridge/Router World.

How it Works

RouteXpander/2 looks like an NDIS-compliant LAN driver to NTS/2. When it gets a packet, it manipulates the LAN header information and converts it to Frame Relay formats, then writes the data to a communications driver, such as the IBM Wide Area Connector (WAC) adapter, through a lower NDIS interface.

You can think of RouteXpander/2 as an NDIS "wedge" that provides an upper-level NDIS appearance to NTS/2 and a lower-level NDIS appearance to the communications driver. The technique of emulating a token-ring LAN allows the protocol products to be configured as if they were communicating with another workstation on the LAN when, in fact, RouteXpander/2 is providing access to multiple workstations and applications that can be reached through the WAN. This wedge technique

is similar to the one used by LAN Distance. The magic, in this case, is to provide Frame Relay routing and bridging.

For routing to occur, a protocol must be routable and the protocol stack must exist on the OS/2 workstation with RouteXpander/2. RouteXpander/2 contains a source route bridge to handle situations where routing is not possible. For example, in the case of NetBIOS (which cannot be routed), the source route bridge is used. The bridge can connect two token-ring LANs. Because the Frame Relay device driver is configured as a token-ring LAN, traffic can be bridged from the LAN to a WAN. It is a source route bridge, so only token-ring LANs are supported for bridging; Ethernet LANs are not supported for bridging. RouteXpander/2 is designed to route packets if possible. If routing is not possible, the packet will be bridged.

System Management

RouteXpander/2 extends the SNMP agent facility of TCP/IP for OS/2 to build and forward alerts to an SNMP manager, such as LAN NetView or NetView/6000. The bridge and Frame Relay Management Information Base (MIB) objects are supported. Performance statistics are maintained as defined in those MIBs. The SNMP GET functions are supported for each of these MIBs. Excuse us if this paragraph doesn't make sense; we explain MIBs and SNMP in Part 8.

RouteXpander/2: What's Coming Next?

The first version of RouteXpander/2 was developed in less than a year by IBM's Network Systems Division. IBM intends to maintain this momentum and support more routable protocols such as IPX and AppleTalk. It is also working on improving performance by supporting larger packet sizes without segmentation. Ethernet bridging support is planned soon. Recent benchmark tests conducted by Data Comm Test Lab show that RouteXpander/2's latest version turned in a respectable performance on T1 tests—an improvement over the first release.[1]

Packaging

RouteXpander/2 sells for $795 and requires less than 1 MByte of RAM and 1.2 MBytes of disk. To create a Bridge/Router, you will also need NTS/2 and a copy of TCP/IP for OS/2. IBM's Wide Area Connector (WAC) card sells for $795.

---

[1] Source: "PC-Based Routers Ready for Remote Sites," **Data Communications** (October 1993).

ANYNET/2: THE APPLICATION TO STACK WEDGE

AnyNet/2, introduced by IBM in September 1993, allows you to run, write, or acquire client/server applications without concern for the underlying transport stack normally associated with the peer-to-peer API. The current product allows APPC, CPI-C, and Berkeley sockets applications to operate independently of the SNA and TCP/IP stacks. AnyNet/2 does that by providing two wedges:

■ *Sockets over SNA* allows existing SNA networks to support the Berkeley sockets API (and applications) without requiring a TCP/IP protocol stack.

■ *APPC/CPI-C over TCP/IP* allows existing TCP/IP networks to support the APPC or CPI-C API (and applications) without requiring an SNA stack.

AnyNet/2 allows you to choose applications independently of the network on which they were designed to run. It allows vendors to migrate their applications to non-native protocol environments quickly and inexpensively (no changes are required). In addition, network managers can pick the protocols that best suit their backbones. This should help them reduce the number of protocols and, as a result, make it easier to maintain their networks. Programmers can focus on writing applications using their favorite network APIs without concerning themselves with the underlying protocol stacks. Client machines can reduce their memory requirements (and complexity) by installing fewer transport stacks.

APPC/CPI-C Over TCP/IP

AnyNet/2 allows any OS/2 APPC or CPI-C application (such as CICS and DB2/2) to communicate over a TCP/IP network by creating a "wedge" between the APPC (or CPI-C) API and the TCP/IP stack (see Figure 17-13). Note that this implementation requires three products to run on every node: Communications Manager/2, AnyNet/2, and TCP/IP for OS/2. AnyNet/2, though, only uses the topmost layer of the Communications Manager/2 product (but don't expect a rebate). Perhaps in the future IBM may take that piece of Communications Manager and bundle it with AnyNet/2, like it does with sockets (see next section).

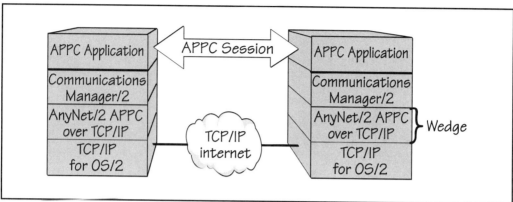

Figure 17-13. AnyNet/2: APPC Applications Over TCP/IP Networks.

Sockets Over SNA

AnyNet/2 allows any OS/2 Sockets application (such as NFS, Telnet, and FTP) to communicate over a SNA network by creating a "wedge" between the Sockets API and the SNA stack (see Figure 17-14). Note that TCP/IP for OS/2 is not required because AnyNet/2 provides a sockets library.

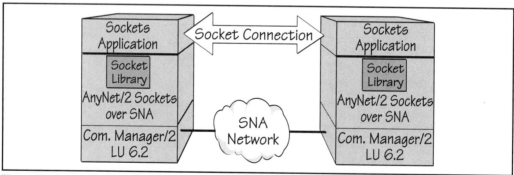

Figure 17-14. AnyNet/2: Socket Applications Over SNA Networks.

How it Works

AnyNet/2 creates a "wedge" that sits below the transport user—that is, the peer-to-peer API—and above the transport layer and its underlying stack (see Figure 17-15). The AnyNet wedge—IBM calls it the *Common Transport Semantics (CTS)*—looks at a call, if it is for a native stack it simply reissues it; otherwise it performs the following magic (see Figure 17-16):

- ■ *It maps namespaces.* The challenge is how to let the application specify a destination address in its native format and at the same time find and access that destination across a different transport network. For example, how does the CTS wedge map a 32-bit IP address to a 17-character SNA name? It does the mapping by either extending the native directory—the directory must support the registration of different address types—or by providing a mapping database (on one of its nodes). In some cases (for example, IP-to-SNA, where the user address is shorter than the transport address) it performs an algorithmic map.

- ■ *It compensates for missing function.* No two protocol stacks are the same. Every stack lacks some function supported in another stack. So the CTS wedge must somehow provide the missing function that satisfies the API call. For example, SNA and NetBIOS are record-based, while sockets are stream-based. The CTS wedge must be able to compensate for that function on both sides.

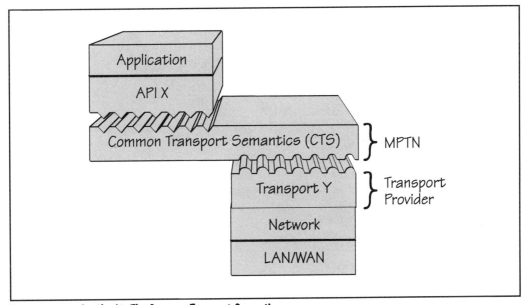

Figure 17-15. AnyNet/2: The Common Transport Semantics.

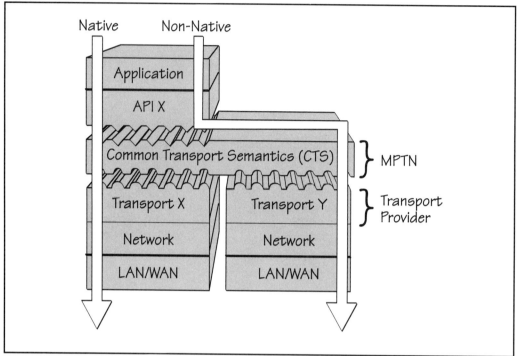

Figure 17-16. AnyNet/2: Native Calls Versus Stack-Redirected Calls.

■ *It lets each environment be managed by its managing platform.* The transport user and transport provider are managed separately using their existing management products and native agents. The CTS wedge correlates among different management protocols—such as SNMP, CMIP, and SNA-MS—to route management information.

Test results reported by IBM show that the overhead introduced by the CTS wedge is negligible. Steady-state send/receive performance is almost equal to the native API running on native stacks.

Unlike other middleware solutions, the AnyNet/2 CTS wedge approach works with existing applications and does not introduce new APIs. Unlike router-based solutions, the AnyNet/2 CTS wedge does not encapsulate data; instead, it uses the full capabilities of the underlying protocol. With AnyNet/2, the application believes that its traffic is being sent on its native transport (see following Briefing box for more information on CTS).

AnyNet/2: Sockets Over SNA Gateway

In January 1994, IBM shipped **AnyNet/2 Sockets over SNA Gateway**, the AnyNet transport gateway on an OS/2 platform. What's a transport gateway and why should you care? A gateway allows applications on one transport network to talk to applications on a dissimilar transport as long as they use the same peer-to-peer API semantics (see Figure 17-17). Gateways provide greater flexibility in designing networks and require no changes to the applications. Applications using different transports communicate through the gateway, which connects the transport networks. For a broader discussion on gateways, refer to the following Briefing box.

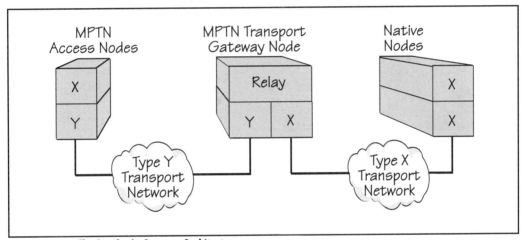

Figure 17-17. The AnyNet/2 Gateway Architecture.

The OS/2 transport gateway allows OS/2 or MVS AnyNet applications running sockets on an SNA network to talk to native sockets applications (on any OS) running on a TCP/IP network (see Figure 17-18). This means that applications traditionally associated with TCP/IP networks, such as FTP, X-Windows and NFS, can now interact with like applications on SNA networks.

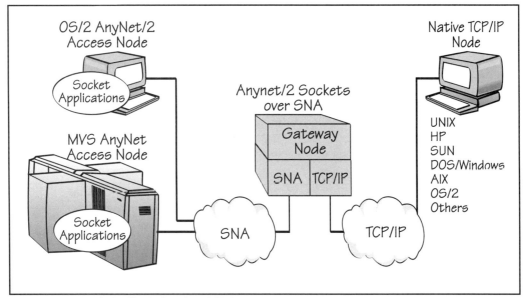

Figure 17-18. AnyNet/2: The Sockets Over SNA Gateway.

In addition, the AnyNet/2 Sockets Gateway can be used to connect isolated TCP/IP networks across an SNA internet (see Figure 17-19). Note that no changes are required within the TCP/IP network besides adding the gateway. In cases where an SNA (or TCP/IP) network already exists, this capability may be very cost-effective and superior to a router that uses tunneling (i.e., it encapsulates the foreign protocol to transport other protocols through the internet). The AnyNet/2 gateway supports up to 100 concurrent network connections. However, it does not support broadcast messages.

Figure 17-19. AnyNet/2: Using Gateways to Tie TCP/IP Networks Over an SNA Backbone.

AnyNet/2: What's Coming Next?

What other protocols can be wedged by CTS? Table 17-1 shows some of the possibilities (or opportunities). IBM intends to provide AnyNet/2 *NetBIOS over SNA*, allowing NetBIOS applications to operate over SNA networks. It is also encouraging third parties to participate in the CTS wedging process. For example, Ki Research is creating a DECnet to SNA wedge (not on OS/2).

Table 17-1. AnyNet/2: Today's Protocol Mix.

	APIs				
Stacks	APPC/CPI-C	Sockets	TLI	NetBIOS	DECnet
SNA (LU 6.2)	Yes	Yes	--	Soon	Ki Research
TCP/IP	Yes	Yes	--	Yes[1]	--
NetBEUI	Soon	Yes[2]	--	Yes	--
IPX/SPX	--	--	Novell	Novell	--
DECNet	--	--	--	--	Yes

1. Packaged with TCP/IP for OS/2 V2.0
2. Packaged with DCE (it is called MPTS)

AnyNet/2 Packaging

AnyNet/2 sells for $170. Its SNA transport stack is provided by Communications Manager/2; its TCP/IP stack is provided by TCP/IP for OS/2. The **AnyNet/2 Gateway** sells for $1,950 and can run in non-dedicated mode on a 80386SX (or higher) machine with 8 MBytes of memory.

The MPTN Architecture

Briefing

Warning! This box is acronym-intensive.

AnyNet/2 delivers pieces of the *Multiprotocol Transport Network (MPTN)* architecture support to OS/2. This architecture was introduced in March 1992 as part of the *IBM Networking Blueprint* (see Figure 17-20). MPTN describes the implementation of the *Common Transport Semantics (CTS)* shown in the figure. IBM is actively soliciting vendor partners to help implement the pieces and is working with standard bodies to standardize MPTN—for example, it's being proposed as an extension of the X/Open Transport Interface (XTI).

MPTN supports communications between two matching peer-to-peer APIs, such as between two CPI-C or two sockets applications, but not between different API types. MPTN calls these APIs *transport user* APIs; it calls the transport stacks *transport providers*. MPTN allows transport users to work with a variety of transport providers. For example, the AnyNet/2 implementation of MPTN allows the sockets *user* APIs to work with SNA—a transport *provider*.

MPTN comes in two flavors:

■ As an **access node**, MPTN runs on the same system as the application. AnyNet/2 is an access node implementation.

■ As a **gateway node**, MPTN can be located on a separate machine from the applications (see Figure 17-17). The three nodes shown in the figure could all be running on the same network. Anynet/2 Gateway is an example of a gateway node.

MPTN is a general solution to the multistack transport problem. It is an attractive solution because it works within the constraint that *our industry will never standardize on a single API or transport stack*. The MPTN solution is more elegant (and flexible) than routing, bridging, or single-API middleware alternatives. MPTN made its "debut" on the OS/2 and MVS platforms in the form of the AnyNet products. Industry analysts expect IBM to provide AnyNet products on other platforms—including DOS/Windows, OS/400, and AIX.

Many networking companies have attempted to develop such an approach and gave up the effort before announcing it. Can IBM succeed where many others have failed? One hopeful sign is that IBM is promoting MPTN to other vendors and will license the full technical specifications. If the industry (i.e., X/Open) accepts MPTN as a standard, the licensing agreements will be provided at no charge. So far, it seems that X/Open loves the MPTN *access node* but is not too sure about the *gateway node*. ❑

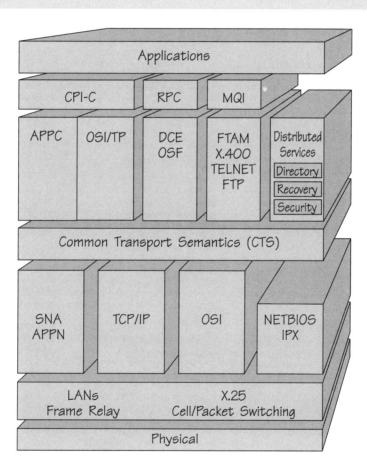

Figure 17-20. IBM's Open Network Blueprint.

Chapter 18

TCP/IP for OS/2: The Unix Connection

TCP/IP is the glue that holds the Internet—or just about any internetwork, for that matter—together.

— *Chip Sparling (October, 1993)*

In this chapter, we explore **TCP/IP for OS/2 Version 2.0**, a product that opens up the OS/2 client/server platform to the Unix world. TCP/IP for OS/2 is more than just a communications stack. The product includes an ONC-compliant NOS, an SNMP-based distributed system management, an IP router, X Windows, multimedia electronic mail, and many popular TCP/IP applications. TCP/IP for OS/2 extends the reach of OS/2 deep inside the world of Unix and provides many levels of *interoperability* between OS/2 and all the Unix variants. It's a very middleware-rich client/server offering.

TCP/IP FOR OS/2

TCP/IP for OS/2 Version 2.0, shipped by IBM in September 1993, provides an extensive TCP/IP protocol suite on an OS/2 platform. In addition, the product incorporates a number of Unix network services such as the Berkeley sockets, SunOS RPC, HP/Apollo's NCS, NFS (client and server), X Windows (client and server), MIT's Kerberos authentication services, SNMP (agent and monitor), and multimedia mail. The TCP/IP product allows OS/2 to play both a client and server role in Unix networks. The product also enables DOS and Windows applications written to the WinSock API to run TCP/IP in the OS/2 environment. As you can tell from the screen shot in Figure 18-1, the TCP/IP product is integrated into the OS/2 Workplace Shell. However, its features will make Unix users and programmers feel quite at home in the OS/2 environment.

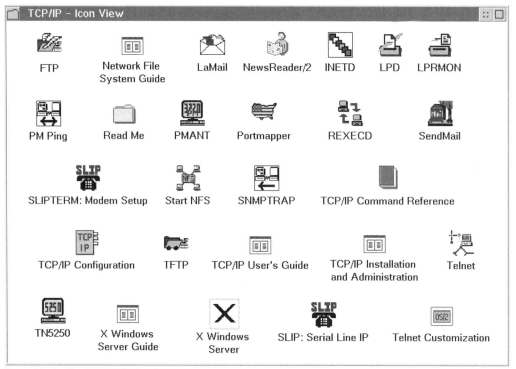

Figure 18-1. The TCP/IP V2 Services.

The TCP/IP for OS/2 Stack

When dealing with communications, you'll always be staring at a layered diagram that shows a protocol stack resembling a wedding cake (Figure 18-2). Unfortunately, the analogy ends there. Instead of chocolate, coconut, and vanilla, you get layers of strange sounding names and acronyms that form the common language of a communication subculture. TCP/IP provides an exotic subculture that has been evolving since the pioneer days of networking. This is the good news. The bad news is that when it comes to acronyms, TCP/IP makes even SNA look pale by comparison. So how do we tell you all there is to know about TCP/IP and its extended network services?

We will present the broad features of TCP/IP for OS/2 by dividing the product into five functional layers: physical network, internet services, transport services, session services, and application services (see Figure 18-2). As usual, we will start at the bottom of the stack and work our way upwards. By the end of this overview, you will be a master of TCP/IP acronyms. Programmers, of course, are mostly interested in the APIs that give their programs access to the services of a particular communications layer. We will briefly cover some of the main APIs after we explain the TCP/IP features.

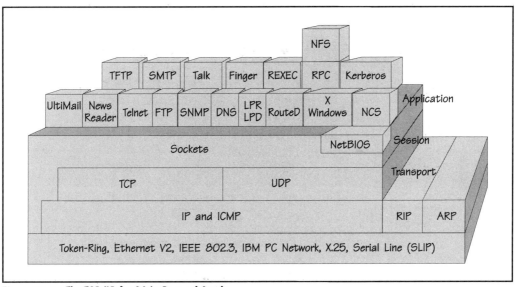

Figure 18-2. The TCP/IP for OS/2 Protocol Stack.

The Physical Network

The TCP/IP protocol does not specify the physical or link layers. These are typically provided by vendor-specific implementations. The OS/2 TCP/IP product provides a very rich set of link layer and physical connectivity options. It does that by using the NTS/2 physical and link layer protocols. The TCP/IP stack interfaces with NTS/2's NDIS drivers and the 802.2 logical link layer. This means TCP/IP will work over any NDIS compliant Token Ring, Ethernet, or FDDI LAN adapter. And, because NDIS allows multiple protocol stacks to access the same adapter, TCP/IP can happily coexist with OS/2's other protocol stacks. TCP/IP, like any NTS/2 supported product, can concurrently support up to four LAN adapters on a single machine.

The **Serial Line Internet Protocol (SLIP)** is a TCP/IP specific ASYNC protocol that lets you set up a point-to-point connection over a serial line using an RS-232 modem connection over a telephone line. You can use SLIP to access a remote TCP/IP network from your local host, or to route datagrams between two TCP/IP networks. SLIP now lets you write REXX scripts to support remote connections that need passwords or dynamically assigned IP addresses. SLIP provides VJ compression for better performance to remote hosts that also have VJ compression.

TCP/IP provides Wide Area Network support using the X.25 protocol. It uses the same X.25 driver as Communications Manager and requires the X.25 Coprocessor/2 adapter. The maximum line speed over X.25 is 64 Kb/s. In addition, TCP/IP supports Frame Relay drivers. Using the Wide Area Card (WAC), the product can interface to a Frame Relay Bridge/Router backbone at T1 speeds.

The Internet Services

The TCP/IP network layer creates a logical network called an *internet* out of one or more physical networks. Each computer on the internet is assigned at least one unique 32-bit internet address consisting of two parts: a network number and a local address. A unique network number is assigned to each network when it connects to the internet. Packets are routed through the internet using this global addressing scheme. A *port* is an endpoint for communication between applications; it provides queues for sending and receiving data. Each port has a port number for identification. A *socket* is a unique address that combines a port number with an internet address. The TCP/IP programs you develop will most likely communicate at the socket level. TCP/IP provides several protocols that support the internet and feed it routing information. Most of these protocols are totally transparent to your applications. But we still should quickly review them because some of the acronyms are culturally significant.

■ *Internet Protocol (IP)* provides the basic mechanism for routing packets in the internet. IP is not a reliable communication protocol. It does not understand the relationships between packets and does not perform retransmissions. IP requires higher-level protocols, such as TCP or UDP, to provide a reliable class of service.

■ *Internet Control Message Protocol (ICMP)* is an internal protocol for passing control messages between gateways, routers, and workstations. ICMP provides general feedback about problems in the internet environment. For example, ICMP messages are used when a packet cannot reach its destination, or when a workstation PINGs to check if another workstation is available.

■ **_Routing Information Protocol (RIP)_** is a dynamic routing protocol for passing routing messages between gateways, routers, and workstations. This is the information that is used to dynamically maintain routing tables that reflect the state of the internet. It is the job of routers to discover the best path from one point to another within an internet. A router must know the location of every node within its domain. This knowledge is obtained dynamically through periodic RIP packet exchanges between the router and the nodes in its domain (every 30 seconds or so). RIP maintains only the path to the next router; it does not store the entire network path to a destination. RIP allows an OS/2 machine to function as a non-dedicated IP internet router.

■ **_Address Resolution Protocol (ARP)_** is another internal protocol used by TCP/IP to maintain and refresh its internet address mapping tables. When an application sends an internet packet, IP requests the appropriate address mapping. If the mapping is not in the mapping table, an ARP broadcast packet (_where is?_) is sent to all the nodes on the network requesting the physical address of the target IP address. The ARP response maps the IP target address to a physical address such as that of a Token Ring or Ethernet adapter. ARPs require network hardware that supports broadcasts. Bridges repeat ARPs, while routers act as "firewalls" that block the flow of ARPs.

The Transport Services

The transport services of TCP/IP consists of two protocols that provide end-to-end transport services.

■ **_User Datagram Protocol (UDP)_** provides a datagram service. Like the NetBIOS datagrams, TCP/IP datagrams are unreliable but fast. Applications that require reliable delivery of streams of data should use TCP instead of datagrams.

■ **_Transmission Control Protocol (TCP)_** provides a reliable, session-based service for the delivery of sequenced packets across an internet.

The Session Services

The Session services provide a friendly environment for programs that use the TCP/IP transport services. The TCP/IP standard does not specify how application programs interact with the transport protocols. TCP/IP for OS/2 provides two interfaces to the transport services: Berkeley Sockets and NetBIOS.

■ **_Berkeley Sockets_** provide a friendly API interface to the services of TCP, UDP, ICMP, and IP. Sockets are TCP/IP's premier peer-to-peer API. Sockets define how an operating system provides network I/O using, whenever possible, a Unix file read/write paradigm. Sockets allow data to be transmitted and received simultaneously (duplex) and provide a peer-to-peer communications service.

■ **NetBIOS** provides a send/receive type of interface to the transport services. The NetBIOS interface makes it easy to port to the TCP/IP environment communications programs that are popular in the PC world. The NetBIOS applications can communicate over a TCP/IP internet with native NetBIOS applications. NetBIOS applications over NetBEUI cannot be routed over WANs; but with TCP/IP for OS/2, they can be routed anywhere. The NetBIOS interface complies with RFCs 1001 and 1002.

The TCP/IP Application Layer

The application layer of TCP/IP for OS/2 includes a long list of network applications and utilities. These applications usually reside on well-known sockets that are reserved for them.

■ **Telnet** is the TCP/IP standard protocol for remote terminal connection. An OS/2 machine can be configured as a Telnet terminal emulator (client) or as a Telnet terminal server. Over seven terminal emulator protocols are supported, including IBM 3270, dumb ASCII, VT100, and VT220. PMANT is a PM 3270 terminal emulator. Telnet uses TCP as its transport mechanism.

■ **File Transfer Protocol (FTP)** is the TCP/IP standard protocol for transferring files from one machine to another. FTP supports the transfer of both binary and ASCII files. FTP also supports OS/2's HPFS file system and its long file names. An OS/2 TCP/IP node can be an FTP client, or server, or both. An FTP client includes a PM front-end that graphically supports functions such as listing remote directories, changing the current remote directory, creating and removing remote directories, and transferring one or more files in a single request. The client also allows simultaneous connections to FTP servers within a single session. The FTP server provides security features such as user account and password validation. FTP uses TCP as its transport mechanism. FTP services can be invoked through API calls.

■ **Trivial File Transfer Protocol (TFTP)**, like FTP, provides a file transfer protocol. Unlike FTP, however, TFTP cannot be used to list or change directories and does not support client authentication. TFTP builds on top of the UDP transport layer.

■ **Simple Mail Transfer Protocol (SMTP)** provides an e-mail protocol for transferring electronic mail messages from a client (sender) to a server (receiver). You do not interface directly with SMTP in the OS/2 environment. Instead, you use **LaMail**, a PM application that provides a user interface to **Sendmail** which, in turn, uses SMTP to send the mail to its destination. The LaMail program allows you to view, create, edit, spell check, sort, and send mail. It also allows you to organize mail in folders and provides an icon that changes when it receives mail.

■ *UltiMail* is the state-of-the-art implementation of electronic mail. It can be used to send electronic mail across a heterogeneous TCP/IP network. UltiMail provides a more sophisticated version of the basic electronic mail capability in Sendmail and LaMail. UltiMail can exchange text mail with LaMail, Sendmail, or with any standard implementation of TCP/IP electronic mail. UltiMail, however, can be used to transmit multimedia messages that conform with the MIME RFC multimedia mail standard. It supports a wide variety of multimedia data, including text, Rich Text Format (RTF), images (BMP, GIF, and TIFF), audio (wave and MIDI), simple video clips, and binary files. UltiMail provides an easy-to-use Workplace Shell interface to implement mail objects (folders, address books, and envelopes) that behave and resemble objects in the more traditional paper world.

■ *Internet News Reader (NR2)* is a multithreaded OS/2 application that lets you tap into the nearly limitless supply of free information provided on *Usenet*—with thousands of conference topics ranging from gourmet cooking to OS debates. With the Reader, you can subscribe to any topic, import and export files, post your comments, and search for articles. Your subscriptions get refreshed automatically.

■ *BOOTP* allows a client machine that knows its hardware address to get an internet address from a server. Both the BOOTP client and server are supported by TCP/IP for OS/2.

■ *Domain Name System (DNS)* is an online "distributed database" system used to map human-readable, symbolic names into IP addresses. DNS servers throughout the IP internet implement a hierarchical naming convention that gives local network administrators the freedom to assign machine names and addresses within their domains. An internet name consists of domain labels separated by periods; each label to the right of a period represents an increasingly higher domain level: *machine.subdomain.subdomain.rootdomain*. You must provide an ETC\HOSTS file containing entries that map symbolic names to internet addresses. You can override that by placing a RESOLV file in the ETC subdirectory. When the name resolver program finds the RESOLV file, it sends the name resolution request to a foreign name server before using the local HOSTS file. The HOSTS file is used on small internets to avoid the hierarchical naming system. The NSLOOKUP function allows a user to interactively query a Domain Name Server for information.

You can establish two types of name servers: a *master server* and a *caching-only server.* A master can function as the *primary* server for its name domain and as a *backup* server for another primary's domain. The backup server takes over if the primary dies. A caching server has no authority for any domain. As it receives queries, it requests information from the master and then caches the data it receives for a period of time, which is determined by the *time-to-live* attribute.

■ ***Simple Network Management Protocol (SNMP)*** is the de facto standard for managing TCP/IP multivendor networks. SNMP separates the job of network management into two types of tasks: agents and managers. The *agent* tasks monitor the network nodes on which they reside and execute remote commands. The agent tasks act on behalf of the network managers. The *manager* tasks run on a network management station and communicate with the distributed agents through remote commands to provide an overall view of the network's status. The manager tasks are the clients. However, agents can also send unsolicited alerts, called traps, to the manager to inform it of important events such as errors, cold starts, and authentication failures (see Figure 18-3). **SN-MPTRAP** is a PM program that displays SNMP alerts received from any agent on the network. **PMPING**, another PM program, can graphically display the status of all workstations defined in a user table. It does that by "pinging" each workstation. **PING**, which stands for *Packet InterNet Groper,* is an echo protocol used in "Are you alive?" type of queries. SNMP defines the protocol for communications between agents and managers. OS/2 SNMP can also act as both a managing system and a managed system.

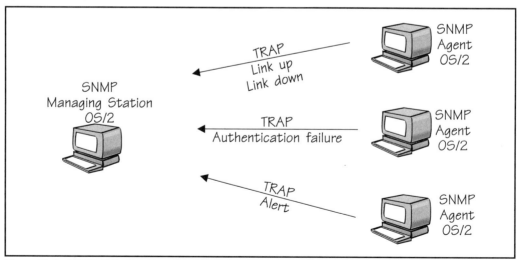

Figure 18-3. SNMP: Collecting Traps From Agents.

The heart of SNMP open management is the **Management Information Base (MIB)**. The MIB defines groups of information fields that the SNMP agents use to store device status. The standard defines the data items that the managed workstation must collect and the operations that are allowed on that data. The information from each agent is kept in the agent's MIB database. The MIB variables are grouped as objects. For example, an Ethernet adapter (agent) may collect statistics on network utilization, CRC errors, and collisions, and then save them in a MIB object. The manager task can query the appropriate MIB objects on the agent to create a report. MIB allows any vendor's management station to access statistics and parameters of any device, regardless of its maker, as long as it supports MIB. Most SNMP products, including TCP/IP for OS/2, implement the MIB-II standard, which specifies 57 additional managed objects. An OS/2 manager task has the ability to obtain values of individual MIB variables using SNMP (see Figure 18-4). The values include performance related statistical variables, network device status, and many others. TCP/IP for OS/2 also supports user-defined MIB data.

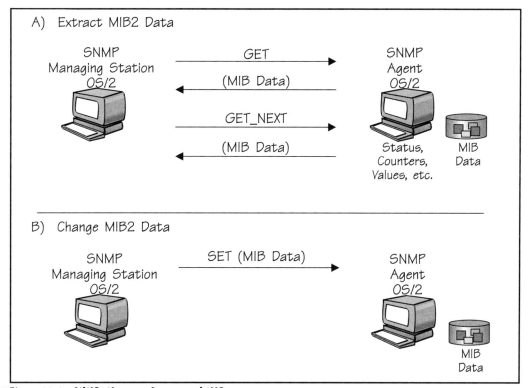

Figure 18-4. SNMP: Manager, Agents, and MIBs.

- **_Kerberos Authentication System_** provides additional levels of security on client/server networks by checking authorization at the user level rather than at the node level. The Kerberos server identifies clients and authenticates connection requests. It then grants an encrypted ticket to the client for a particular service. The key provides a way for authenticated clients to prove their identity to other servers across the network. The client must present its key to the provider of the requested service. Clients must obtain a separate ticket from the Kerberos authentication server for each specific service. Kerberos clients and servers never transmit passwords on the network. They use their password, however, to decode encrypted tickets.

- **_Remote Printing (LPR and LPD)_** provides both client and server support for remote printing. This application allows you to spool files remotely to a line printer daemon (LPD). The line printer client (LPR) sends the file to be printed to a specified printer on the server station.

- **_X Windows_** is a client/server presentation protocol. A "server" in X Windows terminology is a workstation that allows its display screen and mouse events to be monitored by a remote X Windows client. An X server provides a way for remote programs on the network to share the real estate on the server workstation's screen (see Figure 18-5). In this respect, X Windows provides a modern version of the traditional host/terminal arrangement. You can think of the X Window server as a terminal with GUI-like graphics, and the X Window client as the terminal monitoring application. Unlike a traditional terminal, the X server is an intelligent PC that can service many clients at the same time. One client may display a bar chart in a window, another may interact with a user through a menu, and a third client may display an icon to inform the user that the meeting with the boss was rescheduled. TCP/IP for OS/2 supports X Windows clients and servers. The X server function uses PM as the window manager.

- **_Talk_** allows end users to send interactive messages, as opposed to the asynchronous mail capabilities of SMTP. When a local node sends a Talk request to a target node, the user of that machine is immediately notified of the connection request. If it is accepted, the two partners can engage in an electronic conversation. This is a synchronous form of conversation.

- **_FINGER_** provides an interface for querying the current status of a remote host or a user ID on a remote host. FINGER uses TCP as the underlying protocol.

- **_RouteD_**, pronounced "Route-Dee," is a routing server program (a daemon) that uses RIP to dynamically create and maintain network routing tables. The RIP protocol arranges to have gateways and routers periodically broadcast their routing tables to neighbors. Using this information, an OS/2 RouteD server can

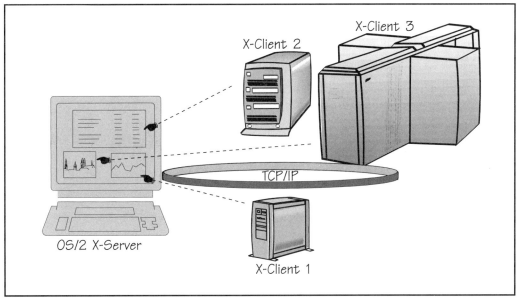

Figure 18-5. X Windows Clients and Servers.

update its routing tables. RouteD can determine if a new route has been created, if a route is temporarily unavailable, or if a more efficient route exists.

■ *Sun Remote Procedure Call (SunRPC)* is a programming interface that allows programs to invoke remote functions on a server machine. With SunRPC, the combination of a server address, program number, version number, and a procedure number specifies a remote procedure. A client makes a procedure call to send a request to the server. The RPC software collects values for the parameters, forms a message, and sends it to the remote server. The server receives the request, unpacks the parameters, calls the procedure, and sends the reply back to the client. The procedure call then returns to the client. The SunRPC uses the *eXternal Data Representation (XDR)*, a machine-independent protocol for representing data. SunRPC, like all RPCs, hides most of the details of the network and extends the local procedure call to distributed environments. The SunRPC is used by NFS and is freely licensed by Sun Microsystems as part of its *Open Network Computing (ONC)* environment. Over 90 vendors offer ports of SunRPC, XDR, and NFS. ONC has been around for quite some time (since 1985) and has an installed base of over a million nodes.

■ *Network Computing System (NCS)* is the Apollo (now HP) RPC toolkit. This toolkit (with extensions and enhancements from DEC) was chosen as the foundation for OSF's DCE RPC implementation. The NCS toolkit consists of three components: the RPC run-time library, the Location Broker, and the

Network Interface Definition Language (NIDL) stub compiler. The NIDL allows programmers to specify the procedures and parameters that a server exports to clients using an interface definition language. The *Location Broker* is a directory service that provides clients with run-time information about the locations of objects and interfaces, including procedure names and calling syntax. The NCS RPC uses sockets for interprocess communications. The location broker makes it possible to bind the address of the RPC server at run time. Servers must register their sockets, objects, and interfaces with the Location Broker. Clients can issue requests for the location of objects by object ID, type, or interface.

■ *Network File System (NFS)* is the OS/2 implementation of Sun Microsystems' very popular distributed file system. NFS uses SunRPC to communicate between the client and the server. NFS supports a hierarchical file structure. OS/2 provides both a full client and server implementation of the NFS system. It allows users to share files (locks are supported) with each other, much the same way that LAN Server/Requester works. It also allows a Unix machine, or any NFS client, to share files with an OS/2 machine. The product also supports software that translates between OS/2 and Unix text file formats (mostly end-of-line format differences).

■ *Remote Execution Protocol (REXEC)* is a protocol for the invocation of commands (and getting back the results) on a remote machine. The OS/2 implementation of REXEC provides automatic logon and authentication.

The TCP/IP APIs

It should be evident by now that TCP/IP for OS/2 is a well-endowed product. Its services and protocols transcend simple connectivity; they allow OS/2 to interoperate with the various operating systems that use the TCP/IP environment. Your programs can take advantage of all this good stuff by plugging into the right APIs. The main API interfaces are Berkeley Sockets, NetBIOS, FTP, SunRPC, NCS RPC, SNMP DPI, Kerberos, X Windows, and Motif.

Berkeley Sockets API provides the least common denominator for writing portable communications programs in the TCP/IP environment. OS/2 supports three socket types: stream, datagram, and raw. Stream and datagram sockets interface to the transport layer, and raw sockets interface to the network layer. In addition to peer-to-peer communications, the OS/2 socket API also provides network service APIs that allow you to obtain internet addressing information, and to convert symbolic names to internet addresses (or domain name resolution). The socket interface can be expanded to provide new socket types for additional services. The OS/2 socket API consists of 57 function calls.

NetBIOS for TCP/IP is compatible with the IBM/Microsoft NetBIOS specifications and also provides facilities for internet operations. The TCP/IP NetBIOS interface supports naming services, datagrams, and sessions. Sessions use TCP; datagrams use UDP.

FTP API allows you to transfer files between FTP clients and servers and between two FTP servers without sending the file to a local machine. You can append information to a remote file, delete files from a remote machine, and manipulate a remote directory. And, you can use two flavors of ping to determine whether a machine is alive before attempting a file transfer. Your applications can use this API to talk to up to 256 FTP servers at the same time. The FTP API consists of 19 function calls.

SunRPC and NCS RPC both provide APIs that facilitate writing client/server applications. The bad news is that you must choose between SunRPC, NCS RPC, and DCE RPC; whatever services you create will not interoperate across these environments. Your choice of RPC will lock you into an RPC compiler environment. The industry is currently standardizing around the DCE RPC, a derivative of NCS. The NCS RPC API set consists of 26 function calls. The combined SunRPC and XDR API sets consists of 83 function calls. Netwise offers SunRPC tools on almost every hardware platform.

SNMP DPI API, an acronym for *Distributed Programming Interface*, is used to dynamically add, delete, or replace network management variables in the local MIB without recompiling the SNMP agent. This lets you create subagents that extend the function provided by the OS/2 SNMP agent. Your subagents can define their own MIB variables and register them with the SNMP agent. When requests for these variables are received from managing stations, the SNMP agent passes the request to the subagent. The subagent returns a response to the agent, which is sent back in a reply packet to the requesting station. The SNMP DPI API consists of 7 function calls.

Kerberos API includes calls that can be used by both your client and server programs. Kerberos provides API calls for creating and reading authentication requests using encrypted or unencrypted messages. The API calls also provide the ticketing services. The Kerberos API consists of 12 function calls.

X Windows and OSF Motif APIs include the standard X Windows API from the MIT consortium as well as the OSF Motif widgets, header files, and GUI APIs. This lets you create and run X Windows and Motif applications on OS/2 or port them from other platforms

TCP/IP for OS/2 Packaging

The **TCP/IP for OS/2 Version 2.0** is packaged as a Base Kit with optional function kits. The *Base Kit* sells for $230. It includes the functions described in this chapter minus X.25, X Windows, NFS, DNS, UltiMail, the Programmer's Toolkit, and NetBIOS. The *Total Kit*, which includes most of the run-time functions described here, sells for $722. The *Programmer's Toolkit* sells for an additional $550. See Table 18-1 for more TCP/IP packaging details.

Table 18-1. TCP/IP for OS/2 Packaging.

Kit	List Price	Function
Base Kit	$230	Provides the protocol stacks and a base set of applications that includes most of the applications described in this chapter. It also provides distributed system management support based on SNMP.
UltiMail Kit	$ 99	Provides a multimedia-enabled electronic mail facility.
NFS Kit	$140	Provides the run time for both an NFS client and server.
Domain Name Server Kit	$495	Provides the name server run-time support.
X Window Server Kit	$195	Provides the run time for displaying and controlling X Window application programs in an OS/2 PM windowed session. The kit conforms with X Windows Version 11 Release 5 (X11R5).
X Window Client Kit	$195	Provides the run time for running X Window client applications on OS/2. It includes the X libraries and Intrinsic libraries.
OSF/Motif Kit	$195	Provides the OSF/Motif V1.2 libraries for client applications on OS/2. The TCP/IP for X Window Client Kit is a prerequisite for the OSF/Motif Kit.
DOS/Windows Access Kit	$85	Provides a run time for DOS applications written to the IBM TCP/IP for DOS V2.1 programming interfaces. Also allows Windows applications written to the WinSock API V1.0 or V1.1 specifications to run in an OS/2 environment on top of TCP/IP for OS/2.
Extended Networking Kit	$197	Provides sockets over SNA support that allows a TCP/IP node to establish sessions with SNA hosts (AnyNet/2). This also includes the X.25 interface support. TCP/IP packets are encapsulated into X.25 packets and are transferred over X.25 switched virtual circuits (SVCs), as described in RFC 877.
NetBIOS Kit	$110	Provides the run time for NetBIOS over TCP/IP.

Table 18-1. TCP/IP for OS/2 Packaging. (Continued)

Kit	List Price	Function
Programmer's Toolkit	$550	Provides the 32-bit APIs and headers for the sockets, Sun RPC, FTP API, NCS, Kerberos, and SNMP DPI functions.
Applications Kit	$175	Provides all the TCP/IP apps without the protocol stack. It allows you to use other vendor stacks (they must be socket-based) with those functions.
Total Kit	$722	Provides a bundled package that includes the Base, NFS, X Window Server, and Extended Networking kits. These are the most often used functions in TCP/IP for OS/2.

Chapter 19

Communications Manager/2: The SNA Connection

APPN tops TCP/IP with a more robust architecture, a richer API, better net management, and tighter integration with SNA.

— *Norman Friedman (February, 1993)[1]*

This chapter introduces Communications Manager/2, an OS/2 product from IBM that includes an SNA communications stack, APPN routing and naming services, CPI-C and APPC interfaces, and many services for communicating with mainframes. We provide a "bird's eye view" of the product, which is enough to introduce you to the awesome amount of communication power that is made available to your client/server applications. It may be hard to believe, but this is a minimum size "architectural overview" that goes one step beyond the marketing literature.

---

1 Source: Norman Friedman, "APPN Rises to the Enterprise Architecture Challenge," **Data Communications** (February, 1993). Norm Friedman is the VP of Engineering at System Strategies Inc.

COMMUNICATIONS MANAGER: OVERVIEW

Communications Manager/2 provides an *all-in-one* subsystem for communicating with almost everything in the mainframe world. The intent was to provide a fully integrated and tested product that provides a "superset" of communications functions. These functions can then be *scaled downwards* to meet a particular machine's communications needs.

"All-In-One" Communications

The Communications Manager/2 supports a variety of communication protocols and communication hardware that can all run concurrently on the same machine. The product consists of modular building blocks with well-defined Application Programming Interfaces (APIs) to many of the popular protocols. The APIs are reentrant, meaning that they can be used simultaneously by more than one user. The support of concurrent communications and the reentrant APIs are a marked improvement over comparable protocols in the MS-DOS environment. In addition, network management support is built into all the elements of Communications Manager, providing another major improvement over similar MS-DOS packages.

The packaging of Communications Manager/2 as a single subsystem ensures that the constituent subcomponents will not interfere with one another, as was so common in the MS-DOS environment. The single package also offers a single user interface for installation, configuration, network management, and common services. From this interface, you can start or stop a communication service, send and receive files, display status and messages, remap your keyboard, and look at traces and alert messages for problem determination.

THE LAYERED VIEW

One glance at Figure 19-1 should help convince you that Communications Manager makes available a kaleidoscope of APIs. These APIs sit on top of layers of communication protocols and services. Each layer builds on top of the services provided by the layers below it. The APIs allow you to tap into the system at selective interfaces. To understand the layers of Communications Manager, we will start at the bottom of Figure 19-1 and work our way upwards.

The lowest layer of software belongs to the device drivers that provide an interface to several types of communication hardware adapters. NTS/2 and the OS/2 kernel sit on top of the device drivers. On top of that are several layers of protocol functions implemented as Dynamic Link Libraries (DLLs). The DLLs provide protocol stacks for SNA, asynchronous communications, and X.25. The functions

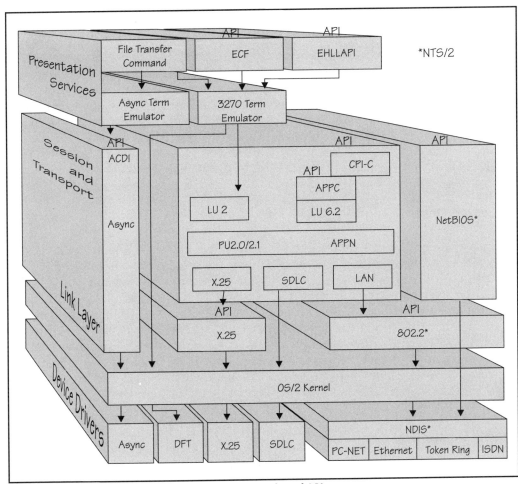

Figure 19-1. Communications Manager/2 and NTS/2: Stacks and APIs.

provided by some of the protocol stacks are roughly equivalent to the OSI Link, Network, Transport, Session, and to some degree Presentation layers. Some of the protocol stacks are far more complete than others; X.25, for example, only partially covers the OSI Physical, Link, and Network layers, while SNA covers all the OSI layers.

The terminal emulators provide user level presentation services that allow you to run your OS/2 machine as a dumb terminal attached to a multiuser host. The screen-driven common services enable you to interactively manage the communications environment. The network management functions that are necessary to monitor and control a communication network are present in all the layers.

Connectivity Options

The first requirement of a communications subsystem is to be able to physically link up with other machines. This rudimentary linkup, or *connectivity*, is the prerequisite for all communications; it forms the platform on which more meaningful forms of information exchange are constructed. Communications Manager provides connectivity through its device drivers and the NTS/2 link layer protocols shown at the bottom of Figure 19-1. The large selection of connectivity options provided by Communications Manager can be divided into three categories: LAN attachment, remote connectivity, and direct attachment to IBM mainframes.

LAN Attachments

LAN attachments provide high-speed local connectivity over a shared LAN cable that serves as the broadcast medium. The media access link layer, which is built into the hardware, arbitrates the access to the cable and allows packets of information to be exchanged reliably over the medium. The Communications Manager depends on the NDIS layer for its LAN support. This means NTS/2 must be installed on the machine; Communications Manager V1.1, shipped in November 1993, now bundles NTS/2. NDIS allows multiple protocol stacks to access the same adapter. NDIS is a standard interface, so fewer drivers need to be installed and maintained. All the OS/2 LAN adapters and protocol stacks, including NetWare, now support NDIS and can share LAN adapters with Communications Manager/2.

Remote Connectivity

The remote connectivity options enable your machine to communicate with the world-at-large. Communications Manager supports remote connectivity over telephone lines through public or private networks using a variety of link protocols, including Asynchronous (ASYNC), Synchronous Data Link Control (SDLC), Integrated Services Digital Network (ISDN) digital telephones, and CCITT's X.25 standard for packet switching. Figure 19-2 shows the various options provided by Communication Manager for programs to "reach out and talk" to other programs over long-distance carriers.

The term *DTE* stands for Data Terminal Equipment in telephony jargon. The DTE is your OS/2 machine, including the adapter hardware. The DTE connects to the Data Communications Equipment (or *DCE*), which provides the long-distance connectivity service through communication carriers.[2] The DCE consists of the

---

[2] This "telephony jargon" use of the term DCE should not be confused with the OSF's Distributed Communications Environment (also called DCE).

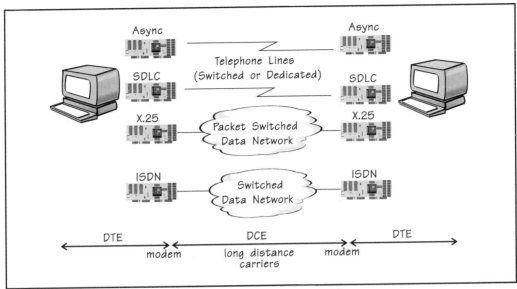

Figure 19-2. Reaching Out Long Distance the Communications Manager Way.

modem and the carrier facilities. ASYNC adapters require asynchronous modems. SDLC and X.25 require synchronous modems, and ISDN requires the ISDN Coprocessor/2 Model 2 adapter (or an NDIS-compliant equivalent). The long-distance carrier may be your ordinary telephone service (switched lines), a dedicated leased line (where speed, connection availability, and noise immunity are requirements), a modem-less ISDN high-speed digital telephone line, or an X.25 Packet Switched Data Network (PSDN). Communications Manager V 1.1 now supports *ISDN Data Link Control (IDLC)*, the native ISDN link layer protocol (this eliminates the need for protocol converters).

ISDN: The LAN's Outer Network

ISDN is a digital telephony technology that supports the high-speed transfer of voice and data over digital telephone lines. Communications Manager/2 supports the more prevalent *Basic Rate Interface (BRI)*, also known as *2B + D*.

Communications Manager/2 allows NDIS-compliant upper-layer stacks—such as NetBIOS, SNA, 802.2, and X.25—to communicate over switched ISDN links. Programmers can write to the APIs provided by these protocols after an ISDN telephone connection is first established. The connection could be done with a REXX command to an IBM-supplied dial utility (CMCALL and CMANSWER). You could also require users to manually place the call, using a PM-based applet, before they start your program. To fully control the telephone connection from within your programs, you must use the **ISDN Connection Manager Interface (CMI) API**.

The CMI API lets you activate a call, obtain status, and accept or refuse incoming calls. *Remember, we're only dealing with the telephone call here.* The real data is passed using peer-to-peer protocols such as NetBIOS, CPI-C, or APPC.

PSDN: The Packet Switched Connection

*PSDN*s provide reliable long-distance service over a shared network of connected computers, as well as an alternative to networks made up of lines dedicated to pairs of users. Packet switching technology allows multiple users to use the same network paths by breaking the information transmitted into intelligent packets that are routed through a network and re-assembled at the destination. PSDNs create permanent or switched virtual circuits between network subscribers and offer various ways of paying for network bandwidth, including schemes where you can literally *pay by the packet*. The term "virtual" in the X.25 context means that you can have multiple logical connections (virtual circuits) over a single physical link. Communications Manager supports up to 128 virtual circuits that can be used concurrently by up to 40 X.25 applications. To use a PSDN, you connect your equipment (the DTE) to the network through the modem (DCE), as shown in Figure 19-2. The X.25 driver works with up to eight concurrent Micro Channel IBM X.25 Coprocessor/2 adapters, which provide bit-synchronous attachment to the Modem.

Direct Attachment to IBM Mainframes

Direct attachment to IBM mainframes is another form of connectivity that is supported by Communications Manager. In fact, Communications Manager transforms a PC into a "great communicator" in the world of IBM host networks. This transformation is accomplished by supporting the old terminal networks as well as the new *peer-to-peer* host/PC connectivity strategies, which are typically LAN-based.

A PC can attach directly through point-to-point coax cable to System/370 terminal controllers (the 3174, 3274, 3X74 series) and the 9370 workstation controller. This type of attachment is called *Distributed Function Terminal (DFT)*. Most IBM customer shops have miles of coax cables on their premises. DFT support can help leverage some of that coax base. The new 3174 Peer Communications network, also known as *LAN over coax*, provides peer-to-peer communications for PCs attached to a 3174 Control Unit using existing coax cable or telephone twisted pair wire. This network allows PCs to communicate with other PCs using APPC, IEEE 802.2, or NetBIOS. It requires the LAN over Coax driver running in the OS/2 workstation and the 3174 Peer Communication Program running in the 3174 Control Unit.

PCs can now be connected to most IBM hosts and their front-end processors (the 37XX series) through Token Ring and Ethernet LANs, ASYNC, SDLC, and X.25.

Upper-Layer Protocol Support

It takes more than link-layer connectivity for two entities to communicate. Additional layers of protocol are required on top of the link. An upper-layer protocol should provide reliable end-to-end service across multiple networks, logical names for network entities, session-based rules of exchange, and common data structures for the representation of information that gets exchanged over a network—including protocols for mail, documents, folders, and images. We could also include common network services such as file transfers, terminal emulation, network management, network authentication and security, network directory services, network time, and electronic mail. Communications Manager supports the SNA and X.25 protocol stacks over the connectivity links that were described. Each protocol stack opens up a communication universe in which your programs can participate.

System Network Architecture (SNA)

Communications Manager/2 implements IBM's System Network Architecture (SNA) in both its old and new forms. The *old SNA* is a hierarchical terminal controller network. This is a network in which hosts reside at the center of the universe and are surrounded by dumb terminals. All the processing power in the network resides at the top of the hierarchy in mainframes running VTAM (in SNA parlance a Physical Unit 5 or PU 5 node). Mainframes are front ended by communication controllers running the NCP program (a PU 4 node), which in turn is front ended by terminal cluster controllers (PU 2 nodes). Terminals talk to the host through terminal controllers. Communications Manager allows the PC to look like a dumb terminal (a Logical Unit type 2 or LU 2 in SNA terminology). A logical unit type describes the characteristics of an SNA session. In an LU 2 session, the entire application runs in the host. The PC can attach to hosts by looking like a terminal through a coax cable or Token Ring. Another option is to have the PC look like a terminal combined with a terminal controller (a PU 2 node) and talk to the host using SDLC.

The New SNA: APPC, APPN, and CPI-C

The *new SNA* is a network of peers, where PC programs can talk to the host programs at a program-to-program level through the use of well-defined *verb* commands (this type of session is called an LU 6.2 type in SNA terminology). Physically, the PCs are endowed with local intelligence to provide parallel session initiation services without VTAM host involvement. A node with those attributes is an SNA PU 2.1 node.

APPN

IBM is evolving SNA into a true distributed operating system that supports cross network directory services, transparent network access to resources (such as servers, applications, displays, printers, and data), common data streams, and integrated network management. *Advanced Peer-to-Peer Network* (or *APPN)* is the network infrastructure responsible for this "true distribution." APPN creates an SNA internet without the mainframe-centric hierarchy of traditional SNA configurations. The mainframe is just another node on the internet. APPN allows LU 6.2 SNA applications, using APPC or CPI-C APIs, to take full advantage of peer networks. It also greatly simplifies SNA configuration, provides better availability through dynamic routing, makes it easier to maintain SNA networks, and meets the flexibility requirements of modern networks.

Communications Manager/2 provides a very complete APPN implementation. It allows OS/2 PCs configured as *Network Nodes (NN)* to act as smart routers that know how to reach any other node on the SNA internet using the best route for a particular class of service. Intermediate routing is supported for nodes that are not on the same physical network. This means that an SNA session can traverse one or more intermediate nodes (these are called mesh networks). The Network Nodes (NNs) know how to reroute traffic if part of the network is down. For example, the Network Node in Chicago (see Figure 19-3) will get to Montreal via Hong Kong if the direct route is down. APPN automatically stores information about all its NNs and their links in a topology database that is replicated on each NN (see next box for details).

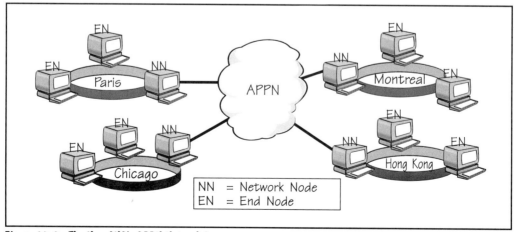

Figure 19-3. The New SNA's APPN Network Layer.

With APPN, an application needs to know its partner's LU name, but not the location. APPN provides a dynamic directory service that discovers, through message exchanges, the destination address and the best routes for getting there (see the following Soapbox). Previously, this information had to be configured manually, a real nightmare. APPN almost makes it a snap to add a new workstation to an SNA network. Programs are not affected any more when machines are moved or when a network adapter's physical address changes.

APPN's Discovery Services

With APPN, no definition of the partner addresses or network routes is required. Each NN keeps a copy of the NN topology (all the NNs in the internet) that it automatically discovers. And each NN is responsible for maintaining a directory of local network nodes. The NNs are part of a distributed network directory (see Figure 19-4).

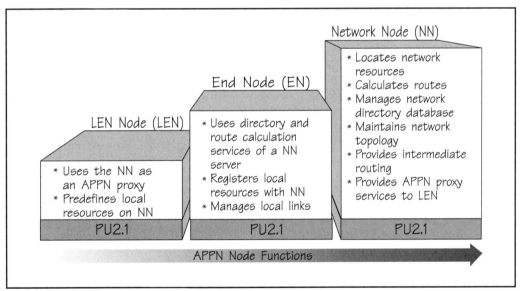

Figure 19-4. APPN Provides a Hierarchy of Network Services on Top of PU 2.1.

APPN **Low Entry Nodes (LENs)** and **End Nodes (ENs)** are clients that use the NN's services to locate partners on the network. An EN is a well-endowed client node that can exchange control messages with an NN. An EN issues a control message to register itself with the NN when it first comes up. It also issues control messages to the NN asking it to locate a remote node. The NN uses those messages to create and maintain a directory of ENs. ENs also maintain a limited directory of local LUs and adjacent LUs. OS/2's Communications Manager provides both EN and NN services. Each NN server can have 100 or more ENs attached to it.

LENs are minimalist clients not endowed with the smarts to dynamically participate in the network by automatically exchanging control messages with NNs. Instead, LENs are manually configured in the NN's database. A LEN is also manually configured with the address of the NN that acts as its proxy on the network. This offloading of function (to the NN) helps the LEN stay skinny, but it creates more work for the network administrator. A LEN node cannot communicate with another node without the presence of an NN on the network. Network Services/DOS is an example of a LEN-only product.

LENs, ENs, and NNs all build on top of PU 2.1's services. They provide the invisible glue that lets an LU discover its partner across an internet when an LU-to-LU session is created. Mercifully, all this dynamic network activity is transparent. We simply issue the verbs that create a session between two named LUs and let the network do all the behind-the-scenes work (see following Soapbox for more information on APPN).

APPN Versus TCP/IP

Soapbox

*I*t is estimated that 65% of today's host-resident, SNA based, mission-critical applications will still be around for another ten to fifteen years.

— Anura Gurugé
August, 1993

The "old SNA is dead...long live the new SNA." But why does the world need a reincarnation of SNA in the form of APPN? Why not simply declare TCP/IP the heir to SNA and go on from there? Indeed, TCP/IP is in the lead as the premier enterprise network. Even IBM fully supports TCP/IP on all its platforms. So why should anybody bother with APPN?

Put simply, APPN provides an excellent migration path from today's SNA networks. In addition, it is a technically superior platform that was designed from the ground up as a *robust* end-to-end enterprise network protocol. APPN has what it takes to support mission-critical applications in distributed LAN environments.

APPN provides a *very scalable* architecture that can start with very small groups and service an enterprise consisting of tens of thousands of nodes. For example, APPN's addresses are alphanumeric, so APPN supports billions of addresses. In contrast, TCP/IP is numeric only. APPN subnets support upward of 10,000 nodes. In contrast, TCP/IP subnets have a 256-node limit. APPN's routing approach is more efficient than TCP/IP's because of its sophisticated *flow-reduction* techniques that conserve the number of discovery packets sent across networks and filter the broadcast of error messages after general failures.

APPN's directory services work with its routing services to create a 17-bit *route label* that gets inserted into every packet. In contrast, TCP/IP creates a great deal of overhead because every packet carries the 32-bit source and 32-bit destination addresses. The APPN directories provide sophisticated hierarchical caching trees that greatly limit broadcast searches. In contrast, TCP/IP's DNS only provides rudimentary caching. APPN's class-of-service routing helps get urgent packets to their destination faster; TCP/IP has the potential to do that, but IP routers support very limited class-of-service criteria.

APPN has better resilience and more "bounce back" characteristics than IP over LAN/WAN internets. According to Anura Gurugé, significant network failures in a modern SNA network may only occur four to five times a year. In stark contrast, a typical TCP/IP bridge/router network may expect to experience a catastrophic failure every month on the average. It seems IBM learned its lesson the hard way by supporting 50,000 SNA production networks.

APPN distributes management and administration to every node on the network and does not require a centralized repository of information. APPN's system management is based on OSI's CMIP protocol (and NetView) and can be centralized or distributed depending on the managing platform's implementation. APPN nodes can be organized into a flexible system of focal points and end points for management information. The entry points forward management events—including statistics, alerts, and events—to focal points. In essence, APPN provides a hierarchy of managers. In contrast, TCP/IP's SNMP is *simpler* but rudimentary, when compared with the CMIP and the APPN management services (SNMP2 removes some of these limitations).

In summary, APPN was developed from scratch as a modern backbone network. It provides the technology that supports today's LANs and tomorrow's multigigabit/s ATM switches. IBM implemented APPN on all its platforms and hopes that by licensing the APPN specification it will transform it from a proprietary protocol to one that enables other vendors to connect to SNA applications (many key vendors support APPN).

If you're in the market for an evolutionary replacement of your SNA networks with great technology base that meets future needs, APPN may be your answer. On the other hand, TCP/IP is winning the popularity contest and has the backing of all major vendors. It's a tough call to make, but client/server means freedom of choice. ❏

X.25

X.25 is an international standard that defines how to connect computers to either public or private packet switching data networks (PSDNs). X.25 support is provided by IBM to primarily extend SNA communications across packet-switched networks and to communicate with equipment from other vendors. X.25 is an SAA supported protocol that provides an alternative network service to SNA's VTAM/NCP. There are no indications, however, that X.25 will replace SNA's VTAM/NCP backbone networks.

Terminal Emulation and File Transfers

The Communications Manager includes the following terminal emulation programs:

- IBM 3270/5250 terminal emulation
- IBM 3101 and DEC VT100 terminal emulation

IBM 3270/5250 Terminal Emulation

IBM 3270/5250 is a "converged" terminal emulator. It provides the same user interface "look and feel" for 3270 (S/370) terminal emulation and the 5250 (AS/400). There is a separate PM window for each terminal emulation session. The total number of active display sessions is 16 for 3270 terminal emulation and 15 for the 5250. You can start and stop sessions, and you can move the session windows using the Presentation Manager controls. Multiple sessions can be viewed simultaneously on the screen, and PM functions—such as mark, cut, paste, and copy—can be used to transfer simple text or bitmaps between windows.

In addition to terminal emulation, an active 3270 session can be used to move files to and from an IBM/370 host on which the 3270-PC file transfer program (IND$FILE) is installed. File transfer to and from IBM hosts running MVS/TSO, VM/CMS, or CICS is supported over any active 3270 session. You can initiate a file transfer from the OS/2 command line with the SEND or RECEIVE command.

IBM 3101 and DEC VT100 Terminal Emulation

The IBM 3101 and DEC VT100 terminal emulation options provide interactive access to hosts that support ASCII terminals via an asynchronous link. Multiple ASCII terminal emulations may be configured, but only one may be active at any time. With the asynchronous services, a user can access a range of data services such as Dow Jones News, CompuServe, MCI Mail, and Prodigy. Three types of file transfers are supported over an asynchronous link:

- With an IBM host (VM/CMS or MVS/TSO) using the 3270-PC File Transfer Program (IND$FILE). ALMCOPY, a superfast multifile transfer program, is provided on an "as is" basis.

- With any host that supports the XMODEM file transfer protocol.

- With any partner that supports a simple Send ASCII Text File function. This works well with systems like MCI Mail.

SNA Gateway

The SNA Gateway is a non-dedicated server PC, which provides its clients a shared link to an IBM System/370 host. Each client workstation thinks it is directly connected to the host, while the host thinks it is communicating with a single terminal controller. The gateway uses a single host communication link to get data from the host and route it to the appropriate workstation. In the other direction, it accepts data from workstations, appends the appropriate control headers, and routes the data to the host. The gateway code emulates the SNA cluster controller 3X74 family. The gateway PC appears to the host as a single PU 2 in SNA terminology.

Up to 254 client PCs can be configured on a LAN supported by the SNA gateway. Clients can have several active host sessions provided that the total number of sessions does not exceed 254. The gateway can transparently extend a 3270 emulation (LU 2) or an APPC (LU6.2) session. The gateway must be linked to the host via SDLC, X.25, or Token Ring. The clients may attach to the gateway via Token Ring, PC Network, Ethernet, SDLC switched links, or X.25 networks. Figure 19-5 shows some of the connectivity options the gateway makes available to workstations. In addition to OS/2 clients, the gateway can support DOS clients running any of the following programs: 3270 Emulation Program Version 3.0, 3270 Workstation Program, and APPC/PC.

PROGRAMMING INTERFACES (APIS)

In this section we describe the programming interfaces Communications Manager/2 brings to the C programmer. Communications Manager/2 makes its whole repertoire of network services and protocols available to the C programmer through API sets. Each of the API sets has a specific purpose, so you can create programs that communicate with many host and PC environments across LANs, WANs, and

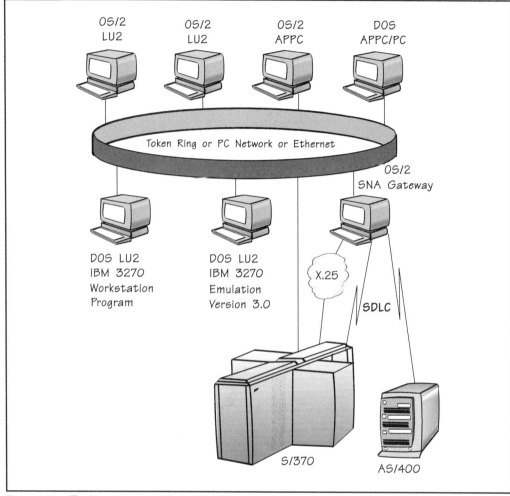

Figure 19-5. The Communications Manager/2 SNA Gateway.

telephone lines. The APIs are accessible from C applications running concurrently under OS/2 user sessions or within the windows of a Presentation Manager session.

Communication API Types

The Communications Manager provides several sets of protocol APIs in addition to an API set to obtain common services. The protocol APIs can be classified into three categories:

■ **Peer-to-Peer APIs** are used to create both cooperative and client/server applications. Any computer can initiate a conversation with any other computer. The protocol tends to be quite symmetric and is sometimes called "program-to-program." The peer-to-peer APIs fall into two categories:

◆ Higher-level APIs that mask the communications and provide associations between two logical programs. The APIs that fall into this category include CPI-C and APPC.

◆ Lower-level APIs that do not quite mask the communications and require that you get more involved with the mechanics of networking, message buffer allocation, session management, and sometimes the direct control of the communication adapter. Protocols that fall into this category include Asynchronous Communications Device Interface (ACDI) and X.25. Both ACDI and X.25 are interface protocols, as opposed to end-to-end protocols. This means that a portion of the API has only local significance and is involved with interfacing to the communications equipment, as opposed to the remote partner.

■ **Client/Server APIs** are used for the remote invocation of services. Communications Manager provides an API for remote host services through the Server-Requester Programming Interface (SRPI), which makes it easier for a PC to share resources on S/370 hosts.

■ **Emulation service APIs** are used to automate and simplify the interaction between a PC user and a terminal-based mainframe application. Unlike the more modern application-to-application protocols (like APPC and CPI-C), emulation service APIs do not require any changes to the numerous mainframe programs designed to work with terminals. APPC, on the other hand, is a more general protocol that provides communications among cooperating programs, but it requires writing new software on the mainframe. Communications Manager supports the Emulator High-Level Language Application Interface (EHLLAPI).

The Communications Manager APIs

In this section, we provide a brief overview of the more important Communication Manager/2 APIs. Refer back to Figure 19-1 on page 329 to understand the underlying protocol stacks on which the APIs build their services.

APPC

Using APPC, an OS/2 program can converse through one of SNA's 50,000 installed networks with peers located anywhere in the world. These peers can run on PCs, RS/6000s, AS/400s, S/38s, and S/370s, as well as on many non-IBM host platforms.

APPC is IBM's architected solution for program-to-program communication, distributed transaction processing, and remote database access across the entire IBM product line. The new Communications Manager V1.1 now supports full-duplex logical conversations over APPC.

Common Programming Interface-Communications (CPI-C)

CPI-C, SAA's official *Common Programming Interface for Communications*, builds on top of APPC and masks its complexities and irregularities. Every product that supports APPC has a slightly different API. CPI-C fixes that problem. Writing to the CPI-C API allows you to port your programs to other SAA platforms such as S/370 and AS/400. Networking Services/DOS (NS/DOS) provides CPI-C/APPC for DOS and Windows using less than 140 KBytes of memory.

Server-Requester Programming Interface (SRPI)

SRPI provides an API that allows an OS/2 client application to request host services through an active 3270 session (LU 2) with a System/370 host server running VM/CMS or MVS/TSO. The calling application first specifies a server name, a function ID, request parameters, and data, and then issues a SEND_REQUEST API call. Communications Manager ensures that the request is routed to the appropriate 3270 session according to the profile you configured. You must also log on to the appropriate 3270 session and start the host router programs (CMSSERV and/or MVSSERV) before using SRPI. Multiple applications can use SRPI concurrently; however, each 3270 session can handle only one call at a time. Calls are queued if a session is busy; however, if SRPI is active, you cannot use the session for interactive work or file transfers.

SRPI's limitation is that it uses 3270 terminal emulation instead of a peer-to-peer protocol such as APPC. Terminal emulation is a very clumsy protocol in unattended client/server environments (that do not have a human sitting at a terminal). The reason for this clumsiness is that your application has to anticipate all the hung-terminal conditions and recover from them without human intervention. IBM made a statement of direction that SRPI will eventually run on APPC. When this happens, SRPI will become a useful client/server protocol for requesting mainframe services (SRPI's design is protocol independent).

Asynchronous Communications Device Interface (ACDI)

The Asynchronous Communications Device Interface (ACDI) provides a low-level programming interface to asynchronous serial ports. ACDI can perform concurrent communications over multiple serial ports, although only one application at a time can use a particular port. However, if an application is waiting for a call-in or call-back, ACDI will give control of that port to another waiting application.

ACDI supports modem commands including AutoDial and AutoAnswer, which you can use to customize and automate dialing procedures such as redialing a busy number. ACDI provides device-independent services for setting line parameters and for device connection control. For example, ACDI allows you to set and read the following parameters: bit rate, word length, flow control, parity, time-outs, stop bits, modem command strings, and AutoAnswer controls. An application can send and receive data through a buffered (block I/O) interface.

ACDI provides a useful LAN redirection feature. Instead of attaching modems to every PC, the ACDI redirection API allows a LAN-attached client machine to use serial ports COM1, COM2, and COM3 on a server as if they were located on the local machine. The *async gateway server* is a non-dedicated PC that provides serial ports, modems, and telephone line connection services to its clients. In addition, the server machine must run IBM's **LAN Asynchronous Connection Server (LANACS)** program. The ACDI redirector communicates with the LANACS server using NetBIOS.

The main benefit of ACDI is that it makes it easy to develop an asynchronous communications program without requiring detailed knowledge of the hardware, device drivers, or the multitasking environment. An ACDI application should work without requiring modification if the hardware or device drivers are changed.

ACDI's main weakness is that it does not provide a reliable session service, such as that provided by NetBIOS, APPC, and 802.2. You will have to code your own packet sequencing and control protocol if you need such a service. However, ACDI does provide some limited error-detection services. It can detect the following error conditions: parity errors, framing errors, overflow and overrun errors, device errors, and line errors.

X.25

X.25's API service provides a low-level interface to packet-switched networks. Much of the X.25 service is concerned with interfacing the local data communication equipment to the packet switched network. Through the API service, you request a virtual circuit and, from then on, you can send and receive information on your virtual circuit. The virtual circuit can be permanent or switched. X.25 allows you to multiplex virtual circuits over the same communication interface (Communications Manager limits you to 128 virtual circuits; the X.25 standard supports 4095). The virtual circuits provide a reliable end-to-end service. Communications Manager allows up to forty X.25 applications to run concurrently. Incoming calls are routed to the appropriate X.25 application. X.25 provides two facilities for recovering from errors: reset and restart. Reset is used to reinitialize a virtual circuit (the sequence counts are reset). Restart causes all virtual circuits to be cleared.

Communications Manager's implementation of X.25 conforms to CCITT's 1980 and 1984 recommendations. Two complementary types of X.25 are provided by Communication Manager:

- *For SNA applications*, the Qualified Link Level Control (QLLC) allows up to 128 SNA switched or virtual circuits. A virtual circuit has a maximum bandwidth of 64 Kb/s. SNA applications such as APPC, 3270 terminal emulation, SRPI, and EHLLAPI may use X.25 through the SNA QLLC protocol to communicate with other SNA remote applications.

- *For non-SNA applications*, the API can be used to support multiple concurrent applications across X.25 virtual network sessions. The X.25 API provides verbs that enable an application to interact with a PSDN. Functions are provided to make and receive calls, allocate and clear virtual circuits, transfer data, and reset the virtual circuit.

Both the SNA and non-SNA applications require, and may share, the same IBM X.25 Interface Co-Processor/2 adapter (the C2X adapter card) to attach to one or more X.25 packet-switched networks. The C2X outboard adapter code is loaded onto the co-processor when X.25 is started as a Communications Manager task. The X.25 DLL can control and manage multiple adapter cards, and it routes incoming calls to the target programs and outgoing calls to the appropriate X.25 virtual circuit.

EHLLAPI

EHLLAPI (pronounced "ee-ha-lap-pee") was introduced by IBM in 1986 as a generic API for accessing terminal emulation functions. EHLLAPI is mainly used by PCs to communicate with existing mainframe applications without altering the code on the mainframe side. It is a cost-effective way to extend the capabilities and lifetimes of the huge inventory of existing IBM 3270 applications. EHLLAPI was designed to be terminal emulator independent. The Communications Manager implementation of EHLLAPI works with 3270 terminal emulators for S/370 mainframes and with 5250 terminal emulators for AS/400 minicomputers. Prior to EHLLAPI, programs had to be tediously written in assembler to manipulate the host data streams. And a program written for a particular terminal emulator would not work with another terminal emulator.

Generally speaking, EHLLAPI applications are not difficult to develop. The API consists of over 30 function calls that handle an assortment of terminal operator functions, from simple, automatic host logon to the complexities of starting and monitoring an unattended host task. Developers can create OS/2 applications to take on tasks formerly performed by a human operator, such as sending keystrokes to the host or capturing information from a 3270 or 5250 "screen."

FYI

The Quick Guide to EHLLAPI

Briefing

When writing an EHLLAPI program, you should think of yourself as an operator interacting with a host through a 3270 or 5250 terminal emulation session. Your program should be able to automate tasks performed by an operator, such as sending keystrokes to the host, requesting host update information, and copying to and from a screen. EHLLAPI API provides calls that perform these functions. You should be able to write applications that automate console operations, filter host messages, and monitor host response time and availability. You can use EHLLAPI to customize PC screens to display only certain fields from a host screen, or you can make a single screen from many screens. You can also run multiple host sessions and display the results on a single composite screen. The data received from the host by EHLLAPI is in the PC memory and is not necessarily displayed on the screen. The EHLLAPI API verbs can be categorized as follows:

- **Operator Services** provide you with controls such as query the system and session status, set session parameters, send_key, wait, pause, reset system, query host update, and start/stop host notification.

- **Presentation Services** allow you to manipulate a block of memory on the PC (the *presentation space*), which represents what the host displays on a terminal screen. It is up to your application to display any, all, or none of the received data. You can use the presentation services to query and set the cursor location, query field attributes, position, and length. You can copy field contents or the presentation space to/from a string. You can search fields or the entire presentation space for string matches or updates.

- **Device Services** allow you to intercept key strokes and to reserve or release a device.

- **Communication Services** allow you to send and receive files.

You should consider EHLLAPI as a useful tool that allows you to work with existing host applications. It is by no means a reliable peer-to-peer protocol that could be used by serious cooperative or client/server applications. ❏

NETWORK MANAGEMENT

Network Management features are built into all the levels of Communication Manager (see Figure 19-6). Errors are detected, logged, and can be forwarded as network alerts to an IBM host running NetView or to a PC-based LAN NetView managing station. NetView allows a network to be remotely managed from a central location and provides tools that allow an operator to stay current on error conditions and monitor network performance. Communications Manager supports the TRANSFER_MS_DATA API call that allows an application to send its own alerts and messages to NetView. Hardware-related errors from SDLC, ASYNC, IBM Token Ring, PC Network, Ethernet, and the X.25 co-processor can be recorded in a local error log and also sent to NetView as a generic alert if a host connection is provided. The generic alert contains information about the type of error detected, probable causes of failure, and recommended action.

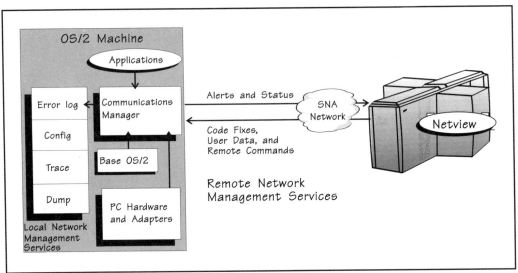

Figure 19-6. Communications Manager/2 Network Management Facilities.

The Communications Manager also supports the receipt of remote commands from Netview. The commands are passed to the program that requests them. For example, a command may be sent to run remote diagnostics on a device and to send back the results to Netview. Netview can also query vital PC data such as machine type, model number, and the name, version, and release of the installed software. The **Service Point Application Router (SPA Router)** is the Communications Manager component that receives commands from a NetView Host and routes them to the appropriate application (any OS/2 program on that machine). The router allows the same command to be broadcast to multiple applications.

A companion process, the **Remote Operations Service (ROP)**, receives OS/2 requests from the SPA Router and executes them on the local OS/2 machine. Currently, ROP executes any OS/2 Command Line Interface program that does not require user input.

The Communications Manager also provides local utilities for problem determination, running traces of the flow of commands and data across interfaces, and displaying and printing error information. The utilities can be run under program control, allowing user-written programs to monitor error incidents selectively and then to take appropriate action. Message pop-ups on the screen can be suppressed making it easy to run unattended diagnostics. Communications Manager V1.1 now includes a *Response Time Monitor (RTM)* that measures response times on terminal emulation sessions. The data can be forwarded to NetView for analysis.

Common Services API

The Common Services API provides general services that can be used with any of the communication APIs. You can use Common Services to gather, process, and send problem determination data. For example, you can use the CONVERT API verb to translate a character string from/to ASCII and EBCDIC. The DEFINE_TRACE verb turns on or off the Communications Manager trace. The LOG_MESSAGE verb allows you to append a message to the Communications Manager's system log file; this message can be displayed through the message services. The TRANSFER_MS_DATA verb allows you to send alerts to a System/370 host running NetView or you could have the alert stored in the Communications Manager error log for local display.

Communications Manager/2 Packaging

The Communications Manager/2 product comes in two flavors:

- *Communications Manager/2 V1.1*—a single user product that provides all the functions described in this chapter. This product sells for $495.

- *Distributed Feature Workstation*—allows the off-loading of most of the Communications Manager's code to a file server. This lets multiple client machines run from a single copy of the code on the file server. The thin client requests its code and configuration from the server when activated and loads it into memory. A Communications Manager Distributed Feature license sells for $295.

Both products are CID-enabled—you can now install and configure Communications Manager remotely. The automatic hardware discovery feature, the ready-to-run defaults, the graphic configuration packages, and the installation response file templates are all very helpful features. A CD-ROM package is also available.[3]

---

[3] To understand some of the thinking that went into the design of the innovative Client/Server Communications Manager/2, we recommend an excellent article by Julie King and Charles Green, "Extending Application Interfaces for Communications: Client/Server" (**OS/2 Developer**, Spring 1993).

Chapter 20

LAN Server and NetWare: The NOS Classics

Choosing a NOS can seem like part blind luck, part mysticism—just like the feeling when you step into a casino. The NOS newcomer must learn the rules of each network offering and discover which vendor requires the steep ante, which game is most likely to pay off at high odds, and which best suits the situation.

— PC Magazine (October 26, 1993)

OS/2 2.X provides client and server support for three of the industry's classical LAN NOSs: LAN Server, NetWare, and LAN Manager. OS/2 clients can also obtain services from a Vines NOS server, which does not run on OS/2. In this chapter, we cover LAN Server 3.X and NetWare 4.X. You will rarely use both products on the same network because they provide an equivalent set of functions. In the final analysis, choosing a NOS is "part blind luck, part mysticism." The purpose of this chapter is to take some of the mysticism out of the process by telling you what each of these two excellent products can do for you. However, you'll still need the blind luck.

IBM LAN SERVER VERSION 3.0

The IBM LAN Server transforms OS/2 into a full-fledged *Network Operating System (NOS)*, which allows applications to become "networked" without being rewritten. The beauty of a NOS is that it lets you get all this network power through your standard OS/2 commands and APIs. The reach of the OS/2 application programmer is now extended beyond the physical boundaries of a single machine, while the network remains transparent to the application.

LAN Server and LAN Man

The IBM LAN Server is the most widely used OEM variant of Microsoft's LAN Manager, popularly known as *LAN Man*. LAN Man makes the network an integral part of OS/2; it also provides interoperability with MS-NET and PC-LAN worksta- tions running MS-DOS and Windows. LAN Manager/X extends the platform to UNIX System V. LAN Man is also bundled with Windows NT Advanced Server. Windows for Workgroups is a peer-to-peer subset of LAN Man. The IBM LAN Server is fully compatible with LAN Man at the API and functional levels. LAN Server supports LAN Man clients (and vice versa). Both utilize the same security system, and the same applications will run on both platforms. LAN Server 3.0 is a 32-bit version of LAN Man that takes full advantage of OS/2 2.X, making it the fastest PC NOS in the industry (see the following Briefing). LAN Server is IBM's "strategic" network operating system product and is developed independently from Microsoft.

With LAN Server, you can write your own network application services as simple OS/2 programs. Your programs can use OS/2's native Named Pipes protocol to communicate with MS-DOS, MS-Windows, and OS/2 clients; one server can support up to 1000 client workstations. Your programs can also take advantage of all the built-in server features such as network security, audit trails, single domain multi- server management, and fault-tolerance. We explain what this all means later in this section.

IBM's contractual rights to Microsoft's LAN Man code end with the current version of the code. IBM intends to continue to evolve LAN Server toward full interopera- bility with NetWare. In addition, LAN Server will continue to interoperate with its LAN Man siblings. Most importantly, LAN Server will implement the powerful OSF Distributed Computing Environment (DCE) on the OS/2 platform.

NetWare interoperability will be delivered in three phases. The first phase (now) provides client coexistence with NetWare. LAN Server and NetWare clients can use the same adapter at the same time. The second phase (very soon) will provide a single client for both NetWare and LAN Server. That client can access either NetWare or LAN Server services. The third phase will provide the transparent

FYI

Benchmarks: LAN Server Versus NT

Briefing

IBM LAN Server 3.0 outperforms Microsoft Windows NT Advanced Server 3.1 (NTAS) and Microsoft LAN Manager 2.2 using nine popular DOS and Windows business applications...At 100 equivalent users, LAN Server was 45% faster than NTAS and 8% faster than LAN Manager. At 300 equivalent users, LAN Server was 16% faster than LAN Manager. Above 100 equivalent users for NTAS and 200 equivalent users for LAN Manager, nearly half the clients failed to complete the test scripts. LAN Server successfully completed 94% of the test scripts at 400 equivalent users. Overall, IBM LAN Server v3.0 supported up to 4 times the number of users and 2.4 times the peak throughput of Microsoft Windows NT Advanced Server V 3.1. Earlier LANQuest Labs application tests showed LAN Server performance to be equivalent or better than other NOSs. Those earlier tests are not as representative as this series.

— LANQuest Labs, September 1993

Other benchmarking groups have reported results that agree, more or less, with the LANQuest results. For example, in a transfer benchmark reported by **PC Magazine** (October 26, 1993), LAN Server came in a close second after NetWare and outperformed LAN Manager, Vines, and NT Advanced Server. In addition, the National Software Testing Labs, or NSTL (November 1992) ran its representative network applications—Wordperfect 5.1, Lotus 1-2-3, dBase IV, XCOPY, and cc:Mail—and gave LAN Server the highest overall performance score: LAN Server 9.3, LAN Manager 8.1, and NetWare 7.1. ❑

integration of LAN Server and NetWare; both will probably use features of the Distributed Computing Environment (DCE) for interoperability. IBM may even provide the NLM version of DCE for NetWare.

IBM has stated that LAN Server will be its DCE-based enterprise server. Future versions of the product will be portable and platform-independent. LAN Server will be ported to IBM's other SAA and AIX platforms and used to create a heterogeneous network operating system layer. The DCE LAN Server will adhere to open systems standards for network naming (by providing multidomain hierarchies), will implement the DCE Distributed File System, and will provide three-way authentication using Kerberos. It will also support the DCE RPC and adhere to OSF's DME standard for system management. This will become clearer after we explain DCE in the next chapter.

LAN Server is the industry's first NOS to support isochronous multimedia traffic on ordinary LANs. It does that by taking advantage of the priority service on network adapters—Token Ring or Ethernet—and uses it to reserve bandwidth for time-dependent multimedia streams. This means we can store our sound and movie masterpieces on the server and share them with others.

The Network Operating System

The LAN Server is a classic implementation of a client/server architecture. The server machine acts as a *central hub* that fulfills work requests from requesters (i.e., clients) all over the network (see Figure 20-1). The server forms the core of the LAN Server application. At least one machine on the network must run the server function before requesters can perform anything useful. Network Servers can be added to the network to provide more resources, remove bottlenecks, and scale an application upward (or downward). Network devices, programs, and data can be centralized on a single server or distributed on multiple servers as the environment dictates. Your LAN Server machines can be dedicated or they can be running other programs concurrently with the server function. The modular capabilities of LAN Server appear to be limited only by checkbook constraints.

From a programmer's viewpoint, LAN Server offers flexibility and the capability to distribute an application easily. You don't have to learn a communication API. In essence, it transforms OS/2 into a powerful Network Operating System. This

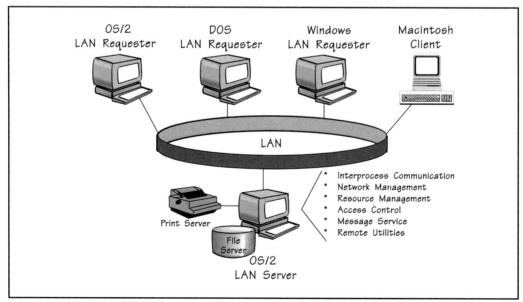

Figure 20-1. The OS/2 LAN Server.

augmented OS/2 opens up a universe of network services. The repertoire of network functions falls into the following categories:

- Transparent access to remote resources
- Network device and queue management
- Remote network applications support
- Single systems image using domains
- Network services
- Network management and administration
- Network security and access controls
- Remote installation using CID
- Peer services
- Remote Named Pipes
- Fault tolerant features
- Multiprocessor support
- Multimedia support
- Open NDIS adapter support
- An open network API

Together these functions provide a very complete Network Operating System. We explain the Network Operating System enhancements in the sections that follow.

Transparent Access to Remote Resources

A client workstation can access the resources of an OS/2 LAN Server workstation as if they were locally attached. The requests are routed from the client workstation to the server by a piece of code called the **LAN Requester**. The LAN Requester makes the physical location of resources (over a network) transparent to an application. Resources that can be shared on a LAN Server include disk directories, disk files, printers and printer queues, serially attached devices and queues, network services, application programs, and Named Pipes. The LAN Requester *redirects* (over the network) API calls for resources that reside on an OS/2 LAN Server; it then passes back the response to the application as if the call were locally serviced.

The LAN Server thus extends OS/2's virtual device support across the network. Practically anything that can be done on a local OS/2 PC can be done remotely and transparently. Basic file sharing is done using logical drives. Users map their own virtual drives to drives and directories on various file servers. Printer sharing is done with virtual printer ports. Users can redirect their serial or parallel printer ports to logical ports on various servers. The network operating system thus extends OS/2 transparently and allows applications written for DOS, Windows 3.x, or OS/2 to become networked without changing a line of code. With **OS/2 LAN**

Server for Macintosh running on an OS/2 LAN Server, DOS, OS/2, and Macintosh clients may access files created by each other. The LAN Server does that by emulating the AppleTalk File and Print server functions over Token Ring or Ethernet.

Network Device and Queue Management

The OS/2 LAN Server allows an application to send its network job to a printer when it is busy. The jobs get queued at the printer and executed in the order received or in the order set by the network administrator. Print jobs can be routed to the first available printer or to a specific printer. Printing can be scheduled for a specific time of day, such as after peak-use hours. Users can be notified of job status with messages. LAN Server also allows you to share character I/O devices such as modems, scanners, and plotters. These devices can be accessed over the network with optional pooling and queuing so that a client will automatically wait for access to the first available device.

Remote Network Application Support

The LAN Server program allows workstations to execute programs that reside on the server. Such programs include standard OS/2 commands, utilities supplied with the LAN Server, or user-supplied programs. You could, for instance, offload compiles, backups, and other processor or disk intensive tasks to the LAN Server machines on the network. The remote program runs on the server with the standard input, output, and error streams redirected back to the requester station that invoked the program. This makes it possible to interactively control a remote program and to receive its output. LAN Server allows you to classify applications as either public or private. *Public* applications can be used by other users in the network; *private* applications are maintained and used solely by the owner of the application. When a user logs on to the network, the OS/2 Workplace Shell network folder is updated automatically with the icons of available network applications (both public and private). The network applications are invoked just like any other application on the Workplace Shell.

Single System Image Using Domains

The LAN Server allows multiple OS/2 LAN Servers to be managed as a single logical system. This capability allows users and administrators to view the network as a single server instead of as a collection of separate resources attached to specific servers. A *domain* consists of the set of servers whose resources are configured as a single logical system. There may be one or more servers in each domain. One server within a domain is designated as the domain controller; this machine provides the view of the OS/2 LAN Server domain to the users. Multiple OS/2 LAN Server domains may coexist on the same LAN. User and machine names can be defined in several domains as long as they maintain unique names. Domain controllers take away some of the headaches associated with managing a growing multiserver LAN. A new user account is added once on the domain controller instead of on each server. The new account automatically becomes available on all servers in the domain. The administrators can control all network resources from a central point. Clients need only one password to access all the resources for which they have permissions within the domain.

Network Services

The bulk of the LAN Server code consists of configurable *services*. These are programs that can be started (installed), stopped (uninstalled), paused, or resumed through LAN Server commands. You can also create your own services by writing programs to a set of simple specifications, which makes it possible to extend the core of LAN Server. You can also individually configure the functional components to provide a certain level of service. Here's a brief description of the standard LAN Server services:

■ The **Workstation Service** enables the redirection of system calls. This service and the operating system work closely together. The redirector packages and passes system calls from the operating system and sends them to a remote server. The server software reissues the call against a local resource, packages the results, and returns them to the redirector. This basic service must be started before any other services can be installed on a client workstation.

■ The **Server Service** handles network requests for disk, printer, and serially attached device services. These primary services can only be provided by servers.

■ The **Message Service** supports the sending and receiving of synchronous messages.

■ The **Netpopup Service** displays received messages as pop-up panels on a user's screen.

■ The **Alerter Service** runs in the server and sends alert notifications to designated users.

■ The ***Netrun Service*** lets a workstation execute a program on a remote server. This service must also be installed on the servers where the programs execute.

■ The ***Remoteboot Service*** runs in the server and supports the remote IPL of MS-DOS, Windows, and OS/2 client machines on all the networks supported by LAN Server. This service is particularly important to users, such as financial institutions, who require diskless PCs. Network administrators can specify through a graphic utility a *Remote Initial Program Load (RIPL)* file information table on the server that describes each diskless workstation's remote-boot requirements. Diskless workstations can have their own individual requirements or the network administrator can specify that multiple machines share the same configuration information.

■ The ***Time Server Service*** allows a domain controller to be designated as the network time server. Clients can then synchronize their time with a designated time server.

■ The ***Replicator Service*** enables a set of files stored on one server to be selectively replicated to other client or server machines. The Replicator service makes it easy to distribute files and programs across the network. It's a great way to propagate new versions of programs and to maintain bulletin boards. A LAN administrator can control the frequency of file replication. For example, the system could be set to replicate at short intervals if the files to be replicated are constantly changing. If the files change infrequently, the system could be set to replicate once a day after everybody goes home.

Other Network services include the network copy and move utilities, as well as extensive online network help.

Network Management and Administration

The administrative and network management facilities of LAN Server are extensive. An administrator can *log on* to LAN Server from any OS/2 requester workstation. A user interface, with context-based help and online hypertext documentation, allows the administrator to control installation and configuration facilities. It also allows the administrator to support daily operations such as Startup, Shutdown, Audit Control, and LAN Usage monitoring. An administrator may browse or update user, group, or resource profiles. The administrator can also manage server print queues, close files, and terminate user sessions. Additionally, the OS/2 LAN Server allows administrators to see at a glance who is using a server, how long they have been connected, what resources they are using, and when they were last active. The new operator rights facility allows an administrator to delegate management capabilities to any user.

In a network environment, it is important to track who has used or misused what resource and when. The LAN Server can capture in an audit trail almost everything that is happening on a network: every file accessed, every attempted access, every connection made, every resource used, every logon and logoff, changes in server states (start, pauses, continued, stopped), and violations in sharing limits or access permission. The network administrator can configure the audit system to only track exceptional events. Audit information may be displayed by the administrator.

Administrators and operators can choose which events are written to the network audit log. For example, to ensure that only pertinent information is captured, an operator can choose to have only failed file-access attempts recorded in the audit log instead of all the file-access attempts.

The LAN Server maintains a set of in-memory statistics that track all network activity. These statistics provide valuable information that help an administrator configure, monitor, and tune the network. LAN Server also provides a disk-based error log that includes comprehensive diagnostic information on errors. A LAN Server can send automatic administrative alert messages to designated users or groups of users when errors that require immediate attention are encountered. Such alerts are generated in case of disk or printer problems—for example, if a printer is out of paper or the server disk is almost full—and when incorrect passwords or excessive error occurrences exceed a threshold. When alerts are sent, all pertinent data is recorded, including the server name, date, and time of the alert. Alerts also provide a description of the problem and the recommended action.

The OS/2 LAN Server provides time-scheduled execution through an **AT** command for automating scheduled functions under time controls. The AT command can run any OS/2 command periodically at a specified date and time. A schedule for periodically executed commands is saved on disk and loaded when the server starts. For example, an AT command may be used to automate a disk backup on a time-scheduled basis.

Network Security: Who Can Do What?

The network security and access controls provided by LAN Server allow practically every aspect of a user's network activity to be defined by the network administrator. The network administrator defines a user's login script and privileges, the files they may use, the resources they may share, the programs they may execute, and the mode in which they perform these activities. Users may belong to groups and are assigned various privilege levels.

The *User Profile Management (UPM)* provides a facility for user and group validation that is common to both the OS/2 LAN Server and the Database Manager. LAN Requester and database clients use the same UPM-defined user and group IDs to control access to resources on a LAN. The passwords for these user IDs are also administered through UPM. A PM interface is provided to help the network administrator maintain all these security features.

OS/2 LAN Server provides two facets of system access controls: logon control and resource protection. A system administrator controls whether a password is required at logon for a specific user and the interval of password expiration. The administrator can specify permitted logon times in weekly intervals and hourly intervals, such as Monday and Friday between 8 a.m. and 5 p.m. A user, by default, can logon from any workstation on the network; however, the administrator can specify one to eight workstations to which a user is restricted.

LAN Server is smart when it comes to passwords. All passwords are doubly encrypted. Passwords are encrypted at the workstation before being sent to the server for validation. LAN Server uses the U.S. Government *Data Encryption Standard (DES)* for encrypted passwords and an equally sophisticated authentication algorithm. The logon dialog is different for every logon attempt. The first time a user enters an incorrect password an *intruder prevention mechanism* is activated to delay password validation for three seconds. This scheme effectively defeats password-finding programs, known as dictionary attacks, that repeatedly try to log on using random passwords.

Resources are controlled by identifying the relationship between the user and the resource. For example, files and directories may be made accessible to a particular user, group of users, or all users. Access authority may be granted to a single user or group of users for a single resource or for a generic resource profile. Access authorities include None, Read, Update, Alter, and Execute. Execute privileges prevent users from copying a program while allowing them to run it. An administrator can specify the maximum number of users who can concurrently execute a program to enforce network license agreements. The category of resources that can be protected using access rights include disk directories, individual files, groups of files (specified with wild cards), application programs, print queues, Named Pipes, and serial device queues.

A local security feature provides file protection for servers that physically reside in public locations (i.e., they're not locked away in a fortress behind barbed wire). A local PC file on a 386 HPFS partition can be protected against unauthorized access. An intruder cannot get around this protection by rebooting the server. The protection is active even if the LAN Server code is not running. Even local applications on the server machine cannot use these protected files without the proper authorization. This local file protection complements other OS/2 local security features. Examples include the power-on password facility, which disables the machines on startup until a proper password is provided; and the *Server Mode* function which automatically disables input at startup but allows the machine to come to full readiness without operator interaction.

Remote Installation Using CID

LAN Server is a showcase for CID installation. Briefly, LAN Server automates the installation of both server and client workstations. It supports *lightly attended install* using NTS/2's pull services, or *unattended install* using NetView Distribution Manager/2's push services. A graphical application helps you install, configure, or remove client or server components on remote nodes (including DOS clients).

Peer Services

Peer services, in theory, allow each workstation to be both a client and a server. But who gets the Pentium with the mirrored disk drive and the Uninterrupted Power Supply (UPS)? What happens when you take your laptop on the road? LAN Server doesn't answer these questions, but its new LAN Requester allows a client workstation to share directories, one printer queue, and one communications-device queue with other LAN Requesters. Yes, you read that right: You don't need the server on the network—a $75 LAN Requester will do fine. So, do we toss away the server? No, because your Requester is limited to a single session. It will only let one client connect at a time to access a shared resource (except for Named Pipes). It's multiuser, but only one user can get in at a time. Is that a problem? Not if you have a small office environment and you don't mind waiting. But what about security, audit trails, fault tolerance, and all the good things we've talked about in this chapter? Most of these features are not included (you currently get what you pay for with peer services).

Remote Named Pipes

Remote Named Pipes extend the OS/2 Interprocess Communication (IPC) mechanism across the network. Named Pipes applications benefit from the network controls provided by LAN Server. For example, access to your server application through a Named Pipe can be controlled by the LAN Server security system so that only specified users can gain access to it. A very important benefit of Named Pipes is that they're part of the base OS/2 interprocess communications service. The Named Pipes interface is identical, regardless of whether the processes are running on an individual machine or distributed across the network.

Fault-Tolerant Features

The LAN Server provides many fault-tolerant features that keep your server running and protect your data (Figure 20-2). This product provides many levels of storage subsystem fault tolerance. At the lowest level, it detects errors that occur while performing hard disk read-and-write operations, and then issues alerts and provides error correction that helps recover and restore data. At the next level, the HPFS file system maps all the defective disk sectors on its hard disks and assigns them "on the fly" to alternate disk sectors. *Disk mirroring* provides the next level of fault tolerance by writing dual copies of the data on separate disk drives. If the primary drive fails, the backup drive takes over and protects against any data loss or interruption of service. *Disk duplexing* extends fault tolerance to the disk drive controller itself. Two disk drive controllers are paired with two hard drives to provide added protection against failure of the controller components.

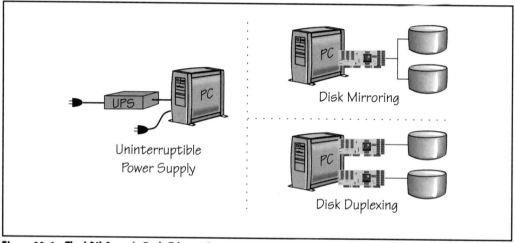

Figure 20-2. The LAN Server's Fault-Tolerant Features.

A complete set of tools is available to help the LAN administrator configure and monitor errors on a server with disk mirroring or disk duplexing. These errors can be monitored and corrected from any workstation on the LAN. For example, a failed mirrored disk can be repaired by the administrator using the FTADMIN PM-based utility.

LAN Server also provides protection against server crashes due to power failures by integrating *Uninterruptible Power Supply (UPS)* support into the product. Depending on the capabilities of the UPS unit, an alert can be sent when the battery first takes over, when battery power gets low, and when server shutdown is about to begin. These alerts can be sent to users, administrators, and to your programs. If power is not restored before the battery runs down, the server flushes its cached data, logs the event, and closes all the open files before shutting down. In the area of communications, LAN Server keeps track of established sessions and rebuilds them automatically if they're lost because of a failure.

Multiprocessor Support

LAN Server can be offloaded to a second processor dedicating the primary processor to the applications. This is an example of *asymmetrical multiprocessing*, and it requires a dual-processor server like the PS/2 Mod 295.

Multimedia Support

LAN Server is the industry's first NOS to support isochronous multimedia traffic on ordinary LANs. It does that by taking advantage of the priority service on network adapters—Token Ring or Ethernet—and uses it to reserve bandwidth for time-dependent multimedia streams. Using the priority service on Token Ring provides nearly 90% bandwidth utilization. LAN Server's multimedia *Resource Reservation Subsystem (RRS)* prioritizes and synchronizes multimedia stream movement on the network with the disk subsystem. RRS detects multimedia data automatically and runs applications unchanged.

For maximum performance, RRS requires an IBM *LAN Streamer* Token Ring card on the server side (see Figure 20-3). The clients can use ordinary 16 Mbit/s adapters. LAN Streamer supports multiple queues, allows direct transfers from the server cache to the adapter memory, and can reserve up to 90% of the network bandwidth for priority multimedia data. Table 20-1 shows the dramatic reductions in discontinuity counts obtained using priorities with 10 multimedia clients sharing a server. IBM is working on technology that can support up to 40 concurrent multimedia sessions on one 80486 server with up to 99% Token Ring bandwidth

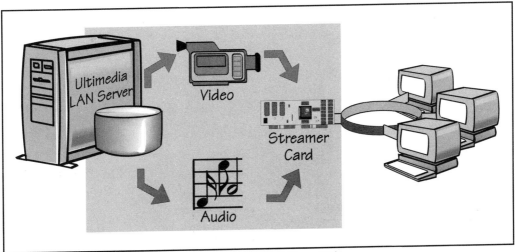

Figure 20-3. LAN Server Ultimedia: Multimedia Services on Ordinary LANs.

utilization. This means we should start thinking about storing our sound and movie masterpieces on the server and share them with others.

Table 20-1. LAN Server Multimedia Performance.

Unreserved Data Frame Size	Without Priority	With Priority
	Discontinuity Counts/5 min	Discontinuity Counts/5 min
2 KBytes	927 to 1397	0
4 KBytes	2684 to 3480	0
8 KBytes	4704 to 5679	0
16 KBytes	6399 to 6777	0

Open NDIS Adapter Support

LAN Server, like TCP/IP and Communications Manager, works with NDIS-compliant LAN adapters and supports up to four LAN adapters per machine. This support means that LAN Server's "Named Pipes over NetBEUI" stack can happily coexist on the same adapter with Communications Manager and TCP/IP stacks. The multiple adapter support allows LAN Server to provide shared services to clients on four logical networks. Remember, the four adapters can be a combination of PC Network, Ethernet, or Token-Ring types. The maximum number of NetBIOS sessions supported is the total available for all adapters installed in the machine (254 x 4 = 1016).

LAN Server APIs

Details

LAN Server provides over 150 API functions; most of these are available to DOS, Windows, and OS/2 clients. With the network API, a C programmer can now explicitly control many of the already described Network Operating System functions through programming interfaces. This makes it easy for your programs to control almost every aspect of LAN administration. Through the DOS Requester component, the API also allows DOS/Windows programmers to use the interprocess communication facilities to exchange data and event signals with OS/2 servers. The DOS Requesters support a subset of the API calls in all the categories except Alerts and Error Logging. The following table provides a quick reference of what these calls do by functional category. ❑

Service	Description
Named Pipes	This service consists of the same 13 Named Pipe API calls that are part of the native OS/2 interprocess communication. They are included here because you must have a running copy of the LAN Server to use Named Pipes remotely. Most of the OS/2 Named Pipe API calls are extended to DOS and MS-Windows Requesters through the LAN Server (or Microsoft LAN Manager).
MailSlots	This service consists of 6 API calls that provide one-way interprocess communications. These calls can come in handy for remote data collection and "I'm alive" heartbeats. Mailslots use NetBIOS datagrams to provide their services. The server side of the communication creates a mailslot for receiving messages (NetBIOS *add name*). The client writes messages to the mailslot. The server side can block waiting for messages to arrive. Mailslots are inherently fast because they do not need to be opened or closed. A process can write to a remote Mailslot with a class and priority attribute. Priority controls the order in which messages are read. *First-class messages* on Mailslots are abstractions of acknowledged datagrams. A sending process blocks (or waits) until its first-class message is delivered and acknowledged or an error occurs. *Second-class messages* are simple datagrams of the "transmit-and-pray" variety. An important feature of second class messages is that they can be broadcast to all workstations in a domain. The full repertoire of Mailslot API calls is available to DOS/Windows Requesters.
Alerts	This service consists of 3 API calls that notify applications of the occurrence of certain network events.

Service	Description
Network Management	This service consists of 23 API calls that do the following: • Control the server's Audit log file • Control the Error log • Collect and reset network statistics on both servers and requesters • Control network sessions, requesters, and servers • Read remote configuration information from the IBMLAN.INI file
Resource Management	This service consists of 23 API calls that do the following: • Control the sharing of server resources • Establish controls and connections between requesters and servers • Control the sharing of serial devices and their associated queues • Monitor the open file, device, and pipe resources on a server • Set or obtain information on a per-handle basis
Access Control	This service consists of 27 API calls that do the following: • Examine or modify user or group access permissions for server resources • Control user and group accounts
Network Services	This server consists of 19 API calls that do the following: • Send, forward, and log messages • Copy and move files • Execute remote programs • Obtain time-of-day from a server • Start and control network service programs

LAN Server: What's Coming Next?

IBM intends to evolve LAN Server to cover a spectrum that spreads from very low-end peer services to the intergalactic full-fledged enterprise NOS (see Figure 20-4). At the low end, the peer services will be repackaged and extended to remove the current session limits. They will provide a very graphical OOUI-based interface for administration services, simple mail, and network DDE. You will also be able exchange information by using the clipboard functions across the network. The *network clipboard* is intended to support DOS, Windows and OS/2 clients.

At the high end, LAN Server will incorporate the OSF DCE functions and package them as an easy-to-use NOS product (see Figure 20-5). This includes easy installation, OOUI-based graphical network administration, UPS support, fault-tolerant features, and all the luxury items NOS users expect. In spite of its 1.1 million lines of code, the OSF DCE is very spartan when it comes to network amenities, utilities, packaging, and user interfaces. It's just a toolkit with a run-time environment. So

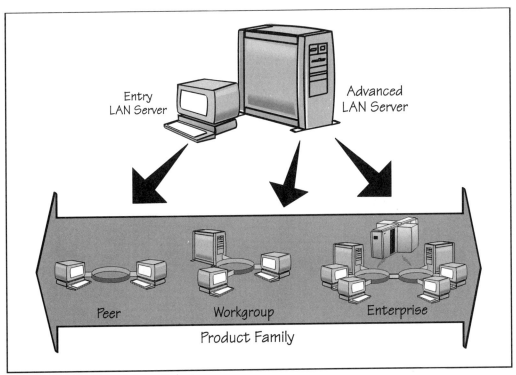

Figure 20-4. LAN Server Futures: Packaging.

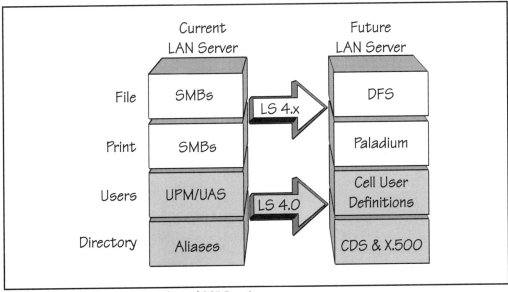

Figure 20-5. LAN Server Futures: Advanced DCE Functions.

DCE needs a shrink-wrapped package like the forthcoming LAN Server 4.X to make it usable—including CD-ROM packaging, CID-enabled installation, user manuals, and graphical system administration.

LAN Server Packaging

The LAN Server 3.0 comes in two packages: Entry and Advanced. Both are 32-bit applications.

■ The **OS/2 LAN Server Version 3.0 - Entry** provides all the functions described in this section, except for the 32-bit HPFS 386 file system, local security, multiprocessing, isochronous multimedia, and the disk mirroring and duplexing fault tolerant capability.

■ The **OS/2 LAN Server Version 3.0 - Advanced** supports all the functions described in this section excluding multimedia. It also provides a highly optimized, Ring 0, 32-bit HPFS file system. It is recommended for servers in high-workload environments where prime performance is critical. It is also recommended for servers that support a large number of remote IPL requesters or that require optimal reliability and security. This product sells for $2,295.

■ The **LAN Server Ultimedia** is an add-on product (shipped January, 1994) that lets users on the LAN access multimedia files from a central file server. It sells for $3,195.

LAN Requesters are available for DOS, Windows, and OS/2. The LAN Requesters work with both entry or advanced LAN Server products. The client programs are distributed with both server packages mentioned here. The client code sells for $75 per client workstation. The **OS/2 LAN Server for the Macintosh** is an add-on package to the LAN Server and sells for $995. No Mac client software is required.

NETWARE 4.X FOR OS/2

Now you can run your NetWare file server right alongside OS/2 on the same machine. Ponder the possibilities.

> — **William Wong,**
> **LAN Magazine (February, 1994)**

Novell has the distinction of providing the world's most popular file server and network operating system. **NetWare 4.X for OS/2** allows NetWare 4.X servers to run in a non-dedicated mode on OS/2 2.X and allows OS/2 servers to service NetWare clients. This means your client/server applications can be developed for OS/2 while taking advantage of the established file and print server capabilities of NetWare. In addition, the **NetWare Requester for OS/2** opens up the vast world of Novell LAN servers to an OS/2 client. What this all means is that you don't have to choose between NetWare and OS/2. You can have them both.

NetWare 4.X Server on OS/2

NetWare for OS/2 consists of "glue code" (add-on drivers) that lets the unmodified NetWare 4.X server program think it owns all the resources on an OS/2 machine. The product uses the same source code and provides the same function that is available in a dedicated NetWare server. A NetWare server on OS/2 can achieve *90-95%* of the native NetWare 4.X performance. That's quite impressive, considering that it's running in a preemptive multitasking environment. The 5-10% overhead is incurred because OS/2 is now handling all the hardware, interrupt, and I/O services that were previously optimized for NetWare. You can divide the CPU processing time between OS/2 and NetWare in any ratio you want by setting a performance ratio parameter.

Who Owns What?

How does it work? NetWare for OS/2 runs as a concurrent operating system on OS/2 dedicated to NetWare. OS/2 allocates a chunk of linear memory address space to NetWare that is not movable, swappable, or available to OS/2. NetWare gets its own disk partition, which it formats, manages, and owns (see Figure 20-6). Unfortunately, OS/2 and NetWare cannot share a CD-ROM drive.

OS/2 owns Ring 0, and from its perspective, NetWare looks like one large device driver that runs in Ring 0. OS/2 treats NetWare as a "trusted app." IBM performed a substantial amount of testing before granting NetWare that privilege. In any case, OS/2 apps are protected from server NLMs and vice versa. An NLM crash won't

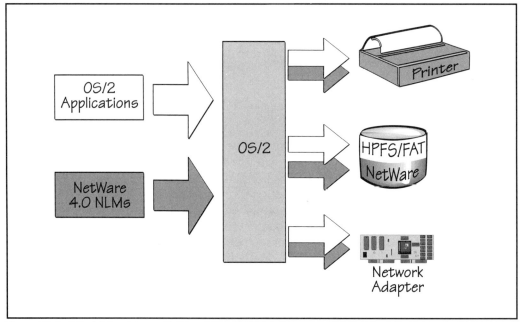

Figure 20-6. Blissful Coexistence: NetWare 4.X and OS/2 2.X.

bring down the machine. But if NetWare or a device driver fails, everything could be brought down.

It's Pure NetWare

OS/2 applications and NetWare services (NLMs) reside on the same server machine. NLMs and NetWare device drivers don't know they're running in an OS/2 environment and can't tell the difference. OS/2 applications can share devices—including printers and network adapters—with NetWare NLMs. To access the NetWare partitioned files, OS/2 applications must use the NetWare Requester.

All the features of NetWare 4.X servers are available on OS/2, including the directory services. After all, we're running the shrink-wrapped NetWare 4.X *server.exe* code on OS/2. The NetWare Server for OS/2 is accessible from all NetWare clients. This packaging is very good news for cost-sensitive environments that can only afford a single server solution and need a common platform for NetWare and OS/2 applications. For example, you can now run Lotus Notes and NetWare on the same server; this can be very useful in small shops.

To get all this to work, you must first install OS/2 and reserve some free disk space for NetWare. You then install NetWare for OS/2 followed by the shrink-wrapped NetWare 4.01 package. The NetWare Requester is bundled with NetWare.

NetWare 4.0 and LAN Server 3.0

NetWare 4.0, as a server platform, offers the same kind of services as LAN Server. Both server platforms are essentially equivalent in the following areas: file and print services, disk duplexing, disk mirroring, UPS support, multiserver domain administration, audit trails, alerts, security features, login scripts, multiple adapter support, Named Pipes support, and remote IPL capabilities for DOS, Windows, and OS/2 clients. NetWare and LAN Server can both be installed and upgraded remotely. And both platforms can support, in theory, a maximum of 1000 clients.

So what does NetWare do better than LAN Server? For starters, it allows you to create monstrous files that can span across multiple disk drives. NetWare can work with a gargantuan amount of total disk storage: 32 Terabytes versus LAN Server's not too shabby 48 Gigabytes. NetWare directly supports Unix clients, while LAN Server relies on third parties. Bean counters are in love with NetWare's meticulously built-in accounting services, which can be used to charge clients for any service used. And NetWare's *Systems Fault Tolerance III (SFT III)* gives you fault tolerance using replicated servers. NetWare 4.0 introduces powerful new features such as the X.500-based directory services, authentication services via encrypted key technology, burst-mode technology for increasing the speed of data transfer over Wide Area Networks and file-by-file compression. It also has built-in routing capabilities for IPX/SPX, TCP/IP, and AppleTalk protocols.

The feature that really makes NetWare wonderful is its multifaceted, chameleon-like file server that can be made to look like everybody else's favorite file system. The NetWare file server stores everybody's files in its own "private-label" Novell format. But depending on what the client wants, NetWare can apply the right magic to make its files resemble MS-DOS FAT, OS/2 HPFS, Sun NFS, or Macintosh AFP. This is how NetWare allows OS/2, Mac, Unix, DOS, and Windows clients to access the same source files.

So what does LAN Server do better than NetWare 4.0? It provides some unique features—such as the file replication service, the network time service, multimedia, multiprocessing, and the remote execution of commands—and it is able to accept commands from NetView. LAN Server, like NetWare 4.0, is gearing up to become an enterprise server platform. Unlike NetWare, LAN Server will be based on an "open" DCE/DME platform for its cell directory, X.500 global directory, Kerberos-based authentication, RPC, network time, and DME-based system management.[1] Both the DCE Toolkit for OS/2 and LAN NetView's implementation of DME's Network Management component are commercially available.

But, what makes LAN Server really *great* is its programming platform. It is safe to say that most of the world's great server applications have yet to be written. LAN Server, because of its affinity to OS/2, provides an ideal platform for creating those applications. When you're programming in the LAN Server environment, you can use any of the software packages described in this book and thousands of others. LAN Server applications can use OS/2's preemptive multitasking, threads, interprocess communications, memory protection, dynamic link library facilities, and demand-paged virtual memory. The LAN Server API package has very consistent semantics because it was designed from the outset as an extension of the OS/2 API set. NetWare, by contrast, added functions piecemeal as the product matured. The OS/2 connection also gives you access to dozens of compilers, programmer productivity tools, Case tools, DBMSs, ODBMSs, ORBs, image and multimedia application enablers, communication stacks, and device drivers for almost anything that can be controlled by a PC.

In summary, LAN Server may not be the world's most ubiquitous server platform, but it gives you everything you need to create 32-bit server "killer apps" on a commodity hardware platform.[2] NetWare 4.0 for OS/2 takes away some of that advantage because you can have both OS/2 and NetWare on the same server machine. Life is tough!

What Is a NetWare Requester for OS/2?

The NetWare LAN Requester for OS/2 provides OS/2 clients transparent access to all the features of NetWare, including advanced file, print and communication services, comprehensive security, fault tolerance, global directory services, security services, and resource accounting. The Requester supports NetWare 2.X, NetWare 3.X, NetWare 4.X, and the NetWare for UNIX environments. Like the OS/2 LAN Requester, the NetWare Requester is integrated into the OS/2 Workplace Shell. This means you can manipulate files and printers that reside on a remote NetWare Server using the familiar PM and Workplace Shell OS/2 interfaces. You can copy files from one server to another by simply dragging them between containers. Likewise, you can print documents on NetWare or LAN Server network printers by simply dragging the document and dropping it on the appropriate icon. This is a good

---

[1] NetWare is semi-proprietary: Its RPC is based on Sun's RPC; its directory service is "X.500 like" but does not interoperate with other X.500 directories; and its authentication service and system management are proprietary.

[2] In terms of popularity, LAN Server (and Microsoft LAN Manager) comes in second-place after NetWare.

example of how the Workplace Shell creates a cohesive online view of distributed resources.

NetWare Requester/IBM LAN Requester Coexistence

DOS, Windows, and OS/2 clients can now access services on both NetWare and LAN Server concurrently using the same adapter card. IBM and Novell solved the famous NDIS and ODI coexistence issue. *Open Data-Link Interface (ODI)* is Novell's version of a "logical network board." ODI, like Microsoft's NDIS standard, allows multiple protocol stacks to use the same network adapter. The good news is that NetWare and LAN Server requesters can now coexist in memory without conflict. We now have *three* miracle pieces of code, affectionately called "shims," for translating between NDIS and ODI and vice versa. The **ODINSUP** shim from Novell (packaged with the NetWare Requester for OS/2) translates from NDIS to ODI and allows NDIS-based software stacks to use ODI drivers. IBM provides two shims that go in the opposite direction:

■ The **LANSUP** shim is packaged with the NetWare Requester for OS/2.
■ The **ODI2NDI** shim is packaged with NTS/2.

Both of the IBM shims translate ODI to NDIS and allow the NetWare Requester to use the same NDIS drivers and adapters as the rest of the IBM OS/2 LAN products. Regardless of which shim you use, you do not have to reboot your machine (like in the old days) to access NetWare when running LAN Server and vice versa. You can have your LAN Server and NetWare too.

NetWare Requester for OS/2: API Categories

We will present a brief overview of the NetWare APIs available to OS/2 applications through the NetWare Requester for OS/2 2. Like the IBM LAN Server, NetWare opens up through its APIs a whole universe of LAN services. The purpose of this section is to give you a feel for what you can do with these APIs.[3] From a programmer's perspective (see Figure 20-7), the NetWare Requester for OS/2 2.1 provides the following API services:

■ *Peer-to-Peer Communications*—including Novell's native IPX/SPX protocol, TLI, and the ubiquitous NetBIOS—allow your OS/2 programs to communicate at the peer-to-peer level with other DOS, Windows, and OS/2 NetWare Requesters as well as Novell servers.

---

[3] The full description of these APIs is in the Novell **NetWare Programmer's Guide for C** (June 1993).

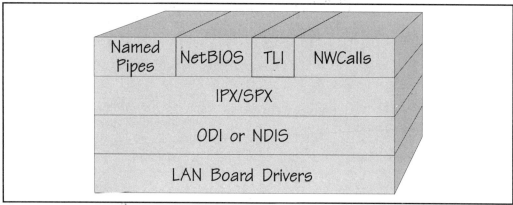

Figure 20-7. NetWare's LAN Requester for OS/2 Protocol Stack.

■ *Network Named Pipes* provide both client and server Named Pipes services without requiring a NetWare server on the network (see Figure 20-8). In theory, this function allows up to 1000 simultaneous Named Pipes connections. This means 1000 DOS, Windows, or OS/2 NetWare clients can simultaneously communicate with an OS/2 NetWare Named Pipes server. Windows and DOS NetWare Requesters do not support the Named Pipes server calls; only the OS/2 NetWare Requesters support those APIs.

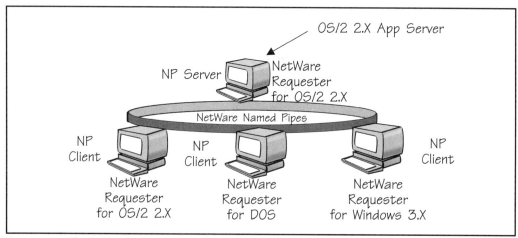

Figure 20-8. The NetWare Implementation of Named Pipes.

■ *NetWare Services*, also known as "NWCalls," provide API calls to NetWare's services like shared file and printer services, login, the bindery, queues, directory, and semaphores. Your programs can use these APIs to access services that run on NetWare server machines. The APIs cover any service that can be invoked interactively using the NetWare Requester's Workplace Shell user interface.

NetWare Requester for OS/2: API Services

Details

The following table provides a quick reference to the NetWare Requester for OS/2 API categories. These services collectively provide over 500 API calls. Some of the services are, of course, only provided on NetWare 4.0 servers. The transition from NetWare's old directory service (the Bindery) to its new X.500 Directory will not be easy. It's a complete paradigm shift. ❑

Service	Description
Peer-to-Peer APIs	
TLI	This service consists of about 25 API calls that provide a reliable peer-to-peer service using Novell's standard Transport Layer Interface (TLI) protocol. TLI is a variant of Berkeley sockets that supports both connection and connection-less API services.
IPX	This service consists of 12 API calls that provide a datagram service over Novell's native Internet Packet Exchange (IPX) protocol. This is a "send and pray" type of protocol with no guarantees. It is used as a foundation protocol by sophisticated network applications for sending and receiving low-overhead datagram packets over the internet. Novell's SPX builds a reliable protocol service on top of IPX.
SPX	This service consists of 16 API calls that provide a reliable, guaranteed delivery service over IPX. SPX stands for Sequenced Packet Exchange. It enables two client processes to exchange messages over a sequenced packet stream. Duplicate packets are detected and suppressed. SPX provides automatic time-outs and retransmissions over a connection-based service. SPX APIs allow two partners to establish a connection, exchange sequenced packets, and terminate the connection. SPX, like IPX, is native to NetWare.
NetBIOS	This service consists of 5 API calls that emulate the NetBIOS interface over IPX/SPX. The actual NetBIOS commands are passed using the NCB control block. The NCBs are submitted using NetWare's **NetBiosSubmit** calls. NetWare supports all the standard NetBIOS commands. This includes general commands, name support commands, session commands, and the datagrams commands. NetBIOS combines the functions of both IPX and SPX and is widely used in PC LAN applications. NetBIOS does not require the presence of a NetWare Server. OS/2 NetWare Requesters can communicate with DOS and Windows NetWare Requesters using NetBIOS.

Service	Description
Client/Server APIs: Network Named Pipes	
Named Pipes	This service consists of 16 API calls. This includes the 13 API calls that are part of OS/2's native interprocess communication and 3 calls that are specific to NetWare. OS/2 NetWare Requesters support both client and server Named Pipes calls. DOS and Windows NetWare Requesters only support the client Named Pipes calls. In theory, an OS/2 NetWare Requester can simultaneously service up to 1000 clients (DOS, Windows, and OS/2). The Named Pipes service does not require a NetWare server on the network. The NetWare-specific Named Pipes calls are used to obtain Named Pipes server names on the network.
NetWare Services: NWCalls	
Accounting Services	This service consists of 5 API calls that allow developers to configure the NetWare server to charge for basic services such as connection time and disk storage. Each user is given an account.
Apple File Services (AFP)	This service consists of 14 API calls that follow Apple Computer's **AppleTalk Filing Protocol (AFP)**. AFP allows a NetWare file server to store both OS/2 and Apple data files. You can write applications to create, access, and delete Macintosh-format directories and files on a NetWare file server.
Auditing Services	This service consists of 39 API calls that support the routine auditing of the network environment by independent auditors. Auditing can be applied to either Bindery objects or Directory Services objects. You can audit network usage, file and directory events, queues, and almost anything NetWare recognizes. The audit will capture events and write them to a file where they can be read by the auditor. Events can be filtered by searching for specific criteria and setting up boolean conditions. *The Auditing Services are only available on NetWare 4.0.*
Bindery Services	This service consists of 23 API calls that maintain information about objects allowed to access a NetWare Server. Each NetWare server maintains a database, implemented as two hidden files, of bindery objects. This special-purpose database is called the *bindery.* A bindery object can be a user, user group, network server, print server, or any other named entity that can access a NetWare server. NetWare records information about each bindery object. The API service allows you to manipulate and query object attributes such as security, password, id, name, and properties (id identifies an objectname.objecttype). **Note:** NetWare 4.0 replaces the proprietary bindery service with a distributed *NetWare Directory Services (NDS)* that provides a global view of the network. This service is object-based (i.e., it supports class inheritance) and complies with the X.500 syntax and naming definitions. The IBM LAN Server naming services will also migrate to X.500.

Service	Description
Connection Services	This service consists of 35 API calls that provide information on the status of connections between client workstations and NetWare servers. The server maintains a table that includes connection ids and passwords for all connected objects. An OS/2 client can obtain information on a connection's id, number, and status. It can query the maximum number of connections available at the requesting workstation (the default is 8). It can obtain the internet address of the connection. This is the address (adapter id and network id) that uniquely identifies the client on a NetWare internet. The service also allows a client to set the primary connection id (this is the connection to the server to which the client originally logged in).
Data Migration Services	This service consists of 8 API calls that move files to an archive store (offline) and bring them back online. If a file is migrated to tape, the system will prompt the user to load the proper tape.
Deleted Files Services	This service consists of 3 API calls that scan for deleted files, recover a deleted file, and purge a deleted file.
Directory Services	This service consists of 91 API calls that allow you to manipulate objects in NetWare's new X.500-based directory service. All the information in the directory is organized by object. Each object belongs to a class and has attributes. The APIs let you create and modify objects and read their attributes. The procedures for accessing an object depend on its class. The directory service includes a standard set of object classes. You can also create new classes using the API. *The Directory Services are only available on NetWare 4.0 Servers.*
Extended Attributes	This service consists of 7 API calls that allow a client to read and write Extended Attributes associated with OS/2 files and to open and close extended attribute files.
File Server Environment	This service consists of 60 API calls that allow a client to "login" and "logout" to/from a file server and attach or detach from a server. Attach creates a connection id (session) with the server. The API calls can also be used to obtain information such as server type, name, and description. An API call returns the network date and time maintained on a specified server. *Warning:* Date and time are not automatically synchronized across NetWare servers, so they may differ on the internet.
File Systems Services	This service consists of 56 API calls that provide NetWare-specific file service functions. These include create, delete, and rename a directory; get, release, and clear file locks and file lock sets; set file and extended file attributes; and copy, rename, and erase a file. **Note:** You may be better off using the native OS/2 file APIs and have your calls transparently redirected to a NetWare file server.
Message Services	This service consists of 8 API calls that enable clients to send broadcast messages to up to 256 specified target workstations. The sending workstation and the target workstations must be attached to the same NetWare file server. The maximum message size is 254 bytes (NetWare 3.11c and above).

Service	Description
Name Space Services	This service consists of 25 API calls that enable DOS, OS/2, Unix, FTAM, and Macintosh clients to create files on a NetWare Server using their own familiar naming conventions. The primary name space is DOS. For example, if you have a DOS file and you load OS/2 (HPFS), Unix, and Mac name spaces, the file would have four entries. The APIs allow you to create name space entries, scan name space entries, and write name space entries.
Path and Drive Services	This service consists of 8 API calls that enable clients to delete or map a logical network drive to a specified directory path; obtain information about specific drives, such as the connection id, path, and drive handle; and parse path strings.
Print Server Services	This service consists of 126 API calls that allow you to manage, configure, control, and define resources on the print servers. The resources include server attributes and the print jobs, print queues, and printers it controls.
Print Services	This service consists of 12 API calls that enable clients to redirect data sent to a local LPT device to a specified NetWare server's print queue. Clients can query the server for the status of the network printer. They can specify the number of copies, tab size, form type, banner page, and so on.
Queue Management Services (QMS)	This service consists of 23 API calls that create, manage, and control network queues. These queues are maintained in special directories on a NetWare file server. One queue can hold up to 250 jobs. Queues are implemented on a server as a Bindery object (they're secure). Clients submit work requests on a queue in first-in, first-out order. Job server applications remove work from the queue and execute it (these applications can also run on an OS/2 client). One queue may be serviced by as many as 25 job servers at a time. Once a job is serviced, its associated file is deleted from the queue directory. Using the API calls, an OS/2 client can create, manipulate, abort, verify the status, and remove queue entries.
Synchronization Services	This service consists of 11 API calls that allow clients to create semaphores on a NetWare server to protect a shared resource, wait on semaphores, and signal on semaphores when they finish using the resource. Wait decrements the semaphore count, and signal increments it. The creator of a semaphore can configure the number of applications that can access the semaphore at one time (1 to 127). If access is restricted to 1, only serial access will be allowed on the resource. A client must first open a semaphore and check its count before using it. If the resource is unavailable, the client is placed in a wait queue for a specified timeout interval or until the resource frees up.
Transaction Tracking Services (TTS)	This service consists of 13 API calls that allow NetWare file servers to track file-based transactions and ensure file integrity by backing out or erasing interrupted or partially completed transactions. Only transactional files are affected. A file is made transactional by setting an extended attribute for transactions. Client applications can explicitly issue begin/end transaction calls to bracket a specific transaction. If the file server fails before all updates to transactional files are committed to disk, the transaction will be backed out when the file server is rebooted. A file server can monitor a maximum of 200 transactions at a time, but only one for each client session.

Service	Description
Volume Services	This service consists of 9 API calls that allow clients to obtain information such as the number of volumes mounted on a file server (64 maximum), the name and size of each volume, the total number of blocks per volume, the number of sectors per block, and the number of available blocks and directory entries.

The NetWare Management Map for the OS/2 Workplace Shell

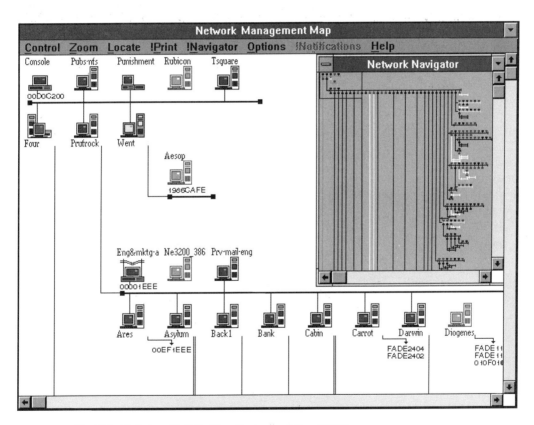

Figure 20-9. The OS/2 Workplace Shell NetWare Management Map (NMM).

The **NetWare Management Map (NMM)** creates graphic displays of a Novell internet using the OS/2 Workplace Shell's object-oriented display facilities. NMM is used primarily by network administrators. It works by automatically discovering all the NetWare servers on a network and then creating a graphic display of the NetWare internet, including even the largest NetWare networks (see Figure 20-9).

Icons are used to represent all the servers, cable segments, routers, and worksta-tions running NetWare. The display continuously updates itself to reflect the status of each node. The interface allows a network administrator to directly manipulate each graphic object by selecting its icon. NMM conducts point-to-point packet transmit/receive tests to isolate communication faults, and it provides online, context-sensitive help that includes probable cause of errors.

In addition to NMM, the OS/2 LAN NetView management platform integrates Novell's **Network Management Services (NMS)**. As you can see, OS/2 is very well integrated with NetWare. Even Novell has a long way to go before it can achieve that close level of integration with UnixWare.

NetWare Packaging

The **NetWare 4.0 Server** from IBM starts out at $1395 (five users) and runs up to $47,995 (1000 users). **NetWare 4.0 for OS/2** costs $300 for the enabling software that makes NetWare run on OS/2. It requires both OS/2 and the NetWare 4.0 Server software.

The purchase of a single $200 NetWare Services for OS/2 license from IBM entitles you to create "as many copies of the NetWare Requester for OS/2 as required within the customer's corporation to access appropriate NetWare network servers."

Conclusion

This concludes our "brief" overview of the two most popular NOSs in the industry: NetWare and LAN Server (a distant second with about 10% of the installed base, but growing very fast). Both NOSs run on OS/2, and they each have their strengths and weaknesses. We hope this short introduction helps you with your choices and takes away some of the "mysticism and blind luck" associated with NOS selections. You will also need to read the next two chapters to understand where DCE and messaging come into the picture.

Chapter 21

DCE: The Postmodern NOS

By 1994, the OSF DCE will be established as the industry standard for client/server computing (0.8 probability).

— Gartner Group (January, 1993)[1]

The dominance of single-vendor software architectures is fading as corporations move into the multivendor world of client/server and enterprise networks. Open Systems is the current buzzword for creating a new world order in distributed computing. The OSF *Distributed Computing Environment (DCE)* is emerging as the de facto standard for client/server computing in an "open" multivendor NOS environment. According to OSF, more than 100 vendors are currently building DCE products, although very few are on the market yet.

DCE is important because it provides the most comprehensive NOS solution for integrating multivendor servers in a *heterogeneous* client/server environment. Although there are some partial NOS solutions for the heterogeneous server

---

[1] Source: **Gartner Research Note**, SAP-222-087 (January 20, 1993). If you're reading this book, it must be 1994 or later. So how good is the Gartner 1993 prediction?

environment, no existing product matches DCE's integration technology. This is because DCE was built on top of the industry's "best-of-breed" commercial NOS technology.

DCE allows a client to interoperate with one or more server processes on other computing platforms, even when they are from different vendors with different operating systems. In addition, DCE provides an integrated approach to security, naming, and interprocess communications. All these pieces are used to create a coherent heterogeneous client/server environment. DCE is the best architectural example of an intergalactic *postmodern NOS*. It is intended to become the "mother of all NOSs." In this chapter, we introduce the OSF DCE and IBM's **DCE for OS/2** product—currently the most complete DCE implementation on PC LANs.

WHAT IS DCE?

The DCE from the Open Software Foundation (OSF) is probably the most significant open systems standard for heterogeneous client/server interoperability. DCE consists of an integrated set of technologies that make it easy to create, use, and maintain applications in a distributed environment. DCE provides the plumbing that enables secure access to distributed resources wherever they are and on whatever operating system they run. In essence, DCE creates an open NOS environment that spans multiple architectures, protocols, and operating systems. The X/Open standards consortium is including the DCE specifications in Version 4 of its *X/Open Portability Guide (XPG)*. The importance of DCE is that *almost* every computer manufacturer is planning to support it (see the following Soapbox).

Who's Not On Board?

Soapbox

As we go to press, Sun, whose RPC was rejected by OSF, has not endorsed DCE. Sun is offering its *Open Network Computing (ONC)* as the alternative to the OSF DCE. A number of third parties are planning DCE ports to Sun platforms. In addition, Novell does not fully embrace DCE but IBM is rumored to be developing NLM versions of DCE. Finally, Microsoft is only implementing parts of DCE (mostly by reverse-engineering the OSF implementation) because it does not want to pay royalties to OSF. Other than these "big three," everyone else seems to be on board the DCE ship. ❏

DCE is the result of a multitechnology and multivendor open selection process. OSF identifies requirements and solicits technologies from the computer industry at large through an open bidding process. The OSF then picks the best submissions and integrates the technology into core software layers for resale by others. OSF member companies receive the core code in "snapshots" that can be integrated into their products. The DCE Release 1.0 package contains more than 1.1 million lines of C code, documentation, and a set of functional tests. Note that DCE is not just for Unix. Its purpose is to facilitate the creation of distributed applications and to enable the transparent sharing of resources across a variety of networks, operating systems, and vendors.

DCE provides key distributed technologies, including a remote procedure call, a distributed naming service, a time synchronization service, a distributed file system, network security service, and a threads package (see Figure 21-1). These six key technologies will be incorporated by IBM (into MVS, AIX, DOS/Windows, and OS/2), DEC (into VMS, Ultrix, OSF/1, and ACE), HP (into HP/UX, Domain, and OSF/1),

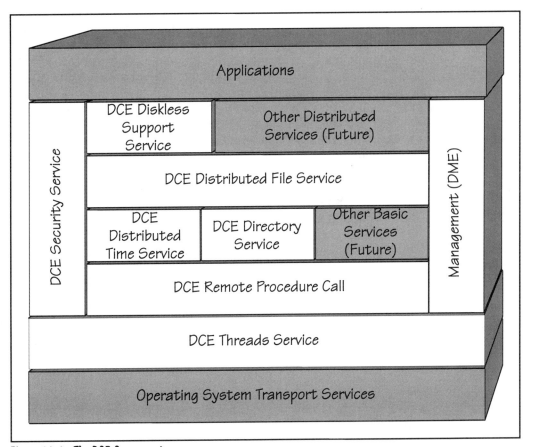

Figure 21-1. The DCE Components.

Gradient (into MS-DOS), Cray (into Unicos), Siemens (into SINIX), and Tandem (into Guardian and Integrity). DCE will also interoperate (at the RPC level) with Atlas, the competing open standard for distributed computing from the now defunct Unix International. The sections that follow contain a brief summary of the main DCE components, including their origins.

DCE RPC

OSF adopted the Apollo RPC with some enhancements from DEC (the multithread server). DCE provides an *Interface Definition Language (IDL)* and compiler that facilitate the creation of RPCs. The IDL compiler creates portable C code stubs for both the client and server sides of an application. The stubs are compiled and linked to the RPC run-time library, which is responsible for finding servers in a distributed system, performing the message exchanges, packing and unpacking message parameters, and processing any errors that occur.

The most powerful feature of the DCE RPC is that it can be integrated with the DCE security and name services. This integration makes it possible to authenticate each procedure call and to dynamically locate servers at run time. Servers can concurrently service RPCs using threads. The RPC mechanism provides protocol and network independence. DCE supports both datagrams and session-based transports. DCE tags the client data types and leaves it up to the server to perform any data conversions. This "server makes it right" approach speeds up client/server interactions on similar machines because data is not always converted into an intermediate network format.

The DCE RPC does not support transactions. To do that means adding context information in the RPC messages that identify the transaction and its status on behalf of which the RPC is doing the work. It also means providing semantics for bracketing transactions (i.e., begin transaction and end transaction). There are currently two competing approaches for adding transactional support to the DCE RPC:

■ X/Open has defined a transaction interface called *TxRPC* that is intended to be used with the DCE RPC.

■ Transarc's Encina product provides its own DCE-based transactional RPC component, including a C-based precompiler.

The OSF DCE SIG TP Working Group is getting ready to issue a TP Requirements RFC that specifies the X/Open API with a DCE-based transaction protocol. Transarc is expected to respond.

DCE: Distributed Naming Services

OSF adopted the DCE distributed naming services from DEC's DECdns product and Siemens' DIR-X X.500 services. The DCE naming services allow resources such as programs, servers, files, disks, or print queues to be identified by user-oriented names in a special-purpose distributed database that describes the objects of interest. Object names are independent of their location on the network.

DCE divides the distributed environment into administrative units (or domains) called *cells*. A DCE cell is a combination of client and server workstations. The cell's domain is defined by the customer. A cell usually consists of the set of machines used by one or more groups working on related tasks. The cell size is dictated only by how easy it is to administer. At a *minimum*, a DCE cell must have one cell directory server and one security server.

As shown in Figure 21-2, the DCE directory service consists of two elements: *Cell Directory Service (CDS)* and *Global Directory Service (GDS)*. This two-tier

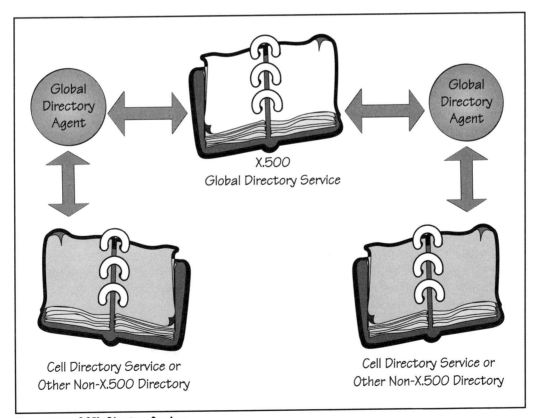

Figure 21-2. DCE's Directory Services.

hierarchy provides local naming autonomy (at the cell level) and global interoperability (at the intercell level). Global access is provided using X.500's "intergalactic" naming system or with TCP/IP's Internet *Domain Name System (DNS)*. All the names in the DCE system taken together make up the DCE *namespace*, which looks like a hierarchical file system. The DCE namespace is used by the different DCE services. For example, the security service uses a part of the namespace to maintain its information on user accounts and principals. The DFS file system uses another part of the namespace for the file system.

The DCE directory structure serves as a model on how to integrate local proprietary directory structures into a cohesive X.500 based global directory. The GDS provides an integration point for information from all the local cell directories. DCE provides a *Global Directory Agent (GDA)* that allows the cell directories to exchange data with the global directory. The GDA will forward any name queries that cannot be resolved at the cell directory level to the GDS. The GDA (and other programs) use *X/Open's Directory Service API (XDS)* to access the GDS. The XDS APIs allow programs to read, compare, update, add, and remove directory entries; list directories; and search for entries based on attributes.

Both the CDS and GDS directories can be distributed across multiple servers. DCE provides replication services that allow administrators to maintain copies of critical data on multiple name servers. DCE maintains a master copy and read-only shadow replicas; it refreshes replicas using both *immediate replication* and *skulking*—a strange-sounding word that means periodic refreshes. DCE also provides directory caching services to improve lookup speeds. The DCE directory services can be queried using different attributes. For example, DCE supports *yellow pages* (attributes to names), *white pages* (name to attributes), *aliases* (name to different names), and *groups* (name to distribution lists).

DCE: Distributed Time Services

OSF adopted this technology from DEC's DECtds time server product. The Time Service provides a mechanism for synchronizing each computer in the network to a recognized time standard. The DCE Time Service provides APIs for manipulating timestamps and for obtaining universal time from public sources such as the Traconex/PSTI radio clock.

DCE synchronizes time on its networks by maintaining agent/server and server/server relationships (see Figure 21-3). Each DCE machine has a *Time Clerk* agent that asks *Time Servers* for the correct time and adjusts the local time accordingly. The agent may consult one or more Time Servers and calculate the probable correct time based on the responses it receives. The agent can upgrade the local time either gradually or abruptly.

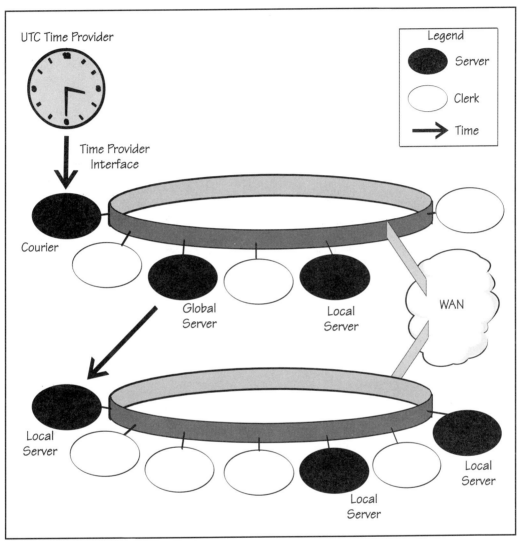

Figure 21-3. DCE's Distributed Time Services.

The *Time Server* is a node that is designated to answer queries about the time. DCE supports three types of Time Servers:

- *Local Time Servers* are only available to clients on the same LAN.
- *Global Time Servers* are available across an extended LAN or WAN.
- *Courier Servers* are local servers who are designated to synchronize time with global servers.

DCE requires at least three Time Servers; one (or more) must be connected to an *External Time Provider.* The Time Servers periodically query one another to adjust their clocks. The External Time Provider may be a hardware device that receives time from a radio or a telephone source. DCE uses the UTC standard, which keeps track of time elapsed since the beginning of the Gregorian calendar—October 15, 1582.

DCE: Distributed Security Services

OSF adopted MIT's Kerberos authentication system and enhanced it with some HP security features. DCE's network security services provide authentication, authorization, and user account management. *Authentication* validates that a client, typically a user or program, is who or what it claims to be. This validation is accomplished through the secure communications capability provided by the RPC and the Kerberos ticketing mechanism (see the following Details box). Each DCE machine must run a security agent.

The DCE *security server* is a physically secured server that stores security-related information such as names and associated passwords. Each DCE cell must have a security server; it is usually a dedicated machine. A cell may have replicated security servers for backup. The DCE *login facility* (see next Details box) enables users (DCE calls them *principals* or *units of trust*) to establish their identity by authenticating themselves using a password. The DCE security system never sends a password in "clear text" across the network.

The security agent works with the authenticated RPC to provide secure access to all the DCE services—not just authentication. The RPC mechanism hides all the complexity of the security system from the user. It obtains the tickets, provides encryption when needed, and performs authenticated checksums if the policy requires it. Under-the-covers, both the RPC client and server must mutually authenticate one another by exchanging tickets (little secrets) with a trusted third party (the Kerberos server). Each party trusts the Kerberos server to identify the other party on the network. This is called *trusted third-party secret-key encryption.* In addition, information is timestamped so that the usefulness of a ticket expires within a relatively short period of time, measured in hours.

Authorization comes after authentication; it determines whether the authenticated client has permission to access a resource. DCE supports authorization through Access Control Lists (ACLs). Each DCE implementation that uses ACLs must implement an ACL manager that controls access to services and resources managed by it (DCE provides sample code that shows how to create an ACL manager).

Data integrity is provided by DCE using cryptographic data checksums to determine whether a message was corrupted or tampered with while passing through the network. In addition, *data privacy* can be ensured by encrypting data that is transferred across a network.

In summary, DCE solves the problems associated with user authentication in distributed networks. Passwords are never sent *in the clear*. The security database (DCE calls it the *registry*) can be propagated across trusted servers. DCE's Kerberos, in addition to solving the authentication problem, helps with the authorization issue. And better yet, the whole scheme can work on heterogeneous systems. No other NOS can match DCE when it comes to security.

Distributed File System (DFS)

For its distributed file server, OSF chose the *Andrew File System (AFS)* from Transarc (and Carnegie Mellon University) and the diskless client from HP (also based on AFS protocols). The DCE *Distributed File System (DFS)* provides a uniform name space, file location transparency, and high availability. DFS is log-based and thus offers the advantage of a fast restart and recovery after a server crash. Files and directories can be replicated (invisibly) on multiple servers for high availability. A cache-consistency protocol allows a file to be changed in a cache. The changes are automatically propagated to all other caches where the file is used, as well as on the disk that owns the file. The DFS file system APIs are based on the POSIX 1003.1a (portable OS interface). DFS is interoperable with Sun's NFS, giving NFS sites an easy migration path to the more function-rich DFS file server.

DFS provides a single image file system that can be distributed across a group of file servers. The DFS file naming scheme is location-independent. Each file has a unique identifier that is consistent across the network. Files use the DCE global namespace just like the rest of the network resources. And the file system is integrated with the DCE security and RPC mechanisms. Because DFS fully exploits the DCE services, it can be administered from any DCE node, which helps keep costs down in a widely distributed system.

Kerberos: The Three-Headed Monster

Details

Kerberos—A three-headed dog that guarded the gates of Hades.

— Greek Mythology

Kerberos, a protocol that Machiavelli would have loved, is based on total mutual distrust. The MIT folks who built it named it after a three-headed mythological monster that guarded the gates of Hades (i.e., hell). Why would anyone want to crash the gates of hell? We'll let security administrators answer that one. The Kerberos monster consists of three "heads" all residing on the same secured server: the Authentication Server, Security Database, and Privilege Server. The MIT three-headed monster gives network administrators the heavy-duty security needed to keep "intruding hackers" from crashing into the network's gates.

The following scenario (see Figure 21-4) is must reading for intruding hackers who think Kerberos is just another security system. It's not. This section will give you a feeling for what you're up against, should you dare mount an assault on a network guarded by a Kerberos three-headed monster. The following scenario starts with an initial login and walks through one secured client/server interaction:

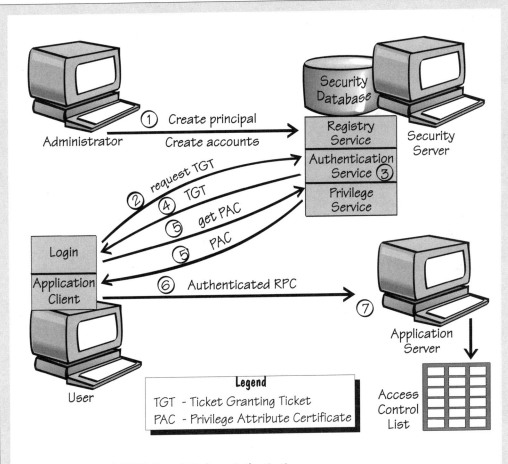

Figure 21-4. A Detailed Walk Through Kerberos Authentication.

1. Administrators must first run a program that creates a Security Database; then they must populate the database with the names and passwords of all the client and server entities on the network (they're known as principals). The Security Database is the only place in the network where passwords are stored. In DCE, the Security Database is part of the Registry Service—a database of users, group accounts, and policies. The DCE Registry may be replicated for enhanced performance and reliability.

2. At login time, once the user name is entered, the client issues a ticket-granting request to the Authentication Server. The client's name (not password) is passed over the network. This prevents hackers with sniffers from capturing the password. In DCE, the password is never sent in "clear text" across the network.

3. The Authentication Server allows two principals to authenticate each other's identities by acting as the trusted third party. It derives secret keys for principals from the passwords stored in their account entries in the Registry Database. It also issues tickets that principals use to access remote services and resources provided by specified servers. In our scenario, the Authentication Server uses the client's name to obtain the password from the Security Database. If the server finds an entry for that name, it generates a *Ticket-Granting Ticket (TGT)* that contains, among other things, the lifetime of the ticket. The ticket is encrypted using a private key known only to the Authentication and Privilege servers. The ticket is also encrypted a second time using the client's password as a key.

4. The ticket-granting ticket is sent back to the client along with a random key for a session with the Privilege server. Next, the user is prompted for a password, which is converted to a Data Encryption Standard (DES) key. If the user can supply the right password, parts of the ticket can be decrypted and accessed by the client's security agent. The login facility has completed its job and verified the user's security credentials.

5. In order for a client to obtain access to a "Kerberized" service, its security agent must get a service ticket from the Privilege Server. The client's security agent sends the ticket-granting ticket along with an authenticator record (with the IP network address, time, and name) to the Privilege Server, which decrypts the ticket, extracts the session key, and uses it to decrypt the authenticator record from the client. It then performs a check to determine if the client's IP address in the authenticator matches the IP address encoded in the ticket. It also makes sure the ticket's time has not expired. This prevents an intruder from reissuing a captured ticket. If all goes well, the Privilege Server has proof that "the client presenting the ticket and the client to whom the ticket was issued are one and the same." The Privilege server then issues a service ticket called a *Privilege Attribute Certificate (PAC)* that contains information—including which authorization groups the client belongs to, a random session key to be used between the client and the requested server, the IP address of the client, and the remaining lifetime of the ticket. The PAC is encrypted using DES with the server's private Kerberos key, which is unknown to the client. The client must obtain a separate PAC for each Kerberized service it requests.

6. An authenticated RPC generated by the client can now obtain access to a "Kerberized" service by presenting a PAC and an authenticator along with the RPC. Note: Authenticators may only be used once; the client must create new authenticators at the moment they issue service requests.

7. The server decrypts the PAC using its private Kerberos key. It then uses the session key obtained from the PAC to decrypt the information in the authenticator. The decryption succeeds if "the client presenting the PAC and the client to whom the PAC was issued are one and the same." The server decides, based on its Access Control Lists, whether the client belongs to a group that can access resources on the server.

In DCE, all the authentication is carried out transparently by the Authentication Runtime. But the level of security—the policy—is determined by the server when it registers itself with the DCE Registry. The client can also demand to have a certain type of security enforced, but the server has the final say.

Based on your policy requirements, the DCE client/server RPC can be conducted at several levels of authenticated protection—including no protection at all; encrypt the first connection exchange between the client and server; attach a verifier to each client call and server response; attach a verifier to each message; attach a cryptographic checksum to each message; and encrypt all user data on each call.

Most of the authentication machinery is transparent to both the user and the programmer. But for intruding hackers Kerberos is pure hell...are you running scared? You'll either have to mend your ways or limit your tampering to networks that don't have a "Kerberos inside" sticker. Of course, if you can gain access to a user's password there is no way Kerberos can distinguish between a user and an attacker. To do that, you'll have to gain access to the security server's disk drive or extort it out of the user at gunpoint. You won't find the password on a network. ❑

The Battle Between Public and Private Keys

Soapbox

A potential weakness of DCE is its security model, which is based on Kerberos, derived from the DES. Rymer notes that many IBM competitors, notably Novell and Microsoft, have openly scorned DES in favor of RSA public key encryption.

— *Andy Reinhardt, Byte Magazine
(November, 1993)*

What John Rymer really said:

NetWare 4.0 uses encryption primarily to authenticate users and sessions. By contrast, OSF offers the option of securing DCE by encrypting messages. IBM also has a general cryptography architecture [DES] that makes encryption services available to application builders.

— **John R. Rymer, Network Monitor**
(May, 1992)

What's going on here? It appears that Andy is confusing two issues: encryption and authentication. We'll clear up this confusion by first giving you a quick level set on public keys, private keys, DES, and RSA. Then we'll speculate on why Novell rejected Kerberos.

Encryption has been used to protect information for at least 4000 years. Today, the two predominant approaches to electronic encryption are based on private cypher keys and public cypher keys:

■ The *private key* approach uses a single key to encrypt or decrypt information. Each pair of users who need to exchange messages must agree on a private key and use it as a cypher to encode and decode their messages. This method works well, as long as both sides maintain the secrecy of the private key. It's their shared "little secret."

■ The *public key* approach uses two keys: a public key and a private key. The public key may be listed in directories and is available for all to see. You encrypt your message with your private key and the recipient uses your public key to decode it. In addition, anybody can send you an encrypted message by using your public key as a cypher (you decode it with your private key). This way, you don't even have to know who the sender is. Again, all this works well, as long as you keep your private key secret.

The *Data Encryption Standard (DES)* is based on this public key approach and has been the official US national cryptographic standard since 1977. DES was originally proposed by IBM as a 128-bit cypher, but the NSA (the U.S. spy agency) insisted that it be trimmed to 56 bits before accepting it as the basis for the national cryptographic standard—the NSA didn't want an algorithm that they could never break. DES has been the encryption algorithm of choice for the U.S. government for doing interbank electronic fund transfers and for most commercial users. In all its years of service, there has not been a reported case of DES cracking. A machine performing one DES decryption per microsecond would take 2000 years to crack a given key. The DES algorithm enables 72 quadrillion possible keys.

Kerberos uses an encryption cypher based on DES. As far as keys go, Kerberos uses a shared, session-specific, private key approach. Remember, Kerberos maintains a list of each client's password (or private key). Because it knows all the private keys (or passwords), Kerberos can generate an encrypted session key that convinces a recipient that the sender is really authentic. The recipient decrypts the session key using its private key, and is satisfied that only Kerberos could have encrypted it using its password. As a result, it accepts the shared session key. And, the sender is happy because it knows the recipient must be authentic because it was able to decipher the encrypted session key issued by Kerberos.

RSA is a public key algorithm invented at MIT. RSA stands for the initials of its three inventors. It is considered the public key algorithm of choice and is used mostly for authentication. RSA can also be used for encrypting very short messages. The problem is that RSA is too slow for encrypting longer messages and requires DES to do that. If the encryption is done in software, DES is about 100 times faster than RSA. In hardware, DES is between 1000 and 10,000 times as fast depending on the implementation (Source: Stang and Moore, **Network Security Secrets**, IDC Books, 1993).

So why would anybody want RSA? Because it lets you encrypt messages without the prior exchange of secrets (or tokens) and it provides an unforgeable electronic signature (see Figure 21-5). Only you can know your private key—there is no "trusted third party" like Kerberos. An RSA signature can be binding in legal courts because there can be no fingerpointing. And if you loose control of your private key, you're the only one to blame. It takes 2 billion years of computer time to break an RSA key. One of the problems with RSA is that the private key part must be delivered to each node on the network without breaching security. They need something like Kerberos to do that.

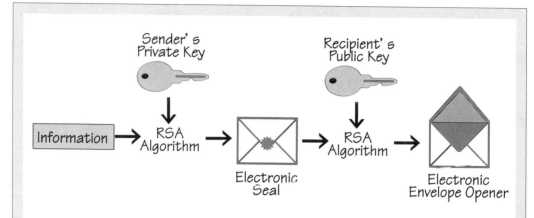

Figure 21-5. Public Keys: The Sealed Digital Envelope.

So with this explanation behind us, let's go back to the Novell, DCE, and Kerberos controversy. Novell does not support encrypted messages; therefore, it does not need DES. But when it came to authentication, Novell chose not to use Kerberos because it felt RSA did the job. It did not require a "trusted security server" that could become a bottleneck in large networks. However, the DCE implementation of Kerberos avoids that problem by replicating the security servers and the password databases. The level of DCE security (and therefore number of exchanges with Kerberos) is based on user-defined policy. It is very hard to imagine a session-level RPC authentication being slower than an RSA encryption/decryption cycle (especially when you factor in the query to the public key server).

The only advantage RSA provides over DCE's version of Kerberos is the "unforgeable" electronic signature. But as far as we know, all the Kerberos security loopholes were eliminated in the HP-augmented version DCE uses. We've never heard of anybody breaking DCE Kerberos, but can it be used in courts? Even though Kerberos does not totally eliminate fingerpointing, somebody should take a Kerberos-authenticated signature to court and find out.

In summary, the DCE version of Kerberos scales well and provides fool-proof authentication. DES is needed for encrypted messages regardless of whether you're using RSA or Kerberos. So why did Novell reject Kerberos? Perhaps Novell, like Microsoft, did not want to pay the OSF licensing fees for the augmented DCE version of Kerberos. Of course, the Novell marketing literature could always claim that NetWare provides electronic signatures that can stand in a court of law. ❑

Threads

OSF chose the Concert Multithread Architecture (CMA) from DEC. This portable thread package runs in the user space and includes small wrapper routines to translate calls to a native kernel-based thread package (like OS/2 or Mach threads). Threads are an essential component of client/server applications and are used by the other DCE components. The DCE thread package makes it possible to provide granular levels of multitasking on operating systems that do not provide kernel-supported threads. The DCE thread APIs are based on the POSIX 1003.4a (Pthreads standard). The DCE threads also support multiprocessor environments using shared memory. DCE provides a semaphore service that helps threads synchronize their access to shared memory.

OSF's DCE Releases

The following is a chronology of the DCE releases from OSF:

- **Release 1.0**, shipped 1Q '92, is a developer's toolkit.

- **Release 1.0.1**, shipped 3Q '92, is a production release.

- **Release 1.0.2**, shipped 2Q '93, fixed hundreds of bugs and integrated DFS into DCE.

- **Release 1.0.3**, shipped December 1993, fixed more bugs. This maintenance release focused on providing an industrial-strength version of the Distributed File System.

- **Release 1.1**, due in September 1994 (it slipped from 4Q '93), is a major DCE release that adds a ton of new function.

Of course, all these releases are for OSF members such as IBM, Tandem, and HP. The members must then take the OSF release code and port it to their respective platforms and do whatever it takes to create a product. You should expect a product lag of at least six months.

THE OS/2 DCE OFFERINGS

DCE is a key part of IBM's distributed computing strategy. IBM shipped its first DCE offerings on the AIX, OS/2, and DOS/Windows platforms. IBM intends to ship DCE offerings for its MVS and OS/400 platforms in mid-1994.

DCE Functions on OS/2 and Windows

In September 1993, IBM introduced the **DCE Software Developer's Kit for OS/2**, an **OS/2 DCE Client**, and a **DCE Software Developer's Kit for Windows**. The kits allow developers to create client/server applications that let DOS, Windows, and OS/2 DCE RPC clients access OS/2 servers that support the DCE Security and Cell Directory Services.

The DCE SDK for OS/2 includes the following components:

■ DCE *Security* Services for OS/2 clients and servers—including support for encryption and authentication

■ DCE *Cell Directory Services (CDS)* for OS/2 clients and servers

■ DCE *RPC* for OS/2 clients and servers (5 licenses)

■ DCE *Threads* and *Time* for OS/2 clients and servers

■ DCE *Threads*, *Time*, and *RPC* for DOS/Windows clients (5 licenses)

■ DCE client/server *application development tools* for OS/2 and Windows— including the DCE Interface Definition Language (IDL) compiler and sample programs

The OS/2 and Windows DCE products are available with *user data privacy* in the United States and Canada and without it everywhere else. The privacy feature uses the *Data Encryption Standard (DES)* to encrypt user data via remote procedure calls and, as such, is subject to U.S. Government export regulations. The products that do not have user data privacy still use the DES algorithm for password encryption and other control information.

The SDK's Client/Server Starter Set

A minimal DCE system consists of a LAN with a number of client workstations, one or more DCE cell directory servers, a DCE security server, and an application server. Because the servers in the network also request services, the client code must be installed on every server workstation. The SDK lets you create a DCE cell with up to five OS/2 DCE clients and up to five Windows DCE clients (see Figure 21-6). Of course, IBM will be glad to sell you more client and server licenses, but it's a good starter kit.

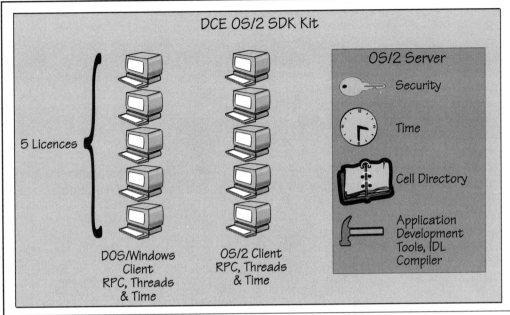

Figure 21-6. What You Get With the DCE SDK for OS/2.

Packaging

IBM sells the following DCE packages for OS/2:

■ The **OS/2 DCE client** sells for $65 (with DES) and requires about 8 MBytes of additional RAM and about 30 MBytes of additional disk space. IBM includes a socket-based TCP/IP transport, AnyNet/2, and NTS/2. The Windows client requires a separate WinSock V1.1-compliant TCP/IP package. The client requires, at a minimum, a 25MHz 80386 PC.

■ The **DCE SDK for OS/2 and Windows** sells for $1,095 including the starter kit. A server that runs the CDS and Directory will require at least 16 MBytes of RAM and about 100 MBytes of disk (including base OS/2). The CDS and Directory add less than 1 MByte of RAM on the client side.

In comparison to other DCE platforms, the DCE for OS/2 package is very reasonably priced.

DCE for OS/2: What's Coming Next?

DCE for OS/2 is based on the latest OSF release 1.0.2. You may have noticed that the GDS and DFS are missing. IBM intends to make all of DCE available on OS/2. But it also needs to provide the type of graphical user interfaces for supporting DCE that the PC community takes for granted. So it takes more time to commercialize DCE on PCs.

If you think about it, many elements of DCE will be buried inside other software packages. For example, LAN Server 4.X may integrate the DCE components— including DFS, GDS, CDS, Security, Time, and RPC—with LAN NetView elements, CID, and an object-oriented user interface and sell the whole Enchilada as a very intuitive turn-key NOS offering for the masses. Likewise, GUI tool vendors will create point-and-click RPC-picker interfaces to the DCE IDL and directory services, which will make it easy to build DCE client/server applications.

In other words, DCE in its SDK incarnation is a substrate NOS technology. The commercial NOSs, application servers, and tool vendors will create value-added DCE products for the masses. In the meantime, you can use the SDK to create one of these tools, by learning how to use DCE at the IDL and API level (about 400 calls). Of course, real programmers only use SDKs.

DCE 1.1: What's Cooking?

DCE Release 1.1, due from OSF in late 1994, will have faster, tighter code and will be easier to manage. The RPC may incorporate the dynamic invocation feature from CORBA and may be more ORB-friendly. We expect to see some load balancing on the server side of the RPC and better availability features. The new auditing and accounting features will help with system management; the DCE environment will be able to track its events. The naming services will support double-byte character sets (for international language support). The release promises to make DCE industrial-strength. These features will not appear in commercial implementations until some time in 1995.

How to Profit From DCE

Soapbox

The intergalactic NOSs are creating brave new possibilities for client/server application developers. There are no limits to the possible system ensembles that can be built on top of an architectural base, such as the one DCE provides. The winners in the software development game will be those who learn how to harness that architectural power and use it to create exciting new software packages. Just think of all the personal agents and network gnomes that can roam through the DCE universe and do all the interesting stuff they can do.

You can think of "intergalactic" distributed architectures (such as DCE) as large shopping malls that rent you space on which to run your software. You create the shops, boutiques, and even department stores that physically reside in the mall and depend on the mall owners to provide parking, common grounds, and a pleasant environment for shoppers. The key is to figure out what services and boutiques will thrive in that mall. You'll have to discover the software server equivalents of bookstores, restaurants, record stores, jewelers, clothing boutiques, hairdressers, and large department stores.

All you need to open shop in this client/server shopping mall is a PC running software components, such as the ones described in this book. The pieces are starting to come together, and there is enough to get you started. The point we're making is that there is a very low barrier to entry in this business. Anybody with a fully-loaded OS/2 PC can play in it and compete effectively. So now that you don't have to worry about the plumbing, lighting, or parking, you have more time to concentrate on what the shoppers in the mall (the clients) really need in terms of services and goods. The ultimate mall will be created using distributed objects on top of DCE's intergalactic services. This is the topic of Part 7. ❑

Chapter 22

MQSeries: The MOM Middleware Products

Every DAD needs a MOM.

— *The Message-Oriented Middleware (MOM) Consortium* [1]

"Every DAD needs a MOM" is the unofficial motto of the MOM Consortium. In this context, DAD stands for *Distributed Application Development* and MOM stands for *Message-Oriented Middleware*. We agree with the motto. MOM is a key piece of middleware that is absolutely essential for a class of client/server products. If your application can tolerate a certain level of time-independent responses, MOM provides the easiest path for creating enterprise and inter-enterprise client/server systems. MOM also helps create nomadic client/server systems that can accumulate outgoing transactions in queues and do a bulk upload when a connection can be established with an office server.

MOM provides a simple approach that dramatically reduces the complexity inherent in communications between programs in a client/server system. So what MOM

---

[1] Source: **Information Week** (November 1, 1993).

products are available on the OS/2 platform? The good news is that OS/2 supports more MOM products than any platform in the industry. The bad news is that we can't cover them all in this short chapter. So which MOM products are we going to present?

The plan for this chapter is to cover, in some depth, products that adhere to IBM's *Message and Queuing Interface (MQI)* architecture. MQI is becoming the industry's "de facto" standard for MOMs and we will tell you all about it. The products that currently implement MQI are the **MQSeries** from System Strategies and IBM. These are the "MQ-ized" versions of System Strategies' **ezBridge Transact** MOM product. We will also cover *very briefly* some of the other major OS/2 MOM products—including Peerlogic's **PIPES**, Covia Technologies Inc's **Communications Integrator**, Horizon Strategies Inc's **Message Express**, and IBM's **DAE** and **LANDP/2 V2** products. There's always so much to choose from in this business!

MQSERIES: EZBRIDGE TRANSACT ON OS/2

In March 1993, System Strategies and IBM jointly announced the **MQSeries**. These are MQ-ized versions of the ezBridge Transact products from Systems Strategies. Both IBM and System Strategies offer the MQSeries on major industry platforms—including DEC VMS, Tandem Computers' NonStop Guardian, HP-UX, SunOS, SCO Unix, UnixWare, Stratus VOS, OS/400, AIX, MVS, Windows, DOS, and OS/2 (see Figure 22-1). The MQSeries product implements the MQI interface along with other pieces of the MQ architecture. In a nutshell, MQSeries supports the delivery of messages between applications running in multivendor computing environments, recoverable queues, and transaction routing.

The Message Queuing Interface (MQI)

IBM and System Strategies are proposing to the MOM consortium a single messaging standard based on their *Message Queue Interface (MQI)* API set consisting of nine simple calls. The MQI is a very high-level interface; it hides the communication protocols from applications that communicate with one another using queues. The MQI API defines an interface between an application program and its local queue manager. The queue manager provides location transparency and handles the delivery of messages by communicating with its fellow queue managers across the network.

The following describes the anatomy of an MQI program:

1. ***Establish a connection with the local queue manager*** by issuing an MQCONN call.

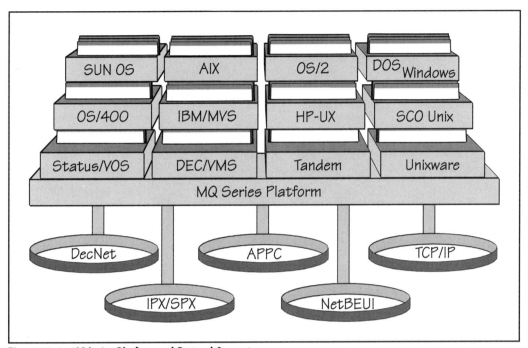

Figure 22-1. MQSeries Platform and Protocol Support.

2. ***Open a queue for exchanging messages*** by issuing an MQOPEN call. A remote queue can be open for output only. Local queues can be open for either input or output. A queue can be shared by more than one application.

3. ***Conduct your business via message exchanges.*** MQPUT puts a message on a local or remote queue. MQGET reads a message from a queue. MQPUT1 combines an open, put, and close in a single command. MQSET is used to control certain queue attributes, including *triggers*, which allow an application to deactivate itself and be invoked when certain events (or messages) occur. Triggering allows a server application to be started when messages are waiting to be processed. Finally, MQINQ allows an application to retrieve queue attributes, such as the maximum message size, the depth of the queue, and how many applications are using the queue.

4. ***Close the queue*** by issuing MQCLOSE. Other applications can still use the queue after you close it. If the queue is *permanent*, its contents are stored on disk and will be there the next time you open the queue. The queue does not have to be empty when you close it.

5. ***Disconnect from the local queue manager*** by issuing MQDISC.

The MQI calls support attributes like priority, message types, and data formatting. Applications written to the common MQI can be created more quickly, changed more easily, and ported readily to other platforms.

MQSeries: How It Works

Figure 22-2 shows the distributed components of MQ-Series. We will demonstrate how they work together by sending a message. The calling application must first address the message by giving it the name of the remote station queue manager and recipient queue (this is the route). It then invokes an MQI API to send the message. The MQSeries takes care of attaching all the routing information in the message header and transports the message using a *Message Channel Agent (MCA)*. MCAs communicate using the *Message Channel Protocol (MCP)*, a high level transport-independent protocol. When the message arrives at the remote system, the MCA delivers it to the remote API, which reads the header and puts the message into the application queue designated by the routing information. A *trigger* is used to notify the recipient that a message was received in its application queue. The recipient then issues a get command to read the message. The transfer is complete.

The MQSeries maintains routing tables that are used to associate inbound messages with their target queues and outbound messages to the proper remote station. *Alias names* may be used to redirect messages to queues other than the one to which they were originally addressed. Aliases allow server applications to be moved around the network transparently.

The MCP protocol supports multihop routes and provides store-and-forward capabilities, if required. MCPs run on top of standard transport protocols. Today, the MQSeries supports APPC (LU 6.2) on all platforms. Some platforms also support NetBEUI, IPX/SPX, and TCP/IP. MCPs can run one stack on one hop and another stack on the next. For example, DOS and Windows clients communicate to a mainframe via an OS/2 gateway, which runs NetBEUI (or IPX/SPX) on one side and APPC (LU 6.2) on the other.

MQI Message Types

The MQI products support four types of messages:

- **Request messages** are used by the client to request something from the server. A request message needs a reply.

- **Reply messages** are used in response to a request message.

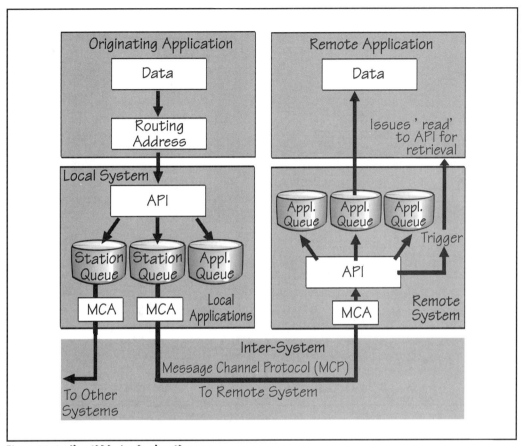

Figure 22-2. How MQSeries Sends a Message.

■ ***One-way messages or datagrams*** can carry data but do not require a reply.

■ ***Report messages*** are used for alerts or when something unexpected happens to other messages.

The message types help the recipient program understand what's expected of it. The queue manager itself doesn't care about the message type. Maximum message sizes are determined by the queue configurations.

Details

MQI Message Attributes

MQI products support very rich messaging semantics. Remember, these products make their living by delivering messages. So it is not surprising that each message they handle can be tagged with attributes that tell the system exactly what to do with it. Every message is special and can be customized to do whatever an application requires. How is that information conveyed between the queue managers? The MQI products do that by encapsulating each message with headers that describe all the unique attributes.

MQI products maintain the following header fields: the *unique id* is generated by the queue manager to ensure that each message is uniquely identified; the *correlation id* matches a reply message with a request; the *priority indicator* specifies the relative priority of the message; the *persistence indicator* identifies which messages are written to disk and are to be protected during restarts; the *format name* is used to indicate the data type of the application portion of the message; the *reply-to-queue* contains the name of the queue to which the reply message is directed; the *reply-to-queue manager* contains the name of the queue manager on which the reply queue resides; and the *report options* specify the messages that must be generated when an error occurs. ☐

MQSeries Message Queue Types

Message queues belong to queue managers. Application programs see two categories of queues:

■ *Local queues* belong to the local queue manager. The local queue is implemented as RAM buffers or as files on disk. The order in which messages are retrieved can be controlled by message priorities.

■ *Remote queues* belong to queue managers other than the one to which the application is connected. A remote queue can only be opened for input. When a persistent message is sent to a remote queue, a store-and-forward mechanism is used to the hold the message at each queue manager along the message route.

Queues can be created either statically or dynamically. Dynamic queues can be either temporary or permanent. Persistent messages must be stored in permanent queues.

How Does MQSeries Protect Your Messages?

How does the MQSeries protect messages from being lost halfway to their destinations with neither side knowing there's a problem? Or, the more general question is: How are messages protected in an asynchronous environment where the sender and the receiver are not directly in touch with one another? MQSeries protects its messages through the following techniques:

■ *Deletion-on-delivery*—the message is removed from the transmission queue only when delivery is confirmed.

■ *Recoverable queues*—a message is safely stored in a local file (or in non-volatile storage), where it will be retained until successfully delivered.

■ *Assured delivery*—if there is no connection between two adjacent queue managers, the message is safely stored until a connection is established and the message is delivered to the destination. This is all done transparently to the application.

■ *Syncpoint participation*—all changes in the queues are synchronized with changes to other resource managers (like DB2) using some form of syncpoint manager (like a TP Monitor).[2]

■ **Message journalling**—all information concerning transfers (including messages, time of transfer, and completion codes) is recorded in the message queues. Old messages may be automatically transferred (after a user-defined period) to a message journal that will hold message information indefinitely.

If the message cannot be delivered for some legitimate reason (such as lack of authority or the destination does not exist), it will be put on a "dead letter queue"; then the application decides what to do with it. A trigger associated with the dead letter queue can be used to call a standard error handler.

MQSeries: The Client/Server Configuration

The **MQSeries for OS/2** can be configured as either a client or server (see Figure 22-3). An OS/2 server provides queues and gateway services to DOS, Windows, and OS/2 MQSeries clients. The OS/2 server must provide a shared file system (such as NetWare or LAN Server) and communication stacks that allow it to act as a gateway to other MQSeries platforms.

---

[2] The syncpoint feature is not currently supported on the OS/2, AIX, and DEC platforms. Instead, a resource locking feature is provided.

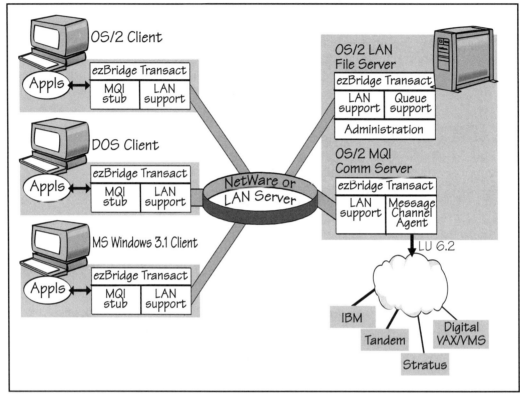

Figure 22-3. MQSeries for OS/2.

The client workstations link to an MQI run-time stub that is downloaded from the OS/2 server. All the queues in the LAN are resident in the file server, not on the client workstations. The client and server LAN configuration is under the jurisdiction of a queue manager. Within the domain of a file server, all queues are local because every client has access to the file server. If a message is destined for another LAN or remote host, the server's queue manager (actually, the MCA) will transmit the message to the appropriate remote queue; in this case, the server is acting as a gateway on behalf of its clients on the LAN.

A single LAN may support multiple servers and/or gateways (see Figure 22-4). These local queue managers communicate outside the LAN via one or more MCAs that act as gateways. We've shown an MCA on each server, but a single MCA gateway can act as a queue manager for multiple file servers. The MCA gateway uses either APPC (LU 6.2) or TCP/IP to communicate with remote queue managers. The protocol on the LAN is based on whatever the file server supports (NetBEUI for LAN Server and IPX/SPX for NetWare).

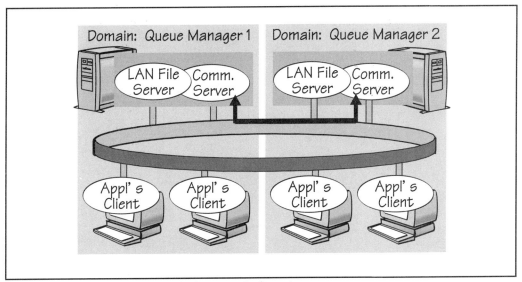

Figure 22-4. MQSeries for OS/2—Multiple Domain Configuration.

System Administration Features

MQSeries provides a user interface that allows administrators to:

■ Configure and change queues
■ Control and monitor the movement of messages from one queue handler to another

As we go to press, the MQSeries is not integrated with a managing platform like LAN NetView.

Packaging

The **MQSeries for OS/2** product—available from IBM or Systems Strategies—includes an OS/2 server and DOS, Windows, and OS/2 clients. A server with a single client costs $2,500; a server with up to four clients costs $4,000; a server with up to 16 clients costs $7,300; a server with up to 64 clients costs $12,100; and a server with up to 256 clients costs up to $25,000. This does not include the communications stacks or file server. Who said MOM was cheap? On the other hand, MQSeries sells for about $90k per node on mainframes, so PCs are cheap in comparison. About all we can say at this point is that the product is brand new (it shipped in the beginning of 1994) and that market pressures will bring the price down.

THE OTHER MOM PRODUCTS

In this section we present a brief overview of five multiplatform MOM products that run on OS/2: Peerlogic's **PIPES**, Covia Technologies Inc's **Communications Integrator**, Horizon Technologies Inc's **Message Express**, and IBM's **DAE** and **LANDP** products.

PIPES From PeerLogic

The PIPES MOM product by PeerLogic comes from a PC LAN tradition. It runs on DOS, Windows, OS/2, AIX, MVS, NetWare, SunOS and Solaris, HP-UX, and ULTRIX (see Figure 22-5). Support for OS/400 and DEC VMS is expected in March 1994. According to PeerLogic, PIPES on OS/2 was installed on 50,000 nodes by late 1993.

PIPES runs on multiple protocol stacks—including IPX/SPX, NetBIOS, TCP/IP, and APPC—and is able to locate the transport protocol at run time. The PIPES kernel can route messages from one protocol to another. For example, an application running on OS/2 using IPX/SPX could establish a peer session with a Windows machine across the world, even though their communications are routed via APPC (LU 6.2) over a corporate SNA network. Programmers do not specify the protocol

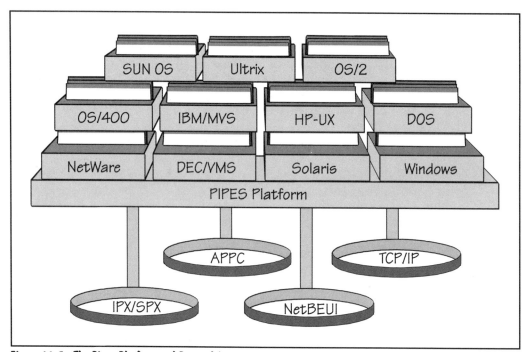

Figure 22-5. The Pipes Platform and Protocol Support.

in their programs; PIPES will discover the best-suited protocol automatically at run time.

All PIPES-based communications involves messages sent on sessions to and from *resources*. A resource is a named piece of executable code with which other processes on the network can converse. The message calls to the PIPES system are *asynchronous* (and non-blocking). They execute triggers (notification routines) supplied by programmers when asynchronous events complete. Messages can be either normal or expedited. Normal messages are sent with guaranteed delivery and sequencing. Expedited messages are sent with guaranteed delivery, but no guaranteed sequencing. The PIPES messaging API consists of 13 functions, callable from C language programs.

PIPES also provides a distributed naming service that uses the following naming hierarchy: *resource @application @machine @area @group @domain @network*. The physical location of a resource is hidden from the user. Resources can be moved from one location to another and PIPES will automatically update all the directories throughout its logical network.

PIPES also provides a highly-available and very comprehensive routing service. If a link goes down, PIPES searches for alternate routes (see Figure 22-6). If no alternate path is found, the session is terminated and the application is informed. PIPES also computes delays on different routes, and does some form of flow control by sending messages along the least congested routes. Each kernel can perform any PIPES function, so there is no single point of failure. PIPES, however, does not provide transactional support.

PIPES V 3.1 for OS/2 2.X supports the following protocol stacks: TCP/IP for OS/2 (by IBM, Novell, FTP or Wollongong), APPC (by IBM), NetBEUI (by IBM), and IPX/SPX (by Novell). PIPES for OS/2 requires 300 KBytes of memory and lists for $365 in single quantities (although very few accounts have been known to pay that price). The PIPES OS/2 Software Developer Toolkit sells for $365. PIPES supports SNMP and provides a MIB. As we go to press, very few tools are available to monitor and tweak system performance. However, PeerLogic announced that by March 1994 it will be supported by management platforms such as HP's OpenView, NetView, Sun, and Legent.

PIPES is distributed worldwide by Texas Instruments (TI)—TI's IEF application development tool uses PIPES as its middleware. Because PIPES does not support general queuing—including file transfers, store-and-forward, and message filters—it complements other MOM middleware products such as MQSeries. PIPES is a lower-level, connection-oriented MOM when compared with MQI. According to PeerLogic, PIPES will soon be able to run with the MQSeries and obtain the support of MQI's store-and-forward messaging and queues. You'll need to purchase the two

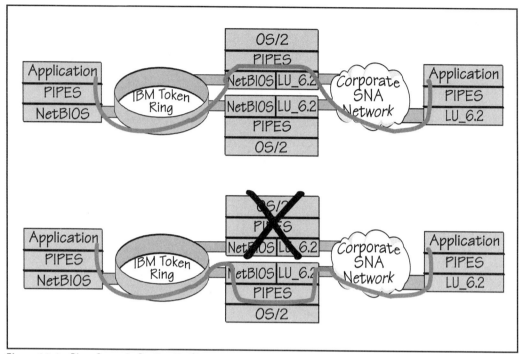

Figure 22-6. Pipes Dynamic Routing Facility.

products to get the combined effect of MQI and the very dynamic PIPES logical network.

Communications Integrator V 3.0 From Covia

Communications Integrator (CI) V 3.0 by Covia Technologies is a high-end MOM product with mission critical pedigrees. Covia Technologies was originally created to support the massive airline reservation system (known as Apollo) used by United Airlines, several international carriers, car rental agencies, and hotels.[3] Covia runs on the following OS platforms: OS/2, MS-DOS, Windows, MVS, Tandem (Guardian), Stratus (VOS), DEC VMS, AIX, OS/400, HP-UX, Solaris and SunOS, and NCR's Unix SVR4 variant (see Figure 22-7). Current protocols supported include APPC (LU 6.2), NetBEUI, IPX/SPX, and TCP/IP.

Each CI provides message routing with full protection (persistent queues), seven priority levels, and many delivery options, including notification on delivery, notifi-

---

[3] Apollo supports 80,000 nodes and handles 1,000 transactions per second, with an average response time of 2.5 seconds.

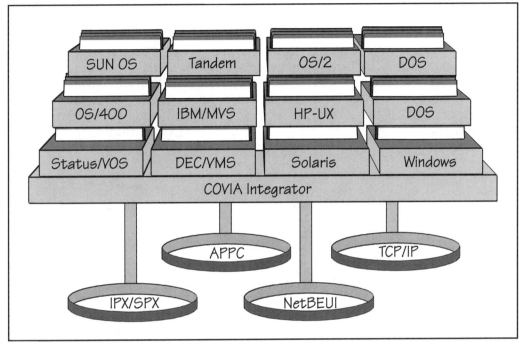

Figure 22-7. The Covia Platform and Protocol Support.

cation on exception, and send-and-pray. It provides "time-to-live" support that stops lost messages and provides critical message assurance (but no syncpointing or transactional support). CI also provides routing, load distribution, and flow control support across networks. Messages can be routed across multiple hops on heterogeneous platforms. A CI provides a simple API consisting of two calls—send and receive.

Now get ready for the shock—Covia charges a whopping $1200 per node for single quantities of its OS/2 or Windows product ($450 per copy in quantities of 16). The good news is that the price goes down by 20% for each additional client after that. It could be worse; Covia charges over $45k per node on some MVS mainframes. Covia thinks it can justify those steep prices because its CIs eliminate the requirement for gateways and routers and they consolidate the number of SNA sessions. It also claims it can save money with its robust CMIP or SNMP2 MIB agents.

Covia provides an OS/2 based console for viewing CIs, configuring them, and creating routing tables (the routes are manual). Its MIB agents also work with standard management tools. In other news, Covia is working with Sun on creating a MOM version of the Sun RPC that is implemented using the CI messaging services.

Message Express From Horizon Strategies

Horizon Strategies was founded in 1989 by two SNA distributed application developers who felt there must be an easier way to develop heterogeneous middleware. Today, they offer a MOM product, **Message Express**, that runs on the following OS platforms: OS/2, DOS, Windows, NetWare, OS/400, Tandem (Guardian), Stratus (VOS), MVS, DEC (VMS), AIX, and various Unix platforms (see Figure 22-8). Current protocols supported include APPC (LU 6.2), TCP/IP, DECnet, Named Pipes, and IPX/SPX.

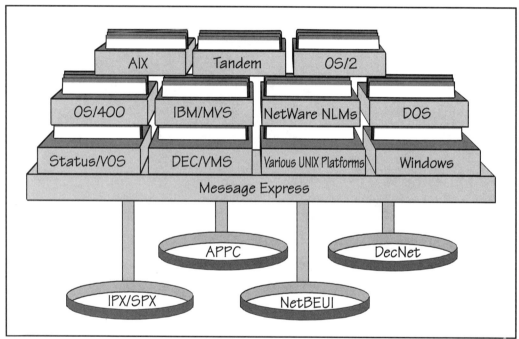

Figure 22-8. The Message Express Platform and Protocol Support.

Message Express is based on an "intelligent" message queue management system that is accessed by four simple API calls: MX_Snd, MX_Rcv, MX_Req_Stat, and MX_Snd_Msg_Conf. So what makes it so intelligent? The latest version of Message Express is designed as a *state machine* that reacts to incoming messages (the events). Each message passed between systems carries its own state information, which helps Message Express decide what to do next with that message. All the concurrency and state information is placed in the message itself, thus improving reliability and performance. As an added benefit, the company claims that this architecture helped create a highly portable message engine (90% of their core code is portable across platforms).

Message Express uses a static naming scheme based on *location tables* to define which application pairs (and their network addresses) can talk to each other. They claim that their customers want this type of tight administration control; they call it "trusted partner management." The product, however, allows you to designate alternate routes, and it will dynamically reroute traffic as needed by conditions in the network and according to message priorities. In the OS/2 product, the location tables are stored on disk using indexed sequential files.

The message queues can be of any size within the limitations of the physical memory. The product supports volatile (in memory) and persistent queues (on disk). The persistent queues are secure and under journal protection (they will survive system outages). Message Express supports five levels of message synchronization: no acknowledgement; acknowledge when message reaches the remote queue; acknowledge when message reaches the application; wait for a confirmation message from the application; and treat the message as part of a chain (but it does not provide syncpointing or transactional recovery). The product can notify applications when certain events occur. In addition, all message traffic can be logged, audited, tracked, and analyzed using system administration facilities.

In addition to messaging, Message Express provides its own RPC and file transfer mechanisms. And they are thinking about adding an SQL capability later in 1994. This "all-in-one" approach is unique and is very convenient in certain situations. The downside is that it locks you into a single vendor implementation. However, that single middleware may eventually run on 22 different hardware platforms and support seven different protocols. The irony is that we may be trading off open hardware for closed middleware.

Message Express for OS/2 sells for $595 in single quantities. (Are you desensitized to price by now?) Mainframe versions can cost up to $35,000. Horizon Strategies is almost ready to release a GUI-based management tool that lets you manage an entire network from a single location.

LANDP/2 V2 From IBM

LANDP/2 V2, introduced by IBM in May 1993, is a rich middleware product with *some* MOM facilities such as "store and forward." LANDP was initially designed for the finance industry, and it includes servers to support specific financial devices. LANDP has a large customer base in the financial industry but is also becoming a platform for cross-industry client/server applications. Its client/server middleware runs on the following platforms: DOS, Windows, OS/2, OS/400, and AIX (see Figure 22-9). Current protocols supported include NetBEUI, TCP/IP, X.25, and SNA.

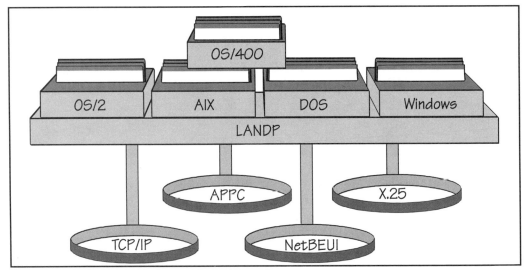

Figure 22-9. IBM's LANDP Platform and Protocol Support.

LANDP creates an environment where each heterogeneous machine on the network can be a client or a server (or both). It provides a general mechanism for servers to register themselves and for clients to obtain services using a set of platform independent APIs across multiple languages (it even provides Smalltalk and C++ class libraries for its services). LANDP is an eclectic product. It provides some of its own services—including store and forward messaging, RPC, a shared ISAM file system, system management, a remote batch command execution facility, and banking services. It acts as middleware for other services—such as access to the CICS OS/2 TP Monitor and submitting SQL queries to an Informix database on AIX. And finally, it acts as middleware for middleware—for example, it enables DDE message exchanges across networks and it interoperates with the DCE RPC on AIX. LANDP makes the access to the physical location of the service completely transparent to the applications.

LANDP's main MOM service consists of a *store-for-forwarding* server and a *forwarding server*. A typical LANDP server consists of a loop; a program calls GETREQ to retrieve a message and the response is passed back to the client via an RMTRPLY call. The store-for-forwarding server stores messages (LANDP calls them transactions) originating in the LAN that cannot be sent to a mainframe (or other LANDP node) because of a failed connection. You can also use this server during normal operations as a queue to transmit all the messages at once or when certain conditions are met. The forwarding server complements the store-and-forwarding server. It retrieves stored data from the queue and transmits it automatically or at periodic intervals. The forwarding server can transmit data while the store-and-forwarding server is adding data. Messages are presented in the order sent. The routing service provides its own directory and namespaces. LANDP currently uses the **DataTrade** MOM model, which is quite popular in the financial industry. But the product is very adaptable; it intends to support the MQI messaging APIs in some future release.

LANDP/2 is CID-enabled and supports the generation of alerts to NetView and distributed security. The **LANDP/2 for OS/2** product sells for $539 in single units. However, the product provides much more functionality than MOM, so we're not comparing apples to oranges. It all depends on how much you value the services LANDP/2 provides.

DAE from IBM

The **Distributed Automation Edition (DAE)**, also from IBM, is probably the oldest heterogeneous client/server NOS in the industry. DAE was initially designed for the manufacturing industry. It provides a full set of NOS services in support of manufacturing devices, robots, workstations, and mainframes. What makes DAE unique is that its entire NOS infrastructure, consisting of hundreds of services, is built on top of a MOM architecture. Everything in DAE communicates via message queues. And they've had many years to perfect their MOM in mission-critical manufacturing environments. DAE runs on the following platforms: DOS, Windows, OS/2, AIX, OS/400, and VM (see Figure 22-10). They also provide an OS for real-time controllers on top of the Artic cards. DAE's MOM isolates all its environments from the lower-level communication stacks, and it runs on top of NetBEUI, MAP 3.0, APPC, DECnet, IPX/SPX, and TCP/IP.

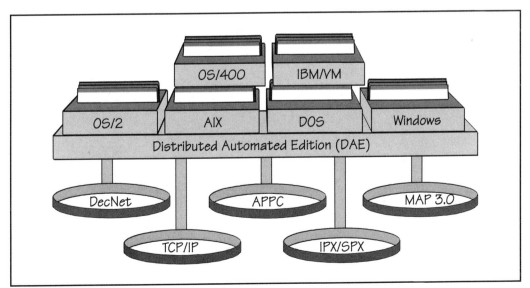

Figure 22-10. The DAE Platform and Protocol Support.

DAE started as a pure-bred MOM product and evolved to provide all kinds of distributed services—including a TP Monitor lite (TxE), a platform-independent GUI-builder, file services, robot support (device services), SQL database access, and queuing support. Like LANDP/2, DAE provides a platform-independent client/server environment (with hundreds of portable APIs) that software vendors can use to create applications that port (and interoperate) across the DAE platforms. Of course, most of the portable DAE-enabled applications—including Paperless, PlantWorks, and PlantControl—are in manufacturing. DAE's most complete client/server offering is on OS/2.

To summarize, DAE is more than a MOM product. Its single quantity pricing starts at $269 per node (for the DOS, OS/2, and AIX clients). Servers start at $930, but the price goes up with number of services required. DAE is in the process of replacing many of its proprietary NOS services (like the security and directory services) with the equivalent DCE components. The modernized DAE will then be in the unique position of offering MOM services that are tightly coupled with DCE. When you add the OS-independent portability layer, it all makes for a strong middleware offering.

Is MOM All Hype?

Soapbox

No, MOM is not all hype. It's a technology developed by early client/server practitioners to solve the real-world communication problems created by connecting heterogeneous platforms. MOM is the easiest way to get all these disparate systems to talk to each other without too much fuss. In many cases, MOM is superior to RPC and easier to use. However, MOM introduces its own set of problems:

- MOM products do not interoperate with each other.

- MOM products do not support a common set of messaging APIs. It would help if they picked a common API, hopefully MQI, and had it anointed by X/Open.

- MOM products use proprietary directory services, distributed security, and naming schemes. Their cause could really be furthered if they were to use some of the DCE (or NetWare) NOS services. Yes, the MOM people had to create their own schemes because there was nothing there to help them. But the times are changing.

■ MOMs are designed to deal with short, structured messages. They do *not* store-and-forward the free format documents and BLOBs created by e-mail, office systems, and multimedia applications. These type of messages are best handled by the groupware-specific middleware we will cover in later chapters.

As MOM products evolve, they may take the DAE route and expand their repertoire of OS-independent APIs. For example, the Message Express product is being evolved to support object associations, database access, and remote file access. In other words, MOM vendors will evolve and become general middleware providers. After all, why stop with MOM when you already have a heterogeneous platform base. Of course, if they do that, they will collide with service-specific middleware vendors.

MOM vendors (with the exception of IBM) are little fish. They face the danger of having their services subsumed by the general NOS products (for example, Novell may bundle a MOM service with NetWare). If that happens, will they survive? MOM products have the advantage of running on more heterogeneous platforms *today*. These products are field tested, robust, and real. That's a big advantage. However, can the MOM vendors maintain their headstart? If they do, can they expand beyond their narrow focus and become the middleware vendors of choice? We don't have the answers. ❑

Part 4
SQL Database
Servers

An Introduction to Part 4

Ah! You're still with us, so you must have enjoyed the "single system illusion" in the last part. NOSs and stacks are great—there can be no client/server computing without them. But the real hot area in client/server today is in SQL databases. Have you Martians heard about Database Valley? That's a strip of highway south of San Francisco where database companies are creating a new California Gold Rush. But in the new Gold Rush, they mine SQL instead of gold.

So pack your luggage: We're heading west. What? You Martians don't have cowboy boots? No problem. They wear sneakers in Database Valley. You won't need mining gear, either. All the modern mining is done on computer screens by looking at SQL tables and relational calculus. The guy who discovered the gold, a guru named Codd, is a mathematician. Yes, an abstract mathematician created a new Gold Rush with tables. No, the tables are not made of gold. They're computer creations that point to other tables and store and organize information. In this part, we're going to visit the gold country and understand how putting SQL databases on client/server networks could have created such a commotion.

Even though all these new database barons live within a few miles from each other, they all speak different SQL dialects. They can't understand each other. And the biggest barons are always charging ahead with new features that bring in more gold. So how do they ever work together? By throwing tons of middleware onto networks. These folks have agreed to create loosely coupled database federations fueled by middleware. The more ambitious are now proposing to pull all the world's data into warehouses and transform it into information. The warehouses could turn into perpetual gold-generating machines.

The plan for Part 4 is to first look at what this SQL stuff is all about: What standards are being created? What awesome new extensions are the barons concocting? We then look at the middleware needed to create the database federations. With all this preparation behind us, we can look at these fabulous warehouses—the new gold-mining machines. We close with an overview of some representative products that give us some form of reality check. When you deal with gold rushes and California dreams, you really need reality checks.

Chapter 23

SQL
Database
Servers

At present the majority of existing client/server-based software is to be found in the area of databases, and it is here that the greatest challenge to any corporation currently lies.

— Richard Finkelstein,
President of Performance Computing

This chapter covers SQL databases from a client/server perspective. SQL servers are the dominant model for creating client/server applications. SQL server vendors—including Oracle, Sybase, Informix, Ingres, and Gupta—have almost become household names. Why is SQL so popular from a client/server connectivity perspective? Can relational databases hold the fort against newer models of client/server computing—including object databases, distributed object managers, and groupware? Are TP Monitors needed, or can we do just fine with the stored procedures provided by the database vendors? In this chapter, we give you a snapshot of where things are in database-centric client/server computing. This sets the stage for answering these questions later in the book.

Our plan for this chapter is to first look at the magic of SQL and the relational model from a client/server perspective. We go over the standards—including SQL-89,

SQL-92, and SQL3. We conclude with the important SQL "extensions" that add active intelligence to tables—including stored procedures, rules, and triggers.[1]

THE FUNDAMENTALS OF SQL AND RELATIONAL DATABASES

Perhaps the most important trend among database servers of any size is the emergence of SQL as the *lingua franca* for the manipulation, definition, and control of data. SQL, now an ISO standard, is a powerful set-oriented language consisting of a few commands; it was created as a language for databases that adhere to the *relational model*.

SQL's Relational Origins

The relational model of database management was developed at IBM's San Jose Research Lab in the early 1970s by E.F. Codd. SQL—pronounced "sequel"—originally stood for Structured Query Language; now the acronym is the name. It was also developed by IBM Research in the mid-1970s to serve as an "English-like" front-end query language to the System R relational database prototype. Even though the SQL language is English-like, it is firmly rooted in the solid mathematical foundation of set theory and predicate calculus. What this really means is that SQL consists of a short list of powerful, yet highly flexible, *commands* that can be used to manipulate information collected in tables. Through SQL, you manipulate and control *sets* of records at a time. You tell the SQL server what data you need; then it figures out how to get to the data.

The relational model calls for a clear separation of the physical aspects of data from their logical representation. Data is made to appear as simple tables that mask the complexity of the storage access mechanisms. The model frees you from having to concern yourself with the details of how the data is stored and makes the access to data purely logical. Using SQL statements, you only need to specify the tables, columns, and row qualifiers to get to any data item.

Oracle Corporation was the first company to offer a commercial version of SQL with its Oracle database in 1979. In the early 1980s, IBM came out with its own SQL products: SQL/DS and DB2. Today, over 200 vendors offer SQL products on PCs, superminis, and mainframes. Most of these products incorporate the SQL-89

---

[1] In spite of its length, this chapter is not a general introduction to programming with SQL. Here's a shameless advertisement: You'll find a lengthy introduction to SQL and 400 pages of detailed SQL programming examples in our book, **Client/Server Programming with OS/2 2.1** (VNR, 1993).

standard features, some include SQL-92 features, and a few have even implemented their proprietary versions of SQL3 functions.

SQL has become the predominant database language of mainframes, minicomputers, and LAN Servers where it provides the focus for a market-share battleground. The emergence of SQL client tools that can work across servers is heating up the competition even more, making SQL a horizontal industry where you can "mix-and-match" front-end tools with back-end servers.

What Does SQL Do?

The SQL language is used to perform complex data operations with a few simple commands in situations that would have required hundreds of lines of conventional code. Physicists might call SQL "the grand unified theory of database" because of the multifaceted roles it plays. Here is a partial list of roles:

- ***SQL is an interactive Query Language for ad hoc database queries.*** SQL was originally designed as an end-user query language. However, modern graphical front ends to SQL databases are much more intuitive to use. And they do a good job hiding the underlying SQL semantics from end users.

- ***SQL is a database programming language.*** It can be embedded in languages such as C, C++, and COBOL to access data or it can be called using the X/Open callable interface API set. Vendors, like Sybase and Oracle, even offer SQL-specific programming languages. SQL provides a consistent language for programming with data. This raises programmer productivity and helps produce a more maintainable and easy to change system.

- ***SQL is a data definition and data administration language.*** The data definition language is used to define simple tables, complex objects, indexes, views, referential integrity constraints, and security and access control. All the SQL-defined objects are automatically tracked (and maintained) in an active data dictionary (that is, system catalogs). The structure and organization of a SQL database is stored in the database itself.

- ***SQL is the language of networked database servers.*** It is being used as a universal language to access and manipulate all types of data. For example, the IBM Information Warehouse uses SQL as the network access standard for both relational and non-relational data (like IMS and Indexed files). Even the object database vendors are adopting a derivative of SQL as a query language for objects.

■ **SQL helps protect the data in a multiuser networked environment.** It does that by providing good reliability features such as data validation, referential integrity, rollback (undo transaction), automatic locking, and deadlock detection and resolution in a multiuser LAN environment. SQL also enforces security and access control to database objects.

SQL provides a number of advantages to system builders because the same language that is used to define the database is also used to manipulate it. The SQL language makes it easy to specify product requirements in an unambiguous manner. This helps communications between customers, developers, and Database Administrators (DBAs).

The ISO Standards: SQL-89, SQL-92, and SQL3

Although many commercial implementations of SQL have existed since 1979, there was no official standard until 1986, when one was published jointly by the American National Standard Institute (ANSI) and the International Standards Organization (ISO). The 1986 standard was revised in 1989 to introduce referential (and check constraints) integrity; it is now known as *SQL-89* or ANSI SQL. In late 1989, a separate ANSI addendum for Embedded SQL was added to SQL-89.

SQL-89

The SQL-89 standard was an "intersection of the SQL implementations of that time," which made it easy for existing products to conform to it. SQL-89 was a watered-down SQL that made the term "SQL compliant" almost meaningless. Vendors (like Gupta, Oracle, and XDB) would usually add DB2 (or SAA) compliance to their checklist of compliances. And even that didn't mean too much, at least in terms of creating a unified SQL.

SQL-92

The ISO *SQL-92* (also called SQL2), ratified in late 1992, is over five times the length of the original SQL-89 standard. SQL-92 standardizes many of the features previously left to the implementor's discretion (i.e., the loopholes) and is essentially a superset of SQL-89. C.J. Date estimates that it's going to take a big implementation effort to bring the current relational databases to SQL-92 standards. To get around that problem, ISO suggests a staged approach with three levels of compliance: entry, intermediate, and full. To help you understand where you're at, the SQL-92 standard introduces the concept of a *flagger*—a program that examines the source code and "flags" all SQL statements that do not conform to SQL-92.

What's New in SQL-92?

Details

Incidentally, the word "relation" does not appear anywhere in the standard. And the word "database" is used only informally (it is formally replaced by "SQL data"). This is a relational database standard?

— C.J. Date (May, 1993)

This section provides a quick summary of what's new in SQL-92 for readers who are already familiar with SQL and the previous SQL-89 standard. If you're not familiar with SQL, first read this chapter and then come back to this box.

The previous SQL-89 standard supports the SQL Data Definition Language (DDL) for creating tables, indexes, views, and referential integrity constraints. The standard also supports GRANT/REVOKE security privileges. The SQL-89 Data Manipulation Language (DML) consists of the SELECT, INSERT, UPDATE, and DELETE commands. COMMIT and ROLLBACK are used for transaction management. A cursor mechanism provides row-at-a-time navigation. The SQL-89 Embedded SQL addendum defines the mechanism for embedding SQL statements in FORTRAN, COBOL, PL/I, and Pascal.

The "new" SQL-92 standard supports all the SQL-89 features and adds the following features:

- ■ *SQL agents*—these are defined as programs or interactive users that produce SQL statements. In the previous standard, SQL statements were associated with Authorization IDs (an ambiguous concept).

- ■ *SQL client/server connections*—before performing any database operations, a SQL agent must ask the SQL client code to CONNECT to some SQL server. A connection establishes a SQL session. SQL-92 supports concurrent connections (or sessions) but only one can be active at a given time. Agents can explicitly switch between connections using the SET CONNECTION command.

- ■ *More granular transaction controls*—using the SET TRANSACTION command, we can specify a transaction as read-only or read/write. A read-only transaction cannot change the state of the database. In addition, we can set the *isolation level* (i.e., the level of automatic lock protection) for a given transaction to *read-uncommitted, read-committed, read-repeatable,* or *serializable.*

- ***Standardized catalogs for describing the structure of a database.*** A catalog, in the new standard, is a collection of *SQL-schemas* describing "one database." The schemas are SQL tables that describe the structure of base tables, views, privileges, constraints, etc. Each SQL-session has one *cluster* of catalogs describing all the data available to that session.

- ***Embedded SQL support for new languages***—including C, Ada, and MUMPS.

- ***Support for dynamic SQL***—including dynamic cursors and the typical commands (with minor surprises) that have been used by most database vendors to generate SQL code at run time.

- ***Support for new data types***—including BLOBs, VARCHAR, DATE, TIME, and TIMESTAMP.

- ***Support for temporary tables***—including local and global tables. Temporary tables are used as working storage and are automatically dropped at the end of a session. Think of them as memory variables created using the SQL DDL statement with the TEMPORARY attribute.

- ***Support for join operators***—including outer join, union join (no matching), cross join (all combinations), and inner join. All of these joins are supported with special operators in the FROM clauses of queries. SQL-89 did not specify mechanisms for creating the different types of joins.

- ***Standardized error codes and diagnostics.*** The use of SQLCODE is not recommended any more; the preferred approach is to use SQLSTATE, which contains a five-character text string with standard values for the different error conditions. A GET DIAGNOSTICS statement was introduced to return more error information.

- ***Domain checks and constraints***—including domain constraints (acceptable values), assertions, and base table constraints. Constraints are rules that a user defines to restrict the values of what goes into the table columns. Any constraint can be defined to be immediate or deferred.

- ***Miscellaneous improvements***—including new string functions, scrollable cursors, commands for altering and dropping objects, refinements to the referential integrity model, support for data type conversions, improvements in revoking privileges, and a CASE statement.

Some of the "new" SQL-92 features are already implemented in existing database products. However, be prepared for a few surprises in almost every area, regardless of how familiar they may seem. ❑

SQL3

Even though it may take vendors many more years to become fully SQL-92 compliant, a new 1000-page SQL3 draft is already in circulation. The specification will be broken into four documents: SQL/CLI, Persistent Stored Modules (or SQL/PSM), SQL/Bindings (with application languages), and SQL3, which covers everything left over. Each document will progress independently—it's a multipart standard. SQL3 adds many new features to an already bloated SQL-92 standard. But we don't expect SQL3 to be ratified until the latter part of the decade. Just to calibrate you, it took three years before the early SQL-92 draft, which appeared sometime in 1989, became a standard. However, it's important to get a cursory understanding of what's being proposed in the SQL3 standard to get an idea of where SQL is heading (see Figure 23-1).

Figure 23-1. The Evolution of the SQL Specification.

The most important new features in the SQL3 draft are the Object SQL features—including encapsulation, methods, user-defined data types, and inheritance. The SQL3 spec refers to these functions as *MOOSE*, which stands for *Major Object-Oriented SQL Extensions*. We will return to Object DBMSs in Part 7.

SQL3 is also developing the specification for stored procedures, triggers, and user-defined functions. It will probably incorporate a revised version of the X/Open SQL *Callable Level Interface (CLI)*, which supports stored procedures. In addition, SQL3 may also include specifications for multimedia SQL (SQL/MM). The ISO group commissioned to look at the implications of "full text" data for SQL recently expanded its charter to include the more general issue of multimedia data—including full text, digitized audio, video clips, spatial and seismic data, and other forms of real-life data structures. SQL/MM, like MOOSE, will use abstract data types to define the operations supported on each multimedia object type. Unlike today's BLOBs, abstract data types provide methods to manipulate each of the multimedia data types. Providing the storage is the easy part; the harder part is providing the methods and enough multimedia-specific data fields that allow us to do something meaningful with these BLOBs (like rotating or playing them). As DEC's Jim Melton, one of the key SQL3 strategists, puts it, "BLOBs and objects are two very different animals."

The SQL3 draft also contains suggested SQL improvements—including persistent (or "held") cursors that remain open after a commit, new join types, temporary views, user-defined roles in security, column specific privileges, and a better definition of how to update views. It also deals with esoteric topics—including syncpoints over sessions, subtables and supertables, and asynchronous SQL statement execution.

WHAT DOES A DATABASE SERVER DO?

In a database-centric client/server architecture, a client application usually requests data and data-related services (such as sorting and filtering) from a database server. The database server, also known as the SQL engine, responds to the client's requests and provides secured access to shared data. A client application can, with a single SQL statement, retrieve and modify a set of server database records. The SQL database engine can filter the query result sets resulting in considerable data communication savings.

A SQL server manages the control and execution of SQL commands. It provides the logical and physical views of the data and generates optimized access plans for executing the SQL commands. In addition, most database servers provide server administration features and utilities that help manage the data. A database server also maintains dynamic catalog tables that contain information about the SQL objects housed within it.

Because a SQL server allows multiple applications to access the same database at the same time, it must provide an environment that protects the database against a variety of possible internal and external threats. The server manages the recovery, concurrency, security, and consistency aspects of a database. This includes controlling the execution of a transaction and undoing its effects if it fails. This also includes obtaining and releasing locks during the course of executing a transaction and protecting database objects from unauthorized access.

Most SQL servers provide, at a minimum, SQL-89 level functionality. Most servers also include some SQL-92 features, but to our knowledge no vendor has yet implemented a fully compliant SQL-92 server. Quite a few servers offer proprietary versions of SQL3 stored procedures, triggers, and rules. Some server engines (for example, Ingres) have implemented some form of SQL Object extensions.

So what is a SQL server? It's a strange hybrid mix of standard SQL and vendor-specific extensions. The leading database-only vendors—including Sybase, Oracle, Informix, and Ingres—have a vested interest in extending the database engines to perform server functions that go far beyond the relational data model. The more diversified system software vendors—including IBM, DEC, Tandem, and Novell—are inclined to stick with SQL standards and offload the non-standard procedural extensions to NOSs (like DCE), TP Monitors, Object Databases, and Distributed Object Managers. Finally, some of the smaller database vendors—including Gupta, XDB, and Watcom—are making their mark by creating "best-of-breed," standard-compliant implementations of SQL.

In this section, we briefly go over the architecture of database servers. We then review some of the major features they provide—including shared data access, transactional protection, referential and domain integrity, and database catalogs.

SQL Database Server Architectures

Figures 23-2, 23-3, and 23-4 show three server architectures that databases use to handle remote database clients: process-per-client, multithreaded, and hybrid. Here are the trade-offs of the three approaches:

- ***Process-per-client architectures*** provide maximum bullet-proofing by giving each database client its own process address space. The database runs in one or more separate background processes. The advantages of this architecture is that it protects the users from each other, and it protects the database manager from the users. In addition, the processes can easily be assigned to different processors on a multiprocessor SMP machine. Because the architecture relies on the local OS for its multitasking services, an OS that supports SMP can transparently assign server processes to a pool of available processors. The disadvantage of process-per-client is that it consumes more memory and CPU resources than the alternative schemes. It can be slower because of process context switches and interprocess communications overhead. However, these problems can easily be overcome with the use of a TP Monitor that manages a pool of reusable processes. Examples of database servers that implement this architecture include DB2/2, Informix, and Oracle6.

- ***Multithreaded architectures*** provide the best performance by running all the user connections, applications, and the database in the same address space. This architecture provides its own internal scheduler and does not rely on the local OS's tasking and address protection schemes. The advantage is that it conserves memory and CPU cycles by not requiring frequent context switches. In addition, the server implementations tend to be more portable across platforms because they don't require as many local OS services. The disadvantage

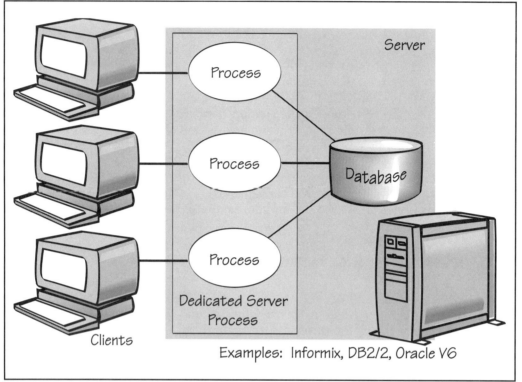

Figure 23-2. Process-per-Client Database Server Architecture.

is that a misbehaved user application can bring down the entire database server and all its tasks. In addition, user programs that consist of long-duration tasks (for example, long queries) can hog all the server resources. Finally, the preemptive scheduling provided by the server tends to be inferior to the native OS's scheduler. Examples of database servers that implement this architecture include Sybase and SQL Server (but SQL Server uses Windows NT's SMP scheduler instead of the one provided by Sybase).

■ *Hybrid architectures* consist of three components: 1) multithreaded network listeners that participate in the initial connection task by assigning the client to a dispatcher; 2) dispatchers are tasks that place messages on an internal message queue, and then dequeue the response and send it back to the client; and 3) reusable shared server worker processes that pick the work off the queue, execute it, and place the response on an out queue. The advantage of this architecture is that it provides a protected environment for running the user tasks without assigning a permanent process to each user. The disadvantages are queue latencies. While this architecture, appears on the surface to be good, its load balancing is not as good as that provided by a TP Monitor. In fact, the queues may get in the way of the TP Monitor's own scheduling algorithms. The

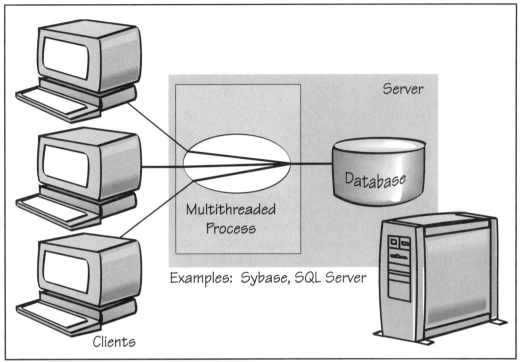

Figure 23-3. Multithreaded Database Server Architecture.

first database server to implement this architecture is Oracle7. According to Rich Finkelstein, you can expect anywhere from 20% improvements to 20% degradation of performance between Oracle V6 and Oracle7.

So which architecture is best for client/server? It's a tough choice. The process-per-client architectures perform poorly when large number of users connect to a database, but they provide the best protection. The multithreaded architectures can support large number of users running short transactions, but they do not perform well when large queries are involved. They also do not provide bullet-proof protection. Hybrid architectures are, in theory, very promising. But are they better than using a TP Monitor with a process-per-client database server?

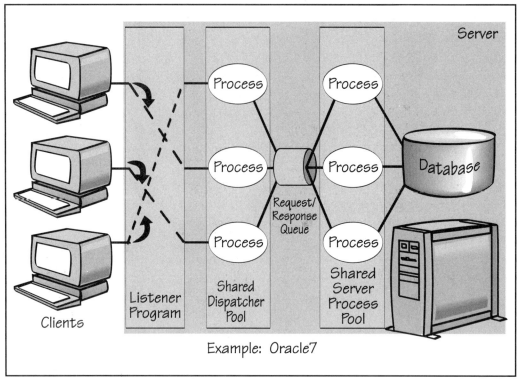

Figure 23-4. Hybrid Database Server Architecture.

Database Servers: Implementing the SQL Language

The primary job of a database server is to execute the SQL commands in a protected environment. SQL commands are divided into three categories:

- ■ **Data Definition Language (DDL)** consists of SQL commands that define database objects such as tables, views, and indexes. The DDL is also used to define the integrity constraints on the objects created. This allows the SQL database server to ensure that the things users do to those objects are correct.

- ■ **Data Manipulation Language (DML)** consists of SQL commands through which users can select, update, insert, or delete rows of information. These data access and manipulation functions are, of course, the principal reason for using a database server. A relational database allows you to access data without knowing its position in the database (no pointers).

■ ***Data Control Language (DCL)*** consists of SQL commands that help the server manage the recovery, concurrency, security, and consistency aspects of a database. This includes transaction controls, lock management, and protecting database objects from unauthorized access.

We will now briefly review some of these SQL language features and what they can do for client/server applications.

Working With Tables and Views

A *table* object, also known as the *base* table, is the most basic database object. Tables are defined as a series of *columns*. *Views* provide "logical tables." These are tables that do not exist in physical storage but consist of data obtained through a query against one or more tables. Views do not contain data; instead, they refer to data stored in base tables. A view is a way of creating "windows" through which data in base tables can be viewed. These windows can be used to simplify the view of data, to reorder columns, or to rename a table. Views can also be used to enforce data security. For example, by creating a view, you can restrict data access to certain rows and columns in the base tables. Views, like base tables, can be used to retrieve, update, or delete data.

Many times, the data you want will not be in one table. A single SQL SELECT command can be used to retrieve data from more than one table through a process called *join*. To join two or more tables, you specify the table names in the FROM clause and the connection between them in the WHERE clause (this is called the *join predicate*). A join predicate based on the equality relationship is called an *equijoin*. In addition, SQL-92 defines outer join, union join (no matching), cross join (all combinations), and inner join. All of these joins are supported with special operators in the FROM clauses of queries. SQL-89 did not specify mechanisms for creating the different types of joins.

SQL Optimizers: Working With Indexes and Plans

The mechanics of SQL data access are handled by the server and vary from implementation to implementation. You simply ask for data and let the server figure out how to find it. You can speed up searches by creating an index on one or more table columns. However, the index from then on belongs to the database server; it decides how to use it. An *index* is a SQL structure that provides rapid access to table data. The index consists of a set of pointers that are logically ordered by the values of a key. A *key* consists of one or more columns that identify one or more rows within a table. An index provides a way for defining keys outside of the table definition. It also stores a pointer to the key values of each row in an indexed table.

The pointers are typically stored in B-Tree format, which speeds up row access and updates. You create indexes on frequently accessed columns to improve performance. More than one index may be defined on a table.

Before a database server executes a SQL command, it must create a *plan* that determines the best strategy for executing that statement. The component in the database in charge of creating the plan is called the *SQL optimizer.* A great deal of the credit for the improved performance of relational databases goes to the optimizer—it's an expert that specializes in minimizing the number of disk accesses for getting to the requested data. Almost all the SQL servers on the market use a *cost-based optimizer* that looks at database-collected statistics to calculate the execution path with the smallest number of disk I/Os. Optimizers create the access plans using sophisticated heuristics; they optimize the data access strategy based on the current state of the database.

The optimizer needs timely and accurate statistics to do its job properly. The information at the optimizer's disposal for making such decisions consists of statistics stored in the system catalog. Based on those statistics, the optimizer will decide whether to use an index or to sequentially scan an entire table. Most SQL servers give you control of when these table statistics are generated. You should refresh those statistics after significant changes have occurred to the database, including the import of a large number of data records, the restructuring of tables, threshold points in the steady growth of a database, and after an index is added or deleted. Statistics are gathered during off hours so that it does not impact database performance.

Because optimizing plans are extremely time-consuming to calculate, the trade-off is to store them with a precompiled SQL statement or stored procedure so as not to recalculate them at run time. These stored access plans are part of a SQL *package.* The process of storing the access plans is called *binding.* You bind packages to the database during precompilation, or do it later through a separate command. You should always rebind your static SQL programs and stored procedures after a refresh of statistics so that they can take advantage of the new statistics.

Your only involvement with indexes is to define them. After that, the database server retains full control of when to use an index for retrieval. The database server is also fully in charge of maintaining the indexes and keeping them synchronized with the underlying base tables. Depending on the run-time conditions, you may be required to issue occasional commands to refresh the statistics, reorganize tables, and rebind static SQL or stored procedure plans. Most database servers support these commands. Some database servers provide an *explain* command that lets you see (and sometimes influence) the optimizer's choice of execution plans.

Protecting the Data's Integrity

Data integrity is concerned with the correctness and consistency of data in a database. The SQL database server's first line of defense is to enforce user-defined integrity constraints on the data. A *constraint* defines the conditions that data must meet to be entered in the database. A constraint is also how you tell the database server "do not let this happen." Integrity checks include entity integrity, validity check constraints, SQL-92 domains and assertions, and referential integrity.

■ *The Entity Integrity constraint* ensures that each row in a table is unique. This is done to reflect "real-world" situations where we deal with unique entities. You can specify, through *primary keys* or *unique indexes*, that each row in a table uniquely identifies the entity represented by that row. The SQL server will prevent rows with duplicate primary keys from being entered accidentally.

■ *Validity check constraints* restrict the values that can appear in a column. When a table is created, each column is assigned a SQL data type; and the SQL server automatically ensures that only data of the specified type is introduced in a column. But what about restricting the set of legal values of the same column type? Most SQL servers provide a *check* option with views, which automatically enforces that each INSERT and UPDATE meets the search criteria (domain restrictions) in the view definition. This search criteria can be used to further restrict the set of values that can appear in a column.

■ *SQL-92 domains and assertions* are two new integrity constraint mechanisms defined by SQL-92. A *domain* is used to restrict the values of data that may appear in a column. You can create, alter, and drop domains. A SQL table column can be declared to be of a domain type rather than a standard SQL data type. Domains provide a more precise way of typing data than what you can achieve with standard data types. The new standard also defines a new type of object called *assertions*. These are simply constraint rules that may be associated with any column in the database. In the old standard, constraint rules were column-specific.

■ *Referential Integrity* is a powerful data integrity feature that ensures cross-references *between* tables are always valid. What this means is that if there is a reference to something, then that something should exist; otherwise, the reference is invalid. The rules for referential integrity are specified as part of the CREATE TABLE statement through two sets of keys: primary and foreign. The server must enforce that foreign key values (in dependent tables) match existing values in *primary keys*. For example, a server can automatically enforce a relation such as "no employee gets assigned to a department that does not exist."

FYI

Referential Integrity SQL-92 Style

Briefing

A **Primary Key** uniquely identifies a single row within a table. The primary key consists of one or more columns; none can be null. Each table can have only one primary key. A unique index is automatically created for the primary key. The primary key ensures that each row in a table is unique. This is done to reflect "real-world" situations where we deal with unique entities. The database server will prevent rows with duplicate primary keys from being entered accidentally.

A **Foreign Key** is a key that points to (or references) a primary key. The foreign key columns must match those of the primary key one for one. However, SQL-92 has now defined a more "relaxed" constraint that allows matches of a foreign key with its primary to be either partial or full. In either case, a foreign key establishes a referential link to a primary key. Each table (including the one with the primary key) can have one or more optional foreign keys. Through these referential links, the database server will enforce, on your behalf, the integrity of dependent data (foreign key data) on parent data (primary key data). Referential constraints may be created between columns on the same table or in different tables. A table is *self-referencing* when it contains both the primary key and the foreign key.

The SQL-92 **referential triggered actions**, known in some products as update or delete rules, specify how to treat rows in dependent tables if a parent row is updated or deleted. For each foreign key, you can specify one of four "triggered actions" on update or delete: 1) The *NO ACTION rule* tells the database server to prevent the deletion of the parent row if that row has any dependents or if an update causes an integrity violation (this is the default rule); 2) The *SET NULL rule* tells the database server to automatically set the foreign key values to Nulls in all the child rows that reference a parent row that is deleted or updated; 3) The *CASCADE rule* tells the server to automatically delete (or update) all dependent rows when the parent row gets deleted (or updated); and 4) The *SET DEFAULT rule* tells the server to set all columns in the dependent rows to the value defined in the default clause. ☐

Transactional Support

A *transaction* is the fundamental unit of recovery, consistency, and concurrency for any type of resource manager. A "database" transaction often consists of one or more related SQL commands that are treated as a single *unit of work*. Either all the commands within the unit of work complete fully or the effects of every command get "undone" fully. A transaction terminates with either a SQL COMMIT, which makes all the database changes permanent, or a ROLLBACK, which cancels the changes and returns the database to its previous commit point state. Figure 23-5 shows the effects of a successful transaction and one that fails. The successful transaction transforms the system from an initial consistent state to a final consistent state. The unsuccessful transaction undoes its work and leaves the system in the previous consistent state (all the intermediate work gets rolled back). A transaction may be aborted by a user program that detects an error and then issues a rollback (i.e., suicide). Or it may be aborted by external events like a power failure or a deadlock tiebreaker, in which case the system issues the rollback (i.e., murder).

Crash recovery requires a clean termination of a program. Transactions provide "all or nothing" protection and ensure that either all of the requested services are

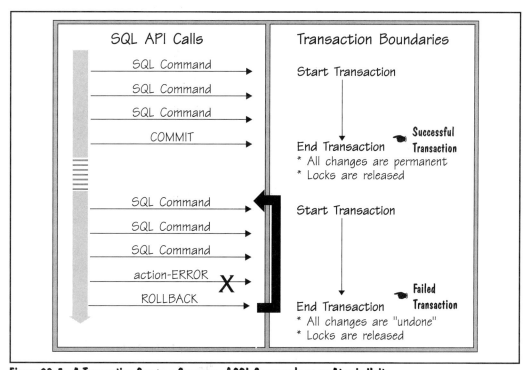

Figure 23-5. A Transaction Groups a Sequence of SQL Commands as an Atomic Unit.

performed or none are. Thus, a program terminates and produces either the intended results or none at all. Most database servers use a write-ahead log technique in which before and after images of the transaction are kept on a log file. If the system crashes or the transaction gets aborted, the system can rollback the unsuccessful updates using the before and after image files.

Another technique called *roll forward* is used to recover a damaged database. This technique requires that all database updates be recorded on a log file that resides on a separate device. In case of a database disk crash, the logged updates are applied against the last backed-up copy of the database to provide a recovered database.

Locking and Data Consistency

Data *consistency* refers to the capabilities of a database server for maintaining the quality and integrity of data in a multiuser environment. In a network environment, requests for database services may be concurrently generated by remote clients. How does a database server protect your data from the inconsistencies that can be introduced in a multiuser environment? There are three kinds of inconsistencies that can happen during the concurrent execution of requests for database services: lost updates (or phantoms), dirty reads, and non-repeatable reads.

■ **Lost updates** are caused by two users who read the same record at about the same time and then each perform an update. Without the proper database consistency protection, one of the updates is lost.

■ **Dirty reads** occur when one user submits a transaction that updates a database but subsequently gets undone or "rolled back." If in the meantime a second user had read the same data before the rollback, that user would be working with "dirty" data (i.e., it does not exist anymore). Obviously, this is an integrity violation.

■ **Non-repeatable reads** occur when one user reads data that subsequently gets altered by another user. If the first user rereads the data, the value read will be different from what was obtained the first time. The implication is that two or more read operations on the same data may yield different results (i.e., non-repeatable reads).

Most database servers solve the problems of data consistency through two techniques: *transaction control* and *locking*.

A database server provides data consistency by introducing various locking techniques down to the row level. The effect of the various locks is to serialize, in one way or another, multiaccess to shared resources. Locking techniques have to provide a sufficient degree of *isolation* for users to maintain control over the data they are working on—without locking out other users for prolonged durations. This is a delicate balancing act.

In addition to being a *unit of recovery*, a transaction is also a *unit of consistency*. At the end of each transaction, the system releases all locks, cursors, and dynamically prepared SQL statements created or acquired during a transaction. A SQL application should always be divided into a number of sequential transactions. In environments where many active transactions are accessing the database at the same time, the number and type of SQL commands that make up a transaction can dramatically affect the concurrency of a system. Consequently, transactions that execute in concurrent environments should be written at a much finer level of granularity while not compromising the consistency of the data. It is your responsibility to define, through transactions, the acceptable units of recovery and consistency for your application. It is the database server's responsibility to automatically provide the right amount of locking to keep the database consistent (at the isolation level you specify) on transaction boundaries. Note that only one transaction at a time can be active on each process or remote application.

The good news is that once you've structured your SQL application into transactions, the database server will then automatically handle locks on your behalf. The server obtains the required locks at the start of a transaction and releases all locks when a transaction ends. It is never necessary (nor desirable) for your programs to explicitly request locks.

Deadlock Detection

Whenever there are locks, the danger of *deadlocks* looms. This "side effect" is caused when two transactions go after the same set of resources and each holds the resource the other needs to complete the job. The result is that both transactions get locked out and wait indefinitely. Database servers overcome this problem by providing a deadlock detection and resolution mechanism. This is a background task that comes to life at a user-specified wakeup interval and then looks for deadlocked transactions. If a deadlock is detected, the deadlock detector breaks it by declaring one transaction the "winner" and the other the "loser." The deadlock detector kills the victim's transaction; consequently, all its locks are released. The "winner" transaction resumes work where it left off. The "loser" transaction will need to be restarted by the application. Most database servers kill the loser. Oracle7 adds a more "gentle" option called "partial rollback" (also see the following Warning box).

SQL-92: Transaction and Isolation Levels

Briefing

SQL-92 defines a new SET TRANSACTION command that lets you to specify transactions as read/write or read-only. A read/write transaction can update a database and is given exclusive lock privileges by the database server. A read-only transaction can indicate how much concurrency it will allow by specifying the level of locking associated with database reads. This is an area where you're given the latitude to specify lesser levels of locking in exchange for higher levels of performance. A SQL-92 compliant database server allows you to specify one of four *isolation levels* or "degrees of isolation" required during database *reads*:

- **Serializable** is the level that provides the most stringent isolation for your reads. In fact, you obtain the same amount of locking that is provided for updates. With this level of isolation, any rows acquired by your transaction cannot be read by another transaction. The trade-off for this higher level of isolation is less overall concurrency. Serializable is the default isolation level specified by SQL-92.

- **Read Repeatable** enforces the second most stringent level of isolation for your reads—any rows acquired by your transaction (for SELECT or UPDATE) cannot be altered (but they can be read) by another transaction. Your transaction will hold locks on any row it touches until it completes. This stringent level of isolation provides maximum protection and guarantees that you will get the same result from a SELECT statement throughout the duration of a transaction.

- **Read Committed** (also known as cursor stability) provides an intermediate level of locking where only the current row pointed to by a SQL cursor is locked instead of all the rows involved in a query. This means other transactions can read or update rows that your transaction previously read. However, you retain exclusive locks for rows on which the cursor is currently positioned. As a result of this more relaxed level of isolation, you can reissue the same SELECT statement at a later point in a transaction, and get a different set of result rows each time. On the positive side, read committed enhances the overall level of concurrency in the system.

■ **Read Uncommitted** provides the least amount of isolation. This is essentially an option to run without "read" locks, which therefore has little effect on transaction processing rates. Any application can read uncommitted data that may subsequently be rolled back. There are two situations where some protection is provided: 1) when the read cursor is for UPDATE; and 2) when an application is about to drop the table. This highly relaxed level of isolation may introduce some mysterious bugs into your programs and should be used only in "safe" situations, such as applications that browse data.

In summary, isolation levels trade off integrity for concurrency. The more the concurrency a database provides, the less it can guarantee the integrity of the data. The more the data is shared, the less integrity it has. The real question is: How much data inconsistency can your application tolerate? What does it mean to you that there's a chance somebody else may be updating your data? Can you live with it? Your answers will determine the isolation level you'll choose for your transactions.

Warning: Some database servers, such as Oracle7, use "no locking" as their *read* default. This exposes the database to corruption (bad data can creep in). To get around that problem, you must manually configure Oracle7 as "Serializable = True." The nice benchmark performance numbers from Oracle will degrade considerably. Ouch! ☐

Wanted! Distributed Deadlock Detectors

Warning

As far as we know, none of the popular database vendors have implemented a distributed deadlock detection scheme. This makes it very problematic to use distributed database technology (even from the same vendor). Given that deadlocks may occur on an hourly basis in production-type database, it is suicidal to use a distributed database that does not support deadlock detection and resolution. ☐

Database Authorization and Privileges

With SQL making access to the data so easy, it becomes important for database servers to provide access protection. You can define the overall framework for securing your data using the SQL language. The enforcement of the security then becomes the responsibility of the database server. SQL-managed database security is based on the interplay of three concepts: *users*, *database objects*, and *access privileges*. The *privileges* define the actions that a *user* can perform on a given *database object*.

The database server controls which objects and resources you can access or create, based on your Authorization ID. Granting rights is done using the SQL **GRANT** command; revoking rights is done through the new SQL-92 **REVOKE** command.

Protection Level	Protection Services	Authority or "Privilege"
Database Manager	Authority to create a database and control any Database Manager resource	SYSADM
Individual Database	Authority to control a database	DBADM
	Authority to connect to a database	CONNECT
	Authority to create tables	CREATETAB
	Authority to create packages (aka plans)	BINDADD
Individual Object	Authority on a table, view, plan or index	CONTROL
	Limited privileges on tables and views	ALL ALTER (table only) DELETE INDEX (table only) INSERT REFERENCES (table only) SELECT UPDATE
	Limited privileges on plans	BIND EXECUTE

Figure 23-6. Authorization and Privilege Hierarchies in DB2/2.

The authorization subsystem maintains a system of privilege hierarchies that closely parallel the object hierarchies you've already encountered (see Figure 23-6). To perform any SQL operation, the user must have the appropriate authority for that operation. More specifically, SQL defines three broad levels of control:

■ Control at the system level specifies the authority needed to create the system itself, including the database.

■ Control at the database level specifies the authority needed to create objects within an existing database. It also specifies the authority required to connect to a database.

■ Control at the individual object level specifies the authority to manipulate specific objects that exist within a database.

SQL-92 allows privileges to cascade up, which means that privileges granted on some object can imply privilege rights to related objects.

The System Catalogs

A SQL server is *self-describing*, meaning that it automatically maintains information about its own structure in the database. These self-describing tables, collectively known as the *catalog tables*, can be accessed (but not modified) through standard queries. This means you can ask a database server to describe its system tables where it maintains its structures for views, columns, privileges, plans, ownership, user comments, and all sorts of useful system information. Database tools can use this information very advantageously (see the following Warning box).

In the SQL-92 standard, a *catalog* is a collection of *SQL schemas* describing "one database." The schemas are SQL tables that describe the structure of base tables, views, privileges, constraints, etc. Each SQL-session has one *cluster* of catalogs that describe all the data available to that session.

SQL Catalogs Are Highly Non-Standard

Warning

Today, all SQL catalogs are vendor-specific. Implementations may vary even within the same vendor family (for example, IBM's DB2 family). Compliance with SQL-92 won't happen overnight. In the meantime, this whole area is highly non-standard, which makes it quite difficult to create database-independent tools. ❏

STORED PROCEDURES, TRIGGERS, AND RULES

Relational databases now have built-in procedural extensions—including stored procedures, triggers, and rules. These extensions are very useful but extremely non-standard. So why are database servers moving into the procedural turf? What are these extensions and what new services do they provide? We answer the first question with an opinionated soapbox. The contents of this section attempt to answer the second question.

Look Who's Cheating

Soapbox

Relational database vendors are cheating big time. They're adding all sorts of procedural extensions to SQL that deviate from the original vision of a "pure declarative language for relational data." Database purists used to scoff at procedural languages for being "relationally incomplete and insecure."

So what are today's newest and hottest SQL extensions? They are procedural constructs of all types—including stored procedures, triggers, rules, and propri-etary scripting languages. So instead of keeping the data separate from the code, the SQL server vendors have simply brought the code to the database. Not only do databases store procedures, but they have also given them the keys to the data kingdom. Procedural constructs, as you will find out in this section, are simply taking over the database.

So the current message we're getting from the relational vendors is: "Procedures are OK as long as they're *ours* and we get to store them on *our* databases." But we believe database vendors are stepping out of their territory. They should stick to managing the data and leave the procedural extensions to the NOS RPCs, MOMs, TP Monitors, Object Databases, and Distributed Object Managers (DOMs). Of course, what will happen instead is that everybody will step into everybody else's turf; most client/server systems will become hybrids of some sort. ❑

What Is a Stored Procedure?

Many database vendors are now offering an RPC-like mechanism for database. This mechanism is sometimes referred to as "TP lite" or "stored procedures." A stored procedure is a named collection of SQL statements and procedural logic that is compiled, verified, and stored in the server database. A stored procedure is typically treated like any other database object and registered in the SQL catalog. Access to the stored procedure is controlled through the server's security mechanisms.

Stored procedures accept input parameters so that a single procedure can be used over the network by multiple clients using different input data. The client invokes a remote procedure and passes it the parameters required to do a job. A single remote message triggers the execution of a collection of stored SQL statements. The result is a reduction of network traffic (compared to remote SQL) and better performance. Table 23-1 shows the results of a TPC-like benchmark we ran on a DB2/2 database to compare the performance of dynamic SQL, static SQL, and two flavors of stored procedures. The results explain why stored procedures are so attractive—they're much faster in client/server situations than the other SQL alternatives.[2]

Table 23-1. Server Network Performance.

LAN Database Servers		LAN Stored Procedures	
Dynamic SQL (RDS/NETBIOS)	Static SQL (RDS/NETBIOS)	Application Remote Interface (RDS/NETBIOS)	Roll-Your-Own Named Pipes (NetBIOS)
2.2 TP1s/sec	3.9 TP1s/sec	10.9 TP1s/sec	11.6 TP1s/sec

---

[2] The benchmarks are from our book: **Client/Server Programming with OS/2 2.1, Third Edition** (VNR, 1993). The book contains about 100 pages of code for running these benchmarks. The benchmarks were run on a slow 486-class machine; they do not represent the best-case performance of DB2/2.

The concept of stored procedures was pioneered by Sybase in 1986 to improve the performance of SQL on networks. Stored procedures are used to enforce business rules and data integrity; to perform system maintenance and administration functions; and to extend the database server's functions. However, the primary use of stored procedures (in all of its variations) is to create the server side of an application's logic. The encapsulation features of stored procedures are well suited for creating performance-critical applications known as Online Transaction Processing or *OLTP.* These applications typically: 1) receive a fixed set of inputs from remote clients; 2) perform multiple precompiled SQL commands against a *local* database; 3) commit the work; and 4) return a fixed set of results.

In other words, a stored procedure is a database-centric, RPC-like SQL entity that is persistent, shared, and has a name. It reduces network traffic, improves response times, and provides an object-oriented flavor of database service that is well suited for OLTP applications. Stored procedures also provide better *site autonomy* because the remote modification of tables can only occur through locally executing programs. If the tables change, you don't need to recompile all your remote applications. In general, stored procedures provide better distribution of intelligence than static or dynamic remote SQL (see Figure 23-7).

Table 23-2 compares the client/server functional characteristics of stored procedures with other forms of SQL programming. You can see that stored procedures offer many advantages.

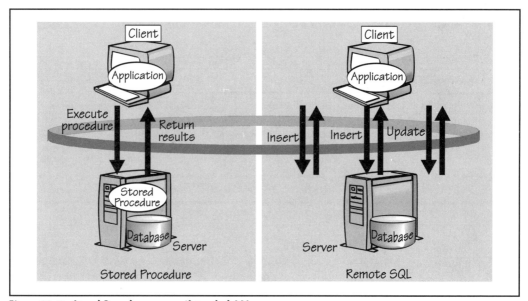

Figure 23-7. Stored Procedures versus Networked SQL.

Table 23-2. Stored Procedures Versus Static and Dynamic SQL.

Feature	Stored Procedure	Remote SQL	
		Embedded Static	**Dynamic**
Named function	Yes	No	No
Shared function	Yes	No	No
Persistently stored on server	Yes	Yes	No
Input/output parameters	Yes	No	No
Tracked in catalog	Yes	Yes	No
Procedural logic	Within object	External	External
Flexibility	Low	Low	High
Abstraction level	High	Low	Low
Standard	No	Yes	Yes
Performance	Fast	Medium	Slow
Tool-friendly	No	No	Yes
Client/Server shrink-wrap friendly	Yes (call procedure)	No (messy)	Yes (CLI calls)
Network messages	1 request/reply for many SQL commands	1 request/reply per SQL command	1 request/reply per SQL command

One drawback of stored procedures is that they provide less ad hoc flexibility than remote dynamic SQL. In addition, stored procedures may perform very poorly if their plans are not refreshed (rebound) to take advantage of the optimizer statistics—dynamic SQL creates a fresh plan with every execution. Another drawback is that there is no transactional synchronization—i.e., two-phase commit—between stored procedures; each stored procedure is a separate transaction.

However, the main drawback of stored procedures is that they're totally non-standard. This results in a number of problems. No two vendor implementations are alike. The language for describing the stored procedures and their functionality vary from server to server; stored procedures are not portable across vendor platforms. There is no standard way to pass or describe the parameters. It is difficult for database tools to create and manage stored procedures. Dealing with the parameters is very messy (there is no standard interface definition language or stub compiler tool).

FYI

Static and Dynamic SQL

Briefing

Static SQL statements are defined in your code and converted into an access plan at program preparation time. The SQL statement is known before your program is run. The database objects need to exist when precompiling static SQL statements. You can think of static SQL as being a compiled form of the SQL language. Static SQL is a performance enhancement feature.

Dynamic SQL statements are created and issued at run time. They offer maximum flexibility at the expense of execution speed. You can think of dynamic SQL as an interpretive form of the SQL language. The database objects need not exist when precompiling dynamic SQL statements. The compilation of dynamic SQL statements is done at run time and must be repeated every time the same statement gets executed again.

Static SQL is used for writing highly optimized transaction programs. Dynamic SQL is used for writing general database programming utilities and by GUI front-end tools that need to create ad hoc queries. ❏

Which Stored Procedure?

The following examples illustrate some of the differences in vendor implementations of stored procedures:

- **Sybase and SQL Server** stored procedures can return multiple rows, but they do not support cursors. They require the use of Transact-SQL, a proprietary procedural language, to create the stored procedures, which are compiled and stored in the catalog. The procedures are invoked using the SQL EXECUTE command and passing it the name of the stored procedure and server on which it resides.

- **Oracle7** stored procedures only return a single row, but they support cursors. They require the use of PL/SQL—a proprietary procedural language. The procedures are invoked by following the procedure or function name with a database link that points to the remote server.

- **IBM's DB2/2** implements stored procedures as ordinary DLL functions written in standard programming languages. The stored procedures (DLLs) reside on the same server as the database, but they are not stored within the database.

The procedures are executed by issuing an Application Remote Interface (ARI) command that uses two buffers (of type SQLDA) to pass self-describing parameters.

- **Gupta's SQLBase** allows a set of SQL commands (known as a *command chain*) to be stored on the server and later executed. SQLBase does not support procedural extensions within the command chain. Three SQL extended commands—STORE, EXECUTE, and ERASE—are used to manage the command chains.

- **Informix** won't let you share stored procedures between transactions.

The list of vendor differences goes on. The bad news is that SQL-92 does not address stored procedures; SQL3 does, but we won't see it soon enough.

Alternatives to Stored Procedures

Soapbox

OK, we'll admit it. Stored procedures are better than the embedded SQL alternative. But now that you've seen what these stored procedures are all about, you may agree with us that they're not a panacea, and they're certainly not the only game in town. Stored procedures (or "TP lite") will face some stiff competition from other types of RPC-like extensions, which offer more sophisticated functions and are further along in their standardized implementations. For example, NOSs and Transaction Monitors have their own architectures for implementing function that is equivalent to the database stored procedures. You've already encountered the NOS's DCE RPC and the MOM implementations in Part 3. In Part 5, we'll go over the "TP Heavy" implementation of stored procedures. You'll discover that Transaction Monitors provide an OS-like environment for scheduling and managing transactions. Transaction Monitors execute stored procedures "in style" by providing message queuing, load balancing, routing, nesting, and two-phase commit synchronization. In addition, distributed object managers are defining their own versions of stored procedures (i.e., method invocations) through the CORBA standard. □

Triggers and Rules

Triggers are special user-defined actions—usually in the form of stored proce-dures—that are automatically invoked by the server based on data-related events. A *rule* is a special type of trigger that is used to perform simple checks on data; triggers can perform complex actions and can use the full power of the procedural language. Both triggers and rules are attached to specific operations on specific tables. In other words, an event tells you something happened to the database; a trigger or rule is an event handler you write to take the proper action in response to the event (see Figure 23-8).

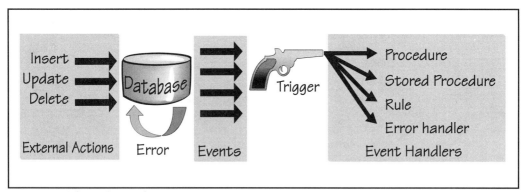

Figure 23-8. The Mechanics of SQL Triggers.

Triggers and rules are typically used to perform tasks related to changes in tables, such as auditing, looking for value thresholds, or setting column defaults. Enabled triggers or rules are executed whenever a table is updated by a SQL DELETE, INSERT, or UPDATE command. A separate trigger or rule can be defined for each of these commands or a single trigger may be defined for any updates to the table.

In general, triggers can call other triggers or stored procedures. So what makes a trigger different from a stored procedure? Triggers are called implicitly by database generated events, while stored procedures are called explicitly by client applica-tions. Server implementations of triggers are extremely non-standard and ven-dor-specific. Here are some examples of vendor implementation differences:

■ **Sybase and SQL Server** support only one trigger per INSERT/UPDATE/DE-LETE operation.

■ **Ingres** supports multiple triggers, but the execution of the triggers is non-de-terministic.

■ **Oracle7** supports up to 12 triggers per table. It does that by allowing you to specify for each INSERT/UPDATE/DELETE the following: a *before trigger* that fires before the SQL statement executes, and an *after trigger* that fires after the SQL statement executes. In addition, Oracle lets you specify the number of times a trigger fires. *Row-level triggers* fire once for each updated row; *statement-level triggers* fire once for the entire SQL statement even if no rows are inserted, updated, or deleted; both can be defined to be active simultaneously. Oracle7's implementation of triggers is close to the SQL3 draft standard (but it's not fully compliant).

■ **Informix** supports before and after triggers and more than one trigger per operation; it uses the column numbers to determine the sequence of trigger firings.

Triggers are written in proprietary SQL procedural extensions. Different implementations limit what triggers can do. For example, Oracle7 will not let you issue commits or rollbacks from within a trigger. Triggers and rules are also used, in a very *non-standard* manner, by Sybase (prior to System 10) and by SQL Server to enforce referential integrity. For example, a trigger associated with a particular table is invoked when data in the table is modified or updated. However, trigger-enforced referential integrity has many drawbacks, and very few database servers use it (see the following Warning box). Instead, most servers implement the SQL-89 defined *declarative referential integrity* standard. In summary, triggers are extremely non-standard, and the situation will not improve until SQL3 becomes a standard.

The Pitfalls of Referential Integrity

Warning

Trigger-enforced referential integrity is non-standard, error-prone, and difficult to implement and maintain. Triggers require programming efforts to implement referential integrity; declarative integrity doesn't. Because a server has no way of knowing that a trigger is being used for referential integrity, it cannot do anything to help optimize it. For example, a transaction that adds 100 new parts to a trigger-enforced relationship between a supplier and parts table will cause the trigger to be executed 100 times. It will check the same key value each time; the execution of triggers is not deferrable. In a server-enforced referential implementation, the value would be checked only once for the entire transaction.

In addition, referential triggers are hard to document (and query) because they consist of procedural code; declarative integrity provides better documentation and clarity by using catalog-based standard DDL SQL statements. Finally, some trigger implementations only support three triggers (or less) per table, which may not be enough to exhaustively cover all the referential constraints and rules that need to be enforced. ❑

Chapter 24

SQL
Middleware

A *client/server database is a waste of hardware and software if there's no way to access its data.*

— *Joe Salemi (1993)* [1]

How does a SQL database client access data that's on multivendor database servers? With database-specific middleware, of course. Why not use straight SQL? Because it's not that simple. A heavy dose of *middleware* is needed to smooth over the different SQL dialects and extensions, network messaging protocols, and vendor-specific "native" APIs. It's sad to report that after eight years of intense standardization efforts, SQL clients cannot talk to SQL servers without layer upon layer of middleware. The best we can do today is to allow a "federation" of loosely-coupled, autonomously-owned, multivendor database servers to communicate using a "least common denominator" approach. The industry calls this compromise *federated database systems*.

---

1 Source: Salemi, **Client/Server Databases** (ZD Press, 1993).

This chapter looks at the middleware that's needed to make SQL clients and servers work across multivendor, heterogenecus, database networks—or more simply put, federated databases. How well does this middleware provide a "single database illusion" in a federated world?

To create the "single database illusion," the middleware must make two sets of customers happy: 1) the developers of applications and front-end tools who need a single OS-independent SQL API to get to any database server; and 2) the IS connectivity people who must make the disparate desktop clients talk to the "federated" database servers on their enterprise networks. The middleware must address difficult issues such as: How does a client program issue multivendor SQL calls? How do federated database desktops interoperate with federated database servers? Can all this be done transparently?

The good news is that the answer to all these questions is a qualified *yes*. Remote access to federated databases is currently one of the hottest new product areas. It's an area that's also getting a lot of attention from the people who create our industry standards, both *de facto* and *de jure*. The bad news is that there are lots of "standards" and hot products from which you can choose. Another piece of bad news is that this middleware cannot be used to create production-strength, federated databases—it does, however, provide an adequate foundation for decision support systems.

SQL MIDDLEWARE: THE OPTIONS

Based on our previous definition, middleware starts with the API on the client side that is used to invoke a service, and it covers the transmission of the request over the network and the resulting response. Middleware does not include the software that provides the actual service. So the questions we need to answer are: What API do SQL database servers provide to clients? And how is the request/reply exchanged with the server? As you will discover, there are too many answers to both of these questions.

Before going into detailed answers, let's first create a common mindset that will help us understand the solutions. We'll start with SQL "Nirvana"—these are the integrated single-vendor offerings. We then look at the problems created in a multivendor, federated SQL environment. Next we give you a quick overview of the two leading architectures for smoothing over the federated database discrepancies. Finally, we give you our two cents worth on what *federated* SQL Nirvana should include.

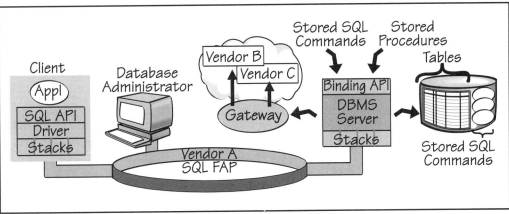

Figure 24-1. The Components of a Single-Vendor SQL Client/Server Offering.

SQL Nirvana: The Single Vendor Option

If a single vendor SQL solution can fulfill all your shared data needs, consider yourself *very* lucky. All you need to do is read this section and then move on to the next chapter. Figure 24-1 shows what a typical single-vendor middleware solution currently provides:

■ *A vendor-proprietary SQL API that works on a multiplicity of client platforms.* Most vendors support DOS, Windows, and OS/2 clients; quite a few also support Macintosh and some Unix variants. Most vendor APIs support SQL-89 with proprietary extensions. Some of the vendor APIs use *Embedded SQL (ESQL)*, and others support a call-level interface (CLI). More on that later in this chapter.

■ *A vendor-proprietary SQL driver.* This is a thin client run-time element that accepts the API calls, formats a SQL message, and handles the exchanges with the server. The format of the SQL message and the handshake are known, affectionately, as the FAP, which stands for *Format and Protocols*. The SQL FAPs are typically vendor-defined.

■ *FAP support for multiple protocol stacks.* As a result of user pressures, most vendors now support multiple protocol stacks. Some vendors bundle the stacks with their drivers; others support a common transport interface (like Sockets or Named Pipes) and require that you provide your own stacks. At the server side, the vendor typically provides "listeners" for the different stacks. However, some vendors provide their own internal protocol gateways. For example, Oracle7 on Unix translates IPX/SPX packets to TCP/IP on the server side.

- *Gateways to other vendor databases.* Some vendors provide gateways that make other vendors' databases look like their own. For example, Oracle, Sybase, Ingres, Gupta, and XDB all provide gateways to DB2. Most vendor-supplied database gateways only provide an intersection of the features supported by the two databases (i.e., the least common denominator). This means that most vendor-supplied database gateways only support dynamic SQL. They are only good for simple data extracts and queries—not for transaction processing (also see the following Soapbox). Most vendor-supplied gateways require two database engines: the vendor's own database, which acts as a middle tier on the gateway server; and the "foreign" database. The middle-tier database server provides a directory of connected databases, catalog services, and handles the shipping and routing of "foreign" requests.

- *Client/Server database administration tools.* Most vendors will let you manage and administer the database from a remote workstation using a graphical user interface. You have a single point of management for the middleware, the clients, and the servers, as long as they're from the *same* vendor.

- *Front-end graphical application development and query tools.* These help you create visual interfaces to the database server. Of course, each vendor supplies GUI tools for their own database servers. Most third-party tools do a good job for a particular database (see the following Warning box).

Tools: Not All Databases Are Equal

Warning

The SQL database server peculiarities and extensions create major headaches for the vendors of multiplatform client/server database tools. As a result, the support of server extensions tends to be highly uneven. Most tool vendors usually do an excellent job supporting their "preferred" server platform, they do a mediocre job on the second platform, and an atrocious job for the rest of the platforms (they provide almost no support for server-specific extensions). Let's face it: front-end tool vendors have their cup full just trying to keep up with the graphical engines on which they run—Windows, Motif, Macintosh, and the OS/2 Workplace Shell—and they can only deal with so many server idiosyncracies. The current darling of the tool vendors is Sybase because its own tools are comparatively weak. However, each database server has its GUI tool specialists. With over 120 GUI tool vendors out there, many are trying to stay alive by becoming best-of-breed for a particular database server (i.e., specializing). ❑

Vendor Gateways: Are They Just a Bandaid?

Soapbox

A vendor gateway solution is not really open. It ties you into the vendor's database offering, and you get whatever gateway connectivity the vendor chooses to implement. Typically, the vendor will not support the smaller platforms (and if they do, support is very spotty). The vendor also has no incentive to create a level playing field for their competitor's databases. Everybody supports data extracts from DB2 and DEC's Rdb; but what incentive does Oracle have to provide gateways to Sybase and Ingres (or vice versa)?

In all fairness, Sybase, Oracle, and Informix are trying to make their gateways more "open" by exposing some of the internal programming interfaces. For example, the Sybase *Open Data Server (ODS)* and the corresponding Microsoft *Open Data Services (ODS)* are general-purpose, event-driven server APIs that can be used by third parties to create gateways. The OS/2-based MDI *Database Gateway for DB2* was developed jointly by Micro Decisionware and Microsoft using ODS as their gateway base. The MDI OS/2 gateway translates Sybase (DB-Library) or ODBC client API calls to DB2 calls. The clients run on DOS, Windows, or OS/2, and use Named Pipes to communicate to the MDI gateway server, which in turn uses an APPC stack to talk to the mainframe (see Figure 24-2). MDI supports, in addition to DB2, Teradata and SQL/DS.

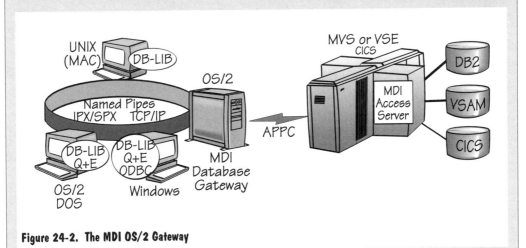

Figure 24-2. The MDI OS/2 Gateway

Some gateways go out of their way to "compensate" for missing functions on the "foreign" database engines. For example, the MDI gateway provides a mainframe component called the *DB2 CICS Access Server.* It uses the CICS TP Monitor to simulate Sybase stored procedures on DB2 (but it doesn't come cheap; count on paying between $24k and $70k for that convenience). Oracle7 and Ingres gateways support some level of two-phase commit for updating foreign data, but it's still a least common denominator approach.

In our opinion (this is a soapbox), if you're already locked into a single vendor database solution, then you might as well enjoy the convenience provided by the vendor's gateways. It's good for occasional decision-support access to foreign databases. And it's highly convenient because you use the same APIs and middleware to get to that foreign data almost transparently. However, you're at the total mercy of your vendor, and it locks you in deeper. But given the chaotic state of "open database middleware," locking yourself into a single vendor solution may not be such a bad idea (you'll understand why after you finish reading this chapter). However, for most large enterprises, a single vendor database solution is not in the cards. They have too many diverse database management requirements that go all the way from PC-based decision support systems to high-volume OLTP production data. ❑

SQL Nightmare: The Multivendor Option

Figure 24-3 shows what happens when you move into a multivendor database world. Here's the short list of obvious inconsistencies that you will immediately face:

- **Different SQL APIs** makes it a nightmare to write a common set of applications. Even if common API semantics were magically to show up later in this chapter, we still need a way to deal with all the proprietary SQL extensions.

- **Multiple database drivers** eat up precious memory space on the client machines (especially for DOS). Can these drivers use the same protocol stacks or do we need duplicate stacks? If multiple stacks are needed, how will they share the LAN adapter? Who do we call when a problem occurs?

- **Multiple FAPs and no interoperability** means that the database protocols from the different vendors are simply sharing the LAN; they cannot talk to one another.

- **Multiple administration tools** means that database administrators must familiarize themselves with a set of managing workstations, each of which have their own semantics and user interfaces.

We have not even addressed some of the thornier issues, such as federated database joins, federated commits, or concurrent access to federated data.

The federated middleware solutions we'll look at concentrate on simple SQL access to a federated database—one connection at a time. More ambitious schemes, such as RDA and DRDA, aim at creating a federated environment that matches the power of a single-vendor distributed database approach. But they're far from accomplishing that goal. The best we can do today is focus on the issues of submitting simple SQL statements against one federated database at a time.

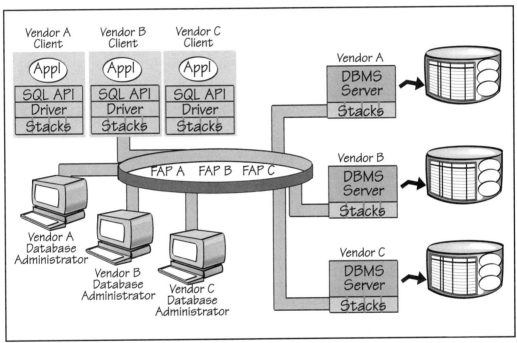

Figure 24-3. The SQL Multivendor Database Nightmare.

Middleware Solution #1: The Common SQL Interface

The first step towards regaining some level of sanity in a federated database environment is to *standardize on a common SQL Interface* (see Figure 24-4). The idea is to create a common SQL API that is used by all the applications and then let the server differences be handled by the different database drivers. This is, of course, easier said than done. Here are the problems:

■ *Which SQL API to standardize on?* You'll soon discover that there are many SQL "standard APIs" on the table. How are stored objects on the server defined and invoked (remember the stored procedures and static SQL)? Should we use a call-level API or the ISO-defined embedded SQL? How do we deal with the non-standard SQL extensions? Will the common interface be slower than the native vendor implementation?

■ **Multiple drivers are still required.** Should the drivers reside on the client or on the server side? Who provides the drivers to the "common APIs"? What's the incentive for the vendors to support a "common" driver over their own "native" driver? Can the drivers coexist on the same stacks? Or on the same LAN adapters?

■ **Multiple managing stations and multiple FAPs are still required.** We still haven't solved those problems, we just made them invisible to the developer. So the system administration people are still not happy.

Later in this chapter, we will go over the contending schemes—including Embedded SQL, the SAG CLI, IDAPI, ODBC, Oracle Glue, X/Open, and the EDA/SQL API—for creating a common SQL interface.

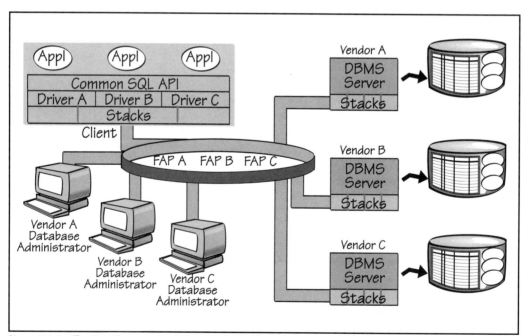

Figure 24-4. The First Convergence: A Common SQL API.

Middleware Solution #2: The Open SQL Gateway

Let's assume that we have all magically agreed on a common SQL interface. What is the next middleware improvement that can be *realistically* accomplished to better articulate the federated database environment? Figure 24-5 shows a middleware solution that's currently in vogue: *the open gateway*. The idea is to standardize on one (or most likely two) open industry FAPs, supply a common client driver for the FAP, and develop a gateway catcher for each server. The gateway catcher will "catch" the incoming FAP messages and translate them to the local server's native SQL interface. The good news is that the industry has at least three "common" FAPs to choose from: the ISO/SAG RDA, IBM's DRDA, and EDA/SQL. Later in this chapter we will spend some time looking at the trade-offs of the three approaches.

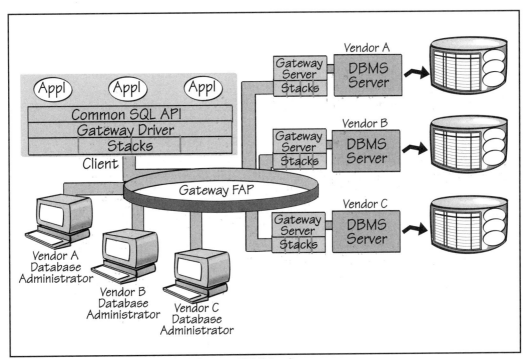

Figure 24-5. The Second Convergence: A Common FAP Using Gateways.

Middleware Solution #3: Federated Nirvana

Let's assume that we have both the common FAP and the common API. What else is needed to create a federated SQL environment that provides the same level of completeness as the single vendor implementation? Figure 24-6 shows what this "ideal" would look like. Notice that we've removed the gateway catchers, which improves server performance, reduces cost, and simplifies maintenance. And, we've created a single database administration interface.

To eliminate the gateway catchers, the common FAP must either support a superset of all the SQL dialects or it must tolerate native SQL dialects (meaning that it must allow pass-throughs). The SQL vendors must also agree to replace their own private FAPs with the common FAP.

The database administration facility will be the last proprietary stronghold to fall. There is just too much variety in the database server implementations to create a common interface. Even if we solved the technological issues, there are still some thorny political issues to be resolved. For example, is there a single point of administration control in a federated database environment? IBM's *DataHub*, an OS/2-based tool, is an example of a federated (but single-vendor) database administration tool. DataHub provides a set of integrated database management functions for DB2/2, DB2/MVS, DB2/VM, DB2/6000, and SQL/400. The database management products from *EcoSystems* are also beginning to address these issues. Finally, the database vendors are working on a DBMS MIB that defines database configuration and control parameters to SNMP management stations.

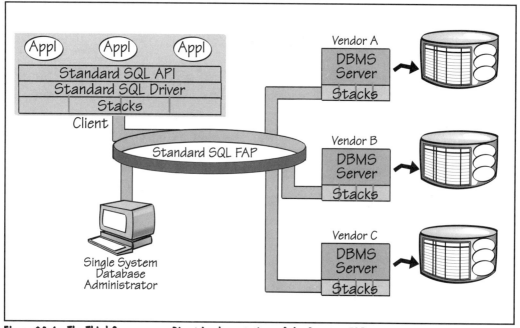

Figure 24-6. The Third Convergence: Direct Implementations of the Common FAP.

WILL THE REAL SQL API PLEASE STAND UP?

How do you access SQL data? Can an application transparently access a system of federated databases? Can an application built for one SQL database be deployed on another? What's the state of the SQL data access standards? The answers, as you will discover in this long section, are a fuzzy yes, no, and maybe.

The early SQL architects felt it was very important to keep the SQL programming language neutral. In fact, SQL was created as a higher-level declarative language that was to isolate us from low-level procedural constructs. Remember, it was designed as an end-user query language. But to create applications that use SQL, it became obvious that SQL constructs needed to be integrated within existing programming languages. Incidentally, "SQL first" people view this process as extending SQL with procedural capabilities, while programmers think of it as providing an interface to SQL services. Two competing approaches are currently in vogue for supporting SQL from within programming languages: *embedded SQL*, and the SQL *Call-Level Interface (CLI)*. Figure 24-7 shows the two approaches.

This section looks at the SQL interface from the point of view of how it helps create a federated middleware solution. We will first look at embedded SQL because it is an ISO standard. We then look at the CLI alternatives, including the SAG CLI and

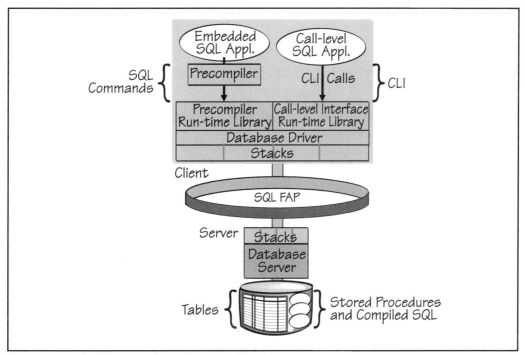

Figure 24-7. SQL APIs Come in Two Styles: CLI and ESQL.

some of its more famous mutants: ODBC, IDAPI, Oracle Glue, and the X/Open SQL CLI. We will defer the discussion of the EDA/SQL CLI to the gateway section.

The SQL-92 Embedded SQL (ESQL)

Embedded SQL (ESQL) is an ISO SQL-92 defined standard for embedding SQL statements "as is" within ordinary programming languages. The SQL-92 standard specifies the syntax for embedding SQL within C, COBOL, FORTRAN, PL/I, Pascal, MUMPS, and ADA. Each SQL statement is flagged with language-specific identifiers that mark the beginning and end of the SQL statement. This approach requires running the SQL source through a precompiler to generate a source code file that the language compiler understands. As an example, for the C-language an embedded SQL statement must start with the **EXEC SQL** keyword pair and end with a semicolon (;). These bracketed statements will be processed by the precompiler and anything else in your source code will be passed through unchanged.

What's Nice About Embedded SQL

Embedded SQL provides the following benefits for doing things the SQL way:

■ The SQL sublanguage is almost independent of the programming language, compiler, and operating system used. This means that you can embed the same sublanguage statements in C, COBOL, or Pascal with only a few minor changes. With some additional minor changes, the same sublanguage program can easily be ported across languages.

■ The precompiler separates SQL processing from the language-specific statements, which means that new SQL features can easily be introduced with minimum impact.

■ We've gained the full power of SQL and the non-procedural discipline it entails.

■ It is remarkably easy and productive to program in the SQL sublanguage.

What's Not So Nice About Embedded SQL

Let's look at the downside of this "almost perfect marriage" from, let's say, a C programmer's point of view:

■ We must run our source code through a precompiler.

■ We must have a running database with fully defined tables as part of the code preparation process. This means that we have to define and create our data tables before we can compile any code. In other words, *the target database must be known at program preparation time. Ouch!*

■ We must store the SQL packages (also known as plans) prepared by the precompiler into a database.

From a client/server packaging perspective, the biggest hurdle with embedded SQL is that the target database must be known (and available) when the program is being developed. This makes it hard to target a client program to a database at run time. In addition, the installation process involves binding applications to each server database they connect to—a process that may be too complicated for the "shrink-wrapped" client/server software market. Finally, precompilers have traditionally been tied to a particular database product; you must recompile your embedded SQL code for each vendor's database server.

In summary, the same features that make precompilers so popular with IS shops and corporate developers have turned into liabilities for the providers of shrink-wrapped client/server software.

What Does a SQL Precompiler Do?

Details

A SQL precompiler provides four functions:

■ It manages the language-specific variables that can be used directly inside SQL statements. These common variables are called *host variables*.

■ It checks the validity of SQL statements, including the user's authority to issue such statements. This includes verifying that the table names and columns referenced in your SQL statements actually exist and that their types are compatible with the host variables declared in your programs.

■ It generates a *modified source language* file. For example, a C-language SQL precompiler generates a (.C) file that can be compiled by a C-language compiler. The embedded SQL statements are changed into comments and the appropriate API calls are generated in their place. For example, the precompiler takes as its input a (.SQC) file containing the C-language source and embedded SQL statements (see Figure 24-8).

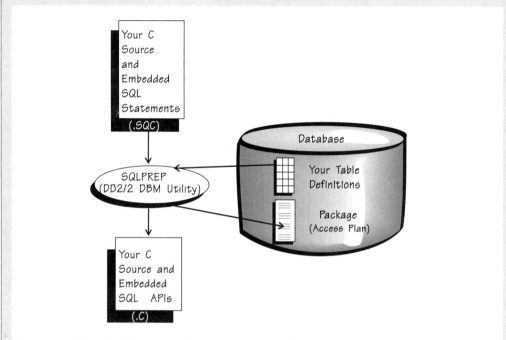

Figure 24-8. The DB2/2 SQL Precompile Process With Immediate Bind.

■ It builds *packages* that contain access plans that tell the database engine how each SQL statement should be executed. These access plans use sophisticated heuristics that optimize the data access strategy based on the current state of the database. The access plans are stored as objects in the database.

The process of storing the access plans is called *binding*. The access plans are part of a package. You can bind packages to the database during precompilation, or you can do it later through a separate bind utility. Figures 24-8 and 24-9 contrast the immediate and deferred bind process for OS/2's DB2/2. If you defer the binding, the precompiler will store the packages it creates in *bind files* with (.BND) extensions. You can bind the (.BND) files at a later time with the production database of your choice (see Figure 24-9). You can even bind OS/2 DB2/2 packages to non-OS/2 databases including DB2 (on MVS), SQL/DS (on VM), DB2/6000, and DB2/400. The packages become portable interchange units of SQL code. The bind attaches the packages to the database environment of choice. ❑

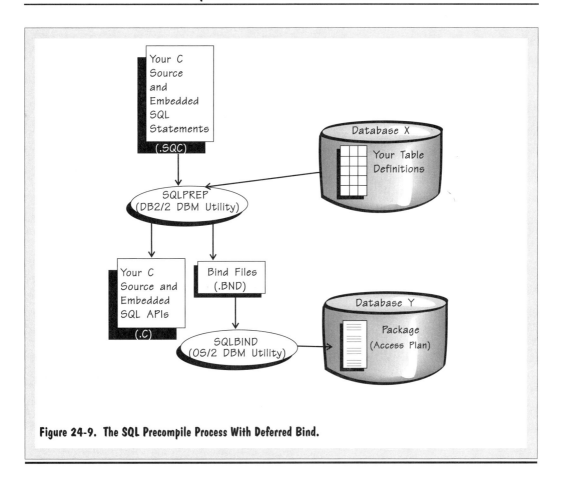

Figure 24-9. The SQL Precompile Process With Deferred Bind.

The SQL Call Level Interfaces (CLIs)

The alternative to Embedded SQL is to use a callable SQL API for database access. An API does not require a precompiler to convert SQL statements into code, which is then compiled and bound to a database. Instead, an API allows you to create and execute SQL statements at run time. In theory, a standard API can help you write portable applications that are independent of any database product. Of course, in practice things are not that simple. In this section, we go over the SAG CLI and some of its more famous mutants: ODBC, IDAPI, Oracle Glue, and the X/Open SQL CLI.

The SAG CLI

In 1988, 44 database vendors created a consortium called the *SQL Access Group (SAG)*, which was to provide a unified standard for remote database access. The original goal of the SAG charter founders—Tandem and DEC—was to accelerate the pace of remote SQL standard development and put in place a multivendor SQL solution that would allow any SQL client to talk to any SQL server. Tandem and DEC were very interested in an open set of multivendor front-end tools for enabling their SQL databases. So they drove the SAG effort, which resulted in one of the industry's most successful "open standards."[2]

SAG focused its efforts on two separate undertakings: 1) An interoperability standard that allows any database client to talk to any database server "at the wire" by using common message formats and protocols, and 2) A SQL *Call Level Interface (CLI)* that defines a common API set for multivendor databases. This section focuses on the SAG CLI; we will return to the SAG interoperability standard in the middleware section.

The *SAG SQL CLI* is a vendor-independent set of APIs for SQL databases; it can be used by applications without requiring a SQL precompiler. In theory, a SQL CLI lets you access any database through the same programming interface. The SAG CLI only supports *dynamic SQL* and provides functions that correspond to the SQL-89 specification. SAG provides common SQL semantics (and syntax), codifies the SQL data types, and provides common error handling and reporting. SAG defines a common set of system catalogs including the table structures they use. SAG's connection management service allows SQL clients to specify connections to remote database servers. The three connection commands defined by SAG—CONNECT, SET CONNECTION, and DISCONNECT—are now part of the SQL-92 standard.

The SAG APIs allow you to connect to a database through a local *driver* (3 calls), prepare SQL requests (5 calls), execute the requests (2 calls), retrieve the results (7 calls), terminate a statement (3 calls), and terminate a connection (3 calls). In December 1993, SAG released a new "preliminary" version of its CLI; the final specification is due later in 1994.

The Microsoft ODBC CLI

Microsoft's *Open Database Connectivity (ODBC)* Windows API standard for SQL is a greatly extended version of the SAG CLI. ODBC defines about 54 API calls; 23

---

[2] The early efforts of Jim Gray (then associated with Tandem Computers, and now with DEC) and of Jeri Edwards (Tandem Computers) led to the formation of the SAG consortium.

(the core APIs) are based on the SAG CLI. Some of the Microsoft extensions are generic; others are specific to the Windows environment. ODBC defines three *conformance levels* for its drivers: core (i.e., SAG), level 1, and level 2. Each of these levels is a superset of the previous level and corresponds to the class of ODBC functions supported by an ODBC database driver (see the next Briefing box). Applications are responsible for making sure that an ODBC driver supports a conformance level. Microsoft provides an ODBC SDK to help developers create database-specific drivers. Some vendors—including IBM for the DB2/6000, Tandem for NonStop SQL, Ingres, and Informix—provide ODBC drivers for their SQL servers (see Figure 24-10).

In addition, third parties—such as Q+E Software—are offering ODBC driver suites on Windows, OS/2, and Unix that run against a variety of database servers. IBM's DB2 CLI (see X/Open CLI section) is almost identical to the ODBC API, which makes it easier to port ODBC-compliant Windows applications to OS/2.

ODBC has many drawbacks. The most serious one is that the specification is controlled by Microsoft and it is constantly evolving. ODBC drivers are difficult to build and maintain. The current drivers are buggy and have different ODBC conformance levels, which are not well documented. The ODBC layers introduce a lot of overhead (especially for SQL updates and inserts) and are never as fast as the native APIs.

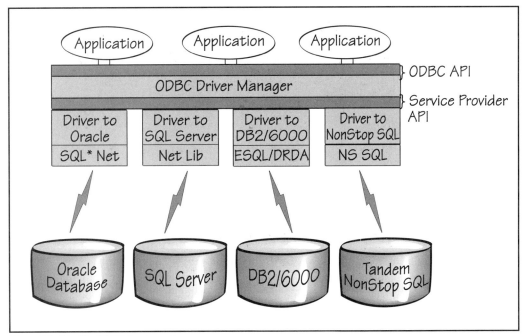

Figure 24-10. The ODBC Components.

What's a Database Driver?

Briefing

CLIs—including ODBC, IDAPI, and SAG—require the use of intelligent database drivers that accept a CLI call and translate it into the native database server's access language. With the proper driver, any data source application can function as a CLI-server and be accessed by the front-end tools and client programs that use the CLI. The CLI requires a driver for each database to which it connects. Each driver must be written for a specific server using the server's access methods and network transport stack. In the future, X/Open and SAG plan to provide a standard driver-to-server protocol, called the Remote Data Access (RDA); it will work with a variety of transport stacks to provide platform independence among database servers (more on that later in this chapter).

Microsoft's ODBC provides a driver manager that routes an ODBC CLI-call to a particular driver (see Figure 24-11). The driver manager talks to the driver through an ODBC-defined *Service Provider Interface (SPI)*. IDAPI goes a step further by providing a networked SPI-like interface, which allows the drivers to reside on a "gateway" machine. This can be very helpful in situations where multiple client workstations need to access multiple servers, each requiring a separate driver. All the driver combinations can reside on a single "gateway" server instead of on every client machine. CLIs may support different levels of compliance; it's up to the driver writer to select the level of compliance provided in an implementation.

Drivers may usually be obtained from database and front-end tool vendors. They are also bundled with some client/server applications that require them. Some database server companies are bundling ODBC (and very soon IDAPI) drivers with their databases and not charging more for it. Drivers may also be purchased from a new-breed of "middleware for middleware" companies. For example, Q+E Software provides a suite of drivers (priced at $199) for more than 15 database servers. Database vendors are not interested in doing drivers unless they have to. As a result, some vendors, such as Informix and Gupta, are directly referring customers who need drivers to Q+E. However, purchasing drivers from a third party introduces one more complication in an already complicated loop. On the other hand, "middleware for middleware" vendors may find themselves becoming the single point of support and contact for federated database integration using CLIs. ❑

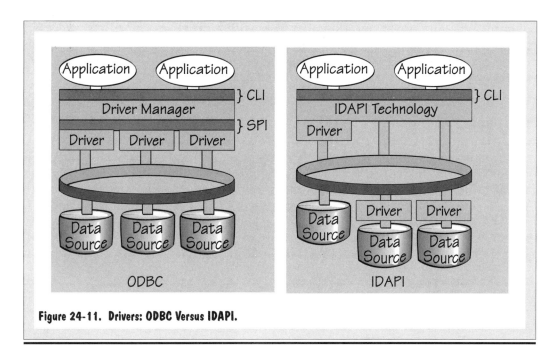

Figure 24-11. Drivers: ODBC Versus IDAPI.

The IDAPI CLI

In February 1993, Borland, IBM, Novell, and WordPerfect introduced a working draft of yet another SAG-based CLI called the *Integrated Database Application Programming Interface (IDAPI)*. IDAPI supports two types of access methods to databases: a SQL CLI based on the SAG CLI, and a record-at-a-time navigational CLI based on Borland's NAV/CLI. The NAV/CLI is used to interface to Xbase and ISAM databases. IDAPI supports advanced SQL features, including cross-database joins, concurrent scrollable cursors on different servers, and query language conversions. These features allow a desktop client to dynamically correlate information from several databases at once. IDAPI promises to introduce less overhead than ODBC. In addition, IDAPI-compliant applications will be able to access ODBC-compliant databases. One of IDAPI's main strengths is that its drivers can reside on the server side, giving clients access to a shared set of database drivers, typically on a gateway server (see Figure 24-11).[3]

IDAPI is key to Borland's strategy. It serves as the unifying interface between Borland's tools—including Quattro and ObjectVision—and its three PC database products: Paradox, dBase, and InterBase. IBM intends to support IDAPI on both OS/2 and AIX. Novell and WordPerfect have pledged to support IDAPI in future releases of their products. In addition, Q+E Software intends to create IDAPI driver

---

[3] The IDAPI working specification may be obtained by calling 1-800-344-4394.

Part 4. SQL Database Servers

suites for Windows, OS/2, and Unix that work with a variety of database servers. In November 1993, Borland claimed that the IDAPI initiative had more than 65 companies behind it. However, as we go to press, no IDAPI drivers are available, and Borland has still not released an SDK for creating them.

Oracle Glue

As the most recent entrant in the SQL "standard" CLI sweepstakes, Oracle announced that its *Glue* would work with everything—including ODBC, IDAPI, Sybase DB LIB, dBase, Paradox, Apple's DAL, and e-mail (see Figure 24-12). Unlike its SQL*Net V2 product, Glue was announced as an Oracle-independent product. A specification document is available that explains how all this will come together. According to Oracle, "Glue fills the gap with an API that's adaptable, portable, and integrated enough to glue the data to the desktop."

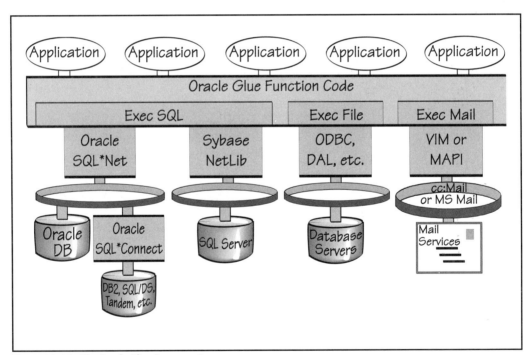

Figure 24-12. The Oracle Glue Components.

The Glue API is invoked through four function calls that can be embedded in application scripts and source code: *execsql* accesses DBMSs; *execfile* works with file servers and Xbase engines; *execmail* accesses mail systems; and *execlink* links applications to Personal Digital Assistants (PDAs). In other words, Glue is supposed to be the universal interface for every type of data-oriented middleware. Glue will even access IBM databases through the *Oracle Open Gateway* for DRDA. Oracle has plans to make Glue available on Windows, Windows NT, OS/2, Macintosh System 7, and various Unix platforms. Unfortunately, the April '93 release of the Glue product only supported Oracle's native APIs.

The X/Open CLI

To counter all these CLI extensions, X/Open became the official "guardian" of the SAG CLI, which is now called the *X/Open CLI*, to differentiate it from IDAPI and ODBC.[4] The X/Open CLI is focused on SQL-89. The next revision is expected to cover the SQL-92 extensions. Figure 24-13 shows an IBM-supplied *DB2 CLI driver* that conforms to the X/Open API (with some extensions) and supports DOS, OS/2, and AIX clients. The DB2 CLI driver translates CLI calls to the native ESQL calls supported by DB2/2.

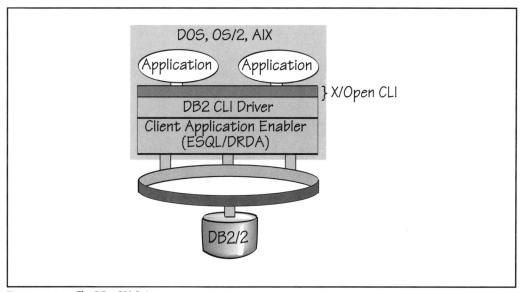

Figure 24-13. The DB2 CLI Driver.

---

[4] The X/Open CLI is documented in the SQL *Common Application Environment (CAE)* specification that is part of the XPG4 package published in late 1992. The CLI spec can be purchased from either X/Open or SAG.

CLI Versus ESQL

Table 24-1 compares the CLI and ESQL capabilities. In general, today's crop of SQL CLIs are flexible but slow. They can only be used for decision support systems. Higher performance systems will require the use of either stored procedures or static embedded SQL. A CLI, like ODBC, may cheat and let you invoke a vendor-specific stored procedure using pass-throughs (you specify the stored procedure name and server as parameters in the EXECUTE SQL API call). X/Open will eventually specify a CLI stored procedure call based on SQL3. But don't hold your breath waiting. In any case, CLIs are still too slow when compared to the performance of native APIs. And as long as vendors don't implement the CLI natively (see the next Soapbox), this will remain the case.

Table 24-1. The X/Open CLI Versus ISO ESQL

Feature	X/Open SQL Call-Level Interface (CLI)	ISO SQL-92 Embedded SQL (ESQL)
Requires target database to be known ahead of time	No	Yes
Supports static SQL	No (future)	Yes
Supports dynamic SQL	Yes	Yes
Supports stored procedures	No (future)	No (future)
Uses the SQL declarative model	No	Yes
Applications must be precompiled and bound to database server	No	Yes
Easy to program	Yes	No
Easy to debug	Yes	No
Easy to package	Yes	No

Which CLI?

Soapbox

Use native (direct) APIs whenever possible. Standard APIs (e.g., ODBC) should be considered as a last resort...not the first.

— *Richard Finkelstein (November, 1993)*

The reason Finkelstein doesn't like "standard" CLIs is that they require too many levels of translations before they reach the native APIs. Any type of layering scheme requires release level synchronizations between the different components, which all come from different vendors. As can be expected, vendors will first support their native API sets and then worry about the "standard CLIs." This means the CLIs will not be synchronized with the latest releases of the database engines and drivers. In addition, the CLI approach on top of database drivers adds layers of complexity. For example, debug is far more complicated. You can expect a lot more fingerpointing between vendors when the NOS, API libraries, database drivers, native OSs, and database engines all have to be in sync for things to work.

But the million dollar question is: Why can't vendors—like Oracle, Sybase, and IBM—make the X/Open CLI the "native API" of their respective databases? The answer is that each database engine offers a unique set of extensions to the native SQL; these extensions require a different set of APIs to invoke their services. Will the vendors ever offer a non-extended version of SQL? Of course not—they're out there trying to differentiate their product! So by definition, the common CLI will always be a "least common denominator" approach that is not optimized for a particular database. Database vendors are not likely to reveal their future "extended plans" to standards bodies, so common CLIs will always trail behind the SQL engine's native API capabilities. And forget portability because even the "standard CLIs" have escape clauses (or pass-throughs) that defeat that goal. The bottom line is that any program that takes advantage of the advanced capabilities of a database engine will not be database-neutral. So much for standards! ❑

What About the Proprietary SQL Languages?

Both the CLI and ESQL approaches let you use your favorite procedural language for writing code. The alternative is letting the SQL vendors introduce new procedural languages for SQL. This is precisely the approach taken by the two leading database vendors: Sybase and Oracle.[5] Sybase requires that you use its proprietary *Transact-SQL* language; Oracle gives you a choice between standard ESQL precompilers or *PL/SQL*, Oracle's own proprietary language.

The benefits of using a vendor-specific proprietary language is that, in theory, all your SQL programs (including the procedural logic) will automatically port to all the platforms these vendors support; you don't have to concern yourself with precompilers and compilers for each platform. But be careful—this is not always the case. The price you pay is vendor lock-in. It's the classic trade-off.

The following is a brief description of three vendor-specific SQL programming environments and what they can do for you:

■ *Sybase Transact-SQL* supports a vendor-specific SQL dialect, which, prior to Sybase 10, did not even support cursors and many of the standard SQL-92 features. However, Transact-SQL includes powerful proprietary extensions that let you create stored procedures, triggers, and rules. *System stored procedures* are used to supplement the server management commands. The execution of a stored procedure on a server can be delayed for up to 24 hours with the *WAITFOR* option. The language supports conditional logic and the declaration and initialization of variables. Error handling in Transact-SQL is cumbersome because the programmer must check the error status after each SQL statement; there is no provision for calling exception handlers automatically when an error occurs.

■ *Oracle PL/SQL* also supports a modified SQL dialect, that is based on the SQL-92 standard. PL/SQL can be used in triggers, stored procedures, or as blocks of SQL statements sent to the server to be executed all at once so as to reduce network traffic. PL/SQL can be used within a host language, such as C or COBOL, or from within one of Oracle's client tools, such as SQL*Forms. PL/SQL provides conditional logic and lets you assign values to variables. In addition, it supports event-driven error handlers; you can use the standard error handler or override it with one you supply. Oracle7 allows you to group PL/SQL procedures within *Stored Packages*. Packages are managed using the regular SQL DDL statements (CREATE, ALTER, and DROP). Objects within a package

---

[5] This approach is not limited to Oracle and Sybase. Ingres provides its proprietary *Ingres/4GL* and Informix supports its own *Stored Procedure Language (SPL)*.

can be *visible*, which means that they are callable from outside the package, or *hidden*, which means they can only be called from within the package.

■ *REXX* supports most of the IBM SQL databases without requiring a precompiler; it processes all the SQL statements dynamically. Of course, REXX is more than just a procedural language for SQL; it's a general programming language. Aside from being proprietary, REXX has two limitations. It is interpreted (also its major strength), and it does not run on all platforms (but that's changing). REXX's major strengths are that it's easy to use, very flexible, and familiar to over one million programmers. Its flexibility and interpreted nature makes it the language of choice for many of the OS/2 front-end tools for databases. If you can live with the interpreted performance, you'll find that REXX provides a powerful and friendly environment for running SQL on both clients and servers. REXX is bundled with OS/2.

In summary, the success of SQL has opened up a plethora of non-standard languages. You'll have to make the decision of which one fits your needs best. You also have the choice of using a standard procedural language with a SQL precompiler. Some database servers, like DB2/2, let you write stored procedures using any language that creates a DLL and supports a SQL precompiler.

OPEN SQL GATEWAYS

In this section, we look at "open SQL gateways" that translate the SQL calls into an industry-standard common *Format and Protocol (FAP)*. The FAP provides the common protocol between the client and the server. As we explained earlier in this chapter, the gateway acts as the broker that translates client API calls into the FAP format, transports them, and then maps them to the appropriate server calls (and vice versa). The open gateway must provide (or support) a standard SQL Interface (CLI or ESQL). It must also be able to locate remote servers and provide catalog services without requiring an intermediary database server. The open gateway must also provide tools for creating the server side of the gateway.

We will look at the three contending architectures (or products) for common gateways: ISO/SAG *Remote Data Access (RDA)*, IBM's *Distributed Relational Data Access (DRDA)*, and IBI's *EDA/SQL*—an open gateway that currently supports more than 50 database server platforms. Gateways are a temporary fix until vendors agree on a common FAP and implement it *natively* on their servers. So we will look at which of the contending FAPs has the best chance of becoming this common standard.

FYI | **RDA and DRDA: More Than Just Gateways**

Briefing

DRDA and RDA are more than just gateway protocols. They both provide end-to-end architectures for creating true federated distributed databases. Most gateways simply pass a SQL statement to a remote database system, generally treating each SQL statement as a separate transaction. DRDA and RDA aim at supporting multisite transactions (though RDA isn't quite there yet). Some gateways handle the character conversion but don't have all the sophisticated features provided by DRDA and RDA for creating common data representations. Gateways typically link two locations; DRDA and RDA are built to support data backbones (with multiple entry and exit points). ❑

IBI EDA/SQL

Enterprise Data Access/SQL (EDA/SQL), from Information Builders, Inc. (IBI), is a family of open gateway products that uses SQL to access over 50 relational and non-relational database servers—an industry record. EDA/SQL is a component of IBM's *Information Warehouse* decision-support solution. In addition, IBI has developed, with Microsoft, an ODBC driver for EDA/SQL gateway servers. EDA/SQL is a continuation of IBI's 10-year experience in developing gateway code primarily for read-only query access. IBI does not provide a database server; the company is focusing on the "glue" business.

Figure 24-14 shows the EDA/SQL components. Here's what they do:

■ *API/SQL* is another "common" CLI that uses SQL-89 as the standard database access language. API/SQL will pass-through SQL calls that it does not recognize. The calls can be issued asynchronously—meaning the client application does not have to block waiting for the call to complete. It lets you query the status of any pending requests. The API/SQL also provides an RPC call that can be used to invoke CICS transactions or user-written procedures. API/SQL is available on DOS, Windows, OS/2, OS/400, AIX, Sun/OS, VAX/VMS, HP-UX, MVS, VM, Wang/VS, and Macintosh.

■ *EDA/Extenders* are utilities that allow API/SQL calls to be issued from within existing products that support some form of dynamic SQL. You can think of the extenders as "redirectors" of SQL calls. Of course, the calls get redirected to API/SQL, which then routes them through the gateway network. Extenders are provided for many popular applications—such as Lotus 1-2-3—and for database

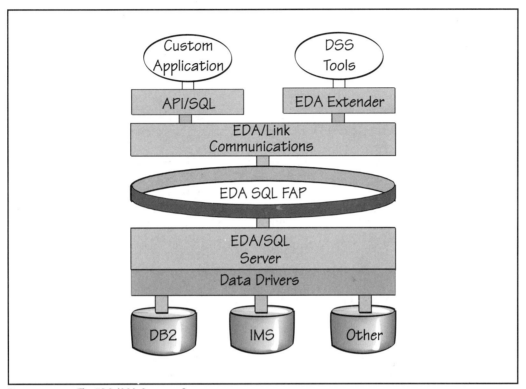

Figure 24-14. The EDA/SQL Gateway Components

front-end tools that work with popular databases (relational or nonrelational). Many popular client tools are being delivered "EDA-enabled" out of the box.

■ ***EDA/Link*** supports over 12 communication protocols including NetBIOS, Named Pipes, SNA, TCP/IP, and DECnet. EDA/Link provides password verification and authentication, and handles message format translations. It lets you create communications profiles using pop-up menus. The stacks it supports vary with different client/server configurations.

■ ***EDA/Server*** is a multithreaded catcher that typically resides on the target database server machine. It receives client requests and translates them into server-specific commands. If the target database is relational, it passes the ANSI-compliant SQL directly to the *EDA/Data Driver*. If the target database is not relational, SQL requests are passed through the *Universal SQL Translator*, which maps the SQL syntax of the incoming request into the data manipulation language that is specific to that server's driver. EDA/Server also handles security, authentication, statistics gathering, and some system management. EDA/Servers are available for MVS, VM, OS/2, RS/6000, DEC VAX (VMS), HP-UX, SUN (OS), and Pyramid. On October 12, 1993, IBI announced additional

EDA/Servers for the following platforms: OS/400 Database Manager, CICS on MVS, and DB2 and IMS via DRDA. It also announced an EDA/SQL "Transaction Server" for CICS and IMS using EDA/SQL RPCs.

■ **_EDA/Data Drivers_** provide access to data in over 50 different formats. These drivers take care of any variations in syntax, schema, data types, catalog naming conventions, and data representation. A specific data driver must be installed for each data source you need to access.

IBI also offers a product called *EDA/SmartMode*. This "smart" element estimates the cost of a request—in time, money, or other user-defined units—before it is executed. The request is rejected if its cost exceeds a user-defined threshold.

All the EDA/SQL components are priced separately. But be warned: The product is not cheap. A complete EDA/SQL setup can run as high as $100k. As a parting note, EDA/SQL is an excellent piece of middleware for decision support systems and data extractions. However, it does not provide the robust transactional support needed for production-type database access. Its FAP is not a candidate for replacing existing vendor-specific middleware. Let's look at RDA and DRDA alternatives to understand why this is the case.

ISO/SAG RDA

The ISO RDA is an emerging standard for universal data access based on the little-used OSI stack. One of SAG's goals is to port (and extend) the RDA FAP to the TCP/IP protocol. RDA provides functionality that is equivalent to the SQL-89 and SQL-92 (entry) specifications. RDA is *not* very tolerant of SQL deviations. The server will reject any SQL command that does not conform to an RDA-defined SQL subset. However, SAG may allow some cheating with pass-through commands.

The current version of RDA only supports dynamic SQL. RDA allows a client to be connected to more than one database server at a time, but it does not support a two-phase commit protocol to synchronize updates on multiple databases. An RDA client may issue asynchronous requests to a server whenever it desires; it does not have to wait for pending requests to complete.

RDA defines a set of SQL catalog tables that are based on the SQL-92 standard; it does not tolerate any catalog deviations. RDA returns error codes using the SQL-92 SQLSTATE return codes. It also supports the SQL-92 subset of SQLCODE return values. All other return codes are rejected. RDA supports a *repetition count* mechanism that lets any operation be repeated one or more times—for example, multirow fetches. Each repetition may use a different set of inputs.

RDA requires that all data exchanged between the client and the server be converted to a common "canonical" format. This means that all data is converted twice—once by the sender and once by the receiver. The benefit is that everybody needs to learn only one common conversion format. The disadvantage is that multiple conversions may result in the loss of data precision and can impact performance, especially when both the client and server use the same protocol.

RDA uses the ISO *Abstract Syntax Notation One (ASN.1)* to define the messages and then encodes (or tags) their contents using the ISO *Basic Encoding Rules (BER)*. BER uses a type/length/value tagging scheme to convey a value. Each data item must be individually tagged, so if a query generates a result set of 20,000 rows, each field in each of the 20,000 rows must be tagged—that's a lot of tagging overhead.[6]

What's coming next? RDA is working on defining a two-phase commit protocol that's based on the *ISO Transaction Processing (ISO TP)* standard. It's also waiting on the final SQL3 specifications for stored procedures before it can incorporate them into RDA. The committee is looking at providing static SQL support along lines that are similar to DRDA packages.

IBM DRDA

IBM's long-term distributed database strategy is known as the *Distributed Relational Database Architecture*, or simply *DRDA*. IBM is promoting DRDA as the standard for federated database interoperability. A number of influential database and gateway vendors—including Oracle, Sybase, Micro Decisionware, IBI, Informix, XDB, Ingres, Borland, Cincom, Progress, Novell, and Gupta—have announced support for DRDA. Six of these vendors have already announced (or are shipping) DRDA-based products. According to IBM, over 100 DRDA-exploitative applications are being developed by different companies using existing products (mostly OS/2's DDCS/2).

DRDA's goal is to provide an interoperability standard for fully distributed heterogeneous relational database environments. To do that, DRDA defines the protocols (or FAPs) for database client-to-server and server-to-server interactions. In DRDA terminology, a client is called an *Application Requester (AR)*, and a database server is an *Application Server (AS)*. The AR-to-AS protocol is used for the typical client/server interactions. The AR-to-AR protocol synchronizes transactions that span across multiple SQL servers; it also used to route SQL commands from server to server.

---

[6] For a more complete explanation of RDA's tagging overhead, refer to Richard Hackathorn's excellent book, **Enterprise Database Connectivity** (Wiley, 1993).

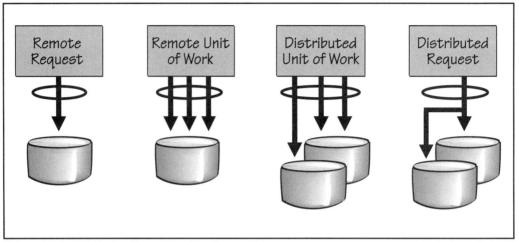

Figure 24-15. DRDA's Four Types of Database Transactions.

Figure 24-15 shows the four levels of database transactions defined by DRDA:

■ **Remote request** means one SQL command to one database. This is used mostly for issuing queries among dissimilar systems.

■ **Remote unit of work** means many SQL commands to one database. This is your typical client-to-single-server transaction. The client can connect to one database server at a time, issue multiple SQL commands against that server's database, issue a commit to make the work permanent, and then switch over to another database server to start a subsequent unit of work.

■ **Distributed unit of work** means many SQL commands to many databases but each command goes to one database. This is your typical multiserver transaction. DRDA handles the multisite synchronization, security, and data integrity functions (two-phase commit). It locates remote data sites and coordinates requests (including the update of data) at several locations in a single transaction.

■ **Distributed request** means many SQL commands to many databases, but each command can execute against multiple databases. With this capability, DRDA can service single requests that span multiple sites, such as a *multisite JOIN*. It can also distribute a single query across multiple servers to improve performance through parallelism.

How much of this architecture is implemented in real products today? The best way to find out is by looking at IBM's own database server products (see Figure 24-16). After all, DRDA's *primary* goal is to allow IBM's own "heterogeneous" database servers to interoperate. Table 24-2 shows where things stand today with the IBM products. We also threw in XDB because they are the first vendor (other than IBM) to offer a DRDA product. The XDB product allows applications to join tables on an XDB server with those on a DRDA server. As you can see from Table 24-2, DRDA is not all fluff. The mainframe version of DB2 just shipped the multisite distributed update capability, and the rest of the DB2 offspring are expected to do the same, soon.

Table 24-2. DRDA: What IBM Has Today.

Product	OS platform	DRDA Client (AR)	DRDA Server (AS)	Highest Level of Transaction Support
XDB with XDB-link	OS/2	Yes	No	Remote unit of work (tables can be joined with those on XDB server)
DB2/2 with DDCS/2 (IBM)	OS/2	Yes	No	Remote unit of work (tables can be joined with those on XDB server)
DB2/6000 with DDCS/6000 (IBM)	AIX	Yes	No	Remote unit of work
SQL/400 (IBM)	OS/400	Yes	Yes	Remote unit of work
SQL/DS (IBM)	VM	Yes	Yes	Remote unit of work
SQL/DS (IBM)	VSE/ESA	No	Yes	Remote unit of work
DB2 (IBM)	MVS	Yes	Yes	Distributed unit of work

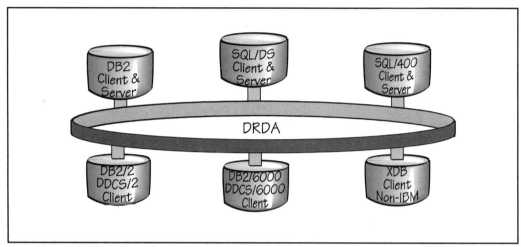

Figure 24-16. IBM's DRDA Implementations.

DRDA Features

What type of additional functions does DRDA provide? It mainly handles the thorny network and code portability issues, including:

- ■ ***SQL Message Content and Exchange Protocol:*** DRDA handles the negotiations between clients and servers for supported server attributes. It only does message translations when needed. There is no concept of a canonical message format; instead, it is a "receiver makes it right" protocol. This means that if data needs to be converted, it is only done once. And no conversion is done if a client and server use the same formats. DRDA uses DDM, an intermediate messaging language, to mediate SQL exchanges across unlike machines; DRDA takes care of dissimilar data representations, catalog structures, and command syntax conversions. DRDA does not tag every field in every row in a multirow result set. Instead, it creates a single descriptor for the entire result set. All these features help reduce network traffic and improve performance.

- ■ ***Transport Stack Independence:*** DRDA supports the MPTN interface, which means that it can run on top of APPC/APPN or TCP/IP (the two protocols currently supported by AnyNet) for client/server communications. DRDA handles data blocking, security, authentication, server routing, and generates alerts for both network and database failures.

- ■ ***Multiplatform Program Preparation:*** DRDA supports under-the-cover, multiplatform program preparation. A program is created locally; its output can be distributed to multiple servers using a remote BIND utility. The BIND process produces executable SQL code (called packages or plans) on the servers.

■ *Static or Dynamic SQL Support:* A DRDA client can invoke the SQL statements on the server one at a time by identifying a package and the statement within it. In addition to dynamic SQL, packages make it possible to execute precompiled static SQL statements on the servers (including support for cursors).

■ *Common Diagnostics:* DRDA returns status information upon completion of each SQL command. DRDA provides a standard set of return codes in the SQLSTATE field (based on the SQL-92 standard). Database specific return codes are still provided in the SQLCODE field. IBM's OS/2 based DataHub product provides an integrated system management approach to DRDA databases. It performs database management tasks across multiple sites. It can trace a transaction through the database network and provide status.

■ *Common SAA SQL Syntax:* DRDA recommends the use of SAA SQL for application portability across platforms. SAA SQL is a subset of SQL-92 (with some extensions). DRDA also supports target-specific SQL commands for situations when it is more efficient to use SQL extensions. In other words, if the client knows that a server supports certain SQL commands, it can issue the calls and DRDA will convey them to the server. Who says you can't have your cake and eat it too?

IBM is licensing both the DRDA specifications and the code to interested parties for a nominal fee. At least six major vendors have licensed the DRDA code. IBM is also adopting the X/Open CLI.

DRDA or RDA?

So why does this industry need two standards? Aside from the political and business issues (see the next Soapbox), there are some compelling technical reasons for choosing DRDA over RDA (see Table 24-3). Many vendors will support both DRDA and RDA. Indeed, many vendors who have announced their intent to support DRDA have also committed to support RDA. Even IBM has made a statement of intent to support RDA (as well as DRDA) should it become the ISO standard. The good news is that some of these vendors will create "gateways" between DRDA and SAG/RDA. And, as usual, this business always has at least two standards for everything!

Table 24-3. RDA Versus DRDA.

Feature	ISO RDA	IBM DRDA
Support for dynamic SQL	Yes	Yes
Support for static SQL and persistent SQL packages	No	Yes
Support for standard SQL (ISO-92 subset)	Yes	Yes
Tolerance for SQL Dialects including dissimilar:		
■ SQL Commands	No	Yes
■ Catalogs	No	Yes
■ Error Codes	No	Yes
Overall performance and efficiency:	Poor	Good
■ Number of format conversions per message for common client and server	2 (to/from canonical)	0 (not needed)
■ Number of format conversions per message for unlike client and server	2 (to/from canonical)	1 (receiver makes it right)
■ Multirow tagging	Every row is tagged.	One tag description per result set
■ Multirow fetches	Using repeated command	Using single row fetch with updateable cursors or multirow fetches.
Two-phase commit and multisite distributed updates	No	Yes
Asynchronous Requests	Yes	No
Easy for vendors to implement	Yes	Not so easy. OS/2 sample code helps.
Transports	OSI and TCP/IP	APPC/APPN and TCP/IP
Integrated management	No	Yes (using DataHub)
Accounting information	No	Yes

Table 24-3. RDA Versus DRDA. (Continued)

Feature	ISO RDA	IBM DRDA
Data encoding	ISO BER/ASN.1	IBM DDM and Compound Object Formats.
Who's behind it?	40 vendors	15 vendors
De jure standard	Yes	No

CONCLUSION

The success of SQL has opened up a plethora of interface and middleware "choices." You'll have to make the decision on which one fits your needs best. As we see it, SQL (with its extensions) will remain vendor-specific for a long time to come. If you're using SQL databases for mission-critical applications, the "mix and match" of SQL database servers can only spell trouble. You might have to accept some form of vendor lock-in, in return for the convenience of getting more SQL power, better support, platform portability, and finding somebody to blame. The situation is better for decision-support systems and information warehouses. There, you have a much better chance of working with data from mulivendor database platforms. The current SQL federated database middleware can easily support these kinds of "non-mission-critical" applications. More on that in the next chapter.

SAG Should Support Both RDA and DRDA

Soapbox

If you think about it, IBM is the only major relational database vendor that must support five different database platforms. The rest of the vendors support a single database engine across multiple platforms. For IBM, DRDA is needed for its survival in the database market—after all, customers rightfully expect total interoperability and portability among a single vendor's database products. So IBM *must* provide a bullet-proof, high-performance, production-strength, distributed, heterogeneous database FAP *immediately*. It can't afford to wait for the standards to evolve. As a result, as long as IBM is in the database business, DRDA will always be ahead of RDA in terms of distributed features. And DRDA products will always be at least two years ahead of corresponding RDA products in terms of features and functions.

According to a persistent industry rumor, SAG was initially ready to endorse DRDA if IBM proposed it. However, IBM, for some strange reason, decided not to attend the SAG meetings (past the first one) and lost a golden opportunity to create a de facto standard. We can't confirm this story. If it is true, SAG also lost—DRDA is a more practical standard.

Another interesting aside: SAG was created to speed up the ISO RDA effort and make its FAP more practical for commercial purposes (remember, it was mired in all these OSI layers). Unfortunately, most of SAG's recent efforts were directed at the SQL CLI. The RDA initiative did not move fast enough (if at all). In theory, RDA may look good with all its canonical conversions and its *absolutist* refusal to deal with anything but the SQL they define. In practice, RDA is totally impractical; it will never replace existing vendors' FAPs (unless these vendors want to go bankrupt). On the other hand, if IBM really makes DRDA open, it can potentially replace existing FAPs. After all, it's the FAP IBM is using for its own commercial products.

Our recommendation—this is a soapbox after all—is that SAG contact the "new IBM" to see if they're interested in making DRDA the "de facto FAP," at least until RDA catches up. Yes, we understand that this may not be the "canonically correct" solution, but it's a question of solid middleware that works today. ❑

Chapter 25

Warehouses: Information Where You Want It

---

*W*ith the new generation of desktop applications, the real database is often perceived to be a personal database that extracts its necessary contents from a myriad of data sources. This trend is causing the fragmentation of enterprise data into numerous isolated presentation-centered islands.

— Richard Hackathorn (1993)[1]

This chapter provides an overview of the technology used to create *information warehouses*—one of the most exciting new developments in client/server databases. "Warehouses" provide the foundation technology for creating intelligent clients that look like Danny De Vito's desktop in the movie *Other People's Money*. For those of you who haven't seen this movie, Danny's closest associate was an information-hungry PC that literally lived on real-time data, which it grabbed (or got fed) from multiple sources. Danny's PC would continuously integrate data, massage it, and present it in dynamic formats—including trends, animations, simulations, and 3-D business graphics—that were relevant to Danny's interests. Danny, of course, was in love with that PC, which he used to make all his investment decisions and

---

1 Source: Richard D. Hackathorn, **Enterprise Database Connectivity** (Wiley, 1993).

lots of money. The poor machine even had to wake him up every morning with an analysis of how his investment portfolio was doing.

WHERE IS THAT OLTP DATA KEPT?

Modern businesses live on data. The total quantity of data on computers currently doubles every five years. With the proliferation of client/server (and multimedia) technology, we expect data to double at least once a year in the future. So who is creating all this data? The answer is modern institutions in the course of conducting their everyday business. The computerized production systems that collect and consume this data are called OLTP systems—these are true data factories that run around the clock.

What Is OLTP?

Database-centered client/server applications fall into two categories: Decision Support Systems (DSS) and Online Transaction Processing (OLTP). These two client/server categories provide dramatically different types of business solutions. These differences need to be understood before we can appreciate what data warehouses have to offer.

OLTP systems are used to create applications in all walks of business. These include reservation systems, point-of-sale, tracking systems, inventory control, stockbroker workstations, and manufacturing shop floor control systems. These are typically mission-critical applications that require a 1-3 second response time 100% percent of the time. The number of clients supported by an OLTP system may vary dramatically throughout the day, week, or year, but the response time must be maintained. OLTP applications also require tight controls over the security and integrity of the database. The reliability and availability of the overall system must be very high. Data must be kept consistent and correct.

In OLTP systems, the client typically interacts with a Transaction Server instead of a Database Server. This interaction is necessary to provide the high performance these applications require. Transaction servers come in two flavors: *OLTP Lite* provided by stored procedures, and *OLTP Heavy* provided by TP Monitors. In either case, the client invokes *remote procedures* that reside on a server. These remote procedures execute as transactions against the server's database (more on this in Part 5). OLTP applications require code to be written for both the client component and for the server transactions. The communication overhead in OLTP applications is kept to a minimum. The client interaction with the transaction server is typically limited to short, structured exchanges. The exchange consists of a single request/reply (as opposed to multiple SQL message exchanges).

Is Client/Server Creating New Islands of OLTP?

In the old days, OLTP applications ran on expensive mainframes that stored massive amounts of data, provided minimum downtime, and were the pride of the enterprise and the MIS shops. Today, the top-of-the-line OLTP applications—such as airline reservations, banking, stock markets, airport control towers, and hospitals—still run on expensive superservers and mainframes and are still controlled by the MIS shops. However, today any department with enough budget to buy a few PCs, hook them on a client/server LAN, and hire a programmer (or consultant) can create its *own* OLTP application. Software packages are also becoming available off-the-shelf. In other words, database-centric client/server technology has lowered the barriers of entry for creating private or departmental-owned OLTP systems. These systems are giving the departments total autonomy and control over the applications that are created and the data that is gathered. At the extreme, an entire OLTP system can run on a single-user desktop database; all the data collected can be kept private (i.e., outside the reach of the enterprise). We all know how easy it is to create ad hoc database systems on stand-alone PCs using spreadsheets and simple database tools.

In general, all the data collected by an OLTP system is of direct use to the application and people that are creating this data. They understand exactly what this data means. And they know how to use it to solve their immediate day-to-day production problems. The application typically provides a sophisticated graphical interface to view and manipulate the data with transactional controls. The members of the organization understand what the data means. They can create sophisticated built-in reports and manipulate the data for their production uses.

What happens if somebody outside the direct OLTP group needs this data? How do they know what data is available? Where do they find it? How do they access it? What format will it be in? And, what will it mean? The last thing the OLTP people want is to give outsiders access to their precious production systems. These outsiders often don't really know what they want, and they may be issuing long ad hoc queries that can slow down the entire production system, corrupt the data, and create deadlocks.

In the old days, the outsiders could ask their MIS representatives to deal with their MIS counterparts that controlled production data to give them an indication of what data was available and how to get to it. With the proliferation of the private one-person and departmental OLTP solutions, even MIS doesn't know what data is available anymore. The data in the enterprise is fragmented, and we've gone back to islands of data processing. Data ends up being all over the place: on the client that originates it, on the departmental server, on one of many federated servers, or on the enterprise server. There is no integrated view.

One of the great attractions of client/server and PCs is the autonomy they provide. Most of us feel disassociated with enterprise data and would prefer local control of our resources. In many cases, our new-found freedom causes us to withdraw into our own little production turfs and ignore the needs of the larger community. We've created a dichotomy between the departmental (or personal) needs and the needs of the organization or larger community. We've also created a dichotomy between production data and informational data.

So who are these "outsiders" we're trying to keep off our turf? They're the people who comb through data looking for patterns, trends, and informational nuggets that can help them make better decisions. Creating barriers to data is like creating barriers to trade. If they can't get to our data and we can't get to theirs, then everybody loses. Precious data is kept out of the reach of those who may need it most.

INFORMATION AT YOUR FINGERTIPS

How do we preserve the local autonomy of production systems and yet allow access to outsiders? How do we make sure the outsiders don't impact the production systems? What data is made available to those outsiders? What data is kept private within the production system? Who owns the shared data? Who can update it? Should we allow direct access to production data or copy it to another database? How is extracted data maintained and refreshed? We'll answer all these questions in this chapter. But first let's look at the informational needs of these outsiders and understand how decision-support systems differ from OLTP production systems.

Information Hounds

Let's give a name to these "outsiders" who want to consume our information. They range from those with compulsive appetites for data—like the character played by Danny De Vito in the movie *Other People's Money*—to those with occasional needs—such as a student researching a term paper. What shall we call them? How about *decision makers*? Or, would you prefer *information hounds*? Let's settle on *information hounds* because it captures the role millions of us will soon be able to play with database warehouse technology. Anyone with a PC connected to an information warehouse will be able do the same types of things the Danny De Vito character did.

Of course, the first to consume this technology are business people making strategic decisions—pricing and market analysis—that depend on the availability of timely and accurate data. The ability to access information and act on it quickly will become increasingly critical to any company's (or individual's) success. Raw data becomes information when it gets into the hands of someone who can put it in context and use it. The data is the raw ingredient, which makes all this possible. There are many parallels between the manufacturing and distribution of goods and the manufacturing and distribution of information. High impact, high value decision making involves risk. Making decisions using old, incomplete, inconsistent, or invalid data puts a business at a disadvantage versus the competition.

Information is becoming a key component of every product and service. For example, analysts use information to spot the trends and shifts in buying patterns of consumers. Information sleuthing is an iterative process. The sophistication of queries increases as the information hound grasps more of the nuances of the business problem. The hound needs the ability to access information for multiple combinations of "what if" situations.[2]

An example may help explain the value of timely information. An unnamed apparel manufacturer was having problems reconciling the fast-moving fashion season with a distribution system that replenished stock based on what was forecast. The manufacturer decided to adopt a different technique and put in a system that collected daily sales information from the point-of-sale registers. The company also invested in analysis tools for knowledge workers and executives who needed to watch the daily sales. As a result, the manufacturer was able to cut costs by $47 million, resulting in a profit increase of over 25%. So timely information is highly valuable to some people.

What Is a Decision Support System?

Decision-Support Systems (DSS) are used to analyze data and create reports. They provide the business professional and information hounds with the means to obtain exactly the information they need. A successful decision-support system must provide the user with flexible access to data and the tools to manipulate and present that data in all kinds of report formats. Users should be able to construct elaborate queries, answer "what if" questions, search for correlations in the data, plot the data, and move it into other applications such as spreadsheets and word processor documents. Decision-support systems are not generally time-critical and can tolerate slower response times. Client/Server decision support systems are typically not suitable for mission-critical production environments. They have poor integrity controls and limited multitable access capabilities. Finding information may involve large quantities of data, which means that the level of concurrency control is not very granular; for example, a user may want to view and update an entire table.

Decision-support systems are built using a new generation of screen-layout tools that allow non-programmers to build GUI front ends and reports by painting, pointing, and clicking. Point-and-click query builders take the work out of formulating the question.

---

[2] We are indebted to Dick Lockert, of IBM Atlanta, for sharing some of his deep insights on how information is used in warehousing applications.

What Is an Executive Information System?

Executive Information Systems (EIS) are even more powerful, easy-to-use, and business-specific than DSS tools. And they're certainly more expensive, which may explain why the "executive" attribute is in the name. In any case, distinctions between EIS and DSS are becoming less clear. The EIS tools have recently expanded their scope and offer a broader range of functions at the enterprise level. Dick Lockert, an information guru, makes a case that the "E" in EIS can now be taken as "Enterprise" rather than "Executive" as such systems now have hundreds of users with many roles such as executive, manager, and business analyst. Another phrase to describe these evolving DSS/EIS systems is *Management Support Systems (MSS)*. If you prefer, let's simply call them the Danny De Vito tools.

Regardless of what they're called, these tools are creating a huge market. The IDC market research firm projects a combined EIS and DSS tools marketplace of $9.9 billion in 1996. These new-breed tools allow information hounds to perform deeper levels of analysis on totally up-to-date, real-time data that is obtained from internal business systems—such as OLTP-driven financial, personnel, and customer information systems—and external data sources—such as Dow Jones and Reuters.

Because the Danny De Vito tools were originally designed for executives, all information is presented in highly visual forms. Extraneous details are filtered out to suit the user's needs. These tools offer unique features—including "hot spot" finders, "slice and dice," "goal seekers," "drill-downs" to related information—and the more mundane features—including graphs, charts, statistical analysis, trends, queries, reports, and project management. They specialize in presenting information using visual metaphors that make it easy to navigate and sift through tons of data. Some of the better tools are used to discover late-breaking news on competitors, suppliers, government legislation, market research, economic conditions, or the latest stock market quotes. Examples of EIS and DSS tools that run on OS/2 include Comshare's *Commander Desktop*, Gupta's *Quest*, Trinzic Corporation's *Forest and Trees*, OpenBooks Software's *OpenBooks*, SAS Institute's *SAS System*, Intelligent Office's *TRACK*, IBM's *PAS/2*, and Lotus tools via *Datalens*.

Comparing Decision Support and OLTP Systems

As shown in Table 25-1, decision-support applications can be created directly by end users. Network administrators are still needed to help set up the client/server system, and Database Administrators (DBAs) may help assemble collections of tables, views, and columns that are relevant to the user (the user should then be able to create decision-support applications without further DBA involvement). The design of client/server systems for OLTP is a lot more involved; consequently, it requires a large amount of custom programming effort. We discuss OLTP system requirements in Part 5 and in Part 9.

Table 25-1. Comparing the Programming Effort for Decision Support and OLTP.

Client/Server Application	Client	Server	Messages
Decision Support	Off-the-shelf decision support tool with end-user programming. Canned event handlers and communications with the server.	Off-the-shelf database server. Tables usually defined for OLTP application. The DBA creates flexible views to make user autonomous.	SQL messages that are being standardized for multivendor interoperability.
OLTP	Custom application. GUI tool lays out screen, but the event handlers and remote procedure calls require programming at the C level.	Custom application. Transaction code must be programmed at the C level. The database is off-the-shelf.	Custom messages are optimized for performance and secure access.

Production Versus Informational Databases

Table 25-2 compares the database requirements of OLTP and decision-support systems. We need to understand the differences to get some better insights into what data warehousing can do for information hounds. The key points of difference is that decision-support data needs to be stable at a snapshot in time for reporting purposes. Production databases reflect the up-to-the-minute state of the business in real-time. Information hounds typically don't want the data changed so frequently that they can't get the same answer twice in a row. So informational copies may be updated less frequently.

Decision support data—or *informational data*—is collected from multiple sources; production data is collected by OLTP applications. The raw data that decision support systems extract from production databases is not normally updated directly. However, information hounds have a high requirement to tailor the informational database to their specific needs. This process is called "derived data enhancement." The informational database may contain derived data that records changes over time and summaries. Information hounds are rarely interested in a specific past event. They're always looking at summaries and trends.

Table 25-2. Database Needs: OLTP Versus DSS.

Feature	OLTP Database Needs	Decision Support Database Needs
Who uses it?	Production workers	Information hounds
Timeliness of data	Needs current value of data.	Needs stable snapshots of data frozen in time. Refresh intervals are controlled by user. May need occasional access to current value data.
Frequency of data access	Continuous throughout workday. Work-related peaks may occur.	Supports knowledge workers and managers.
Data format	Raw captured data	Multiple levels of conversions, filtering, summarization, condensation, and extraction.
Data collection	From single application	From multiple sources including archival data.
Source of data known	Yes, most of it is generated by single application.	No, it comes from different databases.
Timed snapshots versions	No, continuous data. Single version.	Yes, you can key off a snapshot's date/time. Each snapshot is a version unless you overwrite it during refresh.
Data access pattern	Multiple users updating production database	Single-user access. Intense usage on an occasional basis. For example, when a report is due.
Can data be updated	Current value is continuously updated.	Read-only, unless you own the replica.
Flexibility of access	Inflexible, access to data via precompiled programs and stored procedures.	Very flexible via a query generator.
Performance	Fast response time is a requirement. Highly automated, repetitive tasks.	Relatively slow
Data requirements	Well understood	Fuzzy. A lot of detective work and discovery.
Information scope	Finite. Whatever is in the production database.	Very vast. Data can come from anywhere.

THE INFORMATION WAREHOUSE

The "data warehouse" in the client/server environment is the repository of data for decision-support processing.

— **W.H. Inmon (1993)** [3]

Bill Inmon is credited as being the "father of the data warehouse," a concept he started writing about as far back as 1981. Inmon argues that "one cornerstone of client/server applications is the notion of the difference between and separation of operational and decision support processing." In September 1991, IBM announced its *Information Warehouse* framework, an event that "sparked much interest in the industry." In October 1993, IBM announced a series of new products (many on OS/2), which make it very practical to create highly customized "Information Warehouses" on PCs, departmental servers, or mainframes. Many other commercial offerings—including various decision-support tools, Sybase 10's replicated server, Oracle7's replication facility, Teradata, Ingres' Replica Manager, MDI Database Gateway, Trinzic Corp's InfoPump, and DEC's Data Distributor—provide different facets of a warehouse solution. But as we go to press, IBM's implementation appears to be the most complete offering—especially when we include all the IBM business partners.

What's an Information Warehouse?

Bill Inmon and vendors like Teradata define a *warehouse* as a separate database for decision support, which typically contains vast amounts of information. Richard Hackathorn defines a *warehouse* as "a collection of data objects that have been inventoried for distribution to a business community."[4] In our own modest definition, "a warehouse is an active intelligent store of data that can manage information from many sources, distribute it where needed, and activate business policies." In the next section, we present IBM's definition. Hopefully, one of these definitions will ring a bell for you.

IBM's Information Warehouse

IBM defines its *Information Warehouse* as a framework consisting of four components: an informational database, open SQL access, automated copy management,

---

[3] Source: W.H. Inmon, **Developing Client/Server Applications** (QED, 1993).
[4] Source: Richard D. Hackathorn, **Enterprise Database Connectivity** (Wiley, 1993).

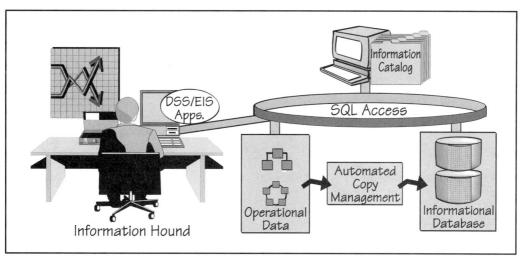

Figure 25-1. The Components of IBM's Information Warehouse.

and an information catalog (see Figure 25-1). These four components are supplemented by an open EIS tools strategy. An explanation of these components follows.

■ ***The informational database*** is a relational database that organizes and stores copies of data from multiple data sources in a format that meets the needs of information hounds. Think of it as the decision-support server that transforms, aggregates, and adds value to data from various production sources. IBM, in contrast to Inmon, does not preclude housing the information database on the same server as the production database. Inmon sees the warehouse as a huge database. In contrast, IBM's informational database can be a personal database on a PC, a medium-sized database on a local server, or a very large database on an enterprise server. IBM's tools support all these environments.

■ ***Open SQL access*** is used to access all databases, whether they're relational or non-relational. IBM supports three SQL APIs: EDA/SQL's CLI, the X/Open CLI, and DRDA's ESQL. IBM encourages an open DSS and EIS tool strategy around these APIs. It also has made alliances with the major tool vendors. IBM's framework does not preclude an information hound from directly accessing a production database. In contrast, purists like Inmon feel that decision-support applications should only be able to access the informational database. IBM provides SQL access to everything and leaves the implementation decision to its customers.

■ ***Automated copy management*** manages the copying of data across databases as defined by the information hound. The hound defines, using SQL SELECT statements, the tables that need to be copied, the source and destination platforms, and the frequency of updates. *Refresh* involves copying over the entire table; *update* only propagates the changes to all the replicas. Everything can be automated or done manually.

- **■** ***The information catalog*** helps the information hound find out what data is available on the different databases, what format it's in, and how to access it. The information catalog gets its "data about data" (or metadata) by discovering which databases are on the network and then querying their catalogs. It tries to keep everything up-to-date. The information hound finds out what's available by consulting the information catalog. Some estimates claim that information hounds in large enterprises spend 80% of their time gathering data and 20% of the time analyzing it. The hounds don't even know the names of the objects they're looking for, where they're located, and how to access them. The information catalog helps alleviate those three problems.

In summary, IBM's Information Warehouse provides a level playing field for all the providers of decision-support tools and components. They've defined SQL as the "lingua franca" of decision support, which is nice, and they defined the components that are needed to automate data gathering. In October 1993, IBM announced *DataGuide/2*—an information catalog that runs on OS/2. Another OS/2 product, *DataHub/2*, is used as the copy manager for all the IBM databases. A third OS/2 product, *FlowMark/2*, can be used with DataHub/2 to further automate multistep processes that transform and move the data. Any relational database—for example, DB2/2—can be used as the information store. Finally, hundreds of DSS and EIS tools that use SQL can participate in this framework.

IBM is the first to admit that information warehouses are too ad hoc and customer-specific to be provided as a single shrink-wrapped solution. The next best thing for everybody is a framework that helps articulate this industry so that we can all contribute a piece of the solution. We think the Information Warehouse framework meets the needs of the OLTP people, while giving information hounds more freedom than ever to get to the information they need. This helps explain why this particular IBM "architecture" was so well-received in the industry.

What's Being Automated?

If you think about it, IBM's Information Warehouse provides a framework for automating all aspects of the decision-support process. Instead of asking the database administrators (DBAs) what information is available, the information hounds can now directly consult the *information catalog*. Of course, like all good DBAs, the information catalog obtains its data definitions from the catalogs of the various database servers.

Instead of asking the DBAs to perform copies of the data, the hounds simply use the *copy manager* to do that. The copy manager keeps the informational databases automatically refreshed (or updated) with changes from the source database. A *workflow manager* can orchestrate the multistep movement of data through the network. For each step of the process—and there can be many steps—the workflow manager knows which tool to invoke and what to do next. Finally, the *information database* is a normal SQL database that replaces all the private schemes that have been used by information hounds to store copies of their favorite data extracts. The Information Warehouse makes it easy for the hounds to get to their data and removes the overburdened DBAs from the loop (now they can focus their attention on the OLTP side of the house).

Replication Versus Direct Access

With the spread of client/server technology and loosely coupled federated databases, it becomes impractical from many perspectives—performance, security, availability, debt-to-history, and local control—to create a single centralized repository of data. Replicated data management will increasingly be used to remove the capacity, performance, and organizational roadblocks of centralized data access.

Automated copy management—or the management of replicated data—becomes a key technology for sharing data in a federated database environment. Decision-support applications using data warehouses are perfect candidates for replicated data technology. These applications usually tolerate a certain amount of obsolescence—the politically correct term is *volatility*—in their data. Data replication for decision support minimizes the disruption of production systems and allows you to tailor the informational databases to fit your needs.

On the other hand, *direct data access* is required by applications—mostly production OLTP—that cannot tolerate any "volatility" in their data. These applications require "live data" that reflects the state of the business. This type of live data is obtained in distributed situations using one of four approaches:

■ ***Using federated databases that support synchronous (or continuous) replication of data***—the target databases must be synchronized within the same transaction boundary as the primary (or source) database. A target database that allows a user to directly update it is called a *replica*. To maintain a single-site update policy, the replica that gets updated becomes the new source database and must immediately propagate its updates. In general, synchronous replicated technology is a risky proposition in federated database environments. It requires support for two-phase commit protocols across heterogeneous databases.

■ *Using a centralized database server*—all the data is kept on one highly-scalable and fault-tolerant server. This solution, if it fits your organizational needs, will give you the least amount of headaches.

■ *Using a single vendor's distributed database multiserver offering*—notice that we did not say multivendor because this technology is still full of holes (see the following Briefing).

■ *Using a TP monitor to front-end multivendor database servers*—the database servers must support X/Open's XA protocol to be managed by a TP Monitor. As you will find out in Part 5, this technology can be very attractive in many situations.

In summary, there's a need for both kinds of data access: replicated and direct. The issues of direct access are well understood by the industry; many commercial solutions are available. On the other hand, the management of replicated data within an Information Warehouse framework is opening up exciting new opportunities. As more PCs become multimedia-enabled, we will start seeing federations of informational databases that include: the desktop client where local information is captured and viewed; the local server, which provides overflow storage; and global servers that collectively contain an infinite amount of information and storage. Efficient replication and copy management becomes the glue that ties together these new federations of databases.

 The Distributed Database Model

Briefing

Our feedback shows that the user community is still more ready for replication today than for multiple site update—except for the adventurous.

— *Marilyn Bohl, VP of Engineering,
Ingres (November, 1993)*

Standard *off-the-shelf* commercial distributed database packages will provide, when they fully blossom, transparent access to data on a network. The distributed database keeps track of the location of data on the network, and will route your requests to the right database nodes, making their location transparent. To be fully distributed, a database server must support multisite updates using a transactional two-phase commit discipline (see Figure 25-2). It should allow you to join data from tables that reside on several machines. It should also *automatically* update data in tables that reside on several machines.

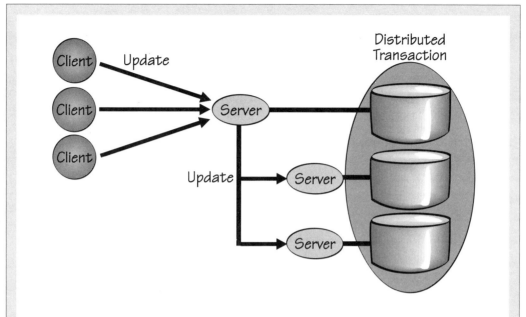

Figure 25-2. The Distributed Database Model.

Distributed databases make it easy to write distributed applications without having to first decompose your applications. With *true* distributed databases, the location of the data is completely transparent to the application. The chief advantage of a distributed database is that it allows access to remote data transparently while keeping most of the data local to the applications that actually use it. The disadvantages of a distributed database are:

■ They currently do not work in heterogeneous database environments. As a result, you're locked into a single vendor solution.

■ They poorly encapsulate data and services. You cannot change a local database table if it is being used by other nodes.

■ They require too many low-level message exchanges to get work done. Distributed databases exchange messages at the SQL level. This is not as efficient as using stored procedures or RPCs managed by a TP Monitor.

■ They are very slow over long wide-area networks. Two-phase commits are very expensive in terms of messages sent, and it is difficult to join tables located on different computers and achieve good performance.

> ■ They are very hard to administer. If one machine is not available, all the distributed transactions associated with it cannot execute. In contrast, with replicated databases, data can be accessed even if one server node is down.
>
> The alternative to distributed databases are *federated* databases, which are more easily adaptable to today's organizational realities. We also believe that eventually millions of desktop machines will come with a standard database. When you start dealing with millions of databases, you're much better off with loose federations that are synchronized using distributed object managers or a new breed of personal TP Monitors—but, now we're talking about the "post-scarcity" client/server scenario. ❏

The Mechanics of Data Replication

It's very common for business people to routinely populate their spreadsheets with data extracted from external sources. The process (see Figure 25-3) consists of the following manual steps: 1) Extract data using a query, 2) Copy the results to a diskette file, 3) Copy the diskette file to the machine with the spreadsheet program, and 4) Import the file into the local database (or spreadsheet). This technique, called *manual extract*, is primitive, labor intensive, and error prone.

Figure 25-3. Getting to the Data Manually.

In this section, we look at the mechanics for the total automation of this extract process (see Figure 25-4). The copy mechanics deal with the following issues: How is the extract specified? How is data from multiple sources blended? Can data be transformed as part of the copy? Who orchestrates the copy process? How is data copied into the informational databases? How are the copies refreshed? How tightly synchronized are the replicas (or extracts) with the source? When can the replicas be updated? What are the transactional boundaries of a copy?

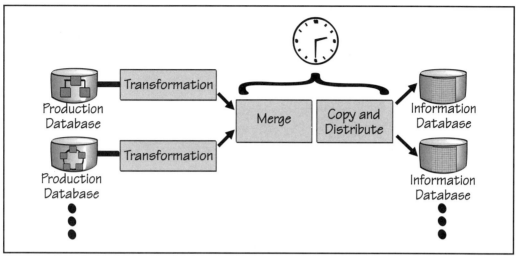

Figure 25-4. The Data Replication and Transformation Process.

Refresh and Updates

The informational databases are populated with data that originates from the various production databases. Typically, the data is copied or extracted using one of two techniques:

■ **Refresh** replaces the entire target with data from the source (see Figure 25-5). This works well when you are moving small amounts of data, which have low requirements for frequency of update (i.e., the data has low volatility). It is also used for doing initial bulk loads to the target database.

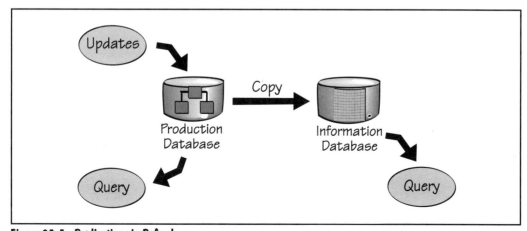

Figure 25-5. Replication via Refresh.

■ *Update* only sends the changed data to the target (see Figure 25-6). Updates can be either *synchronous*, which means that the target copy is updated in the same commit scope as the source table, or they can be *asynchronous*, which means that the target table is updated in a separate transaction than the one updating the source. Synchronous updates are useful in production environments for creating replicated databases that provide high availability. Asynchronous updates are useful in data warehousing situations. You get to specify the level of synchronization that you want to maintain between the source and the target and the interval of updates. This means that you get to control the level of data obsolescence you can tolerate.

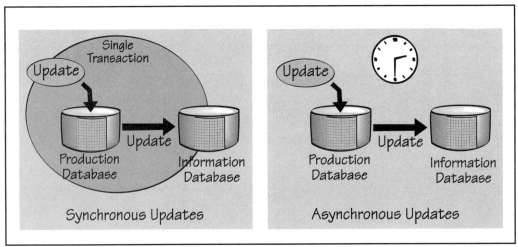

Figure 25-6. Replication via Synchronous and Asynchronous Updates.

Staging the Updates

Some of the warehouse products allow you to finely control the frequency of updates. IBM's Information Warehouse lets you specify the intervals at which you want *asynchronous update* data sent from the source to one or more targets. The changes to the source tables are captured in one or more *staging tables* for subsequent propagation to target tables (see Figure 25-7). At the intervals you specify, all the target databases in the system are updated simultaneously from the staging area.

To be more precise, the *data capture* component takes changed data from the database log and stores it in the *data staging tables* (see Figure 25-7). The *apply* component then takes the data from the staging tables and applies those changes to the target copies.

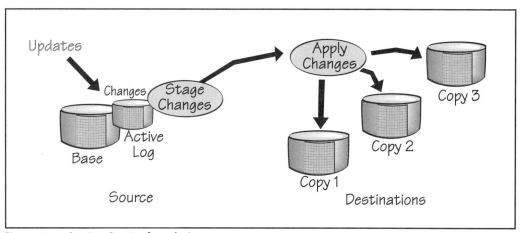

Figure 25-7. Staging: Copying from the Log.

Staging provides users with a consistent view of the data across the copies. It reduces contention on the production database—the copy tool does not interfere with production applications.

Cleaning the Raw Data

One of the attractive features of replicating data in warehouses is that you can control, enhance, and transform the "raw" data before storing it in the target databases. A well-designed warehouse lets you "filter and clean" raw data from production databases and store it in a form that's suitable for your informational needs. In other words, data warehouses are not simply passive collectors of data—they're in the business of creating value-added data from raw data.

As part of the copy, a warehouse translates data from its original raw formats (which may vary widely) into a single common format that's consistent for the informational application. The related data from multiple sites is combined and merged so that the "copy" becomes a single logical database. During this process, data may also be *enhanced*; that is, empty fields may be filled in or records extended. The data may be timestamped and stored in snapshots that capture a moment in time for historical trend analysis. The copy process also takes care of any data format conversions for different targets.

Some of the more sophisticated warehouses may apply user-defined specialized functions to the data to forecast trends; that is, fill in future values or create on-the-fly video presentations. They will also be able to convert data into formats that are appropriate to the decision support, spreadsheet, and multimedia viewing tools on the client machines. In other words, the sky is the limit when it comes to value-added warehousing functions.

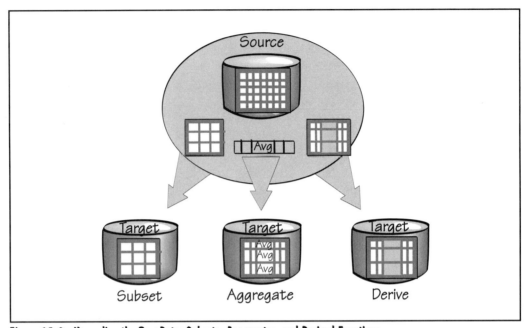

Figure 25-8. Upgrading the Raw Data: Subsets, Aggregates, and Derived Functions.

To give you an idea of what can be done today, let's take a closer look at the transform functions provided by IBM's Information Warehouse (see Figure 25-8). Using the OS/2 DataHub copy functions, the Information Warehouse lets you specify *subsets*, *aggregates*, and *derived functions* that you can automatically apply to data as it is copied between DB2 to DB2, DB2 to DB2/2, and DB2/2 to DB2/2 (refresh only) databases. We explain what this means:

■ *Subsets* allow you to transmit only the rows and columns that are of interest to your informational applications. You use SQL once to define your subsets to the copy tool, and these subsets will be performed automatically as part of the copy. In addition, different views of the same source data can be delivered to different copy targets. Multitable joins can also be used to define the copy transforms.

■ *Aggregates* allow you to transmit only the aggregations of data such as averages, sums, maximums, and so on. Again, you specify this once using SQL, and the copy tool will perform the aggregate every time a transfer takes place.

■ *Derived functions* allow you to specify data that does not exist but is the result of some calculation (or function) on data that does exist. For example, a new column of data may be defined on the target database that is the sum of two columns on the source database. The new column will automatically get created and updated as part of the automated copy process.

In addition to cleaning and merging the data, these functions can help you reduce the network traffic between the targets and the destinations because you only copy the data you want.

True Replicas

Replicas are *copies* of data, that may be updated (see Figure 25-9). When this happens, the updated replica must find a way to resynchronize its state with the original primary database. Normally, updates only take place on a single designated replica, and the primary server must abstain from doing any non-replica generated changes. In other words, the site of update shifts from the primary to the replica. The replica starts off with a full image of the primary database and sends all subsequent updates to the primary, either continuously or on a periodic basis. The primary database is then in charge of propagating the changes it receives to its target databases using the normal processes. The single-site update constraint may be relaxed by using *check-out* versions of replicated data—a technology that is widely used in Object Databases and will be covered in Part 7.

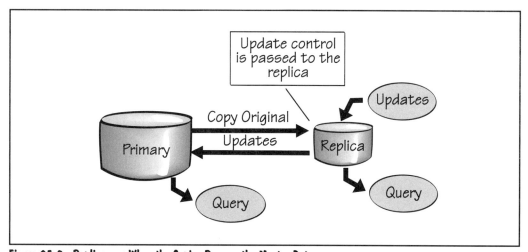

Figure 25-9. Replicas, or When the Copies Become the Master Data.

Ingres implements a database that allows both the master and the replicas to be separately updated and uses a *conflict resolver* to synchronize the data. When the changes in the replica are applied against the master an *update collision detector* resolves conflicts using one of four user-specified policies: the oldest update has priority, the most recent update has priority, a user-specified action is applied, or all replication is halted. Warning: True replicas can corrupt data.

The Future Warehouses

Information Warehouses will pop-up everywhere. We expect most personal computer users to have private data warehouses with hot links to information sources all over the globe. We expect large data warehouses to play an important role as data stores for the information highway. Both Oracle and IBM are investing heavily into database-managed video on demand technology. The replication technology that was presented in this chapter is an embryonic version of what can be done. In addition to moving tabular data, we'll soon be moving BLOBs of video and sound from the large data warehouses in the sky to our private and departmental warehouses (and vice versa). The EIS/DSS technology will help us distill massive amounts of data into a few visual pieces of information that we can quickly understand and use. We expect to see personal versions of these currently expensive tools sell in the volume market for $50 (or less). In addition to business information, we expect the warehouses to package tons of information that deal with personal, educational, and consumer topics.

There's Still Money To Be Made in Database

Soapbox

This concludes our conceptual introduction of SQL Database servers. It was a long tour, which is to be expected from a technology that accounts for the majority of client/server applications that are in production today. Database technology is still in its prime. SQL database servers are becoming commodity items and are now learning how to coexist in federated database arrangements. Mission-critical database systems will continue to be sold in packages that superbly integrate scalable fault-tolerant hardware with software. The new areas of growth will be in the mass markets for database-oriented products. What does it mean to put an information warehouse inside each desktop and mobile laptop? Who will keep these warehouses fed with continuous real-time information? What tools will help us digest all this information in real time?

Yes, there are still fortunes to be made in database technology. Database companies—including Sybase, Oracle, Gupta, Informix, Tandem, IBM San Jose, and Ingres—are transforming Silicon Valley (where your authors live) into "Database Valley." And they did it all with some relational and SQL technology from IBM research. We predict (this is, after all, a soapbox) that the marriage of "data warehouses" and "information highways" will create opportunities in database that dwarf anything we've seen so far. So the best is yet to come. And we certainly expect our valley to be called Database Valley by the end of the decade. ❑

Chapter 26

DB2/2 and Oracle7 For OS/2

---

*T*he problem is that each vendor has probably made excellent, but different, decisions about how to extend the SQL standard.

— Malcolm Colton, Director of Marketing,
Sybase (June, 1993).

It's impossible to do justice to all the relational database products that run on OS/2 2.X in one short chapter. All the major SQL database server vendors—including Oracle, Sybase, Ingres, XDB, Gupta, and IBM—offer database servers on OS/2. The exception is Informix. OS/2 products play a key role in the implementation of IBM's Information Warehouse strategy. *DataHub/2* provides a single focal point for the administration of IBM's databases on all platforms and is the copy coordinator for the Information Warehouse; *DataGuide/2*, announced in October 1993, provides the visual catalog manager for the Information Warehouse. In addition, OS/2 is a great database gateway platform. The MDI Gateway runs on OS/2 and IBM's DDCS/2 product provides the most popular gateway to DRDA databases. Finally, hundreds of database client/server tools—including DSS query pickers, front-end GUI painters, EIS tools, 4-GLs, CASE tools, and report writers—run on the OS/2 platform.

So we had a hard decision: Which of these products should we cover? We decided on Oracle and DB2/2 (and family). **Cracle7** provides an excellent example of an advanced 32-bit database server engine. And we cover the DB2/2 family of products—including **DB2/2**, **DDCS/2**, **DataHub/2**, and **DataGuide/2**—because of the important role they play in DRDA and Information Warehousing. We believe that warehousing deserves a lot of attention as an important up-and-coming database technology. DB2/2 is your average SQL database server; it is *very* affordable, robust, and has a great future. We'll describe both the present functions and the "great futures." We've excluded—except for a soapbox—the very popular Sybase/Microsoft SQL Server because it's not a 32-bit application (the Windows NT version is).

ORACLE7 FOR OS/2

Oracle7 for OS/2 provides the same SQL engine that runs almost identically on more than 80 distinct hardware and operating system platforms. According to Oracle, "OS/2's ease of use and support for Intel hardware, helps you minimize equipment requirements, overhead, and training costs." In general, Oracle is a complicated database to install and administer—the DBA guide is 1500 pages—so any "ease of use" really helps.

In 1992, Oracle produced the first 32-bit database server to support OS/2 2.X. They were able to get a 60% performance improvement from the 16-bit to the 32-bit versions. In May 1993, *Oracle7 for OS/2* was introduced adding many new powerful features. According to Oracle, the new OS/2 database "delivers high performance even under extreme load conditions." In November 1993, Oracle was one the first vendors to run its database in multiprocessing mode on the beta version of *OS/2 2.1 SMP*—the results were impressive.

Oracle7 more than makes up for its complexity with powerful SQL extensions and advanced features. Database engines are continuously leapfrogging one another in terms of new features and how well they run performance benchmarks. 1993 was definitely *the year of Oracle7*. But first position is always shifting in the database world—1994 may be the year of Sybase.

ORACLE7 Features

Oracle V6, introduced in 1988, was one of the first SQL engines to support production-strength database features such as row-level locking, online backups, symmetric multiprocessing (SMP), data clustering—a feature that allows multiple tables to be co-located on the same disk to speed-up joins—and cursors that sequentially access query results.

Oracle7 builds on top of the Oracle V6 foundation and includes all its functionality. The Oracle7 run-time environment is 50% larger than Oracle V6. But what you get for that reads like a catalog of the most advanced SQL database features in the industry. Here's a quick summary of what this includes:

- **Distributed database support**—Oracle7 supports multisite updates through transparent *two-phase commits*. It also supports distributed queries—a single SQL statement can reference data stored on different servers. Oracle allows you to store a link with a password to a remote database in the server catalog.

- **Global database names**—Oracle7 introduces a naming convention that allows database objects to be uniquely identified throughout a distributed environment.

- **Stored procedures, triggers, and alerts**—we already covered in much detail Oracle7's implementation of stored procedures and triggers. An Oracle7 *alert* is a special form of program-generated event. Programs can register their interest in an event and receive notification when it occurs.

- **Shared SQL**—allows precompiled SQL commands and previously submitted dynamic SQL commands to reside in memory cache. If the incoming SQL statement is not already in memory, it is parsed and stored in the cache. This helps expedite the execution of identical dynamic SQL commands.

- **Packages**—these are groups of related SQL procedures that share global data (it's the SQL equivalent of modules). Packages can contain procedures visible only to other procedures in the package.

- **Mirrored log**—the transaction log file can be mirrored for added media failure protection.

- **BLOBs**—these are binary data objects that can be as large as 2 GBytes and are used to store multimedia data types.

- **XA support**—this is an X/Open protocol standard that allows a TP Monitor to synchronize its two-phase commit protocol with a database manager (or other types of resource managers).

- **Declarative referential integrity**—Oracle7 adheres to the SQL-89 specification of referential integrity. Oracle claims that declarative referential integrity is superior in performance to trigger-enforced integrity. Oracle should know because it supports both methods.

- **Transparent network routing**—SQL*Net V2 has a built-in router that does protocol conversions and chooses alternate routing paths across networks.

■ **Replicated tables**—this is an asynchronous form of update copying. Multiple read-only copies of an updateable master table can be refreshed at user-defined intervals. Either the entire table or updates are copied, depending on the snapshot definition. The snapshot to be copied is specified using a SQL query. Oracle also provides extended SQL commands for creating, altering, and dropping snapshots.

■ **Electronic mail interface**—an API is provided to call Oracle*Mail from within your stored procedures. (Oracle is gradually introducing a portable set of APIs that allow applications to be moved across Oracle-supported platforms.)

■ **Security auditing**—simple AUDIT commands can be used to track data access by object and by user.

■ **Role-based security**—this feature, which is similar to the one being proposed in SQL3, groups a set of security authorizations and assigns them as a unit to a user. The grouped features are called *roles*. They take away some of the drudgery in system administration.

■ **Dispatcher-based server architecture**—instead of dedicating a process-per-client, Oracle7 introduces *listener tasks* that queue client requests for database work to any available shared server process. Database administrators can dynamically add or remove dispatchers and adjust the number of server processes to the workload. As we explained in previous chapters, this architecture supports more users with less overhead than process-per-client servers. However, it is not a multithreaded server (a la Sybase).

■ **Parallel server**—Oracle7 provides full read/write access to a single database from multiple nodes of loosely-coupled systems. Oracle implements a "shared nothing" parallel cache management system that uses internode messaging to coordinate the state of the distributed cache. Oracle believes that only massively parallel databases can provide the types of fast access to large amounts of data required by the "Information Highway." Oracle has invested heavily in nCUBE, a manufacturer of massively parallel computers. It hopes that the combination of Oracle7 and nCUBE provides the type of storage needed for accessing multimedia data in real time.

The above list reads like the ultimate "dream list" of features for SQL database servers. It's still too early to judge how well the new Oracle7 features are performing in production environments. Most of the success stories include a TP Monitor—usually Tuxedo—that does load-balancing and keeps Oracle7 running.

Nice Try Oracle

Soapbox

Oracle is very proud of its new distributed database features, which it calls "cooperative server" technology. Oracle's CEO, Larry Ellison, describes the technology as a generation beyond "early client/server" because of its support for multiple servers using SQL. The idea is that a database application can be created once and then deployed to different server topologies without any changes. It's an attractive idea, especially if you're an "all Oracle shop." It's also an architecturally pleasing construct—until reality starts to intrude.

As we pointed out in the last chapter, there are several competing architectures for creating these "cooperative servers." And distributed database is probably the least attractive of the bunch. In the area of decision support, distributed databases compete with federated database architectures and loosely coupled information warehouses. As long as 80% of the world's data is tucked away on non-relational databases, federation is the way to go.

We also can't imagine using raw distributed SQL databases for production-level OLTP applications. As we explained in the last chapter, true distributed databases are notoriously hard to manage (and have other problems too). Even Tandem Computers' customers—who can rely on a fault-tolerant hardware base—avoid writing applications that use the NonStop SQL's distributed database without going through the Pathway TP Monitor. They do that to get better performance, manageability, security, load balancing, and encapsulation of data. In other words, the TP Monitor—and not the database—becomes the coordinator of the multiserver transaction. The TP Monitor in some cases is the consumer of the distributed database facilities. We'll have more to say about TP Monitors in Part 5.

Of course, Oracle7 also supports replicated tables, a key feature of federated databases and information warehouses. However, it only copies from one Oracle7 to another. (Hint: It's easy for an enterprising third party to integrate Oracle's replication facilities into the Information Warehouse framework.) ❑

Oracle's SQL*Net V2 and the Multi-Protocol Interchange

*SQL*Net V2* is used to insulate Oracle applications and tools from the network. It can be used with another Oracle product—the *Multi-Protocol Interchange (MPI)*—to connect separate "communities" of SQL*Net nodes (see Figure 26-1). The MPI is really a gateway that allows transparent connections between SQL*Net applications, regardless of what network protocol is used. In practice, MPI runs on a machine that's separate from the database server. Each MPI can run multiple protocols and more than one MPI can reside on each network. Multiple MPIs give you multiple paths between a client and server pair. According to Oracle, the best two operating system platforms for running MPI gateways between TCP/IP and IPX/SPX are OS/2 and SCO Unix. SQL*Net can be used on its own without MPIs as long as the client and server use the same protocols.

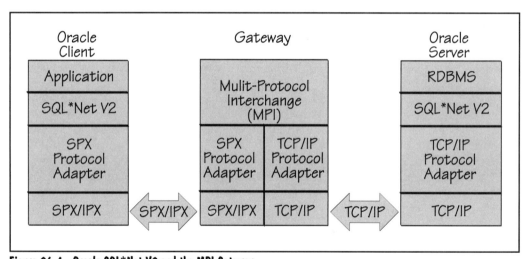

Figure 26-1. Oracle SQL*Net V2 and the MPI Gateway.

SQL*Net sits on top of the protocol stacks. You still need stacks to communicate over the network. SQL*Net supports almost every protocol stack, but only a few are bundled with a DBMS server. Two editions of *Oracle7 for OS/2* are available:

■ **The NetWare Edition** supports running the server on a Novell NetWare LAN using the IPX/SPX protocol stack.

■ **The IBM LAN Server Edition** supports running the server on an NDIS LAN (using NTS/2). The NTS/2 NetBEUI stack supports both the Named Pipes and NetBIOS interfaces. Also available from Oracle—through separate orders—are the TCP/IP, APPC, and DECnet stacks over NDIS drivers.

To take advantage of the new Oracle7's multithreaded dispatching, you'll need to install SQL*Net V2 on your server. The previous version (SQL*Net V1) only supports a process-per-client on Oracle7. This can be a real memory hog—each active process requires about 500 KBytes.

Oracle7 for OS/2 Packaging

Not all the components in Oracle7 are included with a server purchase. Oracle7 servers usually include the core DBMS, a few utilities, and the connectivity software (SQL*Net) necessary to connect a particular client platform to a server platform. The rest of the components are purchased separately. *Oracle7 for OS/2* includes the following components:

■ *The Oracle7 DBMS*—is the server version of Oracle's relational database system.

■ *The Procedural Database Extension*—is an extension of the database server software that supports stored procedures, functions, triggers, and packages; they are written in Oracle's PL/SQL language.

■ *SQL*Net V2*—is a component that allows Oracle tools and applications to communicate over a network. The OS/2 package is bundled with either a NetWare (IPX/SPX) or LAN Server (NetBIOS/Named Pipes) stack.

■ *SQL*DBA for OS/2 and MS-DOS*—is a component that provides a non-GUI menu and command-driven interface for database administrators. It is used for server management, performance monitoring, and interactive SQL entry.

■ *SQL*Loader for OS/2 and MS-DOS*—is a command-driven database loader that reads and converts a variety of file formats and loads them into the database.

■ *IMP and EXP*—are database import and export facilities. They can also be used to backup and restore a database.

■ *OCOPY.EXE*—is an OS/2 utility to make online backups of database files.

■ *CD-ROM Installer 3.0*—is a software utility used to install the server and client software off a CD-ROM drive on an OS/2 or DOS workstation.

The following components are available on OS/2 but must be purchased separately:

■ *The Distributed Database Extension*—is an extension of the database server software that supports distributed queries and updates to remote database servers. This is also the component that provides table replication and transparent two-phase commits.

- *Oracle Call Interface (OCI)*—is a C language CLI to Oracle7.

- *Refsnap*—is a utility used to reset the time intervals for refreshing replicated tables.

- *Oracle Tools*—include a wide selection of tools for developing Oracle7 applications on an OS/2 platform. These are tools such as *Oracle Forms*, *Oracle Card*, *Oracle Graphics*, and *Oracle CASE*Designer*. In addition Oracle is widely supported by third-party tools. C programmers may be interested on Oracle's *Pro*C* precompiler product that works with most OS/2 32-bit C compilers.

Oracle7 requires 16 Mbytes of RAM *minimum* and 60 Mbytes of disk. A 486 (or above) is recommended. A single user version of Oracle7 with the base functions sells for $699; an 8-user version sells for $3,999; and a 96-user version sells for $35,999.

DB2/2: A SQL DATABASE SERVER

DB2/2 is more than just another 32-bit SQL database server on OS/2. It is also being groomed for playing a "kingpin" role in IBM's Information Warehouse and DRDA distributed database. DB2/2 is the designated front end to IBM's DRDA databases, which means that most of IBM's database tools will run on the OS/2 platform. Finally, DB2/2 will become one of the first recipients of some important parallel database technology from IBM Research.

DB2/2: The DRDA Context

The OS/2 DB2/2 is a vital part of IBM's long-term distributed database strategy. This strategy is known as the *Distributed Relational Database Architecture*, or simply *DRDA*. As we explained in earlier chapters, IBM is promoting DRDA as the standard for multivendor database interoperability. A number of influential database vendors have announced support for DRDA, which is the primary vehicle for the interoperation of IBM's five relational database managers:

- *DB2/2* for OS/2 workstations.

- **DB2/6000** for AIX workstations. The AIX implementation is a almost a *twin* of DB2/2. It shares the same common code base; but because it was released five months later than the current OS/2 version, it provides some more advanced functions—including an X/Open compliant SQL CLI, and online backups. The AIX and OS/2 versions will converge in the next release of the two databases. They'll then become true identical twins.

- **SQL/400** for the AS/400 mid-range processors.

- **SQL/DS** DB2 for the S/370 VM Operating System.

- **DB2** for IBM's high end S/370 MVS Operating System. This is the *matriarch* of the DB2 family—the "mother of all DB2s."[1]

While the implementation of each product is tuned for its environment, the commonality of the interfaces is key in realizing the distributed database goal. This goal is to make it possible for the end user to access any DRDA database from an OS/2 machine as if it were a local OS/2 DB2/2. To realize this goal, IBM has stated it will provide the following:

- The OS/2 environment will serve as the primary window for end users to access any of the IBM DRDA databases, including those on the S/370s and the AS/400s. OS/2 also provides the common front end for managing DB2 databases on all platforms.

- The OS/2 DB2/2 will be cognizant of multisite data and provide a logical view of the distributed data that makes the location transparent.

- The OS/2 DB2/2 will handle the multisite synchronization, security, and data integrity functions on behalf of its users and in cooperation with other DRDA Database Managers. This means locating the remote data sites and coordinating requests (including the update of data) at several locations in a single transaction. It also means servicing of single requests that span multiple sites, such as a *multisite JOIN*.

The current implementation of DB2/2 is an embryonic version of the fully distributed DRDA goal described here. DRDA calls this embryonic level the *Remote Unit of Work (RUOW)*. This means that an application can connect to a remote DB2/2 and process multiple SQL statements against that database, issue a commit to make the work permanent, and then switch over to another DB2/2 to start a subsequent unit of work. The DDCS/2 product extends the RUOW function to heterogeneous (or unlike) DRDA DBMSs. In the RUOW model offered today, transactional integrity

---

1 IBM calls its DBMSs the DB2 family. Like Oracle, they are intended to run on all the industry platforms, including Windows NT.

is only provided on a per-site basis. It is up to the application to coordinate the multisite integrity and access of data. However, with the RUOW capability, an OS/2 machine can be used as a *Database Server* that can provide centralized data storage services to multiple users. These multiuser services include security and data integrity.

Why Should I Care?

In summary, the OS/2 DB2/2 is an integral part of IBM's distributed database strategy, both as a database front-end tool and as a database server. IBM customers can scale up their server applications with the OS/2 DB2/2 at the low end and DB2 at the high end. Thus, the SQL code you develop on the OS/2 DB2/2 can be ported to the MVS DB2 with very minor changes. And it also ports in the other direction for those who are downsizing. More importantly, DB2/2 and other DRDA machines will eventually be able to coexist on a network and provide a single logical view of distributed data, with all the necessary integrity and controls that this entails.

This versatility is particularly important for federated database and Information Warehouse environments. DB2/2—especially the single user version—provides a simple solution for extending the federated and warehousing database environments to the desktop where most of today's information is created and consumed. This will become clearer after we explain the DB2/2 components and supporting products.

The Components of DB2/2

DB2/2 consists of three components: Database Services, Database Tools, and Remote Data Services (see Figure 26-2).

Database Services

The heart of OS/2's DB2/2 is *Database Services*, which in industry jargon is typically referred to as a *SQL Engine*. This is the component that controls all accesses to the database, manages the logical and physical views of the data, generates optimized access plans to the data, and provides the transaction management, data integrity, data security, and concurrency support that allow multiple applications to access the same database simultaneously. The Referential Integrity feature provides a consistent level of data integrity similar to DB2. The Database Services is a multiuser database that can be configured either in *standalone* mode or as a network *Database Server* machine. A user application can access multiple local or remote SQL Engines serially.

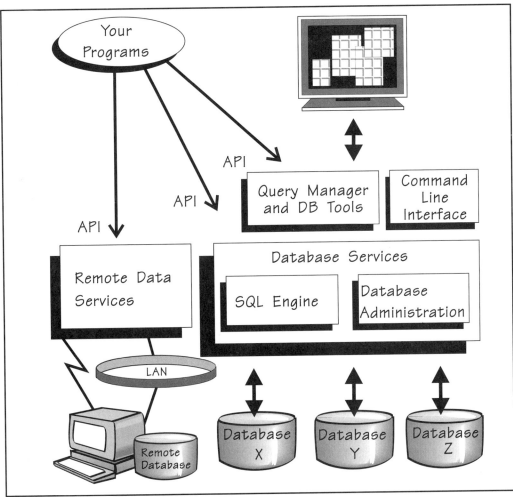

Figure 26-2. The Components of DB2/2.

The Database Services also includes a wide repertoire of service calls for maintaining and fine-tuning a database. These services include import and export of bulk data, backup and restore a database, table reorganization, statistics for query optimization, and operations on database directories. Service calls are also provided to create and delete databases and for connecting to databases on local or remote machines. IBM includes a precompiler with the Database Services that allows applications written in procedural languages such as C to invoke the DB2/2 API. Through the API, you can submit SQL statements, invoke the database utilities, or trigger the execution of stored procedures. IBM also includes the REXX procedures language with OS/2, which requires no precompiler to access the database services. The REXX interpreter can be used in prototyping situations; it is a very handy tool in the OS/2 environment.

Database Tools

Complementing the SQL engine is a suite of DB2/2 tools that are shipped with the product and can be selectively installed on your machine. These tools (see Figure 26-3) collectively allow you to configure DB2/2, backup and restore a database, perform forward recovery, and catalog databases and workstations for client/server and DDCS/2 connections. All the database administration tools have fancy graphical user interfaces that make database administration chores less painful.

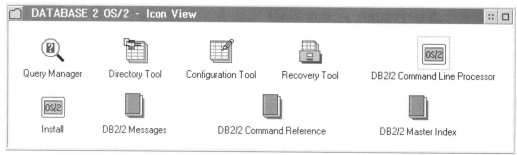

Figure 26-3. The DB2/2 Tools.

The most venerable of these tools, the *Query Manager*, is an interactive end-user tool used to execute database functions and utilities. The Query Manager uses Presentation Manager to provide a front end for creating database elements, submitting SQL queries, editing and entering table data, and for generating reports and procedures. The Query Manager can also be used to create customized applications with forms, menus, queries, reports, and procedures. The customized application can then be executed without the user ever knowing of Query Manager's involvement. Query Manager is the most direct route between an end user and the DB2/2 Database Manager. Through the Remote Data Services, it can serve as a window on either local or remote databases. The Query Manager also provides an API that enables you to call Query Manager functions and commands from within your C programs.

Database administration functions previously executed only through the Query Manager are now available through a separate suite of graphical tools. This unbundling makes it easier for users to replace Query Manager with some of the 20 (or more) excellent DB2/2 front-end tools on the market today. Functions that are still in the Query Manager are import/export, runstats, reorg, operational status, manage authorizations, restore defaults, and open/erase printer name. Forward recovery (also known as roll forward) is not supported within the Query Manager.

Another feature provided by DB2/2 is the *Database Command Line Interface*, which lets you create and run SQL statements, database environment commands, and database utilities from the OS/2 command prompt or from OS/2 command files. The Command Line Interface also includes a REORG check feature that lets you know when your database tables need to be reorganized to improve system performance.

Remote Data Services (RDS)

This is the component of the DB2/2 Database Manager that provides distributed database capabilities to OS/2, MS-Windows, or MS-DOS clients on a LAN. Here's what these capabilities currently include:

- **Transparent SQL access** means that your SQL call is automatically routed to either a local or remote database (see Figure 26-4). This form of remote access is useful for ad hoc SQL calls over networks.

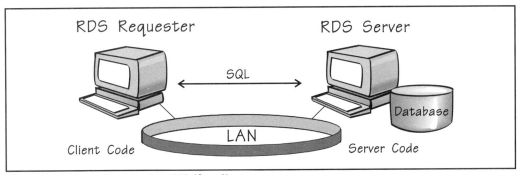

Figure 26-4. Remote Data Services: SQL Client/Server.

- **Remote Procedure Calls** allow you to invoke remote procedures (DLLs) that are stored on the database machine (see Figure 26-5). This form of remote invocation cuts down on network traffic and is typically used for transaction processing.

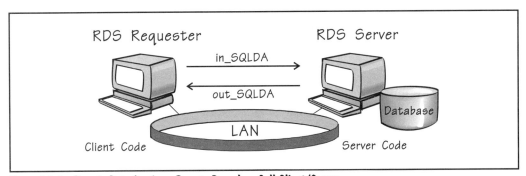

Figure 26-5. Remote Data Services: Remote Procedure Call Client/Server.

■ ***Database consistency across the network*** means that if a remote site fails, the transaction for that application is rolled back and the database is returned to its last consistent state.

■ ***Network directory services***. The current method for achieving local/remote transparency, consists of manually adding information about the physical location of the databases to the system directories. These directories are consulted when an application first connects to the database. The RDS requester routes the non-local database calls to the RDS server where the database resides. The application is not cognizant of whether the database being accessed is local or remote, and the same code can be run in both situations.

DB2/2 Packaging

The DB2/2 product comes in two flavors:

■ ***DATABASE 2 OS/2 (Single User)*** is a low-cost single user version of DB2/2. This product sells for $425. We've seen it promoted for as little as $199 at *DB Expo*.

■ ***DATABASE 2 OS/2 (Client/Server)*** is a costlier version of DB2/2 that provides a networked Database Manager server function for MS-DOS, MS-Windows, and OS/2 clients (see Figure 26-6). This product sells for $2,495.

The database clients only require a separate, "skinny," low-cost program that sells for $75; it's called the ***Database Client-Enabler***. This program requires a NetBIOS communications protocol stack such as the one provided by NTS/2. NetBIOS is the default LAN protocol for OS/2, DOS, and MS-Windows database clients. NetBIOS greatly simplifies the installation and configuration of database

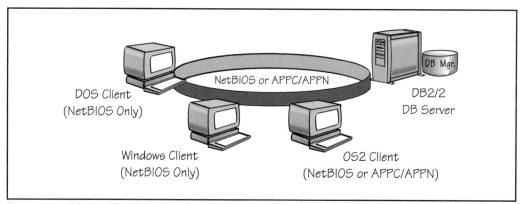

Figure 26-6. DB2/2: Client/Server Configuration.

clients and servers. It keeps the clients "skinny" by using up less memory than APPC/APPN, the other protocol stack option for database clients. You will need APPC/APPN if your database clients require internet routing capabilities, a DB2/6000 server, SNA management, non-LAN attached communications, or direct access to mainframe DBMSs through DDCS/2. The APPC/APPN stack is a component of Communications Manager/2. The Query Manager Client is now packaged separately and sells for $75.

All the components of DB/2 are CID-enabled and can be remotely installed from an NTS/2 code server. The graphical installation program is one of the best for PC DBMSs. DB2/2 can also be managed from LAN NetView.

DB2/2 Futures

The next release of DB2/2 will bring in the new features that are on the DB2/6000. DB2/2 and DB2/6000 will then be concurrent and stay that way. In addition, both DB2/2 and DB2/6000 will incorporate new functions from IBM's Almaden Research lab.[2]

First, what are the missing functions that are already in DB2/6000? There's roughly 20% added functions that provide the following features: an X/Open extended SQL CLI, TCP/IP network support, more DB2 compatibility, online backup, AIX client support, and XA support—an X/Open standard for interfacing TP Monitors with DBMSs.

In addition, IBM intends to incorporate into DB2/2 and DB2/6000 the following Almaden Research-developed features: a new optimizer that will greatly enhance the speed and capabilities of doing joins; support for the SQL-92 BLOB standard; catalog-tracked stored procedures—with the option of storing them in the database; SQL3-like user-defined functions and data types; and parallel database support (see the following Briefing box).

IBM also intends to incorporate DCE NOS features into the database—including security and directory services. More client support will be added—including HP-UX, Sun, and Macintosh. The SQL CLI will support, in addition to X/Open, the IDAPI and ODBC extensions. New LAN protocols will be supported—including IPX/SPX and AppleTalk. You should also expect to see two-phase commit support for multisite updates across DRDA databases. Tables will span across media (64 GBytes per table on each node) and will be able to be backed up and recovered at

---

2   This entire section is based on publicly available information documented in the OS/2 Technical Interchange Proceedings, Orlando, September 1993. Not all the features described here will be in the next release. But, at least, this should give you an idea of where things are going with DB2/2.

the page level. IBM is also putting a big effort on expanding third-party tool and gateway support.

FYI

Almaden's Parallel Database Effort

Briefing

Almaden Research is developing 75% of the code base for the parallel database support that will be provided on both DB2/2 and DB2/6000. The technology creates a single logical database server that runs on multiple machines. Almaden has demonstrated support for both SMP-enabled servers and share-nothing parallel database extensions. The technology shows excellent (almost linear) performance improvements as more processors are added. It also supports the incremental growth in database capacity.

IBM intends to provide 24 x 7 availability—24 hours a day times 7 days a week—using both hardware and data redundancy. It is also working on the administration of such a system—a non trivial effort.

The software version of the parallel database requires no special hardware. The database is simply partitioned across ordinary networked PCs or workstations. The software version provides a distributed optimizer and externally appears as a single database server. The data can span across media and can be distributed across multiple data nodes. This version is expected to go into beta in mid-year 1994.

The hardware version of the parallel database also runs on "off the shelf" workstations, but it uses a high-speed private network for interdatabase communications. However, it's a "shared-nothing" system—the disks are not shared and the processors are not shared. The single system is created by the parallel software that runs on top of the regular database engine. The system is scalable from two nodes up to 256. The parallel systems do not require changes to existing APIs. But under the covers, they introduce parallel queries and transactions, parallel joins, and parallel utilities. ❑

DDCS/2: OS/2'S DRDA PRODUCT

DDCS/2, which stands for ***Distributed Database Connection Services/2 Version 2.0***, is a 32-bit OS/2 DRDA gateway product that allows the OS/2 DB2/2 to interoperate with DB2, SQL/DS, and SQL/400. With DDCS/2, any of those DBMS platforms can become database servers to DOS, MS-Windows, and OS/2 clients (see Figure 26-7). Note that DB2/2 clients can communicate directly with DB2/6000. They don't require DDCS/2.

DDCS/2 is the first PC product to implement the RUOW subset of DRDA. What this mouthful of acronyms means, in a nutshell, is that you can write database server applications on OS/2's DB2/2 and then run them on either OS/2, DB2, SQL/DS, DB2/6000, or SQL/400. You decide where the application runs with a simple directory entry without having to change (or recompile) the code on either the client or server. The choice of a database platform is totally transparent to your application. You just flip the switch by changing a directory entry; you're then connected to DB2, SQL/400, SQL/DS, DB2/6000, or OS/2's DB2/2.

There are a few caveats with DDCS/2, as we will point out in the next section. However, once you get over the caveats and the maze of acronyms, you may discover

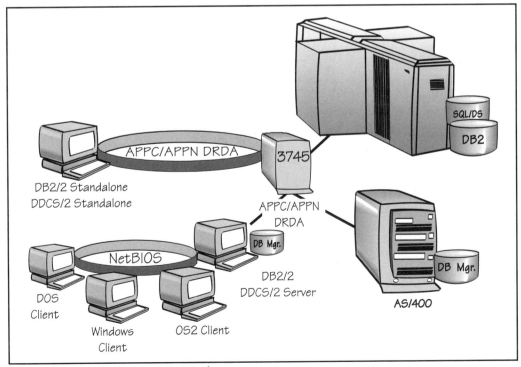

Figure 26-7. DDCS/2: The OS/2 DRDA Product.

that DDCS/2 offers radically new client/server possibilities for environments where the data resides on both PCs and mainframes. With some modification, a mainframe application can be moved to an OS/2 platform, and an OS/2 application can access data without regard to location.

DDCS/2 does not support the Query Manager; instead, it lets you submit queries interactively through the Database Command Line interface. You can submit import and export commands to the host DBMSs (but only the PC/IXF data format is supported). Other administrative functions should be done from the host platform.

Programming DDCS/2

DDCS/2 does not introduce any new programming constructs or functional APIs, except for a couple of APIs used to manipulate the DCS directory (this is better done with a database administration tool). DDCS/2, however, does introduce a programming for portability discipline, which we discuss in this section. Other than that minor caveat, DDCS/2 is totally transparent to programmers. This is quite a feat for a program that provides so much added value at the system level.

DDCS/2 supports connections to DB2, SQL/DS, and SQL/400. In addition, DB2/2 clients can directly connect to DB2/6000. How easy will it be to port OS/2 SQL applications to these platforms? Will they really run unchanged? Where are the pitfalls? What is the development process? What tools are provided? We will attempt to answer all these questions in the remainder of this chapter.

The DRDA Run-time Environment

The DRDA run-time environment is totally transparent to the client/server programs. Here's how it works:

1. Log on to your workstation and provide the password and security information. This information will be used to identify you to the host security subsystems like RACF.

2. Issue a SQL **CONNECT** command to connect to the DRDA server database of choice. The directories are all set up to make the connection transparent to your programs.

3. Run your programs. You're connected in client/server mode with the host. You can run static SQL packages and dynamic SQL.

4. Issue a SQL **CONNECT RESET** when you're done. You can then start using any other DRDA server by repeating the process. It couldn't be easier.

The DRDA Development Environment

Details

The good news is that your friendly DB2/2 environment gives you everything you need to develop portable applications across DRDA platforms. To create your development environment, follow these steps:

1. Install DDCS/2 on a server machine. The installation takes a few minutes. There are no surprises here.

2. Configure the DDCS/2 environment. You must configure Communications Manager and the directory services.

3. Precompile and develop your programs on the local DB2/2 server. Start with the (.SQC) files and run them through SQLPREP with the deferred bind option. This will create (.BND) files that you can later bind to the host database of choice. Compile and link your programs using the C/C++ Tools. This process was explained in earlier chapters.

4. Issue a SQL **CONNECT** (or **START USING DATABASE**) command to connect to the host SAA database of choice. The directories can be set up to make the connection transparent to your programs.

5. Use the DDCS/2 supplied **SQLJBIND** program to bind all the SQL utilities to the host. These include SQLBIND, the Command Line Interface (CLI), REXX (if needed), IMPORT, and EXPORT. We're assuming that you're dealing with a virgin host with nothing installed on it. You must bind the SQLBIND utility to bind your programs to the host; the rest of the utilities are optional.

6. Issue the **BIND** command to bind your (.BND) files to the host database.

The DDCS/2 product provides a set of tools that help you develop and debug DRDA applications:

■ **SQLJSETP** sets environment variables to provide more explicit error messages when you BIND your programs on different host environments. The additional information returned in messages includes the server type, the package type, and the complete SQLCA contents. It tells you in clear terms what error occurred (for example, which column does not exist) and what to do about it.

- **SQLJTRC** traces the DRDA message flows. The trace information is entered in the default SQLJTRC.DMP file. The trace tool is useful for debugging, but should not be used in production environments. It introduces too much overhead.

- **SQLJBIND** binds OS/2 SQL utilities to the host. ❑

SQL Is Not Always SQL

DRDA introduces the first heterogeneous DBMS platform in the industry that supports both static and dynamic SQL across dissimilar operating systems, networks, and hardware platforms. As you can imagine, this complex environment will have some impact on our SQL programming practices. There are also some caveats. This section examines some of those issues.

Different DBMS platforms have introduced their own extensions of SQL. The SQLPREP precompiler was relaxed to accept "unknown dialects." This new level of tolerance means that you can use SQL dialects for other DRDA target machines in your programs. The compiling process leaves it up to the BIND program to check for allowable commands on a target DBMS. IBM's owns DRDA servers have some different SQL tastes and may get different bind results (see Figure 26-8). Notice in the table that only OS/2 (and DB2/6000—not shown) support the DATABASE APPLICATION REMOTE INTERFACE; only DB2 supports TABLESPACES. These differences are detected at bind time.

If you want your programs to be portable across all DRDA platforms, then you must avoid target-specific SQL extensions and use a portable SQL. So what is a portable SQL? For DRDA DBMSs, it is the IBM SAA SQL-92 dialect.[3] There are, in general, two areas where SQL deviates from the standard: the DDL and the advanced SQL extensions. The OS/2 DDL is SAA SQL compliant. However, OS/2 does offer advanced constructs that go above and beyond SAA SQL, like the *Application Remote Interface*—the current DB2/2 implementation of stored procedures. Should you use them? It depends on whether you need performance or portability. There are always trade-offs in this business.

---

[3] See **CPI Database Level 2 Reference**, IBM Order Number SC26-4798. This publication marks in green the DBMS platform deviations from SAA SQL. The current implementation of DB2/2 Database Manager removes most of the green from OS/2.

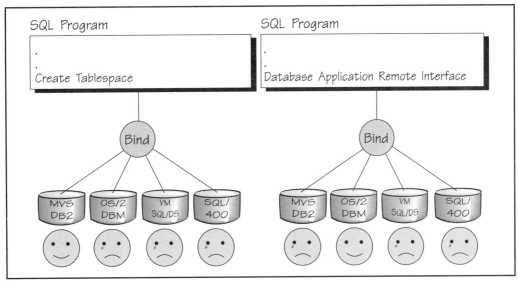

Figure 26-8. Platform Specific SQL Extensions.

How to Handle Sorts

ASCII and EBCDIC sort differently. In ASCII numeric values come first. In EBCDIC, it's the inverse. Your programs may see different ordering results depending on which platform they execute. This will be true for any ORDER BY, GROUP BY, or DISTINCT clause. To get around this limitation, DRDA provides collating sequences. These are tables that allow you to explicitly specify how sorting will occur. You can make "z" come before "a" if you so choose. DDCS/2 provides an ASCII/EBCDIC collating table.

How to Handle "Common" Errors

The different SAA platforms have, over time, created their own error return codes. In OS/2, these are the codes returned in the SQLCODE field of the SQLCA structure. DDCS/2 provides two ways to write portable return codes:

- Using the SQLSTATE field in the SQLCA. This field will return standardized SAA SQL error codes that are consistent across DRDA platforms. This standard complies with SQL-92.

- Using the DDCS/2 error mapping tables. These tables map error codes between DRDA platforms. You can continue to use the SQLCODE field for error returns, and it's business as usual.

System Catalog Variations

Database catalogs is another area where you will find differences in the DRDA DBMSs (see Table 26-1). You can get around this limitation by creating VIEWs that mask the differences between the tables. The DBMSs also use different qualifiers for their system tables. DB2/2 and DB2 use *SYSIBM*; SQL/DS uses *SYSTEM*.

Table 26-1. Differences in System Catalogs Across SAA DBMSs.

DB2/2 DBM	MVS DB2	VM SQL/DS	OS/400 SQL/400
Sysindexes	Sysindexes	Sysindexes	Sysindexes
Sysplan	Sysplan	Sysplan	Sysaccess
Systables	Systables	Syscatalog	Systables
Sysviews	Sysviews	Sysviews	Sysviews

Beware of Locks and Isolation Levels

The DRDA platforms have differences in their locking and isolation level strategies. Locking is transparent to your code. So, there is not too much you can do to protect yourself from these different locking strategies other than to be aware of their existence. Table 26-2 shows the different isolation levels supported by DRDA DBMSs. These isolation levels are specified at BIND time. Table 26-3 shows the different levels of locking support.

Table 26-2. Differences in Isolation Level Support Across SAA Platforms.

Isolation Level	DB2/2 DBM	MVS DB2	VM SQL/DS	OS/400 SQL/400
Read Repeatability (RR)	Yes	Yes	Yes	No
Cursor Stability (CS)	Yes	Yes	Yes	No
Uncommitted Read (UR)	Yes	No	No	No
LCKLVL (ALL)	No	No	No	Yes
LCKLVL (CHG)	No	No	No	Yes

Table 26-3. Differences in Locking Support Across SAA DBMSs.

Lock Support	DB2/2 DBM	MVS DB2	VM SQL/DS	OS/400 SQL/400
Row-Level Locking	Yes	No	Yes	Yes
Page Locking	No	Yes	Yes	No
Table Locking	Yes	Yes	Yes	Yes
Lock Escalation	Yes	Yes	Yes	No

Not All Utilities Are Supported

DDCS/2 only supports the IMPORT and EXPORT utility for exchanging table contents from OS/2 to other SAA DBMSs—and only the PC/IXF interchange format is supported. DDCS/2 does not allow you to issue REORGs, RUNSTATs, or ROLL FORWARDs against other SAA DBMSs. It also does not support the GET ADMIN or AUTHORIZATION commands. You must perform these tasks from within the host environment using SPUFI, QMF, or CICS tools.

DRDA Is Not Perfect, But...

Soapbox

Yes, DRDA is not perfect, but it's a quantum leap toward realizing the SQL dream of seamless access to data across dissimilar platforms. The mainframes contain huge amounts of data. The PCs provide cheap MIPs and ease-of-use. DRDA makes them work together almost painlessly. The DDCS/2 product allows you to get to the mainframe data without writing a line of mainframe code. Your entire development environment is on a PC running OS/2. We've certainly come a long way. ❑

DDCS/2 Installation

DDCS/2 installation is PM-based. The program fits on a single diskette and is CID-enabled. DDCS/2 is always installed on top of DB2/2. On some of the other IBM platforms, DRDA is part of the DBMS itself. DDCS/2 connects to the following DBMS products: DB2 Version 2, Release 3 (or above); SQL/DS Version 3, Release 3 (or above); and SQL/400 Version 2, Release 1.1 (or above). You should make sure that the proper host-based software is installed and that the required communications links and hardware are in place.

DDCS/2 Packaging

So what's left to know about DDCS/2? We need to understand how the program is packaged, how it is installed and configured, and what tools are provided. The DDCS/2 product, like everything else it seems, comes in two flavors:

- ***IBM SAA DDCS/2 V2.0 (Single User)*** is a low-cost product that provides single user access to a host database from a LAN-attached OS/2 workstation. DB2/2 (Single User), Communications Manager/2, and OS/2 must be installed on the machine (see Figure 26-7 on page 531). This product retails for $500.

- **IBM SAA DDCS/2 V2.0 Multiuser Gateway** is a more costly gateway server product that provides concurrent, multiuser access to a host DBMS from LAN attached DOS, MS-Windows, and OS/2 clients (see Figure 26-7 on page 531). The DDCS/2 gateway server runs on top of DB2/2 and OS/2. You can think of it as an ordinary DB2/2 server that has the added capability of being able to redirect requests to the appropriate host database server. This product retails for a hefty $4,680. Welcome to mainframe prices!

There is some good news on the pricing front. The clients use the same software that is used by DB2/2 clients, which is the $75 ***Database Client-Enabler*** program we introduced earlier in the chapter. This means that DDCS/2 does not introduce new costs on the client workstation if you already own (or are planning) a DB2/2 client/server installation.

THE OS/2 INFORMATION WAREHOUSE PRODUCTS

The Information Warehouse is an open platform where any SQL database server and EIS/DSS tool can participate. The two OS/2 products described in this section—*DataHub/2* and *DataGuide/2*—help create an infrastructure for the Information Warehouse. The tools provide open interfaces that allow vendors to plug in their warehouse components. *FlowMark/2* is a general-purpose workflow manager that is only needed if complex multistep operations are required as part of managing the warehouse.

DataHub/2 V1.2: The Warehouse Manager

DataHub/2 is IBM's "strategic" product for federated database management and administration. It provides a set of integrated functions for managing complex heterogeneous database environments that currently include DB2, SQL/DS, DB2/2, DB2/6000, and the OS/400 Database Manager. These databases can all be managed from a single OS/2 workstation control point (see Figure 26-9). In addition, DataHub/2 is the single control point *copy manager* for the IBM Information Warehouse.

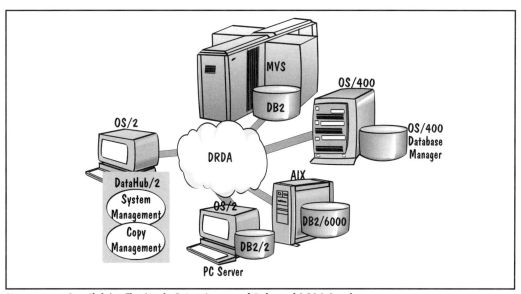

Figure 26-9. DataHub/2: The Single-Point Manager of Federated DRDA Databases.

What Does It Do?

DataHub/2 provides a consistent graphical user interface across an integrated set of tools that mask the differences between heterogeneous databases (see Figure 26-10). The interface allows database administrators, systems programmers, help desk personnel, and application developers to:

■ *Distribute data* across federated databases by copying data between like or unlike servers. As the locations of data become more dispersed, there is a growing need for a single point of administration and control for the various copy management processes.

■ *Perform federated database system management tasks* across multiple like or unlike servers.

■ *Manage authorizations* across federated databases.

■ *Trace and display* **SQL** client/server commands as they execute across platforms. This can speed up problem detection and minimize downtime.

■ *Invoke database utilities* written by IBM, other vendors, and customers. Multivendor utilities are available in the areas of operations, change, configuration, problem and security management.

The consistent user interface shields users from differences in invocation methods across unlike databases. DataHub/2 graphically presents database objects and the relationships between those objects to users. Database objects can be defined on one database system, then copied to like or unlike database servers using simple commands.

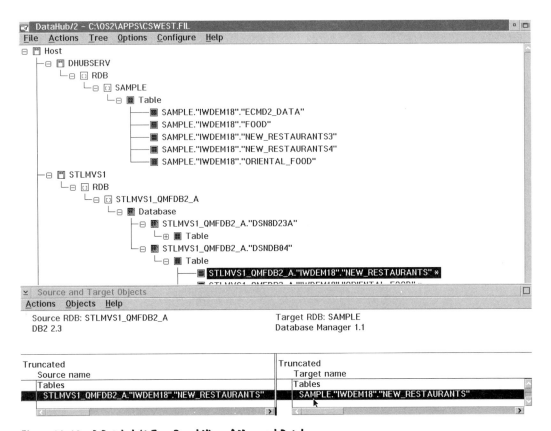

Figure 26-10. A Datahub/2 Tree-Based View of Managed Databases.

DataHub's Role in the Information Warehouse

DataHub/2 provides the control point for defining and administering the copy functions between databases anywhere in the organization. It provides the mechanisms for automating the copying of data between operational and informational data stores. The copy management family of products (from IBM and others) snap into DataHub/2, which gives them the advantage of a consistent interface for data administration.

DataHub/2 integrates with *FlowMark/2* to support workflow-based automation of the copy process. The integration starts with the visual interface that allows DataHub/2 process icons to be dragged and dropped onto FlowMark objects. Database administrators can precisely document their system management tasks using FlowMark's interactive facilities. Once a series of DataHub oriented tasks are documented and verified with FlowMark's process animation facility, they can be automatically executed in unattended environments. We cover FlowMark/2 in Part 6.

A key goal of the Information Warehouse is to provide a structure that allows copy management to be done in an integrated, simple, and automated fashion. You should be able to choose from a variety of products and components when building specific Information Warehouse implementations. A platform—like DataHub/2 V1.2—is needed to bring the pieces together with the following levels of integration:

- *Visual Integration* means the interface is consistent and allows visual objects to interact with each other either directly or through "cut and paste" and other forms of exhanges.

- *Process Integration* means automating the execution of different tools or applications to achieve a particular task.

- *Control Integration* means that if a tool invokes another, it must be done seamlessly. The user must only see one tool even when several are invoked to satisfy a task.

- *Data Integration* means that the sharing of data must be done with minimum effort by multiple tools or applications.

Some examples of copy management products that DataHub/2 integrates are:

■ **DataRefresher** is a newly enhanced product that is designed to refresh relational databases from non-relational sources—including IMS, VSAM, and sequential files (see Figure 26-11). The product only supports *refresh* oriented copies.

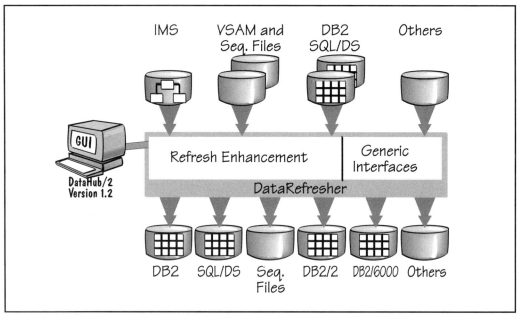

Figure 26-11. The DataRefresher Replication Product.

■ **DataPropagator Relational** is a new DRDA-based product for copying data between relational databases (see Figure 26-12). The version of the product shipped in December 1993 supports enhanced copies between DB2 and DB2/2 (DB2/2 to DB2/2—refresh only). The product provides automated copy capabilities at a level of synchronization tailored to the customers' needs. It supports both *refresh* and *update* oriented copy. Updates are done using the *staging* mechanism described in the last chapter. The product also supports powerful transformation facilities—including subsets, aggregates, and derived data.

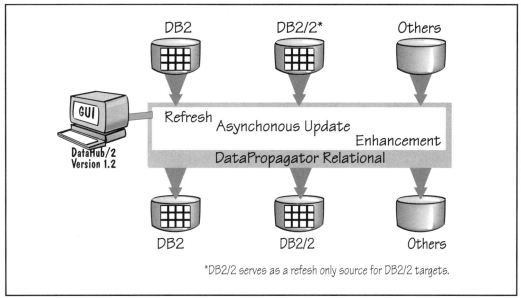

Figure 26-12. The DataPropagator Relational Replication Product.

■ **DataHub's Copy Data tool** is a native DataHub copy facility that provides functions to copy data between IBM relational databases (see Figure 26-13). It can do refresh and some limited data enhancements but no updates.

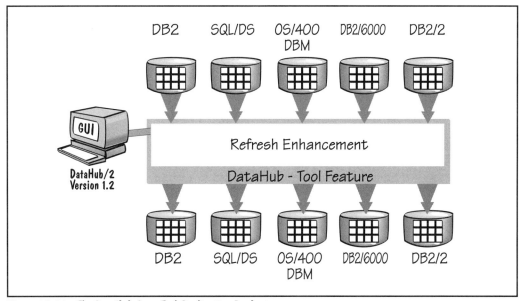

Figure 26-13. The DataHub Copy Tool Replication Product.

■ ***Bridge/Fastload*** is an example of an a non-IBM Information Warehouse product from Bridge Technology that moves data from DB2 directly into DB2/2 or DB2/6000, bypassing the import utility and logging (see Figure 26-14). The Bridge Technology product is good for large refreshes of data and can be up to ten times faster than other data copy methods.

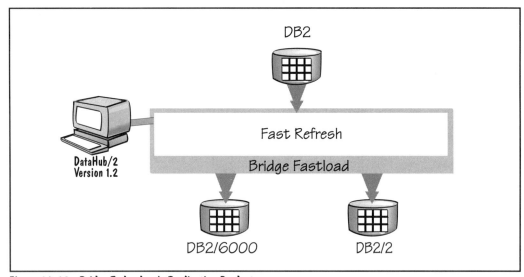

Figure 26-14. Bridge Technology's Replication Product.

In summary, DataHub provides an open platform for federated database management and copy management for warehouses. Twelve system management tool vendors—including Legent, Platinum, Candle, Bridge, and InfoTel—have announced products that integrate with DataHub.

Packaging and Availability

The current version of DataHub does not support DB2/6000, integration with FlowMark/2, and the Information Warehouse copy management. All these features will be part of DataHub/2 V1.2, announced by IBM on October 12, 1993. The new DataHub is scheduled to ship by June 30, 1994. No prices for the new DataHub/2 are currently available. The current version of DataHub sells for between $500 and $6,500, depending on the options.

DataGuide/2: The Information Catalog

DataGuide/2, announced by IBM in October 1993, provides an *information catalog* for end users. It's a component of the Information Warehouse that lets you find out what data is available, information about the data, where is it located, and how to access it. It uses a presentation format that normal mortals can easily understand. The automated collection of "data about data" (also known as *metadata*) becomes important as sources of information start to multiply in a federated database world.

DataGuide/2 is an OS/2 based client/server application that uses DB2/2 as the metadata store. A client application that runs on the OS/2 Workplace Shell provides the graphical interface to the information catalog. The interface is also used to manage and create information object definitions. DataGuide/2 comes with a set of utilities for extracting object definitions from various sources.

What Metadata Is Collected?

DataGuide/2 allows you to look up metadata on information-generating objects—including charts, spreadsheets, reports, and queries—as well as data objects—including files, images, drawings, databases, tables, and columns. Objects are described using everyday names. You can search for an object using keywords, pattern matches on names or descriptions, or by navigating through visual containers and groupings of related objects.

To help you find information, DataGuide/2 provides the following aids: a *glossary* of business terms and descriptions, *people contacts* to identify object owners, *news* items telling you what's new in the information catalog, and *help panels* (see Figure 26-15).

When you find an information object that is of interest, simply click on it; DataGuide/2 will automatically launch the application that handles the data. Even though DataGuide's primary focus is on informational applications—such as DSS and spreadsheets—other applications can be invoked as well—for example, Corel Draw to view drawings. In all cases, DataGuide/2 associates a data object type with the program that can work on it. These can be DOS, Windows, or OS/2 programs running on OS/2 2.X.

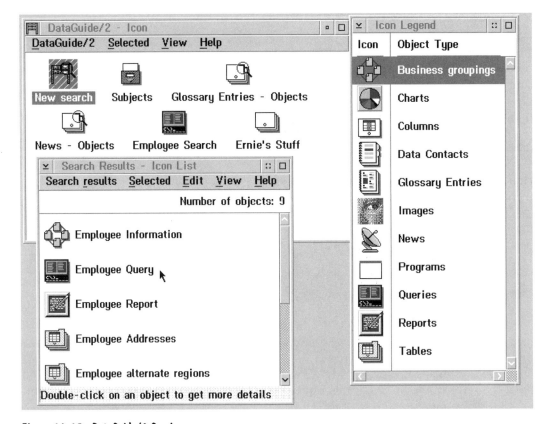

Figure 26-15. DataGuide/2 Services.

Where Does DataGuide Get Its Metadata?

DataGuide captures information about "what's out there" using four techniques (see Figure 26-16):

- **Catalog extractors**—the product includes a set of *knowledge administrator* utilities that can extract "data about data" from database catalogs—including DB2, DB2/2, SQL/400, Oracle on DEC, and Sybase on HP-UX—or from tools such as the Bachman Database Administrator.

- **Imports from other DataGuides**—the product includes an *Import/Export* facility that allows objects to be imported from different information catalogs. The catalog objects are defined in a portable format using a tag language (it's part of the Information Warehouse Architecture). The Export Facility stores catalog objects in the tag format. The objects can be loaded into the DataGuide store with a single invocation of the Import function. This "open" tag language

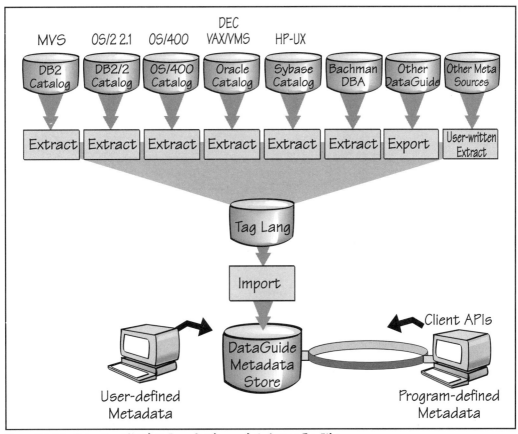

Figure 26-16. Extracting Metadata From Catalogs and via Import Tag Files.

allows third parties to create their own metadata extract programs. For example, you can convert metadata—from sources not yet supported by DataGuide extract utilities—into the tag language format and then import the file into DataGuide.

■ ***User-defined objects***—the product includes starter set of object types and attributes, which you can tailor and extend for your own uses. Object types in the starter set include tables/views, columns, dynamic reports, completed reports, images, programs, business groups, contacts, glossary, and news. You can, of course, create your own object definitions.

■ ***From applications that use embedded APIs***—any program can register its objects with DataGuide/2 using *Information Catalog API*, which is also part of the Information Warehouse Architecture. The API allows an application to access and update metadata, which can be a very useful add-on to existing tools. For example, a query product may use the API to invoke the DataGuide/2 servers on the network and display relevant information to the end user. DataGuide/2, of course, provides its own front-end client to its servers.

Packaging

DataGuide/2 is a classic client/server application package. The DataGuide visual client—the graphical user interface to the information catalog—runs on OS/2 and the DB2/2 client API. The server also runs on OS/2 and requires DB2/2. Networks supported are NetBIOS, APPC, and whatever other stacks are supported by DB2/2. IBM also provides a DB2 version of the DataGuide server; it is accessed by the OS/2 DataGuide/2 visual client (see Figure 26-17).

IBM shipped DataGuide/2 in December 15, 1993, to an already selected set of customers. The general availability dates and prices were not announced when we went to press.

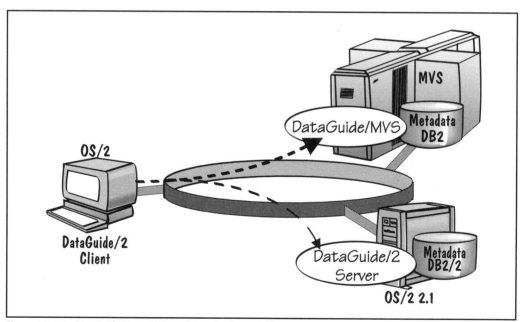

Figure 26-17. DataGuide/2 on LANs and DataGuide on MVS.

The Abandoned SQL Server

Soapbox

Is Microsoft's 16-bit SQL Server on OS/2 an abandoned database? Will Sybase port its powerful new System 10 database to OS/2? What's the future of the Microsoft/Sybase relation? We don't have the answers. But we're certainly ready to indulge in some speculation—this is, after all, a soapbox.

As you may already know, Microsoft is the value-added reseller of the Sybase SQL Server engine on the OS/2 and NT platforms. SQL Server on OS/2 started out as an immensely popular database but lost its luster after Microsoft shifted its focus to the NT platform. SQL Server is based on the Sybase 4.2 code and runs as a 16-bit OS/2 application; it can only address 64 MBytes of memory. Its NT sibling was largely rewritten by Microsoft to take full advantage of NT's 32-bit architecture, native threads, symmetric multiprocessing (SMP), large address space (2 GBytes), performance monitor, and security system including single logon. Microsoft also threw in two new DBA tools: SQL Object Manager and SQL Administrator.

As a result, we now have three SQL Servers on divergent paths: the "stabilized" SQL Server on OS/2, Microsoft's rewrite of SQL Server for NT, and the new Sybase System 10 for Unix and NLM platforms. The Microsoft rewrite of SQL Server is far too radical for it to ever merge with Sybase System 10. However, Sybase may decide to do its own System 10 ports to OS/2 and NT. If it does that, the prospects for the OS/2 port are good because it will compete against a lame OS/2 SQL Server from Microsoft. However, a Sybase System 10 NT port could face some stiff price/performance competition from Microsoft (which Sybase can't win). Microsoft is almost giving away SQL Server to help promote NT, while Sybase's entire revenues come from database. There's never a dull moment in the database business. ❏

Part 5
Client/Server
Transaction
Processing

An Introduction to Part 5

So what did you Martians think of the new California gold country? Oh, you want to start panning for SQL gold. Yes, it's a great business—but they do have earthquakes in California. And we have some other great opportunities to show you. For example, Part 5 is about transaction processing and TP Monitors, another important area of new client/server opportunity. Why? Because client/server computing can't live on shared data alone. The programs that operate on that data are just as important. To create effective client/server solutions, we need the software equivalent of a symphony conductor. That's the guy who waves the little wand to orchestrate all the musical instruments so that they play together.

So where is this client/server software conductor? What little wand can be used to orchestrate programs that don't even know about each other? How do we get these programs to act in unison when it took 200 pages of NOS and middleware just to get them to talk to each other? We've got news for you: The software conductor exists and is called a *TP Monitor*. The wand these software conductors use are called *transactions*. Using these transactions, a TP Monitor can get pieces of software that don't know anything about each other to act in total unison.

No, we're not selling snake oil; TP Monitors have solid credentials—they've been used for many years to keep the biggest of "Big Iron" running. In the mainframe world, a TP Monitor is sold with every database. The folks there discovered that without that conductor they just had some very "inactive" data. If they needed TP Monitors on these single-vendor mainframes, we need them even more on client/server networks where every piece of software only knows how to play its own tune.

Without a conductor, don't expect any client/server music. Yes, an occasional jazz ensemble may spontaneously create music, but it's becoming the exception. We're being deluged with new software every day, and we can't just depend on good luck and Jazz. We need to hire a software conductor for the network. And eventually, every desktop will have a personal software conductor.

So get your tuxedos out—we're going to the symphony. What? You didn't bring them? No problem. The TP Monitor people are not very formal these days; they, too, have discovered sneakers. The plan for Part 5 is to first explore *transactions*. Transactions are to TP Monitors what SQL is to relational databases—it's the commodity that brings it all together. You'll discover that transactions come in all types: flat, chained, nested, long-lived, and sagas. But all transactions have one thing in common: They have ACID properties. What's that? We'll tell you soon. It's good stuff. Eventually, all our software will be ACID-ized.

With transactions in the bag we're ready for TP Monitors: What do they do? What do the new client/server models look like? What kind of standards do they follow? We'll answer all these questions and more. You'll discover that the conductor may save you enough money to more than pay for itself. What a business! The SQL database servers are making gold—the TP Monitors help you save enough so that

some of that gold gets diverted your way. Does this mean you don't move to California? We're not sure yet. The database people are making moves that suggest they may want to keep all the gold in their valley. They've invented something called *TP-Lite*—or "miniconductors" for their databases. You've already encountered some elements of TP-Lite: stored procedures, triggers, and SQL transactions. We'll go over the TP-Lite versus TP-Heavy "miniwar." Do you still have your helmets from the OS wars?

As usual, we close with an overview of some representative products that give us some form of reality check. You'll want to know how real these conductors are and what they can do for you today. However, this time we're going to cheat a bit. We'll present a solid product—CICS OS/2 V2—that is here today. But we'll also present Encina—a product that didn't make it on OS/2 before this book went to the printer; it will be there shortly. Encina is a textbook example of an open TP Monitor. It was designed by professors.

Chapter 27

The Magic
of Transactions

---

*T*he idea of distributed systems without transaction management is like a society without contract law. One does not necessarily want the laws, but one does need a way to resolve matters when disputes occur. Nowhere is this more applicable than in the PC and client/server worlds.

— *Jim Gray (May, 1993)* [1]

Transactions are more than just business events: They've become an application design philosophy that guarantees robustness in distributed systems. Under the control of a TP Monitor, a transaction can be managed from its point of origin—typically on the client—across one or more servers, and then back to the originating client. When a transaction ends, all the parties involved are in agreement as to whether it succeeded or failed. The transaction becomes the contract that binds the client to one or more servers.

---

[1] Source: Jim Gray, "Where is Transaction Processing Headed?" **OTM Spectrum Reports** (May, 1993).

In this chapter we first go over the so-called ACID properties that make transactions such desirable commodities in client/server computing. We then explain the *flat transaction,* which is the workhorse of all the commercial transaction systems—including TP Monitors, Database Managers, transactional file systems, and message queues. The flat transaction is not without its shortcomings; we look at these in some detail and suggest some workarounds. Finally, we go over some of the proposed alternatives to the flat transaction including sagas, chained transactions, and nested transactions.

THE ACID PROPERTIES

Transactions are a way to make ACID operations a general commodity.

— *Gray and Reuter (1993)* [2]

A transaction is a collection of actions embued with ACID properties. In this case, ACID—a term coined by Andreas Reuter in 1983—stands for Atomicity, Consistency, Isolation, and Durability. Here's what it means:

■ ***Atomicity*** means that a transaction is an indivisible unit of work: All of its actions succeed or they all fail; it's a true all-or-nothing proposition. The actions under the transaction's umbrella may include the message queues, updates to a database, and the display of results on the client's screen. Atomicity is defined from the perspective of the consumer of the transaction.

■ ***Consistency*** means that after a transaction executes, it must leave the system in a correct state or it must abort. If the transaction cannot achieve a stable end state, it must return the system to its initial state.

■ ***Isolation*** means that a transaction's behavior is not affected by other transactions that execute concurrently. The transaction must serialize all accesses to shared resources and guarantee that the concurrent programs will not corrupt each other's operations. A multiuser program running under transaction protection must behave exactly as it would in a single-user environment. The changes to shared resources that a transaction makes must not become visible outside the transaction until it commits. Again, this is how the consumer of the transaction sees it.

---

[2] Source: Jim Gray and Andreas Reuter, **Transaction Processing Concepts and Techniques** (Morgan Kaufmann, 1993). This 1000-page book is the Bible of transaction processing. It gives some great insights into the motivation behind transaction processing written by two of the original gurus who have pioneered this field.

Chapter 27. The Magic of Transactions

■ **_Durability_** means that a transaction's effects are permanent after it commits. Its changes should survive system failures. The term "persistent" is a synonym for "durable."

A transaction becomes the fundamental unit of recovery, consistency, and concurrency in a client/server system. Why is that important? Take a simple debit-credit banking operation. You'd like to see all credit to *your* account succeed. Any losses would be unacceptable (of course, any unexpected credits are always welcome). This means you're relying on the application to provide the integrity expected in a real-life business transaction. The application, in turn, relies on the underlying system—usually the TP Monitor—to help achieve this level of transactional integrity. The programmer should not have to develop tons of code that reinvents the transaction wheel.

A more subtle point is that all the participating programs must adhere to the transactional discipline. A single faulty program can corrupt an entire system. A transaction that unknowingly uses corrupted initial data—produced by a non-transactional program—builds on top of a corrupt foundation.

In an ideal world, *all* client/server programs are written as transactions. ACID is like motherhood and apple pie. It's necessary—and you can't have too much of it.

OK, enough preaching. Let's take a look at how software transactions model their business counterparts.

TRANSACTION MODELS

When should a transaction start? When should it end and have its effects made accessible to the outside world? What are appropriate units of recovery in case of failures? Can computer transactions mirror their real-world counterparts? To answer these questions, we will look at the *flat transaction*, go over its shortcomings, and take a quick peek at the proposed extensions.

So What's a Flat Transaction?

Flat transactions are the workhorses of the current generation of transactional systems. They're called flat because all the work done within a transaction's boundaries is at the same level (see shaded area in Figure 27-1).

The transaction starts with *begin_transaction* and ends with either a *commit_transaction* or *abort_transaction*. It's an all or nothing proposition—there's no way to commit or abort *parts* of a flat transaction. All the actions are

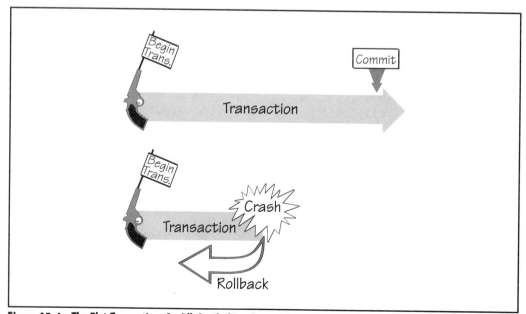

Figure 27-1. The Flat Transaction: An All-Or-Nothing Proposition.

indivisible, which is what we wanted in the first place. Table 27-1 compares the commands used in different TP Monitors to delineate the transaction boundaries.

Table 27-1. Comparing Flat Transaction Delimiters for Major TP Monitors (Adapted from OTM Spectrum Reports; February, 1993).

System	Transaction Delimiter		
	Start	**Commit**	**Abort**
Tuxedo	TPBEGIN	TPCOMMIT	TPABORT
Top End	tx_begin	tx_commit	tx_rollback
Encina RPC	transaction	onCommit	onAbort
X/Open	tx_begin	tx_commit	tx_rollback
OSI TP	C-BEGIN	C-COMMIT	C-ROLLBACK
Tandem RSC	Begin_Transaction	End_Transaction	Abort_Transaction
CICS	SYNCPOINT	SYNCPOINT	SYNCPOINT or ROLLBACK

We Like Our Transactions Flat

Soapbox

The major virtue of the flat transaction is its *simplicity* and the ease with which it provides the ACID features. Thousands of commercial applications were created using the very simple concept of a flat transaction. Historically, the flat transaction was first developed for banking applications—it provides an excellent fit for modeling short activities.

But as the transactional discipline begins to permeate all facets of computing, we're discovering that the flat transaction model does not provide the best fit in all environments. Millions of lines of code have been written to compensate for its shortcomings. The model is particularly weak when it comes to handling business transactions that span over long periods of time—days or even months. It's somewhat weak in the area of batch jobs. And it's a nuisance in situations that require partial rollbacks without throwing away an entire transaction's work—the rigid "all-or-nothing" application of the ACID principle gets in the way.

For political reasons, flat transactions using two-phase commits are usually not allowed to cross intercorporate boundaries—asynchronous MOM may be the preferred approach in such situations. We're also experiencing difficulties with the flat model in client/server environments where the client "think time" is part of the transaction loop. There are workarounds for each of these problems, but they require writing some custom code. Wouldn't it be nice if we could extend the transaction model to automatically take care of all these situations for us?

It turns out that computer scientists everywhere are frantically searching for a "unified theory" of transactions that covers all the complex real-life situations and yet still maintains the ACID properties and the simplicity of the flat model. As a result, the academic literature is flooded with new transaction models that have esoteric-sounding names like Sagas, Chained, Promises, ConTracts, Check-Revalidate, Long-Lived, Multilevel, Migrating, Shopping Cart, and Anarchic and Non-Anarchic Nested Transactions.

With the exception of Non-Anarchic Nested Transactions—implemented in Transarc's Encina—none of these esoterics have found their way into commercial products. They make great reading and are always very clever. However, it's turning out not to be easy to extend the transactional model and still do ACID simply. And the jury is still out when it comes to nested transactions—they may be too difficult to manage in normal commercial applications.

At the risk of sounding too conservative, we still feel there's a lot of life left in that venerable flat transaction. It can be used "as is" in over 90% of commercial client/server applications. And writing a *little* bit of code around them doesn't particularly bother us—at least we can get them to do exactly what's needed. We feel (remember, this is a Soapbox) it's more important to keep pushing the flat transaction discipline into every known program so that they can all participate in TP-Monitor coordinated transactions.

Transactions are here to help simplify our applications and give us better control over the environment in which they run. Some of the proposed extensions may create more problems than they solve. In any case, as Gray and Reuter point out, "no matter which extensions prove to be the most important and useful in the future, flat transactions will be at the core of all the mechanisms required to make these more powerful models work." ❑

Baby Stepping With Flat Transactions

A typical flat transaction does not last more than two or three seconds so as not to monopolize critical system resources such as database locks. As a result, OLTP client/server programs are broken into short transactions that execute back-to-back to produce results (see Figure 27-2). We call this effect transaction *baby stepping*—or getting work done by moving in "baby steps" from one stable state to the next.[3]

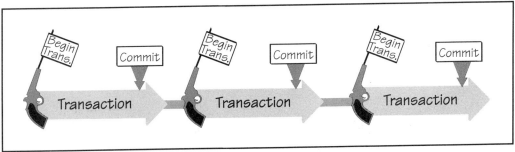

Figure 27-2. Back-to-Back Flat Transactions.

The Distributed Flat Transaction

Can a flat transaction run on multiple sites and update resources located within multiple resource managers? Yes. Even though a high level of parallelism may be involved, as far as the programmer is concerned, it's still just a flat transaction (see Figure 27-3). The programmer is not aware of the considerable amount of "under-the-cover" activity that's required to make the multisite transaction appear flat. The transaction must travel across multiple sites to get to the resources it needs. Each site's TP Monitor must manage its local piece of the transaction. In addition, one of the TP Monitors must coordinate the actions of all its fellow TP Monitors. This is usually done using a *two-phase commit* protocol, which coordinates the transaction's commit or abort across multiple sites (see the following Details box).

---

3 The term "baby step" is adapted from the recent movie, "What About Bob?" Richard Dreyfus played the role of a psychiatrist who advocated baby stepping as a cure-all.

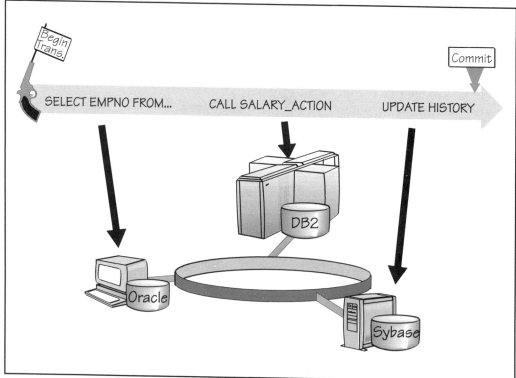

Figure 27-3. A Multisite Distributed Flat Transaction.

What's a Two-Phase Commit Protocol?

Details

The two-phase commit protocol is used to synchronize updates on different machines so that they either all fail or all succeed. This is done by centralizing the decision to commit but giving each participant the right of veto. It's like a Christian marriage: You're given one last chance to back out of the transaction when you're at the altar. If none of the parties present object, the marriage takes place.

It should come as no surprise by now that each commercial implementation introduces its own variation of the two-phase commit protocol. As usual, they don't interoperate. And, of course, there are standards bodies that are trying to make it all work together. In December 1992—after a five-year development cycle—ISO published its *OSI TP* standard that defines very *rigidly* how a two-phase commit is to be implemented (see Figure 27-4). Let's go over the mechanics of this protocol:

1. ***In the first phase of a commit***, the *commit manager* node—also known as the *root node* or the *transaction coordinator*—sends *prepare-to-commit* commands to all the *subordinate* nodes that were directly asked to participate in the transaction. The subordinates may have spawned pieces of the transaction on other nodes (or resource managers) to which they must propagate the prepare-to-commit command. It becomes a transaction tree, with the coordinator at the root.

2. ***The first phase of the commit terminates*** when the root node receives *ready-to-commit* signals from all its direct subordinate nodes that participate in the transaction. This means that the transaction has executed successfully so far on all the nodes and they're now ready to do a final commit. The root node logs that fact in a safe place (the information is used to recover from a root node failure).

3. ***The second phase of the commit starts*** after the root node makes the decision to *commit* the transaction—based on the unanimous yes vote. It tells its subordinates to commit. They, in turn, tell their subordinates to do the same, and the order ripples down the tree.

4. ***The second phase of the commit terminates*** when all the nodes involved have safely committed their part of the transaction and made it durable. The root receives all the confirmations and can tell its client that the transaction completed. It can then relax until the next transaction.

5. ***The two phase commit aborts*** if any of the participants return a *refuse* indication, meaning that their part of the transaction failed. In that case, the root node tells all its subordinates to perform a rollback. And they, in turn, do the same for their subordinates.

The X/Open XA specification defines a set of APIs that work with the underlying OSI TP protocol. In order to participate in an XA-defined two-phase commit, TP Monitors and resource managers (like databases and message queues) must map their private two-phase commit protocols to the XA commands. They must also be willing to let somebody else drive the transaction—something they're not accustomed to doing. The XA specification allows participants to withdraw from further participation in the global transaction during Phase 1 if they do not have to update resources. In XA, a TP Monitor can use a one-phase commit if it is dealing with a single resource manager. We'll have a lot more to say about XA in the next chapter.

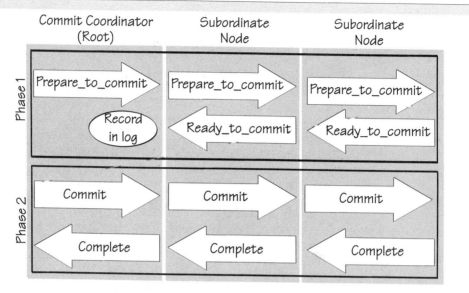

Figure 27-4. The Mechanics of Two-Phase Commit.

The two-phase commit protocol is by no means perfect. Here are some of its more serious limitations:

- ■ *Performance overhead*, which is introduced by all the message exchanges. The protocol has no way of discerning valuable transactions that need this kind of protection from the more tolerant transactions that don't need protection. It generates messages for all transactions, even read-only ones.

- ■ *Hazard windows*, where certain failures can be a problem. For example, if the root node crashes after the first phase of the commit, the subordinates may be left in disarray. Who cleans up this mess? There are always workarounds, but it's a tricky business. It helps to have some fault-tolerant hardware somewhere in the system, and preferably coordinating the transaction.

In the June 1993 ISO meeting, a number of suggestions were introduced on how to improve the two-phase commit protocol—including single-phase commits, read-only optimizations, overlapped transactions, implicit prepares, and delegated commits. We don't expect to see any of these proposals in a final draft soon. However, the *delegated commit* proposal is of practical interest in client/server applications. It means that a transaction originating from an unreliable platform—such as a cellular notebook—can delegate the commit coordination to an alternate node. Most of today's TP Monitors don't allow their clients to coordinate transactions. They prefer to do it for them. "Delegated commit" makes the process more democratic. ❑

The Limitations of the Flat Transaction

The "all-or-nothing" characteristic of flat transactions is both a virtue and a vice.

— Gray and Reuter (1993)

So when does the all-or-nothing nature of the flat transaction become a liability? Mostly, in situations that require more flexibility than the all-or-nothing approach. The following are examples of business transactions that require a more flexible approach:

■ *Compound business transactions that need to be partially rolled back.* The classical example is a complex trip that includes travel arrangements, hotel reservations, and a car (see Figure 27-5). What happens if you simply want to cancel the car reservation but preserve the rest of the reservations? You can't do that within a flat transaction—the entire reservation is rolled back. It's an all-or-nothing proposition. This means you must give up the hotel and plane reservations just to get rid of the car—a real nuisance. The hotel/car reservation problem is used to justify the need for nested or chained transactions. But flat

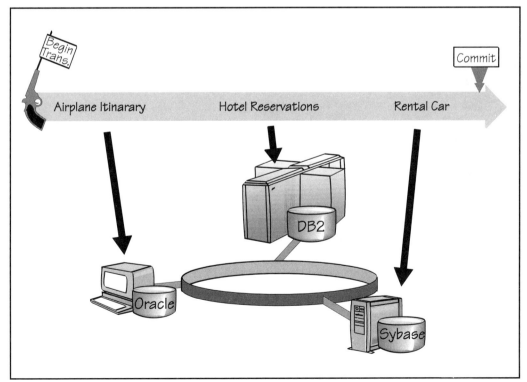

Figure 27-5. Flat Transactions: One Change and You Have to Start All Over.

transaction advocates could make a case that the hotel/car transaction should be broken down into separate hotel and car transactions. In other words, use multiple flat transactions to simulate the compound one.

■ *Business transactions with humans in the loop.* This is a classical GUI client/server transaction where a set of choices are presented to the user on a screen and the server must wait for the decision. In the meantime, locks are held for those records that are on the tube. What happens if we're displaying some airline seats and the user goes to lunch? How long are the seats locked out? If it's executed as a single flat transaction, the seats will be held as long as that user is thinking or eating. Nobody else can get to those seats. This is obviously not a very good way to run a business. The solution is to split the reservation into two transactions: a query transaction that displays the available seats, and a reservation transaction that performs the actual reservation (see Figure 27-6). Of course, the existence of the seats must be revalidated before the update. If the seat is gone, the user must be notified. These extra steps mean more work for the programmer.

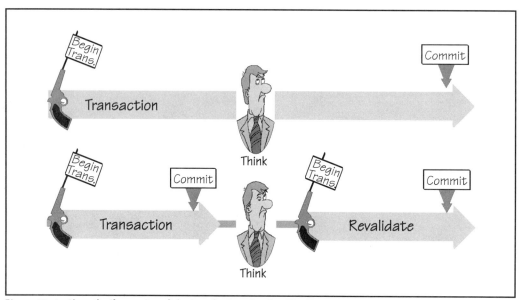

Figure 27-6. Keep the Human Out of the Loop by Creating Two Flat Transactions.

■ **_Business transactions that span over long periods of time._** These are your typical engineering Computer-Aided Design (CAD) transactions that may require CAD-managed components to be worked on for days and passed from engineer to engineer (see Figure 27-7). The CAD transaction must be able to suspend itself and resume after shutdowns, preserve ongoing work across shutdowns, and know where it left off and what needs to be done next. In essence, it becomes a workflow manager. Obviously, flat transactions must be augmented by a workflow program to handle such long-lived work. This is an area where alternative transactional models—including object database check-in check-out transactions, replica management, and workflow—look very promising.

Figure 27-7. Long-Lived Transactions Spanning Days or Weeks.

■ **_Business transactions with a lot of bulk._** The classical problem here is: How do you handle one million record updates under transactional control (see Figure 27-8)? Must the entire transaction be rolled back if a failure occurs after record 999,999 is updated? Yes, it's all-or-nothing if you're using a single flat transaction to do the million updates. On the other hand, if you make each update a separate transaction, it is much slower—a million separate commits are required—and where do you restart after the failure? This is an area where syncpoints or chained transactions have been proposed as a solution. But the solution may slow you down because it introduces more commits and maybe some restart code. We think you may be better off restarting an occasional flat transaction then going with the alternatives. After all, how often can a bulk transaction fail?

Figure 27-8. Flat Transaction: It Failed—Restart That Million Update Job.

■ *Business transactions that span across companies.* The problem here is a political one. Very few companies will allow an external TP Monitor (or database) to synchronize in real-time a transaction on their systems using a two-phase commit. The more politically correct solution may be to conduct an intercompany exchange using loosely coupled transactional message queues. A MOM solution allows organizations to split the unit of work into many transactions that can be executed asynchronously, processed on different machines, and coordinated by independent TP Monitors within each company (see Figure 27-9). You lose instantaneous consistency, but you're able to maintain arm's length controls between companies. From a software perspective, we ended up breaking a single two-phase commit flat transaction into three independent flat transactions that execute on company A's TP Monitor, MOM, and company B's TP Monitor. The MOM transaction ensures that the transaction has safely made it from company A's computer to company B's computer. We're assuming that MOM provides a durable queue that gives you "D" in ACID at commit time.

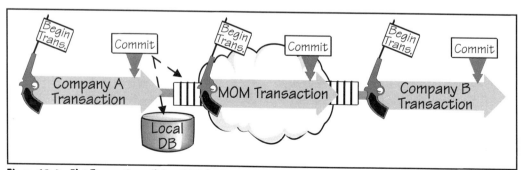

Figure 27-9. Flat Transactions: Using MOM for Intercompany Transactions.

In summary, most of the flat transaction's problems come from the rigidity imposed by the all-or-nothing discipline in situations that require more flexibility. You can work around most of these problems by breaking down transactions into smaller units and developing the control code that synchronizes the several smaller transactions. It's a trade-off: You can write one long transaction that can fail in a big way, or several smaller ones that fail in smaller ways. The designer, as usual, must perform a balancing act.

The Alternatives: Chained and Nested Transactions

Most of the proposed alternatives to the flat transaction are based on mechanisms that extend the flow of control beyond the linear unit of work. Two of the most obvious ways to extend the flow of control are by chaining units of work in linear sequences of "mini" transactions—the chained transaction or Saga—or by creating some kind of nested hierarchy of work—the nested transaction. Each of these two basic approaches have many refinements.

The solution to the long-lived transaction requires some form of control flow language for describing activities that evolve in time. This is more or less the model proposed in some of the more recent research literature under names such as *ConTracts*, *Migrating Transactions*, and *Shopping Cart Transactions*. None of these models are available in commercial applications. We feel that the best commercial solutions available today for long-lived transactions are in workflow managers and object databases, which we cover in Parts 6 and 7. So we will defer this discussion until then.

Syncpoints, Chained Transactions, and Sagas

The chained transaction, as the name implies, introduces some form of linear control for sequencing through transactions. The simplest form of chaining is to use *syncpoints*—also known as savepoints within a flat transaction that allow periodic saves of accumulated work (see Figure 27-10). What makes a syncpoint different from a commit? The syncpoint lets you roll back work and still maintain a live transaction. In contrast, a commit ends a transaction. Syncpoints also give you better granularity of control over what you save and undo. The transaction can be broken into a series of activities that can be rolled back individually. But the big difference is that the commit is durable while the syncpoint is volatile. If the system crashes during a transaction, all data accumulated in syncpoints is lost.

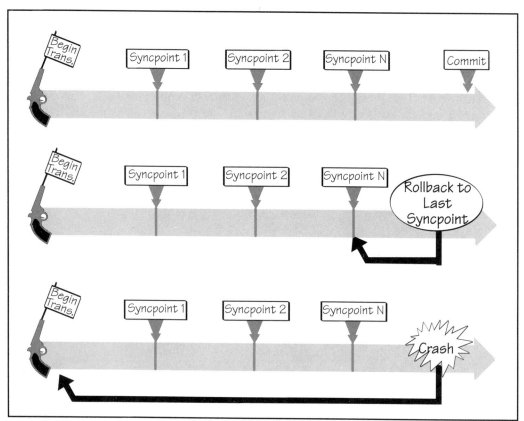

Figure 27-10. Syncpoints Are Not Durable.

Chained transactions are a variation of syncpoints that make the accumulated work durable. They allow you to commit work while staying within the transaction (i.e., you don't give up your locks and resources). A commit gives you the "D" in ACID without terminating the transaction (see Figure 27-11). But what you lose is the ability to roll back an entire chain's worth of work. There's no free lunch.

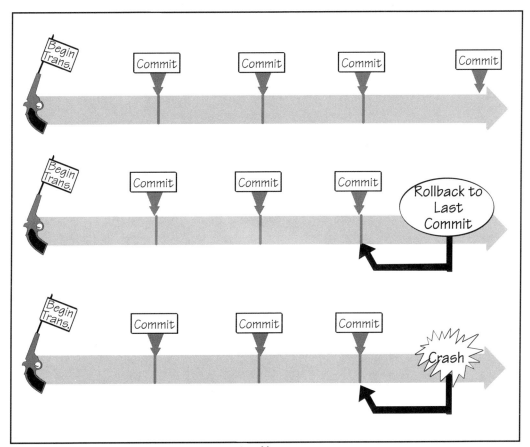

Figure 27-11. Chained Transactions: Commits Are Durable.

Sagas extend the chained transactions to let you roll back the entire chain, if you require it (see Figure 27-12). They do that by maintaining a chain of compensating transactions. You still get the crash resistance of the intermediate commits, but you have the choice of rolling back the entire chain under program control. This lets you treat the entire chain as an atomic unit of work. You can now have your cake and eat it too.[4]

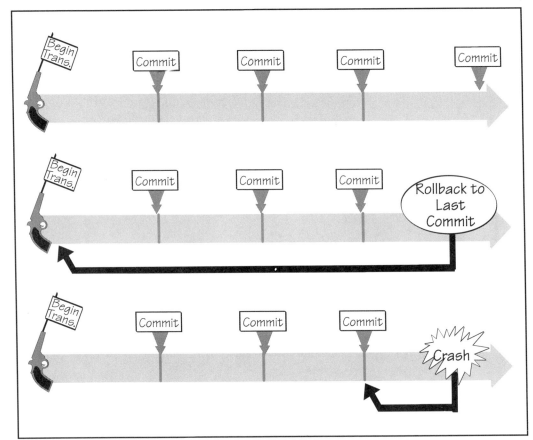

Figure 27-12. Sagas: Commits Are Durable but Can Be Rolled Back.

---

[4] The term Saga was first suggested by Bruce Lindsay of IBM Almaden Research. The concept was fully developed by Hector Garcia-Molina and K. Salem in 1987.

Nested Transactions

Nested Transactions provide the ability to define transactions within other transactions. They do that by breaking a transaction into hierarchies of "subtransactions," very much like a program is made up of procedures. The main transaction starts the subtransactions, which behave as dependent transactions. A subtransaction can also start its own subtransactions, making the entire structure very recursive (see Figure 27-13).

Each subtransaction can issue a commit or rollback for its designated pieces of work. When a subtransaction commits, its results are only accessible to the parent that spawned it. A subtransaction's commit becomes permanent after it issues a local commit and all its ancestors commit. If a parent transaction does a rollback, all its descendent transactions are rolled back, regardless of whether they issued local commits.

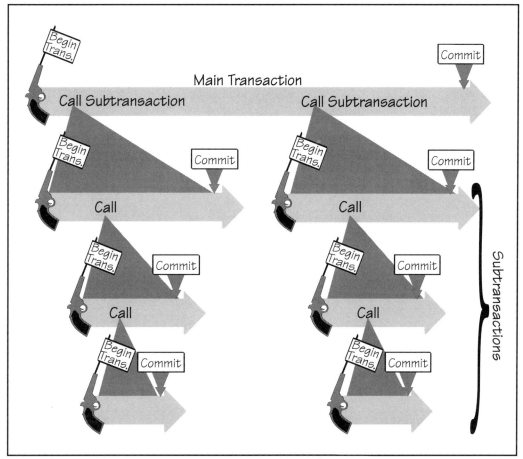

Figure 27-13. Nested Transactions: One Transaction and Many Dependent Subtransactions.

The main benefit of nesting is that a failure in a subtransaction can be trapped and retried using an alternative method, still allowing the main transaction to succeed. It improves the granularity of modularity in writing transactions. The only commercial implementation of nested transactions we know of is the Encina TP Monitor. Encina's Transactional C allows you to declare the nesting directly in your code where it starts resembling regular procedure invocations. We still feel nesting may be an overkill that creates more problems than solutions. Of course, now that the Encina TP Monitor is on the market, you'll have your chance to prove us wrong.

Conclusion

Transactions are important because they give ordinary programs ACID qualities without writing a line of messy code. All you need to do is say begin and end transaction—and suddenly the magic appears. In the next chapter, we explain how the magic wand of TP Monitors provides the robust mechanisms that keep these transactions running under all sorts of conditions. We also noted that transactions are now being used to represent more complex business activities. Eventually, our transactions will be extended beyond their flat origins to cover some of these more complex business activities. The more pressing need is to permeate the simple flat transactions into all our client/server programs and "ACIDify" them. ACID is the best antidote to the inherent complexity in distributed systems.

Chapter 28

TP Monitors: Managing Client/Server Transactions

TP Monitors make a silk purse out of a sow's ear—they turn mundane operating systems into fast, highly reliable, transaction engines.

— *Jeri Edwards, TP Monitor Director,*
Tandem Computers (February, 1994)

TP Monitors specialize in managing transactions from their point of origin—typically on the client—across one or more servers, and then back to the originating client. When a transaction ends, the TP Monitor makes sure that all the systems involved in the transaction are left in a consistent state. In addition, TP Monitors know how to run transactions, route them across systems, load-balance their execution, and restart them after failures.

One of the great appeals of a TP Monitor is that it is the overseer of all aspects of a distributed transaction, regardless of the systems or resource managers used. A TP Monitor can manage resources on a single server or multiple servers, and it can cooperate with other TP Monitors in federated arrangements. Future TP Monitors may reside on every client machine to bring desktop resources—such as the user interface, local data warehouses, or personal agents—within a distributed transaction's reach.

In this chapter we explain in some detail what TP Monitors are and what functions they perform. We go over X/Open's model for how TP Monitors interact with other resource managers in an open environment. We conclude with a list of benefits that TP Monitors provide. We felt this list was needed because the benefits of TP Monitors are not well understood in the PC LAN and Unix worlds. TP Monitors are either treated with awe and left to the "High-Priests" of computer science, or they are dismissed as antiques. Neither is true. TP Monitors are fun to program, and they create transactional magic on ordinary client/server networks. But enough talk; this isn't a soapbox.

TP MONITORS

TP Monitors first appeared on mainframes to provide robust run-time environments that could support large-scale OLTP applications—airline and hotel reservations, banking, automatic teller machines, credit authorization systems, and stock-brokerage systems. Since then, OLTP has spread to almost every type of business application—including hospitals, manufacturing, point-of-sales retail systems, automated gas pumps, and telephone directory services. TP Monitors provide whatever services are required to keep these OLTP applications running in the style they're accustomed to: highly reactive, available, and well managed. With OLTP moving to client/server platforms, a new-breed of TP Monitors is emerging to help make the new environment hospitable to mission-critical applications.

What's a TP Monitor?

It should come as no surprise that our industry has no commonly accepted definition of a TP Monitor. We'll use Jeri Edwards' definition of a TP Monitor as "an operating system for transaction processing." This definition captures the essence of a TP Monitor. So what does an operating system for transaction processing do in life? How does it interface with the rest of the world? What services does it provide? We'll answer all these questions. But, in a nutshell, a TP Monitor does two things extremely well:

- **Process management** includes starting server processes, funneling work to them, monitoring their execution, and balancing their workloads.

- **Transaction management** means that it guarantees the ACID properties to all programs that run under its protection.

TP Monitors and OSs: The Great Funneling Act

Historically TP Monitors were introduced to run classes of applications that could service hundreds and sometimes thousands of clients (think of an airline reservation application). If each of these thousands of clients were given all the resources it needed on a server—typically a communication connection, half a MByte of memory, one or two processes, and dozens of open file handles—even the largest mainframe server would fall on its knees (see Figure 28-1). Luckily, not all the clients require service at the same time. However, when they do require it, they want their service *immediately*. We're told that the humans on the other end have a "tolerance for waiting" of two seconds or less. TP Monitors provide an operating system—on top of existing OSs—that connects in real time these thousands of impatient humans with a pool of shared server processes.

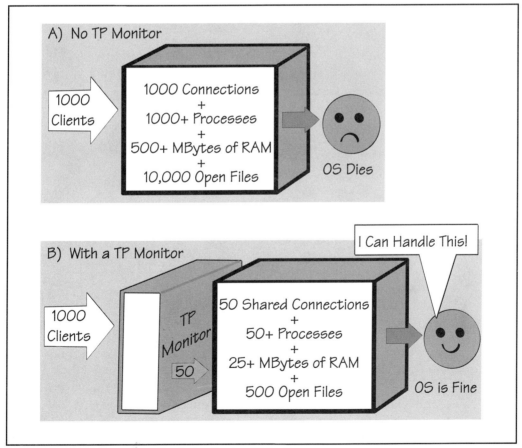

Figure 28-1. Why a Server Operating System Needs a TP Monitor.

How Is the Great Funneling Act Performed?

The "funneling act" is part of what a TP Monitor must do to manage the server side of a user-written OLTP application. In the OS/2 environment, the server side of the OLTP application is typically packaged as a DLL that contains a number of related functions. The TP Monitor assigns the execution of the DLL functions to *server classes*—these are groups of processes or threads that are prestarted, waiting for work. Each process or thread in a server class is capable of doing the work. The TP Monitor balances the workload between them.

When a client sends a service request, the TP Monitor hands it to an available process in the server class pool (see Figure 28-2). The server process dynamically links to the DLL function called by the client, invokes it, oversees its execution, and returns the results to the client. After that completes, the server process can be reused by another client. OS/2 keeps the already loaded DLLs in memory where they can be shared across processes. It doesn't get better!

In essence, the TP Monitor removes the process-per-client requirement by funneling incoming client requests to shared server processes. If the number of incoming

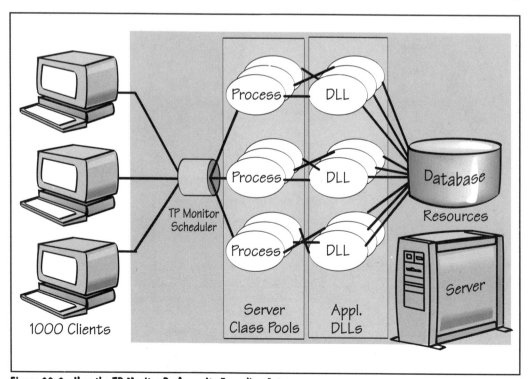

Figure 28-2. How the TP Monitor Performs Its Funneling Act

client requests exceeds the number of processes in a server class, the TP Monitor may dynamically start new ones—this is called *load balancing*. The more sophisticated TP Monitors can distribute the process load across CPUs in SMP environments. Part of the load balancing act involves managing the priorities of the incoming requests; the TP Monitor does that by running some high priority server classes and dynamically assigning them to the VIP clients.

TP Monitors and Transaction Management

The transaction discipline was introduced in the early TP Monitors to ensure the robustness of the multiuser applications that ran on the servers. These applications had to be bullet-proof and highly reliable if they were going to serve thousands of users in "bet-your-business" situations. TP Monitors were developed from the ground-up as operating systems for transactions. The unit of management, execution, and recovery was the ordinary transaction and the programs that invoked them. The job of a TP Monitor is to guarantee the ACID properties while maintaining high transaction throughput. To do that, it must manage the execution, distribution, and synchronization of transaction *workloads*.

With TP Monitors, the application programmers don't have to concern themselves with issues like concurrency, failures, broken connections, load balancing, and the synchronization of resources across multiple nodes. All this is made transparent to them—very much like an operating system makes the hardware transparent to ordinary programs. Simply put, TP Monitors provide the run-time engines for running transactions—they do that on top of ordinary hardware and operating systems.

TP Monitor Client/Server Interaction Types

Ordinary operating systems must understand the nature of the jobs and resources they manage. This is also true for TP Monitors—they must provide an optimized environment for the execution of the transactions that run under their control. This means they must load the server programs, dynamically assign incoming client requests to server processes, recover from failures, return the replies to the clients, and make sure high-priority traffic gets through first.

So what kind of assumptions do TP Monitors make about their client/server transaction interaction types? They typically fall into one of four categories: conversational, RPC, queued, and batch (see Figure 28-3). The batch transactions typically run in low-priority mode. RPC and conversational transactions usually involve a human user that requires immediate attention; they run in high-priority mode. MOM-based queued-transactions can be of either type.

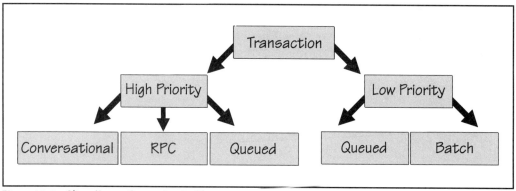

Figure 28-3. Client/Server Transaction Profiles.

In addition, TP Monitors must be prepared to communicate with all the resource managers on which the transaction executes—whether they're on the same machine or across a network. When the resource managers are across networks, the TP Monitor synchronizes the transaction with the remote TP Monitors using a two-phase commit.

Transactional RPCs, Queues, and Conversations

On the surface, transactional client/server exchanges appear to use the traditional NOS communication models: queues, RPCs, and conversational peer-to-peer communications. This is not so. They're using highly-augmented versions of these traditional communication mechanisms. However, most of the value-added elements are made transparent to the programmer—they look like ordinary exchanges bracketed by start and end transaction calls. The transactional versions augment the familiar NOS exchanges with the following value-added extensions:

■ They piggyback *transactional delimiters* that allow a client to specify the begin-transaction and end-transaction boundaries. The actual commit mechanics are usually *delegated* to one of the server TP Monitors because the client is assumed to be unreliable.

■ They introduce—under-the-cover—a three-way exchange between a client, server, and TP Monitor (the transaction manager). A new transaction is assigned a unique ID by the coordinating TP Monitor. All subsequent message exchanges between the participants are tagged with that transaction ID. The message exchanges allow the TP Monitor to keep track of what Jim Gray calls the "dynamically expanding web" of resource managers participating in a distributed transaction. TP Monitors need that information to coordinate the two-phase commit with all the participants in a transaction.

- They embed transaction state information within each of the messages exchanged. This information helps the TP Monitor identify the state of the distributed transaction and figure out what to do next.

- They allow a TP Monitor to enforce *exactly-once* semantics—this means that the message only gets executed once.

- The TP Monitor guarantees that a server process is at the receiving end of the message. Traditional RPCs and MOMs do not worry about this kind of stuff—they assume that a program will "automagically" appear on the receiving end.

As you can see, there's a lot more going on here than a simple RPC or MOM exchange. The literature calls these enhanced services *Transactional RPC (TRPC)*, *Transactional Queues*, and *Transactional Conversations*. The distinguishing factor is that all resource managers and processes invoked through these calls become part of the transaction. The TP Monitor is informed of any service calls; it uses that information to orchestrate the actions of all the participants, enforce their ACID behavior, and make them act as part of a transaction. Traditional RPCs, messages, and queue invocations are between separate programs that are not bound by a transaction discipline. Table 28-1 summarizes the differences between transactional communication mechanisms and their traditional NOS equivalents.

Table 28-1. Transactional Versus Non-Transactional Communications.

Feature	Traditional MOM, RPC, and Conversations	Transactional MOM, RPC, and Conversations
Who participates?	Loosely-coupled client/server programs	Transactionally bound client/server and server/server programs. The message invocation causes the recipient program to join the transaction.
Commit synchronization	No	Yes
Only-once semantics	No	Yes
Server management on the recipient node.	No. It's just a delivery mechanism.	Yes. The process that receives the message is started, load-balanced, monitored, and tracked as part of the transaction.
Load balancing	Using the directory services. The first server to register becomes a hot-spot. No dynamic load balancing is provided.	Using the TP Monitor's sophisticated load-balancing algorithms. Can spread work across SMP machines and dynamically add more processes to cover hotspots of activity.

Table 28-1. Transactional Versus Non-Transactional Communications. (Continued)

Feature	Traditional MOM, RPC, and Conversations	Transactional MOM, RPC, and Conversations
Supervised exchanges	No. It's simply between the client and the server. Exchanges are transient. No crash-recovery or error management is provided. You're on your own.	The TP Monitor supervises the entire exchange, restarts communication links, redirects messages to alternate server process if the first one gets hung, performs retries, provides persistent queues and crash-recovery.

Examples of commercial implementations of a TRPC include the Encina Transactional RPC and CICS OS/2's External Call Interface (ECI). Examples of conversational transactional interfaces include Tuxedo's ATMI, Tandem's RSC, and APPC's Syncpoint features. MQSeries is an example of a transactional implementation of an "open" MOM queue. Some TP Monitors also include their own bundled versions of recoverable queues—in Encina's case it is RQS, and in Tuxedo it is /Q; CICS uses transient queues.

TRANSACTION MANAGEMENT STANDARDS: X/OPEN DTP AND OSI-TP

TP Monitors need standards because they're the ultimate glue software. The applications they coordinate could be running on different platforms with access to different databases and resource managers. These applications are most likely developed using different tools. And they have absolutely no knowledge of each other. The only way to make these disparate pieces come together is through "open standards" that specify how a TP Monitor interfaces to resource managers, to other TP Monitors, and to its clients.

Most of the standards activity around TP Monitors comes from two sources: the International Standard Organization (ISO)—the OSI-CCR and OSI-TP specifications—and X/Open's *Distributed Transaction Processing (DTP)* XTP working subgroup. The ISO-OSI standards specify the message protocols (i.e., FAPs) that allow TP Monitors to interoperate. The OSI-TP specification, which we covered in the last chapter, is the most important of these standards; it defines, among other things, the two-phase commit protocol. The X/Open XTP group has taken the lead in defining the APIs within a general framework for transaction processing. Together, X/Open DTP and OSI-TP form the foundations for "open transaction management."

The X/Open DTP Reference Model—Vintage 1991

*T*he X/Open DTP model is a software architecture that allows multiple application programs
to share resources provided by multiple resource managers, and allows their work to be
coordinated into global transactions.

> — *X/Open, DTP Reference V2*
> *(December, 1993)*

In 1991, the X/Open XTP group published the *Transaction Processing Reference
Model*, which has achieved wide acceptance in the industry. The primary purpose
of this model is to define the components of a transaction-based system and to
locate the interfaces between them. The 1991 model defined three components:
application programs, transaction managers, and resource managers (see
Figure 28-4). In X/Open's definition:

- A *resource manager* is any piece of software that manages shared resources—
  for example, a database manager, a persistent queue, or transactional file
  system—and allows the updates to its resources to be externally coordinated via
  a two-phase commit protocol.

- A *transaction manager* is the component that coordinates and controls the
  resource managers. The transaction manager and resource manager communicate via X/Open's *XA interface* published in 1991. The transaction manager use
  xa_* API calls to interact with the resource managers; the resource managers
  use ax_* API calls to interact with the transaction manager. For example, the
  transaction manager issues an xa_start to tell a resource manager to join a new
  transaction. It issues $xa\_prepare$, xa_commit, and $xa\_rollback$ to tell a
  resource manager to perform a two-phase commit. And it issues xa_end to tell
  the resource manager to leave this transaction. XA defines some additional calls
  for performing the recovery of "in-doubt" transactions. In the reverse direction,
  a resource manager issues an ax_reg call to register its presence dynamically
  with the transaction manager.[1]

- An *application program* uses the general APIs supplied by a resource manager
  (for example, SQL), but issues the transaction bracketing calls directly to the
  transaction manager via X/Open's *TX interface* published in 1992. An application calls tx_begin to start a transaction, tx_commit to commit it, $tx\_rollback$
  to abort it, and $tx\_set\_transaction\_controls$ to set the chaining mode. Transactions can be chained or unchained (the default mode). The tx_info call returns

---

[1] X/Open allows resource managers to become associated with a global transaction only
after the application directly calls them. They use the ax_reg call to dynamically register
their presence.

information about the global context of a transaction. It is important to note that in the X/Open model, the application decides when it wishes to participate in a transaction; the TX interface drives the XA interface when managing global transaction. In theory, this allows an application to be developed independently of the TP Monitor target environment.

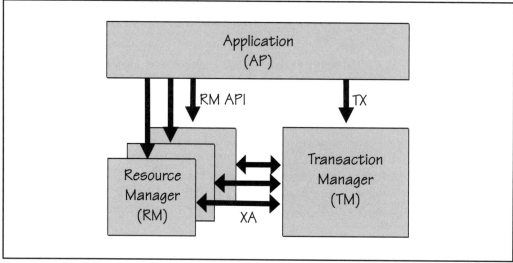

Figure 28-4. The X/Open 1991 Transaction Processing Reference Model.

The 1991 X/Open model only deals with programs talking to their local resource and transaction managers. The transaction can only execute within a single transaction manager's domain. It does not cover how an application requests resources that are on remote nodes and how these remote nodes join the transaction.

The X/Open DTP Reference Model—Vintage 1993

In December 1993, X/Open issued Version 2 of its Distributed Transaction Reference Model that adds a fourth component to the model: the *communication resource managers*. This component controls communications between distributed applications (see Figure 28-5). X/Open also defined a superset of XA called *XA+* that defines the interface between the communication resource managers and the transaction manager. This interface lets the transaction manager know which remote resource managers the transaction is visiting and supports global transaction information flows across transaction manager domains. XA+ is still an X/Open snapshot; it will eventually supersede XA.

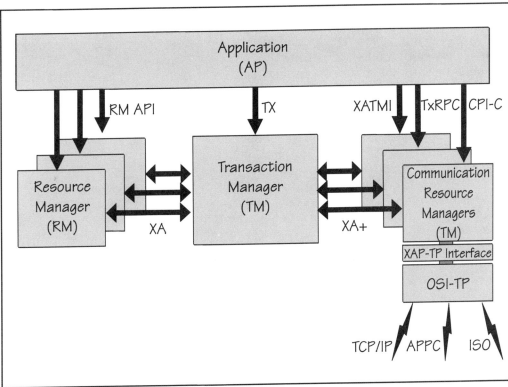

Figure 28-5. The X/Open 1993 Transaction Processing Reference Model.

At the application level, X/Open is in the process of defining *three* interfaces between applications and communication resource managers:

- **TxRPC** is a transactional version of the DCE RPC. An RPC call can either have *transaction-mandatory* or *transaction-optional* attributes that are specified through the IDL. The underlying mechanism for TxRPC is a technology from DEC called *Remote Task Invocation (RTI)* that uses OSI-TP to do the two-phase commit. TxRPC is still in the X/Open snapshot phase (also see the following Soapbox).

- **CPI-C V2** is a peer-to-peer conversational interface based on CPI-C and APPC. An IBM-led working group is in the process of extending CPI-C to support OSI-TP semantics. A preliminary spec is expected in mid-94.

- **XATMI** is a client/server conversational interface based on Tuxedo's *Application/Transaction Management Interface (ATMI)*. The interface allows you to issue a single request/response using the *tpcall* API. Or it can be used in general conversation mode through the *tpconnect, tpsend, tprecv* calls. This interface is in the X/Open snapshot phase.

The target upper-layer protocol for each of these APIs is the OSI-TP FAP. Below the OSI-TP FAP, communication resource managers can support multiple transport protocols—including TCP/IP, ISO, and APPC. Of course, proprietary protocols may be used between homogeneous transaction manager domains. The use of OSI-TP is mandatory for communications between heterogeneous transaction manager domains. In theory, we should be able to achieve some level of multivendor interoperability (this is, after all, the idea behind all these standards). However, note that X/Open does not address the relationship between the different communication APIs—for example, it says nothing about an XATMI application being able to exchange messages with a CPI-C application via the X/Open specified communication resource managers.

Figure 28-6 shows how a global transaction exchange may be conducted. The application on the left node interacts with the remote resource via its communications resource manager. The transaction manager on the node where the request originates acts as the commit coordinator using the services of the communications resource manager. The commit coordinator is the *root* transaction monitor and the remote monitor is a *subordinate*.

Of course, more than two nodes may participate in an exchange. Global transactions that operate across distributed transaction managers are managed using trees of transaction manager relationships (see Figure 28-7). The example shows B to be the *superior* to both C and D, but it is a *subordinate* of A, which acts as the commit coordinator. During the two-phase commit, the superior manages the commitment coordination of its subordinates and reports the results up the chain.

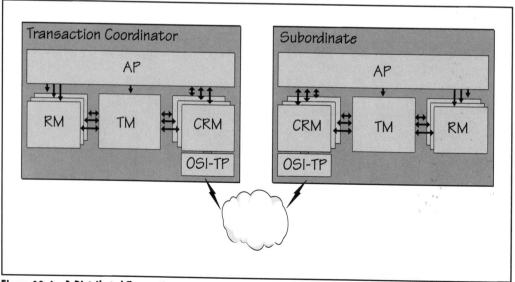

Figure 28-6. A Distributed Transaction.

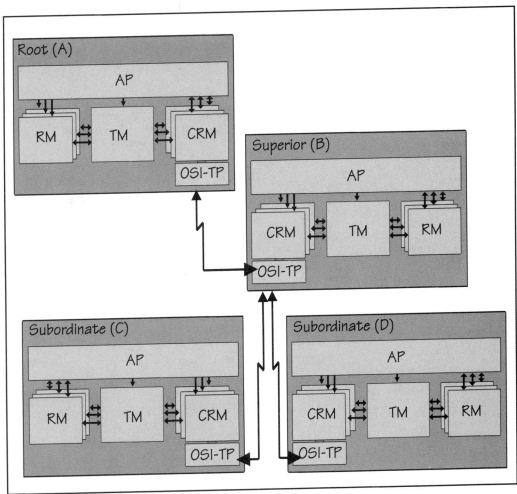

Figure 28-7. A Global Transaction Tree Structure.

Soapbox

Why Three Interface Standards?

So why do we need three interfaces at the application level? Wouldn't a single API make more sense from the portability and interoperability perspectives? We think so, but the "official" X/Open line is that they each bring their own rich set of interapplication communication paradigms. A more likely explanation is that the committee put together a specification that would make its three warring contingents—DCE, CICS, and Tuxedo—happy. This is how most standards are born!

By the way, there's more coming. X/Open is currently looking at adding a message queuing interface. Three base proposals were submitted for consideration: MQI (IBM), /Q (Tuxedo), and RQS (Encina). In addition, there's OSI-MQ. So perhaps we may get four more "standard" interfaces that will make everybody else on the committee happy. And a glaring omission is that nobody's defined a thin client interface that can issue a "delegated commit" and let the closest TP Monitor take it over from there. This may also lead to a few more interfaces!

And while we're on this soapbox, note that OSF is not necessarily endorsing the X/Open TxRPC—remember, it's the one that's based on DCE. OSF's DCE SIG TP Working Group is issuing a Request for Technology for a "DCE-based" transactional RPC that is *not* based on OSI-TP. Transarc is expected to respond to this with a proposal that incorporates its own two-phase commit technology over different transports. Yet another potential standard in the making. Where does it all end? ❑

What the Transaction Standards Do Not Address

The X/Open standard does *not* address many issues that are of practical importance to TP Monitors; for example:

- Process management including starting processes, registering processes, balancing workloads among processes, and so on
- Configuration, installation, and monitoring of transaction processing systems
- Security
- Naming and directory services
- System management and operator interfaces
- Fault-tolerance
- They don't do anything for the desktop where all transactions originate. At a minimum, X/Open should address the issue of thin clients and delegated commits.

The X/Open model *does* address a very small but important subset of a TP Monitor: The transaction interfaces and how transactions are declared. However, it does not address the inner core: *transaction processing*. Yet, we need to standardize a lot of this inner core so that federated TP Monitors can become a reality.

Alternatives to the Standards

The alternative is to standardize on a single vendor's TP Monitor platform—preferably one that runs on many OSs and interoperates with a wide variety of resource managers. For example, IBM offers a "CICS on everything" solution—with CICS provided on MVS, AIX, HP-UX, OS/2, OS/400, and possibly NT. Tuxedo is being ported to all the Unix platforms and to Tandem Computers' highly-scalable Pathway environment. IBM and Transarc are also porting Encina to as many platforms as money and time permits.

The benefits provided by this single-vendor approach are:

- You can pick and choose and even "mix-and-match" resource managers (such as databases). You can do that because most TP Monitors and database managers now support XA and XA+ interfaces.

- Your applications are easier to manage because you're dealing with a single point of management.

- Your applications are easier to port (on your TP vendor's other supported OS/hardware platforms) because you get a large number of portable API calls.

Your applications can take advantage of a much larger number of services than those provided in a least common denominator portability approach.

The negatives of this single-vendor approach are:

■ Your applications are not portable across TP Monitor platforms.
■ Your applications may not interoperate with other TP Monitors.
■ You're locked into a single vendor TP Monitor solution.

It's the typical "catch-22" of client/server computing: single vendor lock-in with peace of mind, or multivendor openness but waiting for up-to-date standards and broader functionality.

DO YOU NEED A TP MONITOR?

Because TP Monitors may be unfamiliar to many of our readers, we will go over a list of benefits that TP Monitors offer to client/server applications. Even though TP Monitors were originally introduced to serve very large "mission-critical" applications, the new versions are well-suited for handling client/server applications that span from a few nodes to thousands of nodes. Eventually, we believe that a TP Monitor component will reside on every workstation that's connected to a network—not just servers.

Here's a list of benefits that can be obtained from using the current crop of client/server oriented TP Monitors:

■ ***Client/Server application development environment.*** Increasingly, visual tool vendors are directly supporting RPCs and making the TP Monitor transparent to the developers. IDL-defined RPCs are easier to integrate with front-end tools than proprietary stored procedures. On the server side, TP Monitors provide general-purpose server shells (server classes) that run your RPCs. The TP Monitor introduces an event-driven programming style on servers by letting you associate RPCs (event handlers) with server events. In addition, the TP Monitor run-time environment enforces the ACID discipline without requiring any specialized code other than begin/end transaction. You can think of a TP Monitor as providing a pre-built framework that helps you build, run, and administer a client/server application (you don't start from ground zero). TP Monitors—augmented with open vendor GUI tools—provide an excellent platform for developing robust, high-performing, client/server applications quickly.

■ ***Firewalls of protection.*** In a client/server world, it is important to protect yourself from everything that can go wrong in the distributed environment. TP Monitors implement "firewalls" between applications and resource managers and between applications themselves. TP Monitors support tightly-coupled firewalls—such as two-phase commits or loosely-coupled firewalls such as those provided by transactional queues. The firewall unit of protection is the ACID transaction.

- *High availability.* TP Monitors are designed to work around all types of failures. The permeation of ACID principles throughout all components helps create self-healing systems. TP Monitors, at all times, are aware of the state of all the client/server resources that are under their control. With ACID you can detect a failure exactly where it happens. A TP Monitor can then restart a failed process or switch over to a process on another node in the event of hardware failures. Architectures with no single point-of-failure are achievable.

- *Load balancing.* TP Monitors specialize in process management and support both static and dynamic load balancing techniques. TP monitors support the prioritization of requests and can *dynamically* replicate server processes on the same server node or on different nodes. In the static case, a pool of server classes may be scheduled to handle certain peak loads (for example, between work shifts) and then scaled down to support other job mixes during the day. The TP Monitor's load balancing software is an excellent match for today's new breed of SMP server hardware.

- *MOM Integration.* TP Monitors complement MOMs very well. Together they can provide support for long-lived transactions and workflow type of applications. TP Monitors can act as the transaction coordinator for work that is exchanged through transactional queues. The queued events can trigger server processes managed by the TP Monitor.

- *Scalabilty of function.* TP Monitors encourage you to create modular reusable procedures that encapsulate resource managers. With a TP Monitor, you export the function call and not the data itself. This means that you can keep adding new function calls and let the TP Monitor distribute that function over multiple servers. TP Monitors allow you to create highly complex applications by just adding more procedures. The TP Monitor guarantees that procedures that know nothing about each other will work together in ACID unison. In addition, the TP Monitor lets you mix resource managers—meaning that you can always start with one resource manager and then move to another one while preserving your investments in the function calls. All functions—even legacy ones—join the TP Monitor managed pool of reusable procedures. In other words, TP Monitors let you add heterogenous server resources anywhere without altering the existing application architecture. The Standish Group calls this "matrix scalability."

- *Reduced system cost.* With TP Monitors you can save money. According to the Standish Group, TP Monitors may result in total system cost savings of greater than 30%—depending on system scale—over a more database-centric approach. In addition, the Standish Group research shows that significant "development time" savings—up to 40% or 50%—can be achieved. In addition, the funneling effect of TP Monitors can result in large savings in the acquisition of resource managers. This is because database vendors charge by the number of active users; funneling cuts down on that number, which equates to lower license fees. For example, the Standish Group estimates that with a TP Monitor you can save between 69% (on a 16-user Oracle) and 62% on a (128-user Oracle). TP Monitors, with their load balancing, also provide better performance using the same system resources; this means that you can run your application on less expensive hardware. Finally, TP Monitors don't lock you into a vendor-specific database solution, which makes the acquisition process more competitive adding to cost savings (instead, they lock you into a TP Monitor single vendor solution).

Chapter 29

TP-Lite or
TP-Heavy?

It is not part of Oracle's declared strategy to build a transaction manager because there are already plenty of known players out there who specialize in this area—Tuxedo, Top End, CICS, plus the Encina Monitor to come.

— Jnan Dash, VP of Database Planning,
Oracle (May, 1993) [1]

You may recall from Part 4 that the SQL database managers are also in the business of managing transactions across their own resources. Some database-centric advocates argue that database transactions with stored procedures is all that's needed in the area of transaction management. They call their approach *TP-Lite*.

In contrast to database managers, TP Monitors extend the notion of transactions to *all* resources, not just data-centric ones. TP Monitors track the execution of functions on a single server or across servers on the network—their approach is called *TP-Heavy*. We will go over the current industry debate between TP-Lite and

---

[1] Source: **OTM Spectrum Reports** (May, 1993).

TP-Heavy. As Jim Gray puts it, "Your problems aren't over by just embracing the concept of RPC or even TP-Lite."

And while these two TP camps are debating, the majority of the PC-centric (and Unix) client/server world is *TP-Less*. There is very little awareness in the PC world today of what transaction management is and why it's even needed. However, transaction management is second nature to most IS people who are "downsizing" from mainframe environments. These folks won't deploy an OLTP application on PC LANs without some kind of TP Monitor. As a result they're creating demand for a new breed of LAN-based TP Monitors. The Standish Group says revenue from the so-called *open OLTP* systems will jump to $6 billion in 1994, which is about double 1993's estimated $3.1 billion; it is expected to reach $21.7 billion by 1996. Even if these numbers are overly optimistic, they still say that a big client/server OLTP market is in the making.

The TP Monitor vendors must be getting the message because they're delivering a new breed of "open" TP Monitor products on Unix—including Tuxedo, Encina, CICS/6000, and Top-End—and OS/2—including CICS and Encina. In addition, some products—for example, Bachman's newly acquired Ellipse client/server tool—now include an embedded TP Monitor.

In this chapter we cover the TP-Lite versus TP-Heavy debate. It's important to understand what's missing from database-centric transaction processing. And, of course, there will be a soapbox that tells you which side of that debate we're on. As Jim Gray puts it, "TP is where the money is: both literally (most banks are TP systems) and figuratively (CICS has generated more revenues than any other piece of software)." So it may be worth exploring which type of TP system—Lite or Heavy—is best for client/server needs.

THE ORIGINS OF TP-LITE

My transaction hopes are pinned on the impact of the distribution of processing—when it is realized that data is not everything and that process is just as important.

— Jim Gray (May, 1993)

In the good old days of mainframes, the divisions were clear: Database servers focused on managing data, while TP Monitors focused on managing processes and applications. The two sides stayed out of each other's turf and kept improving on what they did best. It was a classical win/win situation where everybody prospered. This happy coexistence came to an end in 1986, when Sybase became the first database vendor to integrate components of the TP Monitor inside the database engine.

Sybase Breaks the Truce

How did Sybase do it? You may recall from Part 4 that Sybase funnels all client requests into a multithreaded single-process server. It's an N-to-1 funnel. This may be called a case of *funnel overkill* because the database and user applications share the same address space—a sure invitation for disaster.

But Sybase did not stop with funneling; it also became the first database vendor to introduce stored procedures and triggers—two functions that definitely belong on the procedural side of the house. With its new architecture, Sybase became the uncontested champion of the database benchmarking wars. Of course, most database vendors were quick to follow suit. By now, most of them provide some level of funneling and support for stored procedures in their database engines. Application developers and tool vendors were quick to exploit the benefits of stored procedures, and the *TP-Lite* client/server architecture was born.

Given the popularity of database servers on PC LANs, does this mean TP Monitors are dead? Are they just an anachronism from the mainframe days? Is TP-Lite integrated with database the new platform of choice for application servers and OLTP? The answers to all these questions must, of course, be no; we didn't write an entire part on TP Monitors for nothing. So let's first review the facts in a cool, analytical manner. Then we'll jump on the soapbox and throw in some opinions as to where all this is heading.

What Is TP-Lite?

TP-Lite is simply the integration of TP Monitor functions in the database engines. Currently only a few of the TP Monitor functions are integrated, including function shipping, some level of funneling, single-function transaction management, and RPC-like calls. It is not clear if the database vendors plan to reinvent the wheel and develop all the missing TP Monitor functions in TP-Lite. There's still a long list of unimplemented functions; the TP Monitor people have a ten-year headstart.

What Is TP-Heavy?

TP-Heavy are TP Monitors as defined in this chapter. The new generation of *TP-Heavy* products for client/server LANs includes CICS, Encina, Tuxedo, Tandem's Pathway, Top End, and DEC's ACMS. All these TP Monitors support the client/server architecture and allow PCs to initiate some very complex multiserver transactions from the desktop. All these products are supported by open visual builder tools that let you create the front end separately from the back end.

TP-Heavy includes all the functions defined in this chapter—including process management, load balancing, global transaction synchronization, interfaces to multiple resource managers, and error recovery.

TP-LITE VERSUS TP-HEAVY

TP-Lite systems may not solve all the world's problems, but they solve many simple ones. According to Ziph's law: most problems are simple.

> — *Jim Gray, High Performance Transaction Workshop (September, 1993)*

We won't have an OLTP environment manufactured by a single vendor (TP-Lite), but rather an OLTP environment that comprises of a mosaic of services (TP-Heavy). I think TP-Heavy will win.

> — *Alfred Spector, High Performance Transaction Workshop (September, 1993)*

The competition between TP-Lite and TP-Heavy is painfully unequal. It's like comparing a Harley-Davidson motorcycle with a bicycle. TP-Lite can best be defined by what it lacks, which is a long list of functions. In a nutshell, TP-Lite functions don't execute under global transaction control, there is no global supervisor, and the process management environment is very primitive. TP-Lite server functions only work with a single resource manager (the local database), and they don't support any form of ACID nesting. Like a bicycle, these functions are perfect fits for certain environments. But it's important to understand what you're missing because you'll rarely see it mentioned in the database marketing literature.

TP-Lite Versus TP-Heavy: Scope of the Commit

A *TP-Lite* stored procedure is written in a database-vendor proprietary procedural language—PL/SQL, Transact SQL, and so on—and is stored in the database. A stored procedure is a transactional unit, but it can't participate with other transactional units in a global transaction. It can't call another transaction and have it execute within the same transaction boundary. As shown in Figure 29-1, if stored procedure A dies after invoking stored procedure B, A's work will automatically get rolled back while B's work is committed for posterity. This is a violation of the ACID all-or-nothing proposition. This limitation causes you to write large transactions that put everything within the scope of the commit. It doesn't help the cause of modularization or writing reusable functions.

In contrast, *TP-Heavy* procedures are written using standard procedural languages. They can easily provide all-or-nothing protection in situations like the one shown in the right-hand side of Figure 29-1. For TP-Heavy, dealing with global transactions is second nature.

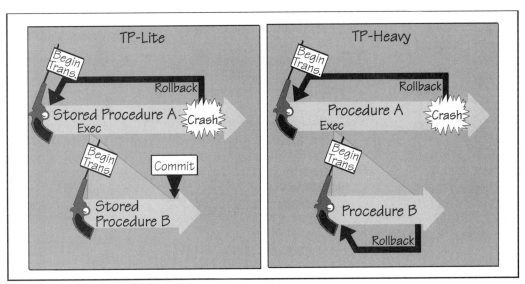

Figure 29-1. TP-Lite Versus TP-Heavy: Scope of the Commit.

TP-Lite Versus TP-Heavy: Managing Heterogeneous Resources

A *TP-Lite* stored procedure can only commit transaction resources that are on the vendor's database or resource manager (see Figure 29-2). It cannot synchronize

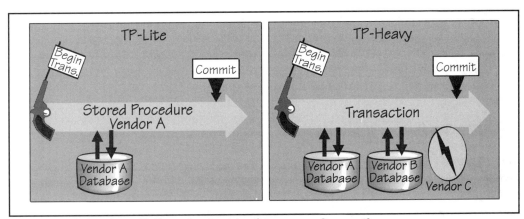

Figure 29-2. TP-Lite Versus TP-Heavy: Synchronizing Heterogeneous Resource Managers.

or commit work that is on a foreign—local or non-local—database or resource manager. In contrast, *TP-Heavy* procedures can easily handle ACID updates on multiple heterogeneous resource managers within the scope of a single transaction.

TP-Lite Versus TP-Heavy: Process Management

A *TP-Lite* stored procedure gets invoked, executed under ACID protection (within a single-phase commit), and *may* then be cached in memory for future reuse. That's about it. In contrast, *TP-Heavy* processes are prestarted and managed as server classes (see Figure 29-3). If the load on a server class gets too heavy, more processes are automatically started. Server classes support priorities and other class-of-service attributes. Server processes have firewalls around them so that the programs that run within them don't interfere with each other. If a server class process dies, it is restarted or the transaction can be reassigned to another server process in that class. The entire environment runs under the constant supervision of the TP Monitor. The server class concept helps the TP Monitor understand what class of service is required by the user for a particular group of functions. It's an intelligently managed environment.

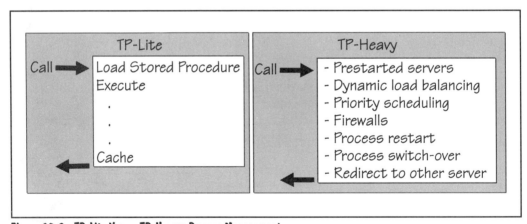

Figure 29-3. TP-Lite Versus TP-Heavy: Process Management.

TP-Lite Versus TP-Heavy: Client/Server Invocations

The *TP-Lite* stored procedure invocation is extremely non-standard. Vendors provide their own proprietary RPC invocation mechanism. The RPCs are not defined using an IDL. And they're not integrated with global directory, security, and authentication services. The communications links are not automatically restarted, and they're not under transaction protection. In addition, TP-Lite does not support MOM or conversational exchanges.

In contrast, the *TP-Heavy* environment is very open to communication styles (see Figure 29-4). The RPC can use DCE as its base. MOM transactional queues can easily be integrated into the global transaction. Most TP Monitor vendors also support APPC/CPI-C for peer-to-peer communications.

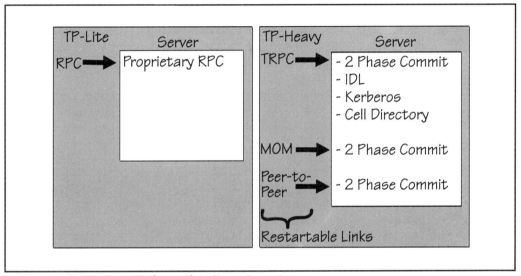

Figure 29-4. TP-Lite Versus TP-Heavy: Client/Server Invocation.

TP-Lite Versus TP-Heavy: Performance

TP-Lite stored procedures are much faster than networked static or dynamic SQL. However, they don't perform as well as TP-Heavy managed procedures, especially under heavy loads. According to the Standish Group, "today, virtually all standardized transaction processing benchmark results (e.g. TPC-A) are executed with a TP Monitor managing the application services in front of a database." Essentially the TP Monitor offloads the database server by multiplexing client requests. It acts as a funnel on top of whatever funnel the database may have already put in place.

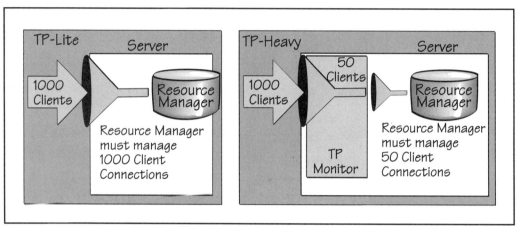

Figure 29-5. TP-Heavy Funneling Into TP-Lite.

Let's see how this can help even the "over-funneled" Sybase Server. In the example shown in Figure 29-5, instead of seeing 1000 clients, a Sybase multithreaded server is made to think it's dealing with 50 clients. The Sybase database server sees a reduced number of database clients, and acts more responsively as a result. The same story applies to other vendors' databases, some more than others. Figure 29-6 shows you how dramatic some of these numbers can be—the benchmarks were run on the same hardware with an Informix database engine (with and without a TP Monitor). In addition, significant cost savings can be achieved because fewer database resources are needed to support a given workload (the Informix example makes the point).

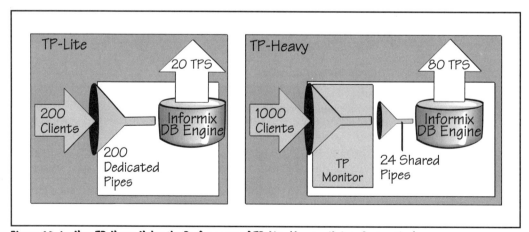

Figure 29-6. How TP-Heavy Helps the Performance of TP-Lite (Source: Unisys Corporation).

Conclusion

The database companies are primarily database-centric; it is unlikely they will solve the complete breadth of the problem.

— Alfred Spector, CEO Transarc Corp.
(November, 1993)

TP-Heavy products were created to meet the process management requirements of mission-critical OLTP environments. They tend to be very robust and have excellent system management facilities. TP-Lite products are newcomers in the area of process management and haven't had time to develop mature field-tested products. It takes years of product incubation to develop the right facilities in areas such as online distribution of new processes, remote debugging, built-in statistics, administration tools, and automatic switch-overs during failures (and later reconciliations). See the Soapbox below for a stronger opinion.

So Is It TP-Lite or TP-Heavy?

Soapbox

TP-Lite or TP-Heavy? Most likely neither. The debate about the need for a TP Monitor is only interesting in the short term, since today's transactional infrastructures are inappropriate for supporting business process re-engineering.

— Gartner Group (November 22, 1993)

Rome wasn't built overnight and neither were TP Monitors. And as far as we can see, TP Monitors have a huge head start over TP-Lite in the area of process management. TP-Lite doesn't even come close to managing environments where a transaction spans across machines or resource managers (i.e., the so-called multidomain transactions). TP-Heavy provides global management and allows multivendor resource managers (including databases) to be plugged into the system; it gives us choice. You can then depend on TP-Heavy to make the "mosaic" whole. In contrast, TP-Lite provides an entry-level, single-domain, single-server solution for transaction processing.

So TP-Lite, like a bicycle, is quite useful in situations where you're dealing with a single vendor database and a small to medium number of users (let's say fewer than 50). And, as bicycles teach us the joy of being on wheels, TP-Lite will teach millions of programmers the joy of transaction programming. TP-Lite is ideal in entry-level situations because it's less complex; you only have to deal with one server component: the database. The TP-Lite vendors also understand how to market to the client/server world—a very important advantage.

However, TP-Heavy technology is extremely important to the future of client/server computing. Think about what you could do with a Harley-Davidson instead of a bicycle. TP Monitors let us mix together components in all sorts of wild combinations; at the same time, they guarantee that everything comes together like clockwork. In other words, TP Monitors let us do the mix-and-match that is the forte of an open client/server world. Unfortunately, the TP monitor vendors are having a very hard time selling this message. They still use a lot of antique terminology that sounds very foreign to the PC LAN culture.

TP-Heavy vendors should focus on putting a "friendly" version of a TP Monitor on every desktop and in every 32-bit operating system. Gartner (see previous quote) would like to see transaction processing move to the next phase and start worrying about workflow—the topic of Part 6. We wholeheartedly agree, and think they should also move to objects. But given the current mindset of the TP-Heavy vendors, we'll be lucky just to get a TP Monitor on an occasional PC or Unix LAN server. The other problem is that they don't have the volume channels or the right packaging for their products. They can't get beyond their "selling to MIS" origins. Yet MIS and the rest of us can greatly benefit if every PC on the network were ACID-ized. Wouldn't it be nice if every PC could participate in a global transaction? We believe that most exchanges in the "post-scarcity future" will be in the form of global transactions.

The situation may improve dramatically after Novell introduces "red box" versions of Tuxedo in mid-1994. CICS OS/2 V2 is also an excellent client/server product (the previous version was almost useless). It could do very well in the mass market, if only it could lighten up on the heavy "CICS-speak" that permeates throughout it. Encina—with its nested transactions, transactional RPC, and DCE NOS base—is the epitome of the postmodern TP Monitor. But it remains to be seen if any of these products can create a mass market that puts TP-Heavy back into the driver seat. If they fail because of poor marketing, database companies will not only steal the show but also end up having to reinvent the transaction wheel. ❑

Chapter 30

TP Monitor Products: Encina and CICS OS/2 V2

At a recent High Performance Transaction Systems Conference, one after another Transarc, NCR, AT&T, and others described how and why their UNIX based transaction processing approaches are technologically open and "standard." All through this, Tony Storey of IBM Hursley remained silent. Eventually he stood up to make these telling points:

- all CICS interfaces are published
- CICS runs on, or will run on, virtually every platform
- more than one third of a million people program against the CICS interface, all over the world
- hundreds of millions, if not billions, of dollars worth of applications run against CICS.
- CICS is coming to UNIX.

If this is not open and a standard, what is? he asked. What could we say?

— **Jim Gray (May, 1993)** [1]

This chapter covers two TP Monitors: **CICS OS/2 Version 2** and **Encina**. With over 55,000 licenses (10,000 on OS/2), CICS is the world's most widely used TP Monitor.

---

[1] Source: **OTM Spectrum Reports** (May, 1993).

CICS is proven and familiar to hundreds of thousands of system designers and programmers.[2] Micro Focus—the leading vendor of CICS application development tools—estimates that *40 million* CICS applications (a truly astounding number if true) were developed over the last 15 years, representing billions of lines of code (85% of which are in COBOL). In addition to IBM, CICS TP Monitors are offered by Micro Focus, VISystems, and Unikix. Tandem Computer's Pathway is implementing CICS "personalities" on top of their TP Monitor engines. An "open CICS" movement is in place to make the CICS API a TP standard. And IBM is porting CICS to many platforms—its own and others.

CICS OS/2 V2 introduces the best client/server implementation of CICS on any platform by providing a new thin client implementation of the *External Call Interface*—for DOS, Windows, and OS/2 clients. The CICS OS/2 V2 server is a true 32-bit OS/2 implementation. It's the first shrink-wrapped version of CICS—meaning that it doesn't require a host computer tape to install. Before shipping in October 1993, the prerelease code was tested for a little under a year at 170 customer sites. This relatively large beta program gave IBM a lot of feedback on usability and ease-of-use improvements. We saw some substantial improvements in performance between the first release of the beta and the version that shipped.[3]

As we said in the last chapter, Encina is a postmodern TP Monitor that implements an "open" architecture based on standards—X/Open DTP and DCE. IBM made statements of direction about its intention to ship an Encina version for OS/2. Unfortunately, as we go to press, Encina for OS/2 hasn't shipped (we were hoping for a mid-December shipment). So we will cheat a bit and describe the Encina architecture as it is implemented on RS/6000. We want to use Encina to demonstrate how the transaction standards, covered in the last chapter, are implemented in a commercial TP Monitor. In addition, Encina has several neat features that will give you a feel for what's coming. But if you really need an industrial-strength TP Monitor on OS/2 today, CICS OS/2 V2 is your best bet.

CICS OS/2 V2

CICS OS/2 V2, shipped by IBM in October 1993, is a PC LAN version of CICS that provides both client/server and server/server TP Monitor services. The server/server facilities allow CICS applications on OS/2 to participate in distributed transactions with applications that run on other members of the CICS family—including CICS/6000 on AIX, CICS/400 on AS/400, CICS/VSE, CICS/MVS, and CICS/ESA on mainframes (and, in the future, CICS on HP-UX and Windows NT). An application that strictly uses the CICS APIs (the CICS/6000 subset to be exact) can easily be ported across platforms.

---

[2] Source: **PC Week** (June 7, 1993).
[3] We were an internal beta site for the product.

The plan for this section is to first go over the CICS OS/2 process management architecture and what it takes to write a CICS server application. We then cover the CICS client/server and server/server transaction communication facilities—including the Extended Call Interface, Distributed Program Link, Transaction Routing, Function Shipping, Distributed Transaction Processing, and Asynchronous Transaction Processing. What a mouthful! But you should be able to tell from this list that CICS has some powerful transaction functions. However, one of our challenges will be to translate them from "CICS-speak" into modern client/server terminology. We conclude with a list of features offered by the CICS OS/2 V2 product.

Process Management

Like all Transaction Monitors, CICS OS/2 provides an environment for running user-written server applications. It does this by making good use of OS/2's native DLL, priority, thread, and process management facilities. Here's how it works:

■ You write your server programs as DLL functions. In CICS terminology, a DLL function is a *transaction*. The DLL itself is called a *program*. A *group* consists of all the programs that constitute an application. A group is a packaging unit.

CICS Transactions Versus Transactions

Warning

A transaction, as we described it in the last few chapters, is a logical unit of work—an ACID unit of code that starts with a begin_transaction and ends with an end_transaction (i.e., commit or rollback). A CICS transaction is a *superset* of this definition; it's a unit of execution—a DLL function that can contain one or more logical units of work. The DLL function, which CICS calls a transaction, does not necessarily end after the first commit. To differentiate the two, we'll call one of them the CICS transaction. ❑

■ You must then register your CICS transactions using an interactive facility in the *Processing Program Table*. Using this facility you can specify the server class—CICS calls it the *task class*—to which this CICS transaction belongs. You can specify the CICS transaction to be secure, meaning that it will require password-secured access. You can also assign a priority to the CICS transaction (0-255). The actual OS/2 task priority will be determined by CICS at run time based on many factors.

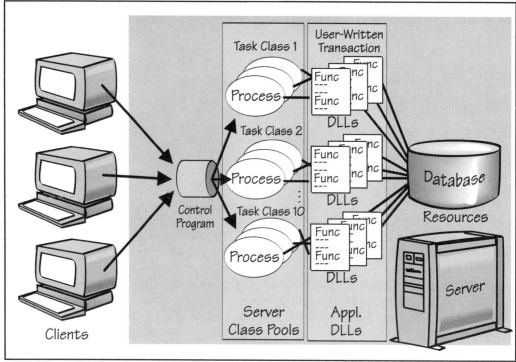

Figure 30-1. The CICS OS/2 V2 Process Management Facility.

- A CICS *task class* consists of a pool of prestarted processes and the DLL functions assigned to them (i.e., the CICS transactions). Because the CICS transactions are written as OS/2 DLL functions, they are reentrant. A CICS OS/2 server supports up to 10 user-defined task classes. Each task class can run up to 99 OS/2 processes. However, the combined number of prestarted processes in all 10 task classes must not exceed 99. You define all these limits using the *System Initialization Table* facility.

- At run time, the CICS main program—the control program—starts all the processes in every task class and waits for incoming work. When a request arrives for a local CICS transaction, it is assigned to a free process in the task class that was associated with this CICS transaction. The process will load the DLL function (if it is not already in memory) and execute it. It then returns to the free pool for that task class.

- In the event of an application failure, CICS OS/2 provides the capability to dynamically backout transactions that were "inflight"—this is called *Dynamic Transaction Backout*. If the PC crashes, CICS has an *Emergency Restart* facility that returns all CICS recoverable resources to their last syncpoint before the interruption.

Figure 30-1 shows the how the different pieces of the CICS OS/2 process management environment come together at run time. It's a typical example of a *static* load-balancing scheme.

Customizing the Server Environment

CICS OS/2 provides server event triggers that let you customize the run-time environment. It surfaces some key server events that you can provide handlers for by writing DLL functions. CICS calls these event handlers *user exits*. Figure 30-2 shows some of the more useful server-generated events:

■ *Startup and Shutdown* events are triggered when CICS first comes up and when it terminates. You can provide special logic that you want executed at both these times.

■ *Task_Created and Task_Terminated* events are triggered when the CICS control program creates or destroys a process that's part of a task class. Usually these processes are all prestarted around startup time and persist as long as the server is up. The *Task_Created* event is particularly useful because it lets you initialize the task's environment and connect to resources such as databases. *Task_terminated* allows you to disconnect in an orderly fashion.

■ *Transaction_Error* event is triggered when a CICS transaction error occurs. You can use it to associate a general purpose error handler.

■ *Unknown_Transaction* event is triggered when the TP Monitor receives a request to execute an unknown CICS transaction. All CICS transactions, even those on remote systems, must be registered with the CICS server.

■ *Syncpoint* event allows an application using both CICS and an external resource manager (such as a SQL Database) to issue a CICS SYNCPOINT and have the SQL COMMIT or ROLLBACK command issued automatically via a user exit. The user exit for DB2/2 is supplied by CICS OS/2. You can use this mechanism to create your own syncpoint synchronizations with resource managers. Note that this is a poor man's version of XA. (IBM intends to implement XA in a future version of CICS OS/2.)

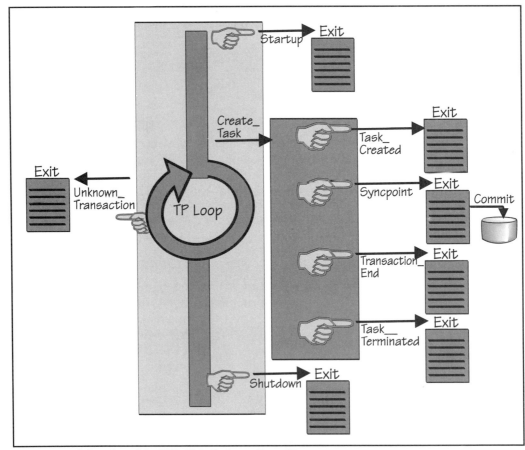

Figure 30-2. A Sampling of the CICS OS/2 V2 Server Event Triggers.

CICS: Server/Server Communications

All the CICS transaction programs execute on servers. CICS provides some very powerful server/server transaction coordination and routing facilities, which are collectively known as the *Intersystem Communication (ISC)* facilities. These facilities can be used to communicate with any CICS TP Monitor, regardless of its platform.

This is an area where the "CICS-speak" really gets in the way. But in a nutshell, ISC lets you route transactions between CICS servers, invoke transactions on remote servers using RPCs or Queues, conduct peer-to-peer exchanges, and transparently access CICS-owned resources on remote systems. We'll now go over these functions one by one:

■ **Transaction Routing** lets you transparently initiate and execute a transaction on any CICS system (see Figure 30-3). The transaction must have been defined previously.

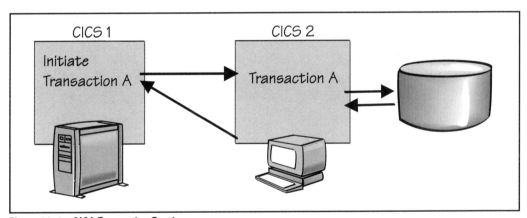

Figure 30-3. CICS Transaction Routing.

■ **Distributed Program Link** is the CICS equivalent of a transactional RPC. The RPC call will load the remote program (CICS calls it a link), execute it, and return the results (see Figure 30-4). Unlike a traditional RPC, the remote program participates in the commit process (CICS calls it syncpointing). The program must have previously been defined as "being remote" to the local server. The *Communications Area* is used to pass the name of the remote program, the parameters, and the transaction ID (it can be up to 32 KBytes in size). Some optional data conversion is handled by CICS OS/2 with user defined templates. The underlying communications stack is SNA LU 6.2.

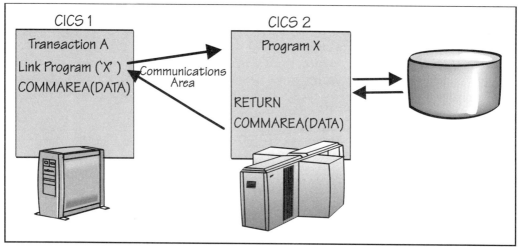

Figure 30-4. Distributed Program Link: The CICS RPC.

■ *Distributed Transaction Processing* is the CICS conversational exchange mechanism based on APPC/CPI-C. The APPC/CPI-C verbs are submitted via high-level CICS commands (see Figure 30-5). This protocol is also used to connect CICS to other TP Monitors because they all support APPC and some level of syncpoint exchange. So until the X/Open protocols become prevalent, APPC is the "lingua franca" of federated TP Monitor exchanges.

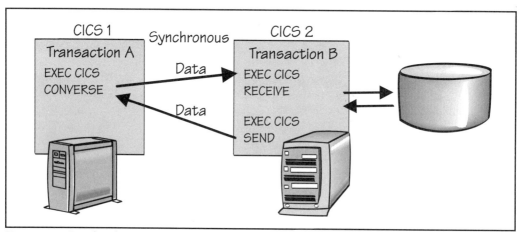

Figure 30-5. Distributed Transaction Processing: The CICS APPC Conversation.

■ *Function Shipping* allows a local CICS program to transparently access resources that are on a remote CICS machine. The call is sent to a *mirror*, a CICS-supplied transaction program that reissues the remote request locally. In addition to fetching remote data, this service can be used to synchronize local and remote updates within the scope of a CICS transaction. For example, a single CICS transaction can be initiated to read a set of remote records and use them to update a local database (see Figure 30-6). The only problem is that the resource managers on both sides must be native to CICS. This limits you to Btrieve, ISAM files, and CICS transient data and queues (a not-too-thrilling choice).

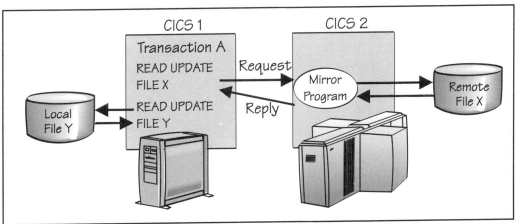

Figure 30-6. Function Shipping: CICS Redirected Access to Remote Resources.

■ *Asynchronous Transaction Processing* allows a CICS program to queue a time-triggered transaction on any CICS system. The request is stored on a CICS queue and triggered at the specified time; the results are shipped back via a queue (see Figure 30-7). CICS allows you to do both Function Shipping and Transaction Routing asynchronously.

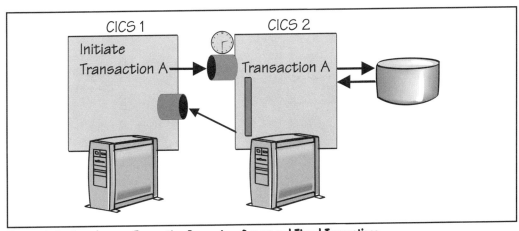

Figure 30-7. Asynchronous Transaction Processing: Queues and Timed-Transactions.

In summary, from within CICS an application can execute a CICS transaction anywhere in the network, submit delayed transactions, access CICS controlled resources and data, invoke RPCs, and perform peer-to-peer communications. Of course, you have to be running the CICS TP Monitor on both sides of the exchange, which is why we call it server-to-server communications.

CICS: Client/Server Communications

So how does CICS allow non-CICS applications to invoke it? In CICS OS/2 V1, this was done using an API called the *External Call Interface (ECI)*. The only problem was that ECI could not be called over the network, which meant that the caller had to be on the same machine as the TP Monitor—a not too useful client/server arrangement. So CICS OS/2 V1 was used as a fat client to host-based TP Monitors— very few installations could afford to put a full-blown CICS TP Monitor on every client machine.

CICS OS/2 V2 fixed this problem by providing a networked version of ECI called the *thin client*; it requires less than 100 KBytes and runs on DOS, Windows, and OS/2 clients (see Figure 30-8). The new ECI works with either the NetBIOS or APPC stacks. The calls can be issued either synchronously or asynchronously by Windows and OS/2 clients but only synchronously by DOS clients. This means that multiple calls can be issued in parallel from a Windows or OS/2 workstation. The control can be returned via a message to the Windows or PM message queues.

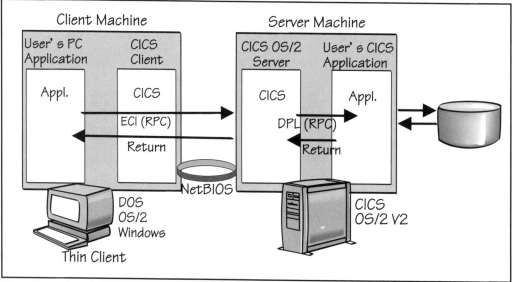

Figure 30-8. Extended Call Interface: The Thin Client RPC.

The extended ECI is just an RPC that passes the name of the transaction to be executed, the parameters, and a Transaction ID. At the TP Monitor end, it looks exactly like a CICS-CICS DPL invocation. The server transaction program gets loaded and executed. The Transaction ID is returned by the server and it is used to identify the response in an asynchronous request/reply exchange and for extended CICS transactions.

Other CICS OS/2 V2 Features

This section provides a summary of the remaining features in CICS OS/2 V2. Many of these features deal with terminals, which is not too interesting from a client/server perspective. CICS carries a lot of historical baggage with it. However, this may turn out to be a benefit in the case of CICS OS/2. The more complete the implementation, the better chance it has of becoming a target platform for porting downsized versions of the mainframe applications. The more complete versions also interoperate better with the existing mainframe CICS applications. The "billions of lines" of CICS code on the mainframes are going to be with us well into the next millennium; so we need to learn how to interoperate with them. As far as CICS platforms go, CICS OS/2 is very complete.

Here's the world's briefest summary of what CICS OS/2 V2 has to offer:

■ *Application portability.* Applications that write to the CICS API can be moved to any server within a CICS network. CICS OS/2 V2 is very close to adhering to the CICS/ESA Version 3.3 API set—the ultimate CICS API standard. This makes it easy to downsize mainframe CICS applications to OS/2 or to port CICS OS/2 applications to other CICS platforms when processor workloads require it. CICS OS/2 Version 2.0 clients support a new programming interface—the *External Presentation Interface (EPI)*—that can be used for front ending existing 3270 terminal applications.

■ *Application interoperability.* CICS OS/2 applications can participate in networks of federated CICS TP Monitors that can span from mainframes to minis to workstations. Functions and data can transparently be moved to where it's most convenient. CICS transactions may be coded as distributed cooperative programs; each runs closer to the data sources it manages—for example, it could be local, regional, or corporate data sources.

■ *Bundled Btrieve resource manager.* CICS OS/2 includes Btrieve technology for its emulated VSAM file management. New improvements include more granular locking of files, a forward recovery capability, and batch data sharing. When combined with LANs using NetWare, CICS applications on an OS/2 server may access data stored in Btrieve files held on the same machine or a NetWare server. CICS applications on both OS/2 and on host systems can access Btrieve data transparently via the CICS file control.

■ *ASCII terminal support*. Yes, you read that right. CICS OS/2 can be used to create multiuser terminal-based solutions. Of course, we don't advocate the use of terminals anywhere; this is, after all, a client/server book. But if you want to turn back the clock, CICS OS/2—combined with ARTIC cards and a separately purchased *Programmable Network Access (PNA)* software package—provides a low-cost solution for supporting clusters of ASCII terminals. The number of ASCII terminals supported is a function of the number of ARTIC cards that can fit in a PC and the number of terminals each of these cards can drive. For example, a PS/2 Model 95 can support up to five ARTIC cards, each can attach eight terminals, giving a grand total of 40 terminals.

■ *Development Workstation*. CICS OS/2 V2 provides a single-user offering for application developers writing applications in COBOL or C, targeted for production in CICS workstation or host environments. These applications can be compiled and tested in a standalone OS/2 system. They can access files and databases that are stored on any CICS system.

■ *Trace and Error Capture*. CICS OS/2 provides facilities to help you develop and maintain your programs. This includes trace formatting, exception tracing, timestamp on trace entries, and system trap handling. It also provides a range of serviceability and problem determination enhancements, which include "sympathetic failure notification" between the client and the server. Additional user exits help you determine where an application has abnormally terminated.

■ *CID-based installation*. CICS OS/2 V2 is now enabled for unattended CID installation.

■ *Security*. CICS OS/2 provides a log-on program that implements password control of user access to programs, data, and other resources. Additionally, user exits are provided to enable users to create their own security procedures if required.

■ *Third party support*. Over 50 ISVs are working on GUI tools, utilities, and products that exploit the CICS OS/2 V2 platform.

A Little Bit of Exciting CICS History

Soapbox

The original (1968) CICS was based on a single process architecture—the TP Monitor and user applications all ran in the same address space. This was the ultimate mixed blessing—part panacea and part nightmare. The *panacea* was that CICS could dispatch threads at about one-tenth the cost of a corresponding operating system call; it was fast and made few demands on the underlying operating system. The *nightmare* was that CICS ran together with all its applications in a totally unprotected environment; a single errant program could bring the entire system down (NetWare NLMs and Sybase have the same dilemma).

On the panacea side, database vendors discovered early on that they too could run their databases as CICS applications. So guess where they landed? In that same overcrowded address space with everyone else—back to the nightmare. The name of the game was who could crash the CICS system first in any given hour. To get rid of some of these unwanted folks, the CICS people invented a cross-memory interface that kept the resource managers (like DB2, Oracle, and IMS) in their own separate address spaces. The CICS idea of an interface to resource managers is the basis for X/Open's XA interface.

As CICS systems grew, they became partitioned into multiple address spaces that communicated through shared memory—the so-called *Multi-Region Operation (MRO)*. Each region ran a separate TP Monitor and separate applications. MRO was not a hit with system administrators who never knew, for sure, in which TP Monitor a piece of an application would end up—they had to manage all this movement and it was not transparent. However, MRO became an *instant hit* with the TP vendor community after it extended its interprocess communications across networks using APPC peer-to-peer communications. Foreign TP Monitors—like Tandem's Pathway and Tuxedo—could masquerade as CICS applications and participate in a CICS transaction via APPC (see Figure 30-9).

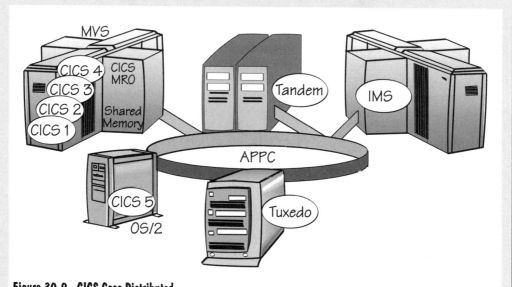

Figure 30-9. CICS Goes Distributed.

In the last few years, the CICS process management model was totally revamped (at least in the OS/2 and AIX implementations). The new process model runs the TP Monitor in its own process (i.e., address space) and assigns each CICS transaction (or application) to a separate server process. This makes the environment much more "bullet proof" than in the wild days. In addition, the client/server version of CICS leaves the implementation of the presentation services to the clients—all they need to do is issue an ECI RPC call to invoke the CICS-managed functions. Figure 30-10 shows the evolution of the CICS model. Jim Gray calls it the one-ball, two-ball, and three-ball models of transaction processing.

It would be nice if customers would let the TP Monitor vendors forget about terminals so that they could devote their full attention to their client/server implementations. Unfortunately, we're in a transition period where the two worlds must coexist for a while. We hear that terminals are getting replaced by PCs at the rate of 50,000 per month or more. But according to Micro Focus, CICS applications have 25 million terminals attached to them. If that's true, it will be many, many moons before we get rid of our existing stock at the current rates of attrition. Please don't add new any new terminals—take our word: PC-based client/server (or peer network) solutions are more cost-effective over the long run than terminals at the low end. We understand that customers worldwide are buying 100,000 PCs every day, so there is hope. ❑

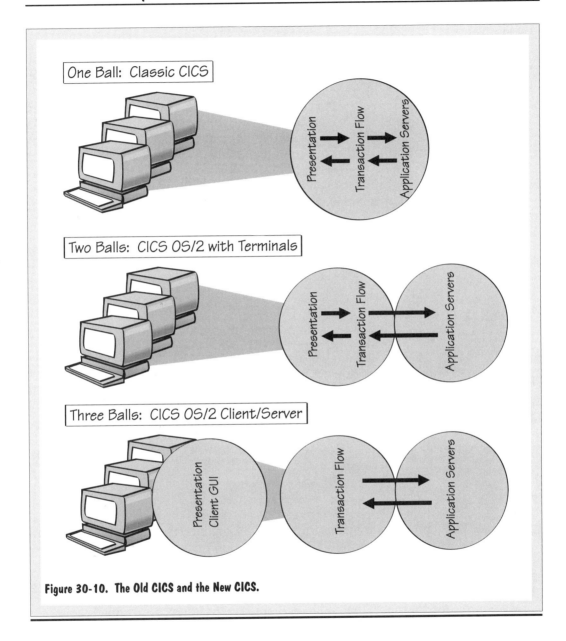

Figure 30-10. The Old CICS and the New CICS.

Packaging

CICS OS/2 Version 2.0 comes in two flavors:

■ A **Single-user** version sells for $795. This version may be used as a standalone development workstation or as a superfat CICS client to a mainframe or a CICS OS/2 multiuser server. It supports all the functions in CICS OS/2 V2 multiuser except for those required for the support of multiple users.

■ A **Multiuser** version sells for $3,995. This is the full-function CICS server we described earlier in this chapter.

The CICS thin client feature for DOS, OS/2, or Windows sells for $150 per workstation. It does not include a transport stack. NTS/2 (for NetBIOS) or Communications Manager/2 (for APPC) must be purchased separately.

CICS OS/2 Futures

By now everybody knows that it's IBM's intention to port CICS to NetWare, NT, and a variety of Unix platforms.[4] This is being done using a 32-bit portable version of the CICS engine written entirely in C. IBM also intends to provide a thin CICS client for Macintosh and Unix. Functional enhancements are expected in the following areas:

■ Better integration with DCE—including the TxRPC, directory, and security services

■ Transactional message routing via the MQSeries

■ X/Open DTP compliance by incorporating XA for interfacing to resource managers and XA+ for interfacing to communication resource managers

■ Standards compliant, single-systems image, management platform to have a single point of control (or distributed control) for CICS configuration, operations, workload/performance management, and problem determination

■ Enhancement of the CICS API set

---

[4] Source for CICS futures: A presentation by Dr. Geoff Sharman of the CICS strategy group at GUIDE.

In summary, CICS plans to keep up with the times and maintain its leadership position through a two-pronged strategy based on portability and adherence to industry standards.

TRANSARC'S ENCINA

Transarc is a privately held Carnegie Mellon University (CMU) spinoff company; a significant share is owned by IBM. Transarc's Encina TP Monitor product was developed from CMU research—the Camelot project. It also includes elements from MIT's Argus project and IBM Almaden Research's Quicksilver. Transarc primarily sells Encina as raw technology (source code). The products are delivered to the users by OEMs. Transarc has lined up a solid list of OEMs that includes IBM, HP, Stratus, NEC, and Hitachi. These companies port, test, package, and distribute the Encina product. Database vendors—including Sybase, Oracle, Informix, and Ingres—have also expressed interest in certain parts of the Transarc technology.

Encina: Creating the Standards

Because it adopted a standards-based technology and started with a "clean slate," Encina can focus solely on the issues of transaction processing and leave everything else to the standards bodies. This means Encina does not have to be concerned with the issue of portability; it has no portable API set to push. If an API is needed, it will push to get one through either OSF or X/Open. Encina does not have to worry about NOS level functions—including directory services, security, authenticated RPC, IDL compilers, and so on. It gets all these by pointing to the DCE standards, which it helped create. So what's left to do? Mostly the integration of transactions into the NOS plumbing. In the future, Encina may do more standards work in the area of TP Monitor process management—a real orphan when it comes to standards. In summary, Encina is the ultimate embodiment of the "open" paradigm. This is both a strength and weakness. For example, what happens if DCE fails in the mass market?

The Encina Two-Tier Architecture

Encina is a two-tier family of transaction processing products (see Figure 30-11):

- **Tier 1: The Toolkit** provides the basic infrastructure components for transaction processing. The toolkit sits on top of DCE.

- **Tier 2: The Extended TP Services** includes a modular collection of TP products that sit on top of the toolkit base. The Services include a TP Monitor, two transactional resource managers (a file system and a queue system), and a communications resource manager based on APPC and SNA.

The idea is to let ISVs mix-and-match the pieces they need based on this flexible foundation. For example, CICS/6000 replaces the Encina TP Monitor with the CICS engine (to get the CICS API support).

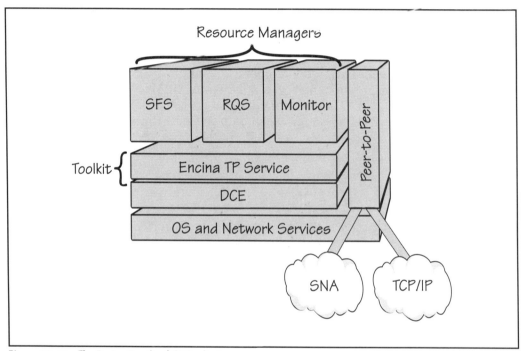

Figure 30-11. The Encina Family of TP Products.

The Encina Toolkit: The Base TP Services

The Encina toolkit extends the services of DCE at the transactional level and provides core transactional services such as a transaction log and the interface to XA-based resource managers (see Figure 30-12). These are components that can be used by all the extended TP services. Here's a quick summary of what these components do:

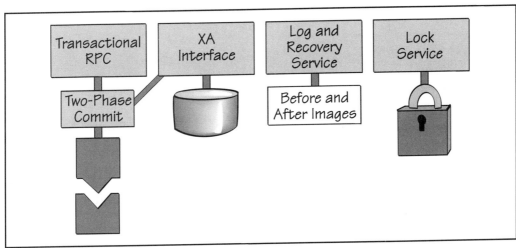

Figure 30-12. The Encina Toolkit.

- ■ **_Transactional RPC_** includes C-language APIs for adding transaction semantics to the RPC (see Figure 30-13). It also includes DCE IDL extensions for transactions (i.e., to specify an RPC as transactional).

```
transaction { ...
        debit (salaryExpense, amount);
        credit (accountsPayable, amount);
        enterAuditData (employee, amount, date);
        ...}
onCommit
        printf ("Transaction succeeded.");
onAbort
        printf ("Transaction failed.");
```

Figure 30-13. An Example of Transactional RPC C Code.

- ■ **_Two-phase commit run time_** is used by the different transactional services to commit their distributed transactions. It is a proprietary implementation of a two-phase commit, but Transarc _may_ offer it to OSF as an alternative to the more complicated OSI-TP. It is highly unlikely that X/Open will accept an alternative to OSI-TP. However, OSF may be in the market for such an implementation.

- ■ **_X/Open XA interface_** is an API library and run time for interfacing to external resource managers that are XA-compliant.

- **_Log recovery service_** provides a write-ahead log, which can be used to rollback failed transactions.

- **_Locking service_** provides a locking library to serialize calls.

These foundation elements can be used by the higher-layer services. They are all quite useful in their own way.

The Encina Extended Services

Transarc has developed its own family of TP products based on the foundation services of its Toolkit. These products include:

- **_The Encina Monitor_** is a full-feature TP Monitor that supports process management, administration, and development. The _process management_ environment includes the load balancing and scheduling of server processes across heterogeneous computers; it uses DCE-based authentication and access control lists to provide security. The Monitor coordinates resources that are invoked using the TRPC, XA, or APPC calls (see Figure 30-14). The _administration facilities_ make heavy use of the DCE cell directory services. The development environment is based on transactional C.

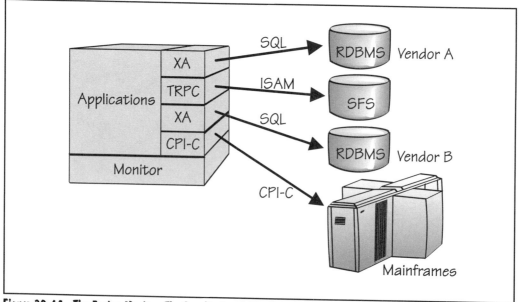

Figure 30-14. The Encina Monitor: The Coordinator of Distributed Transactions.

■ *Structured File Server (SFS)* is a record-oriented file system that provides transactional integrity and log-based recovery. It can be managed by an external two-phase commit coordinator.

■ *Recoverable Queuing Service (RQS)* is a transactionally protected queue service that allows tasks to be queued for later processing. But it ensures that system failures do not result in lost information. RQS supports multiple levels of priority.

■ *Peer-to-Peer CPI-C Services* is a transactionally protected CPI-C conversation service. Encina supports the syncpoint level 2 APPC two-phase commit service. This means that your SNA conversations participate in a two-phase commit with the rest of the resources that are participating in the transaction.

■ *Peer-to-Peer TCP/IP Services* is a transactionally protected TCP/IP conversation service. Encina provides a proprietary form of two-phase commit over TCP/IP. You'll have to run Encina on the two sides of the line for this to work.

It's hard, at this stage, to tell how well these features work in production environments. How's the performance? How's the quality? Very few Encina TP Monitors have been deployed. However, the beauty of this architecture is that it's a textbook implementation of the standards. All the pieces fit neatly in their places. The TP Monitor is like an orchestra conductor that brings it all together.

So Is It CICS or Encina?

Soapbox

Why is IBM supporting Encina when CICS is the dominant TP Monitor platform in the industry? Of course, we don't have an official answer. But if we were to speculate, this is after all a soapbox, here's what Encina brings to the CICS party:

- **Standards-based TP Monitor technology.** Even though Encina had the technology (Camelot) to create its own distributed infrastructure, they decided to bet-the-shop on DCE. They also went all the way with the X/Open standards—including of XA, XA+, and CPI-C. And they're at the bleeding edge of the transactional RPC technology and all the standard wars that surround it.

- **Interoperability with mainstream CICS.** Encina accepts requests from CICS to synchronize its resources (with Synclevel 2 APPC support).

- **Layered packaging.** Encina solves some of the tough layering issues associated with the placement of function in an "open" TP Monitor.

- **New transaction semantics.** Encina is the first platform in the industry to support nested transactions.

On the other hand, we feel that mixing two TP Monitor paradigms creates its own level of complexity. Industry observers have complained that CICS/6000 with its Encina and DCE layers is far too complex. It is also difficult to administer and manage. Everybody is for "openness" until they get the bill. In contrast, CICS OS/2 V2 is getting rave reviews for its modern integrated packaging, which doesn't include Encina or DCE technology. Eventually, all this technology may somehow get seamlessly integrated, and the Encina/CICS marriage may start making more sense. ❏

Part 6
Client/Server
Groupware

An Introduction to Part 6

Well, if you Martians think that ACID transactions and TP Monitors were fun, wait until you see groupware. Oh, by the way, we have an Earthling game for you to play—its called the blind men and the elephant. We're going to put some blindfolds on you and let you guess what groupware is. The winner gets a night on the town. Are you ready?

OK, so what's groupware? Martian number one says "it's e-mail." Martian number two thinks it's a multimedia "document store." And Martian number three says they're both wrong: "it's clearly workflow." Do we have any more takers? Does anybody think it's got something to do with electronic conferencing? How about group calendaring and scheduling? As you can see from the cartoon, the groupware elephant is all of the above. OK, so you all won a night on the town. Do you need a party guide? We have a volunteer.

Part 6 is about this amorphous client/server category called groupware; it's amorphous because it's so new, and we don't yet fully understand its potential. The groupware proponents claim that their technology allows us to create new classes of client/server applications that are unlike anything we've seen on mainframes or minis. It does that by enabling the people-to-people elements in client/server communications. The PC revolution was built around *personal* computing; groupware may create an analogous software revolution around *interpersonal* computing. Yes, of course it includes Martians. So where is Groupware Valley? You Martians are always one step ahead of us.

We'll start by defining groupware (don't laugh). We then go over what makes groupware different from SQL databases and TP Monitors. Next, we explore the constituent technologies that make up groupware—including multimedia document processing, workflow, e-mail, conferencing, and group calendaring and scheduling. However, with groupware the whole is more than the sum of the parts, so we need to explore where that synergy comes from. We conclude with some groupware products—including Lotus Notes, ImagePlus/2, and FlowMark/2. Are you all packed and ready to go exploring the new frontier?

Chapter 31

Client/Server Groupware

> *O*ur groupware technology can serve to alienate and isolate people, or it can serve to forge a community. It is our choice.
>
> — *Carol Anne Ogdin,*
> *Deep Woods Technology (August, 1993)* [1]

Client/server groupware is a collection of technologies that allow us to represent complex processes that center around collaborative human activities. It builds on five foundation technologies: multimedia document management, workflow, e-mail, conferencing, and scheduling. Groupware is not another downsized mainframe technology; it's a genuinely new form of computing. It provides an excellent example of how client/server technology can be used to extend the computing envelope into uncharted territory. Of course, this also means that groupware doesn't neatly fit into predefined software categories. So we'll have some explaining to do.

---

[1] Source: **GroupWare'93 Proceedings** (August, 1993).

Our plan for this chapter is to first define groupware and the problems it solves. We'll then place groupware in the client/server model we've been building throughout this book. This won't be easy—groupware is an elusive concept that's continuously redefining its role as well as its relationship to the more established technologies. In addition, no single groupware product incorporates all the technology pieces. After we get a working definition, we'll look at the foundation technologies and how groupware combines the pieces within a client/server setting. We'll conclude with a classification of groupware that will help us pick the representative OS/2 products to cover in the next chapter. OS/2 is the original home of Lotus Notes—the industry's most successful groupware product.

WHY IS GROUPWARE IMPORTANT?

People don't talk about operating systems; they simply assume they're there. Eventually, groupware will evolve the same way.

> — **Esther Dyson,**
> **Editor of Release 1.0 (December, 1993)**

The Workgroup Technologies market research firm believes the groupware market will grow to almost $2.9 billion by 1996 from a modest $430 million in 1993. Lotus Notes—an amorphous groupware product that escapes definition—has sold more than 500,000 licenses to 2000 companies. Notes revenues have soared more than fourfold—from $21 million in 1991 to an estimated $90 million in 1993. That's not counting the sizeable mini-industry, which has developed around Notes. So what's causing all this sudden interest in groupware? According to David Coleman, editor of the newsletter "GroupTalk", the rapid growth is occurring because groupware can transform a company by changing the way people communicate with each other and, as a result, the business processes. For example, groupware may be used to automate customer service and make a company more responsive. Groupware also has the potential to flatten organizations and remove layers of bureaucracy (see the following Soapbox).

Groupware allows direct contributors—wherever they may be—to collaborate on a job using client/server networks. We anticipate the growth of "virtual corporations" that get formed by unaffiliated groups of people to collaborate on a particular project. Groupware helps manage (and track) the product through its various phases; it also allows the contributors to exchange ideas and synchronize their work. It keeps track of the "collective memory" of the group.

Groupware, in many cases, allows departments to develop and deploy their own applications. Anyone who can create a simple spreadsheet can learn how to create a Lotus Notes application—few programming skills are required. The ability for departments to develop and create their own client/server groupware applications is leading to phenomenal returns on investment. Lotus quotes an independent study of 17 Notes customers that shows that their initial investment was recovered in three months (average). The groupware phenomenon—like spreadsheets or Macintosh Hypercards—is self-feeding. The difference is that groupware is a self-feeding client/server application; it is networked and interpersonal. Most groupware products also support open APIs that allow third parties (and IS shops) to add new functions on top of the foundation.

Groupware and Re-Engineering

Soapbox

Are we investing in groupware to infuse the organization with collaborative energy? Or are we investing primarily to staunch the bleeding?

— *Michael Schrage, Fellow,*
MIT Sloan School (September, 1993)

Bureaucracy in most organizations is very resilient; it will take a lot more than groupware to get rid of it. In fact, groupware can be misused to automate bureaucracy and make it more permanent. The current "re-engineering" movement thinks it has found the problem: We've been applying Ford's assembly-line processes to business operations. We need to rethink the way we work—that is, re-engineer the process. We wish them luck. Hopefully, they'll leave a few jobs behind after the re-engineering.

The re-engineering movement asserts that throwing technology into a poorly performing process won't help. We agree; nobody can quarrel with the fact that it doesn't make sense to automate a process that shouldn't be there in the first place. However, groupware is a secular technology; it can automate any type of process, including bad ones. You can use it to automate inefficient processes and make them more "efficiently inefficient." Or you can automate the re-engineered structures and shoot to attain the order of magnitude improvements the gurus preach about. But we'll probably see a great deal of misuse of the technology until people learn this lesson. It's a lot more effort to rethink the way we work than to throw a shrinkwrapped package of groupware at it. Groupware vendors will make the same amount of revenue either way, but its value to the companies that buy it will be radically different. ❑

What Is Groupware?

If you were to put twelve groupware experts in a room, you would get twenty definitions.

— **David Coleman (August, 1993)**

In a contest for the most fuzzily defined client/server software category, "groupware" would be the hands down winner. Over 200 products call themselves groupware. So let's cut the suspense and propose the following working definition: "Groupware is software that supports the creation, flow, and tracking of non-structured information in direct support of collaborative group activity."

There are other terms used as synonyms for groupware—collaborative computing, workgroup computing, and the academic-sounding "computer supported cooperative working." Groupware is the easiest of these terms to remember; vendors like the way it sounds because of the "ware" attached to it. So groupware it is.

Our definition implies that groupware is involved in the management of both information and activities. The "million dollar" question is: What makes groupware different from database managers and TP Monitors? For a change, we have some ready and straightforward answers.

HOW IS GROUPWARE DIFFERENT FROM SQL DATABASES?

Using an RDBMS to support documents is like teaching an elephant to fly.

— **Frank Ingari, VP Marketing, Lotus (February, 1993)**

The relational databases we covered in Part 4 deal with highly structured data that is accessed using SQL. They are excellent for managing applications that require high concurrency controls—including locking and isolation features—that are needed for immediate updates. They also provide excellent ad hoc query facilities. In contrast, groupware deals with highly unstructured data—including text, image, graphics, faxes, mail, and bulletin boards. Groupware provides the tools to capture this data at the point of entry and organize it in a nebulous thing called a *document*. You can think of a document as the container of diverse types of information. The document is to a workgroup what a table is to a SQL database: It's a basic unit of management. Groupware helps end users create document databases. It can move these documents via electronic mail and database replicas. And it provides everything you need to query, manage, and navigate through document databases. Documents are the currency of groupware.

Using OLE, DDE, OpenDoc, or native editors, groupware lets you view the components of the documents by launching the tools that created them in the first place. This means that if the document contains an image, movie, or sound clip, the groupware software will find it for you and let you view it. But can't we do that kind of stuff using SQL database BLOBs? Absolutely not (see the following Soapbox). SQL databases are great for providing access to structured data that's organized in table formats, but when it comes to multimedia and non-structured data, they're almost hopeless. Groupware-style document management fills this gap very well.

What About BLOBs?

Soapbox

In their current form, BLOBs are a lousy tool for handling advanced datatypes. They buy little or no leverage over storing data in a flat file. The RDBMS acts as little more than a very expensive flat file server.

> — Wayne Duquaine, Sybase,
> HPTS Workshop (September, 1993)

A BLOB, at least in a SQL database, is nothing more than up to four GBytes of uninterpreted binary data. All the rich semantic information is buried in the binary headers that the SQL database couldn't care less about. The headers describe the various sub-types and components that make up the BLOB including the data type (image, voice, text, and so on), the compression type, and the various indexes. The SQL database throws back at the application all the navigation tasks that are required to move through the BLOB's components.

SQL does not specify a self-describing data standard for BLOBs. Determining what's in the BLOB has to be reinvented by each application. GUI tools are left blind and clueless as to what each BLOB contains and how it should be processed. When it comes to BLOBs and multimedia, a SQL database is just a glorified and expensive file server with no value added. In contrast, the groupware document servers have made great strides toward providing some kind of a multimedia client/server solution. □

How Is Groupware Different From TP Monitors?

The TP Monitors we covered in Part 5 deal with management of transaction processes across client/server networks. So how do they compare with groupware? When it comes to document stores, TP Monitors can complement groupware software very well. The TP monitor treats the document store like any other resource manager; if it supports a two-phase commit the TP monitor will gladly coordinate a distributed transaction that includes the document store. However, TP Monitors and groupware compete in the area of workflow. We believe that the groupware workflow is a much more developed technology than the TP Monitor long-lived transaction (but it's less protected).

The current workflow model—and groupware in general—is not transaction-oriented in the ACID sense. Groupware is good at reflecting the changing states of information over time, but it does not do very well when it comes to reflecting the current state of the data in real time. For example, groupware (and workflow) does not use two-phase commits to synchronize distributed changes across resource managers. It would be nice if TP Monitors and groupware combined efforts to infuse workflow with ACID properties (if it can be done). We cover workflow later in this chapter.

THE COMPONENTS OF GROUPWARE

As we said earlier, groupware builds on five foundation technologies: multimedia document management, workflow, e-mail, conferencing, and scheduling (see Figure 31-1). Groupware achieves its magic by combining these technologies and creating new synergy. The technology for multimedia document management and workflow comes from electronic document imaging systems; e-mail and scheduling

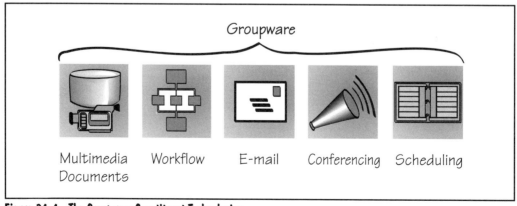

Figure 31-1. The Groupware Constituent Technologies.

come from office automation; and conferencing is native to groupware. Before we get into groupware proper, let's quickly review what these component technologies have to offer.

From Electronic Imaging to Multimedia Document Management

Groupware document management technology has its roots in electronic imaging. If we want to be purists, electronic imaging is just another form of special-purpose groupware. Of course, electronic imaging people—who have created a huge multi-billion dollar industry—can make the claim that groupware is just an imaging spin-off. In either case, we need to look at electronic imaging because it's an important client/server industry that is a precursor to groupware.

Electronic imaging started small. In the 1960s many businesses replaced large information paper warehouses with microfilm and computer-aided retrieval systems. By the mid-1980s, the appearance of PCs, LANs, scanners, compression, and optical disk juke-boxes allowed the automation of image storage as well as the data-centered tracking systems that locate those images. The new technologies made the online storage and display of images economical. In some applications, the cost savings associated with reduced staff and faster online access to documents (in seconds rather than days) justified the incremental expense for the new client/server systems. It costs $25,000 to fill a four-drawer paper file cabinet and $2,160 annually to maintain it. More importantly, 3 percent of paper is lost; the average cost to recover a document is $120. It is estimated that 3 billion paper documents are buried in US businesses alone; it's those kind of numbers that gave birth to the electronic imaging industry.

Electronic Imaging Client/Server Architecture

Electronic imaging systems are inherently database-oriented, client/server applications (see Figure 31-2). The client PCs capture and manipulate the images; they serve as front ends to the data stored in the image servers. The client PC typically does the following:

■ The scanner attached to the client's PC digitizes the image through a process similar to that of a fax machine. (Not so coincidentally, fax machines sometimes serve as remote scanners.

■ After being digitized, the image is displayed and checked for quality; it is rescanned if necessary.

■ While the image is displayed, information is extracted from it by an operator who enters the data in the fields of a GUI form. At a minimum, the document is assigned a simple index and identification code so that it can be retrieved later. More sophisticated (and costly) applications automate the extraction of information from the image into the GUI form using intelligent character recognition or bar-code readers.

■ The images are compressed by software or a hardware coprocessor and then sent to the server where they get stored.

■ The client can always access the documents in the server and visually display them. An image can be reviewed, printed, faxed, annotated with red lines or electronic notes, and so on.

The server side of an imaging application manages a shared database of images. Image servers typically store all the structured information in an SQL database; the document itself (i.e., the BLOB) is stored in a file server. Large image servers can handle 200,000 documents or more per day. Images are big: the average compressed digitized image weighs in at about 75 to 100 KBytes, but they can be as large as 2.5 MBytes for medical X-rays and engineering drawings. Consequently, many imaging applications may require terabytes of online storage.

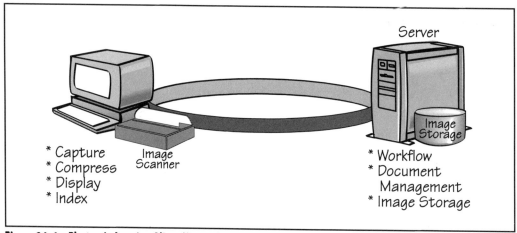

Figure 31-2. Electronic Imaging Client/Server Systems.

The image servers manage the workflow, security, image indexing (or metadata), and the pointers to the file systems where the BLOBs are physically stored. Here are some of their key functions:

■ Servers manage electronic renditions of file cabinets, which contain drawers and folders comprising documents. A document comprises a series of multimedia pages.

■ Workflow automates the movement of documents by moving them from one business operation to the next according to customer-defined rules and routes. Rules are used by the image server to control the routing, which may be based on document content, age, priority, workload balancing, external events, the day you need a document, database triggers, and other user-defined criteria.

■ User profiles and work queues are created and maintained on the server to specify the type of work users receive.

■ Reporting facilities allow managers to monitor the volume and types of work-in-process in the system, and to note its progress.

■ Documents are stored on various media; the server moves them around to optimize the delicate trade-off between storage cost and performance.

Groupware Multimedia Document Management

The groupware document management paradigm is a generalization of the electronic imaging file cabinet. The basic unit of storage in groupware such as Lotus Notes is the *document*. A Notes document has an extremely flexible structure; it can be tagged with properties such as *client*, *region*, and *subject*. A Notes document can have any number of BLOB-like *attachments* (or embedded objects). Notes supports a compound document architecture, which means that it can handle multiple data types—including text, images, graphics, voice, and video.

Related collections of Notes documents are stored in *databases* that can then be indexed and retrieved by any of the documents' properties, or by the actual contents of the documents. It also supports full-text indexing. Notes created its own document database technology from scratch; unlike the image vendors, it does not build on top of existing file and SQL database servers. We're dealing with a *new* groupware-specific, document-centric, multimedia-enabled, database technology.

Workflow: What Is It? Where Does It Come From?

Imagine submitting a home mortgage application and having it go through in a matter of hours. Workflow is the "up and coming" client/server technology that can be used to automatically route events (and work) from one program to the next in structured or unstructured client/server environments (see Figure 31-3). The "classical" workflow paradigm is a river that carries the flow of work from port to port and along the way the value gets added. Workflow defines the operations that must be visited along the way and what needs to be done when exceptions occur. The original work item may be merged with other work, transformed, or routed to

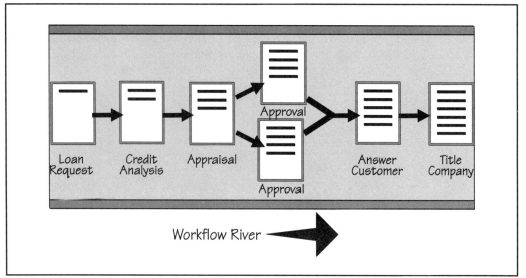

Figure 31-3. The Workflow River.

another workflow. It's quite a dynamic environment. Some workflows may be fuzzy and not understood very well; others are deterministic and highly repetitive. In all cases, these workflows are there to help us collaborate in getting work done.

To appreciate what workflow is all about, you must understand its origins. Workflow technology has its historical roots firmly planted in the world of image management and computer-integrated manufacturing technology. FileNet Corporation—an imaging vendor—was a pioneer of this technology in 1984. FileNet and other electronic imaging companies—including Viewstar, Sigma, and IBM's Image-Plus/2—discovered that workflow could be used to automate the high-volume, formerly paper-based processes (see Figure 31-4).

Workflow is especially applicable to "paper factories," large offices that routinely process documents representing business transactions (for example, loans, claims processing, and tax returns). Paper to these factories is what raw material is to manufacturing: "grist for the mill" that produces the organization's product. When the paper became an electronic image, workflow automated the movement of documents from one image processing operation to the next; both the workflow controller and the work are electronic renditions of real-life factory constructs.

The imaging workflow systems are costly, rigid, centralized, and typically require a highly-skilled IS professional to do the design and integration. These systems tend to be proprietary and cannot interface well with other applications. On the positive side, they can handle very large workloads and have excellent built-in security and

Chapter 31. Client/Server Groupware

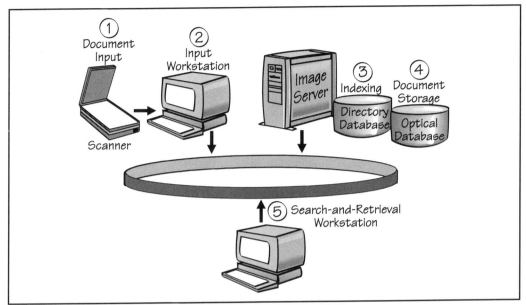

Figure 31-4. Workflow in Electronic Imaging Systems.

version controls. They are very good at scheduling document-related tasks and tracking them to completion. The cost of such systems start at $5,000 per seat.

The New Workflow Systems

Groupware introduces a new breed of client/server workflow software for the masses. The new workflow packages go beyond their imaging counterparts in the following areas:

■ **Support for ad hoc user needs.** The new workflow packages address both structured and unstructured process automation needs. They can automate well-understood processes as well as more nebulous ones.

■ **Low-cost.** The new workflow packages sell at PC software prices—expect to pay between $100 to $500 per seat.

■ **Integration with other applications.** The new workflow packages can integrate with existing applications by either spawning a process, or sending them some type of message-based event notification when their intervention is needed (using DDE, e-mail, and so on). For example, the FlowMark/2 workflow package can be used to schedule Datahub/2 tasks and automate some very complicated database management operations. Applications can also call the workflow manager to participate in or initiate a workflow process.

- ***Programming with visual metaphors.*** The new workflow packages support drag-and-drop iconic manipulations for creating workflows and defining business rules. They typically provide tools for designing forms (or importing them from a GUI-Builder); designing sequential or conditional routes; and scripting languages to specify the business logic. The routes and workflow definitions are sometimes stored in SQL databases. Templates are provided to help "jump start" the creation of a workflow application.

- ***Integration with e-mail, MOM, or RPC.*** The new workflow packages use loosely coupled forms of communication, such as e-mail or MOM message queues, to inform humans or programs that their intervention is required. Action Technologies, for example, defines a set of message formats that can be conveyed using all the popular mail transports. These formats are used to convey, capture, or initiate workflow commands and actions. Action also supports the transmission of workflow commands using DDE, Named Pipes, RPCs, and peer-to-peer protocols.

- ***Provide facilities for tracking work-in-progress.*** Most of the packages allow you to query the status of work-in-progress and what stage of the workflow it's in. Some of the better packages help you identify inefficiencies in the routes and bottlenecks.

- ***Provide users with tools to complete an action.*** In addition to notifying users that an action is required, some of the better tools provide users with help panels that tell them how to complete the action and sometimes even the tools to perform the requested action. The user may also be able to obtain information about where the task fits in the overall process.

- ***Provide APIs that let developers customize workflow services.*** Of course, no standard APIs for workflow exist, so this feature is very implementation-specific.

The heart of a workflow system is the server that receives requests and events from the various client workstations and interprets them according to a user-defined workflow. The client agents are programmed to execute the repetitive parts of a user-defined script. The workflow server acts as a clearinghouse that determines what needs to be done next based on the global state of the system (and the rules). It usually maintains a database that dynamically tracks the work-in-progress and contains instructions (and rules) for what needs to be done at a given instance of a workflow process.

Workflow Models

*T*he *three R's of workflow are: Routes, Rules, and Roles. In order to qualify in my book as a true workflow development tool, the product must offer a way to define and automate these three things.*

— *Ronni T. Marshak, Editor, Workgroup Computing Report (May, 1993)*

The workflow software must create electronic renditions of real-world collaborative activity. The "real world," however, covers a wide spectrum of activities from tax return processing to co-authoring a paper. These activities differ radically in their structure, number of users, flow of control, and process predictability. Almost any workflow can be represented using raw code; however, the trick is to minimize custom development using shrinkwrapped workflow models. The workflow packages must be able to visually define who does "what, when, and to what"; parallel routes; logic for dynamically determining routes at run time; and the exceptions to any rules. It must deal with Ronni Marshak's three R's: routes, rules, and roles.

- **Routes** define the paths along which the object moves. They also include definitions of the objects—documents, forms, events, electronic containers and parts, messages, and so on—that are to be routed.

- **Rules** define what information is routed and to whom. Rules define both the conditions the workflow must meet to traverse to the next step and how to handle exceptions: "If loan is over $100,000, send it to the supervisor or else send it to the next hop."

- **Roles** define job functions independently of the people who do it. For example, the "supervisor" role can be handled by users "Mary" and "Jeri." Any one of these people can do the job; just put the job on the next available supervisor's queue.

Groupware packages must provide the three R's for automating well-defined applications—*process-oriented workflow*—as well as the more ad hoc spontaneous type of applications—*ad hoc workflow*. Here's the differences between the two models:

- ***Process-oriented workflows*** are used to automate business systems that have definable, repetitive, and well understood policies and procedures. For example, a mortgage loan is an understood business process that goes through a prescribed set of procedures. Loans are processed in the same way every day. The routing of the work is automatic and requires very little user involvement. It's like taking a train. This type of workflow is a natural candidate for TP Monitor initiated sagas or long-lived transactions.

■ *Ad hoc workflow* deals with short-lived and unstructured work processes. They can involve task forces of people working on a common problem. Consider, a short-duration project with a deadline. The workflow is used to assign roles, track and route work-in-progress, monitor deadlines, and track who got what and when. It's an excellent tool for tracking work among people who are physically dispersed. This type of workflow is like driving a car. The navigation is driver-centric, but you need road signs and a map to figure out where you're going. The driver also needs to know the set of options available at every turn. Ad hoc workflow is used for incremental automation—leaving anything the system can't handle to humans. It takes full advantage of desktop power to help humans navigate through the country roads.

Workflow Routes

Modern workflow packages support the same type of topologies that are common in human communications (see Figure 31-5). Typically, these packages let you specify a route that defines the set operations a unit-of-work traverses. They also let you define rules that specify acceptance conditions for moving from one operation to the next. You can create sequential routes, parallel routes (alternate paths), routes with feedback loops (for example, rework), circular routes, wheel-spoked routes, and fully interconnected routes. The first four routes are used in process-oriented workflows, while the last two are used in more ad hoc workflows.

Workflow Splits and Joins

Workflow objects can go off on different routes and then merge back into a single route at a "rendezvous" point. In addition, a workflow object can be split into multiple parts and merged back into a single part as it moves down the workflow river (see Figure 31-6). This is done using splits and joins, as explained in the following examples:

■ *And-Splits* are used to explode an object into many parts. For example, a set of chips on a wafer are tracked as a group until the chips are split with each going their own way.

■ *Or-Splits* are used to peel off a few parts from a group. For example, a few chips may be split off the wafer for random testing; they rejoin the group later using an Or-Join.

■ *Or-Joins* allow certain members to rejoin the group. For example, in a manufacturing line, a defective part can go to a rework operation and it can then rejoin the group when it's fixed using an Or-Join.

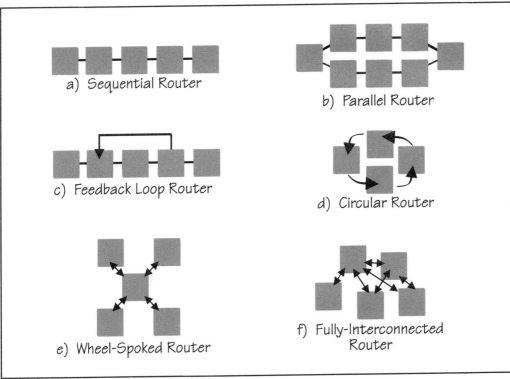

Figure 31-5. Workflows Come in All Patterns.

- **And-Joins** are rendezvous points that are used to group together objects so that they move in a route as a group. For example, an And-Join can be used to package many units into a container that can be shipped as a unit.

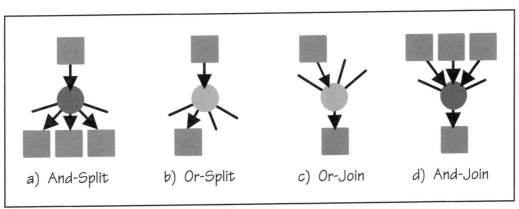

Figure 31-6. Workflow: Splitting and Joining Work.

FYI

The Action Workflow Model

Briefing

Action Technologies Workflow Model—an innovative Windows and OS/2 work-flow product—is based on research by Terry Winograd and Fernando Flores on how people communicate to make an action happen. Action identifies for each unit of work in a workflow the *performer* who is doing the actual work for a *customer*—the person for whom the work is being done and who must be satisfied. Each step in the workflow involves a negotiation loop between a customer and a performer (see Figure 31-7). At the end of each step the conditions must be fulfilled to have a satisfied customer.

According to the Action Technologies methodology, every action in a workflow consists of four phases in which customers and performers coordinate with each other (see Figure 31-8):

1. *Preparation* is when the customer prepares to ask for something—often, for example, by filling out a form or preparing an e-mail.

2. *Negotiation* is when the customer and performer agree on the work to be done and on the conditions of satisfaction—exactly what must be done to complete this job to the satisfaction of the customer.

3. *Performance* is the phase in which the actual job is done. At the end the performer reports to the customer that the work requested has completed.

4. *Acceptance* of a job or task is not considered complete until the customer signs off and expresses satisfaction to the performer.

At any phase there may be additional actions, such as clarifications, further negotiations, and changes of commitments by the participants. The Action Technologies approach does more than just coordinate between tasks: It helps specify the client/server contract and does it all very recursively. The entire application is a client/server task that gets broken down recursively into sub-tasks as defined by the workflow. The application is a series of "who is getting what done for whom" steps and the conditions of satisfaction. Action provides a set of visual tools to help capture the negotiation semantics and automatically generates the scripts from them. □

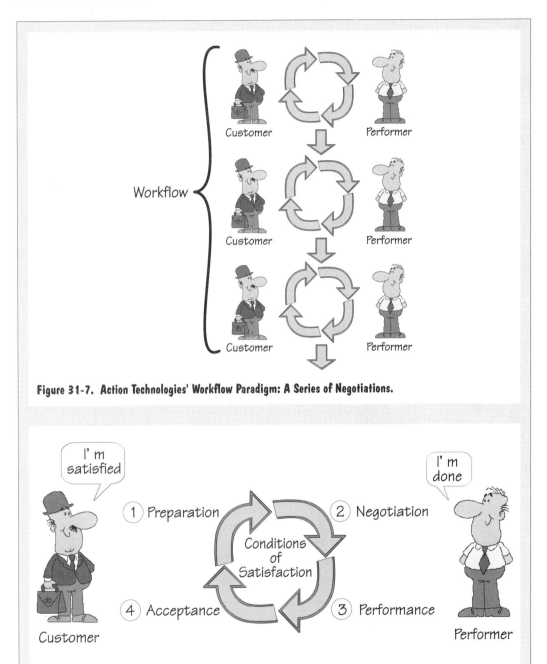

Figure 31-7. Action Technologies' Workflow Paradigm: A Series of Negotiations.

Figure 31-8. Action Technologies' Workflow: The Negotiation Details.

Workflow: The Bottom Line

Workflow helps bring the information to the people who can act on it. It coordinates existing software and tracks the processes to make sure the work gets done by the right people. Workflow by itself cannot do too much; but with other software—such as e-mail, databases, and desktop productivity tools—it can create some dynamite combinations.

The Electronic Mail Component

For many organizations, all the groupware they need may be an e-mail package that's closely tied to group calendaring and scheduling features. This is the philosophy behind *WordPerfect Office*, which has more than one million copies in use. Of course, groupware allows you to do much more with electronic mail; it uses it to extend the client/server reach. Why is e-mail so important to groupware? Because it matches the way people work. E-mail can be used to send something to others without making a real-time connection; the recipients don't have to respond to senders until they're ready to do so. In addition, it's one of the easiest ways for electronic processes to communicate with humans. And it's ubiquitous.

According to IDC, there were 50 million electronic mailboxes in 1992—over half of them on PC LANs. IDC foresees that the number of LAN e-mail users will grow tenfold by 1997. Mail-enabled groupware applications can take advantage of this very extensive mail infrastructure to send and receive information and communicate directly with users—electronic mail is one of the most hassle-free forms of distributed interactions. E-mail front ends are not the only way to send messages. The new mail APIs, such as VIM and MAPI, are designed to let any application work with the mail messaging infrastructure. Most electronic mailboxes will soon be interconnected through mail backbones and gateways.

The Lotus cc:Mail Success Story

Soapbox

Lotus's cc:Mail is the industry's most popular and easy-to-use mail package (four million seats). It's the only e-mail product that runs on all major client platforms including DOS, Windows, OS/2, Macintosh, and Unix. The OS/2 version of cc:Mail is seamlessly integrated with the Workplace Shell (see Figure 31-9). You can drag-and-drop any Workplace Shell object and e-mail it. Or you can right-click on an object and e-mail it using its pop-up menu. It doesn't get any easier. The market seems to know a good product when it sees one—the OS/2 version of cc:Mail sold over 200,000 copies. ❑

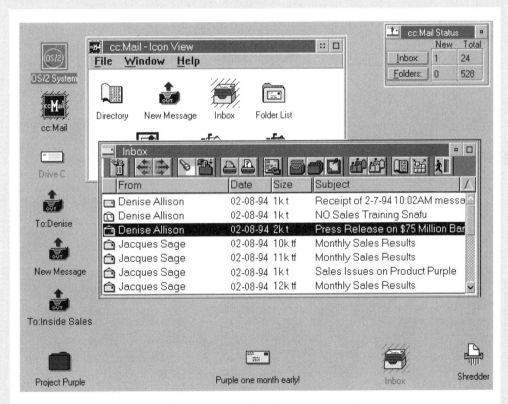

Figure 31-9. Lotus cc:Mail—Full Integration With the OS/2 Workplace Shell.

The Electronic Mail Infrastructure

Most LAN-based e-mail systems are very good at handling mail within workgroups and departments. However, these networks are still poor at providing intergalactic mail capabilities. Fortunately, most of the infrastructure components required to create ubiquitous mail backbones are coming into place. It's important to note the distinction between the mail application—the front end—and the mail infrastructure—the back end. Ideally, the front end and back end should communicate along client/server lines—this is what Lotus Notes does today (see Figure 31-10). Unfortunately, most LAN-based e-mail packages bundle the front end and the back end in the same process and use a file server on the LAN for the mail store. This is the approach used by Lotus cc:Mail, the most popular e-mail product in the industry. Most PC LAN e-mail products follow the cc:Mail file server approach, but that's changing. For example, Lotus is redesigning cc:Mail along client/server lines. Both cc:Mail and Notes will eventually share the same back-end mail server.

However, it takes more than cc:Mail or Notes to create an intergalactic mail infrastructure. How do you connect cc:Mail or Notes to other mail networks? There are two ways to do that:

■ *Gateways*—you'll need one gateway for each different e-mail system you need to access. But this could quickly turn into a management nightmare. Gateways also limit some functions like the capability to search for an address. They're also poor at providing synchronized directory management services, efficient message routing, global system management, and so on. **LAN Gateway/2** is an example of an advanced e-mail gateway product that runs on OS/2. It will eventually support the exchange of e-mail between the following products: Lotus Notes, cc:Mail, PROFS, SNADS, OV/400, OV/MVS, and OV/VM. The main benefit of this product is that it works with existing e-mail systems without requiring any gateway code to be installed on the mainframes.

■ *Mail backbone*—you'll need one gateway to the backbone, period. But the question is: Which backbone? The contenders are X.400, an international standard, Novell's Message Handling Service (MHS), and the Internet's Simple Message Transport Protocol (SMTP) mail service. The pendulum seems to be swinging in X.400's favor—it is much simpler and less expensive than it once was (see the following Details box). Of course, MHS, SMTP, and X.400 backbones will most likely be interconnected via gateways. So all the backbones may win.

The separation of mail functions along client/server lines will facilitate the creation of front-end clients that are totally independent of the back end mail engines. We'll now look at the mail API standards that will help bring this about.

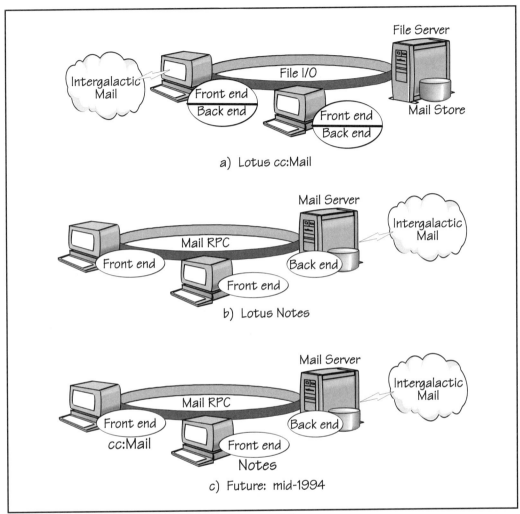

Figure 31-10. Client/Server E-Mail: Lotus Notes Versus cc:Mail.

The New E-Mail APIs: VIM, MAPI, and CMC

A new hot area in our industry is *mail-enabled applications*. The primary purpose of these applications is not mail, but they still need to access mail services. Most groupware products fall into that category. E-mail becomes just another form of client/server middleware. *Electronic Data Interchange (EDI)* is becoming an important source of mail-enabled business transactions (see Details box). Personal agents will be making extensive use of EDI to pay your bills and do your electronic shopping. And e-mail by itself supports the exchange of faxes, files, BLOBs, documents, and workflow events at an application-to-application level—it's a pow-

X.400 Mail Backbones

Details

The X.400 mail protocol is finally hitting the critical mass as the common mail backbone for the industry. It has been adopted by all the major public service providers across the world. Most e-mail vendors—including Lotus, Microsoft, HP, IBM, and SoftSwitch—are coming out with X.400 products. Several large vendors, such as IBM and DEC use X.400 as a way to link their messaging systems. An X.400 version of cc:Mail should be available by the time you read this book—it will give X.400 a friendly look on all platforms. X.400 provides the following features:

- **Support for BLOB exchanges.** X.400 defines a way to exchange images, fax, and other binary attachments to messages.

- **Electronic Data Interchange (EDI) support.** EDI defines the contents and structures of messages that are used in electronic business exhanges (for example, invoices, billing forms, and so on). X.400 consolidates both e-mail and EDI on the same backbones. It maintains audit trails of EDI exchanges as required by the X.435 EDI standard.

- **Support for distributed directories.** The X.500 standard, developed as part of the X.400 1988 specification, defines how a single system image is provided using directories that are distributed over multiple nodes.

- **Security.** X.400 adheres to the X.509 security standard that specifies the mechanisms for password identification, digital signatures, encryption, and audit trails.

- **Mail API.** The X.400 Common Mail Calls (CMC) API combines subsets of MAPI and VIM, and it has been adopted as a "compromise" API by both parties. We'll have more to say about that in the mail API section.

Clearly X.400 offers a secure, standards based approach to creating electronic mail backbones.

We'll now look at what it takes to put an X.400 backbone together using commercially available products that run on an OS/2 platform. An X.400 backbone consists of a network of *Message Transfer Agents (MTAs)*. The MTA is a piece of server software that stores, forwards, and routes X.400 messages across a backbone of MTAs (see Figure 31-11). The *User Agent (UA)* is the X.400 client component that talks to the MTA. A mail client application talks to its local UA, which in turn talks to the MTA. The MTAs talk to each other and create a mail backbone.

Retix provides a UA/MTA client/server package that runs on OS/2 (it sells for $6000). Outside clients can communicate with X.400 mailboxes using gateways. Lotus (Link), Retix, and Notework provide gateways to Novell's MHS backbone. Gateways to the Internet's SMTP are available from Retix and Notework. So you can create a relatively low-cost X.400 mail backbone—including gateways—using OS/2. ❏

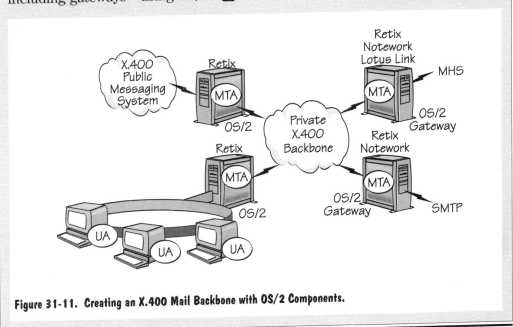

Figure 31-11. Creating an X.400 Mail Backbone with OS/2 Components.

erful form of middleware that may already be in place in an organization (in that case, it's free and ready to be exploited). One of the main advantages of using e-mail over lower level APIs—like NetBIOS or RPC—is the store-and-forward capability that's built into the mail system.

So how does an application become mail enabled? By using e-mail APIs that allow programs to directly access mail transport services, mail directories, and message stores (see Figure 31-12). This used to be the *private domain* of mail vendors. The newly-exposed APIs are making it easy for developers to mail-enable their applications without becoming e-mail experts. What kind of functions can we expect from an open e-mail API that can work across multiple mail transports?

The following is a composite of functions provided by the three leading contenders for the "common" mail API:

- **Simple messaging services.** These are functions for addressing, sending, and receiving a mail message—including files and enclosures—an optional user interface is provided for logon, addressing the mail, and text entry.

- **Message store manipulation.** This includes opening and reading messages delivered to a message store, saving messages, deleting messages, navigating through the contents of the store, searching for messages, and moving messages across containers. The message store can be external to the mail package. For example, a message store could be an SQL database, a Lotus Notes document database, or an Object Database. The same APIs should work across all stores. Message stores contain a wealth of information that is of interest to groupware applications. We expect to see a lot of exciting developments in this area.

- **Address book and directory services.** An address book is a collection of individual or group—i.e., distribution lists—recipients. Address books can be personal (i.e., cached on the local system) or part of a global directory. The API should let you read and write directory information as well as navigate through hierarchies of address books. You should be able to add/remove groups or members from address books and search through them.

- **Mail object manipulation.** The APIs should let you access the subcomponents of a mail object. For example, a message may consist of heading fields and various data items.

- **Authentication and security services.** This includes APIs that lets an application log on to the mail system and authenticate its users.

- **Service provider interface.** This interface allows service providers to supply their own back-end services to the front-end mail APIs. For example, a Lotus Notes mail server is accessed through the proprietary Lotus RPC. We've already encountered the concept of the service provider interface in the SQL CLI section in Part 4 (both IDAPI and ODBC support one). The service provider interface creates an open environment for the providers of mail services; it doesn't do much for the developers of mail-enabled applications.

The separation of the mail front end from the back end allows a single API set to work with multiple mail back ends. In addition, different vendors can offer their own specialized plug-in services (for example, message stores). So what is the common API set that gives us access to all this mail server power?

Surprise, the e-mail industry has more than one common, open, API set. Remember, we *always* choose from more than one standard. In the case of e-mail, we started

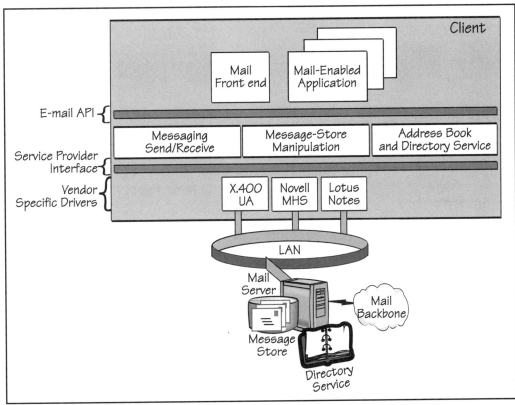

Figure 31-12. A Generic API for E-Mail.

with five standards. However, Novell and Apple may be gravitating toward VIM, so that leaves us with three key ones: VIM, MAPI, and CMC. Let's find out what these standards can do and who is behind them.

■ **Vendor Independent Messaging (VIM)** is an interface that is jointly backed by Lotus, Apple, IBM, Borland, MCI, Oracle, WordPerfect, and Novell. VIM was designed from the ground up as a cross-platform interface. Apple will provide a version of VIM for Macintosh; Novell will support VIM on MHS; and Lotus provides it on all the cc:Mail and Notes client platforms. VIM consists of 55 API calls—10 of which are optional—that support simple mail, message store, and address book services. VIM also provides a *Simple Mail Interface (SMI)* that consists of two calls: SMISendMail and SMISendDocuments. The main strength of VIM is its cross-platform support and the vendors who are behind it. Its main weakness is that it does not provide a Service Provider Interface (SPI).

■ **Messaging API (MAPI)** is Microsoft's WOSA offering for e-mail. MAPI is a Windows first client API—it's a Windows DLL—that works primarily with

Microsoft Mail back ends. MAPI is also getting endorsements from mail server vendors including DEC, HP, Banyan, CompuServe, and SoftSwitch. The MAPI front-end APIs are written to the Windows *Mail Spooler*. Mail server providers can redirect the Mail Spooler calls to their back-end services using the MAPI Service Provider Interface. Simple MAPI consists of 12 API calls that provide simple mail, message store, and address book services. *Extended MAPI*—a future technology that will be included in Chicago—will support 100 API calls that allow applications to handle large numbers of messages, filter through mail, manage message stores, and access complex addressing information. Extended MAPI exposes the Service Provider Interface (SPI) to the application; it defines three types of SPIs: Transport, Address Book, and Message Store. MAPI's strength is in its Windows packaging; its weakness is that it is specific to Windows.

■ ***Common Mail Calls (CMC)*** is the X.400 API Association (XAPIA) interface. It was published in June 1993 as part of a negotiated truce in the mail API wars— both the VIM and MAPI camp endorse it. Microsoft provides a free DLL library for CMC, and Lotus will do the same for VIM developers (it will also be included in cc:Mail and Notes). CMC consists of 10 API calls—a subset of the VIM and MAPI calls (see Figure 31-13). It does not include the advanced VIM functions or Extended MAPI functionality. CMC only does simple mail.

The first round of the mail API wars is over—everyone won. Round two of the mail API wars is just starting. On the VIM front, work is continuing on advanced e-mail functions; Lotus, IBM, Action, and Plexus are working on Workflow VIM APIs and a VIM-aligned consortium is working on VIC (see next section). Meanwhile on the MAPI front, Microsoft is working on Extended MAPI (see the next Soapbox).

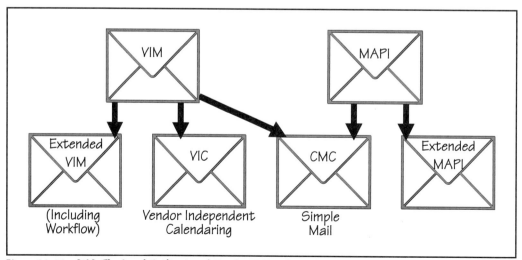

Figure 31-13. CMC: The Grand Unification of Simple MAPI and Simple VIM.

Soapbox

Thank You for CMC

CMC is a very positive development in our industry. It's an example of how user power can stop the mindless proliferation of standards. Apparently the mail API debate irked enough users that it forced vendors to agree to work together through the revived X.400 API Association (XAPIA). XAPIA was originally formed to create an API to X.400 services. The result of this revival was the CMC standard—a poor man's e-mail API. CMC can only do simple tasks like reading or sending messages or looking up an address. Unlike VIM and MAPI, it doesn't support fancy mail tasks like enclosures and interfacing to message stores. But we are still very thankful for CMC—a "baby step" in the right direction.

CMC frees developers from having to write separate versions of their programs for MAPI and VIM. However, the mail API wars are not over yet. In fact, they're just starting. Groupware, calendaring, data collection, and personal agent applications still need the advanced mail functions that MAPI and VIM are defining: interfaces to message stores, message filters, calendaring, scheduling, and advanced directory services. These are the "crown jewels" of e-mail—it's literally where all the big e-mail client/server money is going to be made. Unfortunately, these functions are not part of CMC. And they will be much harder to unify than simple mail. The good news is that at the 1993 XAPIA conference, key participants discussed the merging of VIM with CMC to provide CMC with the needed functionality. So we may have more to be thankful for. ❏

Scheduling and Calendaring

Scheduling is a native groupware technology. There's an extensive technology behind the electronic scheduling of meetings, sharing calendars and "to do" lists, and all that good stuff. This technology was built from the ground up on a solid client/server foundation. The client front ends make excellent use of GUI facilities; the servers use background tasks, shared data, and triggers to manage and schedule group events. Now imagine if we could combine this scheduling and calendaring technology with workflow managers, e-mail, and multimedia document stores. This could result would be some dynamite combinations of groupware. A workflow manager would be able to automatically add a meeting to the calendars of all the participants, schedule a meeting room, and send them reminder notices. Or a workflow manager could consult the group calendars to discover who is on vacation and route (or re-route) work accordingly.

So how do we get to the services provided by the scheduling and calendaring servers? Using APIs and client/server exchanges, of course. But which APIs? This is where the *Vendor-Independent Calendaring (VIC)* API effort comes into the picture. The VIC effort spearheaded by IBM and Lotus allows VIM-compliant programs—such as Lotus Organizer 1.1, WordPerfect Office 4.0, and IBM's Time and Place/2—to seamlessly exchange scheduling and calendar data. The proposed VIC standard is based on the client/server calendar and scheduling APIs of the OS/2 *Time and Place/2* product (see the next Briefing box). Of course, VIC is not the only game in town; Microsoft is developing similar group-scheduling and calendaring capabilities for Chicago's Extended MAPI. In addition, XAPIA launched an effort to define a standard for LAN-based calendar and schedule exchanges. However, XAPIA is moving in the direction of a "common file format" as an interim solution until APIs are defined. The good news is that the standards competition is heating up, and we may end up with some sort of "open" calendar and scheduling service API on client/server LANs.

Time and Place/2 Version 2.0

Briefing

Time and Place/2 is a client/server group scheduling and calendaring application. The clients can run on DOS, Windows, or OS/2; the server is a 32-bit OS/2 application. Time and Place screens use GUI renditions of daily, weekly, and monthly paper desktop calendars. The LAN-based calendar lets you schedule events and "to do" reminders for yourself and for other users on the network. An event definition window lets you specify and describe an event such as a meeting; select a date, start, and stop times; search a directory for names of individuals or groups to include; reserve a room; and even assign a repeating status (see Figure 31-14). A notification function informs the group of the new events or tasks that have been added to their calendars. A VIM e-mail interface allows notifications to be sent to users who are not part of the shared calendaring network.

Time and Place/2 provides simple calendaring APIs that enable programmers and ISVs to develop client applications that can access the group calendaring and event databases. These are the APIs that are being proposed for the VIC standard. In addition, Time and Place/2 supports the synchronization of address books with Lotus Notes and cc:Mail. It can also link with the calendar functions of host-based users via Time and Place Connectivity/2, an OS/2 based program that links with PROFS, OfficeVision/VM, and OfficeVision/MVS. This link supports free-time searches, interactive calendar viewing, and calendar updating across all these environments. This is all done in real time. Host and LAN users can all see and use the calendars in each other's environments. In summary, this may be the first federated group calendaring and scheduling application on client/server LANs. ☐

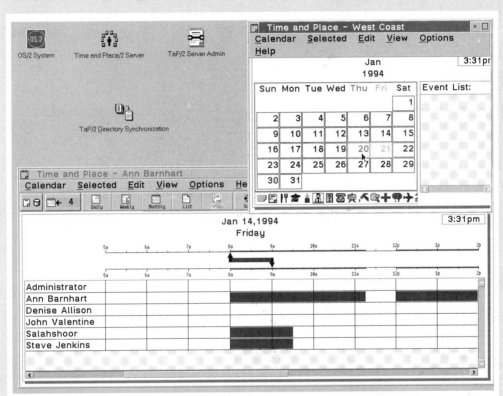

Figure 31-14. Time and Place/2: Client/Server Event Management and Calendaring.

Conferencing

Conferencing, or "electronic meetings," is another native groupware technology. Millions of PC users are now discovering the wonders of conferencing through electronic bulletin boards on CompuServe, Prodigy, and Internet. We can divide client/server conferencing technology into two types: realtime and anytime.

Realtime Conferencing

Realtime conferences allow groups to interactively collaborate on a joint project using instantly refreshed document replicas, electronic whiteboards, different-colored cursors with the initials of each participant, and a designated chairperson that controls access to the shared document. Participants can speak on their microphones and see each other in video windows on their computer screens. Eventually—when we get the cheap bandwidth—we will be able to augment these conferences with movie clips. Conferencing packages, like IBM's Person to Person/2 and FutureLabs TalkShow, are selling for as little as $250 per seat, making this technology affordable for the first time.

Anytime Conferencing

Anytime conferences allow people to participate in the group discussion when and where they want. You can join the discussion, add your own two cents, and leave at anytime. And because you can jump into an ongoing discussion at anytime, you can see the entire discussion in context. This flexible environment helps articulate spontaneous groups around a topic of interest—customer support, operating system advocacy, shared problems, and tracking projects. The medium is open and democratic. Everyone gets the opportunity to express themselves—ideas are never lost.

Using replicas, the system makes all the contributions available to all participants in close to realtime. The contributions then become part of the group memory—they are stored for posterity in the document databases that manage this wealth of shared information. As these conferences flourish and multiply, tools are provided for viewing and navigating through the mazes of information they contain. Lotus Notes is the premier technology for the creation of these electronic discussion groups. Its enormous popularity is an indication of the mass acceptance of the asynchronous electronic meeting place paradigm.

Conferences provide one more technology that helps articulate the "group" in groupware. Electronic meeting environments provide an almost bottomless set of opportunities for client/server technology. We're just seeing the tip of the iceberg.

GROUPWARE: BRINGING IT ALL TOGETHER

This was a long chapter that dealt with many of the emerging technologies that form a new genre of client/server software called "groupware." What's new is the synergy gained by bringing the pieces together on client/server networks. Groupware supports the asynchronous distribution of information to groups. It's a flexible technology that can adapt to the way people do business in both structured and ad hoc settings. The e-mail foundation helps bring humans into the loop. The information that is collected and distributed can be highly unstructured and rich with meaning. Workflow allows the creation of highly intelligent "routing clouds" that deliver information to the points where it can be processed. It also creates what Forrester calls "value-added rivers" as information moves from one point to the next along an intelligent route.

Soapbox

Groupware: Is It Hype?

Groupware lets us move from personal applications to interpersonal applications. In so doing, it's creating new client/server markets and new types of applications.

— **Jeri Edwards (February, 1994)**

Like every new client/server technology, groupware is getting its share of high-decibel marketing hype. What makes it worse is that any multiuser piece of software can be called "groupware." All client/server software deals with group communications in some form or another. Even though we carefully defined the constituent technologies in groupware, there is still a tremendous amount of fuzziness associated with the term. You can't find two people—even from Lotus—that can give you a common definition of Lotus Notes; yet Notes is selling like hot cakes. So it must be fulfilling some need somewhere.

We believe that any new technology will be fuzzy at first. The trick is to sort out reality from marketing hype, and understand what we can do with the technology. In the case of groupware, the opportunity is in creating client/server applications—unlike any we've ever seen—using multimedia document databases, e-mail, workflow, conferencing, calendaring, and scheduling technology. The groupware industry is creating the common interfaces between these disparate pieces. All we need to do is learn how to use them and perhaps even integrate them with database warehouses, TP Monitors, and the distributed object technology that we will be covering in Part 7. ❑

Chapter 32

Lotus Notes, FlowMark/2, and ImagePlus/2

Notes enables rich forms of human communications by exploiting the true potential of client/server technology; it helps create more than just reborn, downsized versions of traditional apps.

— **John Landry, Lotus Senior VP and Chief Technologist (September, 1993)**

Again, we're faced with a quandry: Which of the hundreds of OS/2 groupware products should we cover in this chapter? The first pruning decision was not to cover any of the *basic* groupware component products—including e-mail, multimedia servers, group calendaring, group scheduling, and conferencing. Instead, we decided to pick three products that cover the three key facets of client/server groupware applications: multimedia-document database management, workflow automation, and electronic imaging.

Picking the multimedia database product was a no-brainer; it had to be **Lotus Notes**—95% of Lotus Notes servers run on OS/2, and there's no other product on any platform that compares with it. When it came to workflow and imaging, there were plenty of excellent choices, and we could only pick one for each category. Our representative workflow product is **FlowMark/2,** a new kid on the block from IBM. It could have just as easily been **Floware** from Recognition International, **TeamWare** from Decathlon Data Systems, **Quality at Work** from Quality Decision Management, **TeamFlow** from ICL, **Electronic Workforce** from Edify, **Action-Workflow** from Action Technologies, or **Keyfile** from Keyfile Corp. Our representative imaging product is **ImagePlus/2** from IBM, which is in the process of being ported to all the IBM platforms and several Unix variants. We could have picked **Omnidesk** from Sigma Imaging Systems, **Docutrieve** from Image Automation, **Lotus Document Imaging** from Lotus, **AdaptFile 5000** from Adaptive Information Systems, and many others.

LOTUS NOTES 3.0

The combination of the maturing of Notes Release 3 and the competition's inability to understand the Notes phenomenon virtually assures Notes' domination of the client/server workgroup applications for the foreseeable future...Notes is still breakthrough technology and is still without real competition.

> — David S. Marshak, Seybold Group
> (March, 1993)

Lotus Notes—now in its third release—is the premier client/server groupware product in the industry. Even though Notes has been in the field for over three years and has sold over 500,000 seats, it still remains a mystery to the vast majority of PC users. It's even a mystery to its competitors. Some call it a "cute bulletin board," others label it as "glorified e-mail," and some SQL purists pooh-pooh it as—heaven forbid—an "unstructured database." In reality, Notes is a multifaceted, client/server groupware product. And as we know from the last chapter, it is hard to define groupware in 25 words or less. The secret of a good groupware package is that it creates a whole that is *much* more than the sum of the parts. Notes does this very well.

So What Is Lotus Notes?

Lotus Notes allows groups of users to interact and share information that can be of a highly unstructured nature. It provides a client/server application development and run-time environment that provides the following functions (see Figure 32-1):

■ *A document database server* stores and manages multiuser client access to semi-structured data—including text, images, audio, and video.

■ *An e-mail server* manages multiuser client access to mail.

■ *A backbone server/server infrastructure* supports both mail routing and database replication. The replication mechanism synchronizes copies of the same database, which can reside on multiple server (or client) machines. Notes comes with a mail backbone infrastructure; X.400 is available as an optional component.

■ *A GUI client environment* presents views of the document databases and provides an electronic mail front end. Users can navigate through the databases and their document contents. Views are stored queries that act as filters for the information in the databases. The e-mail front end is just a specialized view of a mail database. Notes can attach GUI forms (private or public) to the various databases that are used for data entry.

■ *Distributed services* include electronic signatures, security and access control lists, database administration services, system management, and an X.500 based global namespace.

■ *Application development tools* include a GUI forms generator, tools and templates for creating databases, a primitive scripting language consisting of *formulas*, and an open API set—including the Notes API, VIM, and DataLens (SQL access). ODBC support is in plan for mid-1994 release.

All Notes communications—client/server and server/server—are done using a proprietary RPC. Notes supports client/server drivers for NetBEUI, TPC/IP, IPX/SPX, and AppleTalk stacks. Optional APPC and X.25 drivers are available for server/server communications.

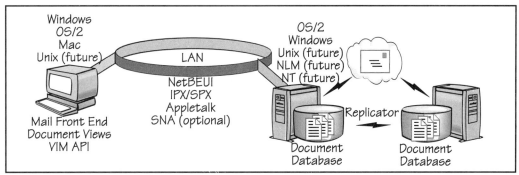

Figure 32-1. The Components of Lotus Notes.

The Multimedia Document Database

Ray Ozzie, founder of Iris Associates, a company that developed Notes under contract to Lotus, describes the foundation of the Notes architecture as a "database engine for semi-structured and unstructured information." Ozzie's model of a database is more akin to computer conferencing than Online Transaction Processing (OLTP). The Notes database was designed as a vehicle for gathering and disseminating all types of information; it was not meant to be a "database of record" that reflects the real-time state of the business. In this respect, Notes is more like an Information Warehouse except that the data tends to be highly eclectic. Another way of putting it is that Ray Ozzie was more interested in adding and capturing real-time information than providing synchronized access to shared data for updates. You'll get a better feel for this after we explain the Lotus Notes replication model.

The primary commodity in a Notes system is a semi-structured, multimedia *document* that can contain a variety of data types—including voice, BLOBs, video, and multifont text (see Figure 32-2). A Notes system organizes, stores, replicates, and provides shared access to documents. Related collections of Notes documents are stored in a *database*, which can then be indexed and retrieved by any of the documents' properties, or by the actual contents of the documents. Notes supports full-text indexing and searching (see next Details box). A Notes *document* consists of a set of fields, also known as *properties*; each has a name, type, and value. For example, a Notes document can be tagged with properties such as *client, region, subject*. The regions can contain any number of BLOB-like *attachments* (or embedded files). Embedded files are managed and organized as part of a Notes document.

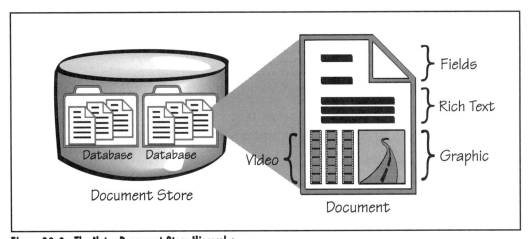

Figure 32-2. The Notes Document Store Hierarchy.

Notes Release 3 supports databases that can be up to 1 GByte in size (up from 300 MBytes in Release 2.1). More importantly, Release 3 removes any limitations on the number of documents in a database (the limit was around 20,000 documents in Release 2.1). Notes stores an entire database in a single file. A Notes application typically consists of many databases that are organized by topic. Again, the Notes concept of a database is more akin to conferencing (data is organized by topic) rather than relational DBMSs (all data is organized in a single database consisting of multiple tables).

Notes Database Replication

Like information warehouses, Notes allows databases to be replicated across servers (and clients). Unlike the warehouses we covered in Part 4, Notes has no notion of a master database—it uses replicas. The *replicator* is responsible for bidirectionally adding, deleting, or updating documents among all *replicas* of the database. Notes uses replication as a means to disseminate (or broadcast) information across geographically distributed locations.

The Notes replicator supports both full and partial replication and has a tunable level of consistency based on the desired frequency of replication. Notes time-stamps all new and edited (i.e., updated) documents that are known to have replicas. Unattended servers can dial each other up, compare notes, and swap changes at times configured by an administrator. You can also store replicas on client workstations and initiate swaps from there.

Notes Release 3 introduced *background replication*, which allows Notes laptop clients to continue working in Notes while replication is taking place in the background. Laptop users will find replication to be very helpful for on-the-road activity. You copy a Notes database, work on it, and then swap changes with the server when you can make a connection (see Figure 32-3). *Selective replication* limits the sections in documents that get replicated. You can choose not to replicate binary attachments to save on local disk space. You can also limit the size of each document to be replicated (for example, the first 200 characters). Or you can choose to only replicate unread messages from your boss.

This loosely synchronized style of information update is adequate for most conferencing applications, but it is a far cry from the synchronous two-phase commit updates used in OLTP applications. So how are concurrent updates handled? Prior to Notes Release 3, if two users simultaneously updated a server-based document, the first save was accepted and the next save was notified that it was overwriting someone else's changes. The decision of whether or not to overwrite the data was left to the user (not a very comforting thought if you were the first user). Notes Release 3 introduced a versioning capability that lets an edited document become

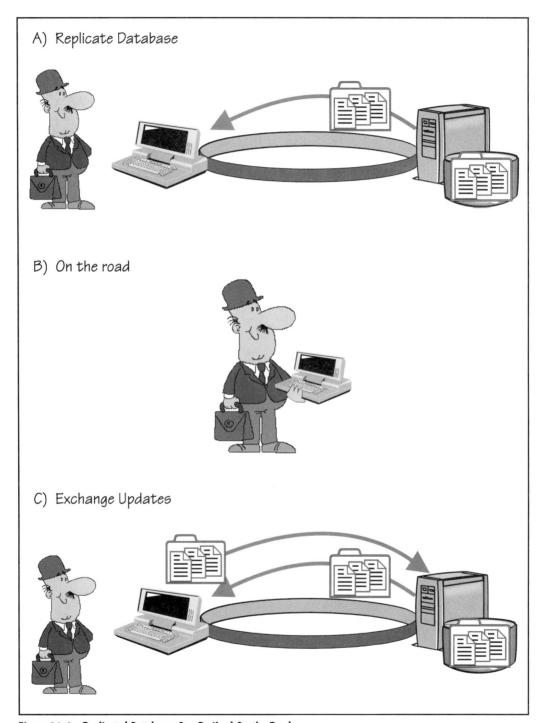

Figure 32-3. Replicated Databases Can Be Used On the Road.

a response to the original document, or the last updated version can become the main document with all previous versions displayed as responses.

Versioning does not guarantee that the last version is the most accurate, and it cannot merge changes into a single copy of the data. So even Release 3 of Notes is not a suitable technology for OLTP database applications or applications that require high concurrency controls involving immediate updates. However, versioning eliminates the loss of data through concurrent updates or through replication. It's quite useful for its intended use: document-centric groupware applications—an area that OLTP doesn't even touch.

How to Build a Notes Application

A new Notes *database* is typically created by using one of the Lotus-provided templates and customizing it. A database is simply a new file; it can be given an identifying icon, a title, help panels, and a *policy document* that explains what it's all about. *Forms* are used to enter information or view information in a database. To create a form, you can start with one of the pre-existing forms and modify it using the GUI editor. Forms provide data entry fields, text fields, and graphic areas where pictures or other sources of multimedia data can be pasted (or attached). Lotus provides a scripting language—it's like 1-2-3 spreadsheet formulas—that allows you to associate commands with specific events and actions. The forms you create are associated with the database. You can designate them as either *public*, which means they're available to all client applications that have access to the database; or you can make them *private*, which means only the creator can use them.

Views are stored queries that display the contents of a database or of a particular document. They're used for navigation and for the filtering of information—examples are display documents less than one month old "by region" or "by salesperson." The view will display the list of documents in a tabular or outline fashion. Any database has one or more views that the designer creates for easy access to information. Users also can create *private* views to provide a listing or access criteria that the database designer didn't anticipate.

On the client side, a user has a visual *workspace*—a notebook-like visual that organizes databases by topics (see Figure 32-4). A notebook consists of six color-coded workpages; each has a folder-like tab that identifies a category into which you want to organize your databases. Each workpage can contain from zero to hundreds of databases. Each database is represented by an icon and a title. You must associate a new database to a workpage. You then double-click on it to open it and work with its views. Release 3 lets you open multiple databases and gives each its own window. However, you still can't join documents from different

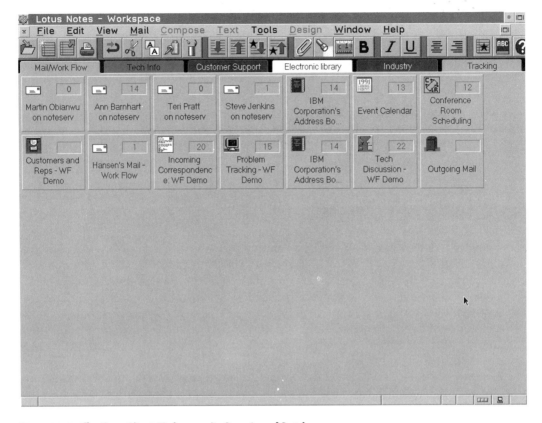

Figure 32-4. The Notes Client Workspace: An Organizer of Databases.

databases into a single view. But you can create hypertext links from any document in any database to any other database.

The process of creating a new Notes client/server application and tailoring forms and views can take less than an hour. It's that simple. For the more adventurous, the Notes scripting language—or *formula macro language*—provides about 200 functions to control almost everything from field input validation to database queries and document routing. A prompt command can be associated with any event to display a dialog box that prompts users to enter data or to select an entry from a list-box. Release 3 provides *periodic macros* that can be used to launch macros at a specific time interval or as a result of a particular action or condition— for example, when a document is deleted. This is the Notes equivalent of a trigger.

The Lotus Notes API

Notes also provides a C programming API, which developers can use to store and retrieve Notes documents; it also gives you broad access to many of the features of the Notes user interface. The API allows you to:

- Create or delete databases
- Read, write, and modify any document and any field in the document
- Create and use database views
- Control database access with access control lists
- Gather and report server performance statistics and register new workstations and servers
- Write custom tasks that you can add to the Notes server software and specify the schedule under which the custom task executes
- Create, read, and run Notes macros using the API
- Perform full-text searches using the new search-engine
- Issue calls to restrict what documents get exchanged during replication
- Obtain the list of names and address books in use locally or on a server
- Issue mail gateway calls

In addition, Notes supports an e-mail client API based on VIM—an open industry "standard." You'll need to purchase the separate Lotus VIM Developer's Toolkit ($395). But the Notes VIM run-time libraries are part of the product. You cannot use the APIs to modify or remove features of Notes including the "Notes Desktop."

Notes and SQL Databases

An external database API based on DataLens drivers is available free of charge. It lets Notes users access data stored in external databases using Notes' keywords and lookup capabilities. The foreign data can be displayed in Notes fields. However, still missing is a way for programs to access the Notes database using an open SQL CLI. This may change when Lotus provides its relational database interface using the ODBC CLI (mid-1994). The ODBC drivers will allow Notes programmers to write SQL queries that can be translated into Notes queries. And, it will provide the capability to bring Notes data into a relational database. In other words it will provide bi-directional Notes/SQL capability (see Figure 32-5).

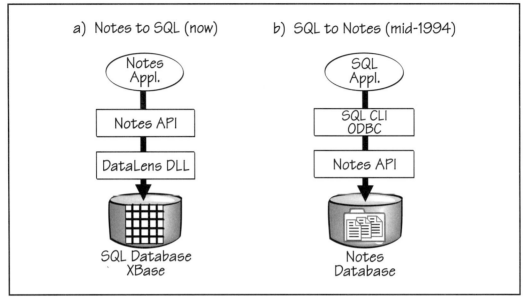

Figure 32-5. Bidirectional Data Exchanges Between Notes and SQL Databases.

Notes E-Mail

We want to enhance Notes as the place to live on the network.

— *Jim Manzi, Lotus CEO (October, 1993)*

From a client workstation's perspective, e-mail is just another Notes database that contains a collection of mail documents. The procedures to read incoming mail, sort through mail, or create a mail document are the same ones used to create and read documents in any Notes database. You simply use forms and views that are tailored to your mail documents. Of course, one of the differences is that the mail documents you create will be sent to somebody else's mailbox. Notes provides visual indicators to let you know that you have incoming mail. You then open the database and read it. Ray Ozzie's design seems to be very consistent.

The Notes e-mail server is open. If you don't like the Notes mail front end, you can use the VIM API to create your own. Or you can simply use VIM to mail-enable your applications using the Notes server as a back end. By mid-1994, cc:Mail clients will be able to use the Notes mail server. So what kind of services does a Notes Mail server provide? It provides mail backbone functions with the following features:

■ **_Routing optimization._** The techniques include outbound message prioritization and dynamic adaptive route selection based on link costs.

■ **_Separate OS/2 router threads._** Release 3 uses OS/2 threads to handle routing. All server to server communications are handled by separate transfer threads. Threads allow multiple concurrent transfers to occur on different backbone routes. In addition, threads prevent large mail messages from delaying other server tasks.

■ **_Delivery failure notification._** Senders can be notified when delivery isn't possible (including the reasons).

■ **_X.500 namespace support._** Notes Release 3 supports the full X.500-compliant hierarchical naming as its native means of identifying _users_ within the system. This makes it straightforward for Notes directories to interoperate at the naming level with other X.500-compliant systems. It avoids naming conflict headaches.

■ **_Electronic signatures._** Notes uses the RSA public key cryptography for all aspects of Notes security, including encryption. (In Part 3, we explained that RSA was good for electronic signatures but very slow when it came to general encryption.) If you sign a message, it takes Notes a few seconds longer to send it because it must generate an RSA electronic signature. If it takes a few seconds just to encrypt a name, how long does it take to encrypt a medium-sized document?

■ **_VIM open client support._** Notes Release 3 supports VIM calls, which means that Notes users can select their mail clients independently from the server. Of course, the mail clients must be VIM-compliant.

■ **_Mail gateways and directory services._** Notes provides e-mail gateways to the most popular e-mail networks, including X.400, SMTP, cc:Mail, MHS, PROFS, VinesMail, FAX, VAXmail, and SoftSwitch (see Figure 32-6).

As we explained in the last chapter, the Notes mail engine will serve both Notes and cc:Mail front ends in mid-1994. Notes provides a true client/server e-mail architecture. The clients and servers communicate via RPC. VIM provides the call level interface on the client side.

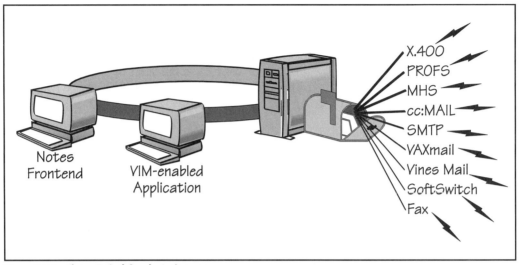

Figure 32-6. Notes E-Mail Reach via Gateways.

The Notes Text-Search Engine

Details

Lotus Notes Release 3 adds some very sophisticated text search and retrieval capabilities. The good news is that text can now be searched across more than one database. The bad news is that the search engine user interface is still not very intuitive. Before you perform a search, you must first create a content index on all the databases that you're going to target. This process consumes time and eats up disk space. The content index can now be created in a background process that incrementally indexes the words found in a database's documents. Once you've indexed the databases, you can specify your query using the following search criteria:

- The target databases for the search

- Boolean search operators (AND, OR, NOT)

- Wild-card operators and pattern searches

- Text strings that are within the same sentence or in relative proximity to each other

- Text searches that are limited to a specific field

- Text searches that are limited to a specific document

- Searches on numeric and date fields using the operators (>, <, <>, >=, and <=)

- Sort results by date or relevance—you can also set the maximum number of matches to be returned

Queries that are submitted using the expanded Query Bar can be saved by title, run periodically, and associated with scripting actions. Developers can also access the search engine using APIs. ❏

Systems Management

A multiserver system with replicated databases and a mail backbone is an invitation for disaster—a management nightmare. Notes Release 3 addresses some of the distributed management needs by providing the following aids:

- ***Remote management and configuration.*** Release 3 lets an administrator monitor a Notes server from any client workstation. Any Notes server can be managed and configured remotely.

- ***Stored views and forms.*** By treating forms and views as stored database objects, Notes can distribute applications through its server replication facilities. This makes it easier to deploy applications.

- ***Statistics and thresholds.*** Notes maintains statistics on peak and average mail traffic (per port and per server pair), for server usage by time of day, and on performance degradation. The collected statistics can be sent to a database that compares the new values against thresholds. If problems are detected, an alert may be generated and sent via the e-mail system.

- ***X.500 distributed naming support.*** X.500 hierarchical naming makes it easier for administrators in different locations to create unique user names in address books, access control lists, digital signatures, and author fields in Notes documents. The downside is that names are longer (and more complex) than in the previous release but aliases (or nicknames) can help alleviate that.

- ***Access control lists.*** Notes provides the ability to grant or deny access to shared databases, documents, views, forms, and fields.

■ ***Template inheritance.*** Notes Release 3 allows databases to inherit the design of other databases. Each class of database can have a "design template" that contains forms and views for all other databases of the same class. If administrators want to modify a standard form or view, they only have to make the changes in one place. Notes will automatically propagate the changes to all the applications that have created derived objects from these templates.

■ ***Field dictionary.*** Notes Release 3 allows fields to be shared among applications, giving administrators some control over a data dictionary.

■ ***Alerts and preventive maintenance.*** Notes servers can proactively generate alerts that can be fed to network administrators through electronic mail. Alerts can be generated before disk space and swapfile limits are reached, when security access is violated, and when mail routing or replication errors occur (see Figure 32-7).

Lotus is working with third parties on providing an SNMP MIB and agent support for Notes.

Figure 32-7. Notes Alert Notification via E-Mail.

Packaging

At first, Notes was priced to appeal only to large organizations, but with Release 3.0, Lotus is trying to broaden Notes' acceptance in the mass market. The list price of a Release 3 license (either client or server) is $495. (Yes, it's still too expensive on the client side, and Lotus is getting a lot of complaints). Notes requires an OS/2 server with over 12 MBytes of RAM and over 100 MBytes of disk space. An OS/2 Notes client can live comfortably in 8 MBytes of RAM and 40 MBytes of disk space. Lotus is preparing a 3.1 version of Notes that corrects some the 3.0 incompatibilities with OS/2 2.1.

Lotus is working with 150 third-party vendors who are developing companion Notes products including mail gateways, SQL database integration tools, multimedia products, electronic imaging, workflow, and system management utilities. There is also a powerful network of Notes Value-Added Resellers—including IBM—who are selling and supporting Notes.

How Revolutionary Is Notes?

Soapbox

Notes is a very exciting product that makes you want to jump in and create a client/server application just for the fun of it. Notes databases have the tendency of proliferating like rabbits. Once you get the hang of them, they're contagious. With Release 3, Notes starts to address the client/server needs of mobile users and intergalactic enterprises. You can carry your Notes databases in a laptop or have them replicated to the far corners of the universe. Lotus is also doing more to open up the Notes environment at the API level so that ISVs and IS programmers can jump in and provide add-ins. So in many ways, Lotus Notes may be a "killer app" that does for client/server what Lotus 1-2-3 did for PCs and DOS.

We like Notes and highly recommend it for certain classes of applications. But it's important to understand what it can and cannot do. Notes is a very good fit for applications that collect multimedia information, perform very few updates, and need to be integrated with e-mail. But Notes is not very good at handling applications that deal with structured data, are query intensive, and require multiuser updates with high-levels of integrity. Notes does not do very well with transactions and does not even know how to spell ACID. These types of applications are best handled by TP Monitors, Information Warehouses, transactional MOMs, and SQL and Object databases. ❑

FLOWMARK/2: AN OS/2 WORKFLOW PRODUCT

We already encountered FlowMark/2 in Part 4, where we explained that it could be used to automate complex Information Warehouse copy management tasks. Flow-Mark/2 is a client/server workflow-management system that runs on OS/2. The product provides a highly visual interface for designing, simulating, and animating workflow applications (IBM calls it the build time). Flow-mark run-time clients provide a GUI environment to display worklists and manage desktop programs that perform the work. The FlowMark server uses an object database—ODI's Object-Store—to model, track, store, and execute the workflow. The client and server communicate using a proprietary RPC.

The FlowMark/2 Workflow Model

FlowMark is an example of a process-oriented workflow model; it is suitable for automating business systems that have definable, repetitive, and well-understood policies and procedures. The routing of the work is automatic and requires very little user involvement. FlowMark uses *to-do lists* and *procedures graph* meta-phors. You create the workflow with a visual tool to define business activities and draw lines to interconnect them (see Figure 32-8). The tool lets you specify the order in which the activities are done, the people that perform them, the programs that support the people, and the flow of control and information between activities. FlowMark also lets you assign the activities to roles (i.e., job titles). These roles can then be assigned to people who can fulfill them at run time. You can also specify help screens and instructions that guide run-time users through an activity.

The workflow information is stored in an ObjectStore ODBMS. The entire model is stored as object classes that can be reused, inherited, and derived to create new processes or rearrange existing ones. This makes the design environment very flexible and intuitive. So even though we're dealing with a rigid process model, the design tool makes it easy to put together workflows using ad hoc reusable process arrangements. You create complex business processes from elementary reusable object classes.

Workflow Animation

FlowMark provides an animation facility that lets you test-drive the workflow to get the wrinkles out of the design. You can navigate through the different activities and simulate the different roles without leaving your development workstation. Anima-tion helps you uncover design errors such as loops, unused paths, and dead spots, which are otherwise hard to find. It's better to find these errors during the design than at production time, when they are expensive to find and correct.

Chapter 32. Lotus Notes, FlowMark/2, and ImagePlus/2

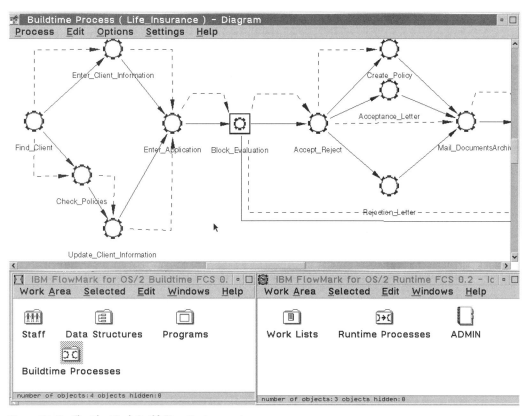

Figure 32-8. The FlowMark Build-Time Environment.

Animation is especially useful when you're dealing with large activity networks consisting of multiple operations with feedback loops. You can think of the animation as a form of visual simulation of the workflow that helps you perform "what-if" experiments, remove the bottlenecks, and optimize the design. The animation facility also helps you demonstrate the workflow to potential customers to get their feedback. You can simulate an entire client/server workflow network on a single laptop, which makes it easy to carry around and demonstrate to the interested parties.

The FlowMark Client/Server Run Time

Once you're satisfied with the workflow definition, you can deploy it on a client/server network (see Figure 32-9). The Flowmark/2 client and server run-time elements run on different networked machines. The server simply executes the workflow model that was created by the build time and stored in the object database. Here's what a FlowMark server does:

■ It schedules and dispatches units of work according to the activity model that's stored in its object database and according to the state of the work-in-progress.

■ It stores and tracks instances of the work-in-progress in the object database.

■ It follows the progress of each unit of work and orchestrates its movement from activity to activity based on workflow model.

■ It handles concurrent requests from multiple clients. The processes execute concurrently on the server machine.

■ It maintains an audit trail that keeps a full record of the activities and their execution time. This can be used to track results and to help find and eliminate bottlenecks in the workflow processes.

The server code is a 32-bit OS/2 program that runs on top of an embedded ODBMS—the ODI ObjectStore product. The ODI product provides very fine levels of concurrency and locking controls.

So what does a FlowMark run-time client do? It acts as a remote agent that helps a server manage the activity on a client machine. Here's a list of what a FlowMark run-time client does:

■ It requests from the server the list of activities that need to be performed by a user (or role) on a client machine.

■ It directly executes the activities that do not require human intervention. This is done by starting and stopping programs that are associated with the activity and passing them required parameters.

■ It assists a human user in performing an activity. It does that by displaying a personalized work list in a list-box of activities as part of a GUI front end. The client interacts with the user and helps get the job done by starting local programs that are needed to complete an activity.

■ It sends an event notification to the server at the completion of an activity and receives its marching orders on what to do next.

The FlowMark clients and server cooperate to keep the process moving. When an activity is completed the next activity on the worklist appears right away. The human doesn't need to worry about having to find and start programs. This gets done automatically as part of workflow management. Data items that are used repeatedly—such as file names, customer names, and account numbers—are only entered once; FlowMark keeps track of these variables in its object database and makes them available to downstream operations as needed.

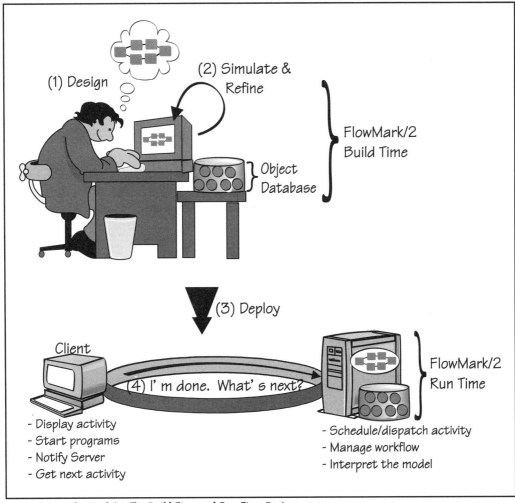

Figure 32-9. FlowMark/2: The Build-Time and Run-Time Environments.

Packaging

IBM shipped the Flowmark/2 product in September, 1993 to a select group of customers. The general availability date was not announced as we went to press. The server sells for around $10,000. The run-time client sells for $200 per workstation. The build-time client with the visual builder interface sells for $800. You will also need the Prolog/2 run-time facility if you plan to do any simulation or animation. The ODI ObjectStore run time is included in the server price. The build time requires a fast 80486 class machine with about 25 MBytes of RAM (for running the client and server on the same development machine and doing simulations). The run-time client runs comfortab'y on a 33-MHz 80386 class machine and requires 5 MBytes of RAM. The run-time server requires 15 MBytes of RAM and an 80486 class machine.

FlowMark/2 clients and servers are CID-enabled. You can install all the components of FlowMark selectively, either for a stand-alone workstation or for a client/server scenario. You can also selectively install, restore, or delete components and fixes. The product does not currently support server-to-server communications. You cannot, for example, execute remote sub-processes on a second server as part of a workflow. A FlowMark/2 server can comfortably support approximately 20 concurrent run-time clients.

IMAGEPLUS/2: AN OS/2 CLIENT/SERVER IMAGING PRODUCT

ImagePlus/2 is the OS/2 member of IBM's "strategic" document imaging product family. It provides a complete client/server imaging solution on PC LANs. ImagePlus/2 interoperates and exchanges documents and routing information with other members of the ImagePlus family—including ImagePlus on MVS, ImagePlus/400, and future ImagePlus implementations on AIX, HP-UX, and other Unix platforms. The product runs on PCs and LANs and uses ordinary PC hardware attachments—including document scanners, facsimile, high-resolution displays, magnetic and optical storage, and image printers. ImagePlus/2 was jointly developed by IBM and Eastman Kodak.

ImagePlus/2 Components

The ImagePlus/2 product, which shipped in January 1992 and was upgraded in 1993, provides a complete imaging solution on OS/2 clients and servers. The product allows you to enter, store, and retrieve image documents online. It organizes images using an electronic document and folder paradigm. And it provides image workflow management and document routing capabilities.

ImagePlus/2 is a classical client/server imaging product (see Figure 32-10). The client component provides a user interface for capturing, displaying, and retrieving images and documents. The server component manages an image store on optical or magnetic disk media, organizes and maintains the folder/document hierarchy, provides an indexed search facility for locating documents, and supports a workflow engine that specializes in the routing of electronic documents. Both the client and server components provide APIs and "user exits" that let other applications hook into the system. We'll go over these functions in a little more detail.

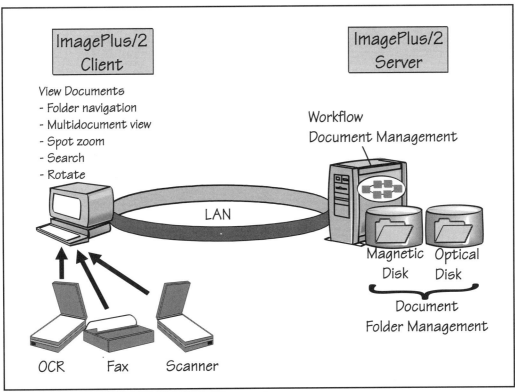

Figure 32-10. ImagePlus/2: The Client/Server Components.

ImagePlus/2 Client Functions

The ImagePlus/2 client uses a CUA-89 GUI interface to provide image capture, display, and document search and retrieval functions. Here's the details of the functions it provides:

■ *Image capture.* The client can capture images from attached scanners, fax machines, and optical character readers. It supports a wide variety of devices from IBM and other vendors. Scanner settings can be set via a pop-up window. The images are captured in either the *Tagged Image File Format (TIFF)* or the *Mixed Object Document Content Architecture (MODCA)* formats. TIFF is a widely accepted industry standard; MODCA is an ImagePlus family standard.

■ *Image display.* The client software lets you scale, scroll, zoom, rotate, and reverse images. Spot zooming provides the capability of enlarging a particular section of an image. ImagePlus/2 supports a variety of image hardware including large screen portrait, landscape, and ordinary VGA and XGA graphics monitors.

- *Image indexing.* The client provides GUI dialogs for indexing captured images. The required index fields are highlighted to help the operator. Help can be associated with any field. Indexing helps you find images faster. Multiple index fields—for example, employee name and personnel number—provide even greater flexibility in accessing a document.

- *Folder and document views.* The client provides views for navigating through electronic folders and their document contents. ImagePlus/2 lets you combine image pages into *documents* that can be stored, retrieved, copied, printed, deleted, or archived (see the following Briefing box).

- *Workflow front-end functions.* The client provides a menu-driven workflow processing front end. The visual metaphor used is an electronic inbasket—ImagePlus/2 calls it the *workbasket*. A workbasket holds a sequence of folders and/or documents for processing by an individual or a group (i.e., role). A user is presented with a prioritized list of items for selection, or the system may be configured to assign the highest priority item automatically. A folder can be placed in *suspended mode* for a period of time—for example, while waiting for additional information needed to complete the work on it.

ImagePlus/2 Server Functions

The ImagePlus/2 server is an OS/2 application that provides image storage management, indexing, and workflow multiuser services on ordinary PC LANs. Here are the details of what's provided:

- *Mass storage management.* The server provides a hierarchical storage subsystem using RAM caching, magnetic storage, and optical mass storage. ImagePlus/2 supports a large selection of optical disk subsystems, including juke boxes from IBM and Kodak.

- *Document and folder hierarchies.* The server implements and tracks the image containment relationships—page, document, folder, and fileroom—using a DB2/2 SQL database. The actual images are stored in the mass storage subsystem; the relational database keeps track of the pointers, index, and containment relationships.

- *Document workflow.* The server implements the workflow model, tracks and routes documents, and manages work-in-progress. Users can define workflow routes for a standard business process. The documents or folders are then passed from workbasket to workbasket in the predetermined sequence. As work

ImagePlus/2 Docs, Folders, and File Rooms

Briefing

The ImagePlus/2 document paradigm is an electronic version of the familiar office environment. The basic unit of storage and manipulation is a *document* consisting of a variable number of pages in scanned image form. Associated with a document are:

- **Textual notes** which can be added online to documents and folders. These are like "post-it" notes (or yellow stickers) that are used in offices.

- **Index information** that make it easier to store and retrieve documents.

- **Multiple-document views** that allow several documents to be opened and stacked in one window so that you can page through them faster. This function simulates paging through a paper file folder.

- **An activity log** that records the document processing activity.

Documents may be collected, manually or automatically, into *folders*. Folders and documents are stored in a *fileroom* database. You can search the filerooms to retrieve a sorted list of folders and documents. Wild-card searches are also supported. ❑

is completed on a document or folder, it is routed to the next workbasket automatically. A user can dynamically alter this sequence to handle exceptions.

The server's performance was recently improved and it can now comfortably handle up to 40 concurrent clients—it's at least twice as fast as the original release. And it does all this as a 16-bit OS/2 application. So we should be able to obtain even better performance when the application is upgraded to 32-bit OS/2.

ImagePlus/2 System Administration

ImagePlus/2 provides online, menu-driven system administration facilities. A client front end provides the functions that you need to administer and configure an image system. This includes functions for:

- Providing online help documentation
- Defining workflows and workbaskets
- Creating document and folder classes

- Creating index formats and dialogs
- Creating access control lists that define user access to image resources

Together, these functions allow you to personalize an image system and configure it to meet your needs.

ImagePlus/2 APIs and Document Content Formats

ImagePlus/2 provides over 150 API calls that make it easy for other applications to interface to it and use its services. The APIs allow outside programs to control the user interface, query the index database, access image objects, and invoke imaging functions. ImagePlus/2 also provides sample code and APIs for controlling OCRs. The product supports standard image document content architectures—including MODCA-P.1, MODCA-P.2, and TIFF Revision 5.0—and compression formats.

Packaging

The ImagePlus/2 server sells for $2,495; the clients sell for $395. The servers require 16 MBytes of RAM and 320 MBytes of disk (minimum). The clients require 8 Mbytes of RAM and 60 MBytes of disk (minimum).

Over 50 ISVs and IBM business partners provide complementary ImagePlus/2 applications, functional extensions, and support for a variety of image devices.

Part 7
Client/Server With
Distributed Objects

An Introduction to Part 7

So did you all enjoy that night on the town? Oh, you want to play elephant and blind men again? We can't afford it—you Martians party too hard. But, we have a great new adventure ahead of us, and it's going to be fun. We're going to explore the uncharted territory of distributed objects. No, we're not talking about *Unidentified Flying Objects (UFOs)*—that's Martian stuff. Sorry, that was rude: Of course you Martians are not objects and, yes, you have identities. What we're dealing with here are computer objects. Do they fly? Yes, some do over wireless networks. And, we know of roaming objects that live on networks and their brokers who organize communities of objects. Yes, it's another new frontier and there may be a pot of gold there, too. Are you all packed and ready for another adventure?

Part 7 is about distributed objects. The word *distributed* is important because it means we're dealing with objects that participate in client/server relationships with other objects. More plumbing? Yes, but this is supposed to be the "mother of all plumbing." Objects can do everything we've covered in this book, and, supposedly, *they do it better*:

- **Objects** themselves are an amazing combination of data and function with magical properties like polymorphism, inheritance, and encapsulation. This magic works wonders in distributed environments.

- **Object brokers** provide the ultimate distributed system. They allow objects to dynamically discover each other and interact across machines and operating systems.

- **Object services** allow us to create, manage, name, move, copy, store, and restore objects.

- **Object TP Monitors** may emerge as the most powerful and flexible transaction managers yet. Objects and transactions are a dynamite combination.

- **Object groupware** may change the way we interact. The new groupware will be built using roaming objects, intelligent event managers, and object replication services.

- **Object databases** provide the ultimate management system for BLOBs, documents, and almost any type of information—especially new information types.

- **Object linking** technology allows us to create highly flexible webs among programs that don't know about each other. The webs emanate out of ordinary looking desktop documents.

- **Object frameworks** promise to revolutionize the way we build our distributed systems. They provide flexible, customizable, prefabricated software subsystems.

Objects may provide the ultimate infrastructure for building client/server systems. We say "may" because success depends on more than just great technology. What products are available? Are the major players lined up behind the technology? Are the key standards in place?

We think you Martians will love this distributed object stuff. It has all the elements of a new gold rush. But first we must clearly understand what makes this 25-year old technology finally ready for prime time. The answer is CORBA. You'll have to read the ORB chapter to discover what's behind CORBA magic. Complementing CORBA are distributed object services, compound document technology (including OLE and OpenDoc), object databases, and object frameworks. We devote a chapter to each one of those topics. We conclude the part with the normal product reviews that give us a "reality check" on the technology. So we have an exciting (but long) journey ahead of us. Pack lots of trail mix and energy bars—you'll need it all. And yes, it's new frontier country. So bring along all your exploration gear and let's hope we don't lose any of you in those uncharted and potentially treacherous mountain passes and ravines.

Chapter 33

Object Request Brokers

If we could combine the power of objects with the reliability of transactions, we would catapult commercial computing into a new era.

— *John Tibbets and Barbara Bernstein*
(November, 1993)

By now, anybody associated with computers knows that objects are wonderful—we simply can't live without them. SmallTalk can be used to create GUI front ends, C++ is the only way to write code, and the literature is full of articles on the wonders of encapsulation, multiple inheritance, and polymorphism. But what can these things do on a client/server network? Where do objects fit in a world dominated by SQL databases, TP Monitors, and Lotus Notes? What happens when we stray away from the cozy single-address space of a program and try to get objects to talk across a network? What happens to inheritance in a world of federated operating systems separated by networks? In a nutshell, we need to understand how object technology can be *extended* to deal with the complex issues that are inherent in creating robust, single-image, client/server systems.

The purpose of the next few chapters is to describe exactly what objects can do for client/server systems. The key word is *systems*—or how objects work together across machine and network boundaries to create client/server solutions. We're not going to rehash the marvels of Object-Oriented Programming (OOP), SmallTalk, and C++ because we assume you've heard about them all before. We're moving on to the next step: objects in client/server systems. We strongly believe that this is the area where objects will realize their greatest potential; in the process, they will become the new "mainstream computing model." We also believe that client/server technology needs objects to fulfill its promise of plug-and-play computing across networks and dissimilar operating systems. Finally, we believe that without a strong distributed object foundation the management of client/server systems is a lost cause (more on that in Part 8).

In this chapter, we go over *Object Request Brokers*—or "ORBs," as the natives call them. The ORB is the mechanism that allows objects to communicate with each other across a network. We will look at the OMG's CORBA specification for ORBs and put the whole thing in a familiar client/server perspective. You may have noticed in reading the Tibbets and Bernstein quote that some key distributed object pieces are still lacking. So we will also look at what's brewing in the upcoming OMG specifications and how they plan to address the marriage of distributed objects and transactions.

WHAT DISTRIBUTED OBJECTS PROMISE

> *Data will be encapsulated in objects that will in some cases be able to roam to where they are most needed.*
>
> — *Peter Wayner, Byte Magazine*
> *(January, 1994)*

Object technology radically alters the way software systems are developed. The promise is compelling: We will be able to put together complex client/server information systems by simply assembling and extending reusable software components. Any of the objects may be modified or changed without affecting the rest of the components in the system or how they interact. The components may be shipped as collections of class libraries preassembled in *frameworks*, where all the pieces are known to work together to perform a specific task. Frameworks are working subsystems that revolutionize the way we create client/server systems. They promise to provide the ultimate in mix-and-match capabilities. And flexible mix-and-match is the heart and soul of client/server.

Snapping Together Distributed Objects

For objects to be successful, they must reside in open client/server environments and learn how to "plug-and-play" across networks and operating systems. In theory, object technology is well-suited for creating client/server systems because the data and business logic are encapsulated within objects, allowing them to be located anywhere within a distributed system. The *granularity* of distribution is greatly improved. Objects can easily mask the platform-specific elements and make the pieces appear to interoperate seamlessly.

Object-oriented client/server applications can afford to be much more flexible than traditional vertical applications—frameworks allow end users to mix-and-match components without making the distributed application *less* robust. Objects have the inherent potential to become intelligent, self-managing entities; this allows us to manage very complex systems by broadcasting instructions and alarms. In summary, distributed objects allow granular components of software to plug-and-play, interoperate across networks, run on different platforms, coexist with legacy applications through object wrappers, roam on networks (a la General Magic), and manage themselves and the resources they control (see Figure 33-1). What more could we want?

Are Objects Ready for Prime Time

A recent IDC study of 800 corporations indicates that 12% of those surveyed are using object technology, while 44% are exploring object technology benefits and 73% of those moving to objects are using them to build client/server solutions. Why is there this sudden interest in a technology that's been around for 25 years? One answer is that the stars are aligning and the pieces may finally be coming together. The more likely catalyst was the formation of the *Object Management Group (OMG)* in April 1989. This non-profit, international consortium, which now has over 300 members, is dedicated to establishing standards for distributed objects. The best way to understand client/server object technology is to look at the OMG's distributed object management standards.

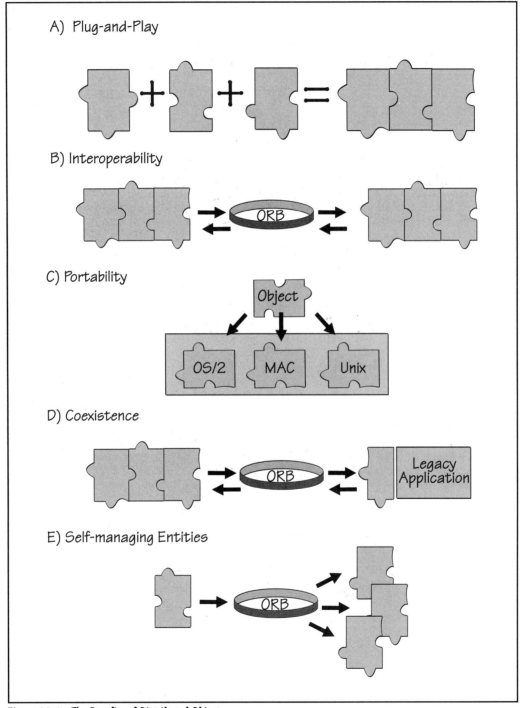

Figure 33-1. The Benefits of Distributed Objects.

The World's Shortest Tutorial on Objects

Briefing

If you want to shrink something, you must first allow it to expand. If you want to take something, you must first allow it to be given. This is called the subtle perception of the way things are.

— Lao Tzu

An *object* is a piece of code that owns things called *attributes* and provides services through *methods*. Typically, the methods operate on private data—also called instance data—that the object owns. A collection of like objects make up a *class*. A class also acts as a template for describing the behavior of sets of like objects. Technically speaking, objects are run-time *instances* of a class. This all sounds pretty straightforward, so why all the fuss about objects? First, they provide a better programming model for representing the world. We can create intelligent software objects that mirror the things around us. Second, objects have three magical properties that make them incredibly useful: encapsulation, inheritance, and polymorphism. In our book, **Client/Server Programming with OS/2 2.1**, we call them "the three pillars of object-oriented programming." They allow us to create reusable objects without distributing the source code. They form the essence what Lao-Tzu calls "the subtle perception of the way things are."

Encapsulation

Encapsulation means "don't tell me how you do it; just do it." The object does that by managing its own resources and limiting the visibility of what others should know. An object publishes a public interface that defines how other objects or applications can interact with it (see Figure 33-2). An object also has a *private* component that implements the methods. The object's implementation is encapsulated—that is, hidden from the public view. Instance data can be declared private—usually, the default—or public. Private instance data can only be accessed by methods of the class. Public instance data, on the other hand, is part of the published external interface. The public methods and instance data are the permanent interface between the object and the outside world. Old methods must continue to be supported when an object changes. The public interface is a *binding contract* between the class providers and their clients.

Method 1

Method 2

Method 3

Method 4

Instance Data

Figure 33-2. The First Pillar of OO Wisdom: Class Encapsulation.

Polymorphism

Polymorphism is a high-browed way of saying that the same method can do different things, depending on the class that implements it. Looking at Figure 33-3, you can see polymorphism in action (hit the "accelerator" on a Corvette and on a Volvo, and then compare notes). Objects in different classes receive the same message yet react in different ways. Polymorphism is also the mechanism that allows subclasses (see next paragraph) to override an inherited method—and "do their own thing"—without affecting the ancestor's methods.

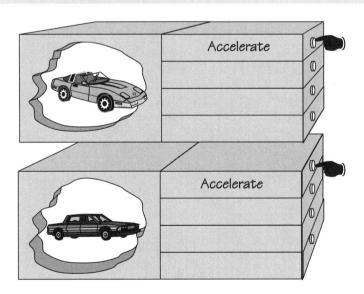

Figure 33-3. The Second Pillar of OO Wisdom: Polymorphism.

Inheritance

Inheritance is the mechanism that allows you to create new child classes, also known as *subclasses*, from existing parent classes. Child classes inherit their parent's methods and data structures. You can add new methods to a child's class or *override*—that is, modify—inherited methods to define new class behaviors. The parent's method is not affected by this modification. Figure 33-4 shows a typical class family tree—start with a generic "car" class and derive from it Volvos or Maseratis.

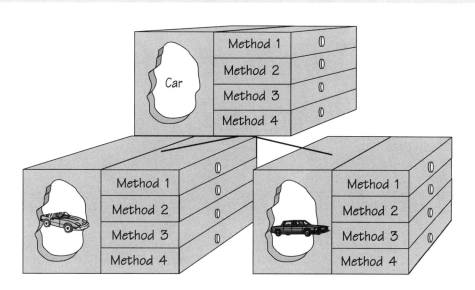

Figure 33-4. The Third Pillar of OO Wisdom: Inheritance and Subclassing.

Frameworks and Class Libraries

The three pillars of OO provide the foundation for creating, assembling, and reusing objects. The first generation of OO relied on *class libraries* to package objects for reusability. A more promising approach is the use of *object frameworks*. These are preassembled class libraries that are packaged to provide specific functions. Frameworks will make it easier to assemble objects; they raise the level of abstraction. We cover frameworks in more detail in a subsequent chapter. ❏

OMG'S OBJECT MANAGEMENT ARCHITECTURE

If objects are to be assembled, they must be compatible with one another. This is rarely a problem when writing a single program because all the objects are written in the same language, run on the same machine, and use the same operating system. But building entire information systems out of objects is quite a different matter. Objects have to interact with each other even if they are written in different languages and run on different hardware and software platforms.

— *David. A Taylor* [1]

Clearly, we need standards for objects to interoperate in heterogeneous client/server environments. Fortunately, this time around the industry anticipated this need and the Object Management Group (OMG) was founded specifically to create distributed object standards *before* any major products were introduced—a truly amazing phenomenon in our industry. As a result, over 300 vendors (and corporate associate members) are working on CORBA-compliant software products. The noticeable exception is Microsoft. But even that may change soon—OMG is in the process of creating a compound document architecture standard that may include both OLE and OpenDoc. We expect the remote object links in the compound documents to be managed via CORBA-compliant ORBs (OpenDoc supports this feature, and DEC may provide the same support for OLE). But we're getting ahead of our story.

In the fall of 1990, OMG first published the **Object Management Architecture Guide (OMA Guide)**; it was revised in September 1992. Figure 33-5 displays the four main components of the architecture:

■ ***The Object Request Broker*** is the mechanism that lets objects transparently make requests to—and receive responses from—other objects located locally or remotely. The client is not aware of the mechanisms used to communicate with, activate, or store the server objects. The ORB serves as the *foundation* for building distributed object applications. In the words of OMG, "the ORB component will guarantee portability and interoperability of objects over a network of heterogeneous systems." The current specification includes a generic *Interface Definition Language (IDL)* that is used to define the interfaces to objects that communicate via the ORB. However, we'll have to wait for ORB 2.0 (late 1994) to get a solid interoperability standard (it's work in progress). The ORB component is also commonly referred to as *CORBA*—which stands for *Common Object Request Broker Architecture*. Like the rest of the industry, we'll use both names interchangeably.

---

[1] Source: David A. Taylor, **Object-Oriented Information Systems** (Wiley, 1992). This book provides an excellent introduction to object technology.

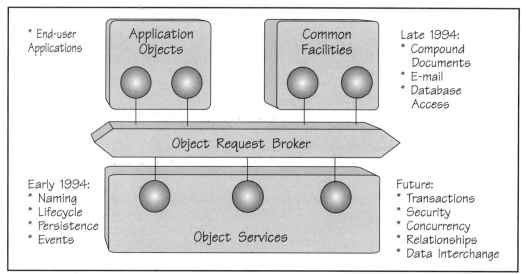

Figure 33-5. The Object Management Architecture Components.

■ ***Object Services*** are collections of services with object interfaces that provide basic functions for using and implementing objects. You can think of object services as augmenting and complementing the functionality of the ORB. The object services that are close to becoming standards include object naming, event notification, persistence, and object lifecycle management. A bit further on the horizon are object services for transaction management, security, concurrency control, relationships, data interchange, change management, trading, licensing, query, and properties.

■ ***Common Facilities*** are collections of end-user oriented services. Examples include e-mail, compound documents, database access, services that specifically support the construction of word processors, and network management applications. The dividing line between Common Facilities and Object Services is imprecise. Object Services *must* be implemented on every ORB, while Common Facilities are optional. Most of the OMG activity is currently in the object services area. But in December 1993, the OMG created a Common Facilities Task Force to look at compound documents and other components.

■ ***Application Objects*** are objects specific to end-user applications. These objects must be defined using the Interface Definition Language if they are to participate in ORB-mediated exchanges. An application is typically built from a large number of basic object classes; some of these may be provided by the OMG's Common Services.

FYI

Are ORBs the Mother of All Middleware?

Briefing

Orb—A jeweled globe surmounted by a cross that is part of a sovereign's regalia and that symbolizes monarchical power and justice.

— American Heritage Dictionary

Orb—Putting down some pavement on the dirt road called distributed computing.

— Chris Stone, President of OMG

The ORB becomes the "mother of all middleware" by providing granular levels of interoperability between objects in heterogeneous distributed environments. OMG hopes to achieve this ambitious goal by following two steps: 1) It will turn everything into nails, and 2) It will give everyone a hammer.

■ The "nail" is the CORBA *Interface Definition Language (IDL)*. The IDL allows object providers to specify in a standard definition language the interface and structure of the objects they provide. An IDL-defined *contract* binds the providers of distributed object services to their clients. For one object to request something of another object, it must know the target object's interface. The CORBA *IDL Repository* contains the definitions of all these interfaces.

■ The "hammer" includes the set of distributed services OMG providers will supply. These services will determine which objects are on the network, which methods they provide, and which *object interface adapters* are supported. The location of the object should be transparent to the client and object implementation. It should not matter whether the object is in the same process or across the world.

Does this all sound familiar? It should. We're describing the "object wave" of client/server computing; this time it's between cooperating objects as opposed to cooperating processes. The goal of this new wave is to create multivendor, multiOS, multilanguage "legoware" using objects. Vendors such as Sun, HP, IBM, and NCR are all using CORBA as their standard IDL-defined interface into the object highway. The IDL is the *contract* that brings it all together. We'll spend the next few sections digging into the details of how this all comes together. ❑

THE OBJECT REQUEST BROKER

The ORB is the middleware that establishes the client/server relationships between objects. Using an ORB, a client object can transparently invoke a method on a server object, which can be on the same machine or across a network. The ORB intercepts the call and is responsible for finding an object that can implement the request, pass it the parameters, invoke its method, and return the results (see Figure 33-6). The client does not have to be aware of where the object is located, its programming language, its operating system, or any other system aspects that are not part of an object's interface.

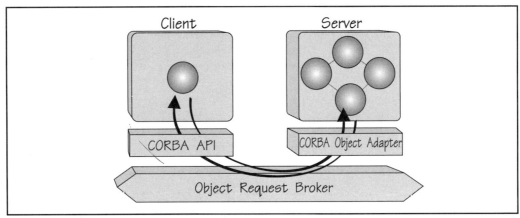

Figure 33-6. The Client/Server Request Using the ORB.

The Structure of a CORBA ORB

Figure 33-7 shows the client and server components of an ORB. Even though there are many boxes, it's not as complicated as it appears to be. This section provides the big picture of what these components do. We then go into more details in the sections that follow. The key is to understand that CORBA, like SQL, provides *both* static and dynamic interfaces to its services. This happened because the OMG received two strong submissions to its ORB Request For Proposal (RFP): one from HyperDesk and DEC that was based on a dynamic API, and one from Sun and HP that was based on static APIs. The OMG told the two groups to come back with a single RFP that combined both features. The result was CORBA. The "Common" in CORBA stands for this two-API proposal, which makes a lot of sense because it gives us both static and dynamic APIs.

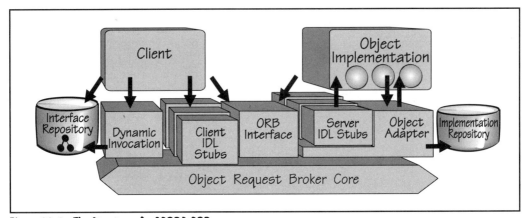

Figure 33-7. The Structure of a CORBA ORB.

Let's first go over the ORB components on the client side:

■ **The client IDL stubs** provide the static interfaces to object services. The precompiled stubs define how clients invoke corresponding services on the servers. The services are defined using the Interface Definition Language (IDL), and both client and server stubs are generated by the IDL compiler.

■ **The Dynamic Invocation APIs** let you discover the method to be invoked at run time. CORBA defines standard APIs for obtaining the service definitions, generating the parameters, issuing the remote call, and getting back the results.

■ **The Interface Repository APIs** allow you to obtain descriptions of all the registered classes, the methods they support, and the parameters they require. CORBA calls these descriptions *method signatures*. The Interface Repository is a run-time database that contains a machine-readable version of the IDL-defined interfaces. The APIs let your programs access this information.

■ **The ORB Interface** consists of a few APIs to local services that may be of interest to an application (the calls are not part of the client/server invocation mechanism).

The client and server components communicate using the *ORB Core*, which is implementation-specific (i.e., not defined by CORBA). The idea is that CORBA provides the interfaces above the ORB Core that mask the differences between vendor implementations. Vendors may use any transport they want for the networked ORB traffic and for the basic representation of objects in their system. Sun's DOE uses the ONC RPC over TCP/IP, HP's DOMF uses DCE RPC, HyperDesk's DOMS supports Netwise's RPC over TCP/IP, and IBM's DSOM supports sockets over TCP/IP, NetBIOS, or IPX/SPX (IBM is also working with HP on a DCE-based ORB). The result is that the different vendors' ORBs don't interoperate. The ORB 2.0 committee is leaning towards a gateway solution for ORB interoperability—the proverbial compromise. Vendors are also resorting to bilateral technology exchanges to make their ORB Cores interoperate (for example, the IBM/HP common DCE-based ORB Core).

CORBA-defined components appear on the server side between the ORB Core and the object implementations. Here's a quick explanation of what the pieces do:

■ **The server IDL stubs** (also known as skeletons) provide the static interfaces to each service exported by the server. These stubs, like the ones on the client, are created using the Interface Definition Language compiler. The server cannot tell the difference between incoming static or dynamic invocations. They're both invoked through server stubs.

FYI

ORB versus RPC

Briefing

Brokers of all types—stock brokers as well as object brokers—exact a price for their services.

— *Bill Andreas,*
Chief-Architect, HyperDesk

So how are ORB method invocations different from RPCs? The mechanisms are very similar, but there are some important differences. With an RPC you call a specific function (the data is separate). With an ORB, you're calling a method within a *specific* object. Different object classes may respond to the same method invocation differently through the magic of polymorphism. Because each object manages its own private instance data, the method is implemented on that *specific* instance data (see Figure 33-8).

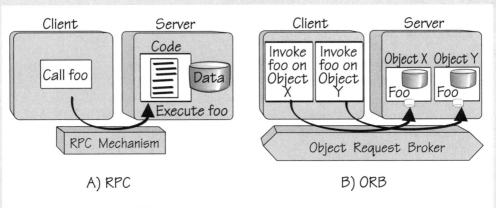

Figure 33-8. ORBs Versus RPC.

ORB method invocations have "scalpel-like" precision—the call gets to a *specific* object that controls *specific* data, and then implements the function in its own *class-specific* way. In contrast, RPC calls have no specificity—all the functions with the same name get implemented the same way. No differentiated service here. Of course, the ORB is usually built on top of an RPC service, so you end up paying a performance penalty for this "refined" level of service. It's worth every penny if you're taking advantage of new levels of distributed granularity provided by objects. Otherwise, you just bought yourself another layer of middleware—with all the costs and headaches that come with it. ❑

RPC = remote procedure call

■ **The object adapter** interfaces with the ORB's core communication services and accepts requests for service on behalf of the server's objects. It provides the run-time environment for instantiating server objects, passing requests to them, and assigning them object IDs—CORBA calls them *object references*. The Object Adapter also registers the classes it supports and their run-time instances (i.e., objects) with the *implementation repository*. CORBA specifies that each ORB must support a standard adapter called the *Basic Object Adapter*. Servers may support more than one object adapter.

■ **The Implementation Repository** provides run-time directory information about the classes a server supports, the objects that are instantiated, and their IDs. It also serves as a common place to store additional information associated with the implementation of ORBs. Examples include trace information, audit trails, security, and other administrative data.

■ **The ORB Interface** consists of a few APIs to local services that may be of interest to an application (the calls are not part of the client/server invocation mechanism).

This concludes our panoramic overview of the ORB components and their interfaces. If you're confused, keep reading—the next level of detail may help clarify things.

CORBA Client/Server Requests

Figure 33-9 shows the two types of client/server invocations that are supported by a CORBA ORB: static and dynamic. In both cases, the client performs a request by having access to an *object reference* (i.e., object ID) and invoking the method that performs the service (see the following Details box). The dynamic and static interfaces for performing the service satisfy the same request semantics. The receiver of the message cannot tell how the request was invoked. In both cases, the ORB locates a server object adapter, transmits the parameters, and transfers control to the object implementation through the server IDL stub (or skeleton).

Clients see the object interfaces through the perspective of a language mapping—or *binding*—that brings the ORB right up to the programmer's level. Client programs should be able to work without any source changes on *any* ORB that supports the language binding with *any* object instance that implements the interface. The implementation of the object, its object adapter, and the ORB used to access it is totally transparent to both static and dynamic clients.

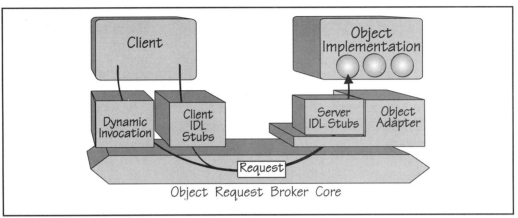

Figure 33-9. The ORB-Based Static and Dynamic Invocation Services.

What's an Object Reference?

Details

An object reference provides the information needed to uniquely specify an object within a distributed ORB system—it's a unique name or identifier. The implementation of object references is not defined by the CORBA specification, which means it is implementation specific. Two CORBA-compliant ORBs may have different representations for object references. So how is client/server program portability maintained in such an environment? By using language bindings to insulate the programs from the actual representation of the object references (see Figure 33-10).

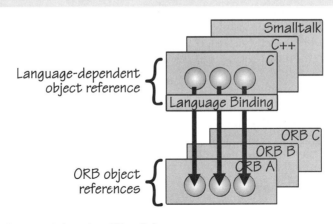

Figure 33-10. Language-independent Object References.

All ORBs must provide the same language binding to an object reference (usually referred to as an *Object*) for a particular programming language. This means that the language provides the portability and allows you to reference objects that run on different ORBs from within your programs. What happens if your program is accessing object references on two different ORBs? According to CORBA, your programs should still work fine; it is up to the vendors to resolve any object reference conflicts that may be encountered by the client code.

How do the client programs obtain object references? They usually receive them from directories or invocations on other objects to which they have references. An object reference can be converted to a string that can be stored in files. Or it can be preserved or communicated by different means and then turned back into an object reference by the ORB that produced the string. We also expect the OMG to get into the business of allocating "well-known object references." Somebody's got to do it. ☐

The CORBA Process: From IDL to Interface Stubs

Figure 33-11 shows the steps you go through to create your server classes, provide interface stubs for them, store their definitions in the Interface Repository, instantiate the objects at run time, and record their presence with the Implementation Repository. Let's go through these steps one-by-one and see what's involved:

1. ***Define your object classes using Interface Definition Language (IDL).*** The IDL is the means by which objects tell their potential clients what operations are available and how they should be invoked. The IDL definition language defines the types of objects, their attributes, the methods they export, and the method parameters. The CORBA IDL is a subset of ANSI C++ with additional constructs to support distribution. The IDL is purely a declarative language. It uses the C++ syntax for constant, type, and operation definitions, and it does not include any control structures or variables.

2. ***Run the IDL file through a language precompiler.*** A typical CORBA-compliant precompiler processes the IDL files and produces C language *skeletons* for the implementation server classes. By the time you read this, the OMG may have also published specifications for C++ language bindings.

3. ***Add the implementation code to the skeletons.*** You must supply the code that implements the methods in the skeletons. In other words, you must create your server classes.

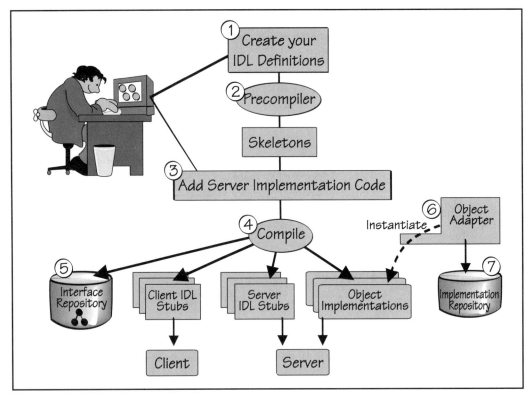

Figure 33-11. Defining Services: From IDL to Interface Stubs.

4. **Compile the code.** A CORBA-compliant compiler is typically capable of generating at least four types of output files: 1) *import files* that describe the objects to an Interface Repository; 2) *client stubs* for the IDL-defined methods—these stubs are invoked by a client program that needs to statically access IDL-defined services via the ORB; 3) *server stubs* that call the methods on the server—they're also called *up-call interfaces*; and 4) the code that implements the server classes. The automatic generation of stubs frees developers from having to write them and frees applications from dependencies on a particular ORB implementation.

5. **Bind the class definitions to the Interface Repository.** Typically, a utility is provided to bind—or, if you prefer, compile—the IDL information in a persistent store that can be accessed by programs at run time.

6. **Instantiate the objects on the server.** At startup time, a server *Object Adapter* may instantiate server objects that service remote client method invocations. These run-time objects are instances of the server application classes. CORBA specifies different Object Adapter strategies that are used to create and manage the run-time objects (more on that in later sections).

7. ***Register the run-time objects with the Implementation Repository.*** The Object Adapter records in the *Implementation Repository* the object reference and type of any object it instantiates on the server. The Implementation Repository also knows which object classes are supported on a particular server. The ORB uses this information to locate active objects or to request the activation of objects on a particular server.

The seven steps we just outlined are typical of most CORBA implementations. CORBA, of course, allows deviations. For example, it is not a requirement for IDL source code to be available, as long as the interface information is available in stub form or in an Interface Repository. It is not necessary for the server objects to be implemented as classes as long as they're encapsulated by IDL stubs. The separation of the interface from the implementation makes it possible to incorporate existing (legacy) systems within an ORB environment.

How Methods Are Dynamically Invoked

CORBA's *Dynamic Invocation* APIs allow a client program to dynamically build and invoke requests on objects. The client specifies the object to be invoked, the method to be performed, and the set of parameters through a call or sequence of calls. The client code typically obtains this information from an *Interface Repository* or a similar run-time source. The dynamic invocation provides maximum flexibility by allowing new object types to be added to the distributed system at run time. Visual tools will use this API to create interfaces through point-and-click interactions with a user.

To invoke a dynamic method on an object, the client must perform the following steps (see Figure 33-12):

1. ***Obtain the method description from the Interface Repository.*** CORBA specifies about ten calls for locating and describing objects within the repository. After an object is located, a *describe* call is issued to obtain its full IDL definition.

2. ***Create the argument list.*** CORBA specifies a self-defining data structure for passing parameters, which it calls the *NamedValue list*. The list is created using the *create_list* operation and repetitive *add_arg* calls to add each argument to the list.

3. ***Create the request.*** The request must specify the object reference, the name of the method, and the argument list. The request is created using the CORBA *create_request* call.

4. ***Invoke the request.*** The request may be invoked in one of three ways: 1) the *invoke* call sends the request and obtains the results; 2) the *send* call returns

control to the program, which must then issue a *get_response* or *get_next_response* call; and 3) the *send* call can be defined to be "oneway;" in this case, no response is needed.

As you can see, it takes effort to dynamically invoke a method. You're trading off complexity and performance for added flexibility.

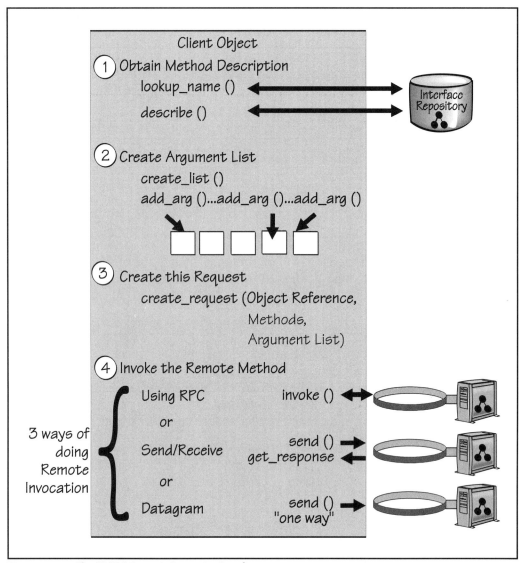

Figure 33-12. The CORBA Dynamic Invocation Interface.

Static Versus Dynamic Method Invocations

The static APIs are directly generated in the form of stubs by the IDL precompiler. It is perfect for programs that know at compile time the particulars of the operations they will need to invoke. The static stub interface is bound at compile time and provides the following advantages over the dynamic method invocation:

- *It is easier to program*—you call the remote method by simply invoking it by name and passing it the parameters. It's a very natural form of programming.
- *It provides more robust type checking*—the checking is enforced by the compiler at build time.
- *It performs well*—a single API call is issued to the stub, which takes it from there.
- *It is self-documenting*—you can tell what's going on by reading the code.

In contrast, the dynamic method invocation provides a more flexible environment. It allows you to add new classes to the system without requiring changes in the client code. It's very useful for tools that discover what services are provided at run time. You can write some very generic code with dynamic APIs. However, most applications don't require this level of flexibility and are better off with static stub implementations.

CORBA Servers

A *primary CORBA goal was to permit a wide variety of implementations. The specification does not rule out any of the different approaches to an ORB.*

— *Geoff Lewis, Chairperson of OMG Object Services (May, 1993)*

CORBA *represents the least common denominator. It treaded on nobody's product.*

— *Anonymous vendor* [2]

What does an object implementation need from an ORB on the server side? It needs a server infrastructure that registers the application's classes, instantiates new objects, gives them unique IDs, advertises their existence, invokes their methods when clients request it, and manages concurrent requests for their services. If we want to get more sophisticated, we could add transaction management, load

[2] Source: Robert E. Shelton, "OMG's CORBA 2.0," **Distributed Computing Monitor** (May, 1993).

balancing, and fine-grained security to the list. In other words, we need a program that takes raw class libraries and transforms them into a multiuser server environment. We're talking about the equivalent of a TP Monitor for objects. So who does this type of work? The answer is the *Object Adapter.*

What's an Object Adapter?

The Object Adapter is the primary mechanism for an object implementation to access ORB services (see Figure 33-13). It provides a total environment for running the server application. Here are some of the services provided by the Object Adapter:

1. ***Registers server classes with the Implementation Repository.*** You can think of the Implementation Repository as a persistent store that is managed by the Object Adapter. Object Implementation classes are registered and stored in the Implementation Repository.

2. ***Instantiates new objects at run time***. The Object Adapter is responsible for creating object instances from the implementation classes. The number of instances created is a function of the incoming client traffic loads. The Adapter is responsible for balancing the supply of objects with the incoming client demands.

3. ***Generates and manages object references***. The Object Adapter assigns references (unique IDs) to the new objects it creates. It's responsible for mapping between the implementation-specific and ORB-specific representations of object references.

4. ***Broadcasts the presence of the object servers.*** The Object Adapter may broadcast the services it provides on the ORB—or it may respond to directory type queries from the ORB core. It is in charge of letting the outside world know of the services it manages. Eventually, we expect to see some tight levels of integration with global directory services such as X.500.

5. ***Handles incoming client calls.*** The Object Adapter interacts with the top layer—typically, an RPC—of the ORB core communication stack, peels off the request, and hands it to the interface stub. The stub is responsible for interpreting the incoming parameters and presenting them in a form that's acceptable to the object's method invocation.

6. ***Routes the up-call to the appropriate method.*** The Object Adapter is implicitly involved in the invocation of the methods described in the stubs (or the skeleton). For example, the Object Adapter may be involved in activating the implementation or authenticating the request.

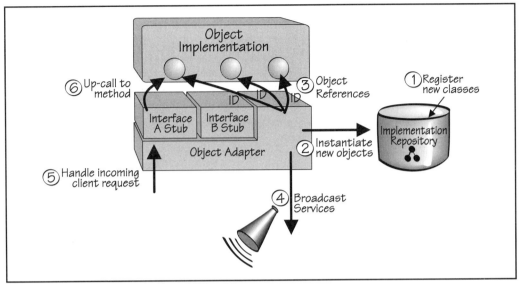

Figure 33-13. The Structure of a Typical Object Adapter.

An Object Adapter defines how an object is activated. This can be done through the creation of a new process, through the creation of a new thread within an existing process, or through the reuse of an existing thread or process.

BOA and Other Object Adapters

A server could support a variety of object adapters to satisfy different types of requests. For example, an Object Database (ODBMS) may want to implicitly register all the fine-grained objects it contains without issuing individual calls to the Object Adapter. In such a case, it doesn't make sense for an Object Adapter to maintain a per-object state. The ODBMS may want to provide a special-purpose Object Adapter that interfaces with the ORB core, and at the same time meets its special requirements. However, OMG prefers not to see a proliferation of Object Adapter types. To avoid this proliferation, CORBA specifies a *Basic Object Adapter (BOA)* that "can be used for most ORB objects with conventional implementations."

CORBA requires that a BOA adapter be available in every ORB. Object implementations that use it should be able to run on any ORB that supports the required language bindings. CORBA requires that the following functions be provided in a BOA implementation:

■ An Implementation Repository that allows the installation and registration of applications. It also contains information describing the application.

■ Mechanisms for generating and interpreting object references; activating and deactivating object implementaticns; and invoking methods and passing them their parameters.

■ A mechanism for authenticating the client making the call. BOA does not enforce any specific style of security. It guarantees that for every object or method invocation, it will identify the client (or principal) on whose behalf the request is performed. What to do with this information is left to the implementation.

■ Activation and deactivation of implementation objects.

■ Method invocations through stubs.

BOA supports traditional and object-oriented applications. It does not specify how methods are packaged or located—this could be done through DLLs or a system call at startup that identifies the location of the methods. To get the widest application coverage, CORBA defines four activation policies that specify the rules a given implementation follows for activating objects. Think of them as scheduling policies. The four policies are: *shared server, unshared server, server-per-method*, and *persistent server.*

BOA Shared Server

In a *shared server* activation policy, multiple objects may reside in the same program (i.e., process). The server is activated by BOA the first time a request is performed on any object implemented by that server (see Figure 33-14). When the server has initialized itself, it notifies BOA that it is prepared to handle requests by calling *impl_is_ready.* All subsequent requests are then delivered to this server process; BOA will not activate another server process for that implementation. The server handles one request at a time and notifies BOA via a *deactivate_obj* call when it finishes processing a request. When the process itself is ready to terminate, it notifies BOA by issuing a *deactivate_impl* call.

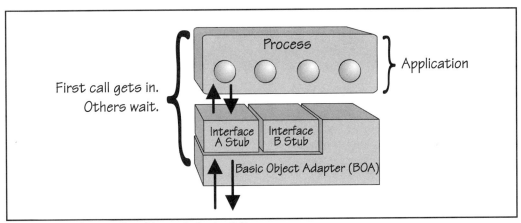

Figure 33-14. The BOA Shared Server Activation Policy.

BOA Unshared Server

In an *unshared server* activation policy, each object resides in a different server process. A new server is activated the first time a request is performed on the object (see Figure 33-15). When the object has initialized itself, it notifies BOA that it is prepared to handle requests by calling *obj_is_ready*. A new server is started whenever a request is made for an object that is not yet active, even if a server for another object with the same implementation is active. A server object remains active and will receive requests until it calls *deactivate_obj*.

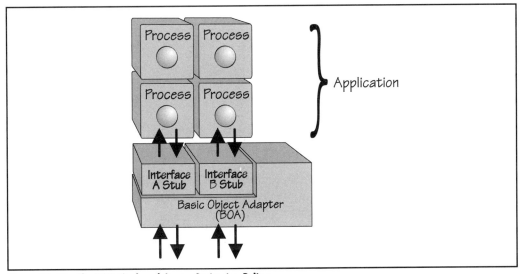

Figure 33-15. The BOA Unshared Server Activation Policy.

BOA Server-per-Method

In a *server-per-method* activation policy, a new server is always started each time a request is made. The server runs only for the duration of the particular method (see Figure 33-16). Several server processes for the same object—or even the same method of the same object—may be concurrently active. A new server is started for each request, so it's not necessary for the implementation to notify BOA when an object is ready or deactivated. BOA activates a new process for each request, whether or not another request for that operation or object is active at the same time.

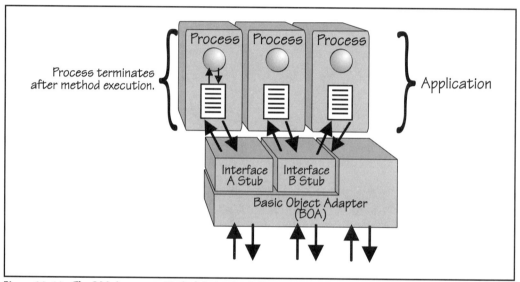

Figure 33-16. The BOA Server-per-Method Activation Policy.

BOA Persistent Server

In a *persistent server* activation policy, servers are activated by means outside BOA (see Figure 33-17). BOA may start the server application, which then notifies BOA that it's ready to accept work by means of an *impl_is_ready* call. BOA treats all subsequent requests as shared server calls; it sends activations for individual objects and method calls to a single process. If no implementation is ready when a request arrives, an error is returned for that request.

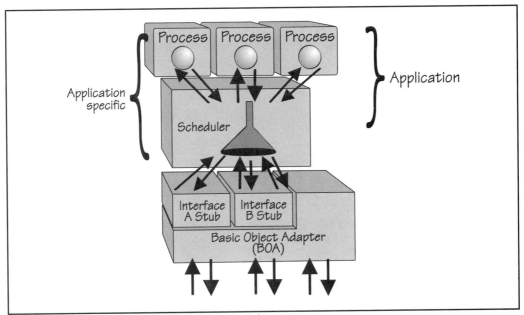

Figure 33-17. The BOA Persistent Server Activation Policy.

The CORBA Interface Repository

The Interface Repository is an online database of object definitions. These definitions may be captured directly from an IDL-compiler or through APIs—CORBA doesn't care how the information gets there. The CORBA specification, however, details how the information is organized and retrieved from the repository. It does that in a *very creative* fashion by specifying a set of classes whose instances represent the information that's in the repository. The class hierarchy mirrors the IDL specification. The result is a highly flexible object database that keeps track of collections of objects organized along the same lines as the IDL. Of course, all the objects in the repository are compiled versions of the information that's in an IDL source file.

Why Is an Interface Repository Needed Anyway?

An ORB needs to understand the definition of the objects it is working with. One way to get these definitions is by incorporating the information into the stub routines we introduced earlier. The other way to get this information is through a dynamically accessible Interface Repository. What does an ORB do with the information in the repository? It can use the object definitions to do the following:

■ ***Provide type-checking of request signatures***. The parameter types are checked regardless of whether the request is issued using dynamic APIs or through a stub. Signatures define the parameters of a method and their type.

■ ***Assist in the creation of inter-ORB gateways***. The information in the repository can be used to translate requests that go across heterogeneous ORBs.

■ ***Provide information to dynamic clients and tools***. Clients use the interface repository to create on-the-fly method invocations. Tools—such as class browsers, application generators, and compilers—can use the information to obtain inheritance structures and class definitions at run time.

Interface Repositories can be maintained locally or managed as departmental or enterprise resources; they serve as valuable sources of information on class structures. An ORB may have access to multiple Interface Repositories.

The Interface Repository Classes

The Interface Repository is implemented as a set of objects that represent the information in it. These objects must be persistent, i.e., they must be stored on a nonvolatile medium. CORBA groups them into modules that represent naming spaces. The repository object names are only unique relative to a module. CORBA defines a class for each of its eight IDL structures:

■ ***ModuleDef*** defines "namespace" modules.
■ ***InterfaceDef*** defines the object class.
■ ***OperationDef*** defines the methods of an object class.
■ ***ParameterDef*** defines an argument of a method.
■ ***AttributeDef*** defines the attributes of an object class.
■ ***ConstantDef*** defines constants that are associated with an object class.
■ ***ExceptionDef*** defines the exception handlers that are associated with an object class.
■ ***TypeDef*** defines the named types that are part of an IDL definition.

In addition to those eight classes that represent IDL structures, CORBA specifies a **Repository** class that serves as the root for all the modules contained in a repository namespace. Figure 33-18 shows the *containment hierarchy* for these classes. You'll notice that some of the classes—for example, repository—contain other classes. Others—for example, ModuleDef—are contained in other classes (repository) and at the same time are containers of classes. Finally, some classes—for example, ExceptionDef—are always contained in other classes but don't contain classes of their own.

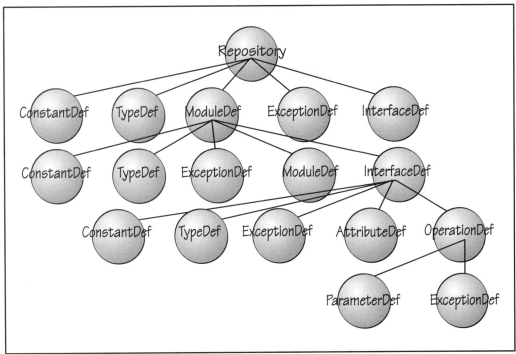

Figure 33-18. The Containment Hierarchy for the Interface Repository Classes.

The CORBA Interface Repository architects noticed these containment hierarchies and defined two *abstract classes*—i.e., classes that cannot be instantiated—called **Container** and **Contained**. The Container class defines the behavior of objects that contain other objects; the Contained class defines the behavior of objects that are contained in other objects. Having done this, the CORBA people proposed the class *implementation hierarchy* shown in Figure 33-19 (we used an example from SOM). The figure shows an *inheritance* hierarchy as opposed to a *containment* hierarchy. According to CORBA, all the repository classes can be derived from Container, from Contained, or from both through multiple inheritance. This clever scheme allows the repository objects to behave according to their containment relationships.

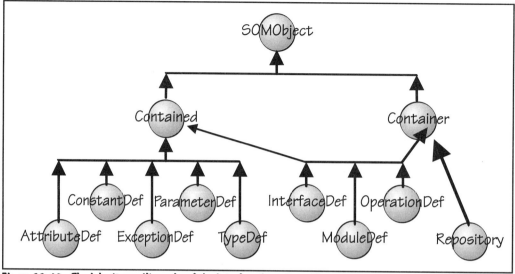

Figure 33-19. The Inheritance Hierarchy of the Interface Repository Classes.

The Interface Repository Operations

The Interface Repository is accessed by invoking methods on different object types. Because of that clever design, only nine methods are required to navigate and extract information from the repository objects (see Figure 33-20). Five of these methods are defined on the ancestor classes: Container and Contained. The other four are method overrides that adapt the base methods for specific object types. Here's a description of the five basic methods:

■ **Contents**—when this method is applied on Container objects, it returns a sequence of pointers to the objects it contains. The method provides options for limiting the search by excluding inherited objects or by looking for a specific type of object (for example, of type InterfaceDef).

■ **Describe_contents**—when this method is applied on Container objects, it returns a sequence of pointers to *ContainerDescription* structures that contain IDL information; this information "describes" each object within the container.

■ **Lookup_name**—when this method is applied on Container objects, it returns a sequence of pointers to objects of a given name.

■ **Describe**—when this method is applied on a target Contained object, it returns a *Description* structure containing the IDL information that "describes" the object.

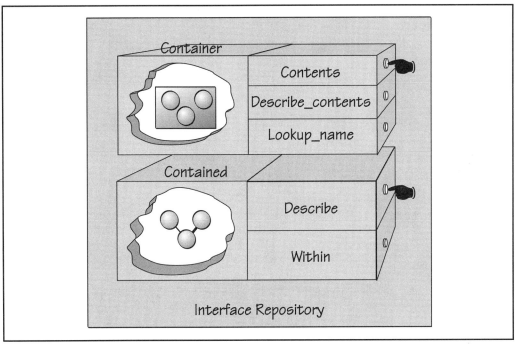

Figure 33-20. The Container and Contained Interface Repository Classes.

■ **Within**—when this method is applied on a target Contained object, it returns a sequence of objects which contain the target.

These method calls allow you to navigate through a repository global container or the namespaces of specific modules looking for objects that meet your search criteria. When an object is found, the *describe* method invocation is used to retrieve the IDL information that defines it. In summary, CORBA defines an object database—the Interface Repository—to keep track of user application object descriptions. It's all very recursive.

Is CORBA Ready for Prime Time?

Soapbox

Interoperability is the customer organizations' single most requested upgrade to CORBA.

> — *Richard Soley,*
> *VP of Technology, OMG (May, 1993)*

Transactions are the primary concern of our customers, seconded by interoperability, after they get the basic distributed object transparency the ORB provides.

> — *Cliff Reeves,*
> *Director of Objects, IBM (May, 1993)*

The best way to answer the question is to look at what's missing from CORBA, when the missing pieces can be expected, and what, if any, are the showstoppers in the technology. Richard Soley and Cliff Reeves started a list of what's missing in CORBA; now let's complete it:

■ ***Interoperability standards for ORBs.*** CORBA took an "anything goes" approach to creating ORBs. Now they have the problem of how to get these ORBs to communicate with each other. CORBA must deal with the typical NOS level communication stuff—including authentication, object FAPs, directory services, federated naming, and stacks—and it must deal with object naming and representation issues across the different vendor implementations. OMG would have been much better off building on top of DCE or some existing NOS platform.

■ ***What happened to ACID motherhood?*** In Part 5, we established that it would be insane to build client/server systems without transaction protection. The anemic BOAs are nowhere close to providing the functionality of a TP Monitor: process management, load balancing, transaction protection, high availability, etc. They're obviously not ready for mission-critical prime time.

■ ***Where's MOM?*** MOM is extremely important in heterogeneous environments. We absolutely need object messaging queues on both the client and the server.

■ ***BLOBs.*** The current CORBA standard has almost nothing to say about BLOBs and multimedia objects.

■ ***Broadcast.*** The current CORBA standard does not support broadcast or multicast, which are needed in groupware applications, for systems management and for the creation of ORB-mediated object bazaars.

■ ***Shared object concurrency control, locking, versioning, and replicas.*** CORBA needs to address these issues to be on par with other client/server architectures.

■ ***Persistent object support.*** How is the object state saved and restored between machine shutdowns? The Implementation Repository is a first step, but it is nowhere close to providing a persistent store for objects.

■ ***Object interchange standard.*** In the future, objects will be able to roam across machines. General Magic does some of that today. We need standards that specify object interchanges.

■ ***Certification suites.*** What does it mean to be CORBA-compliant? What are the levels of compliance? Who's going to provide the seal of approval?

■ ***Support for fine-grained objects.*** How does CORBA deal with millions of small objects? Who manages the object references? How are these references stored persistently?

That's a pretty nasty list of deficiencies in the current CORBA 1.1 specification. So what's OMG doing about it? This may come as a surprise, but they're really on top of many of the issues. Most of the action is outside the ORB; it has shifted to the Object Services—including naming, event services, lifecycle management, concurrent access, persistent stores, object replication, and transactions. We'll be covering Object Services in the next chapter. The ORB is limiting itself to providing the basic distributed infrastructure. The ORB 2.0 committee is addressing the interoperability question (through gateways). OMG is subcontracting X/Open for a set of CORBA-certification test suites. In addition, it is working on more complete definition of the Implementation Repository, and is looking at broadcast and MOM (but we don't expect them until ORB 3.0).

Are there any showstoppers? As far as consortia go, OMG is very proactive and has an excellent technical staff. But it's still a vendor-dominated consortium—it costs $50k per year to be a full-voting member—and vendors have their own agendas of what standards should cover and, more importantly, not cover. For example, vendors prefer to provide interoperability through gateways to preserve their current product investments. For the same reason, vendors don't want any changes to the ORB or APIs; the major architectural changes go into the Object Services.

In the long run, these are all minor issues. Are there any real technical showstoppers? From our vantage point, there appears to be solutions to all the issues we raised, with one exception: Can ORBs handle fine-grained objects? We don't have enough experience at this time with ORBs to answer this question. The current BOA is certainly not capable of dealing with millions of fine-grained objects. For example, how do you handle a database of one million bank accounts where each account is an object? The ODBMS people have working solutions, but they did that by bypassing BOA and even the ORB itself. We will return to this issue after we cover ODBMSs.

So are ORBs ready for prime time? They're getting there. You can use the current generation of ORBs in homogeneous environments to develop a better understanding of distributed object technology and encapsulate some of your key legacy applications with object wrappers. The current ORBs will help you create and manage a consistent set of distributed interfaces to all your important networked applications, tools, utilities, and medium-grained objects. The ORB becomes the "great integrator." Object-oriented production applications with fine-grained distributed objects will come *later*. These are the applications that will ultimately revolutionize the way we do client/server computing. ❑

Chapter 34

Distributed Object Services

OMG envisions a day where users of software start up applications as they start up their cars, with no more concern about the underlying structure of the objects they manipulate than the driver has about the molecular construction of gasoline.

> — *Object Management Architecture Guide*
> *(September, 1992)*

An ORB by itself doesn't have all it takes for objects to interoperate at the *application* level. The ORB is like a telephone exchange—it provides the basic mechanism for brokering object requests. All other services are provided by objects with IDL interfaces that reside on top of the ORB. The IDL and ORB provide the function of a "software bus"; the services and end-user object applications plug into this bus. We've finally reached a point where we don't have to introduce more layers of infrastructure—you simply plug your objects into the ORB and play them.

As we explained in the last chapter, OMG is working hard on defining object services. Its *Object Management Architecture* separates services into two categories: the system-oriented *Object Services* that each ORB must provide, and optional *Common Facilities* that are more end-user oriented. Vendors are expected to package both types of services in *system frameworks*. A budding object component "cottage industry" is expected to provide application object classes (or even frameworks) that plug directly into CORBA-compliant ORBs. All these services take advantage of the inherent self-describing nature of objects and the uniform interfaces they provide.

This chapter provides a brief introduction to the OMG Object Services (the white area in Figure 34-1). We first cover the Object Services that became OMG standards in late 1993 and early 1994—including Lifecycle, Naming, Persistence, and Event Notification. These services provide very basic functions that are needed by all distributed object applications (and services). We then briefly look at the next wave of services (late 1994)—including Security, Relationships, Transactions, and Concurrency Control. We also speculate on what's coming beyond that.

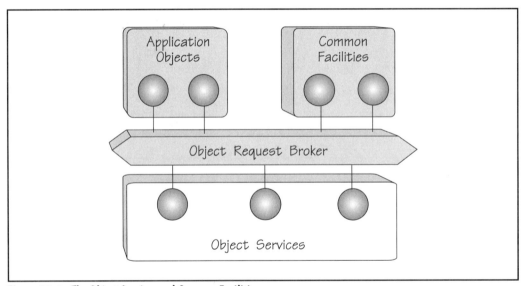

Figure 34-1. The Object Services and Common Facilities.

DISTRIBUTED OBJECT SERVICES

In CORBA-compliant ORB environments, distributed object services are classes of IDL-defined objects that provide useful middleware functions for all objects. These are functions that each application would have to recreate if they didn't already exist. More specifically, these functions help manage, distribute, store, exchange, find, copy, protect, and version objects on a network. Some of the services—for example, directory and protection—may already be provided by NOSs. If that's the case, they may simply be encapsulated with IDL-defined wrappers and used "as is." In other words, OMG is not trying to reinvent *all* the client/server middleware;

however, it wants all the relevant existing services to be "objectified" so that they can be accessed via ORBs. This is classical "hammer and nails" OMG stuff.

WHICH DISTRIBUTED OBJECT SERVICES?

Table 34-1 provides a list of object services OMG is currently working on (or considering). The "objects" in the table refer to code that responds to an IDL-defined interface. In addition to the object services described in the table, the OMG *Object Services Architecture* identifies a need for *system-related* object services including archive, backup/restore, startup, installation, operational controls, replication, threads, and time. These services may end up in a future ORB specification. Some of these services are also being addressed by NOS and distributed system management standards.

Table 34-1. The OMG Object Services.

Service	Function
Object Lifecycle	Provides functions for managing object creation, deletion, copying, and equivalence.
Object Persistence	Makes an object instance live (or persist) beyond the lifetime of the process that created it or the client applications that access it.
Object Events	Sends event notifications to interested objects.
Object Naming	Supports the mapping of meaningful names to objects.
Object Security	Provides access control list protection on objects and interfaces.
Object Relationships	Supports associations between two or more objects and defines containment relationships.
Object Transactions	Extends ACID properties to objects.
Object Concurrency Control	Mediates the concurrent access to one or more objects by one or more objects.
Object Externalization	Deals with the issues of external and internal object representations.
Object Data Interchange	Supports the exchange of some or all of an object's state information between two objects.
Object Licensing	Provides hooks for enforcing license management on object classes (for example, how many objects of a given class can be instantiated).
Object Trading	Matches available services to the services needed by a client.

Table 34-1. The OMG Object Services. (Continued)

Service	Function
Object Query	Supports operations on sets and collections of object attributes. The queries return sets and collections. The service also supports the indexing of objects.
Object Change Management	Manages the consistent evolution of objects, including versioning and configuration management.
Object Properties	Provides dynamic named attributes associated with an object.

SO WHEN CAN WE EXPECT THESE SERVICES?

The Event, Lifecycle, and Naming Services became OMG standards in September 1993. The Object Persistence Service was approved by the OMG Technical Committee and is being finalized as we go to press. Figure 34-2 is our best guess for when the next set of standards may be adopted. The following Briefing box roughly explains the OMG standard selection process. This should give you an idea of when these services will be offered in commercial implementations. RFP1 services should appear in product form in mid-1994; RFP2 services may appear in the early part of 1995; and the services in RFP3 and RFP4 may appear in late 1995. So why is there this interest in services, which, at best, may start to hit the streets in mid-1994? Because they give us a clear idea of the real power that's in distributed objects and what they can do for client/server systems.

The object services bring together some of the best distributed technology in the industry. For the first time, a common IDL language is used to define services that can incrementally be added to CORBA-compliant ORBs. A wide coalition of vendors are using this common language and infrastructure to build the next generation of distributed services. Vendors use the IDL to define the interfaces and protocols they can all live with; they can then compete with implementations.

To better appreciate the services that are being built on top of ORBs, we'll give you a "sneak preview" of the standards. We will first look at the RFP1 services because they provide foundation building blocks for the other services; they've already been adopted as standards. We'll also look at the joint proposal by Tandem, Transarc, and IBM for Object Transaction Services (it's one of five proposals on the table, but it's the most likely one to be adopted). This very preliminary information should give you a good idea of how the distributed object infrastructure is being built brick by brick.

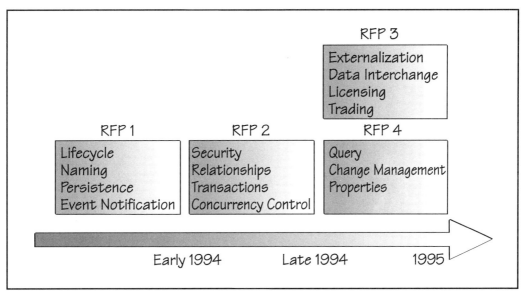

Figure 34-2. A Best Guess for When OMG Will Deliver What Object Services.

 FYI

How the OMG Creates Its Standards

Briefing

The OMG is not your *typical* standards organization; it's an extremely creative organization that seems to be able to effect change proactively. The charter of the OMG is to develop architectures and specify standards for objects to interoperate across heterogeneous network computers. The organization consists of 300 members; 75 are corporate members. The OMG has a Board of Directors and a Technical Committee (TC) consisting of individuals appointed by the board. The standards work gets done by standing groups composed of members of the TC and invited guests with a mandate to provide a recommendation to the TC in some area. These groups are known as Subcommittees (SC), Task Forces (TF), and Special Interest Groups (SIG). The worse thing about the OMG is having to deal with all these acronyms.

After the OMG and members magically pick a subject area that needs to be standardized within the *Object Management Architecture*, they follow these steps:

1. The OMG *Technical Committee (TC)* either forms a new *Task Force (TF)* or hands the job to an existing one such as Object Services, ORB 2.0, or the newly formed Common Functions.

2. The TC and TF release a *Request for Information (RFI)*, asking the vendor community at large for input on the standard.

3. Based on the RFI response, the TC releases a *Request for Proposal (RFP)*, asking the community for existing technology (beta products are accepted) to fulfill the requirement. It takes the TC and TF about four months to create and review an RFP, and they typically expect the community to respond to it within two or three months.

4. The TF selects one or more RFP responses and may ask for revisions or a merger of responses. This process takes about four months.

5. The TF votes on the final RFP response and submits it to the TC, which must vote on it within a month (there's a "three-week rule").

6. The TF recommends the standard to the OMG Board of Directors, which usually adopts the specification within a month.

In practice, it takes OMG from one to two years to adopt a standard (depending on the number of revisions requested by the TF). To speed the process, RFPs may include a group of proposals and they may be issued in parallel.

The OMG, unlike OSF, does not create technologies or working code; it simply creates the IDL specifications and models. The vendors can implement the IDL specification in any way they please. Note that IDL interfaces are object-based, so they can be extended, customized, and subset; it's more than a standard API. Because of all this freedom, compliance testing becomes very important in an OMG environment. ❑

THE OBJECT EVENT SERVICE

The *Object Event Service* allows objects to dynamically register or unregister their interest in specific events. An *event* is an occurrence within an object specified to be of interest to one or more objects. A *notification* is a message sent to the interested parties informing them that a specific event occurred. Normally, the object generating the event doesn't have to know who the interested parties are. This is all handled by the Event Service, which creates a loosely-coupled communication channel between objects that don't know much about each other. Events are more loosely-coupled than RPC but less loosely-coupled than MOM.

The event service defines two roles for objects: suppliers and consumers. The *suppliers* produce events and the *consumers* process them via event-handlers. Events are communicated between suppliers and consumers using standard CORBA requests. In addition, there are two models for communicating event data: push and pull. In the *push model* the supplier of events takes the initiative and initiates the transfer of event data to consumers. In the *pull model*, the consumer takes the initiative and requests event data from a supplier. An *event channel* is an intervening object that is both a supplier and consumer of events. It allows multiple suppliers to communicate with multiple consumers asynchronously and without knowing about each other. An event channel is a standard CORBA object that sits on the ORB and decouples the communications between suppliers and consumers.

The event channel supports both the "push and pull" event notification models (see Figure 34-3):

■ With the **Push model**, the supplier issues a *push* method invocation on the event channel object; the event channel, in turn, pushes the event data to the consumer objects. A consumer can stop receiving events by invoking a *disconnect* method on the event channel. The consumer invokes an *add_push_consumer* method on the event channel to register its interest in some event type.

■ With the **Pull model**, the consumer issues a *pull* method invocation on the event channel object; the event channel, in turn, pulls the event data from the supplier. Using the *try_pull* method, the consumer can periodically poll for events. A supplier can stop accepting requests for supplying events by invoking a *Disconnect* method on the event channel. The supplier issues an *add_push_supplier* method on the event channel to register its object reference and offer its services.

An event channel can communicate with a supplier using one style of communication, and communicate with a consumer using a different style of communication.

The generic event channel object does not understand the contents of the data it's passing. It leaves it up to the producers and consumers to agree on common event semantics. However, the Event Services also support a *Typed Event* model that allows applications to describe the contents of events using the IDL. The parameters passed must be input only; no information is returned. Typed events support both the pull and push model. Using the IDL, you can define special event types— for example, document or system management events. Consumers can then subscribe to a particular event type; typing becomes a powerful means of filtering event information. You can track the exact events you're interested in (it's a rifle instead of a shotgun).

The event interface supports multiple levels of service (for example, different levels of reliability). A persistent store of events may be supplied by the event channel object as part of its service (for example, some key events may be stored for up to a week or whatever). The event channels are *well-known objects*. They can serve as anchor points to help objects discover each other at run time. The consumers

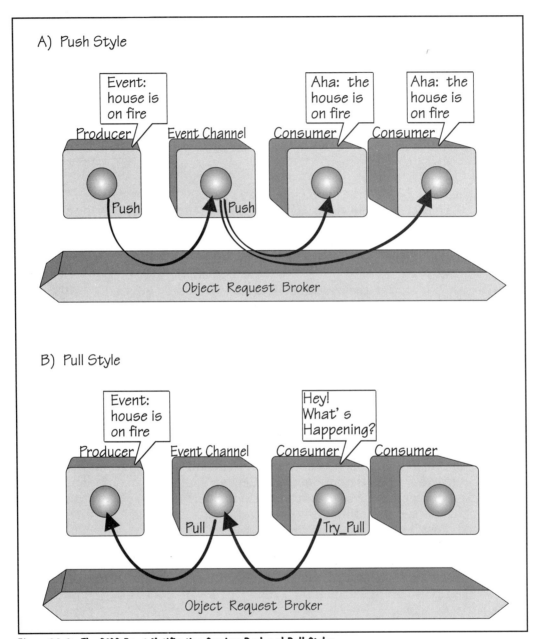

Figure 34-3. The OMG Event Notification Service: Push and Pull Styles.

and suppliers of events use the standard CORBA IDL interfaces—no extensions are required.

In summary, the Event Service introduces a minimalist form of MOM communications into CORBA. It is minimalist because it doesn't support message priorities, filters, rich message typing, transaction protection, reception confirmation, time-to-live stamps, or sophisticated queue management. The channel objects make it easier to develop groupware applications and to help objects discover each other. Event typing allows you to zoom-in on the events of interest. The fan-in and fan-out capabilities of event channel objects can serve as a broadcast or multicast system, which can help create online object bazaars. The Event Service is extremely useful; it provides a foundation for creating a new genre of distributed object applications.

THE OBJECT NAMING SERVICE

The Object Naming Service is the principal mechanism for objects on ORB-based systems to locate other objects. *Names* are humanly recognizable values that identify an object. The naming service maps these human names to object references. A name-to-object association is called a *name binding*. A *naming context* is a namespace in which the object is unique. To *resolve a name* means to find the object associated with the name in a given context. To *bind a name* is to create a name-to-object association for a particular context. In other words, we're creating federated naming services for objects. It should be "deja vu" for readers of this book (if not, see Part 3). The Object Naming Service was originated by 15 companies that go under the name of JOSS, which stands for Joint Object Services Submission. It became an OMG standard in September 1993.

The Object Naming Service does not try to reinvent the wheel. It was designed to be built on top of existing name and directory services such as the DCE CDS, ISO X.500, or Sun NIS+. The service supports naming hierarchies that allow clients to navigate through different naming context trees in search of the object they're looking for. Objects can register their characteristics with the Naming Service to help clients locate them through searches on attributes.

Figure 34-4 shows the two classes—**NamingContext** and **BindingIterator**—that implement the Naming Service and the methods (or interfaces) they export. The binding methods add and destroy names and contexts within a naming hierarchy. After they're named, objects can be found using the *resolve* method. The *list* method allows a client to iterate through a returned set of names; the iteration is done using *next_one* and *next_n*; and *destroy* frees the iteration after it is complete.

In summary, the Object Naming Service is provided by instances of two object classes that export methods for managing namespaces and querying and navigating

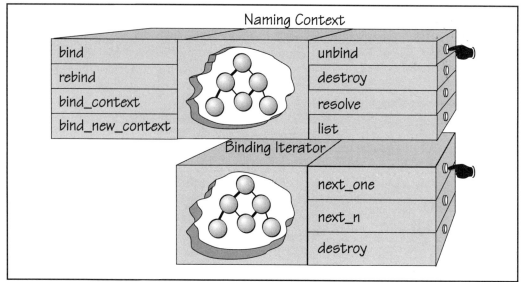

Figure 34-4. The OMG Object Naming Service.

through them. These objects live on the ORB and can be implemented by encapsulating existing procedural naming services with CORBA wrappers. The OMG simply
defines the interfaces to these services, not the implementation.

THE OBJECT LIFECYCLE SERVICE

The Object Lifecycle Service provides operations for creating, copying, moving, and
deleting objects. All the operations must handle associations between groups of
related objects. This includes containment and reference relationships, as well as
the enforcement of referential integrity constraints between objects. The lifecycle
services provide an important element of the infrastructure required to support
nomadic objects.

Let's walk through an example of how the lifecycle operations are implemented on
an object that has explicit associations with other objects. Figure 34-5 shows a
document object that contains one or more page objects, which in turn contain
multimedia and text objects. The document is stored in a folder object and
references a catalog object that contains an entry for it. The Lifecycle Service
maintains a graph of all these associations.

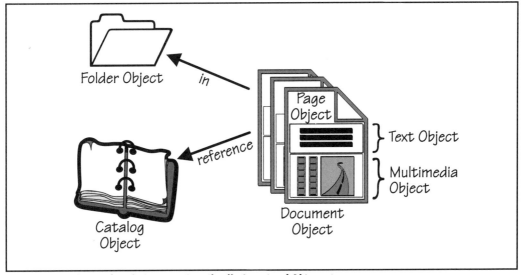

Figure 34-5. Object Lifecycle Services Must Handle Associated Objects.

A "deep move" causes the document to be moved along with all its dependent objects (the pages and their contents); the reference in the catalog is updated; and the document gets removed from the source folder and gets inserted into the target folder (see Figure 34-6). Likewise, when the document is externalized to a file, all the objects it contains go with it. When the document is deleted, its page objects and the graphic objects they contain are also deleted. The references to the document are removed from both the catalog and the folder (see Figure 34-7).

Clients have a simple view of Lifecycle operations. In the example in Figure 34-5, the clients simply invoke methods to move, copy, delete, externalize, and internalize the document object; all the associated objects are handled transparently. The lifecycle service implementation must be able to handle simple containment and reference relationships.

To create a new object, a client must find a *factory object* (meaning an object that knows how to instantiate an object of that class), issue a create request, and get back an object reference. A client can also create an object by cloning an existing object using a template. The factory objects must allocate resources, obtain object references, and register the new objects with the Object Adapter and Implementation Repository. When an object is copied across machines, the factory object on the target node is involved.

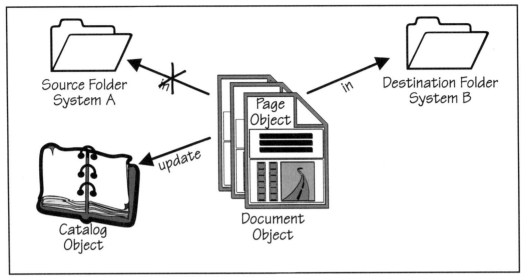

Figure 34-6. A "Deep" Move Handles All the Associations.

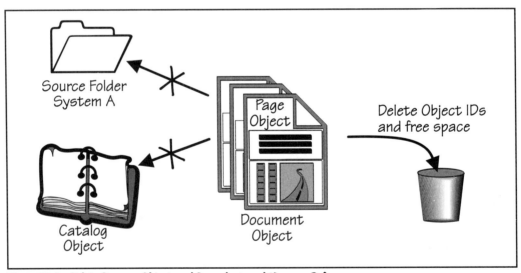

Figure 34-7. Delete Removes Objects and Dependents and Manages References.

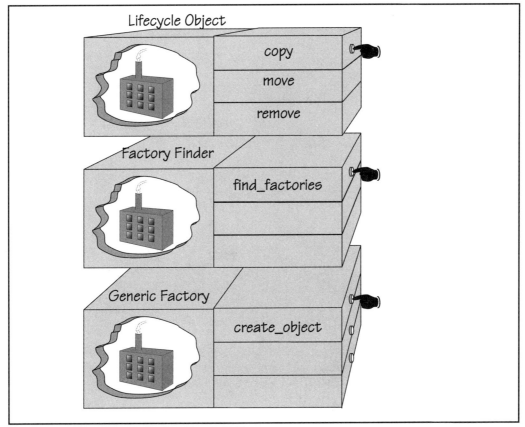

Figure 34-8. Object Lifecycle Services Class Definitions.

Figure 34-8 shows the three class interfaces defined by the OMG specification for providing Lifecycle services. The **LifeCycleObject** defines the copy, move, and remove operations; it provides the client's primary view of lifecycle operations on target objects. The *copy* operation makes a copy of the object and returns an object reference; the *move* operation allows the object to roam to any location within the scope of the factory finder; and the *remove* operation deletes the object. The **FactoryFinder** defines an interface for finding factories. Because every object requires different resource information for its creation, it's impossible to define a single factory interface for all objects. The **GenericFactory** simply defines a general *create_object* operation.

THE OBJECT PERSISTENCE SERVICE

The Object Persistence Service allows objects to "persist" beyond the application that creates the object or the clients that use it. The lifetime of an object could be relatively short or indefinite. The service allows the state of an object to be saved in a persistent store and restored when it's needed (see Figure 34-9). The state of the object can be cached in local memory; data access speeds in this case are comparable to a native programming language. The caching is done transparently.

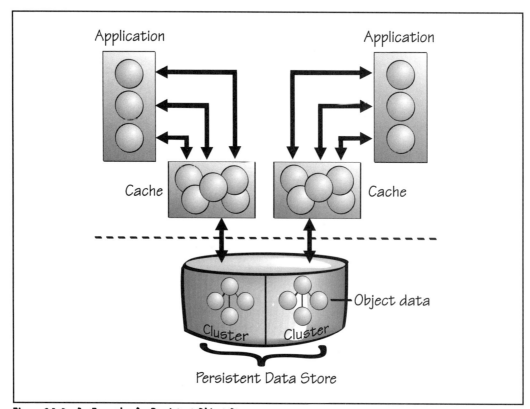

Figure 34-9. An Example of a Persistent Object Store.

The Object Persistence Service is the result of the merging of the IBM and SunSoft submissions to the OMG (see the next Soapbox). The result is a specification that can accommodate a variety of storage services including SQL, Object Databases, document filing systems (like Bento), and others. The Persistence Service defines the interface to data as a collection of objects using IDL-defined interfaces. The implementations of the interface can be lightweight file systems or heavyweight full-featured SQL or Object Database systems. The idea was to create an open implementation that meets the different persistent storage requirements of objects—it encompasses the needs of large-grained objects (such as documents) as well as fined-grained objects (such as SQL table rows).

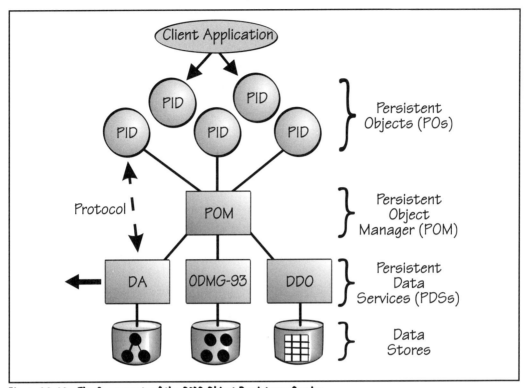

Figure 34-10. The Components of the OMG Object Persistence Service.

The Object Persistence Service can accommodate different levels of client involvement. At one extreme, the service can be made transparent to client applications. At the other extreme, client applications can use storage-specific protocols that surface all the details of the underlying persistence storage mechanism. Again, the idea is to accommodate different object needs: Some objects need a fine-grain level of control over their persistent store, and for others ignorance is pure bliss. The object has the choice of how much persistent data management it wants to delegate to the service.

Figure 34-10 shows the components of the Object Persistence Service. Let's quickly review what they each do starting from the top down:

■ ***Persistent Objects (POs)*** are objects whose state is persistently stored. Objects can be made persistent by inheriting (through the IDL) the **Persistent Object** class behavior. The service also provides a "back door" to persistence using *persistent factories* instead of the IDL (i.e., all objects created through these factories are persistent). Every persistent object has a *Persistent Identifier (PID)* that describes the location within a datastore of that object using a string identifier.

■ ***Persistent Object Manager (POM)*** is an implementation-independent inter-face for persistence operations. It insulates the POs from a particular Persistent Data Service. The POM can route the calls to the appropriate Persistent Data Service by looking at information that's encoded in the PID. A Persistent Storage Service has a single POM that typically sits between the objects and the Persistent Data Services.

■ ***Persistent Data Services (PDSs)*** are interfaces to the particular Datastore implementations. The PDSs perform the actual work for moving data between an object and a datastore. The PDSs export a set of uniform IDL-specified interfaces and an implementation-dependent *protocol*. The protocol provides a mechanism for getting data in and out of an object. The Persistent Object Service specifies three protocols: *Direct Attribute (DA)*, *Object Database Management Group (ODMG-93)*, and *Dynamic Data Object (DDO)*.

■ ***DataStores*** are the implementations that store an object's persistent data independently of the address space containing the object.

In a nutshell, the Persistent Storage Service provides different levels of abstractions that hide different storage implementations (see Figure 34-11). For most applications, the persistent mechanism will be totally transparent. If you need more data intimacy, the POM provides a generic interface that allows different PDSs to

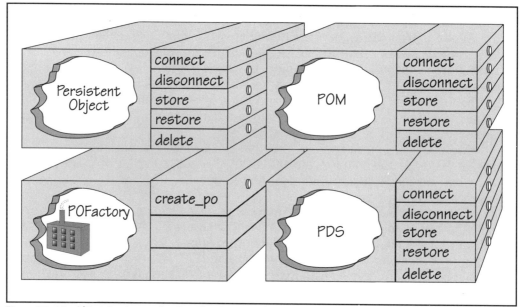

Figure 34-11. Object Persistence Service: The Main Interface Classes.

plug-and-play transparently. The PDSs provide three generic interfaces coupled with implementation-specific protocols—that's where the rubber meets the road:

- The Direct Access (*DA*) *PSM protocol* is the basis of the original JOSS proposal; it provides direct access to persistent data using an IDL-like *Data Definition Language* (see Briefing box that follows).

- The *ODMG-93 protocol* provides direct access from C++ using an ODMG-specific DDL. We cover ODMG in the Object Database chapter.

- The *Dynamic Data Object (DDO) protocol* is a datastore-neutral representation of an object's persistent data; it defines a structure that contains all the data for an object. We cover a current version of DDO in the chapter on DSOM.

The Direct Attribute PSM Protocol

Briefing

The Direct Attribute (DA) protocol defines an interface for directly accessing a Persistent Data Store (PDS). It's meant to support very "fine-grained" objects that are comparable in size and complexity to typical C++ data structures. The design is the brainchild of the *Object Database* vendor contingent of JOSS. It's is an upwardly compatible subset of the *Object Database Management Group (ODMG)* standard that we cover in a later chapter. The service allows OMG-compliant object applications to easily upgrade to Object Databases as their object storage needs evolve.

The service uses an IDL-like *Data Definition Language (DDL)* to define persistent data. It also employs an IDL-like language binding approach to provide client API support from within C and C++. To provide compatibility with Object Databases, access to persistent data is done using native programming language operations. For example, C and C++ data structure components can be accessed using the dot notation. The DDL only supports data structures defined in CORBA 1.1; the only *collection* data type supported is an IDL *sequence*—an element array of variable length. In contrast, Object Databases support a wide range of container types (more on that later).

To store an object's persistent state, the designer of a CORBA object implementation first uses the *Persistent Storage Manager (PSM)* DDL to describe the object's persistent state as one or more *data object* interfaces. Each data object provides persistent storage for the list of attributes defined by its interface. A *schema* is a group of data objects that defines the persistent storage for an application. The schema bindings are created by a standalone DDL compiler.

A *data store* may service many schemas (i.e., applications); each is given its own *cluster* of storage (see Figure 34-9 on page 736). Changes to data within a cluster are under ACID transaction control. However, the cluster store can only deal with single-user transactions. The design is predicated on the idea that only an object should access its private state. Concurrency control is achieved via ORB calls between objects. The persistent store does not support fine-grained concurrent access to persistent data; this functionality is provided by a full-fledged Object Database. However, the data store supports concurrent activity on different clusters—they're treated as totally independent databases that share a physical store. Each cluster is isolated from the concurrent changes occurring elsewhere in the data store. ❑

How Standards Are Really Created

Soapbox

*T*hose IBM guys gave us a hard time.

> — **Unnamed friend,**
> **JOSS (January, 1994)**

*Y*ou're lucky we were persistent (no pun intended). We've done the world a service by standing up for the idea that objects can be stored in any form of persistent storage.

> — **Roger Sessions,**
> **IBM (January, 1994)**

The combination of the JOSS and IBM proposal for Object Persistence Services is more than just the merging of two proposals—it really combines the best of two worlds. The original JOSS proposal was centered around providing a transparent persistent store for C++ objects. The emphasis was on data objects not CORBA objects. It was very much in line with the strategy of the Object Database vendors. The JOSS proposal even abandoned the IDL in favor of direct APIs to the objectstore. The idea was to maximize the persistent store performance of fine-grained C++ objects.

The IBM proposal (the work of Roger Sessions and Dan Chang) was a more traditional CORBA object approach that used the IDL to encapsulate the Persistent Object Services. It decoupled the client from the service and allowed different persistent stores to plug-and-play behind the interface. This means that the service could be used to encapsulate any persistent store—including SQL databases, Bento-like containers, file systems, or Object Databases. It's the standard OMG encapsulation stuff (hammer and nails).

The merger of the two proposals—an effort that lasted over six months—gave us the best of all worlds. This includes CORBA persistent objects with IDL interfaces, a wide choice of objectstore implementations, and fine-grained object performance. These are the components that we covered in this section.

But since we're on a soapbox, let's give Roger and Dan a hand. They were really the underdogs, who as Spike Lee would put it, "did the right thing." JOSS had the formidable endorsement of 17 vendors. The IBM people couldn't even agree among themselves; they came in with two separate proposals—one from Roger (from IBM, Austin) and one from Dan (from IBM, San Jose). Even after Roger and Dan joined forces, everybody (even at IBM) felt their cause was totally hopeless. But they persevered (Roger can be tenacious). Eventually, about half the JOSS contingent, in a tumultuous meeting in Paris, felt there was enough technical merit (and benefits) in the Roger/Dan proposal to warrant a merger. As a result, we have another great OMG standard. ❑

THE OBJECT TRANSACTION SERVICE

We made the case in Part 5 that transactions are essential for building reliable distributed applications. So it should come as no surprise that transactions and distributed objects are getting married. This marriage will be cemented by the Object Transaction Service. It will provide ORBs with a service that supports the ACID properties of transactions and an environment for running transactional applications. The service allows both ORB and non-ORB applications to participate in the same transaction; it provides interoperability between object transactions and transactions that adhere to the X/Open DTP standard.[1]

---

[1] The Object Transaction Service is still in the early discussion phases of the OMG adoption process (with five contending proposals). We present in this section the joint proposal submitted to the OMG by IBM/Tandem/Transarc in November 1993. The proposal was created by the top TP Monitor architects in the industry; it has a very good chance of becoming the standard (0.8 probability). The key architects included Tony Storey, Ed Cobb, and Iain Houston from IBM; Pete Holman and Wilfried Kruse from Tandem; and Graeme Dixon from Transarc. They produced an excellent design for marrying transactions with objects. However, be warned that what you read in this section is not final.

The Object Transaction Service manages the transaction on behalf of the application and guarantees system-level integrity. This means that the service must be aware of the propagation of the transaction so that it can reliably implement the ACID semantics. It must track all transaction activity and ensure the all-or-nothing properties. Transactions can include multiple, separately-defined ACID objects. The Object Transaction Service provides the functions that allow multiple objects to be involved in a single transaction, to coordinate the completion of the transaction, and to allow objects to include changes in their internal state as part of a transaction.

Figure 34-12 shows the elements of the Object Transaction Services. The service itself consists of two classes: *Transaction* and *Transaction Manager*. The objects that are involved in the transaction can assume one of three roles: *Transactional Clients*, *Transactional Objects*, or *Recoverable Objects*. Let's go over these pieces and see what they do:

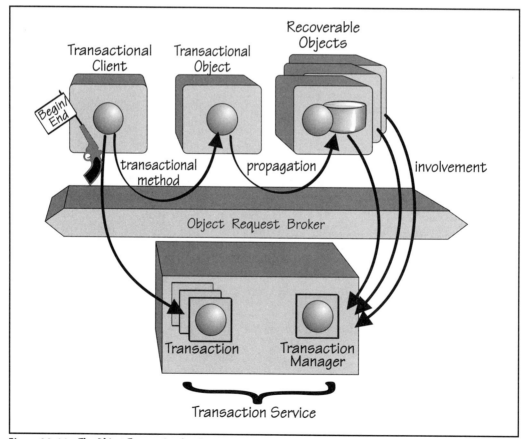

Figure 34-12. The Object Transaction Services.

■ A **transactional client** issues a set of method invocations that are bracketed by begin/end transaction *demarcations*. The calls within the bracket may be for both transactional and non-transactional objects. An object is declared transactional through an attribute in its IDL definition. The ORB intercepts the *begin* call and directs it to the Transaction Service, which creates an object instance for the new transaction and returns an ID. The ORB propagates the ID in all subsequent communications among the participants in the transaction. The ORB also gets involved when the client issues a commit or rollback and notifies the Transaction Service. A client is totally oblivious to all this under-the-cover activity; it simply starts a transaction, issues its method invocations, and commits or rolls back the transaction.

■ A **transactional object** is an object with at least one IDL-declared transactional method. When a transactional method is invoked, the transaction ID is *propagated* from the client to the transactional object. The object in turn propagates this ID when it calls other transactional objects or recoverable objects. Transaction IDs are not propagated on ordinary method invocations (the IDL default).

■ A **recoverable object** is the object-oriented version of a resource manager. It's an object whose internal state has ACID properties; the state changes at transaction boundaries. A recoverable object is a transactional object with ACID resources to protect. It uses the *register* method invocation to tell the Transaction Manager that it has just joined the transaction whose ID was propagated in the client call. The recoverable object also exports four methods that are used by a transaction coordinator (the coordinator is the Transaction Manager whose client originates the transaction) to orchestrate an ORB-mediated two-phase commit protocol (see Figure 34-13).

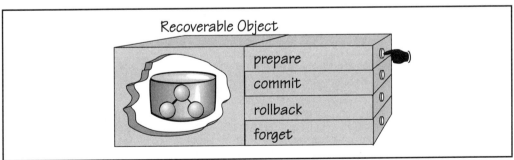

Figure 34-13. The Recoverable Object Two-Phase Commit Methods.

■ A ***Transaction Service*** consists of two classes: Transaction and Transaction Manager (see Figure 34-14). An instance of a *Transaction object* is created for each active transaction in the system. The transaction object exports methods—begin, commit, and rollback—that allow the transactional client to *demarcate* the begin and end of a transaction. The *rollback_only* allows clients to change their minds in the middle of a transaction and mark it for subsequent rollback. *Suspend* and *resume* attach the current transaction to an object. An object can have multiple transactions associated with it, but at any one time, only one of these transactions is the active, current transaction. There is only one *Transaction Manager* object associated with a Transaction Service. It provides a *register* method that allows objects to record their *involvement* in a transaction.

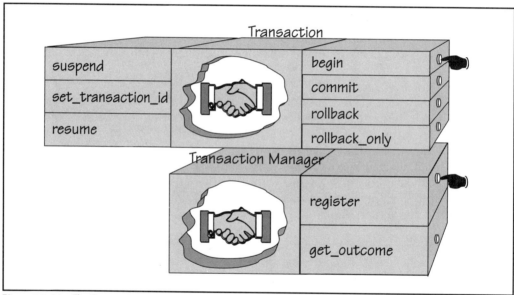

Figure 34-14. The Transaction Manager Classes.

The first phase of the Object Transaction Services will support flat transactions only for compatibility with the X/Open model. Nested transactions, Sagas, and long-lived transactions will come later. The transaction service does not support all the ACID properties directly; it simply provides the protocol engine for coordinating a global transaction (it's the orchestra conductor). Still needed are the ACID persistent stores, the logging services that record the old and new values of an object during a transaction, and object adapters with TP Monitor-like scheduling services. However, this section should give you an idea about how all the pieces come together in an object setting.

Chapter 35

Compound Documents: OLE 2 and OpenDoc

By 1997 enterprise business documents will become the primary paradigm for capturing corporate information, challenging the dominance of record-oriented data. Compound document technology will become the overall framework for managing various non-record oriented information.

— **Meta Group** *(February, 1994)*

The OMG's *Common Facilities* will provide standards for objects that are closer to the end user. However, there's been very little activity from the OMG in this area—they were waiting for the first wave of Object Services to finalize so that they could build on top of that foundation. However, this is all changing. OMG fearlessly accepted the mission of standardizing *Compound Object Architectures*. As a result, the Common Facilities standardization effort may find itself in the midst of the *OpenDoc versus OLE 2.0* mini war. For most users, their first interaction with objects will be through these compound documents. So it is important to understand how this technology and the distributed CORBA infrastructure come together. In this chapter, we explain the compound document approach for objects. We then go over OLE 2 and OpenDoc (the two de facto standards for compound object documents), and finally, we see if it all fits with CORBA. It's like building a railway starting at the two ends of a continent—eventually, you want the rails to seamlessly come together at some intersection point.

WHAT'S A COMPOUND DOCUMENT?

A compound document is a *container* for data that comes from a variety of sources, including other applications. The container provides the appropriate hooks to activate the foreign applications (or objects) that are associated with the separate data elements. It does that by directly *embedding* the foreign data within a document or by maintaining pointers—or *links*—in the document to the external data sources. In either case, the document is still editable by various applications; each sees its data in native format.

End users work with a single document in a single-viewing window. Multiple tools—such as editors, forms, database query dialogs, and paint programs—magically take over the document window when needed—that is, when their portion of the data needs to be worked on. For example, if you're working on a document within WordPerfect and double-click on a spreadsheet object, the WordPerfect menus magically become those of Excel—the editor becomes a spreadsheet right in the same window frame (see the following Soapbox). Users can create compound documents with data of different formats and focus on the data rather than on the applications responsible for it. The compound document preserves the identity and behavior of the information it contains.

Compound document technology facilitates this type of integration by defining a set of interfaces and run-time facilities through which applications can exchange data and invoke each other's services. They also provide protocols for sharing the viewing window and for navigating within the shared file container. A file becomes more than a stream of bytes; it must be divided into units of ownership and navigation that all the applications can understand. A simple file is transformed into a container system. Microsoft calls it "creating a file system within each file."

In summary, compound document technology provides the protocols that let the applications that manage a document communicate with the applications that own objects within the document. They must also let these applications effectively share resources such as a document and a window on the screen. The trick is to make these protocols general enough so as to allow independently developed applications, with no prior knowledge of each other, to discover each other's existence and collaborate at run time.

Are OOUIs No Longer Needed?

Soapbox

The compound document model provides a *document-centric* paradigm to user interfaces that allows users to manipulate information in an intuitive manner—they don't have to hunt for multiple applications and use the clipboard to pass information between them. The user benefits by never having to leave the document viewing context. The world becomes less application-centric and more document-centric. This is definitely a step in the right direction. But does it mean that compound documents are replacements for Object-Oriented User Interfaces (OOUIs)?

Some of the extreme proponents of document-centric architectures advocate the use of documents as containers for anything and everything—they become the primary user interface. Users of OOUIs, however, understand that there are many visual object paradigms, one of which is the document. As we explained in Part 2, OOUIs provide desktop level views for directly manipulating documents and other visual objects. Document-centric technology complements OOUIs very well. The OOUI serves as the container view of desktop objects—including documents and folders—while the compound-document supports inside navigation *within* a detailed document view. You can have your cake and eat it, too. ❏

OLE 2.0 AND COM

OLE 2 is the first step in the evolution of Windows from the function call-based OS we have today to an object-oriented operating system in the future.

> — *Kraig Brockshmidt,*
> *Author, Inside OLE 2,*
> *(Microsoft Press, 1993)*

In 1990, Microsoft introduced *Object Linking and Embedding (OLE)* technology as its basic strategy for integrating multiple applications and multimedia data types within a compound document framework. OLE 1 was a clumsy and slow protocol built on top of DDE. When an application was launched from within a compound document, it was given its own window and the data it needed was copied into its address space. There was no way for the application to directly access the document. OLE 2.0, introduced in 1993, fixes many of these shortcomings with a new object-encapsulation technology called the *Component Object Model (COM)*.

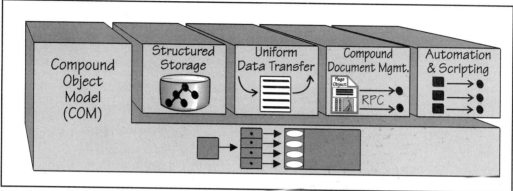

Figure 35-1. The Components of OLE 2.

COM is the foundation of "Window Objects" and is a single-machine version of the technology that will be used in Cairo.

OLE 2.0 has over 350 COM-based API calls organized into 42 *interface classes*. Some of these calls introduce new functions; some simply mask the Windows API surface with a COM encapsulation layer—for example, the clipboard and file systems can now be classes through COM. OLE is a complex product that provides a variety of functions that don't easily fit into a simple classification scheme. Having said that, we offer Figure 35-1 as our best shot for what constitutes OLE 2.0 (it seems we enjoy living dangerously). Let's go over the constituent pieces and see how they relate:

- The ***Compound Object Model (COM)*** specifies interfaces between *component objects* within a single application or between applications. COM, like CORBA, separates the interface from the implementation. Like CORBA, it provides APIs for dynamically discovering the interfaces an object exports and how to load and invoke them. Like CORBA, COM declares that all shared code will be declared using object interfaces (Microsoft even provides its own proprietary Interface Definition Language). Unlike CORBA, COM only provides *local* RPC facilities and does not support remote method invocations or distributed objects (i.e., it does not provide an ORB). COM provides an object factory, but its class model is very limited in the sense that it does not support inheritance. COM is mostly an encapsulation mechanism (see Figure 35-2). Clients use pointers to an array of function pointers known as a *virtual table (VTBL)*. The functions that are pointed to by the VBTL are the object's implementation methods. Each OLE object has one or more VBTLs that define the contract between the object implementation and its clients. COM provides the foundation on which the rest of OLE is built.

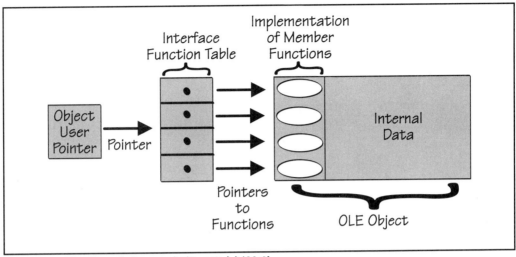

Figure 35-2. The Microsoft Compound Object Model (COM).

■ The **Structured Storage System** provides a file system within a file (also known as DocFiles). It breaks the file into *storages*—that is, directories—and *streams*—that is, raw files. This internal directory system can be used to organize the contents of a document. OLE allows objects to control their own storage in the compound document. The directories describe the streams (BLOBs); the hierarchical structure makes it easy for OLE objects to navigate within the document. The Structured Storage System is packaged as 7 COM interface classes.

■ The **Uniform Data Transfer Model** allows users to transfer data uniformly with drag and drop, copy/paste, or through API calls. The data can be represented in a variety of formats. OLE associates two types of data with a compound document: *presentation data* and *native data*. The presentation data is needed to display the object, while the native data is needed for editing. The Uniform Data Transfer is packaged as 6 COM interface classes (including drag and drop).

■ The **Compound Document Management** is implemented as a document within a *container application* that seamlessly integrates data of different formats, such as bitmaps or sound clips. Each piece of integrated data, referred to as a *compound document object*, is created and maintained by its *object application* (Warning: The term object used in this context is misleading. We're not dealing with OO objects or even COM objects). Document objects can either be linked or embedded in the document. Embedded objects can be edited or activated *in place*. OLE 2 allows object applications to be invoked via local RPCs across address spaces or via DLLs in the same address space. The container applications manage storage and the window for displaying the document. The Compound Document Management function is packaged as 16 COM interface classes (including drag and drop).

■ The *OLE Automation and Scripting* component allows applications to expose their COM interfaces for other applications and scripting languages to use in building custom solutions. An object can expose a set of commands and functions through its interfaces. Each command can take any number of parameters. OLE 2 provides a way for these objects to describe their interfaces. This function is particularly useful for creating system macros from within tools or scripting languages.

In summary, OLE 2 is much more than a compound document architecture. It includes a foundation for defining object interfaces independent of the implementation; it also introduces a primitive form of method invocation and object encapsulation.

OPENDOC

OpenDoc allows developers to move their existing applications to the compound document world and provides interoperability across Macintosh, OS/2, DOS, Windows, Taligent, and UNIX.

— *David Nagel, Senior VP,*
AppleSoft (September, 1993)

OpenDoc is a set of APIs and software for doing compound documents. It is similar in scope and function to OLE 2, but it comes from Apple rather then Microsoft. Apple developed the technology, and has gathered partners to form a consortium for the care and feeding of this technology across multiple platforms. In September 1993, Apple—along with IBM, Novell, Oracle, Taligent, SunSoft, WordPerfect, and Xerox—announced the *Components Integration Laboratories (CIL)*. The purpose of CIL is to establish, promote, and certify OpenDoc and related compound document technologies. CIL technology will integrate multimedia, three-dimensional models, text, graphics and other types of information in any application.

The initial CIL technology includes Apple's OpenDoc software for Windows, OS/2, Macintosh, and UNIX; Apple's Bento technology for the storage and interchange of multimedia information; Apple's Open Scripting Architecture (OSA) for the coexistence of multiple scripting systems; and IBM's System Object Model (SOM) architecture, a platform and language-independent run-time mechanism for dynamic object linking. We offer Figure 35-3 as our best shot for what constitutes OpenDoc's answer to OLE 2. Because of the immaturity of the OpenDoc standard as we go to

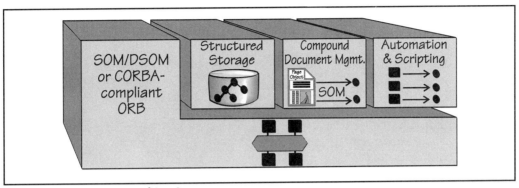

Figure 35-3. The Components of OpenDoc.

press, this is another one of those fearless attempts. Let's go over the constituent pieces and see how they relate:

- **SOM and DSOM** provide local and remote interoperability for OpenDoc objects. SOM is a language-independent, CORBA-compliant protocol for objects that communicate in a single address space or across address spaces on the same machine. DSOM allows SOM objects to communicate across networks— it's a CORBA-compliant ORB. SOM and DSOM support both static and dynamic method invocations. Static invocations using IDL stubs are for objects that know about each other at compile time; dynamic invocations are for objects that know nothing about each other at compile time and end up discovering each other's services at run time. DSOM will eventually support the Object Services introduced earlier in this Part. SOM/DSOM allows OpenDoc objects to communicate using powerful industry-standard protocols across address spaces in a single machine or across machines on a network. SOM/DSOM also support multiple inheritance on object classes. We cover SOM/DSOM in the product chapters.

- **Bento Object Containers** provide a system of structured files; each file contains many streams. Each container may contain a number of document objects; each object can contain one or more draft objects. Bento—named after Japanese plates with compartments for different foods—defines a container format that can be used in files, network streams, clipboards, etc. Bento also defines an API that reads and writes the container format very efficiently. The Bento API is implemented in a library that currently runs on Macintosh, Windows, OS/2, and several Unix systems. A Bento container allows applications to store and retrieve collections of objects. The container format is platform-neutral and can store data regardless of its content. In a Bento document, each object has a persistent ID that moves with it from system to system. Bento also supports references between objects in different files (documents). If there are several drafts of a document, Bento only stores the incremental changes.

All this makes Bento a good protocol for the interchange of compound documents, or groups of objects, between different platforms and applications.

■ ***OpenDoc Compound Document Management*** provides a container in which *parts* can be inserted. Parts are the fundamental building block of OpenDoc. Every part contains data—for example, spreadsheet parts contain spreadsheet cells with formulas, and video parts contain video clips. Every document has a top-level part in which all other parts are embedded. A part can contain other parts. *Part handlers* are the independent programs that manipulate and display a part type. Part handlers are divided into two types: editors and viewers. *Part editors* display a part's contents and provide a user interface for modifying that content. *Part viewers* allow a user to display and print a part's content but not edit it. *Frames* are areas of the display that represent a part. They also represent the part in the negotiations for space during the layout of a document. Bento gives each part its own data stream in persistent store. References can be made from one stream to another, enabling parts to be integrated into a single document. The parts call each other using SOM/DSOM.

■ ***Open Scripting Architecture (OSA)*** is modeled on the Mac's AppleScript. It defines about 14 polymorphic commands that tell a part what to do. For example, "next" can mean the next cell or the next word, depending on the type of part that receives the command. Each part is scriptable, allowing users to customize their applications with user-specific tasks. This is called *content-centered* scripting. A part handler must be prepared to provide at run time the lists of objects it contains and the operations it supports. In addition, OpenDoc can deliver event messages from the scripting system to the part handlers. Scripting provides a medium for coordinating the work of parts in documents, and allows users and parts to work together to perform tasks. OpenDoc supports recordable macros that allow an application to record a user's actions and then save them to a user's preferred scripting language for later use.

CIL plans to make source code available to the industry for these technologies, and its sponsors plan to support the technologies across multiple platforms. Initial target platforms include Microsoft Windows, Macintosh, and OS/2, with plans to support UNIX systems. The CIL Consortium plans to make OpenDoc compatible with OLE. This means that an OpenDoc container would see an OLE object as an OpenDoc part and vice versa. The translation layers are being developed by Wordperfect with help from Borland, Apple, and Lotus. The OpenDoc products will start becoming widely available in mid-1994.

COMPARING OPENDOC AND OLE

Microsoft views the OMG's CORBA as the chief obstacle to OLE 2.0's success. And so, during most of 1993, Microsoft sought to demolish CORBA.

> — **John R. Rymer, Editor, Distributed Computing Monitor (January, 1994)**

Table 35-1 provides a comparison of OpenDoc and OLE 2, based on the best information we have today. Clearly, OLE has the advantage of being here today. OpenDoc has the advantage of being vendor-independent and more open. We expect OpenDoc to be implemented simultaneously on many platforms. OLE will always be implemented on Windows first (the Mac implementation is always lagging). The strongest proponent of OpenDoc is WordPerfect—it seems the folks there did not like being in the position of having to reveal their OLE plans to the Microsoft Word competition. OpenDoc, at least on paper, has a stronger object model: All objects are CORBA-based. Eventually, the two technologies may interoperate, meaning that users may be spared the pain of having to go through another vendor standards war. However, developers will have to choose between a Microsoft standard and a multiplatform, multivendor standard.

Table 35-1. A Preliminary Comparison of OLE 2 and OpenDoc.

Feature	OLE 2	OpenDoc
Availability	Now	Late 1994
Ease of programming	Low	Low
Support for inheritance	No	Yes
Support for recordable macros with script generators	No	Yes
Platforms	Windows and Mac	Windows, OS/2, Mac, and Unix
Networking	Late 1994 using DEC's CORBA ObjectBroker	Built-in using SOM/DSOM or other CORBA-compliant ORBs.
Source code licensing	Controlled by Microsoft	Available to anyone via CIL consortium
Content shape support	Non-overlapped rectangles only	Overlapped rectangles, circular objects, and other irregular shapes—text can wrap around a variety of shapes.
Storage subsystem	Hierarchical structure within a DOS FAT file CAIRO will provide true object store in 1995	Bento containers—here today

COM Versus CORBA

Soapbox

Microsoft's labeling of COM as an object model has drawn jeers from some corners of the industry. To many, the definition of object oriented includes support for inheritance. The object-purists have a point: Some developers value inheritance as a way to speed development of code. However, COM is aimed at construction of interfaces, not objects.

> — **John R. Rymer, Editor,**
> **Distributed Computing Monitor**
> **(January, 1994)**

Underlying OLE and OpenDoc are two competing object models: Microsoft's COM and OMG's CORBA via SOM/DSOM. They're both trying to provide an infrastructure for objects to communicate. Currently COM only operates within a single machine, while CORBA defines an elaborate architecture for ORBs and distributed Object Services. CORBA supports inheritance; COM doesn't. COM takes the unique position that inheritance is dangerous, citing the "fragile base class problem." COM's solution is to encapsulate a group of procedures with an array of pointers. For the rest of the industry, inheritance forms the basis of OO and frameworks; without it, you have simple encapsulation without object reuse. Inheritance allows an object to reuse code without duplication and without code redundancy. Paradoxically, Microsoft supports inheritance in its standalone class libraries—for example, its C++ Foundation Class Library.

In a bizarre turn of events, Microsoft and DEC announced (in late 1993) that they are linking OLE and DEC's CORBA-based ObjectBroker to provide distributed OLE 2. Client applications using OLE 2 will be able to access remote ORB-based servers via ObjectBroker V3 (available late 1994 as part of the Cairo Beta). When all this comes together, Microsoft will provide three object models: language-based class libraries for small objects; COM for larger objects; and indirectly ObjectBroker for CORBA. Which do you choose? And how do they play together? The beauty of the OpenDoc/CORBA marriage is that the same object model is used for all objects—whether they're local or remote, fine-grained, or large-grained. It scales very gracefully from local to distributed objects.

The COM versus CORBA debate transcends OLE and OpenDoc. Even though COM is currently single machine based, Microsoft plans to carry COM (and most of OLE 2.0) *in toto* to Cairo. OLE and COM on Cairo will provide the basis for Microsoft's future distributed computing environment. Chicago will participate as a client. The OLE 2.0 *Local RPC (LRPC)* will become a true RPC in Cairo and Chicago; it will allow OLE calls to be transparently routed over the network. We still don't know how these distributed OLE objects will be stored, located, secured, replicated, and managed; Microsoft has not revealed its plans for an ORB. We may get a better idea of what's "in plan" after the first beta of Cairo ships. What is clear, is that Microsoft is putting some form of distributed objects in its next generation of Windows products and it will be document-centric. It also looks like our industry is heading for a great distributed object showdown: COM versus CORBA. DEC will provide the proverbial gateway. ❑

Chapter 36

Object Database Management Systems

---

*T*he biggest problem with relational databases is that they deal with an intermediate level of data abstraction. Users want to browse the real world and record the transactions of an enterprise...This requires adding a new schema, a higher-level application programming interface. The way we're doing this [in Oracle8] is by decomposing the data from the object and storing it in two-dimensional tables.

> — *Larry Ellison, CEO of Oracle*
> *(May, 1993)*

*T*he practical commercial problem is that most people have just moved to relational databases and don't want to even think about moving to object databases.

> — *Paul Harmon, Object Oriented Strategies*
> *(May, 1993)*

Object Database Management Systems (ODBMSs) provide a client/server architecture that is significantly different from Relational Database Management Systems (RDBMSs). ODBMSs take a revolutionary approach to shared data that's totally centered on the management of persistent objects. We encountered some of this

technology in the OMG Object Services. Today, the ODBMS vendors claim they can provide efficient client/server access to fine-grained objects. The major ODBMS vendors recently released their *ODMG-93* standard; it is intended to become the SQL of ODBMS. Of course, with a common standard, the market for ODBMSs may take off like its SQL-based RDBMS counterpart. Many people in our industry—including Oracle's CEO Larry Ellison—believe that object databases may ultimately become the successors of RDBMSs.

So will ODBMSs replace RDBMSs, in the same way relational vendors replaced their hierarchical predecessors ten years ago? This is one of the questions we'll try and answer in this chapter (in a Soapbox, of course). But just to give you a preliminary idea, the Cowen Market Research firm believes the market for ODBMSs will grow to $430 Million by 1997 from $32 Million in 1992. In contrast, the RDBMS market is expected to grow to $6.8 Billion in 1997 from $2.7 Billion in 1992.[1] The numbers show that ODBMSs will grow very fast; however, their market size is dwarfed by RDBMSs. ODBMSs will grow in areas like multimedia, object repositories, and groupware—the next wave of client/server technology. The RDBMS vendors won't sit still either. All the major relational vendors have declared that they will incorporate support for objects as it's being defined in the SQL3 standard. According to Larry Ellison, Oracle8 will be fully object-based.

In this chapter, we first look at what an ODBMS is and what it does well. We look at it through the composite technology that's provided by five small but very dynamic ODBMS vendors (together, they own over 90% of the object database market). Then we go over the ODMG-93 standard that was created by these five vendors—incidentally, they all pledged to make their products ODMG-compliant in 1994. We'll look at how ODMG-93 compares with OMG's Object Services and SQL3. As part of living dangerously, we end the chapter with a soapbox on RDBMSs versus ODBMSs.

WHAT'S AN ODBMS?

> We define an ODBMS to be a DBMS that integrates database capabilities with object-oriented programming language capabilities. An ODBMS makes database objects appear as programming language objects, in one or more existing programming languages.
>
> — *Rick Cattel, Chairman ODMG-93,*
> *(Morgan Kaufman, 1993)*

---

[1] Source: **Cowen Research Report**, "Object Development Strategies" (September 15, 1993).

An ODBMS provides a persistent store for objects in a multiuser client/server environment. The ODBMS handles concurrent access to objects, provides locks and transaction protection, protects the objectstore from all types of threats, and takes care of traditional tasks such as backup and restore. What makes ODBMSs different from their relational counterparts is that they store objects rather than tables. Objects are referenced through *Persistent Identifiers (PIDs)*, which uniquely identify objects, and are used to create referential and containment relationships between them. Objects also enforce encapsulation and support inheritance. The ODBMS combines object properties with traditional DBMS functions such as locking, protection, transactions, querying, versioning, concurrency, and persistence.

Instead of using a separate language like SQL to define, retrieve, and manipulate data, ODBMSs use class definitions and traditional OO language (usually C++ and SmallTalk) constructs to define and access data. The ODBMS is simply a multiuser, persistent extension of in-memory language data structures (see Figure 36-1). In other words, the client is the C++ program; the server is the ODBMS—there are no visible intermediaries like RPCs or SQL. The ODBMS integrates database capabilities directly into the language.

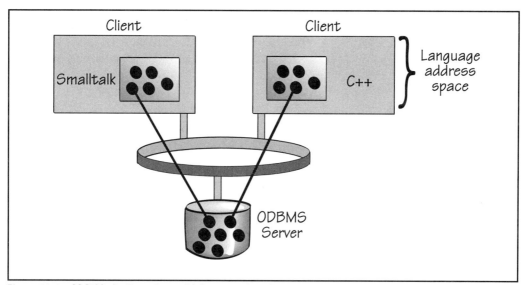

Figure 36-1. ODBMS: An Extension to OO Language Data Structures.

Of course, not everything is transparent to the language. By necessity, the ODBMS introduces extensions to the OO language such as container classes and operations that help navigate through the containers. The ODMG-93 specification includes a full-blown *Object Manipulation Language (OML)* that supports queries and transactions. In an attempt to make the data-definition language neutral, the

ODMG-93 specifies a generic *Object Definition Language (ODL)*. As a result, the ODBMS, like SQL, requires a precompiler to process the object definitions, language extensions, and queries. The output of the compiler, like SQL plans, must also be linked to the ODBMS run time. So we've come a full circle.

WHAT'S AN ODBMS GOOD FOR?

Object databases have evolved more rapidly than any other database approach in history.

> — Dick Loveland,
> Director, Digital Consulting,
> (January, 1994)

ODBMSs were for a long time an area of great interest to academicians and OO researchers. The earliest commercial ODBMSs made their appearance in 1986 with the introduction of Servio and Ontos. The three firms that currently lead the industry—Object Design (ODI), Versant, and Objectivity—all entered the market in 1990. The ODBMS niche is in applications that deal with complex data structures and long-lived transactions—including computer-aided design, CASE, and intelligent offices. With the emergence of multimedia, groupware, and distributed objects, the esoteric features of ODBMSs are now becoming mainstream client/server requirements. ODBMS technology fills the gap in the areas where relational databases are at their weakest—compound data, versioning, long-lived transactions, nested transactions, persistent object stores, inheritance, and user-defined data types.

Here's a list of the features that were pioneered by the ODBMS vendors (see Figure 36-2):

- *Freedom to create new types of information*—ODBMSs give you the freedom to create and store any data type using standard object descriptions. The data type is part of the object class definition. You can easily store arbitrarily complex data structures in an ODBMS (like container hierarchies). In contrast, traditional databases offer a limited number of hard-wired data types; complex structures must be converted into artificially "flattened" table representations.

- *Fast access*—ODBMSs keep track of objects through their unique IDs. A search can move directly from object to object without the need for tedious search-and-compare operations using foreign keys and other associative techniques.

- *Flexible views of composite structures*—ODBMSs allow individual objects to participate in a multiplicity of containment relationships, creating multiple

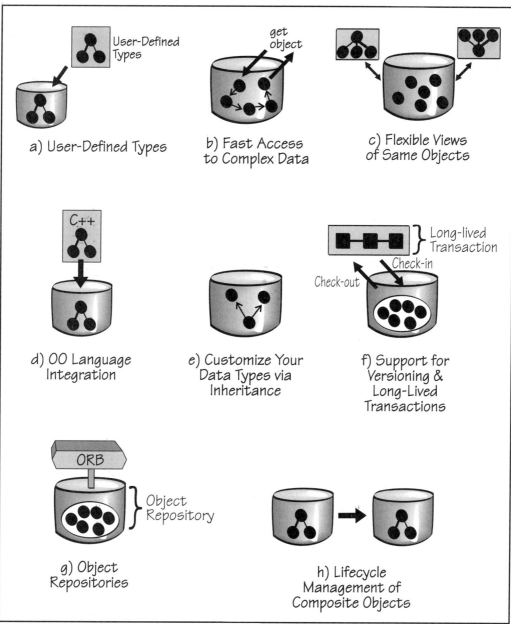

Figure 36-2. The Eight Wonders of ODBMS.

views of the same objects. Objects can maintain pointers to other objects in a very recursive manner; there's no limit to the different container relationships that can be assembled. A container typically maintains references to object IDs as opposed to the objects themselves—it's a form of *linking* as opposed to *embedding*.

- **Tight integration with object-oriented languages**—ODBMSs present themselves as persistent extensions of the OO language's in-memory data structures. This allows them to minimize the impedance mismatch between programs and data while maintaining the strong encapsulation features that are inherent in OO languages. OO programmers may find an ODBMS to be a natural extension of their paradigm. ODBMSs provide the fastest and most direct access to objects they store; they also do a good job preserving the intact characteristics of these objects. In contrast, all types of mappings are introduced to bridge between the tabular nature of relational data and the complex in-memory data structures of an OO language. Relational systems can store objects, but they must first break them down into components and flatten them into structures that can fit in tables. SQL people, of course, may think that chasing corporate data via in-memory C++ pointers is a travesty. (We'll resume this discussion in the Soapbox).

- **Support for customizable information structures using multiple inheritance**—the ODBMS data types are defined using object classes. This means that any class can be subclassed to create custom structures that meet exceptional data needs. In addition, the ODBMS allows you to mix desirable characteristics from different classes and combine them using multiple inheritance. So the ODBMS extends the concept of object reuse through inheritance to the database.

- **Support for versioning, nesting, and long-lived transactions**—many commercial ODBMSs (including ObjectStore, Ontos, and Objectivity) support nested transactions and versioning for long-duration transactions. Objects can be grouped in configurations and managed as one transaction. ODBMSs are most popular in engineering design applications that require the management of complex documents. A typical Computer Aided Design (CAD) system also depends on version control to track the progressively more enhanced versions of an engineering design. Because of their long involvement with CAD, ODBMSs have perfected the art of versioning and long-lived transactions. ODBMSs have introduced the concept of *configurations*—meaning a collection of objects that are managed as a locking and versioning unit. CAD users typically *check out* a configuration of objects from the ODBMS, work on it, and *check in* their configuration as a new version.

- **Repositories for distributed objects**—ODBMSs provide natural multiuser repositories for run-time objects. We believe the ODBMS vendors have a huge lead in providing solutions for concurrent access to large numbers—in the millions—of fine-grained objects with ACID protection. Eventually ODBMSs will provide true stores for *roaming objects* (a la General Magic); they serve as object store-and-forward servers for roaming objects—think of it as an object Hilton.

■ ***Support for life-cycle management of composite objects***—ODBMSs have also perfected the art of managing composite objects as a unit. For example, a composite object can be assembled, disassembled, copied, stored, restored, moved, and destroyed. The ODBMS automatically maintains the relationships between the parts and treats the aggregate as a single component. This is also a result of their long involvement with CAD.

In summary, ODBMS vendors have had the luxury of being able to create pure object databases without being encumbered by debt to history. As a result, they were able to provide some missing pieces of technology needed to create the new generation of multimedia intensive databases with flexible data types. An ODBMS has the advantage over a relational database of knowing the overall structure of a complex object (like a document, for example) and sometimes its behavior (i.e., methods) as well; it can refer to any constituent object by its ID. In contrast, Relational vendors are attempting to provide object technology (meaning SQL3) by using a hybrid approach that decomposes the data from the object and stores it in tables. This is an area where relational databases are at a disadvantage, but we'll defer that discussion to a soapbox.

ODBMS CLIENT/SERVER IMPLEMENTATIONS

Most ODBMSs store the data part of an object but not the behavior [methods]...An object without behavior is just a complex data structure. It is not an object.

— *Dr. Raymond Vorwerk,*
Object Magazine (January, 1994)

There are several architectural alternatives to implementing ODBMSs on client/server networks. The effects of the architecture show up in various ways, even though the underlying programming model is the same. Mary Loomis, VP of Technology at Versant, defines two basic approaches for splitting the application between ODBMS clients and servers:

■ The ***object server*** balances the load between the client and the server. The client and server communicate by moving objects from the server's persistent store to the client's memory (see Figure 36-3). Clients request objects by specifying their Persistent IDs. The client component manages the object in the local memory; the server provides a multiuser ODBMS with transaction protection and locking. The unit of locking is an object. Methods can be executed on either the client or the server, depending on the location of the object. The processing of queries is done on the server.

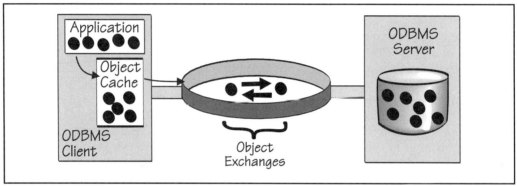

Figure 36-3. ODBMS Object Server Architecture.

■ The *page server* is a fat client approach that treats the ODBMS as a shared multiuser virtual memory store. The server pulls pages off the disk and moves them to the client's memory cache (see Figure 36-4). There are no persistent object IDs. All the intelligence and the object model is on the client. The page server locks pages, not objects. The methods are executed on the client where the object's logic resides. Queries are processed on the client, requiring the movement of candidate objects to the client's address space before applying selection criteria.

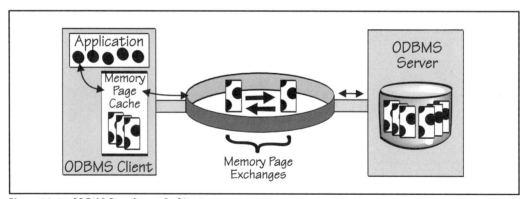

Figure 36-4. ODBMS Page Server Architecture.

We believe the object server is the better implementation. It allows objects to be moved to where they're needed. The access can be made transparent to the application (but it's done via RPCs). In contrast, a page server application needs to be aware of the distribution of objects across database systems. References within a single database are traversed as C++ pointers. However, references across databases require the use of remote functions or RPCs. This means that objects cannot be moved around to improve performance without changes to the application's code.

ODMG-93: THE NEW LINGUA FRANCA FOR ODBMS

The ODMG-93 standard, published in September 1993, is the ODBMS answer to SQL. The standard is the result of work done by the *Object Database Management Group (ODMG)*—a consortium that includes all the major ODBMS vendors. The ODMG is a working subgroup of the OMG and intends to submit its standard to both ISO and ANSI. In theory, the adoption of ODMG-93 should allow applications to work with ODBMSs from any of the major vendors. Today, most of the ODMG vendors are shipping systems that are compliant with large subsets of the specification. But the ODMG members have committed to bring their systems into *full* compliance within 18 months of the publication of the standards document.

ODMG-93 and CORBA

ODMG-93 is an extension of the OMG Object Persistence Service that defines how to implement the components of an efficient *Persistent Data Service (PDS)* for fine-grained objects. The standard uses the OMG object model as its basis. If you haven't done so, please review Chapter 34, "Distributed Object Services," for an explanation of where an ODBMS fits in the OMG Persistent Object Service architecture. The ODBMS's role in an ORB environment is to provide concurrent access to persistent stores capable of handling millions of fine-grained objects. To do that, the OMG refers to a special PDS protocol called ODMG-93. This protocol supplements the IDL-defined RPC invocations with direct API calls to the objectstore for fast access to data.

The ODBMS vendors are also actively promoting within the ORB 2 committee a *Library Object Adapter (LOA)* that provides direct API access via the ORB to specialized high-speed APIs. ODMG-93 states that the ODBMS vendors would like CORBA to standardize on a specialized version of LOA called the *Object Database Adapter (ODA)*. Figure 36-5, adapted from ODMG-93, shows the differences among BOA, LOA, and ODA—yes, more TLAs (three-letter acronyms) to impress the folks back home.

ODA should provide the ability to register subspaces of object identifiers with the ORB—instead of all the millions of objects that are stored in the ODBMS. From the client's point of view, the objects in the registered subspace appear just as any other ORB-accessible objects. The ODA should allow for the use of direct access—as in

Part 7. Client/Server With Distributed Objects

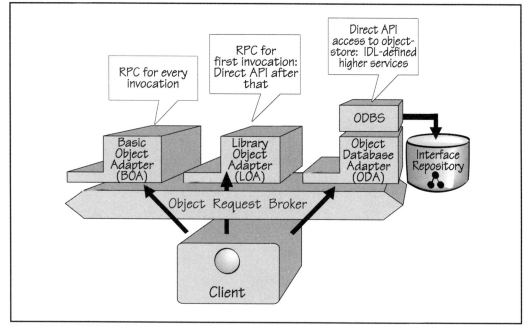

Figure 36-5. ODMG-93: ODBMS as Object Manager on an OMG ORB.

the LOA—to improve the performance of ORB/ODBMS applications. To summarize, the ODBMS vendors are pushing CORBA to be more flexible when it comes to dealing with applications that manage millions of fine-grained objects. The new Object Persistence Service specification indicates that OMG got the message. But it remains to be seen if OMG will extend this new permissiveness to the ORB itself.

The ODMG-93 Components

The ODMG-93 standard consists of three major components (see Figure 36-6):

■ *Object Definition Language (ODL)*—ODMG-93 uses the OMG IDL as its data definition language. ODL is a "clean" superset of IDL in the sense that it defines elements that are not in IDL such as new collection classes and referential relationships. The ODL provides a programming language-independent way of describing metadata. The ODL is processed through a precompiler, which generates stubs that get linked to the ODBMS and the client language (C++ or SmallTalk). ODL provides interface and data definition portability across languages and ODBMS vendor platforms.

■ *Object Query Language (OQL)*—ODMG-93 defines a SQL-like declarative language for querying and updating database objects. It supports the most

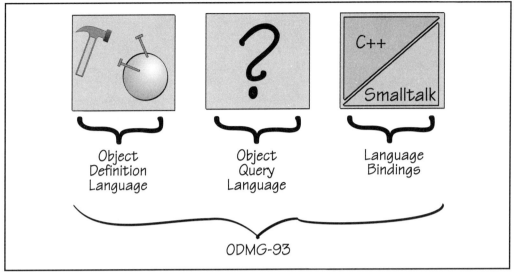

Figure 36-6. ODMG-93 Components.

commonly used SQL SELECT structures including joins; it does not support SQL INSERT, UPDATE, or DELETE (it uses C++ or SmallTalk extensions for that). ODMG-93 purposely did not use the SQL3 semantics for objects because of "limitations in its data model and because of its historical baggage." However, they "hope that OQL and SQL3 can converge at a future date." How nice! OQL provides high-level primitives to query different collections of objects—including *sets*, which means unordered collections with no duplicates; *bags*, which means unordered collections with duplicates; and *lists*, which are ordered collections. OQL also supports structures in queries—a very powerful construct.

■ *C++ and SmallTalk language bindings*—ODMG-93 defines how to write portable C++ or SmallTalk code that manipulates persistent objects. The standard defines C++ *Object Manipulation Language (OML)* extensions. The C++ OML includes: language extensions for OQL queries, iterations for navigating through containers, and transaction support. The ODMG-93 people do not believe exclusively in a "universal" Data Manipulation Language (a la SQL). Instead, they propose "a unified object model for sharing data across programming languages, as well as a common query language." According to ODI's Tom Atwood, "The OML should respect the syntax of the base language into which it is being inserted, so that programmers feel they are writing in a single integrated programming language that supports persistence." In theory, it should be possible to read and write the same ODBMS from both SmallTalk and C++, as long as the programmer stays within the common subset of supported data types.

Figure 36-7 shows the steps involved in using an ODMG-compliant ODBMS. The process is very similar to the CORBA IDL, except that the stub bindings are for an ODBMS and the OO Language application that manipulates persistent objects.

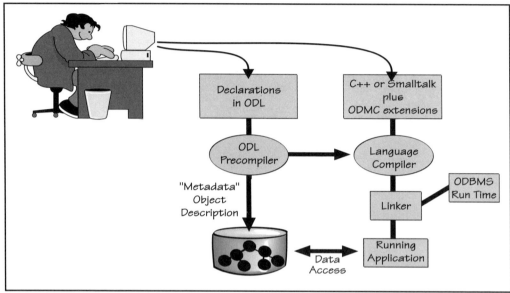

Figure 36-7. The ODMG-93 Process.

So, Are ODBMSs Perfect?

*P*ure *ODBMSs are mere pretenders to the DBMS throne.*

— *Michael Stonebraker (February, 1994)*

Stonebraker notes that pure ODBMSs still lack functionality in the areas of complex search, query optimizers, and server scalability. Furthermore, many ODBMSs run their products in the same address space as user programs. This means that there is no protection barrier between a client application and the ODBMS. In addition, ODBMSs have a minuscule market penetration when compared to relational DBMSs. The debate continues in the following Soapbox.

The Future of Database: Object or Relational?

Soapbox

Object Mania has taken over the industry. Proponents of object orientation are heralding object databases and ODBMSs as a cure for the purported weakness of relational technology. Poppycock...Applying object orientation directly and indiscriminately at the database level reintroduces problems that took the relational approach two decades to get rid of.

— Fabian Pascal, Author of
Understanding Relational Databases
(Wiley, 1994)

Among users, few doubts remain that ODBMS will ultimately be the successor to RDBMS...In the imagery of the poet William Blake, the young god of revolution Orc has begun to age into the icy tyrant Urizen—keeper of the law and standards.

— Thomas Atwood, Chairman,
Object Design (October, 1993)

We can have our cake and eat it, too! The point is to marry the two technologies instead of throwing mud at each other...It would be a great shame to walk away from the experience gained from more than 20 years of solid relational research and development.

— Chris Date (June, 1993)

Date and Pascal both acknowledge that current SQL database implementations have weaknesses; however, they both feel the relational model per se can handle the problems that ODBMSs solve. The power of ODBMS can be approximated in the relational world using nested relations, domains (or user-defined encapsulated data types) and a more powerful set-oriented language than SQL. These features can do the job without chasing after object pointers or manipulating low-level, language-specific, record structures. We don't have to mitigate the associative powers of relational theory. Developers won't have to resort to manual methods to maximize and reoptimize application performance—setting the clock back. Date believes that a domain and an object type are the same; the solution is for relational vendors to extend their systems to include "proper domain support."

The ODBMS people feel that there's more to this than just extending the relational model. In fact, they've rejected the SQL3 extensions (due in 1995) as being insufficient. ODBMS diehards believe that they're creating better plumbing for a world where information systems will be *totally* object-based. Relational databases are an impedance mismatch in a plumbing consisting of ORBs, object services, OOUI front ends, powerful OO languages, and OO frameworks. A pure ODBMS is exactly what's needed. Why keep extending a legacy foundation like SQL with BLOBs, stored procedures, and user-defined types? They prefer to stick to objects all the way and sometimes borrow a few things from SQL (such as queries). They're also recreating the multiuser robust foundation that includes locking, transactions, recovery, and tools.

What about all these great SQL tools with their pretty GUI front ends, query pickers, and fancy reports? No problem. The ODBMS people will recreate this whole foundation and do it much better using objects. If you have any doubts, a look at the Servio toolset should give you an idea of how objects can seamlessly integrate everything from the client OOUI to the ODBMS. Of course, Servio is currently a proprietary and expensive tool. However, we may not be too far from the day when CORBA Interface Repositories replace database catalogs; method invocations replace stored procedures; transactional BOAs replace TP Monitors; and ODBMSs replace RDBMSs. It could be a total paradigmatic shift.

RDBMS vendors may someday heed to the criticisms they've been receiving over the years from the likes of Chris Date, Fabian Pascal, and E.F. Codd, and do something about domains. Will it be too late? It all depends on the state of the distributed object infrastructure. If information systems shift to ORBs and CORBA, if C++ replaces Cobol and C, if OOUIs replace GUIs, and if OO frameworks become the craze, then ODBMSs will be kings. There's no way "legacy" RDBMSs will be able to compete effectively with ODBMSs on a distributed object turf—the impedance mismatch is just too big.

Of course, we're talking about David and Goliath here. SQL databases are the current kings of the hill. They have the big development budgets and wide commercial acceptance from MIS shops to the low end of the client/server market. Will the king of the hill be deposed because of a few BLOBs, inheritance, and ORBs? We don't really know. Larry Ellison's Oracle8 may simply gobble up objects and multimedia as we know them today and create a new de facto standard. But it's highly unlikely, given the incredible amount of intellectual energy that seems to be gravitating in the direction of distributed objects and CORBA. Can Ellison co-opt that technology? It remains to be seen. But as Esther Dyson puts it, "Using tables to store objects is like driving your car home and then disassembling it to put it in the garage. It can be assembled again in the morning, but one eventually asks whether this is the most efficient way to park a car." ❑

Chapter 37

Object Frameworks: A Closer Look

---

*T*he clearer the view of our dreams, the greater our cohesion.

— *Carlos Castaneda,*
The Art of Dreaming

The real pay-off of CORBA technology will be provided by the object "frameworks" that are starting to come our way. The migration from procedural system APIs to object frameworks will eventually revolutionize the way client/server applications are developed, deployed, and managed on *all* operating system platforms—OS/2 happens to be at the leading-edge of this technology. Think of these frameworks as the "software backbones" of client/server. Distributed objects, like all client/server software, will greatly benefit from the use of frameworks. In this chapter, we explain what a framework is and what problems it solves. We compare frameworks with traditional API sets and object-oriented class libraries. We then take a closer look at the type of frameworks we can expect from IBM and Taligent. We conclude with some examples on how frameworks will be used in client/server environments.

YOUR GUIDE TO OBJECT FRAMEWORKS

In this section, we define object frameworks, explain what they do, and what benefits they provide. You'll discover that frameworks are a packaging technology for object classes. They're ideally suited to work with ORBs. It's the next level of object abstraction.

What Are Object Frameworks?

In their 1991 paper, "Reusing Object-Oriented Designs," Ralph Johnson of the University of Illinois and Vincent Russo of Purdue offer this widely accepted definition of frameworks:

"An abstract class is a design for a single object. A framework is the design of a set of objects that collaborate to carry out a set of responsibilities. Thus frameworks are larger scale designs than abstract classes. Frameworks are a way to re-use...high-level design."

Still confused? Let's try an explanation from Taligent's 1993 White Paper:

"Frameworks are not simply collections of classes. Rather, frameworks come with rich functionality and strong *wired in* interconnections between object classes that provide an infrastructure for the developer."

The "wired-in" interconnections among the classes are meant to provide the right level of abstraction to the consumer of the framework. Think of a framework as a fully debugged software subsystem, that you can customize to create your own applications. It's like buying a hardware board instead of individual chips (see Figure 37-1). But unlike a hardware board, the "software board" can be extended and further customized to fit your needs.

How Do Frameworks Work?

So how do you customize a framework? You tell it which key events you want to personalize and provide the code that handles those events. The framework will then call your code when that event occurs; your code doesn't call the framework. Your programs don't have to worry about structure, flow of execution, and calls to system-level API libraries; the framework does all that for you. All your code does is wait to be called by the framework (see Figure 37-2).

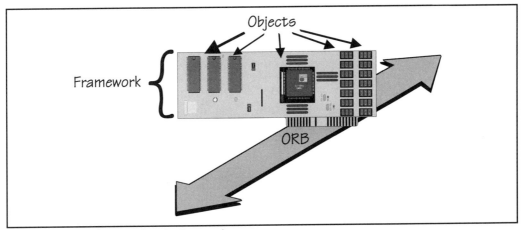

Figure 37-1. A Hardware Analogy for Frameworks.

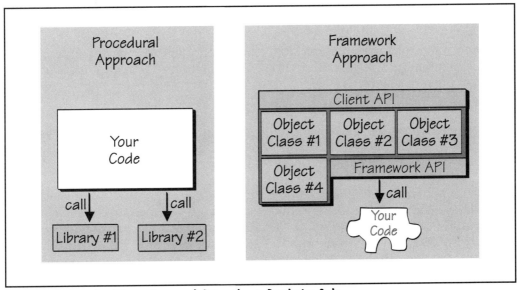

Figure 37-2. Procedural Versus Framework Approaches to Developing Code.

Frameworks, unlike traditional operating systems, are very malleable. If you don't like a particular part of the subsystem, just change it. You can also customize a framework by replacing some of its classes with your own. This is done using traditional object-oriented approaches such as multiple inheritance and method overrides. Of course, frameworks can also play tricks and change their underlying structure to take advantage of new hardware (or software) in a manner that's totally transparent to your software.

Frameworks and Subclassing

Details

How does the framework call your code? Technically, what you do is subclass *certain* framework classes and override specific methods. Overridden methods will be called by the framework when an instance of that subclass is invoked at run time. Your method executes and returns control to the framework. ☐

What else can frameworks do? They integrate well with other frameworks. Going back to the hardware analogy, hardware boards can be plugged into a motherboard (a board with a system bus) to interoperate with other hardware boards and create a system. For example, a system could consist of a motherboard with a microprocessor, a LAN Adapter card, a memory card, and a printer card. Frameworks do the same for software.

But where's the software motherboard? How do frameworks (in separate address spaces) communicate with one another? The framework "software motherboard" consists of two mechanisms:

■ *The framework service interface* provides a set of APIs that are simple abstractions of the services provided by each framework. We show in Figure 37-3 that interface as a layer on top of the frameworks. A CORBA-compliant framework would use IDL-specified interfaces.

■ *An inter-framework object request broker* is used to pass the requests across address spaces. Figure 37-3 shows the software bus (the broker) that carries the traffic across frameworks. A CORBA environment would use regular ORBs.

But aren't we going back to APIs and procedural calls? No, because most of the code you write runs within individual frameworks (the little puzzles in the figure). These little puzzles of code are invoked directly by the framework. The APIs are used to invoke services on other frameworks where you may also have some code (another little puzzle).

Key Benefits of Object Frameworks

You may have already surmised that frameworks provide a very powerful approach for creating complex systems. Here's a list of the advantages frameworks provide:

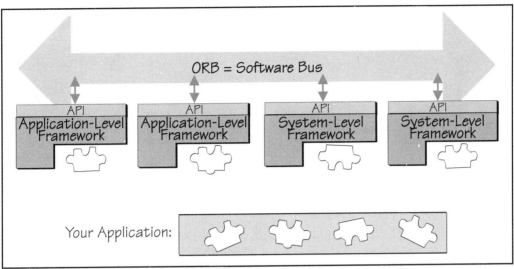

Figure 37-3. An Application in the Era of Frameworks.

■ **A prefabricated infrastructure.** Frameworks reduce coding, debugging, and testing by providing working subsystems. This is code that you don't have to write yourself.

■ **Architectural guidance.** Frameworks are wired and ready to go. All you need to know is where the hooks are and tap into them to extend the system's behavior. You don't have to wade through thick manuals that describe APIs. And if you're an object-oriented programmer, you won't have to spend half your time shopping for classes, providing the interconnections between classes, discovering which methods are available, and then trying to figure out which ones need to be called and in which order. Frameworks hide all this complexity by providing a higher level of abstraction.

■ **Less monolithic applications.** Frameworks encourage you to write small pieces of applications that plug into their appropriate frameworks. When you need a function in another framework, you simply call that piece of the application that runs there (or the framework itself). Instead of writing one monolithic application, you write little pieces of custom code that run in different frameworks.

■ **A foundation for a software components industry.** Well-designed frameworks allow third-party software companies to provide parts or entire components that can be assembled or modified by end users or system integrators. Frameworks will create the "critical mass" for software part catalogs. We will see the software equivalents of hardware motherboards, cards, chips, printers, and modems.

■ **Reduced maintenance.** Frameworks provide the bulk of the code that goes into applications—a line of code you don't write is one you won't have to maintain. Because of inheritance, when a framework bug is fixed or a new feature is added, the benefits are immediately available to derived classes.

The overall benefit of frameworks is that they enable a very high level of code and design reuse in the development of complex systems. Their main weakness is that they're not here. APIs appear first and frameworks will come after. It would be nice if vendors delivered both at the same time. But we're getting ahead of our story.

Frameworks, APIs, or Class Libraries?

The line of code that costs the least is the line of code you don't write.

— Steve Jobs, 1993

Yes, you've heard it before. Structured programming, then OO-class libraries, were supposed to save the world from programming drudgery. None were a panacea. Why are frameworks any different? Table 37-1 provides a quick summary of the features that distinguish frameworks from procedural API programming and object-oriented class libraries.

Table 37-1. Comparing Frameworks, OO-Class Libraries, and Procedural APIs.

Feature	Frameworks	OO Class Libraries	Procedural APIs
Application model	Frameworks are the application. The frameworks handle all the control flow.	You must create the control flow of the application and the glue that ties the different class libraries together.	You must create the control flow of the application and the logic that invokes the APIs. The system knows nothing about your code.
Application structure	Multiple cooperative frameworks.	Single monolithic application consisting of class libraries.	Single monolithic application linked to API libraries
How services are obtained?	The frameworks are the service.	By inheriting function from the class libraries.	By calling API libraries
How the system is customized?	The frameworks call your code. You can subclass parts of frameworks.	By subclassing or creating new classes.	By writing new code and calling additional APIs.

Table 37-1. Comparing Frameworks, OO-Class Libraries, and Procedural APIs. (Continued)

Feature	Frameworks	OO Class Libraries	Procedural APIs
Granularity of control	Medium. You can only subclass parts of frameworks.	High. You can subclass any class.	High. You can write everything from scratch.
Abstraction of services	High. Hides complexity. Automates standard features. You program by exception	Low. Hides APIs but creates its own layer of complexity—you must determine which methods are available to call and in which order.	Very low. You need to deal with raw APIs and determine the order in which to call them.
How much code do you write?	Very little	A Medium amount	Lots
Maintenace costs	Low	Medium	High
Reduced Complexity	Yes. You write small pieces of code within multiple frameworks. Frameworks call you only when necessary. Frameworks provide architectural guidance.	No. You must shop for classes and develop the program. You must integrate the different class libraries.	No. You must develop the entire program and understand how the APIs work together.
Client/Server support	High. Using interframework communications.	Low. You must use the native OS's interprocess communications.	Low. You must use the native OS's interprocess communications
Time to develop an application	Low	Medium. Depends on class reuse.	High
Component reuse	Very high	The design gets reused.	Medium. Some functions get reused.
Is the model familiar?	No	Yes	Yes

Procedural Frameworks: Look Ma, No Objects

Not all frameworks are object-based. Many of the middleware services—including transports, NOSs, and transactions—are provided using *procedural frameworks*. Why do we need procedural frameworks? Because the bulk of existing system code was written without the faintest notion of objects. DCE, for example, consists of more than two million lines of procedural "legacy" code. It will take some time to rewrite DCE into a "true" object framework. In other cases, object standards are still being defined. For example, the OMG is working on a specification for transaction services that will be built around some type of object framework. In the interim, we have *procedural* TP Monitor frameworks.

Procedural frameworks are very useful. They encapsulate heterogeneous services with CORBA-defined interfaces. Figure 37-4 shows an example of a SOM encapsulated procedural framework for OS/2. Each framework provides configuration and installation support for its services. In addition, frameworks register their services with a CORBA-compliant Interface Repository that lets applications discover which services are available and how to invoke them at run time. The OS only has to load the framework itself and handle version control.

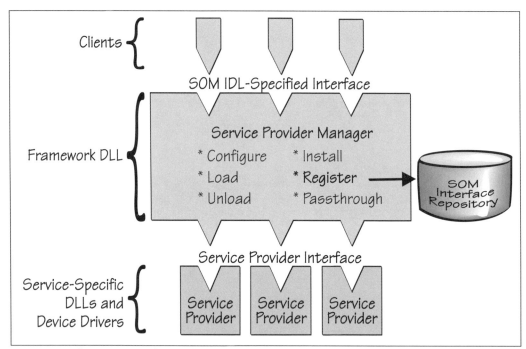

Figure 37-4. The Components of a Procedural Frameworks.

Procedural frameworks are very useful as object-wrappers. They allow us to transition to objects gradually from the existing base of legacy system software. The object wrappers make the legacy code appear object-like to the object-oriented programs, tools, and frameworks. So what do procedural frameworks lack? Their two major limitations are: 1) they don't allow you to modify the service itself using subclassing (for example, you won't be able to modify DCE); and 2) they are still API-based.

IBM/TALIGENT: FRAMEWORKS EVERYWHERE

We will deliver everything we do in frameworks.

— Cliff Reeves, IBM Director of Objects

If IBM and Taligent succeed, almost every piece of system software they deliver will be wrapped into some kind of framework. The IBM plan calls for layering a series of object frameworks in the place of each of the procedural APIs that make up OS/2. Larry Louckes, the IBM Fellow and chief OS/2 strategist, estimates that the application frameworks alone consist of 1.2 million lines of code. When the frameworks all come into place, OS/2 will provide developers a platform on which they can more easily create applications. OS/2 will also give users an environment where all applications are seamlessly integrated. The OS/2 frameworks will be plugged into SOM, which provides a language-neutral repository for exchanging services between applications created using different tools. DSOM goes even further—it allows applications created on different platforms to interoperate.

So how do we classify these frameworks? Figure 37-5 shows a recent IBM/Taligent classification that breaks frameworks into two general categories: Desktop and System. The Desktop frameworks (also called Application Frameworks) deal with the business logic of an application and provide the tools to build the visual components. The System frameworks cover everything else—including device control, file and print systems, every aspect of intergalactic client/server middleware, and distributed objects. We break down the system frameworks into two categories: Middleware (IBM calls it NOS) and OS. Did that help? Probably not, so let's continue to peel the framework layers until we get to some more familiar ground.

The Names May Change

Warning

These classifications may change with time. Don't get hung up on the names. What's important is to get a feel for what these frameworks can do. We need to keep peeling the layers until we get to something recognizable. ❑

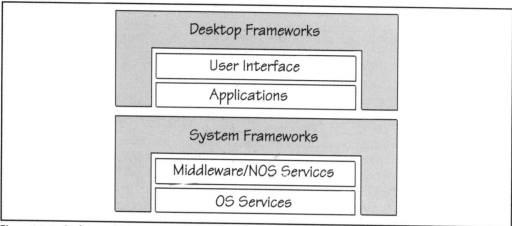

Figure 37-5. Desktop and System Frameworks.

The Desktop Frameworks

Figure 37-6 shows a combination of IBM and Taligent desktop frameworks that promise to change the way visual applications are developed. Cliff Reeves, the director of objects at IBM, predicts a ten-fold increase in programmer productivity with the new desktop programming model. Desktop frameworks cover compound documents, multimedia, mail, groupware, international text, graphics (2D and 3D), OOUI/GUI builders, and decision support systems. Some of the frameworks will allow end users to wire together some applications, but most of the frameworks are productivity tools for programmers.

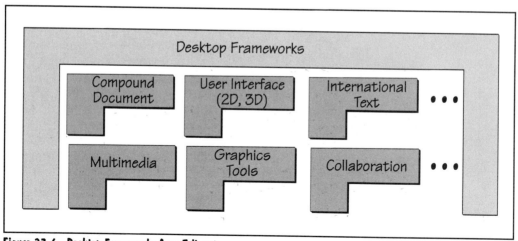

Figure 37-6. Desktop Frameworks from Taligent.

The Middleware Frameworks

Figure 37-7 shows some of the middleware frameworks.[1] This is a very comprehensive set of frameworks that cover all aspects of client/server middleware. As shown in Figure 37-7, IBM intends to provide frameworks that handle the middleware for transaction processing (TX), telephony (CMI), transport-independent calls (Sockets), E-mail (VIM), directory services (DCE, XDS/NSI), database access (IDAPI/ODBC), licensing (NetLS), authentication (DCE/GSS, OMG), System Management (XMP/DMI, SNMP, and DME objects), Print (COSE), Access Control Lists (DCE), etc. Sorry for the new acronyms—remember, we're dealing with client/server middleware! The system management acronyms will be explained in Part 8.

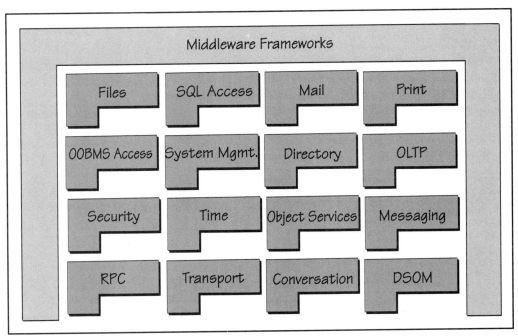

Figure 37-7. Middleware Frameworks from IBM and Taligent.

Most of the middleware frameworks are created by putting SOM-based object-wrappers around existing system software. IBM calls these wrappers *procedural frameworks*. Some of the middleware functions—like object services and mail—will be provided by true object frameworks that support subclassing. Frameworks, both procedural or object-based, make it easier to create client/server applications.

---

[1] IBM provided the first detailed descriptions of its frameworks in September 1993 at the *OS/2 Technical Interchange* in Orlando, Florida. The information on the middleware frameworks is based on a presentation given by John Wilson, a senior architect with OS/2's LAN Systems.

They promise to mask the complexity of the middleware. And some of the frameworks make it unnecessary to learn hundreds of APIs.

The OS Frameworks

With its frameworks, Taligent is creating an object-based operating environment from the bottom up. *Everything is an object* built on top of foundation classes that interface with the IBM Microkernel (see following Briefing box).

What Is Taligent Up To?

Briefing

In Taligent, we are dealing with a system optimized for a very large number of small objects...We don't move a few big objects. We move a lot of very little things around, so we have a tremendous amount of tasking going on.

> — Joe Guglielmi,
> Taligent CEO, 1993

Taligent, a joint venture by IBM, Apple, and HP, is creating an environment that is built from the ground up with object-oriented technology. The Taligent environment runs as a set of foundation classes on top of the IBM Microkernel. Everything in the system is an object. The Taligent personality will provide an OOUI with a deep object foundation behind it.

Frameworks are central to the Taligent operating environment. Taligent is in the process of creating frameworks that span the entire system—from application frameworks that assist in developing the user interface to lower level frameworks that provide basic system level software such as communications, printing, and file systems support. Taligent will also provide a set of development tools that are intimately connected to the framework approach of software design.

One advantage of applying frameworks at the lower levels is that frameworks allow the system to be extended to add new kinds of hardware devices. In traditional operating systems, developers who need to support new types of hardware devices have to write entire device drivers for each new device. However, with frameworks, developers only supply the characteristics and behaviors specific to each new device.

Taligent will first make its frameworks available on the OS/2 2.X, AIX, System 7, and Workplace OS platforms. The Workplace OS with the Taligent personality will provide frameworks that permeate objects into virtually every component of the system.

What Object Request Broker (ORB) will Taligent use for interframework communications? We don't have a firm answer to that question. Joe Guglielmi, in an interview we did with him, said "We will support DSOM, which is CORBA compliant to deal with objects across networks." Within the Taligent system we speculate that they may use the IBM Microkernel as their ORB. The quote from Joe at the top of this Briefing may give you some clue why this may be the case. They need a lot of bandwidth to handle thousands of minute objects like semaphores or the high-speed requirements of interactive 3-D graphic devices. Taligent is stretching object technology to its outer limits. ❑

What Do Frameworks Do for Client/Server?

Integrating client/server technology from 2500 competitors is as much fun as having a root canal.

— *Jim Cannavino, 1993*

Today's client/server industry provides a bag of "piece parts" that must be painfully assembled by skilled system integrators. The thousands of choices quickly become nightmares. How do you integrate and manage multivendor software across networks and disparate operating systems? How much glue code is required? How much of that complex and tricky code gets reinvented with each system integration contract?

Frameworks improve our ability to deal with the complexity of client/server systems. They help coordinate middleware elements that run on distributed heterogeneous platforms. The frameworks create a client/server infrastructure of communicating system objects. Each system object is defined using the CORBA-compliant interface definition language. Each service registers itself at run time with a CORBA-compliant interface repository. The entire system is self-describing. And the best part is that the components have been certified to work together. The integrator simply provides the "last snippets" of code that customize the system at a very fine-grained level.

Eventually all client/server applications will live within frameworks. All the communications between applications will be handled by the frameworks themselves.

Visual programming tools will allow us to create and manage client/server applications by wiring together prefabricated software building blocks. This is how hardware is built today; frameworks will extend these techniques to complex system software. In summary, frameworks will provide the software backbone of the client/server infrastructure. They will help pull the multivendor puzzle pieces together.

Conclusion

Personal computing changed the way people worked. Object computing will change the way the world works. It is the wave of the future and it is here today."

— Philippe Kahn, 1993

In summary, a continuum of object frameworks—from the very simple to the very powerful—is coming our way. The IBM frameworks aim at solving an immediate problem: how to create intergalactic client/server solutions across heterogeneous systems. Taligent is trying to solve a less-immediate problem: how to effectively use objects "from the bottom up." IBM and Taligent will create layers of objects and class libraries on top of procedural operating systems. Everything about objects should be "open" and extendable by third parties. Object frameworks are an essential component of the client/server infrastructure. These frameworks will help us realize the vision: *ubiquitous client/server computing*. The smart money will go to distributed objects now.

Chapter 38

DSOM and SOMobjects

SOM is the cornerstone of an emerging multiplatform, comprehensive, distributed object computing environment that IBM plans to roll out during the next several years...IBM's reward for its efforts is a large lead over its major competitors in delivering a state-of-the-art distributed object computing technology.

— **John R. Rymer (March, 1993)**

There is a field of dreams approach to this technology—if we build it will they come?

— **Cliff Reeves, IBM Director of Objects (January, 1994)**

OS/2 has great object technology. This chapter covers the **Distributed System Object Model (DSOM)** and some of the "Frameworks" and tools that are part of the **SOMobjects Toolkit**. SOM became famous with OS/2 2.0 when programmers discovered that the entire Workplace Shell was written as a SOM class library; some—for example, the cc:Mail developers—even figured out the *magic* of inheriting the Workplace Shell's graphical capabilities. In fact, every object in the Workplace Shell is an instance of a SOM class. Your applications can use the

Workplace shell class library "as is" to create containers, context menus, folders, and notebooks. You can also create new classes that inherit characteristics from existing Workplace Shell classes. If this is not enough, you can extend and modify the functions of any SOM class by substituting (overriding) the class-provided methods with your own.

With the release of the DSOM ORB and SOMobjects, SOM is moving into object "prime time" and may become the "killer app" that OS/2 has been craving. The new DSOM extends SOM communications across address spaces and machines. In fact, it is emerging as the industry's premier implementation of the OMG's CORBA specification for an Object Request Broker (ORB). With the release of the C++ class bindings, SOM could set in motion a whole new objectware industry—object providers can now sell language independent object components. In this chapter we will look at the implementation of SOM/DSOM on OS/2; the AIX implementation is almost identical. SOM/DSOM will be ported to many platforms—including Windows, System 7, OS/400, and MVS.

WHAT'S THE SOMOBJECTS TOOLKIT?

SOMobjects are professional programming tools for OS/2's System Object Model (SOM) and Distributed System Object Model (DSOM) technologies. This is the toolkit for creating objects for that famous Object Request Broker (ORB) and CORBA specification (see Figure 38-1). Here's what you get with this toolkit:

- **The SOM/IDL Compiler** provides language neutrality using OMG's Interface Definition Language (IDL). IDL is how objects tell potential clients what operations are available, and how they should be invoked. SOM provides language bindings for C and C++ that let programmers in those languages use SOM objects and create new SOM object classes. SOM provides emitter utilities that let you create bindings for additional languages.

- **The DSOM ORB Services** let objects communicate across processes in a single workstation or across multiple machines on a TCP/IP or NetBIOS LAN. DSOM is a CORBA-compliant ORB; it also includes a fully CORBA-compliant Interface Repository.

- **A Replication Framework** lets you create copies of objects and synchronize changes made by multiple clients. Updates are automatically propagated to all the object copies. This is great for creating groupware-like applications.

- **A Persistence Framework** lets you save and restore SOM objects to and from a repository that can be a file system, database, or object database.

■ **A Framework of Collection Classes** lets you create compound objects (that is, objects that point to other objects) and navigate through the elements. SOM provides the following object container types: lists, sets, queues, and dictionaries. You can inherit from and use these SOM classes in your applications.

■ **An Event Management Framework** lets you organize application-level events into groups and to process all events in a single event-processing loop.

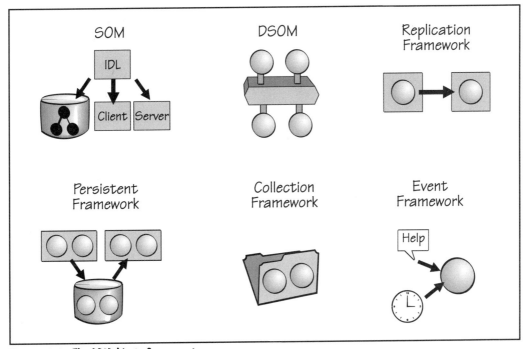

Figure 38-1. The SOMobjects Components.

THE SYSTEM OBJECT MODEL (SOM)

SOM provides the industry's first implementation of a CORBA-compliant, language-neutral environment for defining, manipulating, and releasing class libraries. SOM objects are language-neutral in the sense that they can be implemented in one programming language and used by applications or objects written in another programming language (see Figure 38-2). SOM makes it possible for objects and classes to be shared and ported across OO languages. It does not compete with C++, Smalltalk, C, or any programming language; it complements them. SOM provides a solution to this very real and pressing problem: *How do you develop class libraries that have properties similar to our current procedure libraries?*

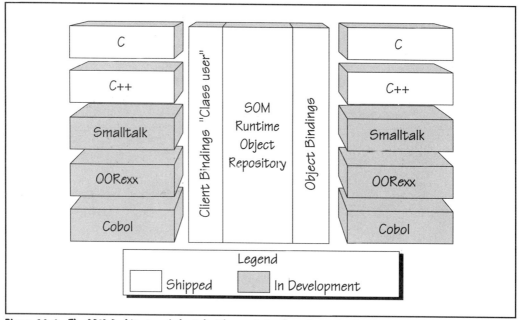

Figure 38-2. The SOM Architecture (adapted with permission from Roger Sessions).

What Problems Does SOM Solve?

Today, SOM allows a developer to define classes and methods using C (or C++). This means that C programmers should be able to use SOM quickly to develop object-oriented programs without having to learn a new language syntax. SOM, however, is specifically designed to work with both procedural (non-object-oriented) languages and object-oriented languages such as C++. Why do I need SOM when I have C++? Now that it is available, 32-bit C++ is becoming the language of choice for programmers wanting to build system class libraries. However, C++ without the SOM run time is not usable for building binary class libraries because:

■ The binaries of one C++ compiler are not acceptable to another.

■ An application that binds to a C++ DLL will need to be recompiled if the DLL is replaced with a new release, unless the developers make almost no changes to their implementation.

■ The use of the libraries from any other language (even C) would be almost impossible.

When C or C++ is combined with SOM, these problems are removed. SOM makes object technology binary (just like DLLs for procedural languages). It's the first commercial technology that makes it possible to package objects as sharable "dynamic binary modules." SOM does that by packaging "neutral" object classes in standard binary library formats—DLLs for Windows and OS/2 and shared libraries for Unix. This makes it possible to ship objects as ordinary DLLs—a technique that's very popular with other forms of shrinkwrapped commercial software. Table 38-1 compares the packaging features of procedural libraries (DLLs), traditional class libraries, and SOM class libraries.

Table 38-1. Comparing Packaging Features for Code Libraries.

Packaging Feature	Procedural DLLs	Ordinary Class Libraries	SOM Class Libraries
Language neutral classes	Yes	No	Yes
Can ship classes as binaries	Yes	No (frequently requires shipping the source code)	Yes
Sharable classes	Yes	Almost never	Yes
Supports inheritance	No	Yes	Yes
Clients must be recompiled when implementation changes	No	Yes	No

The table makes it clear why we haven't achieved *object* code reuse. SOM fixes this problem. For example, in Figure 38-3 SOM lets you change the implementation of the car class without having to recompile the clients. In addition, multiple clients written in different languages can share the same class. SOM classes can be distributed as DLLs or Unix shared libraries. SOM also provides hooks for exchanging class libraries with other object-oriented languages. SOM's language neutrality makes it possible for a Smalltalk object written in SOM to inherit attributes from a C or C++ object. This also means that objects written in different languages can communicate using SOM's common object interface.

SOM class libraries (present and future) are designed to be part of the operating system (OS/2 and AIX today). The promise of SOM is to make *OO technology part of the operating system, not part of a programming language*. SOM allows the integration between operating-system objects and user-supplied objects to be as efficient as possible without requiring users to recompile their programs when the next version of the operating system appears.

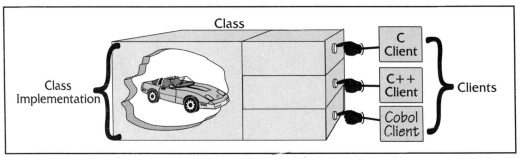

Figure 38-3. SOM Provides Language-Neutral, Sharable, Class Packaging.

What Does SOM Do?

SOM is not a language; it is a complete system for defining, manipulating, and releasing class libraries. The system includes the following components: a CORBA-compliant IDL compiler and Interface Repository complemented by an emitter-framework for creating new language bindings; a run time that provides flexible method resolutions and dispatching; and a unique implementation that treats classes as ordinary objects. The pieces jointly provide a CORBA superset for creating IDL definitions independently of the object implementation. Let's briefly go over the pieces to give you an idea of what they provide.

SOM IDL Compiler and Interface Repository

SOM provides a CORBA-compliant IDL compiler that lets you create class libraries with any language you choose (although in the current release, only C and C++ are supported). You use the SOM IDL to define object-oriented classes and their interrelationships (including multiple inheritance, encapsulation, and method over-rides). An IDL definition of a class specifies the methods available to their clients, their return types, and parameters; the parent classes; public data attributes that clients can set and get; exception handling; and SOM-specific extensions. The methods themselves are written in C or C++. Like any CORBA-compliant compiler, SOM provides the bindings for individual languages for mapping the public class interfaces to the language's native format for creating objects.

Figure 38-4 shows the output of the SOM compilation process. SOM generates the typical CORBA-compliant client IDL stubs for static method invocations, server interface stubs, and the class implementation skeletons. To produce class imple-mentations, a developer needs to add the class implementation code to the SOM-generated skeletons and run it through the native language compiler. SOM also registers the class definitions in a CORBA-compliant Interface Repository. The

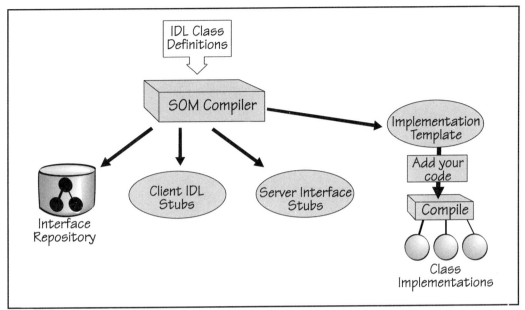

Figure 38-4. The SOM IDL Compiler and Interface Repository.

Interface Repository is accessible to client applications that need to invoke SOM methods dynamically. The query interface to the repository is 100% CORBA compliant and uses the methods we described in Chapter 33, "Object Request Brokers". SOM extends the CORBA specification by defining a write interface to the repository. The ORB 2 committee is working on a standard interface for repository updates, but until then we have the SOM extensions.

SOM provides an *emitter framework* for creating bindings for new languages. This framework is being used by Digitalk and ParcPlace to provide SOM bindings for Smalltalk. IBM and Micro Focus are using it to create COBOL bindings. And it was used by the C and C++ compilers from MetaWare, Borland, and IBM to provide the existing C and C++ bindings. In general, the emitter framework is only of interest to language providers. The language bindings they create make SOM transparent to ordinary programs.

SOM Flexible Method Resolution

The SOM run time provides the environment for creating objects, resolving which method to call, finding objects, querying parent/child relationships, and debugging the run time (see Figure 38-5). SOM supports both the static and dynamic CORBA standards for method invocations. The language IDL stubs constitute the static interfaces to SOM objects. Clients simply access the method implementations

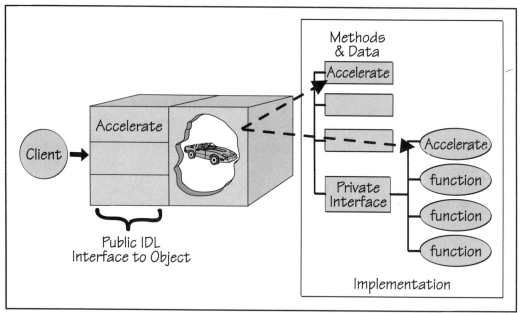

Figure 38-5. Method Resolution: Mapping an Interface to an Implementation.

through the bindings of their programming languages as defined in the IDL. The static stubs invoke SOM APIs that are transparent to the programmers.

SOM also gives clients the ability to dynamically invoke methods on other objects by assembling their own messages using the Interface Repository. The SOM dynamic API and Interface Repository are visible to programmers—and are used to implement the interface standard described in Chapter 33, "Object Request Brokers".

Method resolution—meaning mapping a method name to an address—is a key feature of object-oriented systems because polymorphism and inheritance allow the same method name to be defined in several classes. OO languages like C++ and SmallTalk support radically different styles of method resolution. To be language-neutral, SOM must be flexible and provide support for a broad latitude of method resolutions styles. A SOM method can be invoked using one of three resolution styles:

■ **Offset resolution**, the SOM default, looks up the method in a table and returns the offset location that points to the method implementation. This table look-up is done transparently to the program using the *somResolve* API call. This type of look-up is similar to the C++ virtual method mechanism. It tends to be very fast (about 5 machine instructions) and can satisfy most programming environments. John Pompei—an independent DSOM consultant—quoted a figure of

160,000 SOM method invocations per second on a 486 class machine (the invocations are within the same machine).

■ *Name resolution* allows a programmer to explicitly obtain the method's address by invoking *somFindMethod*. This type of resolution is significantly slower than offset resolution; it is used in SmallTalk like situations where the parameters of the method are known at compile time but the method to be called can only be resolved at run time. You can also instruct the compiler to generate the resolution code automatically by adding the modifier *Name Lookup* to the method in the IDL.

■ *Dispatch resolution* allows a programmer to discover the method and create a message with arguments at run time. SOM allows dynamic dispatching to be done using either the CORBA dynamic method invocation APIs (and Interface Repository) or through the more convenient SOM Dispatch proprietary extensions. In either case, you're trading off flexibility for speed.

SOM also allows programmers to override SOM's dispatch methods—defined in the SOMObject class—and create their own method resolution implementations. Table 38-2 compares the SOM method resolution alternatives.

Table 38-2. Comparing the SOM Method Resolution Schemes.
(Source: Roger Sessions and Nurcan Coskun of the SOM development team.)

Resolution Scheme	Offset Resolution	Name Resolution	Dispatch Resolution
Resolution Speed	Very fast	Fast	Very slow
Ease of Use	Yes (single call-like invocation)	Medium (call-like or explicit invocation)	No. Several explicit calls to discover at run time what's available and how to invoke it
Method Name	Specified at compile time	Discovered at run time	Discovered at run time
Parameters	Specified at compile time	Specified at compile time	Discovered at run time

SOM's Object Management Services

The SOM run time consists of three SOM root classes and a class manager object that gets created during SOM initialization (see Figure 38-6). The purpose of the class manager is to dynamically load and register new SOM classes into the system. The classes that make up the SOM run-time environment—**SOMObject**, **SOMClass**, and **SOMClassMgr**—are packaged in a DLL named SOM.DLL. This library also contains a collection of related functions for initializing and customizing the SOM run-time environment. A single instance of a special **SOMClassMgr** class is created during SOM initialization; it is the **SOMClassMgrObject**. Its job is to maintain a *registry*—that is, a run-time directory—of all SOM classes that exist within the current process, and to assist in the dynamic loading and unloading of class libraries packaged as OS/2 DLLs. When a class is referenced for the first time, the **SOMClassMgrObject** will load the appropriate OS/2 DLL and construct a run-time instance of the class.

The basic unit of organization of SOM programs is the object. All SOM objects are descendants of the **SomObject** class. A SOM *object* consists of instance data and the *methods* that can be performed on the data. An object has a public IDL-defined interface that tells other objects or applications how to interact with it. An object also has a private component that implements the methods. *Instance data* (i.e., object variables) can be declared private (the default) or public. Private instance data can only be accessed by methods of the class. Public instance data, on the other hand, is part of the published external interface.

The public methods and instance data are the permanent interface between the object and the outside world. Old methods must continue to be supported when an object changes. The public interface is a *binding contract* between the class providers and their clients. SOM allows you to change the object's internal implementation—including adding new methods, changing unpublished instance variables, relocating methods upward in the class hierarchy, and inserting new classes above your class in the hierarchy—without affecting the applications that use your objects. In fact, the client applications don't even need to be recompiled. This is one of SOM's great strengths.

SOM supports multiple inheritance. A SOM class—unlike C++—cannot inherit data from its ancestors. However, like C++, it does inherit all the methods from its ancestor classes. A SOM class can override any inherited method that does not have a *no-override* modifier attached to its IDL definition. How does SOM resolve multiple-inheritance ambiguities? It does that using the *left path precedence* rule. Figure 38-7 shows a parent class CAR A with an accelerate method that gets overridden by CAR C. CAR D inherits accelerate methods from its CAR B and CAR C parents. Which accelerate does CAR D end up with? The IDL parents were declared as CAR B and CAR C (in that order). So CAR B wins—CAR D ends up with its ancestor's CAR A accelerate method.

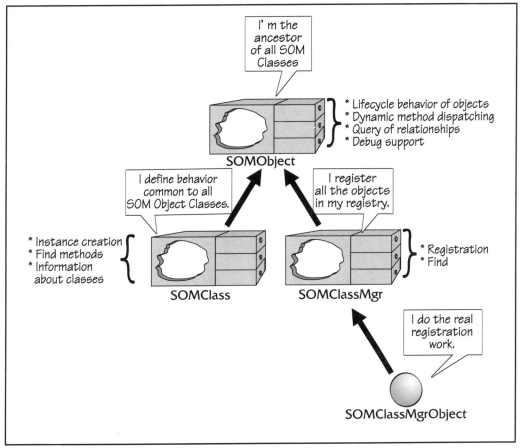

Figure 38-6. The Basic SOM Run-Time Object Management Services.

SOM Classes Are Objects

Another key feature of SOM is that its classes are real objects that play an active role in the run-time environment. **SOMClass** provides the methods for manufacturing object instances; it is the root class for all SOM *metaclasses*. The *metaclass* is a class description of an object that creates other objects. This very useful SOM feature is not as intuitive as the rest of OO programming. As a result it may take some time to grow on you. The trick is to understand that every SOM class is itself a real object. Because SOM classes are real objects and all objects are instances of some class, it follows that a SOM class object must also be an instance of some other class. SOM calls this special class a *metaclass*. Let's further explore this concept.

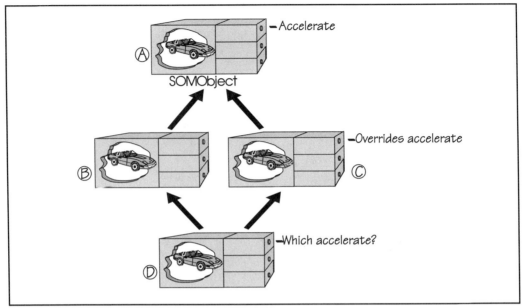

Figure 38-7. SOM Multiple Inheritance.

A SOM class is defined at compile time. A SOM *class object* is a run-time implementation of a SOM class. Objects that are instances of the class are also created dynamically at run time by the application. The methods that an object responds to are called *instance methods* because any object instance can perform them. But before instance methods can be used, an object instance must exist. Who creates the object instances?

The answer is the *class methods* (also called factory methods or constructors). These are methods that an object's class responds to. But all object instances must belong to a class. So what is the class of an object class? It belongs to its *metaclass*. What is a metaclass? It's a SOM class that defines factory methods for classes. Metaclasses are classes of classes. The class methods for an object are listed in the description of its metaclass (just like an object's instance methods are given in its class description). The relationship between objects, classes, and metaclasses is shown in Figure 38-8. (see following Details box for more information).

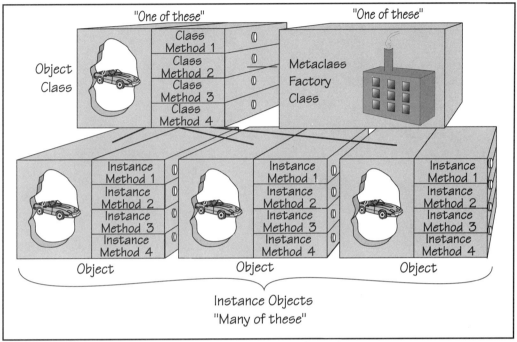

Figure 38-8. The Relationship Between Objects, a Class Object, and Metaclasses.

SOM's Metaclasses and Class Hierarchies

Details

Don't confuse the notion of a "parent class" with a "metaclass." The parent of a class is another class from which instance methods are inherited. The metaclass, on the other hand, provides the factory methods for a class, not instance methods. The parent class and the metaclass of a class will always will be different. In addition, a metaclass has its own inheritance hierarchy.

The example shown in Figure 38-9 should help clarify these relationships. The left-hand side of the figure shows the parent-child relationships between user-written classes (**vehicles** and its descendants) and the built-in SOM classes. The right-hand side shows the class (and metaclass) relationships. This elaborate class hierarchy (ours and SOM's) is used to create two types of object instances: sports car objects and family car objects. The instances of these objects belong to the **sports car** class and **family car** class. Both these classes are descendants of the **automobile** class, which in turn is a descendant of **vehicles**. And **vehicles** is a descendant of **SOMObject**. The buck stops there.

Part 7. Client/Server With Distributed Objects

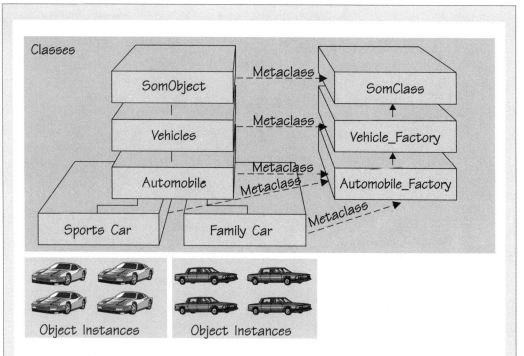

Figure 38-9. Hierarchies of Classes, Metaclasses, and Objects.

Looking at the top right of Figure 38-9, you'll notice that **SOMClass** is the root class for all SOM metaclasses. It defines the essential behavior common to all SOM class objects. If a metaclass is not explicitly specified, it automatically defaults to the one associated with its parent's class. Notice that we've created our own hierarchy of user-written metaclasses (**vehicle-factory** and its descendants). Why?

Typically, you create your own metaclasses to define new class methods for your objects, or to override the behavior of the generic class methods supplied in SOMClass. Here's some reasons why you would want to supply your own metaclasses:

■ To create metaclass instance data (by overriding the methods somInit, somUninit, and somDumpSelfInt).

■ To intercept the constructor methods (somNew, somRenew, and somClassReady) and add your own hooks at creation time. For example, you may want to log information about new objects in a database for persistent object storage.

■ To track object instances and provide object management information that is global to a set of object instances. For example, you can create your own object broker and have it communicate with other brokers to provide distributed object directory services. However, if you can wait, SOM/CORBA will provide these services in future releases.

■ To allocate and deallocate memory and provide your own automatic garbage collection services.

SOMClass provides the methods for manufacturing object instances (somNew and somRenew), which you may want to override to create your own metaclasses. These metaclasses can be used by your applications to dynamically obtain (and provide) information about a class and its methods at run time. ❏

DISTRIBUTED SOM (DSOM)

Distributed SOM (DSOM) is the CORBA-compliant ORB element that allows SOM objects to talk to other SOM objects across address spaces on the same machine or across networks. SOM insulates clients from the object implementation; DSOM adds to that object location insulation. As we go to press, DSOM is the most comprehensive implementation of OMG's CORBA standard for ORBs. It currently allows OS/2 objects to interoperate with AIX objects. DOS/Windows may also be supported by the time you read this book. Eventually, DSOM will interoperate with every ORB via gateways.

DSOM: Workstation Versus Workgroup

DSOM is simply distributed SOM. It uses the standard SOM IDL compiler, SOM APIs, language bindings, and dynamic object model. *Workstation DSOM* supports client/server object interactions among processes on the same machine; it uses existing interprocess communication facilities (IPCs). *Workgroup DSOM* supports client/server object exchanges across networks of OS/2 and AIX machines. It uses socket-based TCP/IP, IPX/SPX, and NetBIOS stacks, and it can be customized to other stacks. DSOM programs run unchanged in both environments (see Figure 38-10); they use the same language bindings and stubs. DSOM is packaged as a client and server DLL addition to SOM.

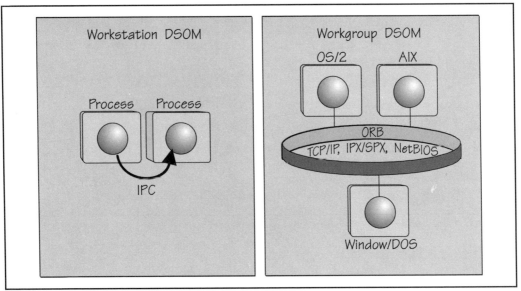

Figure 38-10. DSOM: Workstation Versus Workgroup.

The DSOM ORB

If you haven't done so yet, please read Chapter 33, "Object Request Brokers"—otherwise, you're in for some very strange reading. DSOM is a CORBA-compliant ORB. Like all good ORBs, it makes its living by providing interobject client/server communications (see Figure 38-11). This includes creating, destroying, identifying, locating, and invoking methods on remote objects. It also includes managing object references. The default Basic Object Adapter that ships with DSOM—it's called *SOM Object Adapter (SOMOA)*—only supports the CORBA *shared server activation policy.* SOMOA's multithreaded implementation supports multiple objects within the same server process.

DSOM supports both the CORBA Interface and Implementation Repositories. The Interface Repository describes the behavior of objects; the Implementation Repository deals with their location and packaging. DSOM provides a very open architecture that let you subclass and modify the classes that provide the proxy client, server, and socket functions. As a result, you can tailor the key pieces of the ORB implementation to suit your needs. Of course, it takes some serious programming to do that.

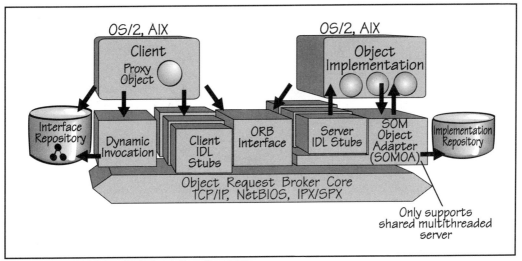

Figure 38-11. DSOM Is a CORBA 1.1 Compliant ORB.

DSOM Implementation Details

Details

The DSOM architecture is very much that of a traditional CORBA ORB with a shared server BOA. This box goes into the next level of detail of how the DSOM ORB is implemented in the OS/2 environment. In Figure 38-12, we walk through a scenario that includes starting DSOM on both the client and server and invoking a method on a car object. We then watch its execution on the server, and what happens at each step:

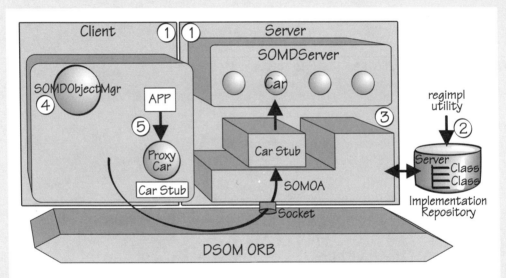

Figure 38-12. A Detailed DSOM Scenario.

1. ***Set environment variables.*** The DSOM clients and servers must set environment variables that give the path names of the directories (local or remote). These directories contain the implementation and interface repositories and the location of the class DLLs.

2. ***Register the class implementations.*** *Regimpl* is an interactive tool that lets you query and update the contents of the Implementation Repository. Use it to define the server's program name, the class implementations it supports, and the location of the server machine.

3. ***Start the DSOM daemon, SOMDServer, and SOMOA.*** Issue *start somdd* on the server to start the SOM daemon, which starts the a default server program object of class **SOMDServer** and a **SOMOA** object adapter. The program registers the classes it implements and the active object IDs in the Implementation Repository; it then notifies SOMOA that it's ready to accept requests by invoking the *impl_is_ready* method. Each DSOM server must contain an Object Adapter of class SOMOA (see Figure 38-13). The SOMOA object registers the socket port with the DSOM location daemon, handles communications with the ORB, executes the main server loop, dispatches the next method request to the SOMDServer object (see Figure 38-14), and keeps running until the SOMDServer program invokes the *deactivate_impl* method.

4. ***Start the client Object Manager.*** This is an object of class **SOMDObject-Mgr** that knows how to find objects on the network (see Figure 38-15). For example, it can find a server that implements a particular class of objects or find a remote object given its ID. It also provides Lifecycle services for proxy object creation and destruction on the client workstation.

5. ***Invoke the method on the client proxy.*** Remote server objects are represented in the client by local proxy objects. Methods invoked on the local proxy are transparently redirected to the remote object. The proxy object inherits the interface of its target object; each method call is automatically overridden with a remote dispatch call. The dispatching logic is inherited from **SOMDObject** and **SOMDClientProxy** (see Figure 38-16). The proxy object call cooperates with the local Object Manager to find a server, marshals method arguments, converts object pointers in the clients, sends the method to the server, and later receives the method results.

6. ***Invoke the method on the server.*** SOMOA receives the request, demarshals the arguments with the help of the IDL stub, authenticates the message, calls SOMDServer to convert the target object ID to a SOM object pointer (SOMDServer loads class DLLs and creates/locates objects as needed), executes the method by invoking the *somdDispatchMethod* on SOMD-Server, marshals the method's return values to the client, and sends the response back to the client.

It should be apparent by now that the entire DSOM ORB is built using objects. This type of design creates well-defined interfaces between the components; the system can be extended and modified at will. The system objects blend with the customer objects and they both feed on each other through inheritance webs. We're getting our first glimpses at the client/server system "objectware components" of the future. Your authors are still evaluating the performance implications of client/server system design by inheritance. But we're getting ahead of ourselves; this is the topic of our next book—**Client/Server Programming with Objects** (VNR, 1995). ❑

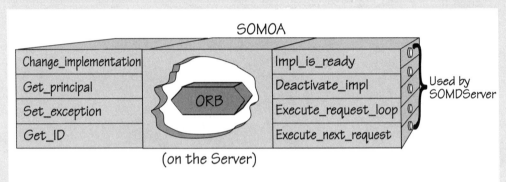

Figure 38-13. The SOMOA Object Adapter Class (on the Server).

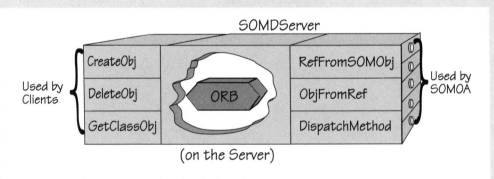

Figure 38-14. The SOMDServer Class (on the Server).

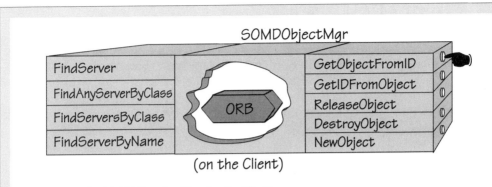

Figure 38-15. The SOMDObjectMgr Class (on the Client).

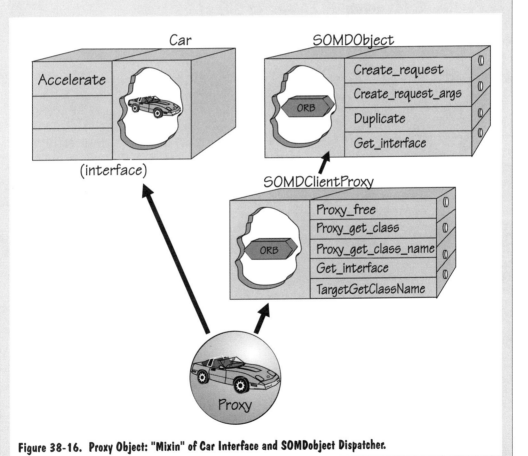

Figure 38-16. Proxy Object: "Mixin" of Car Interface and SOMDobject Dispatcher.

THE SOM PERSISTENCE FRAMEWORK

The Persistence Framework is an object service for making SOM/DSOM objects persistent—meaning that the state of objects can be preserved beyond the lifecycle of the process that created them. Functionally, the Persistence Framework replaces the file system interface of a programming language. The Persistence Framework, like any Object Database, must "flatten" the objects by removing pointers, store the objects on a non-volatile media, and assign them IDs that can be used to restore them to an active state. Like the rest of the SOM/DSOM system, the Persistence Framework is implemented as SOM classes, which means that it can be extended and modified. In this way it is open.

The Persistence Framework Versus an Object Database

So how is the SOM Persistence Framework different from an Object Database? It isn't. Think of it as a "poor person's" Object Database. It provides a simple way to declare objects persistent and then manage their storage and retrieval. However, it lacks the multiuser locking and concurrent access facilities that are inherent to Object Databases. Note, though, that the Persistent Framework is slimmer in both size and price than an Object Database. Table 38-3 offers a perspective of how the SOM Persistent Framework differs from an Object Database.[1] Interestingly, the SOM group is also working with ODI (see next chapter) to create an Object Database version of the Persistent Framework.

Table 38-3. The SOM/DSOM Persistent Framework Versus an Object Database.

Feature	Object Database	SOM Persistent Framework
Storage of complex objects	Yes	Yes
Cost in memory and dollars	High	Low
Optimized for single user	No	Yes
Multiuser	Yes	Limited support (cooperative)
Transaction protection and recovery	Yes	No
Query and reporting capability	Some	None

---

[1] The source for some of this information is Roger Sessions of the SOM development team. We added our own biases to a comparison chart Roger presented at *Colorado OS/2* (November, 1993).

The Persistence Framework Functions

The Persistence Framework can store complex objects. In addition, the objects can contain *persistent pointers* to other objects. When an object is saved, its persistent embedded objects are also saved. For example, the car object (see Figure 38-17) maintains persistent pointers to four wheels, one assembly, and one engine. When the car is saved, so are its embedded objects. When the car object is reactivated from persistent store, so are its embedded objects.

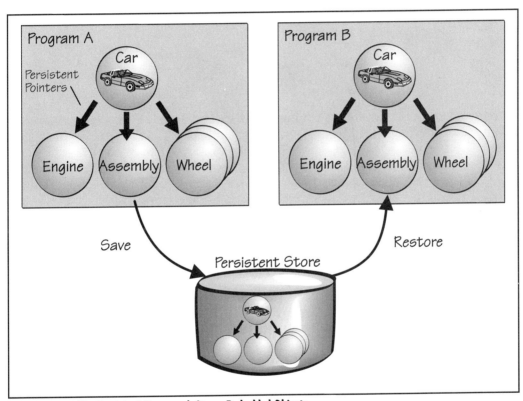

Figure 38-17. The Persistent Framework Stores Embedded Objects.

The Persistence Framework consists of a set of abstract classes that define the framework and a set of classes that manage the object store using standard files (With some effort, a programmer can override them to make them work with an Object or SQL Database.) Objects can be *grouped* together in files or stored individually. Objects that are grouped together are said to be *near* each other. The application can define how the objects are grouped. The framework by default stores near objects in the same file. To be stored, an object must have an ID. Any IDL-supported data type can be declared persistent.

THE SOM REPLICATION FRAMEWORK

We covered replication in the context of document and SQL databases in Part 6; the SOM Replication Framework is the first implementation of replicas using objects. It provides the functions needed to synchronize multiple copies of a single object in the address spaces of several processes distributed across a network. This type of function is very useful in multiparty applications such as groupware. Replication provides the foundation for collaborative online activities such as distributed whiteboards, group editing, and games.

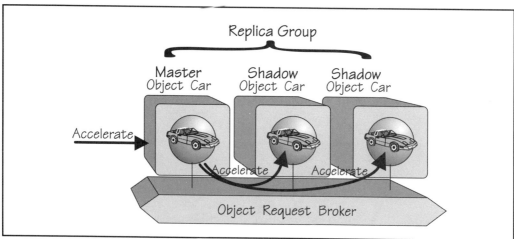

Figure 38-18. The Car Object Is Replicated on Three Nodes.

The Replication Framework supports many advanced "true replica" features. It's the most developed form of replication we've covered in this book. Updates are communicated in real time without the use of secondary store (see Figure 38-18). The replicas are totally transparent in the sense that none of the participants knows how many object replicas exist or where they're located. In addition, any participant object is free to join or leave the replica group at any time. The following is a summary of the additional features the framework provides:

■ *True replica updating*—meaning that any copy of the object can be updated. The framework guarantees that the updates are serialized and propagated by providing a protocol that orders the update sequence. In reality, there is a master/shadow relationship. However, any object can be the master and if the master goes away the other processes hold an election and elect a new master.

■ *No delay for readers*—reading is fast however a delay is experienced by writers when they obtain a lock.

■ *Network support*—the framework supports one replica per process on processes that can be distributed across machines on WANs or LANs.

■ *Security*—the framework provides file-level security for readers and writers.

■ *Fault tolerance*—the framework is tolerant of a single failure resulting from either a process crash or a network failure. As part of its recovery, the failed replica resynchronizes its data objects with the rest of the group.

How is this magic provided? Through inheritance, of course. All the replicable classes must be derived from the **SOMRReplicbl** class (see Figure 38-19). The subclass objects—like our Corvette—can then be replicated. There are two ways changes can be propagated among replicas: operation logging and value logging. In *operation logging*, each method invocation that modifies the data also executes at the site of the other replicas. In *value logging*, the updated data is propagated after the method invocation to the other replicas; it's the programmer's responsibility to provide a description of the updates.

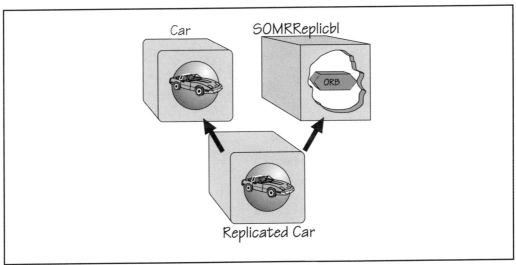

Figure 38-19. The Car Object Is Made Replicable Using Multiple Inheritance.

THE SOM EVENT FRAMEWORK

The SOM Event Management Framework (also known as "EMan") is a facility for registering the events an application is interested in and the callback methods to handle each event. EMan then loops forever to handle events and distribute them to the callback methods. It's very similar to the PM or Windows event loop, except that events can be routed across the network and EMan uses method invocations for callbacks. Both the replication framework and DSOM use EMan to notify them of events that are of interest.

The EMan framework consists of an Event Manager class, a registration class, and several event classes. The programming consists of initializing EMan, registering the events of interest and the callbacks, and handing over control to EMan to loop forever and to dispatch events. An application can register (or unregister) events, even after control is turned over to EMan.

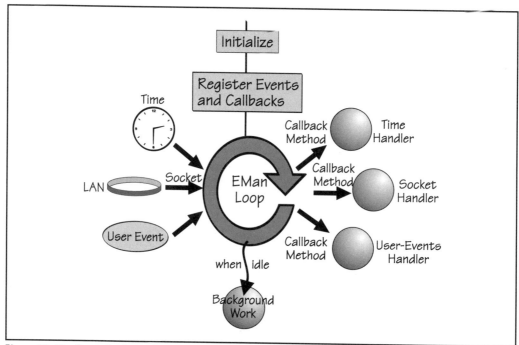

Figure 38-20. Eman: An Event Management Framework for Objects.

EMan currently supports four event types: *timer events*, *sink events* such as socket calls, *client events* that are application-specific, and *work procedure events*—these are background tasks that can be executed when the event loop is idle (see Figure 38-20). Like the rest of SOM, EMan is extendible via subclassing so you can add anything that meets your needs.

COLLECTION CLASS FRAMEWORK

The Collection Classes are a large group of SOM classes that originated from Taligent; they provide container objects that are frequently used by programmers. Table 38-4 summarizes the container types that are provided by the Framework.

"Mixin" classes allow you to extend the collection by creating combinations of containers. The framework also includes classes that provide methods for navigating through the various containers.

Table 38-4. The Container Objects Provided by the SOM/Taligent Collection Classes.

Container Class	Description
Hash tables	A table of key/value pairs that provides fast access by hashing on the key.
Dictionary	A table of key/value pairs that is similar to the hash table. However, objects with equal keys can only appear once within the dictionary.
Set	An unordered collection of objects where the objects can only appear once.
Queue	A list of objects where the elements are inserted and removed in FIFO order.
Deque	A double-ended queue; insertion and removal can occur at either end of the list.
Stack	A list of objects where the elements are inserted and removed in LIFO order.
Linked list	A list of objects where each object is linked to the one in front of it and also to the one behind it.
Sorted sequence	A collection of objects where the order is determined by how those objects relate to each other.
Priority queue	A special case of the sorted sequence where ordering is based on priority.

SOMOBJECTS PACKAGING

The SOMobjects Developer Toolkit for OS/2 sells for $365. The Workstation and Workgroup run time is heavily discounted in quantities greater than one (see Table 38-5).

Table 38-5. SOMobjects Run-Time Pricing.

Package	SOMobjects Workstation	SOMobjects Workgroup
1-Pack	$75	$235
5-Pack	$135	$450
20-Pack	$300	$1000

The Developer Toolkit requires 10MBytes of memory (including OS/2) and 14 Mbytes of disk space. The run times (Workstation or Workgroup) require 9 MBytes of memory (including OS/2) and 3 MBytes of disk space. One of the following communications transport facilities is required: TCP/IP, IPX/SPX, or NetBIOS. In addition, a shared file system is required for the Replication Framework.

SOM/DSOM FUTURES

ORB technology, object services, and object frameworks are the infrastructure of postmodern operating systems—they provide flexible and highly adaptive plumbing. The object model is also extensible in a first class way; its underlying client/server model scales very well in every direction. This means distributed objects make great middleware. SOM started out as a technology to package operating system services. According to IBM's Cliff Reeves, future versions of SOM will be packaged with OS/2 2.2 (October, 1994). Perhaps AIX will do the same.

The next release of SOMobjects will include the new CORBA Object Services—Persistence, Lifecycle, Event, and Naming. It's not clear that all these services will be in the operating system. We expect the ORB to be incorporated first. In other words, the SOMobjects kit becomes the vehicle for the early introduction of new SOM technology. However, when the technology matures, it ends up in the operating system—where it really belongs. Taligent Frameworks are also being introduced in a similar way. The first set of frameworks will be shipped in toolkit form until it gets integrated into OS/2 proper.

In 1994 we expect to see *Enterprise DSOM*—a version of DSOM that integrates with the DCE NOS. The following are target schedules for SOM/DSOM platform shipments in 1994: Windows (April), Macintosh System 7 (July), OS/400 and MVS (late 1994), and COSE (end of 1994). In addition, we expect to see shipments of SOM visual tools and an Interface Repository class browser. We also expect to see more "Direct to SOM" compiler support—for example, the MetaWare C++ compiler can produce SOM objects and IDL descriptions. SOM will also be supported in interpreter languages like OO REXX and Basic. Finally, IBM is expected to ship a large number of procedural frameworks with SOM class wrappers for almost every type of middleware described in this book, including system management. So 1994 may be the year of SOM/DSOM.

Chapter 39

ObjectStore for OS/2: An ODBMS Product

Object Design is not only the leader in the ODBMS market, they are rapidly becoming an industry standard.

> — **Steve Jobs, Chairman, NeXT**

Object Design is the leader in this field.

> — **Bill Gates, Chairman, Microsoft**

Object Design's ObjectStore is the market leader, but the race is by no means over.

> — **Cowen Market Research
> (September, 1993)**

With all the major ODBMS products running on OS/2, we had to make the usual decision of which one to pick. We settled on Object Design's (ODI) **ObjectStore for OS/2** because it leads in marketshare and because we spent time playing with it. In the process, we developed a good feel for its strengths and weaknesses—we know it has a ravenous appetite for memory. As you will find out, we don't consider ourselves fans of ObjectStore's "fat client" architecture. On the other hand, many love this architecture: ObjectStore was selected by Sun's project DOE and NeXT to be their core object-oriented file system. It's also IBM's ODBMS of choice (ODI tells us that ObjectStore is being embedded in over 40 IBM products).

ObjectStore has sold over 60,000 licenses, which accounts for over 33% of the ODBMS marketshare. And most importantly, it got the endorsements of *both* Steve Jobs and Bill Gates! So it *must* be doing something right. OK, we'll admit it: It's not very pretty—you get a "no frills" ODBMS engine core; and it's not elegant—we like persistent object servers better. But it's superfast, robust, C++ friendly, and has great server features. ObjectStore runs on Windows, OS/2, Solaris, SunOS, AIX, HP-UX, and NetWare NLM.

OBJECTSTORE'S VIRTUAL MEMORY MAGIC

In an ideal world, a developer would simply allocate objects and they would persist until they were no longer needed. This sort of transparency requires intimate connection between the compiler and the database.

— David Siegel (February, 1993)

ObjectStore comes close to meeting David Siegel's ideal and at the same time provides safe multiuser client/server access to a common ODBMS. The ObjectStore magic is a by-product of its page server architecture—the one we're not too fond of architecturally.

How Does It Work?

ObjectStore uses virtual memory as the means for providing relatively transparent access to the ODBMS objects. It literally takes over a portion of the virtual memory, which it organizes into a local page cache. ObjectStore then maps persistent objects into the page cache it manages. Its unique design uses the CPU's virtual memory handler to detect access and changes to persistent objects. When a *pointer* "dereferences" an object that's not in the client's cache, a page violation occurs. ObjectStore then retrieves the object from the server and places it into the client's cache. Now you understand why ObjectStore is so fast; it gets right down to the metal.

With this virtual memory approach, the theoretical limit of an ObjectStore database system is 2 to the 89th power bytes (this is practically an unlimited virtual address space). A pointer can reference any other object in this virtual address space. The address space is OS-independent; it can be distributed across multiple disk volumes and machines on a network. ObjectStore divides a database into areas called *segments*. When you create a new persistent object, you can specify the segment to which it belongs. Segments make it possible to *cluster* objects that are tightly-coupled. Clusters maintain the locality of reference on the client's cache, which translates into improved performance. If you have many closely related objects, you should choose to make segments the unit of caching allocation (see Figure 39-1). If you're dealing with small unrelated records, you're better off making a page the unit of network movement and cache allocation.

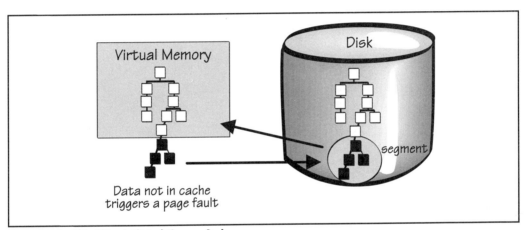

Figure 39-1. ObjectStore's Virtual Memory Cache.

In summary, ObjectStore creates its magic by extending virtual memory to the network, which makes it persistent and provides an infinite virtual address space. The highly optimized caching system makes it possible to move things (segments or pages) quickly between the server and the cache; it taps into the OS's paging mechanism to obtain raw speed.

C++ Programmers Love It

Why not have a single type system that spans both the programming language and the database?

— Malcolm Atkinson

C++ programmers love the product because it is unobtrusive, blends well with their language, and provides a *single-level store* view of the system (see Figure 39-2). ObjectStore also makes it painless to deal with persistence and transaction protection from within a C++ environment. The heart of the design is the C++ pointer—

it is virtualized across networks and persistent stores. For C and C++ programmers, chasing after pointers (or "dereferencing" them) is second nature. ObjectStore was designed with the idea that you can program a database using a regular OO language. You don't need to learn a second language like SQL. As they put it, "Programmers don't have to manage the incompatibilities between the two languages (SQL and C++), and they can reap the benefits of a full OO data model."

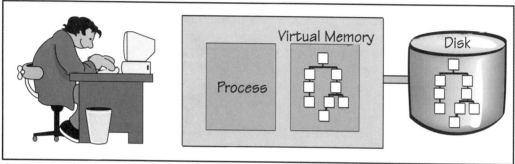

Figure 39-2. ObjectStore Creates a Single-Level Store View.

ObjectStore: Speed Versus Elegance?

Soapbox

We believe ObjectStore's greatest strength—the virtual paging system—is also its greatest weakness. We already explained in Chapter 36, "Object Database Management Systems," the architectural limitations of a paging server compared to an object server alternative. The trade-off is speed (and C++ transparency) versus a more balanced client/server distribution of function. If you like fat clients, you'll love ObjectStore—let's face it, our industry is divided on this question. We're not sure that a "pointer dereferencing" paradigm is the ultimate client to an object persistent store. However, we like ObjectStore's goal of making the "speed of dereferencing pointers to persistent objects the same as that for transient objects—namely the speed of a single load instruction." As we said earlier, it's not very elegant but it's sure fast. Of course, fat clients are not cheap either. ❑

SO WHAT DOES OBJECTSTORE DO?

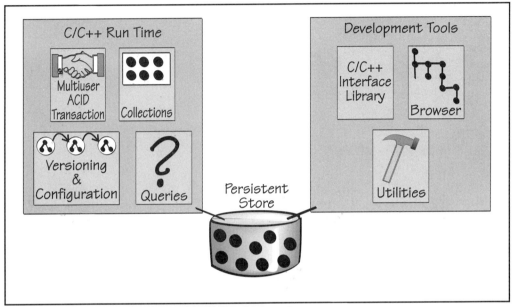

Figure 39-3. ObjectStore's Run-Time and Build-Time Components.

In a nutshell, ObjectStore extends the in-memory language data structures to the network and persistent store. It adds DBMS-like server protection and some unique versioning support features. You can then access ObjectStore using library extensions to popular C and C++ compilers, including C Set++ on OS/2. The libraries augment C++ with powerful container classes, associative query, collection navigation aids, index management, transactions, clustering, versioning, and referential integrity management (see Figure 39-3). This section provides a quick explanation of the main features.

The ObjectStore Collection Classes

ObjectStore augments C and C++ with powerful containers for managing large numbers of objects. A *collection* is an object that groups other objects. ObjectStore supports four collection classes—including sets, bags, lists, and arrays (see Figure 39-4). For each class it provides functions for inserting, removing, and retrieving elements of a given collection. It also supports methods for doing unions and intersections among elements of different collection. Collections may also be *embedded* within other collections creating nested relationships. Typically, collections are used to group objects of the same type and organize containment hierarchies.

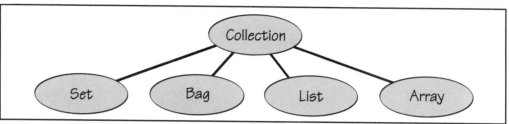

Figure 39-4. ObjectStore's Collection Classes.

ObjectStore's ACID Transaction Support

ObjectStore provides ACID protection for running database transactions in a multiuser client/server environment. It provides two approaches for handling simultaneous access to objects:

■ *Conventional transactions*—ObjectStore provides language constructs for defining transaction boundaries. A conventional transaction may be of type *read-only* or *update*. ObjectStore also provides support for nested transactions. All transactions execute with "all or nothing" semantics. Any object that's been updated by a transaction is written to persistent store when the transaction commits (see Figure 39-5). ObjectStore supports a proprietary two-phase commit protocol for doing distributed updates across multiple servers. The system automatically manages locks on information that's cached in both the client and server. A copy of the object in a client cache is marked as either shared or exclusive. The system keeps track of the objects that are in the client's caches. The server sends messages to clients holding locks on objects that are requested by other clients. ObjectStore also supports deadlock detection and resolution.

■ *Long-lived transactions*—ObjectStore does not provide direct mechanisms for supporting long-lived transactions. It does, however, provide a versioning and configuration management service that allows long transactions to *collaborate* around some form of concurrency control (we cover versioning in the next section).

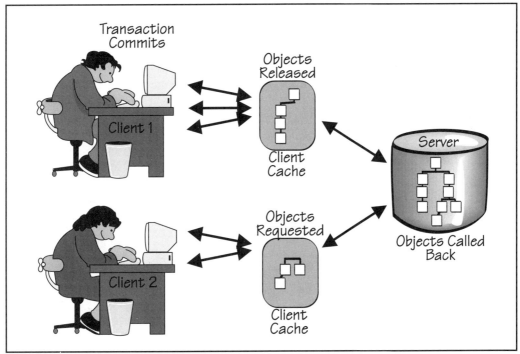

Figure 39-5. ObjectStore's Transaction and ACID Protection.

ObjectStore's Versioning and Configuration Management

ObjectStore provides the ability to store and manipulate multiple versions of the same object simultaneously. A user can *check out* a version of an object or group of objects, make changes, and then *check in* the updated object. In the interim, other clients can continue to use previous versions of the object without creating concurrency conflicts. Typically, this check in/check out activity is related to long-duration transactions that span over hours or days. ObjectStore also supports *alternative versions*—a special type of versioning that allows independent versions of an object to be *merged* back together with some form of difference reconciliation.

ObjectStore also supports *configurations* that allow you to group related objects that evolve together as part of a version. An example is a document object made of many smaller objects (such as pages, text, and graphs) that is treated as a single unit evolution and concurrency control. The *ObjectStore Browser* supports a history graph that you can use to visually track versions. This facility is mostly used for tracking large-grained objects through their evolutionary phases.

Queries on Collections

ObjectStore collections have properties that are similar to a relational database in that they allow you to find related objects without chasing after pointers. You can create query expressions that select objects based on the values they contain or based on their relationships with other objects. ObjectStore treats queries as ordinary expressions in C or C++ (it does not currently support SQL-like semantics). The system allows you to create indexes that help a query optimizer find results using the least expensive search path. ObjectStore queries can execute anywhere on the network.

Relationships and Referential Integrity

Relationships are useful in modeling complex objects such as a bill-of-materials, a document, or a city streetmap. An ObjectStore *relationship* consists of two or more objects that are constrained to be consistent with each other in a particular fashion. Of course, you get to declare the constraints between the members. This is the primary mechanism by which ODBMS provide *referential integrity*. If you declare two objects to be *inverses* of each other, the ODBMS will automatically enforce update dependencies. When an object is deleted, the inverse relationship pointer is automatically deleted as well. In addition to specifying referential integrity, relationships are ideal for expressing parent child associations (i.e., *containment*). You may recall that ODBMSs are especially good at dealing with complex object hierarchies and other complex structures.

OBJECTSTORE C++ AND ODMG-93

*T*he ODMG rallying cry is: "No API."

— *Thomas Atwood, Chairman,*
Object Design (January, 1994)

ODI's C++ language extensions form the basis for ODMG-93 C++ level-2 bindings. The philosophy of ODI (and ODMG) has always been no APIs and no separate data manipulation language (a la SQL). Instead, they would like to extend C++ and SmallTalk to support multiuser persistence, transactions, containers, and the navigational constructs required to traverse complex structures. Currently, these extensions are offered in the form of libraries (or through a precompiler). Eventually, the ODMG would like to see them integrated into the language itself (i.e., no precompiler and no separate libraries).

ODMG-93 does not want to duplicate functionality that's already in C++ or SmallTalk (the base languages); it only adds the ODBMS extensions needed for transactions, persistence, collections, inverse relationships, and navigation. The rest is your normal programming environment. As a result, ODMG hopes to avoid the complications that SQL3 is getting itself into—a 700-page specification that defines a "language-neutral" programming language. The current ODMG reference is about 100 pages.

In the remainder of this section, we discuss the current ObjectStore C++ extensions that are also part of the ODMG-93 standard:

- **Relationships**—the Object Definition Language extends the C++ class definition syntax with the keyword *inverse*, which is used to establish referential or containment relationships between classes.

- **Object creation**—objects are created in C++ by calling *new*. The new operator has been overloaded in the ODMG-93 specification to allow three additional arguments—the first specifies that the object is persistent; the second specifies the database name; and the third (optional) specifies a cluster to which the object belongs (for improving locality of reference).

- **Object manipulation**—after a persistent object is created, it is manipulated and updated by the same code used in the programming language.

- **Queries**—because they're not supported by C++, ODMG-93 introduced the Object Query Language (OQL) extensions to C++ that define container classes and associative query constructs. Queries in the C++ bindings can be used to identify transient as well as persistent objects.

- **Transactions**—because they're not supported by C++, ODMG-93 introduced a transaction class with the methods *transaction::begin*, *transaction::commit*, *transaction::abort*, and *transaction::checkpoint*. Commit writes the results of a transaction to disk and releases locks; checkpoint writes to disk but does not release locks (it is used for chaining). Transactions can also be nested.

- **Database creation**—commands are needed for creating an ODBMS, opening it at run time, and managing it. As a result, ObjectStore provides a set of proprietary C++ commands.

In summary, all these ODMG-93 functions are currently provided in ObjectStore. The syntax may be slightly different because of the macros ObjectStore introduces to mask some of the underlying constructs. These extensions require very modest changes to traditional C++ practices. If anything, they reduce the amount of programming by making it easier to do searches, I/O, and transactions.

OBJECTSTORE TOOLS

ODI provides a barebones ODBMS engine; it relies on third parties to provide query and reporting capabilities (refer to the *Object Design Partner Catalog* for what's available). ODI provides a *class browser* with a *schema designer* to help you visualize your classes and their inheritance relationships. A schema is the set of class definitions for all objects stored in the ODBMS. The schema designer shows diagramatic representations of classes in one window and their corresponding C++ definitions in an adjacent window. Arrowheads indicate whether the relationship is one-to-one, one-to-many, or many-to-many.

ObjectStore provides some raw utilities (or API calls) to help administer the ODBMS—including disk management, access/control, performance statistics, on-line backup, archive logging, and restart/recovery. It does not provide a graphic user interface for performing these functions. For developers, ObjectStore offers a choice of three applications interfaces:

■ A **C++ library** call interface.

■ A **C library** call interface.

■ A **Data Manipulation Language (DML)** that is embedded in the host language and preprocessed into native compiler code. As we go to press, this feature is still not available in the OS/2, Windows, and NLM versions of the product.

We anticipate that the ObjectStore environment will evolve to become totally ODMG-93 compliant (before the end of 1994). Some of the C++ extensions are already in place.

PACKAGING

ObjectStore for OS/2 is available in both standalone and client/server configurations. The client/server implementation allows a client to access multiple databases on many servers; a server can also be resident on the same machine as a client. Clients can connect to ObjectStore servers via TCP/IP (IBM's TCP/IP for OS/2 works fine). ODI recommends IBM C Set++ but they're also working with Borland and other vendors. The ObjectStore development environment requires a minimum of 16 Mbytes of RAM (32 MBytes is recommended).

Part 8
Distributed System Management

Before DSM

After DSM

An Introduction to Part 8

You Martians have so far been getting the scenic tour of client/server computing. You've seen all the cool stuff—objects, groupware, database, and NOS. But there's also a seamy side to client/server—the nasty little secrets that are normally kept out of the grand tour circuit. So what are these nasty little secrets? In a nutshell, the first generation client/server applications were "systems from hell" when it came to keeping them up and running. These client/server projects were either single-vendor based or kept very small until we could figure out the kinks. Many of the early "Kamikazes" who attempted to build large scale open systems often fell prey to the technology; some never returned to talk about it. We call this nasty secret "Client/Server burnout."

So what is the cause of client/server burnout? The root cause is that we all got the scenic tour and fell in love with the promise of client/server. However, no one ever told us that we were *totally* on our own after we unwrapped the glossy packages from the different vendors. There was no single number to call when something went wrong. Yes, the different vendors gave us some rudimentary tools to manage their products, but these tools did nothing to help us manage the *sum of the products*. When something went wrong it was always "the other vendor's fault."

We were left in the great "no vendor's land" of client/server, trying to make our systems work or face loosing our jobs. Many of us burned the midnight oil trying to learn how to read the bits and bytes that flew over the network using Sniffers and other protocol analyzers. These early tools were real lifesavers—without them, we would have been totally blind. However, this was not the answer. We can't expect every client/server installation to have its resident TCP/IP, SQL, and object guru.

OK, you want us to get to the point—enough of this early "pioneer" talk. But we have news for you: we're *still* in the pioneer days of client/server. The *Distributed System Management (DSM)* technology—the topic of Part 8—*may* be the cure to "client/server burnout." We say "may" because DSM products are just coming out of the labs; most are still untested in the battlefield. In addition, the success of a DSM platform depends on how easy it is for third-party tools to "snap into" it; that won't happen overnight. So the good news is that there is a cure: DSM platforms. The bad news is that DSM platforms are in their infancy; you may have to pack a Sniffer back to Mars and be prepared to look at some bits and bytes.

Part 8 starts out by going over DSM platforms and what they can do for you today. Next, we spend time going over DSM standards and middleware. DSMs can only succeed by creating an open-platform based on standards. Standards allow management applications to "plug and play" into the DSM and access their agents anywhere in the intergalactic client/server universe. As usual, there are many standards from which you can choose. We will review the Internet, OSI, and CORBA-based standards for system management; they're also called the neoclassical and postmodern standards. We end the part by looking at a commercial DSM platform and the system management applications that run on it. So welcome to

the seamy side of client/server. We hope that this won't be a Conrad-like journey into the "Heart of Darkness."

Chapter 40

Client/Server Distributed System Management

*N*ow that my applications have moved off the mainframe, how am I going to manage this mess?

— *Anonymous MIS Manager*

*T*he mere existence of a problem is no proof of the existence of a solution.

— *Yiddish proverb.*

Client/Server has applied a giant chainsaw to centralized systems; they have been sliced into pieces that are spread all over the network. How do we manage the pieces? Management and support issues are the Achilles heel of client/server computing. Even though the benefits of client/server systems are real—lower hardware and software costs, more flexible systems, easier to use front ends—we're discovering that administration and support is far more costly than for centralized systems. Client/server computing disperses applications across multiple systems on a network and creates daunting problems for all types of administrators concerned with keeping these systems running. The gap is widening between what users expect and what the support organization can deliver. It obviously doesn't make economic sense to ship a database and network administrator with every new client/server application that we deploy. So the rapidly escalating support burden of client/server systems must be brought under control, or the entire edifice may crumble.

Are we in a no-win situation like the one described by the Yiddish proverb? Is there a solution to the problem of distributed system management in multivendor client/server environments? Until *very* recently, client/server management tools and products were totally inadequate for dealing with the complexities of distributed environments—they were always far less developed than their mainframe counterparts. You had to be a total masochist (or suicidal) to deploy a client/server solution in intergalactic environments. Departmental-sized solutions had slightly better success rates because somebody local was willing to put in the long hours of "volunteer" work. The first generation of client/server systems were mostly a "labor of love" by people who were willing to put in long hours to gain control over their local computing environment.

Fortunately, the situation may be turning around. Some very creative solutions to systems management are starting to come on the market. Most of them use client/server technology to help manage client/server systems. It's very recursive in that sense. Vendors of all sizes have finally come to the realization that no single system management product (or suite) can solve all the world's problems. The new trend is for vendors to create products that plug-and-play in one of the "open" distributed system management platforms—including LAN NetView, OpenView, SunNet Manager, NetView/6000, Tivoli, and the NetWare Management System (NMS).

These open management platforms can exchange management information with almost anything that lives on the network—including low-level devices, system software, and user applications—using standard protocols such as SNMP and CMIP. The distinction between network management and system management disciplines is quickly fading. Object-oriented user interfaces are providing single views of the managed environment; management information databases are providing common views of the managed data. Finally, management platforms can interoperate in all sorts of flexible arrangements, ranging from peer-to-peer to complex manager-of-manager relationships. This chapter looks at the distributed management problem: Why the chaos? What needs to be managed? Then we explain the popular management/agent paradigm for solving the world's problems. Following that we take a quick look at the services that management platforms and applications provide. We briefly introduce some open management platforms such as HP's OpenView, LAN NetView, and Tivoli.

NEW WORLD DISORDER

In many large companies the network control center room seems as complex as the bridge deck of the starship Enterprise. Many systems are linked into the control center, but few are integrated...As a result, operations staff must be rocket scientists to integrate fault, performance, configuration, and other information gleaned from multiple management systems.

— *Gartner Group (March, 1993)*

System management is, of course, much more complex in distributed environments—especially heterogeneous ones. Unlike past generations of computers, client/server systems consist of three logically integrated but physically dispersed types of components: computer nodes, networks, and applications. The health of the system is dependent on the individual health of its component parts, as well as their interrelationships. All the problems associated with managing a typical computer system exist, and they are exacerbated by a substantial set of problems unique to the network itself.

Ironically, the multivendor diversity that's inherent in client/server solutions is also the primary obstacle to effective and affordable system management. You save money by buying components "a la carte," but you must turn around and spend what you just saved, making these components "whole" again. The great variety of vendors, networks, software packages, and system configurations make each cli-

ent/server system different from the last one. And, until quite recently, vendors' management tools were customized for their own set of products and were generally targeted at the workgroup or departmental level.

As a result, client/server control centers in large organizations *do* look like the bridge deck of the starship *Enterprise*. So who does the correlation between the different management platforms? The operators, of course. They must learn a different set of commands for each user interface and product. And they must continuously correlate information—such as fault, configuration, and performance—from the different management consoles. Because each system has its own separate management database, it's not unusual for the same information to be re-keyed multiple times. A single error may cause hundreds of different messages to flash on all the different consoles at the same time. In many cases, functions may overlap leading to more confusion. The first generation client/server systems were much too complex to manage—even in limited configurations with only a few vendors involved.

DEALING WITH CHAOS AND LEARNING TO LOVE IT

Sometimes the most vexing questions have simple answers: Distributed applications need distributed management.

— *James Herman,*
VP Northeast Consulting Resources Inc.

By 1990, the industry began to realize that multiplying incomplete tools by multiple vendors created an unmanageable mess that threatened to derail the entire client/server movement. Something had to be done fast; the industry met that challenge and introduced many innovations very quickly. In the last four years, *three* generations of management architectures were introduced in rapid succession: *Manager of Managers, Distributed System Management (DSM)*, and *Open DSM platforms* (see Figure 40-1). We cover these architectures in the rest of this section.

Manager of Managers

IBM's NetView was one of the first attempts to solve the problems of distributed system management at the enterprise level. NetView introduced the concept of *manager of managers*, which made it possible for a "mainframe in the sky" to oversee an entire enterprise. The idea was to create a single system image using a three-level hierarchy of management elements: low-level *Entry Points* that collect management information and send it upward; middle-manager *Service Points* that

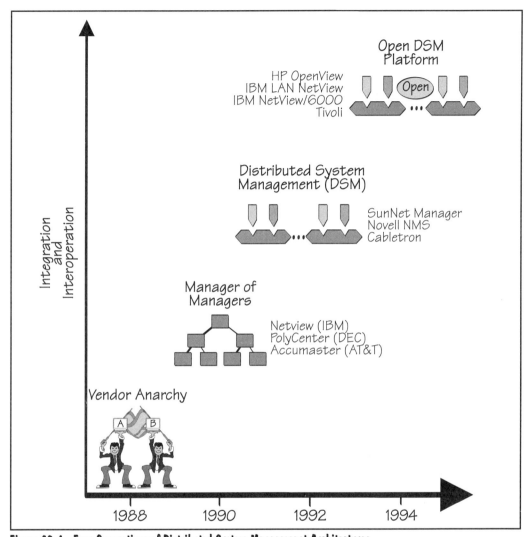

Figure 40-1. Four Generations of Distributed System Management Architectures.

act on some of the information and send the rest upward; and *Focal Points* at the top that maintain a central database of management information and present a unified view of all the distributed resources. NetView/PC—the first *Service Point* product introduced by IBM—also served as a gateway that could convert management information from non-SNA devices into a format the mainframe Focal Points could understand: using the SNA Network Management Vector Transport (NMVT).

It didn't take long for DEC and AT&T to introduce their own manager of managers: *PolyCenter Framework* and *Accumaster Integrator*. Each product was based on a proprietary distributed management architecture. So the race was on between IBM, DEC, and AT&T to see who would be the first to manage the entire universe. It quickly became apparent that no one vendor—not even IBM, DEC, or AT&T—could possibly anticipate all the customer needs and requirements for a manager-of-managers product. There was just too much diversity for any one vendor to absorb—it was a huge and costly undertaking. IBM, DEC, and AT&T must have come to the same conclusion because they're now among the strongest proponents of open management platforms.[1]

Distributed System Management Platforms

The next step in the evolution of management systems was the *Distributed System Management (DSM)* platform approach pioneered by Sun Microsystem's *SunNet Manager*, Cabletron's *Spectrum*, and Novell's *NetWare Manager System (NMS)*. These systems introduce two innovations:

■ ***The use of client/server technology in system management.*** Instead of a hierarchy of managers, these systems split up management applications along client/server lines. A GUI-based client workstation can work with any management server using RPCs to obtain management information. The servers collect their information from agents all over the network. The client workstation can provide a single view of the LAN by visually integrating management information that resides on multiple servers. The back-end data can be managed by peer-to-peer or manager-of-managers arrangements among servers—the architecture is very flexible.

■ ***The use of "toaster" platforms***. The new DSM systems pioneered the concept of the "toaster" model that allows management applications to plug into the platform and play. They accomplished that by creating a "barebones" management infrastructure consisting of published APIs, a starter kit of system management middleware, a system management workstation with integrated graphical utilities, and a management database on the server. The infrastructure was designed to entice third-party management application providers to write to the platforms. The success of a platform is measured by the number of applications that it supports, the type of services these applications provide, and how well they integrate with other applications.

---

[1] Source: **Management Platforms for Networked Systems**, Gartner Group (March 31, 1993).

The combination of client/server and toaster platforms caused a massive migration by third-party management application developers to the DSM platforms. The flexible client/server architecture provided scalability from entry level LANs to enterprise systems.

Open DSM Platforms

The most recent step in the evolution of distributed management systems is *open DSM platforms*. Simply put, this is a DSM platform model that uses industry standards for its main interfaces. So where do these industry standards come from? The usual places, of course. Here's the list of standard bodies and consortia that *together* provide all the pieces needed to create a working distributed management platform: X/Open for management APIs; UI-Atlas and OSF-DME for conceptual frameworks and working technology; OMG for ORBs and object services; and OSI and the *Internet Engineering Task Force (IETF)* for specialized middleware.

MANAGER TO AGENTS: WHAT'S GOING ON OUT THERE?

Mirror Worlds are software models of some chunk of reality, some piece of the real world going on outside your window. Oceans of information pour endlessly into the model (through a vast maze of software pipes and hoses): so much information that the model can mimic the reality's every move, moment-by-moment.

> — **David Gelernter, Author, Mirror Worlds**
> **(Oxford, 1992)**

In his fascinating book, **Mirror Worlds**, David Gelernter defines five key ingredients that make up a mirror world: A deep picture that is also a live picture, agents, history, experience, and the basic idea that knits these all together. We found the "mirror world paradigm" to be very applicable to distributed system management. To make sense out of a chaotic distributed environment, we need to be able to grasp the whole and then move selectively into the parts. This is done by creating a mirror world of the client/server environment. Even though Gelernter does not mention it in his book, today's open management platforms provide the most advanced mirror world implementations.

So what does an open management platform do? It manages mulivendor devices and applications on the network, runs management applications, interoperates with other managing stations, provides an integrated user interface of the managed components, and stores management data. How does it do it? By running an elaborate network of agents—it's like the CIA. The agents reside on the different managed entities on the network and report on their status. The management station can "parachute" its software agents anywhere on the network to look after its interests and gather the data it needs. The agents are also capable of executing commands on its behalf.

The agents help the manager create a "mirror world" of the client/server universe to be managed. Each agent monitors one piece of the universe. Potentially, there may be thousands of agents parachuted throughout the network. They all run simultaneously, never stopping to take a break, always on the lookout for what may go wrong, and always gathering data that may be of use to some manager. The manager software sifts through the massive amounts of real-time information it collects looking for the nuggets—the trends and patterns as they emerge. It must make sure the operator isn't overwhelmed with data. To do that, it must create a data model of the "chunk of reality" it manages. "Data refineries" must convert the data into useful information. A managing workstation should include either a relational or object database for managing and organizing the information that's collected and to remember past occurrences.

A mirror world isn't a mere information service—it's a *place*. You can stroll around inside the mirror world. To allow you to do that, the managing station uses iconic images to create visual computer representations of "what's going on out there." Multiple views allow you to zoom in, pan around, and roam through the network. You can read the screen like a dashboard when you need to see the status of a system at a glance, or you can wade through massive amounts of information organized in

many views when you need to do some serious detective work. At every level the display is live; it changes to reflect the changing conditions of the system as you watch. The way things are presented is a very important aspect of system management. Ideally, you should be able to see and control every aspect of a managed system from a single managing workstation. System management has the visual look and feel of an electronic arcade game, but in the background it deals with real agents that collectively control every aspect of a distributed system.

A management platform also provides the middleware needed for communicating with all types of agents. This includes simple agents that manage hardware devices such as routers to complex agents that chase after objects that roam on networks. The simple agents may be reached using a simple protocol like SNMP; the complex agents may be invoked via an ORB. In between, we have traditional agents for client/server applications that communicate using RPCs and MOM. In summary, distributed system management uses client/server technology to manage client/server systems. It's all very recursive. Mirror worlds are examples of how client/server technology will be used in the years to come. We can get a jump start by understanding the workings of the system management mirror world.

THE COMPONENTS OF AN OPEN DSM PLATFORM

Figure 40-2 shows the main components of an open management platform. It's a composite of the OSI, OSF-DME, UI-Atlas DM, and IBM SystemView conceptual models of distributed management. More importantly, the figure is also a good composite model of commercial open management platforms such as HP's Open-View, IBM's LAN NetView on OS/2 and NetView/6000 on AIX, and Tivoli. Because of the common standards, the main commercial platforms are starting to converge at the implementation level. For example, HP's OpenView is the basis for the OSF-DME implementation of network management technology. LAN NetView and NetView/6000 contain large amounts of code that IBM licensed from HP's Open-View. Tivoli provides object technology that's used in both the OSF DME and UI-Atlas. The irony is that LAN NetView and NetView/6000 have much more in common with HP's OpenView than their mainframe namesake, NetView. A more appropriate name would have been "OpenView for OS/2" and "OpenView for AIX/6000."

Let's quickly introduce the management components of an open management platform before getting into the details. We start at the top of Figure 40-2 and work our way downward:

■   The *OOUI User Interface* provides visual representations of managed objects. The managing workstation should be able to automatically discover the topology of agents on a network and display them in a top view. Background maps can be used to indicate the geographic locations of agents. Clicking on an icon

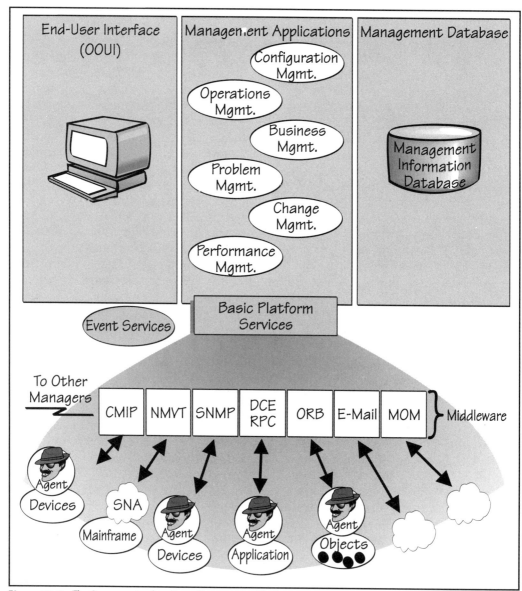

Figure 40-2. The Components of an Open Management Platform.

representing a managed object displays a view of its current status and options for observing and controlling its state. You should be able to visually define event/action combinations. Query dialogs are provided to view information in the management database. Tree views can be used to traverse information that's stored on any remote agent.

■ The ***Management Applications*** are typically provided by third parties on top of the management platform's underlying facilities—including the user interface, the management database, the topological discovery services, and the facilities for communicating with remote agents and other managing applications. The management applications fall into the following categories: problem management, change management, configuration management, performance management, operations management, and business management.

■ The ***Management Database*** is a database of information collected from the agents under the managing workstation's control. It can be implemented using an RDBMS or ODBMS. The database engine may provide active backgound daemons that monitor the historical data for trends and unusual developments. Triggers can be used to proactively launch corrective actions. It's important to note that a portion of the real-time management data is maintained by the agents themselves and stored in the local nodes they manage—the MIBs. So in a sense, we're dealing with a distributed database of hierarchical information that's spread on MIBs throughout the network. The managing workstation maintains aggregate snapshots of this distributed data. However, the data in the central database is not as up-to-date as the data kept in the remote MIBs (the point of capture).

■ The ***Basic Platform Services*** provide high-level APIs that allow a managing application to communicate with agents, other managing applications, other managing platforms, and the event management service. These APIs conform to open industry standards.

■ The ***Middleware Stacks*** provide the elaborate communication infrastructure needed by a management workstation and its applications to talk to distributed agents, other management workstations, and operators via e-mail. A good management platform should support all the industry standards for agent to managing station communications—including SNMP, CMIP, DCE, and CORBA. It should also support legacy management protocols such as SNA NMVT alert packets. E-mail and MOM services are needed for sending asynchronous alerts and notifications. Finally, either SNMP2, CMIP, RPC, or CORBA may be used for communications between management stations.

In summary, the management platform isolates the managing applications from the distributed environment and provides the common OOUI, database, and event services needed to create a single-system image of client/server management. The managing applications themselves are written by third parties. The more standard the APIs supported by a platform, the easier it is for third parties to port their applications. Of course, the real management work is done by their management applications—the platforms just provide the necessary plumbing and the install base.

MANAGEMENT APPLICATIONS: COPING WITH DIVERSITY AND COMPLEXITY

With standardized APIs and what we believe will be the convergence to a small number of management platforms, an entirely new market is being created. A major opportunity now exists for the development of best-of-breed management applications.

— Gartner Group (March, 1993)

Management applications do the real work in distributed system management. They help us answer the following questions: How is my client/server system doing? What is out there and where? Who is doing what to whom? How do I install new software? What went wrong? How do I fix it? Is everything being backed up? Can my system survive an 8.0 earthquake? In this section, we take a quick look at the categories of system management software that help us answer these questions.

How Is My Client/Server System Doing?

Collecting real-time information from various system components in a client/server environment and pinpointing the causes of performance problems can be a real headache for system and database administrators. The management software must be able to collect extensive data, in real time, from different sources in a client/server environment. It must then act on that data or present it in graphical or numerical form for further analysis. You should be able to correlate the performance data with information collected from configuration management tools and proactively identify system bottlenecks.

Performance monitoring tools gather statistical data on resource utilization levels of key components in a client/server system, and then generate alarms when some administrator-defined criteria are not met. Some of the tools may even provide scripting facilities for generating repair actions or doing preventive maintenance. The tools monitor utilization levels on typical resources—including networks, CPUs, disks, memory, file space, processes, server transactions, e-mail, modems, routers, and so on. The better systems use histograms and standard deviations to monitor the response time of servers. Performance monitoring tools maintain a database on the historical performance of the system so that trends can be discovered. You should be able to obtain graphical displays of usage data on any computer, network, or database resource. The tool should be able to automatically collect relevant data over a period of time so that resource utilization during peak hours can be analyzed before making hardware or software capital expenditure decisions.

Unfortunately, very few generic tools can be used to automate the corrective actions in the areas of performance tuning. In this case, what's needed are tools that automate load balancing in response to varying loads. Some of that is done by specialized system components such as TP Monitors and routers.

What Is Out There and Where?

Inventory management tools, also known as "asset managers," keep track of what programs run on which machines, what levels of software they run, and the like. They also keep track of hardware inventory and maintain a database of inventory information. Most tools can automatically notify you when they detect changes to the hardware and software on the LAN. Some of the more "authoritarian" tools may do more than just report changes; they may automatically revoke and restore files to the parameters that an administrator sets—for example, login files.

In theory, an automated inventory manager should be able to automatically deter-mine all the software, workstations, peripherals, routers, and servers directly attached to the LAN. Unfortunately, most tools require you to key in some data; there is no way to automatically gather information such as the serial number of devices. In addition, it is hard to track all the software that's used on the LAN because no single comprehensive list of software exists. Vendors typically rely on a list from the Software Publisher Association (SPA). This list is updated twice a year and contains only the software of vendors that have paid to have their applications included. Some tools can isolate unknown software by checking the file size and version number, and then making educated guesses as to what the application is.

Configuration management tools can set software parameters and fine-tune complex systems such as relational databases or operating systems. Fortunately, generic software management tools are becoming less scarce. However, hardware configuration tools are still what most people think about in terms of configuration control—they've been around longer. These tools can set device thresholds and tuning parameters. They can also collect configuration information from any managed system via its MIB. You should be to track changes in the configuration of the client/server environment over time and use that information to perform crucial maintenance and tuning work such as identifying and balancing the load around bottlenecks. For example, a database management tool should be able to monitor database resource utilization, database space fragmentation, application deadlocks, application throughput, computer resources, dead processes, and resource "hogs."

The client/server computing environment is always in flux as new clients and applications log on and off the network. *Topology management tools* keep track of how the network is interconnected, what nodes are out there, and how to best reach them. They make it easy for an administrator to continuously monitor the changes in the client/server environment. The administrator can graphically display crucial information, such as which client is using which server, which database resource resides on which server, and which applications are available on each server.

Who Is Doing What to Whom?

Security tools monitor access to resources and manage who can access what. These tools provide a friendly interface that help you maintain user and group account information as well as access lists and the like. The NOS provides the middleware that does the actual authentication and access protection. The management tool provides the user interface and the environment to manage passwords, run virus scans, and track intruders. The idea is to provide an integrated view of client/server system management. So it makes sense to have the NOS services (such as security and directories) managed through the open system management platform.

How Do I Install New Software?

The number of programs on each individual machine has risen dramatically over the last few years. Administrators have had a hard time managing this explosion; it's one of their top five headaches. *Software distribution and installation tools* let you download, update, track, and deinstall software packages on any networked machine. These packages can include anything from new operating system releases to end-user applications. Most of these tools can track the version number and status of the software. The better tools can perform unattended pushes from the code server to a particular client machine. *Software license management* tools can meter and enforce the use of licensed software. They typically support a wide range of licensing policies. This is an area where proper standards are important.

Users can subscribe to a particular software package and have it automatically delivered and installed on their machine. Of course, this delivery must be coordinated with the license metering application. A typical installation tool is divided into three components: clients or recipients of a delivery, the software package to be distributed, and the delivery schedule. You should be able to create distribution lists of recipients making it easier to send software updates to a group of users. The delivery can be scheduled for a particular date and time. Clients can also perform installations on their own time—the *pull method*.

You should be able to define software distribution packages and subscription lists using a GUI (or preferably an OOUI). The "management by subscription" approach is used to automatically push the packages to all the subscribers. An OOUI allows a subscription list to be created by simply dragging and dropping individual host icons on a software package. The package typically consists of two component types: the files and directories that make up the software to be distributed, and the name of a program to be executed after the software is copied on each subscriber machine. Adding a new subscriber to a distribution list is just a matter of dragging a new icon and dropping it on the package.

Still missing is a "software vending machine" concept that lets clients browse from a wide selection of applications available on the server and try out an application before they buy. If they want to buy, the system should generate a purchase order, inform the licensing tool that it's OK to use this application, and update the inventory tool.

What Went Wrong? How Do I Fix It?

The number one headache of any administrator is, of course, how to deal with faults. The distributed nature of client/server systems—different transports, OSs, and databases—add several degrees of complexity. Failures can be caused by any single component or from mysterious combinations of conditions. *Fault management and help desk tools* receive alarms, identify the failure, and launch corrective actions. The best tools can combine network, systems and application-level management views. They help break down walls between database, network, and system management functions, making it easier to correlate failure symptoms. The tool should maintain error logs and issue *trouble tickets* to the people who need to know about the problem.

If an alarm occurs, a tool should be able to perform any combination of the following: send a notification, send an e-mail message, call a beeper, invoke a user-supplied program, update a log file, flash an icon, and pop up an alarm window. The better management systems provide scripting facilities that make it easy to automate the known corrective actions. Some tools provide mechanisms for associating events with actions (event handlers). It's a typical event-driven system—for each failure event, there is an event-handler action script. The event-handler script language should be able to call on other managing applications (for example, the configuration control tool) to perform some corrective action or to gather information on what went wrong. It's also important to provide sophisticated filters for events to narrow down the conditions that require intervention.

Most tools do a good job gathering real-time data on device and connection status, but fall short on tasks like trend analysis, trouble ticketing, and reporting on network elements. The management software should continuously monitor the system for potential problems and be able to automatically launch preventive or corrective actions to resolve problems before they occur. Instead of relying on problem *autopsy* and after-the-fact repair actions, potential problems should be avoided without requiring human interaction. This makes managing client/server systems less tedious and less susceptible to human error.

Can My System Survive an 8.0 Earthquake?

It's not just for disaster recovery anymore. Network backup is becoming part of a storage-management strategy that removes the weak link: you.

— *Michael Peterson, PC Magazine*
(September, 1993)

Data on the network is continually growing, leaving the administrator with another big headache: How can you manage this growth within the allocated budget, while keeping the data safe from disasters? Disaster recovery includes everything from scheduling daily backups to maintaining hot-standby sites. *Disaster backup, archive, and recovery tools* can initiate the backup or restore action where the source and destination of the operation can be located anywhere on the network. These tools provide a user interface for scheduling the operations in unattended mode. The backup can be performed on any type of media. The better tools provide *hierarchical storage management* for multiple levels of storage—including memory caches, file servers, and an archive medium such as an optical juke box or tape drives. The tool should allow you to monitor where all the data resides and let you set policies like backup times. The best tools have the ability to learn from access patterns; they have some understanding of how information is related.

Chapter 41

Distributed System Management Standards

As we move to this new distributed client/server relationship, the question is: Are we going to have to put an administrator in each location? At $100,000 a year or so for each person, that gets expensive.

— Gary Falksen, DBA with XES Inc.

This chapter introduces about a dozen distributed management standards and a gaggle of new acronyms. We cover the traditional manager/agent standards—including SNMP, SNMP2, RMON, XMP, and XOM—a standard for tiny desktop agents—the DMTF's DMI—and two CORBA-based system management standards—the OSF's DME and UI's Atlas-DM. Of course, there is a soapbox that gives you *our* opinion on system management in client/server environments. What would life be without soapboxes?

Two "standard" management protocols have been defined: the Internet's SNMP and OSI's CMIP. Both are manager/agent protocols. Each of these protocols defines its own way of describing management information. The two approaches have much in common (including a confusing similarity in terminology), but they differ in a number of important ways. SNMP's approach is simple and straightforward, while

CMIP's is both more powerful and more complex. The SNMP2 protocol introduced in 1993 fixes many of the "simple" SNMP's shortcomings, but it cannot be called simple any more—the specification is now over 400 pages. To isolate developers from the underlying management protocols, X/Open defines the *X/Open Management Protocol (XMP) API* that works on top of either SNMP or CMIP. The other contending standard is based on the use of distributed objects (of the CORBA variety) for system management.

THE INTERNET MANAGEMENT PROTOCOLS

The impact of adding network management to managed nodes must be minimal, reflecting a lowest common denominator.

> — *Marshall T. Rose, Chairman of the SNMP Working Group*

In 1988, the *Internet Engineering Task Force (IETF)* decided it needed an immediate stopgap solution to system management. The *Simple Network Management Protocol (SNMP)* was created to fill that need. IETF originally planned to pursue a two-track approach: SNMP in the short term, and the OSI *Common Management Information Protocol (CMIP)* in the long term. The OSI CMIP was far too complex for the needs of most devices; SNMP was simple and easy to implement. To help the transition, it was originally intended that the SNMP *Management Information Base (MIB)* and *Structure of Managed Information (SMI)* be subsets of those for the OSI systems management. Eventually, that requirement was dropped, and each protocol went its own way; but they still retain a lot of common terminology. SNMP is the dominant network management protocol today. However, SNMP has a lot of deficiencies—it cannot meet modern system management needs. SNMP2, introduced by the IETF in 1993, is intended to remove some of these deficiencies. In the meantime, many large corporations, telephone companies, and governments are committed to the OSI approach.

Defining Management Information: SMI and MIB-II

The Internet and OSI have introduced their own versions of a Data Definition Language for system management; in the process, they've also introduced a lot of strange and confusing terminology. To put it simply, the OSI and Internet people have created a language for defining the structure of the data that's kept on the managed devices. Their language defines a hierarchical (tree-based) database and names the components within the tree. The managing workstation uses this information to request data via a protocol such as SNMP or CMIP. The two protocols use the same type of architecture and terminology; however, CMIP is much richer and more complex than SNMP. CMIP uses richer data structures, more object-oriented data definition techniques, and a more sophisticated protocol for exchanging the data.

Both SNMP and CMIP use object-oriented techniques to describe the information to be managed; each resource to be managed is called a *managed object*. The managed objects can represent anything that needs to be managed—an entire host, a program, or just a variable maintaining a counter of received TCP packets. A *Management Information Base (MIB)* defines a structured collection of managed objects. The *Structure of Management Information (SMI)* defines the model, notations, and naming conventions used to specify managed objects within a particular protocol (such as CMIP or SNMP). If you view the MIB as a database, then the SMI provides the schema.

SMI identifies the data types and the representation of resources within a MIB as well as the structure of a particular MIB. The ISO *Abstract Syntax Notation One (ASN.1)* is a formal language used to define MIBs for both SNMP and OSI management systems. ASN.1 describes the data independently of the SMI encoding technique used. The Internet's RFC 1155 defines a simple SMI to be used with SNMP MIBs; it only supports a subset of simple data types consisting of scalars and two-dimension arrays of scalars. (In contrast, OSI supports complex data structures and inheritance relationships for data.) An *object identifier* consists of a left-to-right sequence of integers known as subidentifiers. The sequence defines the location of the object within a MIB tree.

RFC 1123 defines MIB-II, which is a superset of MIB-I (RFC 1156). MIB-II adds additional groups of managed objects. Figure 41-1 shows the structure of managed objects that are defined in MIB-II. Objects are defined by their hierarchical location in the tree—for example the IP object group is 1.3.6.1.2.1.4. New objects are always added "down and to the right." The ten object groups defined by the Internet are essential for either fault or configuration management. All devices that claim to be Internet managed nodes must implement the MIB; however, not all functions need to be present on all nodes. The *group* provides a convenient way to organize management objects according to the functions they provide. All objects within a group must be supported to be MIB-II compliant. For example, an implementation must include all objects within the IP group if it implements the IP protocol. The *experimental* node is used to introduce and debug new Internet-defined object categories before they become official MIB objects. The Internet believes that ideas must be proved in a working environment before they are considered for standardization.

The ten MIB-II object groups are not particularly thrilling. They contain several hundred low-level objects that perform TCP/IP based network management functions (from the transport layer down). The interesting system management stuff is left to the private MIB extensions.

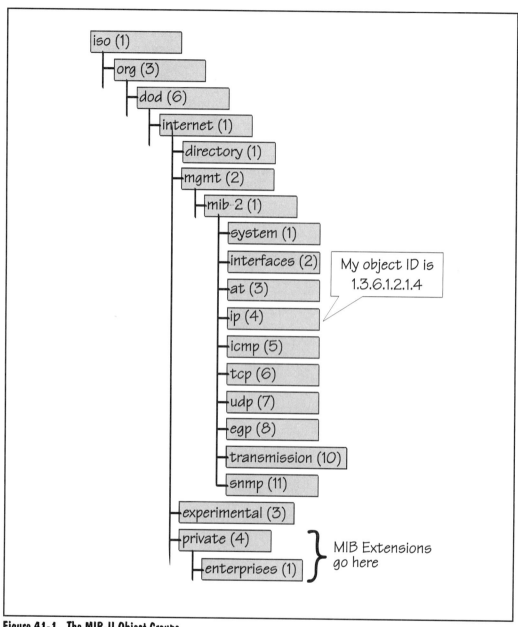

Figure 41-1. The MIB-II Object Groups.

New management objects are typically defined as MIB extensions in the *private* subtree; they allow vendors to create extensions that make their products visible to a managing station. The *enterprises* node is used to allocate *enterprise object IDs* to each vendor that registers for one. Vendors must describe their MIB extensions using formal descriptions—as defined in RFC 1155 or RFC 1212—inside a text file. Enough information must be provided to allow a managing station to load and compile the vendor-specific MIB definition and add it to the library of managed object descriptions. The managing station can only access information it knows how to ask for. The private MIB extensions are the heart of SNMP and OSI system management, but they're also the areas of greatest confusion. Users must make sure that the management platforms they select can handle the private MIB extensions for their systems. Different managing systems are known to produce different results when managing the same MIB data; it's scary stuff.

MIB Tools

Most management platforms provide tools that make MIBs friendly. A MIB is, in essence, a form of hierarchical database that's distributed across managed stations. Like any database, it requires tools that make it accessible. Here are the typical tools that make it easier to work with MIBs:

■ A *MIB compiler* takes a file in RFC 1155 format and converts it to a format that can be used by the management station. The compiler is also used to update an existing MIB and add new vendor-specific definitions.

■ A *MIB browser* displays the MIB tree in a graphical manner; it allows you to search for objects by groups or attributes. You can refresh instance data from any managed node. The browser should allow you to create aliases for MIB objects (i.e., give them names that you find meaningful). The browser is really nothing but a specialized query tool for MIB databases. Some vendors allow you to overlay the MIB information on maps or on pictures of the objects you're interested in.

■ A *MIB report writer* allows you to graphically create reports of the managed data. These reports may be augmented with business graphs, maps, and other forms of visual presentation.

MIB tools are typically integrated with other visual management tools. For example, an agent discovery tool can display the location of the agents on the network and the MIB query tool can be used to browse through the data they contain.

The Internet's SNMP

The *Simple Network Management Protocol (SNMP)* is the most widely implemented protocol for network management today—it is supported by a constantly growing number of network devices. SNMP, as defined in RFC 1157, is designed to do exactly what its name suggests—it performs relatively simple management of the components in a network. It is used to alter and inspect MIB variables. SNMP is an asynchronous request/response protocol that supports four operations (see Figure 41-2):

- **GET** is a request issued by a managing station to read the value of a managed object. The get operation is atomic; either all the values are retrieved or none are. SNMP only supports the retrieval of leaf objects in the MIB.

- **GET-NEXT** is a request made by a managing station to traverse a MIB tree; it reads the value of the "next" managed object in the MIB.

- **SET** is a request issued by a managing station to modify the value of a managed object. This operation is often not supported because SNMP provides no effective security or ways to control who is allowed to perform SETs. The last thing you need are intruders causing havoc on the network using unprotected SNMP SETs.

- **TRAP** is a notification from a managed system to a managing station that some unusual event occurred. SNMP traps are very limited; they report one of seven events: cold start, warm start, link down, link up, authentication failure, external gateway neighbor loss, and enterprise specific trap. The traps use unacknowledged datagrams.

SNMP exchanges use TCP/IP's *User Datagram Protocol (UDP)*—this is a very simple, unacknowledged, connectionless protocol. It is also possible to support SNMP over the ISO stack using the connectionless transport system. Most SNMP agents are implemented as TSRs or Daemon background tasks.

SNMP's Limitations

So what are the limitations of SNMP? The list is long; it's a classical tradeoff between simplicity and the complex requirements of modern management systems. Here's a quick of summary of SNMP's more blatant shortcomings:

- ***SNMP is not secure.*** The protocol provides a very trivial form of authentication; it is child's play for an intruder to break into the system. Most network managers do not allow the use of the SET command. This can be very limiting.

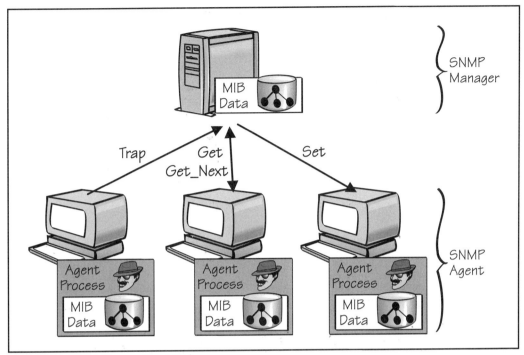

Figure 41-2. SNMP Manager/Agent Exchanges.

- ***SNMP is inefficient.*** The protocol is not suited for retrieving bulk data; you must send one packet for each packet of information you want returned. SNMP relies on polling, which can swamp a network with traffic. Because the event traps cannot be extended, they cannot be used to create an event-driven environment. The server calls the agent and not the other way around. Polling limits the number of variables that can be monitored by a managing station, which translates into more cost.

- ***SNMP lacks important functions.*** The protocol cannot be used to create new instances of MIB variables; it cannot execute management commands; and it does not support manager to manager communications.

- ***SNMP is unreliable.*** The protocol builds on the UDP, which is an unacknowledged datagram mechanism. The traps are unacknowledged, and the agent cannot be sure they reach the managing station. The SNMP designers believe that a datagram may have a better chance of reaching its destination under catastrophic conditions (that may be a bit far-fetched).

In summary, SNMP is excellent at its intended task—simple network management. However, it is too limited to handle the more complex functions of systems management.

Stretching SNMP's Limits: The RMON MIB-II Extensions

The *Remote Network-Monitoring (RMON)* standard defined in RFC 1271 is a very significant extension of MIB-II that stretches SNMP to its limits. The moving forces behind RMON were the network monitor vendors; they needed extensions to SNMP that would allow their equipment to participate in the management of networks. A *network monitor*—for example, Network General's *Sniffer*—is a "promiscuous" device that sits on the network and can capture and view any packet, regardless of who sends it to whom. Clearly, these sniffer-like devices collect a tremendous amount of information that can be very useful to an SNMP managing station. Monitors are the ultimate "secret agent." They're tapped into the network and can see anything that moves on it. So the question is: How does a managing station obtain this massive information using SNMP? The answer is through the RMON MIB-II extensions.

What makes RMON so interesting is that it is the most intelligent entity ever defined by the Internet; it breaks the mold of the simplistic, simple-minded, and brain-dead managed device. A monitor must have enough intelligence to filter and act on the information it collects without directly involving the managing station for every action or swamping the network with massive amounts of bulk data transfers. Through *preemptive monitoring*, the sniffer continuously runs diagnostics on the network traffic, notifies the managing station when a failure is detected, and provides useful information about the event. This activist style is a far cry from the typical SNMP philosophy that views each managed node as a set of remote MIB-defined variables.

RMON defines the conventions, using MIB-II extensions on standard SNMP, for telling a remote monitor what data to collect. Remember that SNMP does not support imperative commands and it cannot create new instances of objects. So, RMON does it all via conventions that allow a MIB variable to represent a command and other variables to represent the parameters to the command; it's all very clumsy, but it shows what can be done in desperation. RMON defines a number of new MIB-II objects that represent commands. The monitor executes the command when the managing station writes to them (changes the state) using the SNMP SET command. The RMON specification defines how rows are to be added, deleted, or modified in a MIB setting.

The bulk of the RMON defines nine MIB-II object group extensions that are used to store data and statistics gathered by a monitor (see Figure 41-3):

- **Statistics** is a table that stores statistics for each monitored Ethernet network. Each column in the table is a counter.

- **History** is a single table whose entries contain the results of running periodical statistical samplings of the information gathered in the statistics table.

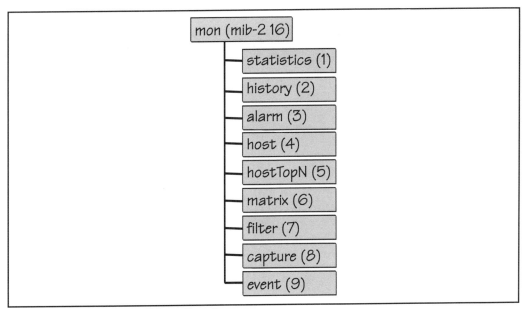

Figure 41-3. The RMON MIB-II Group Extensions.

■ **Alarm** is a single table whose entries define a set of thresholds on MIB variables. If the threshold value is exceeded, the monitor generates an alarm trap and sends it to the managing station. The managing workstation can create a new alarm threshold by adding a new variable to the table. It can also specify the frequency interval for comparing a monitored variable's data against its threshold value.

■ **Host** contains a set of tables that maintain information on traffic to and from each discovered network node. The information includes the number of errors, broadcast packets, in and out packets, and the time when the node was discovered on the network.

■ **HostTopN** contains a sorted list of statistics about a set of hosts (or network nodes) that top a list based on some specified criteria. For example, the list could keep track of the ten PCs that generate the largest number of transmission errors during an interval.

■ **Matrix** records information about traffic exchanges between a pair of nodes. You can use this information, for example, to discover which client conducts the most exchanges with a server.

■ **Filter** contains tables for instructing a monitor to filter network traffic based on some specified criteria. The monitor can be instructed to record all the packets that pass the filter or simply record statistics on those packets.

■ *Capture* contains a table that specifies the buffering scheme to be used with the data captured by the filters. Each row defines one buffer to be used with a particular filter channel. In addition, data tables contain one row for each packet captured.

■ *Event* contains a table where each row describes an event to be generated when certain parameters are met. It also includes an event log table that contains a timed entry of each event occurrence that is recorded.

Each of the nine RMON groups provide a set of control variables that allow a managing workstation to remotely control the operation of a monitor agent. These can be seen as state tables that tell the monitor what to collect and how to handle the events it generates. In a more modern setting, all of this could have been done using RPCs, MOM, or ORB invocations. RMON is a weird data-centric protocol that uses MIB variables to pass instructions, parameters, and control information between a managing station and an agent. It's a "kludge."

SNMP2: What's New?

SNMP Version 2 (SNMP2) is the creation of Jeffrey Case, Keith McCloghrie, Marshal Rose, and Steven Waldbusser—the designers of the original SNMP and related Internet management standards. SNMP2, adopted as an Internet standard in March 1993, is designed to fix some of the more blatant problems in the original SNMP. The new specification consists of 12 RFC documents that total over 416 pages. SNMP2 improvements over SNMP include a new security protocol, optional encryption, manager-to-manager communications, bulk data transfer, new SMI data types, new MIB objects, and the ability to add or delete table rows (a la RMON).

SNMP2 Operations

An SNMP2 node can now be both a managing and a managed object. This makes it possible to create manager-of-managers arrangements, and it allows SNMP2 to share management information with its fellow managers. A new *Manager-to-Manager (M2M)* MIB is provided to support this topology. SNMP2 is a "proper extension" of SNMP.

Chapter41. Distributed System Management Standards

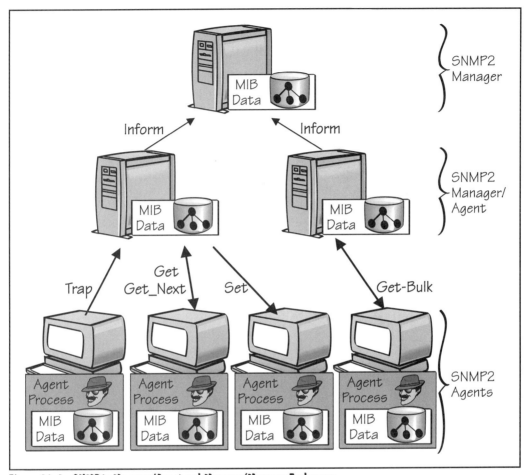

Figure 41-4. SNMP2: Manager/Agent and Manager/Manager Exchanges.

Here's the list of the old and new operations SNMP2 supports (see Figure 41-4):

■ **GET** is identical to SNMP. The only difference is in the way responses are returned. SNMP2 removes the atomic constraint, meaning that it will return whatever values can be returned—partial results are allowed. In contrast, SNMP either returns all the required variables or it posts an error.

■ **GET-NEXT** is identical to SNMP except that the atomic requirement is relaxed.

■ **GET-BULK** is a new command issued by a managing station. It is similar to GET-NEXT. However, instead of just returning the next variable, the agent can return as many successor variables in the MIB tree as will fit in a message.

■ **SET** is identical to SNMP. It is a two-phased operation. The first phase checks that all the variables in the list can be updated; the second phase performs the update. Like SNMP, it's an all-or-nothing proposition.

■ **TRAP** performs a role similar to SNMP, but it uses a different packet format (the SNMP trap header only recognizes a TCP/IP address type; SNMP2 is more general). And, like SNMP, the trap is unacknowledged.

■ **INFORM** is a new command that's sent by an SNMP2 manager to another manager. It is used to exchange management information. The messages can be sent to all the manager nodes specified in the M2M MIB or to a particular manager. The M2M MIB allows a superior manager node to define the subordinate events it's interested in.

Like SNMP, SNMP2 is connectionless; it uses a datagram service. The specification includes mappings to UDP, IPX, AppleTalk, and the OSI connectionless service.

THE OSI MANAGEMENT FRAMEWORK

Many of SNMP's deficiencies are addressed by OSI network management. Some, however, see this as a case of the cure being worse than the disease, given the complexity and the size of OSI network management.

> — **William Stallings, Author,**
> **SNMP, SNMPv2, and CMIP**
> **(Addison Wesley, 1993)**

OSI distributed system management is defined by over 30 standards. Are you ready for a new dose of acronyms? In the OSI worldview, network management is divided into five application-level components called *System Management Functional Areas (SMFAs)*. These include fault management, accounting management, configuration management, performance management, and security management (see Figure 41-5). SMFAs rely on the services of 13 OSI-defined *System Management Functions (SMFs)*, which can be used by one or more SMFAs. The SMFs rely on the *Common Management Information Services Element (CMISE)*. CMISE is a combination of the protocols defined by the *Common Management Information Services (CMIS)* and the *Common Management Information Protocol (CMIP)*. CMIP, like SNMP, performs the actual exchanges between a managing station and an agent on the managed system. And like SNMP, it relies on a MIB to understand the capabilities of the managed agents and the data they store. OSI, of course, has its own CMI that defines information using ASN.1 notation; the basic unit of information is an object.

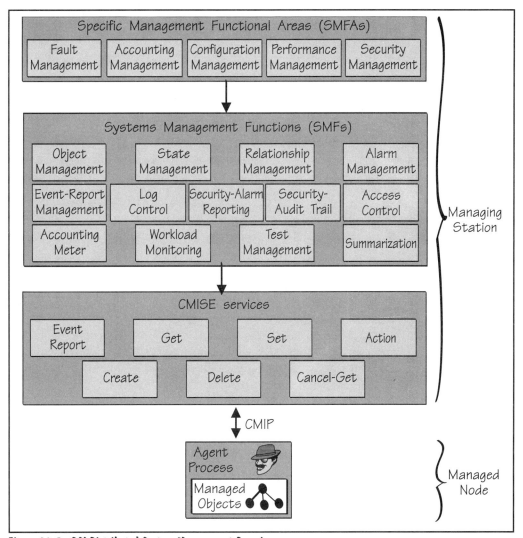

Figure 41-5. OSI Distributed System Management Overview.

What's an OSI Object—and What Can It Do?

While SNMP was intended to be simple, immediately useful, and quickly deployed, the groups developing OSI management took a different approach. The goal of OSI management is to provide a comprehensive solution to the broad problems of network (and, to some extent, systems) management. Because of its ambitious goals, OSI provides a comprehensive framework for defining *managed objects* borrowing heavily from object-oriented technology. The OSI notation used for

describing managed objects is much richer than that used by SNMP. CMIP relies on a series of *templates* for defining managed objects and their attributes. You can specify the following characteristics for each managed object:

- **Attributes** are variables that represent the data elements in a managed object. Each attribute represents a property of the resource the object represents.

- **Operations** are the actions that can be performed on the attributes of an object or on the object itself. The actions that can be performed on the object's attributes include *get, replace, set, add,* and *remove members*. The actions that can be performed on the object itself include *create, delete,* and *action*. OSI does not provide the semantics for defining the behavior of an object (i.e., method implementations or inheritance).

- **Notifications** are events that are emitted by a managed object. For example, when some internal occurrence that affects the state of the object is detected. ISO defines a number of notification types, including the format of the data carried in a CMIP *event-report* and an object ID that uniquely identifies the source. Notification types include various alarms and violations, attribute value changes, object creation and deletion, and object state changes.

- **Inheritance** is a managed object class that inherits all the characteristics of its parent class. ISO defines a number of object classes that can be used as parent classes for the purposes of inheritance, including an *alarm record, log, system, security alarm reports,* and an *event forwarding discriminator*.

The notation for defining objects is defined in *ISO 10165*, a document entitled **Guidelines for the Definition of Managed Objects (GDMO)**. The notation is commonly referred to as GDMO templates; it is substantially more powerful (and complex) than the simple language for defining SNMP objects. As we explained, ISO objects have a rudimentary level of object-oriented characteristics; in contrast, SNMP MIB objects are just glorified variables in a hierarchical tree. The GDMO is closer in intent to the CORBA IDL. However, CORBA provides much more advanced and complete object semantics.

Surprisingly, no widely agreed upon ISO MIB has yet been defined; we do not have the equivalent of the Internet MIB-II. The good news is that a number of groups are working on such MIBs—including ISO itself, the *National Institute of Standards and Technology (NIST)*, the *European Workshop on Open Systems (EWOS)*, and the *Network Management Forum* (a consortium of vendors interested in developing vendor-neutral network management solutions). It remains to be seen when these groups will have completed a set of object definitions that don't conflict.

OSI Management Protocols: CMIP, CMOT, and CMOL

CMIP is really an abbreviation for the (overly) Complex Management Information Protocol.

> — Marshall T. Rose, author,
> The Simple Book
> (Prentice Hall, 1991)

CMIP is the OSI protocol for manager-to-agent and manager-to-manager communications. In sharp contrast to SNMP, *CMIP* is a connection-oriented protocol that runs on top of a complete seven-layer OSI stack. *CMIP over TCP/IP (or CMOT)* provides a skinnier version of CMIP for TCP/IP networks. *CMIP over LLC (or CMOL)* is the skinniest CMIP yet; it was designed by IBM and 3Com to run directly on top of the IEEE 802.2 logical link layer. CMIP is much richer in functionality than its SNMP counterpart. The CMIP protocol provides the following services:

■ **Get** requests data from the agent's management information base. The request may be for a single managed object or a set of managed objects. For each managed object value, one or more of its attributes can be requested.

■ **Event-Report** is a notification sent by an agent to a managing system indicating that some event has occurred. The service can optionally request a confirmation. Five parameters are passed with the notification event to specify the class of object and instance where the event originated, the type of event, the time it was generated, and any user information about the event.

■ **Action** is a request that directs a managed object to perform some particular action. The action is implemented by a procedure that's specified as part of the managed object. The *action-information* parameter, if present, can be used to pass input parameters and other information.

■ **Create** is a request made by a managing system to create a new instance of a managed object class.

■ **M-Delete** is a request made by a managing system to delete an instance of a managed object class.

All the CMIP services may be optionally performed with confirmation. To specify the context for the management objects of interest, CMIP employs two constructs: *scoping* and *filtering*. Scoping marks a node within the information tree where the search tree starts; filtering is a boolean search expression applied to the attributes of the scoped objects.

TINY AGENTS: THE DESKTOP MANAGEMENT INTERFACE (DMI)

Intel's winning strategy is to get a management agent on every X86. We opened up that technology to the world and created the DMTF.

> — *Ed Ekstrom, Intel Corp.*

Not a single vendor adapter should be sold without a MIF...MIF everything in sight. MIFing now means users will be a lot less miffed later.

> — *Jamie Lewis, PC Week*
> *(February 14, 1994)*

At the other end of the spectrum, an industry consortium called the *Desktop Management Task Force (DMTF)* is creating a lightweight agent to manage all components on a PC—including hardware, OSs, applications, storage, and peripherals. The DMTF consortium includes DEC, HP, IBM, Intel, Microsoft, Novell, Sunconnect, and Synoptics. DMTF is developing a set of agent APIs called the *Desktop Management Interface (DMI)* that will allow different vendors' desktop management applications to share common memory space on a PC. About 70 other companies, including Apple Computers, are working with the DMTF on DMI specifications. In October 1993, DMTF released version 1.0 of the *DMI Service Layer* for DOS, Windows, and OS/2 at its first developer's conference. Over 35 vendors demonstrated beta implementations of the technology. Both IBM and Microsoft announced they would build the DMI into future releases of their OSs by the end of 1994. DMI, however, is a protocol-independent multiplatform interface.

The DMI agent will be able to communicate with any type of *management system*, including those based on SNMP and CMIP, without implementing SNMP or CMIP. IBM has already demonstrated CMIP/CMOL support for DMI. The idea is that SNMP or CMIP are simply impractical when it comes to managing a DOS or Windows PC. They require anywhere from 40 KBytes to a MByte—that may be unacceptable on DOS PCs. So DMTF is trying to create an agent that's skinnier and simpler than even SNMP. Using a concept called "slushware," the DMI agent can load and unload different pieces of code on demand, never taking up more than 6 KBytes. The DMI agent is packaged as a terminate-stay-resident (TSR) program for DOS and as a DLL for Windows and OS/2; it only consumes RAM when activated. The agent loads on demand the code needed to manage a device. After that the DMI software agent unobtrusively collects information while other applications are running.

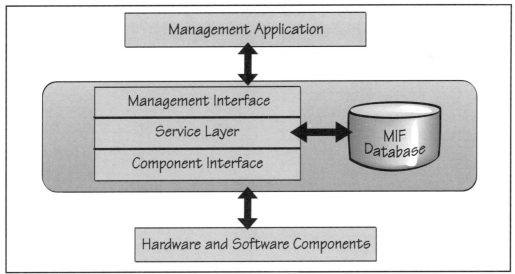

Figure 41-6. The DMTF Architecture.

The DMTF architecture (see Figure 41-6) consists of four components:

■ The ***Component Interface*** allows vendors of PC components such as memory boards, CD-ROMS, LAN adapters, and modems to register their devices and interfaces with DMI.

■ The ***Service Layer*** provides generic agent services. This device-independent layer interfaces to the local MIF database to deal with device-specific issues.

■ The ***Management Interface File (MIF)*** contains descriptions of the managed devices; it's similar in function to a MIB. The MIF is interpreted by the Service Layer, which uses the information to determine what actions to take on a managed device. The idea is that each of the 10,000 or so PC components will have a MIF provided by the component vendor. The vendor supplies the MIF and DMI handles the management.

■ The ***Management Interface*** provides a platform-independent API to the DMI services. The DMI agent can be externally accessed via SNMP, CMIP, or local applications; it provides the protocol to get to the MIFs.

DMI solves a real problem: It makes it practical to manage the 10,000 PC add-ins. One of the reasons management hasn't proliferated down to the PC components through SNMP is *cost*. To be SNMP-compliant, add-in vendors had to create a private MIB, work out the interfaces to SNMP agents, and negotiate with vendors of management platforms to have their MIBs interpreted. In addition, most PCs

running DOS and Windows don't have enough RAM to support multiple SNMP agents or their protocol stacks. To compensate, proprietary agents were sometimes placed in adapter cards—for example, Ethernet cards from 3Com or Cabletron. With DMI, component vendors only have to "MIF" their device; DMI does the rest. DMTF is also working with the Internet task force to add a *Host Resource* MIB group that manages objects on the PC.

X/OPEN MANAGEMENT STANDARDS

Wherever there are APIs, there's an X/Open standard lurking. So of course there are some X/Open standards for distributed system management calls. The idea is to provide a set of standard management APIs that isolate applications from the underlying management protocols (such as SNMP or CMIP). It's a very strange business we're in—we need standards to isolate us from other standards. X/Open defines two API sets: *XMP* and *XOM* (see Figure 41-7).

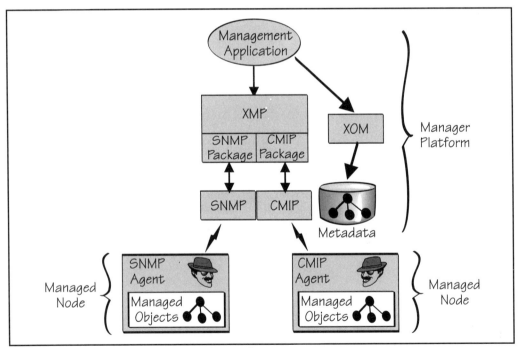

Figure 41-7. X/Open's XOM, XMP, and Metadata Database.

The X/Open XMP API

The *X/Open Management API (XMP)* is derived from an earlier interface called the *Consolidated Management API (CM-API)* from Bull and HP. The XMP API is used for standards-based, process-to-process communications between a managing system and a managed system. XMP defines a set of C API calls that allow access to both SNMP and CMIP. The interface semantics are more like CMIP than SNMP. Because of the differences in the representation of managed data, XMP does not make SNMP or CMIP totally transparent to the application. But as a compromise solution, XMP provides different XOM-based "packages" for use with the different protocols (XOM is explained in the next section). One package is defined for standard SNMP operations, and one is defined for standard CMIP operations.

The X/Open XOM API

XMP relies on another X/Open-defined API called *X/Open Object Manager (XOM)*. The XOM API is used to manipulate the data structures associated with managed objects. The XMP data structures are prepared using XOM API calls. The current version of XOM provides a way to deal with complex ASN.1-defined types in C. Both SNMP and CMIP use ASN.1. XOM is general enough to be used by protocols that are not even related to system management. For example, DCE uses XOM in its Global Directory Services.

To support the more complex CMIP object hierarchies, X/Open includes a *Package Development Kit (PDK)*. The primary component of the PDK is a *metadata compiler*, capable of reading GDMO definitions and producing a package (which is actually a set of C data types). These C structures can then be used with XMP and XOM. The metadata compiler populates a local database with information derived from GDMO definitions. The information about CMIP managed object classes includes their superior and subordinate object classes, the attributes of the class, and whether a given object class supports create and delete requests. The metadata database can be accessed using normal XMP calls. This process is similar in nature to the CORBA IDL compiler and Interface Repository. But the CORBA architecture is generally much more consistent; and it provides more advanced functions.

THE OSF DME STANDARD

In July 1990, the OSF issued a request for technology for a *Distributed Management Environment (DME)*, which was to provide a total solution for system and network management in heterogenous multivendor environments. Anyone, OSF member or not, could respond. 25 organizations submitted technologies. In September 1991, OSF announced the winners, which included HP's OpenView,

Tivoli's WizDOM, IBM's Data Engine, Groupe Bull's CMIP and SNMP drivers, and a few others. In May 1992, OSF published a very comprehensive architecture that combined a traditional network management framework with a postmodern CORBA-based object framework. As we go to press, it appears that OSF is scaling down its DME effort. Instead of using the Tivoli ORB, OSF now specifies management interfaces to any CORBA-compliant ORB. It also appears that OSF is putting most of its efforts in the management of DCE and interfacing DCE to ORBs (see following Soapbox). As a result, open platform vendors are acquiring parts of the DME technology directly from its originators and incorporating them into their products. For example, IBM licensed parts of OpenView from HP, which got incorporated into NetView/6000 and LAN NetView.

Regardless of what happens to DME (again see following Soapbox), its architecture remains of great interest. It provides a comprehensive framework for understanding distributed system management in its classical and postmodern approaches. The DME architecture uniquely reconciles these two approaches by using object wrappers and a CORBA-compliant IDL and ORB. This section provides a brief overview of DME's two design points:

■ The ***Network Management Option (NMO)*** takes a classical manager/agent approach to system management.

■ The ***Object Management Framework (OMF)*** provides a "postmodern" object-oriented solution based on CORBA.

In addition, DME includes a *Distributed Services* component that provides an infrastructure for services in a distributed environment. It also includes a user interface component.

The DME Network Management Option (NMO)

DME's *Network Management Option (NMO)* provides a traditional management platform for applications that wish to access SNMP and/or CMIP. DME augments the traditional X/Open components with an *Instrumentation Request Broker (IRB)*; see Figure 41-8. The IRB provides additional services on top of SNMP or CMIP. These services include the use of the DCE directory services to locate agents on the network, configurable retries, and a gateway service to the future DME CORBA-based management environment. Via the IRB, objects will be able to access SNMP and CMIP managed resources.

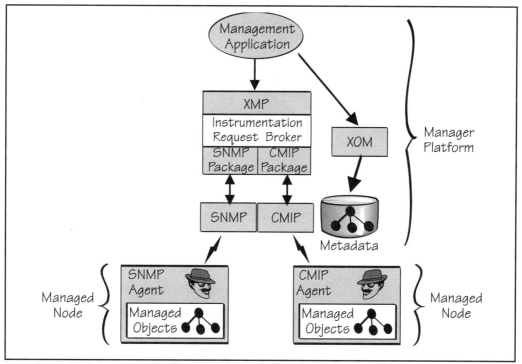

Figure 41-8. DME's Instrumentation Request Broker.

The DME Object Management Framework

DME's *Object Management Framework (OMF)* takes a radically new approach towards unifying network and system management; it builds on CORBA and the OMG services. The DME OMF is composed of multiple objects that cooperate and share information. The new framework goes beyond the traditional manager/object relationship. Instead, an object may at any time take either of two roles: a client requesting a service or a service provider. The DME *I4DL*—an upwardly compatible CORBA IDL with some extensions for event management and installation instructions—is used to describe the interfaces, attributes, and inheritance relationships of any management object. The communication between objects takes place over any standard CORBA ORB that uses DCE for its core communications (see Figure 41-9). DME calls this DCE-based ORB the *Management Request Broker (MRB)*.

How does the postmodern object-oriented DME incorporate devices that are managed using traditional protocols such as SNMP and CMIP? The answer is through special DME encapsulators called adapter objects (not to be confused with the CORBA object adapters used on servers). The I4DL is used to encapsulate legacy

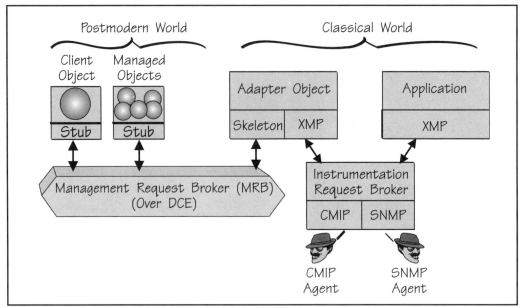

Figure 41-9. The DME Object Management Framework.

protocols and bring them to the object world. The adapter object looks like any other IDL-defined object. An application object can invoke operations on the adapter just like it does on any object using the typical remote invocations. Proxy methods invoked on the adapter call XMP to perform SNMP or CMIP functions. The adapter may define a set of operations that emulate the corresponding CMIP or SNMP calls, or it could augment them in some useful ways. For example, a CMIP adapter object might aggregate several CMIP operations on some managed object into one, providing a higher level of abstraction to the legacy object.

In summary, DME's OMF uses objects to encapsulate the implementation of any management resource. A managed object can only be accessed through an IDL-defined set of interfaces. The combined network and system management is modeled as the communication and interaction between objects that represent the resources of the system and objects that represent the user interface and managing applications. DME primarily deals with communication between management objects. Object adapters are used to encapsulate standard management protocols—such as SNMP, CMIP, and DCE. The DME Management Request Broker (with the help of the DCE directory services) provides a uniform naming space for all its objects (legacy or postmodern) and knows how to find them and invoke their services. DME may extend its security services to cover SNMP and other vulnerable spots in the system. So welcome to the postmodern world of system management with distributed objects.

Is DME Dead?

Soapbox

The ultimate goal of DME is unchanged: To provide a platform for integrated system and network management. Much of its work is aimed at providing better integration with DCE, but the scope of DME remains broader than simply managing DCE.

> — Michael Goulde
> Distributed Computing Monitor
> (January, 1994)

After the demise of UI, the trade press has been ripe with speculation about the long term viability of OSF (the other Unix consortium). The press started reading the tea leaves when the Tivoli-based ORB technology was dropped from the DME plans. Is DME really dead? To paraphrase Mark Twain, "the rumors of DME's death have been greatly exaggerated." It appears that DME is alive and well and has simply been redirected.

The "redirected DME" has adopted a secular approach to the management ORB—any CORBA-compliant ORB will do. The original *Management Request Broker (MRB)* was based on Tivoli, which was not CORBA-compliant. When OSF members decided to move to a CORBA-compliant management ORB, they made the decision that OSF should leave the ORB business to OMG. Any CORBA-compliant ORB now qualifies as an MRB. DME was restructured (late 1993) to define management services on top of the MRB. The OSF was also chartered to provide lower-level interfaces between any CORBA-compliant ORB and DCE. (For example, DCE needs to provide a dynamic invocation API to support CORBA and the DCE IDL needs to be made more compliant with CORBA's).

According to the new plan, OSF will release (in late 1994) management services that run on any CORBA 1.1 compliant ORB. These services will include discovery agents, maps, collections, and topology displays. OSF will also define a set of management APIs to those services. The OSF is submitting its APIs for the future enhanced DCE to the OMG as part of the CORBA 2.0 RFT. OSF would like DCE to become the future basis for interoperability between ORBs. In addition, OSF is working with OMG on the management services. In a separate move, Tivoli is submitting its management APIs to X/Open; OSF may also end up adopting these APIs. (Source: **Distributed Computer Monitor**, January, 1994). ❑

UI-ATLAS DISTRIBUTED MANAGEMENT FRAMEWORK

Unix International (UI) was the industry's other Unix consortium; its 270 members defined the requirements for the evolution of distributed software for Unix within an architecture framework called *Atlas*. In July 1991, UI published its *Atlas-Distributed Management (Atlas-DM)* requirements—distributed objects were the key unifying concept. USL elected to implement the first release of Atlas using existing Tivoli technology. The second release, which was due in 1994, was to be CORBA-based. The UI requirements, in the pre-Novell acquisition days, were implemented by USL (or whomever USL contracted out for the job). We're using the past tense because UI was dissolved on December 31, 1993. We still cover Atlas-DM in this section because it's an important architecture that may still end up being implemented in some variant of Unix.

Architecturally, UI went even further than OSF's DME in its support of objects—the first release of Atlas didn't even bother with SNMP and CMIP. Atlas-DM, like the postmodern DME, defines management applications as collections of objects that interact with each other and with objects that represent the managed resources. The UI *Management ORB (MORB)* provides transparent access to managed objects across the network (see Figure 41-10). The objects represent generic resources in the distributed environment—including hosts, users, LANs, DBMSs, applications, disks, files, and OSs. A single dynamic API call—the Tivoli *objcall*—is used to invoke methods on objects (all parameters are passed as ASCII character strings). Object references can be passed at run time. In addition, Tivoli allows the dynamic discovery of objects and the operations they support. The second release

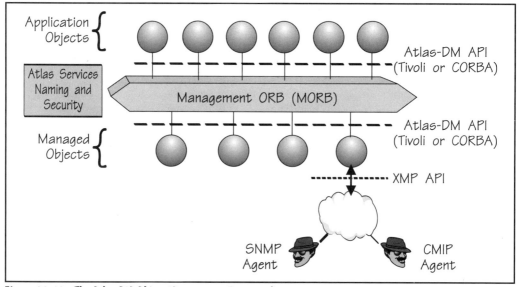

Figure 41-10. The Atlas-DM Object Management Framework.

of Atlas-DM would have used CORBA IDL stubs, dynamic method invocations, and a CORBA-compliant ORB. It was going to implement the X/Open XMP API for interfacing to SNMP and CMIP.

COMPARING CMIP, SNMP, SNMP2, AND CORBA

Table 41-1 compares the features of SNMP, SNMP2, CMIP, and CORBA. SNMP and SNMP2 place a minimum amount of event-emitting logic in the agents so as to keep the managed nodes simple; the smarts are in the managing station. As a result the traps are infrequently used and the managing station must poll the agents to find out what's happening. In contrast, CMIP and CORBA are event-driven, which means the agents are smarter; the managing station doesn't have to poll as much. As a result, a CMIP managing station can handle a much larger number of managed objects. In general, CMIP or CORBA are better suited for the management of large, complex, multivendor networks than SNMP. Of course, SNMP's simplicity allows it to be deployed on more devices, which, in turn, makes it easier to manage large networks. The designers of SNMP understood these trade-offs very well. They opted for the least common denominator approach and were willing to live with the consequences. SNMP2 makes the same architectural trade-offs as SNMP. It looks like the Internet designers still feel that their original assumptions are valid. But looking at the comparison table, we're not so sure SNMP is still the way to go (see the following Soapbox).

Table 41-1. Comparing SNMP, SNMP2, CMIP, and CORBA Objects.

Feature	SNMP	SNMP2	CMIP	CORBA Objects
Installed base	Huge	Small	Small	Small
Managed objects per managing station	Small	Small	Large	Large
Management model	Manager and agents	Manager and agents	Manager and agents	Communicating objects
View of managed objects	Simple variables organized in MIB trees	Simple variables organized in MIB trees	Objects with inheritance defined in MIBs	Objects with IDL defined interfaces, attributes, and multiple inheritance
Manager/agent interactions	Polling. Infrequent traps,	Polling. Infrequent traps	Event driven	Event driven
Explicit manager to agent command invocations	No	No	Yes	Yes

Table 41-1. Comparing SNMP, SNMP2, CMIP, and CORBA Objects. (Continued)

Feature	SNMP	SNMP2	CMIP	CORBA Objects
Security	No	Yes	Yes	Yes
Manager-to-manager exchanges	No	Yes	Yes	Yes
Bulk transfers	No	Yes	Yes	Yes
Create/delete managed objects	No	No (but can add table rows)	Yes	Yes
Communication model	Datagram	Datagram	Session-based	ORB
Standards Body	Internet	Internet	ISO	OMG
Approximate Memory requirements (in KBytes)	40-200	200-500	300-1000	300-2000

Soapbox

SNMP, CMIP, or Objects

A network-management system is limited by the capabilities of the network-management protocol and by the objects used to represent the environment to be managed.

— William Stallings, Author,
SNMP, SNMPv2, and CMIP
(Addison Wesley, 1993)

We believe CORBA provides a modern and natural protocol for representing managed entities, defining their services, specifying instance data, and invoking methods via an ORB. The CORBA Interface and Implementation Repositories can be used to discover and dynamically invoke methods on these managed objects at run time. The managed objects can directly call the managing station when they have something significant to report (in contrast, SNMP relies mostly on polling). The CORBA Event Manager service is ideal for distributing asynchronous system management events. And the CORBA object services are providing a ton of useful functions that would have to be reinvented by SNMP or

CMIP (lifecycle, naming, transactions, persistence, etc.). Using CORBA, Distributed System Management becomes just another service on the ORB. Objects can manage themselves. Management applications provide views on collections of self-managing objects.

Unfortunately, many of today's managed devices don't have the memory or processing power to support a full ORB; these devices can only support the "simple" version of SNMP or, better yet, DMI. However, hardware is getting cheaper while the cost of administering systems isn't. In addition, "simple" SNMP is too limiting for the requirements of total systems management—it needs to be replaced. This means that in the next few years we'll be experiencing a large migration to more sophisticated agent software.

The three contenders for replacing SNMP are SNMP2, CMIP, and CORBA. All three require more memory and smarter processors than SNMP. So the question is: Which one do you choose? In our opinion it should be CORBA. SNMP2 and CMIP are both antiques and incredibly clumsy to program. MIBs are an anachronism in the age of IDL and object persistent stores. SNMP2 does not allow you to register operations on managed objects; CMIP does it in a very clumsy fashion. We feel the "simple" SNMP was a wonderful, basic protocol that solved many real problems in the age of scarcity and simple network management. But now that we're moving to total systems management, the sooner the world moves away from SNMP, SNMP2, and CMIP and replaces them with CORBA, the better off system management will be. ❏

Chapter 42

LAN NetView: The OS/2 DSM Platform

The large number of desktops and the growing support costs for PC LANs are making system management a key factor in the battle for the next-generation desktop and server software.

— **James Herman, Vice President,
Northeast Consulting Resources Inc.**

OS/2 is emerging as one of the industry's best-managed platforms. Because of its OOUI, rich middleware, and 32-bit OS on PCs, OS/2 can be an attractive and low-cost system management platform. With OS/2, you could potentially manage an entire enterprise from a laptop. But an operating system by itself is not sufficient to create a great managing platform. You also need the open *Distributed System Management (DSM)* software base and the middleware that comes with it. In November 1993, IBM shipped the **LAN NetView** product. It provides an open DSM platform that runs on OS/2. LAN NetView uses HP's OpenView and DME as its base, with many OS/2 specific enhancements. For example, it makes good use of the Workplace Shell's OOUI facilities to display views of dynamically discovered managed objects. It also replaces OpenView's closed interfaces with X/Open's XMP API set.

LAN NetView was designed to manage DOS, OS/2, Windows, and NetWare PC LANs. It even incorporates Novell's *NetWare Services Manager* as a managing application. The platform supports both SNMP and CMIP middleware; it can also send alerts to mainframe NetView via a gateway application called *LAN NetView Tie*. Over 15 vendors are preparing plug-and-play applications that run on the LAN NetView platform—including Microcom, ProTools, Shany, and IBM. This chapter covers the LAN NetView DSM platform and some of the key applications that run on it. Here are some examples:

■ *NetWare Services Manager* is a Novell-written application that lets you manage Novell clients and servers from within the LAN NetView environment.

■ *LAN NetView Monitor* is a performance monitoring tool from IBM; it can monitor key resources such as the disk, CPU, and RAM on any OS/2 workstation on the network.

■ *LAN NetView Fix* is a problem management tool from IBM; it incorporates Help Desk and Trouble Ticket facilities. You can use this tool to automate recovery procedures by associating events with error management actions. The events are generated by the LAN NetView DSM elements.

■ *LAN NetView Tie* is a gateway service to IBM's mainframe NetView; it converts OSI and SNMP alerts to the NMVT format and sends them to NetView.

■ *LAN NetView Scan* is a configuration management tool from IBM; it collects and monitors configuration data on PCs. It is visually integrated with the LAN NetView topology and discovery services.

■ *NetView Distribution Manager/2* is a software installation and distribution tool from IBM. It complements software distribution tools such as NTS/2 and LAD/2.

■ *LANlord* is an inventory management and metering tool from Microcom Inc. It was designed to fully integrate with LAN NetView.

■ *AlertVIEW* is a management product from Shany; it provides asset management, virus detection, and configuration management. The product is designed to be integrated with LAN NetView.

■ *Network Analysis Series* is a complete management subsystem from ProTools. The product provides an SNMP RMON MIB for performing real-time monitoring and performance analysis. It will integrate with LAN NetView at the user interface level; it will also share data obtained from the topology and discovery services.

- *LAN NetView Management Utilities (LMU)* is a low-cost extension to LAN NetView from IBM. The product acts as a proxy agent to LAN NetView; it can manage OS/2, DOS, Windows, and Macintosh workstations.

- *NetFinity* is a hardware management environment from IBM; it reports detailed information on a wide variety of hardware adapters. The product can be launched from LAN NetView.

- *Adstar Distributed Storage Manager/2 (ADSM/2)* is a disaster backup, archive, and recovery tool from IBM. It backs up data from clients running on OS/2, NetWare, Windows, DOS, Macintosh, and Unix to a backup server running on OS/2. The product can be launched from LAN NetView.

The list of DSM products on OS/2 can continue for many more pages (but our book can't). The products we chose are representative of what you should expect from a modern DSM platform. Let's find out what they can do to help us with our system management problems.

THE LAN NETVIEW DSM PLATFORM

Figure 42-1 shows the components of the LAN NetView DSM platform. Like any modern DSM platform, LAN NetView provides a framework for running system management applications. The LAN NetView framework includes manager and agent components. The manager is provided by the **LAN NetView Manage** product (see top of Figure 42-1). The agent components are provided by three products: **LAN NetView Enabler**, which includes OS/2 and LAN Requester agents; **LAN NetView Agents for DOS**, which includes agents for DOS and Windows; and **LAN NetView Agents Extended**, which includes agents for LAN Server, DB2/2, and Communications Manager/2.

In this section, we cover LAN NetView Manage and its agents. From a management application's viewpoint, the LAN NetView framework provides services for discovering agents, APIs for communicating with them, event management, and services for storing and viewing management information. It also provides APIs for communicating with SNMP, CMOT, and CMOL agents. A management application can use whatever services it needs. However, the more services it uses, the better it integrates with LAN NetView. A loosely integrated application may simply use LAN NetView to launch it from a common user interface. The fully integrated applications use the topology, user interface, event, metadata, and agent services.

Management applications that plug into the LAN NetView DSM platform are sold separately; you buy what you need to manage your client/server systems. For example, you'll need the *NetWare Services Manager* to talk to NetWare agents,

LAN NetView Tie to talk to mainframes, and so on. We cover management applications in more detail later in this chapter.

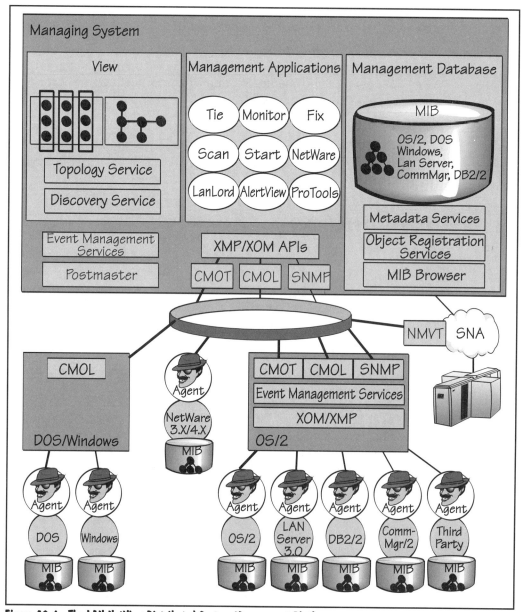

Figure 42-1. The LAN NetView Distributed System Management Platform.

LAN NetView Manage

LAN NetView Manage provides the core DSM functions required by a managing system—including a communications infrastructure, event management, metadata and topology/discovery services. The product supports the X/Open XMP API industry standard. Management applications can use this API to communicate with agents using SNMP or CMOT/CMOL. The View component provides a graphical interface to the LAN NetView platform. The Manage product includes an OS/2 agent and a LAN Requester agent. These agents make it possible for the managing station to manage its local components. LAN NetView Manage also bundles two managing applications: a MIB browser called the *Request Manager* and a remote command invocation program called the *Remote Command Line Interface*. We go over some of these functions in more detail.

The View Service

View provides an OOUI-like interface for managing client/server systems (see Figure 42-2). The interface lets you navigate through a hierarchy of containers or a topological map of the system. When you find a managed object of interest, you can open it to display its "views" in progressive layers of detail. You can then invoke an action on this object from a pop-up menu—an action will typically launch a management application. Alarm situations are indicated with a visual cue such as a change in the object's icon.

You can choose the icon to represent a resource. View presents a list of tools that can operate on that type of resource. The tool list includes any application that can be invoked from the command line. View will transparently invoke the tool and pass it the relevant parameters, including the object name of the icon selected by the user. All applications that can be invoked from a command line may be integrated at this OOUI level, whether they use any additional Manage facilities or not. The following hierarchy of views can be used to represent the distributed environment:

- The *topology view* displays the current topology of managed systems on the network; it lets you navigate through the various levels of detail concerning the underlying objects. The topology view includes the collection of managed objects obtained from the distributed agents using SNMP, CMIP, and IPX (via Novell NetWare Services).

- The *management collection view* displays a logical grouping of related systems—such as departments, locations, building floors, or systems to be managed as a group. View lets you define background maps and provides the facilities for automatically positioning systems on the map. The map is an "intelligent bitmap" that is divided into named regions; objects are automatically placed on the map based on the value of their location attribute.

- The ***system view*** displays the resources associated with a particular machine on the network; it provides the next level down the hierarchy of views. It shows you what's inside a particular system.

- The ***resources view*** displays the objects contained within the systems. Groups of resources are selected and displayed graphically. You can select an individual resource to view its subresources or to invoke a function that is supported by that resource. The invoked function is provided by the agent for the resource or by a systems management application that utilizes information about the resource.

View helps you find and act upon managed resources (for example, file servers) within complex configurations. Resources are presented as graphical collections. You can apply *filters* to any management collection; filters are "snap in" modules that can be applied to any LAN NetView collection. Resource objects are presented from the viewpoint of the task being performed, instead of from the viewpoint of a specific application. So you are able to perform functions on these objects based on the task to be accomplished (for example, get performance statistics on a server) without having to directly access the underlying application.

View lets you open multiple views on a set of related objects. When changes are made to one view (window), the changes are reflected automatically in all other relevant views. The graphical presentation of multiple views helps you recognize and effectively solve problems. View's pervasive support for direct object manipulation using drag and drop makes the interface very intuitive to use.

View provides a programming library of System Object Model (SOM) based objects that can be used by third-party applications to provide a consistent look and feel to their management applications; it also gives them access to all the View services. A management application can register to manage a collection of systems, an individual system, or managed objects (resources). The application must provide the menu items and methods for the objects it manages. View Managers are "snap in" modules that are used to determine hierarchical relationships and links between systems.

The Topology and Discovery Services

Topology information helps you understand what devices are on the network and how they're related. The Manage *Topology and Discovery Service* discovers the physical and logical systems on the network and collects data about them; it also

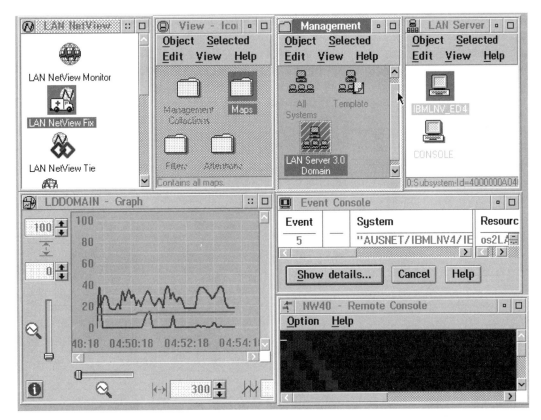

Figure 42-2. View: An Object-Oriented User Interface (OOUI) for DSM.

monitors any changes in the client/server system. The service consists of three components:

- The **discovery processes** work independently to discover and identify systems on the network. They can discover networked machines using SNMP, CMOT, CMOL, and IPX protocols. You can also write your own discovery processes for finding systems that are not using these protocols. The discovery process will attempt to gather as much information as possible about the systems it discovers; the information that can be gathered is determined by the agents installed on the discovered systems.

- The **discovery database** stores information about the discovered devices. An application can query the discovery database through the topology agent to obtain information about the devices. If it needs more information, an application can establish direct contact with the agent on any remote device.

■ The ***topology agent*** manages the discovery database. It collects information from the discovery processes and stores it in the discovery database. The topology agent also consolidates information collected by different discovery processes. For example, a single OS/2 system could be using both the CMOL (HLM driver) and TCP/IP stacks; two discovery processes may have reported finding the same physical system—a double entry. The agent can fix that problem.

Management applications can access information in the discovery database via the discovery agent. View, for example, constantly queries the discovery database so that it can display the most current topology of the managed network.

The Event Management Services

In DSM environments, agents are constantly notifying managing systems of key events that are happening on their managed nodes. The event management service must be able to efficiently route agent events to the appropriate management applications without involving the agents directly. It must also provide a way to filter event information so as not to swamp a network with notification traffic. Notifications should only be sent to applications that are prepared to handle them. The event service should be able to separate noise from real information.

The LAN NetView *Event Management Service (EMS)* addresses these requirements by running an EMS component that can optionally reside on managing and managed stations. The EMS components provide two functions:

■ The ***event sieves*** filter and examine each event generated by an agent and then route it to the appropriate management station (or application). Event sieve agents can reside on both managing and managed systems. On a managed system, the event sieve processes all events generated by any agent that is running on the managed system. Events that pass through the sieve's filter are then forwarded on to the managing systems that have registered an interest in such events. On the managing system, an event sieve filters all the incoming events and routes them to the managing applications that have registered for the particular event type.

■ The ***event log agent*** records all events received at a particular system. Logging allows management applications to asynchronously retrieve their event notifications. For example, an application could retrieve events that occurred before it was started.

The Event Management Service supports two types of event sieves: *static* and *dynamic*. Here's the difference:

■ **Static sieves** require no programming. They can only exist on managed systems, and they don't do any filtering. Events that go through a static sieve are forwarded to a specific set of managing systems, as specified by an administrator.

■ **Dynamic sieves** are created using XMP programs; they can contain very specific filters that are used to limit network traffic and extract relevant information. Dynamic sieves can be created on managed systems as well as managing systems; they can route event notifications to specific applications (static sieves don't do that). Typically, a management application will place dynamic sieves on both the managing system and on managed systems. By doing this, the managing application can ensure that all events of interest will be sent to it.

To limit network traffic, a *filter* can be specified as part of an event sieve. Events can be filtered by object class, object instance, event time, event type, and SNMP trap. In addition, events can be filtered by frequency; that is, a filter could specify that a single event be forwarded only if a certain number of those events are generated during a specified time interval. You can create more complex filters by combining events using AND, OR, and NOT operators.

The Communications Infrastructure

The LAN NetView communications infrastructure allows managing stations to exchange information with their agents and with other managing systems. The communications infrastructure is provided by the X/Open Management API's (XMP/XOM) and two underlying components: *Postmaster* and the *Object Registration Service*. These two components provide routing and naming functions that are equivalent to those defined by the DME Instrumentation Broker. Here's a description of what the different components provide:

■ The **Postmaster** is primarily a message switch; it directs management information between managers and agents. The routing information is obtained from user-specified addresses or from routing tables configured through the Object Registration Services. The Postmaster knows which management protocol to use and hides many of the differences between CMOT/CMOL and SNMP requests. Note: While the Postmaster completely hides CMOT/CMOL differences, certain functional differences between CMOT/CMOL and SNMP will still surface to the programmer.

■ The ***Object Registration Service*** provides a directory that maps managed object instances to specific physical addresses in the network. The service creates and maintains a global directory of agents. It includes the location of each agent, the objects it manages, and the management protocol that it uses. The registration database resides on both managing and managed systems. On a managing system, it is used to locate objects. On a managed system, it is used to determine which agent controls the object being addressed so that the request can be passed to the appropriate agent.

■ The ***X/Open Management API's (XMP/XOM)*** are used to issue requests on specific object instances. The Postmaster daemon handles these requests with the help of the Object Registration Database. The Postmaster will make sure that associations between managing and managed systems are created for CMOT/CMOL. In the SNMP environment where there are no associations, the Postmaster uses timeouts and retries to provide a better quality of service than raw datagrams.

In addition, the XMP API provides program access to most management services in the Manage product (for example, Topology, Metadata Service, and Event Management Service). The XMP APIs may be accessed using C or C++.

Metadata Service

The *metadata service* allows developers to create and delete managed-object class definitions in the Management Information Base (MIB). The MIB is the metadata database; it contains a collection of managed-object definitions that explain what agents can do. Both SNMP and CMIP use the metadata database. Management programs use the XMP API to retrieve managed-object class definitions from the metadata database. The metadata provides an abstract view of all the object classes in the network that can be managed; it allows new object types to be defined and registered with the MIB. The service also allows management applications to query the MIB so that they can dynamically build and invoke requests on managed objects. The metadata service consists of three components:

■ The ***metadata manager*** provides a MIB compiler (METACOMP.EXE) that takes ASCII files containing GDMO definitions of managed object classes and stores the object definitions in the metadata database.

■ The ***metadata agent*** controls access to the metadata database; it performs the requested actions against the metadata database.

■ The ***metadata database*** is the LAN NetView's MIB; it is accessed through the metadata agent.

The metadata service allows you to write dynamic management applications (such as browsers) that learn about the objects they manage at run time. You can add new types of managed objects to the metadata database without recompiling the applications.

Request Manager: A MIB Browser

The *Request Manager*—bundled with Manage—lets you browse, and in some cases set, attributes associated with MIB objects on managed systems. It is fully integrated with the View component of Manage (see Figure 42-3). The tool allows you to query any value accessed by a *get request* from CMIP or SNMP, set values controlled by the *set request*, and register for any notifications emitted by the agent. The tool is general; it can be useful in situations where the agent provides needed function that is not available in the management applications.

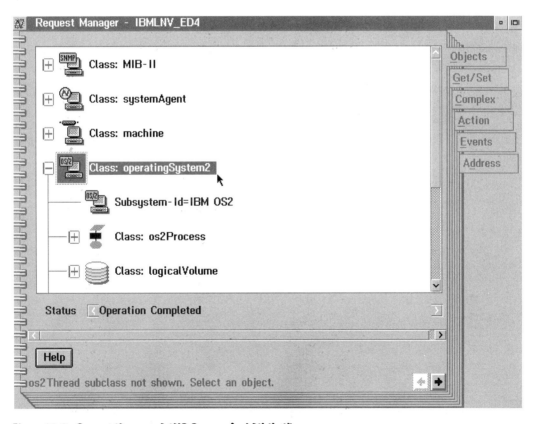

Figure 42-3. Request Manager: A MIB Browser for LAN NetView.

The Request Manager supports the following SNMP MIBs out of the box: MIB-I, MIB-II, RMON, and the IBM 6611 router. These are provided as sample MIBs. (Note: No SNMP agents are shipped with these MIBs; vendors must provide agents for their products). The LAN NetView Manage product also includes examples that demonstrate how to convert other SNMP MIBs into a format usable by Manage. It displays object hierarchies based on SNMP or CMIP MIB definitions. Finally, the Request Manager allows you to create event sieves on managed systems.

LAN NetView Enabler for OS/2

The **LAN NetView Enabler** product provides a *managed* system platform for OS/2. The product is packaged with two agents: one for the OS/2 operating system, and one for the LAN Requester. These two agents make it possible to manage networked machines that run OS/2 and the LAN Requester. The product also provides the XMP/XOM programming interfaces that let you develop your own agents on the OS/2 platform. The agents you develop may use either the CMIP or SNMP protocols. Finally, the product provides a filtering capability for agent-generated events.

The *OS/2 agent* acts as a resource manager on behalf of the management applications; the resource it manages is OS/2 itself. The OS/2 managed data is described using GDMO object definitions. Management applications can use the metadata database to read the OS/2 object definitions, the actions that are supported by the OS/2 agent, and the notifications it emits. The management data collected on OS/2 includes:

■ Operating system process, thread, and spooler information.

■ Performance data on the CPU, memory, files, FAT, HPFS, etc. Examples of the data gathered for the CPU include busy time, number of threads in the ready queue, number of interrupts, and so on.

■ Physical machine information such as the model ID, serial number, type, owner, and so on.

■ Adapters such as Token Ring, SCSI, and so on.

■ Peripherals such as floppy drives, hard disks, processor, coprocessor, printers, keyboard, serial/parallel ports, pointing device, and logical volumes.

The agent for the OS/2 *LAN Requester* allows managing applications to control and monitor the state of the requester, get and set both initial and run-time configuration attributes, gather statistics about the requester's operation, and gather requester vital product data.

LAN NetView Agents for DOS and Windows

This product provides agents for IBM DOS 5.0/6.1, Microsoft DOS 5.0/6.0, and Microsoft Windows 3.X. The agents manage operating system resources on behalf of management applications running on the LAN NetView Manage product. DOS, Windows, and OS/2 agents share many common object definitions. This allows management applications to be written once to access all three.

LAN NetView Agents Extended

The **LAN NetView Agents Extended** product includes agents for LAN Server 3.0, DB2/2, and Communications Manager/2. Managing applications use these agents to manage resources in the LAN Server, Communications Manager, or DB2/2. The object definitions for these agents are documented in Object Catalogs, which allow vendors and customers to write applications that can access the data in the agents.

The agents generally support the starting and stopping of the resource manager, the modification of configuration parameters, gathering of statistics, and changing the operational state. They also emit notifications when certain errors, potential errors, or other significant events occur, such as performance thresholds exceeded. All the agents support topology applications; they return information about the resources they control on demand. The following is a brief summary of the functions each specific agent provides:

- The *OS/2 LAN Server agent* allows managing applications to start, stop, configure, and monitor most LAN Server and LAN Requester services. It also lets them gather statistics and monitor the state of the different services. The agent emits notifications when errors occur—for example, an authentication failure, disk near capacity, UPS power low, and audit log almost full.

- The *DB2/2 agent* allows managing applications to backup, restore, and roll forward a database. It also lets them catalog a database entry in the directory. Managing applications can use the agent to collect database status—such as the time of the last backup, the location of the database, and the number of users connected. They can also retrieve and update DB2/2 configuration parameters. The agent emits DB2/2 error notifications.

- The *Communications Manager/2 agent* allows managing applications to query the communications adapter addresses. It also lets them control and monitor APPN nodes, APPC transactions, and LU 6.2 sessions and conversations. The agent monitors faults and emits error notifications for the APPN, LAN, and SDLC components that it manages.

LAN NetView Agent Summary

To summarize (and recapitulate), an SNMP or CMIP agent is an "object manager" that represents management information and functions on a set of managed objects. The agent represents the objects to the managing applications. The managing applications represent the objects to end users; they interact with agents to get their information. Agents run as background processes (daemons) on the managed stations. The agent generates notifications, invokes operations on the objects it manages, and returns attribute information.

Agents and their objects are typically provided by vendors of hardware devices, system software, and applications. The managed objects on these agents must be registered to a managed station via the MIB (and metadata compiler). The LAN NetView agents provide object definitions for OS/2, DOS, Windows, DB2/2, LAN Server, and Communications Manager/2. It allows these systems to be managed via CMOT and CMOL agents. To a managing platform, these are just more MIBs for managed objects—they just happen to be MIBs for OSs and software subsystems. Table 42-1 gives you an idea for how extensive these MIBs are.

Table 42-1. NetView-Provided Agents Summary.

Agent	Number of Managed Objects	Number of Object Attributes	Number of Object Actions	Number of Object Notifications
DOS	13	192	2	4
Windows	3	59	1	2
OS/2	20	524	12	40
LAN Server and LAN Requester	4	275	19	40
DB2/2	6	131	10	16
Communications Manager/2	14	289	15	252

LAN NetView Packaging

The **LAN NetView Manage** product sells for $1,839. It requires three MBytes of memory over and above OS/2 and other software. As a minimum configuration, IBM recommends a workstation with an 80486SX or equivalent processor and 16 MBytes of memory (this includes one managing application and the TCP/IP protocol stack). The managing server requires as prerequisites OS/2 and NTS/2 (or equivalent).

The **LAN NetView Enabler** product sells for $89 (it includes the OS/2 and LAN Requester agents). The Enabler product is a prerequisite for all OS/2 2.X-specific agents; it must be present on the same machine. The **LAN NetView Agent for DOS and Windows** sells for $75. The **LAN NetView Agents Extended** sell for $75. The agents require one MByte of additional memory on the managed workstation. DOS and Windows managed agents require some form of memory extender.

LAN NetView Directions

The LAN NetView code base will increasingly converge with that of its sibling NetView/6000. The statement of directions from IBM mention future support for the DME Object Architecture, DMI, SNMP2, and the "leveraging of object technology present in new operating systems." Facilities will also be provided to create a single image of the management data in federated management systems. IBM is also working on attracting more third-party support for the platform.

SYSTEM MANAGEMENT APPLICATIONS

The real value of any network management system is derived from its management applications.

— *Gartner Group (March, 1993)*

LAN NetView provides an umbrella platform for system management on OS/2. It creates a single system image for running system management applications. Some of the applications we cover in this section are extensive management subsystems in their own right; others are simply utilities that depend on LAN NetView for an infrastructure. Ideally, View and its topology service should provide the top view for all management applications. View's object-oriented user interface lets you focus on managed objects and not on management applications—they should run transparently and seamlessly. An application that's launched from View receives as a parameter the name of the object that was selected when the launch occurred.

Many of the applications we cover were designed specifically to work on top of LAN NetView; these applications make full use of the event, XMP API, View, agent, and topology services. Why reinvent the management wheel?

NetWare Services Manager

The **NetWare Services Manager** is a Novell-written OS/2 application (marketed by IBM and Novell) that lets you manage NetWare clients and servers from within the LAN NetView environment. This application, which can be launched from the View user interface, provides the following functions:

■ *Server and workstation schematics* display views of the services, software, and hardware resident on the server and its configuration. For example, double clicking on a NetWare server icon opens a window that displays graphical views of the available RAM, disk utilization, and the types of network interface cards that are installed on the server.

■ *User-defined alert thresholds* let you define thresholds for a variety of parameters relating to server performance and configuration, such as number of open files on the server and client/server transactions. When these thresholds are exceeded, alarms are automatically generated and appear on the map.

■ *Printer and printer queue configuration and status* automatically locates NetWare printers and their print queues and displays associated information, such as active jobs in the print queue.

■ *NLM monitor* automatically displays a list of NLMs actively running on the server. It provides the following information on NLMs: memory utilization, names, version numbers, and copyright information.

■ *Automatic server fault and alert notifications* let you monitor the health of an entire NetWare environment at a glance. Network managers can quickly isolate network problems, whatever the source, and respond to the problem.

NetWare Services Manager also includes a NetWare agent. The agent supports a CMIP-like protocol over IPX/SPX. It is packaged as an NLM; it can be used to manage NetWare 3.11 and NetWare 4.0 servers.

LAN NetView Monitor

LAN NetView Monitor is a performance monitoring tool from IBM; it can monitor key resources such as disk, CPU, and RAM utilizations on any OS/2 workstation on the network. It also monitors LAN Server and Requester resources. The application is fully integrated with LAN NetView Manage. It uses the XMP APIs and the View interface to automate performance management. You can specify what information is to be collected, collection schedules, and threshold and data transfer times. NetView Monitor uses DB2/2 as its embedded SQL database engine. It provides a SQL interface that lets you query the performance data it captures.

LAN NetView Monitor provides threshold-based alarm notifications that can be associated with actions such as the display of a message, logging the alarm in the database, or running a corrective action program. Logging the alarm in the database makes it possible to generate an alarm report (or trouble ticket) at a later time. You can specify the threshold value and severity for any of the resources you're monitoring. Threshold-based notifications help you "manage by exception"— meaning that you can ignore the managed systems until an event of interest occurs.

LAN NetView Monitor provides facilities that let you graphically display performance data in real time; it also lets you playback past performance information from the database. You can access the graphing facility from a LAN NetView Monitor folder. Up to 15 resources can be displayed on a single graph. You can specify the width, type, and color of each individual resource line on the graph.

The SQL database provides daily, weekly, and monthly summaries on the data that's collected. "Old data" can be automatically deleted from the database according to retention periods you define. The product comes with the following predefined reports:

■ **Resource reports** provide information on OS/2, LAN Server, and LAN Requester resources.

■ **Application reports** provide application, file, and thread-level information.

■ **Policy reports** list the attributes of all the user-defined policies.

■ **Alarm reports** list all the threshold alarms that are stored in the database.

Of course, you can create your own customized reports using SQL to access the database. The SQL interface makes it easy to generate resource utilization, trend-analysis, and workload reports on the captured data. You can also export the data from the database in ASCII Delimited and Lotus worksheet formats and use the graphing facilities of tools that support these formats.

LAN NetView Fix

LAN NetView Fix is a problem management tool from IBM; it incorporates help desk and trouble ticket facilities. You can use this tool to automate recovery procedures by associating events with error management actions. The product receives and processes notifications that are emitted by CMIP and SNMP agents. It also stores these notifications in an embedded DB2/2 SQL database. The tool is totally integrated with View; it lets you display events associated with an object in an event folder.

Here's the features provided by LAN NetView Fix for handling error notifications:

■ Retransmits events so they can be received by other managing applications on the same workstation or on remote workstations.

■ Calls a pager, displays a message pop up, or invokes user-specified programs when a specified event is received.

■ Provides an *Event Log Browser* that lets you selectively retrieve and display events from the event log.

You can control the events to be received and the actions to be taken by creating entries in an action table. You can specify in that table the recovery actions for the received event in terms of the resource class, event type, time range, and the system from which the notification was emitted. You can also specify a priority for an event type. Upon receipt of a notification, LAN NetView Fix compares the incoming event with the criteria specified in the action table. If the received event matches an entry in the action table, LAN NetView Fix automatically invokes the action or actions associated with that entry.

LAN NetView Tie—The Mainframe Connection

LAN NetView Tie is a gateway service to IBM's mainframe NetView; it converts OSI and SNMP alerts to the *NMVT* format and sends them to mainframe NetView. Non-alarm notifications are wrapped in an *Event Major Vector*. Both types of notifications are sent to the host system via the Communications Manager/2 SNA/MS service. In addition, LAN NetView Tie receives commands sent via mainframe NetView's *Remote Operations (ROP)* services. This includes Register and Deregister commands that let the mainframe administrator selectively specify the notifications they want.

LAN NetView Scan

LAN NetView Scan is a configuration management tool that collects and monitors configuration data on PCs. It is visually integrated with the LAN NetView topology and discovery service. The product also provides inventory management control for LAN-attached PCs running OS/2, DOS and Windows. Here are some of the features this product provides:

- *Stores the inventory and configuration data in an embedded DB2/2 SQL database*. The data is readily available via database query tools or custom applications. It can be used for planning purposes and to keep track of "what's out there."

- *Monitors the status of PC files selected by an administrator*. This includes monitoring the files for changes and tracking versions of the file and information about them (size, date/time) in the SQL database. You can use this feature to manage critical PC configuration files such as CONFIG.SYS or AUTOEXEC.BAT. The monitoring of files on OS/2 machines can be scheduled to take place at designated times. But you cannot do the same for DOS and Windows; the best you can do is to schedule the monitoring via initialization procedures such as AUTOEXEC.BAT or a login profile.

- *Provides a command scheduler*. At regularly scheduled times, it will run programs or commands at selected OS/2 workstations to perform such tasks as software inventory, system backup, virus checking, system diagnostics, and report generation.

- *Provides event triggers*. For example, if you need to post-process data after it is collected, you can do so by having the tool call your programs—including custom DLLs, command files, REXX routines, or executables (EXEs).

The product was still in beta as we went to press. Its strongest feature is the integration of inventory collection and configuration management with LAN NetView and an SQL database.

LAN NetView Management Utilities (LMU)

LAN NetView Management Utilities (LMU) is a low-cost ($995 for a server, no run-time license for agents) extension to LAN NetView. The product acts as a proxy agent to LAN NetView; it can manage on its behalf OS/2, DOS, Windows, and Macintosh workstations. LMU provides its own topology view of the network (see Figure 42-4). It lets a designated workstation manage both servers and requesters on LAN Server and NetWare networks.

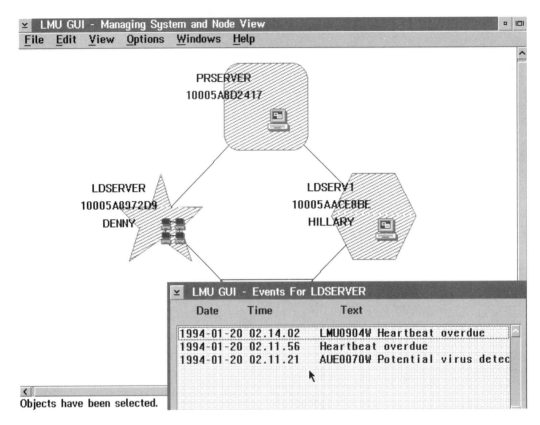

Figure 42-4. LMU: Low-Cost System Management.

LMU provides a graphical display of the LAN, a private manager/agent protocol, a set of bundled management applications (configuration, performance, and fault), and an LMU OS/2 database for data collection. You can also "snap in" your own applications. LMU performs the following management services:

■ Maintains proprietary (but very skinny and license-free) agents for collecting vital product information about OS/2, DOS, Microsoft Windows 3.1, and Macintosh workstations, as well as NetWare and LAN Servers. This data is either displayed on the managing station screen, placed in a central OS/2 database, or made available to LAN NetView.

■ Maintains a change log in the managing station, and optionally generates an alert when a managed station's configuration changes.

■ Remotely executes programs or procedures on managed OS/2, Windows, or NetWare server stations. OS/2 and Windows console text output can be optionally redirected to the administrator workstation or to IBM NetView. Some

LMU functions can be remotely executed on a Macintosh system. It can also schedule the execution of programs on OS/2, Windows, Macintosh, and NetWare server workstations on a scheduled basis.

■ Shuts down in an orderly manner all functions on a managed OS/2 system or NetWare server. It can also reboot the system.

■ Collects OS/2 and NetWare statistics and performance data; it sends the collected information to a central OS/2 database. LMU optionally generates generic alerts when user-specified thresholds are reached; it can forward alerts to LAN Network Manager or LAN NetView.

LMU acts as a proxy agent for SNMP managing workstations (such as LAN NetView or NetView/6000). From a function and cost standpoint, LMU is particularly suitable for low-end PC LAN environments.

NetView DM/2 and LAD/2

This section reviews two "top of the line" products from IBM for automating the distribution and installation of software from an OS/2 code server. **NetView Distribution Manager/2 (NetView DM/2)** uses a "push method" to automate the installation and distribution of software packages on OS/2, DOS, and Windows PCs; it pushes the packages to the clients from a central OS/2 code server. **LAN Automated Distribution/2 (LAD/2)** complements NetView DM/2; it provides visual facilities for generating *Configuration, Installation, and Distribution (CID)* response files for a variety of software products.

You may recall from Part 3 that CID is IBM's strategy for automating the installation and configuration of products on LANs. CID-enablement is not tied to a specific code distribution mechanism. In Part 3, we covered NTS/2, which is a low-cost pull-based code server. "Pull" means that the code distribution is initiated from the client workstation. Network administrators may prefer the convenience of a different approach called "push," which initiates the code distribution from the code server—this can save them a lot of walking.

So what makes NetView DM/2 a "top-of-the-line" code distribution package? It has advanced push capabilities and it allows software packages on OS/2, DOS, and NetWare clients to be managed and controlled from an OS/2 code server (versions of the product support RS/6000 and mainframe code servers). The code server manages change and version control without requiring local intervention from a user at the client workstation. NetView DM/2 tracks changes applied at each target workstation by recording history information in a central repository. The code server can also preserve user customizations and unique system configurations on the clients. It does that by invoking the install program of the system or program being installed and supplying individualized CID response files. NetView DM also provides the capability for removing software from a client workstation.

A NetView DM/2 GUI interface provides dialogs for installing or removing software and for initiating and canceling software distributions. The interface allows you to create distribution lists and software packages. You can then route the software package to a particular distribution list. The distribution of software can be scheduled for a particular time of day. The interface is also used to manage software level controls and track status (change control). The product tracks in its database distribution and change control requests and related results; you can monitor the database entries via the user interface.

We found LAD/2 to be complementary with NetView DM/2. LAD/2's forte is its GUI facility for creating CID *response files*. These ASCII files contain responses to any anticipated installation questions. Response files remove the need for all users to know what the installation and configuration parameters mean. The LAN administrator can tailor the response files for CID-enabled products and for individual workstations. LAD/2 provides response file generation menus (and configuration aids) for OS/2, NTS/2, LAN Server 3.0, DB2/2, TCP/IP for OS/2, NetView DM/2, DOS, Windows 3.1, NetWare Requester, and many other products. In OS/2 environments, the response files adhere to the CID architecture. LAD/2 provides a centralized configuration repository, which it can share with LAN NetView DM/2. The product also generates change files and install control procedures; it can directly read and update NetView DM/2 tables with the information it generates. The two products play together well.

Adstar Distributed Storage Manager/2 (ADSM/2)

Adstar Distributed Storage Manager/2 (ADSM/2) is a new disaster backup, archive, and recovery product from IBM. ADSM/2 backs up data from clients running on OS/2, NetWare, Windows, DOS, Macintosh, Sun Solaris, AIX, DEC Ultrix, HP-UX, and SCO Unix to a backup server running on OS/2 (other versions of the product provide backup servers on AIX and MVS). ADSM/2 maintains its own client/server network of agents. The agents can automate the backup process based on policies created by a workstation user or centralized policies established by an administrator. In both cases, you interact with the backup server using an intuitive user interface that lets you schedule backup times and monitor the storage hierarchy (see Figure 42-5). You can perform administration and backup tasks directly from the client workstation using its native GUI (or a command line facility). Ease of use and automation facilities are very important features for PC-based backup servers—if the interface is not intuitive to the PC end users (or administrators), they simply won't perform any backups.

ADSM/2 provides many advanced client/server features that allow you to create almost infinite backup stores on OS/2 servers. The product allows you to protect data from disasters, making it highly available in a multiuser LAN environment. Here are some of the key features:

■ *Automated scheduled backups.* End users or administrators can schedule (or archive) complete file systems, directories, and individual files for automatic backup. They do this scheduling by using the ADSM/2 GUI facilities or through a command line. You can request that files be restored using the same interface.

■ *Smart agents.* ADSM/2 agents are multifaceted. They can interface with the user on a client workstation via a GUI, they can monitor the client's file system, they can receive callback commands from the backup server, and they can compress data before sending it over the network. They provide this rich set of functions on *all* the popular PC, Macintosh, and Unix workstation operating systems.

■ *Hierarchical storage management.* The backup server stores the data on a hierarchy of storage devices—including disk drives, optical drives, and tape systems. The administrator sets the policies for the storage hierarchy. The backup server automatically migrates "older" data from disk to lower-cost bulk-storage devices, thus providing optimum cost/performance trade-offs. A *collocation feature* places all files associated with a client close to each other in the bulk storage device. Because user files are consolidated, tape mounts are reduced when restoring or retrieving large numbers of files from tape. This provides significant time savings.

■ *Data inventory management.* The backup server maintains a database of inventory information for all of the backup and archived data. The same database contains information about registered clients, policies assigned to those clients, and access control.

■ *Disaster recovery and high availability.* The backup server runs on ordinary OS/2 PCs; however, it provides a highly available data store by maintaining a recoverable log with optional mirroring. If you choose to mirror the database and log, the server will automatically manage all the replicas of the data and bring the system back to a consistent state in case of a catastrophic failure.

Is the ADSM/2 backup server overkill? According to Dataquest, the time spent administering storage on an end-user's workstation is 4.1 hours per month (just for backups). You decide if it's overkill—the good news is that mission-critical backup and archive servers have become affordable and friendly. You can now obtain these mainframe-like, robust management features on ordinary PCs running OS/2.

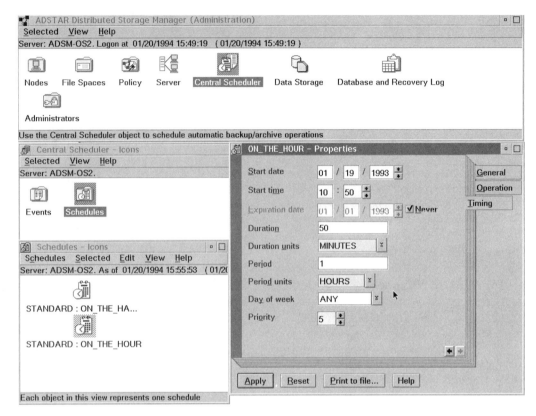

Figure 42-5. The ADSM/2 Administrator User Interface.

LANlord for LAN NetView

LANlord is an inventory management and metering tool from Microcom; it specifically addresses the unique requirements of managing personal computers in PC-based LANs. The product offers an integrated and complete solution for managing hardware, systems, applications, and user and network resources. Specifically, the following LANlord features are planned on the LAN NetView platform:

■ Hardware and software inventory.

■ Centralized and remote monitoring of hardware, software, and network resources. This includes statistics and data collection.

■ Real-time alerts and exceptions based on predefined thresholds and events.

■ Software metering.

■ Reports and data export.

LANlord applications will coexist with other LAN NetView offerings.

AlertVIEW

AlertVIEW is a management product from Shany. It provides asset management, virus detection, and configuration management. Shany plans to deliver a version of the AlertVIEW product for the LAN NetView framework. The LAN NetView version will act as a network "sniffer" for applications. It uses agents to look inside the software to detect and analyze errors or potential error conditions. The agents forward alerts along with hardware and software configuration data to the managing programs. Relevant data is then automatically reported with standard protocols to both LAN NetView and AlertVIEW's proprietary management console.

AlertVIEW provides a program to monitor the incoming messages. It can automatically launch an application on a remote workstation, which runs in the background to correct a problem. This allows corrective actions to be taken immediately, sometimes even before users are aware of the problem. Other capabilities provided by the AlertVIEW product include filtering of events, automatic discovery of new agents, virus detection, asset management, and an SNA-Gateway function.

Network Analysis Series

Network Analysis Series is a complete management subsystem from ProTools. The product provides an SNMP RMON MIB for performing real-time monitoring and performance analysis. It will integrate with LAN NetView at the user interface level and will also share data obtained from the topology and discovery services. ProTools provides two products in its Network Analysis Series:

■ The *Foundation Manager* is a central console for monitoring and analyzing data from up to 256 remote networks; it provides powerful network analysis capabilities for both Token Ring and Ethernet environments. The Foundation Manager product is a full-function network management system in its own right; it can monitor and control subnets throughout an enterprise.

■ *Cornerstone Agent* is an SNMP RMON (Remote Monitoring MIB) agent, which also acts as a real-time, stand-alone network monitor.

The two products work together to analyze an organization's internetwork traffic. They allow LAN NetView users to monitor and analyze local or remote networks from a single platform. Foundation Manager can be invoked from View; it also shares data from LAN NetView's topology and discovery services. By combining these three products, you can monitor and filter network activity, analyze protocol traces, setup alarms, display network traffic statistics, and pinpoint problems before they occur. All this activity is represented with intuitive and visual formats; you don't need to decode protocols such as TCP/IP and NetBIOS to discover what's happening.

NetFinity For OS/2

NetFinity For OS/2 is a hardware management environment from IBM. It reports detailed information on a wide variety of hardware adapters. NetFinity is a flexible, low-cost tool that manages Intel-based PCs; it complements LMU/2 and LAN NetView. Like everyone else, NetFinity has its own agents on the network and a managing application that provides a very visual interface (see Figure 42-6). Together, they detect and report detailed information on a wide variety of hardware including SCSI adapters, disk drives, CPU utilization, PCMCIA cards, memory cards, and system partitions. NetFinity discovers the hardware on the network; its agents generate alerts in response to user or administrator-specified thresholds.

Other OS/2 Management Products

This "not-too-brief" overview should convince you that OS/2 is a well-managed platform. However, there are many in this business who feel that you can never get enough system management: "If you can't totally control it, then it doesn't belong on the network." So we end this chapter by mentioning a *few* more OS/2 management products in case your needs haven't been met yet. If your needs have been met, then we'll see you in Part 9. Here's a list of more OS/2 management tools:

- *IMPACT* is an open architecture data center automation tool from Allen Systems Group; it supports change management, inventory control, critical problem reporting, and notification. A version of IMPACT for LAN NetView is being developed.

- *SUPPORTlink* from Allerion Inc. provides an integrated set of network management tools for LAN NetView.

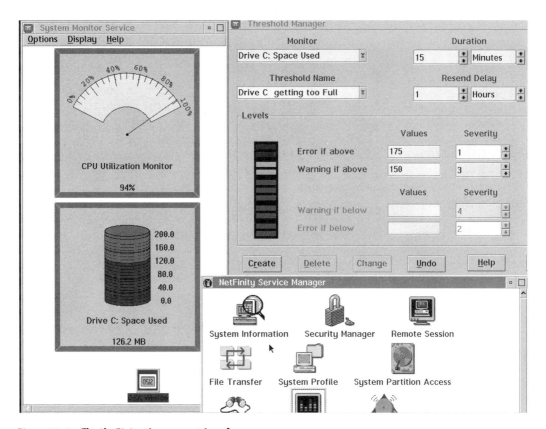

Figure 42-6. The NetFinity Management Interface.

- **BEST/1-Visualizer for OS/2** from BGS Systems Inc. provides a performance and capacity planning tool that processes data obtained from LAN NetView Enabler; it provides graphical bottleneck analysis and trend graphs.

- **CA-UNICENTER** from Computer Associates International provides an integrated OS/2 tool that covers five DSM areas: security, help desk, file backup and archive, workload scheduling, and console management. It lets you distribute OS/2 Workplace Shell administrative clients throughout the network based on job function and geographic requirements while maintaining central control of all management policies.

- **iFOR/LS** from Gradient Technologies is a distributed software license management tool; it can be administered from within the LAN NetView framework.

- **ManageView** from HiTecSoft Corp. provides simple commands that allow systems administrators to quickly create utilities to automate network management tasks on the LAN NetView platform.

■ *NetWorker* from Legato Systems is a backup and recovery product; the calendar-driven administrative front end will be integrated with View.

■ *Net-F/X* from Telesis Inc. provides a "panoramic" view of network performance under real and projected conditions. The system has the unique capability of proactively generating end-to-end traffic and correlating the round-trip response times with network statistics. It can be used to measure the effect of varying conditions on remote LAN service levels. From LAN NetView View, an operator can configure Net-F/X LAN agents to check response times and availability. The traffic generation facility is particularly beneficial in three major areas: performance analysis, capacity planning, and change verification.

■ *Tower* from Pragma Systems provides a network and systems management solutions based on both SNMP and CMIP; it manages PCs, servers, bridges, routers, and gateways in an enterprise. The Tower product family for OS/2 is integrated with the IBM LAN NetView platform and makes use of its topology database and display capabilities.

■ *LAN Network Manager* from IBM, together with the complementary IBM LAN Station Manager, manages Token Ring media and adapters on the LAN.

As you can see, the list goes on. Half the problem is to figure out how much management you really need and how much you're willing to pay for it. The DSM products are finally coming together in "snap in" packages; most will coexist nicely on the same DSM platform. But again, its like buying components for your stereo: How much is enough?

Part 9
Bringing It All Together

An Introduction to Part 9

Are you Martians still with us? All that talk of problem management and disaster recovery didn't faze you? We're reaching the end of our journey. We realize this tour was really long, but client/server is a broad topic. You probably want us to net it all out for you: Which technology do I pick? How do I get an application out in record time? What help can I expect? It turns out these are the one million dollar questions of client/server.

Which technology do I pick? This is like predicting the future. Anybody can predict it, but the trick is getting it right. We'll give you our two cents worth on where we think this technology is going. You Martians now know how to surf, so we'll throw in a wave theory of client/server. The idea is to look at technology cycles and figure out which wave to ride. If you read this book, you won't be too surprised by the answers.

How do I get an application out in record time? This takes us into the subject of tools. Here on earth, we've had tools since the dawn of our civilization to help us with our work. The job of toolmakers is to look at all the raw technologies and create the tools that ordinary mortals can use to get a job done. With tools we can develop client/server applications quickly. The better tools can help us deploy and manage our client/server applications. Toolmakers are constantly trying to keep up with the information presented in this book; they use it to decide the raw technology on which to build their tools. Picking a tool is not easy. It locks you into a client/server paradigm. And we know that there's more than one way to do client/server; in fact, there are hundreds of ways to do it. So we'll answer the question by throwing at you a few models on how to pick a tool. Then you'll have to decide which tool is best for your job.

What help can I expect? You'll need a good tool, a working methodology, and lots of good luck. You'll mostly be on your own—and that's when the real fun starts. This book provides a survival guide; it's just one more aid that will help you filter the signal from the noise in this overhyped field. Of course, you can always get the advice of consultants and attend seminars. But good advice doesn't come cheap. This final part gives you an overview of tools and methodologies. Are you Martians ready for your return trip home? Time does fly when you're having fun.

Chapter 43

Client/Server Tools and Application Development

Sitting quietly, doing nothing, Spring comes, and the grass grows by itself.

— A Zen poem

This is the chapter that's going to bring it all together. We'll bring out our infamous crystal ball and speculate on where client/server technology is heading. We may even jump on a soapbox and give you a fearless forecast of which technology wave looks most promising. The million dollar question is: Which magic tool can take the pain out of client/server application development and deployment? And a related question is: Does client/server require a new approach to application development? All these questions are very dear to your authors' hearts. For the last five years, we've been building client/server application development and visual programming tools. Our elusive goal has always been to create the perfect tool for developing, deploying, and maintaining client/server applications *quickly*. However, we learned the hard way that you have to make some serious compromises. There is no such thing as a "one size fits all" client/server tool. And there is no magic tool (including ours), so the next best thing we can do is leave you with a model for how to evaluate them. We'll even throw in our two cents on client/server development methodologies.

THE WAVES OF CLIENT/SERVER TECHNOLOGY

Figure 43-1 offers our fearless "wave forecast" of where client/server technology is heading. The first wave of client/server was brought about by NOSs. The NOSs make it easier for applications to share files, printers, and other networked devices; they perform their magic by extending the reach of the operating system. We should call the first wave of client/server the "NetWare wave." We're well into the second wave of client/server—the wave of database-centric applications. The predominant technology in the second wave is the "SQL database server." However, we're also experiencing two other major technology ripples around groupware and TP Monitors. The third wave of client/server is the distributed object wave. We devoted over 150 pages of the book to this technology, which we feel is almost ready for prime time. Objects encompass all the technologies of the first and second wave and add considerable new value. They have the unique potential of distributing intelligence among clients and servers to where it's needed most.

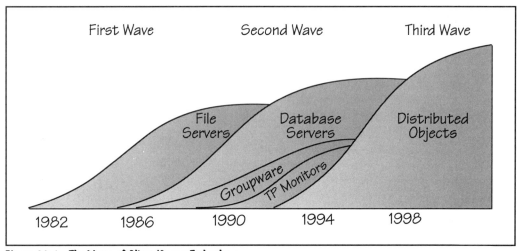

Figure 43-1. The Waves of Client/Server Technology.

Which Wave Should I Ride?

We shouldn't have to get on a soapbox to state the obvious: Distributed objects are the future of client/server technology. Objects encompass all aspects of distributed computing including OOUIs, compound documents, transactions, groupware, database, and system management. So the million dollar question is: Should you invest in interim technologies, or should you just catch the object wave? It's a trade-off between using proven technologies and the ones that are at the "bleeding edge." We constantly face this same dilemma as client/server tool providers: Should we build our tool around proven SQL databases and TP Monitors, or should we go to ORBs and ODBMSs? We're really at a painful technological juncture. Mixing paradigms typically gives you the worst of both worlds. However, in some cases, if you know what you're doing you can also get the best of both worlds. We recommend that you get your feet wet now. There's enough raw technology for you do that. Unfortunately, you can't depend on open distributed object development tools—they're nowhere in sight. (Yes, we know about Forte, but its ORB is proprietary).

The Client/Server Scalability Issue

In addition to technology waves, we must factor the issue of scalability into the choice of a client/server platform. It is much easier to deploy client/server in small enterprises and departments. Over 80% of the existing client/server installations are single server and have less than 50 clients. The small installations are typically easier to deploy and manage. Almost all of the existing client/server tools address that market. These tools can successfully be used to create client/server applications for decision support, e-mail, and groupware. They provide excellent facilities for building GUI front ends and are adept at working with shrink-wrapped middleware and server packages (mostly SQL DBMSs and Lotus Notes). However, even at the low end, we don't have adequate tools for creating mission critical solutions. By this we mean applications you can depend on to run your everyday business operations. These type of applications, especially at the low end, must support transactions, built-in system management, and high-availability. It is also sad to report that with over 200 hundred front-end tools on the market, not a single one can create a decent OOUI interface (they all do GUIs).

Intergalactic client/server is much more complex. It requires the sophisticated middleware described in this book—including DCE, MOM, distributed transactions, and ORBs. It requires proven tools that can take advantage of this middleware. Intergalactic client/server is by definition multiserver. So the tools should be able to deploy applications on multiple servers, manage transactions that are distributed across them, perform some form of load balancing, deploy the software to the clients and servers, and manage the multiserver environment. To be open, these tools are expected to do all this on multivendor operating systems, multivendor resource managers, and multiple GUI front ends.

In short, MIS is demanding the level of cohesiveness and scalability it was accustomed to on single vendor mainframe platforms, but now they want it for an open client/server world. Of course, we're nowhere close to meeting these expectations. As we explained in this long book, much of the technology and standards that are needed to make this happen are finally coming together; it will be another few years before the tools can catch up. Perhaps massive downsizing is a bit premature. It can be done, but using raw third-generation languages and some rudimentary tools that help build the front-end clients. It won't be a picnic. However, some tool vendors seem to understand the requirements and perhaps in a few years we'll have the luxury of being able to create intergalactic client/server applications by pointing and clicking (or better yet, dragging and dropping).

The Secret Shame of Client/Server

Soapbox

There's another scam in progress. People are stampeding toward client/server because they're being told it's easy, and that's just not true. No matter what application development tools you choose, it's extremely difficult to design a high performance client/server application. It's worse than black art.

> — *Patricia Seybold, "The Secret Shame of Client/Server Development," ComputerWorld (August, 1993)*

The real secret is that there are two client/server paradigms: PC LAN client/server and intergalactic client/server. Some call it "Small Client/Server" and "Large Client/Server." Let's face it, client/server started as a PC LAN phenomenon and has done quite well there. It doesn't take a rocket scientist to deploy a NetWare server or write a Lotus Notes application. Tools like Gupta's Quest allow a novice to create a front end to a SQL database in a matter of hours. And how difficult is it to write a client application using VisPro/REXX, Digitalk Parts, or Visual Basic? In general, the PC world has been babystepping into client/server from the bottom up, and most of us have been quite happy with the pace of progress.

The current technology frontier for PC LAN development tools is grappling in the following two areas:

- ■ **Stored procedures.** How do you visually create stored procedures on the server and associate their parameters with the visual elements on the client side?

- ■ **Preloaded client/server.** How do you package, deploy, and manage turnkey client/server applications? And, how do you bundle the system components—including middleware and an SQL database—with the turnkey application?

If client/server is to succeed in the PC market, it must be sold through regular PC software marketing channels. So we need to find ways to easily create shrinkwrapped client/server applications that match the rest of the PC software packages in terms of price, ease of use, and installation. We think these problems are solvable. So there is really no "secret shame of client/server" in the PC LAN side of the house—things are on track and we're moving at a fast pace.

The secret shame may be in the intergalactic side of the house. Perhaps all the relentless client/server hype has led some to believe that they could junk all the mainframes that couldn't fit on a desktop and instantly recreate their 100,000 terminal-based airline reservation systems using Visual Basic. Of course, we can't do that right now.

But you can see from the extensive technology we covered in this book that a solid foundation for intergalactic client/server is coming together. The important standards are behind us. The DCE and MOM infrastructures are almost ready for prime time, SQL servers are in their second generation, open TP Monitors are now a reality, and open platforms for distributed system management are here today. A little bit further out on the horizon are CORBA-based distributed objects and all the services that surround them. And, we're finally getting ready for object frameworks that promise to revolutionize the way client/server applications are written and deployed. So there is not much to be ashamed of. The one exception, of course, are intergalactic client/server development tools—as we said earlier, don't expect to see any soon.

We believe that client/server for PC LANs is ready for business today. You would be at a disadvantage not to make immediate use of the technology PC LANs provide. The tools are not stellar, but they're adequate (we can always do better when it comes to tools). We also believe that you should start laying out some of that intergalactic client/server foundation we've talked about in this book. You can do that by introducing some pilot projects to keep you abreast of the technology as it evolves.

Pssst...Here's the Real Secret to Client/Server Success

But since we're on the topic of "secrets," we'll offer you an opinion that may sound like heresy. (Hopefully, it's too late for a refund now.) With our deep apologies to the open movement, we believe that the *real secret* to client/server success today is to apply the KISS (Keep It Simple Stupid) principle. Pick a single client/server platform, limit the number of vendors, limit mix-and-matching, keep the project simple, use a single server, and get the system up and running fast. Don't think in terms of posterity. Instead, think in terms of *disposable* client/server solutions.

If it takes six weeks to develop and deploy an application that runs on PCs, then it won't hurt you to dispose of it when something better comes along (the PCs can be salvaged). Of course, you should also stay on top of all that "strategic" intergalactic client/server stuff. However, only deploy it when it's as easy and simple as the "disposable" client/server technology. The rule is: If it's easy, then it's ready for prime time. The corollary is: If it's that easy, then it's disposable. So you're constantly introducing new technology by rapidly creating and deploying "disposable" client/server applications. ❑

CLIENT/SERVER APPLICATION DESIGN

Mainframe application designers and programmers have had it easy. In the past, user interfaces were simple constructs driven by simple terminals. The primary focus was on the database and transaction code, leaving the human to simply respond, like an extension of the application. But with client/server applications, the tables have turned. The ultimate goal of client/server solutions is to provide mission-critical applications that have the ease-of-use and responsiveness of stand-alone PCs. In this section, we present a methodology for designing OLTP-based client/server applications.

Client/Server is primarily a relationship between programs running on separate machines. As such, it requires an infrastructure to do things standalone PCs never had to worry about. For example, robust interprocess communications over LANs must be included in the design. Graphical interfaces using GUIs and OOUIs must be exploited to make applications look and feel more like real-world objects instead of programming processes. User interfaces are becoming complex, responsive, ad hoc environments that put the emphasis on the work of the human. OOUI clients bring humans into the distributed loop, which inevitably adds a host of complications. Humans make lots of errors, do unexpected things, and typically require lots of information from diverse sources. The more advanced OOUIs will introduce a new breed of *superclients* that turn the client workstation into multimedia "work-places" where many parallel dialogs are conducted with a variety of servers.

OOUIs also give the user much more freedom than GUIs or terminal-based systems. Users are free to organize their visual objects (and desktop) in any way they please. They are not tied to the rigid logic of task-oriented applications. OOUIs have no main panels and navigation screens. In fact, with the Workplace Shell, it is hard to tell where one application starts and another ends (or what an application object is versus a system object). There are just visual objects everywhere. This begs two important questions: Does client/server require a new approach to system development? Where design used to predominantly start at the database, which comes first now: the client or the server?

What Makes Client/Server Different?

Traditional (terminal-based) system design started with the data. The screens were developed primarily to drive the process of filling in the database, so they were designed after the transactions and tables were defined. Client/Server OLTP applications, on the other hand, require a far more complex design approach:

■ The interface is more flexible than terminals, and the user is allowed more latitude.

■ The object-based, front-end designs place a lot more intelligence on the client side of the application.

■ The messages between the client and the server are custom-built and application-specific.

■ The design must be optimized to take advantage of the parallelism inherent in the distributed application.

This leads us to a design approach unique to client/server applications: You must start your design with both the client and the server. So, you have two starting points in a client/server application: the GUI/OUUI and the data (unless the data for a business process is already in place). The GUI/OOUI and data designs come together at the transaction level. The transaction maps the screen to the database and vice versa. Does this sound complex? Let us assure you right now that it's not nearly as ominous as it sounds.

Rapid Prototyping Is Essential

One way to avoid a "chicken and egg" situation from developing—like the one in Figure 43-2—is to use a rapid prototyping methodology. Rapid prototyping allows you to develop your system incrementally. You start with the client and work your way iteratively towards the server. You always move in small steps, constantly refining the design as you go along. Make sure to involve your end user during all the stages of the interface design. In this form of delta development, the system is incrementally refined until you develop a working prototype that is mature enough to be placed into production. This approach may place a larger burden on the programmer than the traditional approaches, which rely on up-front analysis and design. And, with rapid-prototyping, you also run the risk that a cost-cutting management decision may place a non-optimized "working" prototype prematurely into production. At the other extreme, you may encounter another risk: the perpetual prototyping syndrome.

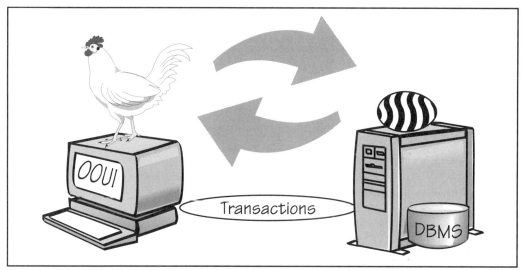

Figure 43-2. The Client/Server Chicken and Egg.

These risks are easily outweighed by the benefits that "rapid prototyping" provides in developing a OOUI client/server system. In client/server environments, it is difficult to determine before hand how the system is supposed to work (the OOUI design, the network performance, and multiuser loading). It has been our experience that user specs cannot anticipate all the needs of the users. Specs cannot adequately convey the potential OOUI technology offers. If you ask the users for guidance, the chances are that they'll give you the wrong answers based on existing solutions (manual or terminal-based solutions). Instead, you should show them what the technology can do for them and what new visual dimensions OOUIs offer; then work with them on developing the application.

Invariably, OOUIs can capture more of the business process than either GUIs or terminal-based front ends. A rapid prototype will help in the discovery of the application objects (or business objects). Users will find it easier to discuss visual business objects, and the visual prototype will help develop the design specifications.

Build a prototype; try it out. The trick is to be able to build the application many times. It is easier to talk about something that can be demonstrated live and used. Moreover, it is important that the prototype be developed in an environment where the issues of client/server performance, network overheads, system management, and transaction server design can be tested live. Client/Server systems require a lot of monitoring, fine-tuning, and administration. It is better for you to get acquainted with these issues early in the game.

From Prototype to Working System

The OOUI objects permeate the entire application and determine its shape. An application can be seen as a collection of visual business objects. The design of the application starts from the objects (and views) the user sees on the screen, and then works its way towards the server and the database structure. Prototypes are used to identify, with your customer's participation, the user model: What business objects are needed, and what do they do? Prototyping is an iterative activity with many false starts. Here is how the typical prototype evolves:

1. ***Understand the business process***. It is a prerequisite that you understand what the application is all about at the business level. So gather the requirements and study the tasks: What does the customer really want?

2. ***Define your business objects***. What the user sees in an OLTP application are objects containing views that react to user input and actions. The objects are manipulated according to the requirements of the business process. You should create user objects that correspond to real-life entities; for example, a seat on an airplane. What are the main object types in the application? What other objects do they contain? What are the attributes of the objects? What functions do they have? How do they behave? What are the relationships between objects? What are the "composed of" relationships (is-part-of)? What are the dependency and collaboration relationships (is-analogous-to, is-kind-of, depends-upon)?

3. ***Work on the detailed object views***. What context menu actions apply to each object? What views are required? Are business forms views required? Can the views be grouped in Notebook pages? What widgets controls—including input/output fields, list boxes, pushbuttons, menus, sliders, value-sets, and so on—will appear in the views? What level of help is needed? What data validation at the field level is required? What level of triggers are required (on error, on message, etc.)? How are external procedures and RPCs invoked?

4. ***Develop dry run scenarios***. You can create your screen objects and animate the application (OOUI tools should provide this capability). Use the scenarios to validate the object model of the user interface. The scenarios should also help you identify the major event-driven interactions.

5. ***Walk through a system scenario***. Such a scenario should follow a transaction from its source through its execution. Identify the protocols that link the different elements. Blow up this scenario in areas that require more detail. Run an application scenario for each business object. Identify redundant behaviors. Which objects can be reused?

6. ***Identify transaction sources***. A client/server system can be thought of as a client-driven event system. The server is, in a sense, passively waiting on

requests from clients. The client, in turn, is driven by the user who is at the "controls" within the confines of the business process. The drag and drop of visual objects is typically the source of transactions. Information required upon opening a container or view may also be the source of a transaction. Object/action intersections almost always lead to the generation of a transaction. There is also a high probability that events such as data entry, menu selections, pushing a button, and action dialogs will generate transactions. The visual client interface will eventually be "brought to life" by writing the transactions that are triggered by the user interaction. OO purists can think of transactions as methods that manipulate persistent data.[1]

7. ***Define your database tables***. You are now in a position to take a first stab at defining the database objects that correspond to the visual business objects you just created. Iterate on this step until you get it right. Many trade-offs are involved. The object/action orientation of the client design can help transform the visual objects into an entity-relationship model for database objects. The actions translate into transactions on database entities. A database entity, in turn, consists of a structure of relationships and constraints between database tables. Publish the resulting CREATE TABLE statements, and then use them to document the data types and the relationships between tables (such as referential integrity constraints).

8. ***Publish the client/server messages***. Messages are the methods by which the clients execute transactions on servers. Define the major transactions and the request/reply messages associated with them, including any required file transfers. The messages provide the only coupling between the clients and the server. The publication of the messages advertises to the world what a server does. It is a *binding contract* between the server and its clients. A message typically has a command field and a data field, which contains the command parameters. In our scheme of things, we divide transactions (or commands) into two broad categories based on the type of responses they produce:

    ◆ ***Request/reply transactions*** are transactions that generate short replies. These transactions are usually updates, inserts, deletes, or single-row queries against database objects.

    ◆ ***Bulk response transactions*** are transactions that generate one or more result files. Think of a result file as a BLOB, which may result from a multirow SELECT or from the request for a metafile or bitmap.

---

[1] In strict OO terms, a raw transaction server is a single object that encapsulates the entire database (as its private instance data). A back-end application could be written as a set of objects that export methods (the transactions). You will eventually hit a design point where SQL's shared data tables and OO's encapsulation discipline don't mix very well.

Another way to create a binding client/server contract is by using an *Interface Definition Language (IDL)*. The IDL defines the functions exported by the server. It provides a higher-level of abstraction than messages. For example, you could use the DCE RPC IDL or better yet CORBA, whose *Interface Repository* offers a way to discover services dynamically.

9. ***Develop your code one object at a time***. Write the SQL code for each transaction. Do that one object at a time. There are typically many transactions per business object. Validate the user interface and the performance of the system with your customer.

10. ***From prototype to working system***. A working system is the sum of all the business objects it contains. You are developing your system incrementally, so you will have a full working system when you've coded your last business object.

We're not done yet. After a suitable prototype is developed, you can involve the user with writing the reports and the decision support forms, and then try them out against the prototype. This may lead to some changes in the design of the system. In the final production system, it may be wise to provide a separate server for decision support. The decision support server can then be fed replicated snapshots of the production data at predetermined intervals (remember all that Information Warehouse stuff we covered in Part 4).

Walking On Two Feet

Client/Server technology offers developers the potential to create revolutionary new visual applications. Creating these kind of applications requires the seamless integration of OOUI technology, operating systems, network architectures, and DBMSs. To succeed, we will need new approaches to systems development that emphasize rapid prototyping and the end-user involvement. Doing that will allow us to exploit the synergy between database objects and OOUI objects. We will also be in a better position to understand early in a project the opportunities (for example, parallelism) and pitfalls (for example, performance and error recovery) introduced by splitting an application across a network.

This prototype-based approach to design eliminates the need for lengthy specifications. More importantly, this approach allows the customer to participate in the specification of the product and its stepwise refinement. The approach also lends itself well to the design of distributed applications, because you can refine and fine-tune the distribution of function as you learn more about your system's real-life behavior.

So, the successful OLTP design starts in parallel with both the client and the server. The two starting points are the OOUI objects and the data objects. The "glue" that ties them together are the transactions using network RPCs or ORBs. Start with the client and move towards the server, or vice versa. In either case, move in small steps and iterate. The visual prototype brings the design to life early. So, which comes first: the client or the server? They both come first!

CLIENT/SERVER APPLICATION DEVELOPMENT TOOLS

Development tools are the hot issue in client/server today. We predict that the U.S. market will grow from 35,000 development seats shipped in 1992 to almost 700,000 seats shipped in 1996.

— *Forrester Research "Client/Server Power Tools Future," (April, 1993)*

Development tools are the linchpin in client/server. Tools encapsulate the client/server technology described in this book and make it easier for users to write applications. The best tools are highly visual. Most of today's client/server tools are used to create departmental decision support systems. Over the next four years, Forrester believes that "improvements in client/server infrastructure, vendor viability, and the tools themselves will set the stage for the power tools to blast out of departmental bunkers." So how do we classify those client/server tools? Which is the right tool for the right job? Like everything else in client/server, it seems everyone has an opinion on tools. In this section, we present two tool classification schemes: Forrester's and ours.

The Forrester Model of Client/Server Tools

Forrester Research breaks down client/server tools into five categories:

- *Purebred client/server.* These are GUI-centric client/server tools that were designed from the ground up for client/server development. Examples include SQL Windows, Enfin, PowerBuilder, HockWare, Visual Age, and Digitalk Parts.

- *Born-again 4GLs.* These tools grew out of the high-end minicomputer market. Examples include Cognos, Progress, FOCUS, Uniface, and Oracle's SQL*Forms.

- *Desktop wannabes.* These tools started out as standalone database development tools, but their new GUI releases reposition them as power tools. Examples include Paradox and dBASE from Borland, and FoxPro and Access from Microsoft.

- **CASE retreads**. These tools grew out of the mainframe market. They provide data modeling, code generation, lifecycle tracking of projects, and multiuser repositories. The leading tools are KnowledgeWare's Application Development Workbench, TI's Information Engineering Facility (IEF), and Andersen Consulting's Foundation for Cooperative Processing.

- **Facelifters**. These tools let you strap a GUI on a terminal-based legacy application. The code for the legacy server remains unchanged. The leading tools in this category are Easel and Mozart.

We found the Forrester classification to be quite useful but somewhat limiting. Instead, we propose the alternative classification that is covered in the next section.

The Latest and Greatest Model of Client/Server Tools

Tool evaluation is fun. There are literally hundreds of products. How do you make a decision? One possibility is to stay in tool evaluation mode until you're told that the decision is due tomorrow, then just pick one!

> — *Anonymous MIS Developer,*
> *HPTP Proceedings (September, 1993)*

Yes, client/server tool evaluation can be a lot of fun. You're probably being bombarded with tons of glossy advertisements for tools that all promise to deliver instant and hassle free client/server solutions. At trade shows, you've probably watched those slick demonstrations that seem to create entire client/server applications with a few mouse clicks. But with over 200 tools on the market, which do you pick for evaluation? These days, we could probably safely assume that you don't have an infinite budget for tools or the time to evaluate all 200 of them. So you could start pruning tools by platform, but most seem to run on OS/2. Or you could prune them by price, but you could end up getting what you paid for. Or you could prune them by brandname and miss out on the most avant-garde tools with the latest and greatest features.

To help you with your evaluation, we propose a simple model that breaks the tool market around four axes (see Figure 43-3):

- **Roots.** What's the tool's ancestry? At one end of the axis are tools that originated on mainframes; they tend to have a CASE-centric focus. At the other end of the axis are tools that originated on PC LANs; they tend to have a GUI-centric focus. Somewhere in between are the supermini 4GL tools. The approach (or paradigm) a tool uses for application development is intimately tied to its roots.

■ **Distributed Technology.** What's the client/server technology? What applications does the tool create? The axis moves from fat clients with thin servers that specialize in decision support to thin clients with fat servers that do OLTP. In the middle are Groupware and Distributed Objects that split the logic more evenly.

■ **Scope.** How much of the client/server function does the tool provide? The axis ranges from tools that specialize in the client, the server, or the middleware to tools that provide all three. Some tools may even go as far as bundling a run time that includes system management, resource managers, and single point of installation.

■ **Scalability.** How well does the tool scale for enterprise solutions? The axis moves from single-server tools to multiserver intergalactic tools. The middleware that the tool targets becomes an important factor in the more intergalactic tools.

You'll need all four axes to understand where a tool fits in the scheme of things and what it can do for you. We will briefly go over these four axes and tell you what to consider. Because your authors are in the tool business, we will refrain from naming tools and making any endorsements. We don't want this section ending as one big Soapbox for our product.

Roots: What's the Tool's Ancestry?

Tools have been around ever since we started writing applications for computers. Over the years, some great tools have emerged around the leading methodologies of the time. When it comes to tools there are "different strokes for different folks." From the dawn of history, people like to work with the tools they are familiar with and that help them get the job done quickly. When it comes to client/server tools, you have choices that span many architectural eras—including COBOL Workbenches, CASE tools, 4GLs, SmallTalk, and object-oriented client/server purebreds. The purebred client/server tools that originated on PC LANs tend to provide event-driven visual programming environments, and they encourage rapid prototyping on PCs. The CASE, 4GL, and Workbenches reflect their mainframe ancestry's emphasis on group development, up-front design and analysis, and structured methodologies (see Figure 43-4).

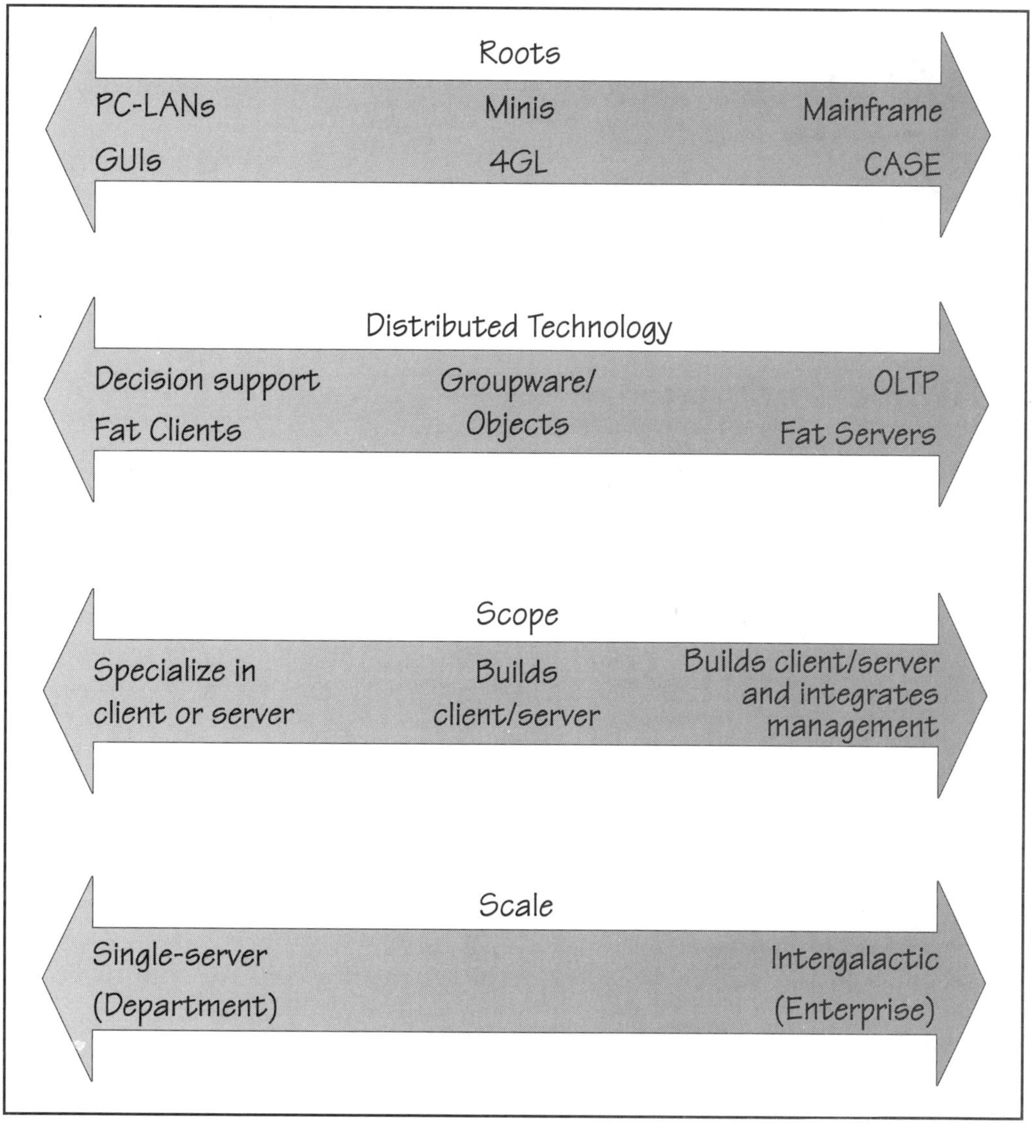

Roots

| PC-LANs | Minis | Mainframe |
| GUIs | 4GL | CASE |

Distributed Technology

| Decision support | Groupware/ | OLTP |
| Fat Clients | Objects | Fat Servers |

Scope

Specialize in	Builds	Builds client/server
client or server	client/server	and integrates
		management

Scale

| Single-server | | Intergalactic |
| (Department) | | (Enterprise) |

Figure 43-3. The four Axes of Client Server Tools.

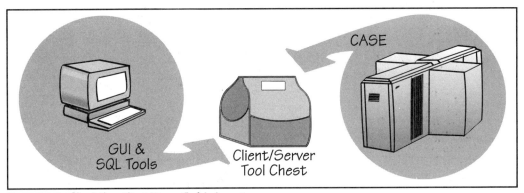

Figure 43-4. Check Your Client/Server Tools's Ancestry.

So what's a 4GL? It stands for a *Fourth Generation Language.* A 4GL is typically a vendor proprietary scripting language that's less procedural than a 3GL (like C or C++). It is also frequently tied to a database. Some 4GLs are associated with a forms generation package. Almost all 4GLs are interpreted; the best are compiled to some intermediate level. In the PC world, Basic, REXX, and the Lotus Script language play an equivalent role to 4GLs. The 4GLs offer increased programmer productivity at the expense of application performance; the intermediate code must be re-interpreted for each function (the performance is about five times slower than a 3GL).

The ancestry of a tool tends to determine how it uses the 4GL. Tools with a mainframe ancestry use the 4GL as the main program. The 4GL calls the visual forms and controls the interaction with the user; it maintains control at all times. In contrast, tools with a PC ancestry call 4GL code snippets when GUI events occur; the GUI is in control at all times.

We recommend the use of 4GLs for rapid prototyping and to write the event handlers for the client side of an application. But remember: They're slow; you'll need a 486 type machine on the client side. At some point, parts of the 4GL code should be converted to a 3GL on the server to improve performance.

Another point to consider is that tools with a mainframe ancestry encourage you to do a lot of design up-front. They provide Entity-Relationship diagrams and all types of methodologies for doing analysis and for documenting the design. These tools are also heavy into version control and team development; they tend to make use of repositories for tracking shared objects. The better tools can directly generate 4GL code from the top-down design. In contrast, tools with a PC ancestry encourage you to build the application visually using GUI painters. The design tends to be client-centric. The code is broken down into small event handlers that are associated with GUI events; the application is the GUI. The code is just an appendage of the GUI objects. Rapid prototyping is essential.

Distributed Technology: Is it SQL, OLTP, Groupware, or Objects?

Tools can be classified according to the underlying client/server technology and the applications they create. Until recently, almost all the PC-based client/server tools were used to create decision-support applications and Executive Information Systems (the Danny De Vito tools). Some of the newer tools provide facilities for creating OLTP-Lite applications via stored procedures; a very small number of tools can even be used to create OLTP-Heavy applications using TP Monitors (the number is less than six). Groupware tools mostly center around Lotus Notes. But some non-Groupware tools provide mail-enabling facilities. Finally, a few vendor proprietary tools are available for creating applications that work with ODBMSs (the number is less than three). ORB-based tools are currently non-existent (there's a lot of chartware in this area).

So what's a Decision Support tool? Decision Support Systems (DSSs) are built using dynamic SQL on database servers. The client side of the application is typically built using a screen-layout visual editor; non-programmers can build GUI front ends and reports by painting, pointing, and clicking. These tools are database-aware; they let you combine graphical objects like radio buttons, check boxes, menus, and scrollbars to create sophisticated display panels that integrate directly with the database. Most of these GUI tools have built-in capabilities to automatically generate forms that can be used to add, update, and delete database records. They provide the ability to create multitable queries (joins) and display the results in one record-per-form format or multiple-record columnar forms with pick lists. The tools make use of the database catalogs to map table columns to fields on a screen. SQL statements can be built "on-the-fly" and associated with a particular push button or menu item. Point-and-click query builders take the work out of formulating the question. The tools provide visual facilities for creating base tables and defining relations between tables. All this is done with "canned" event handlers provided by the tool vendor.

Most decision-support tools allow you to create links with other applications on the desktop using the clipboard, DDE, OLE, or drag-and-drop. Cut-and-paste through the clipboard is used to transfer information into other applications under user control. DDE is used to automatically update documents and spreadsheets with the results of a query. It lets you automate scripts such as "Place the output of this query into this spreadsheet; then run it through a graphics package, print the report, and send the results to a distribution list through electronic mail."

So what's an OLTP tool? As stored procedures became popular, some tools branched out into the server generation side; they allow you to create stored procedures and associate them with client events (via RPC pickers). The tricky part is generating efficient code on the server—most tools are lacking in this area. Another tricky area is how to associate the RPC parameters with the visual fields—most tools are also lacking in this area. Most tools are poor at managing the stored procedures on the server side; they leave that to the database engine or TP Monitor. In summary, OLTP tools (Lite or Heavy) are still in their infancy.

So what's a groupware tool? We covered groupware tools in the Lotus Notes chapter in Part 6. We expect that most ordinary GUI tools will soon provide canned forms for creating mail messages and reading mail as well as mail APIs. Mail-enabling will become a checklist item for most tools.

So what's a distributed object tool? We covered object frameworks in Part 7. The object tools should allow you to wire together those frameworks using visual elements. Object chartware promises ten times (or more) improvements in productivity; it all remains to be seen. We still don't know how to create the server side of a distributed object application. The CORBA-IDL and Interface Repository will play a major role in tying the client and server sides of the equation; they will do for objects what the database catalog does for decision support tools.

Scope: Does it Do Clients, Servers, or Both?

Tools can be broken down by how much of the client/server function they provide. They range from tools that specialize in the client, the server, or the middleware to tools that provide all three (see Figure 43-5). Some tools may even go as far as bundling a run time that includes system management, resource managers, and a single point of installation. This may sound like heresy, but the more bundling the tool provides the less integration you have to do. Integration is a major headache in client/server systems.

The question is: Do you want to spend your time developing applications or integrating the base client/server and middleware components? Many tools, especially on the low-end, will have to provide a totally bundled package that takes care of installation, system management, and configures the required middleware and resource managers. The more creative tools may even provide a run time component that integrates a TP Monitor like facility. The TP Monitor should provide cross-overs in case of failures, ACID protection, dynamic load balancing, and help with system management. This is called *preloaded client/server.* We do not know of any tool with these capabilities (Bachman/CSI's Ellipse came closest). With the current state of the technology, we're lucky just to find a tool that can generate both the client and server sides of an application and take care of some middleware; most tools only do the client side of the application.

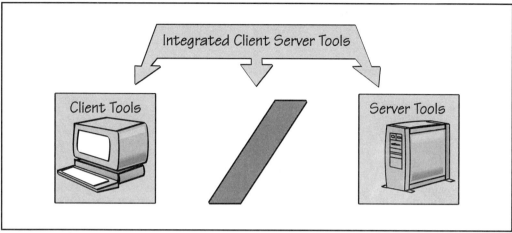

Figure 43-5. How Much Client/Server Coverage Does the Tool Provide?

Scalability: Can it Create Enterprise-Wide Applications?

Enterprise client/server tools are the current vogue (but only in literature). We haven't seen too many of them lately. The industry seems to have an idea of what functions such tools should provide. Briefly, enterprise tools must do the following:

■ **Provide flexible application topologies**. The tool should provide lego-like facilities that let you split the application (at many different points) between the client, the server and, more importantly, across servers.

■ **Provide portable applications**. The tool should spit out code for OS/2, Windows, Macintosh, and Unix front ends and all the known server platforms. You should be able, at run time, to transparently deploy the right version of code to the appropriate machine.

■ **Version control**. The tool should track the versions of code running on the clients and servers and make sure they're consistent.

■ **Load balancing and cross-over facilities**. The tool should keep track of client/server performance and dynamically reroute traffic across applications as required by workloads and failure conditions.

■ **Create compiled code on the server**. The tool should be able to automatically compile the 4GL code on the server to obtain maximum performance.

■ ***Work with a variety of resource managers***. The tool should adapt itself to the resource managers that exist on the network; its interaction with resource managers should be negotiable at run time.

■ ***Work with a variety of middleware***. The tool should adapt its client/server communications to the existing middleware. For example, it should know when an ORB is present and how to exploit it. It should also figure out when MOM is better than RPC. At a minimum, the tool should adjust time-outs based on whether the traffic is moving over a LAN or WAN.

■ ***Team development and a group repository***. The tool should allow groups of programmers to work on a common project; it should provide check-in/check-out facilities for tracking forms, widgets, controls, fields, business objects, DLLs, and so on.

We could keep that list going. But what are the odds of getting all these facilities in our current lifetimes? We know that the demand for such tools exists in the high-end of the market. Much of the technology for creating such tools exists. But it's still a very big project. However, we know of at least three well-funded tool efforts that are headed in that direction. We believe that the best way to get this type of intergalactic distribution is through ORBs and distributed object technology.

Which Tool Should You Use?

We can't answer this question. However you can; now that you have two models to guide you. Start with the type of application you want to build. Is it decision support? Is it OLTP? What do you really want? Next, decide on which methodology you feel more comfortable with: Is it top-down design or visual prototyping? Finally, decide on the scope of your application and its scalability requirements. Is it intergalactic? Or is it single server? These simple questions will help you narrow down your decision on tools to at most two or three (unless you picked decision support). Now you can play the evaluation game until the decision is due, then "just pick one." Can you create client/server applications without tools using raw 3GLs? Yes, but the size of our book, **Client/Server Programming with OS/2 2.1** (1100 pages), should give you an idea of the magnitude of effort required (Sorry, but we couldn't resist another shameless advertisement.)

IT'S TIME TO SAY GOOD-BYE

Yes, the journey was a long, tumultuous one. We hope you enjoyed the guided tour as much as we enjoyed playing guides. To our friends from Mars, we hope you have a safe trip home—it was a pleasure having you here. We hope you'll find that client/server gold somewhere. Don't forget to tell your friends in Mars about our guided tour. We also have a shorter version for those who can't afford the long tour. It's called the **Essential Client/Server Survival Guide**. If you read this guide, you won't need it but your friends may.

We're scratching our heads trying to come up with some words of wisdom to leave you with at the end of this long tour. But we don't have much to add that wasn't already said. We just want to say that this was our attempt to make some sense out of this traumatic shift our industry is going through. It's a very painful shift for many of us; for others, it's the start of a new dawn in computing with the sky being the limit. OK, enough of that fluffy stuff. We'll say good-bye with a *parting* Soapbox on where things are going.

Can We Survive the Client/Server Revolution?

Soapbox

Yes, but to do that we need 100,000 new applications. How did we come up with that number? Client/server technology makes it possible to redeploy most of our computer applications on commodity hardware where the profit margins are razor thin. If we keep recomputerizing the same application base, using PC LANs instead of mainframes, most of us will end up without jobs. This is because we're going after a downsized pie where the profits are dramatically lower. If our profits are lower we cut down on the research that helps us create those new technologies. Our customers won't get new applications or technology and everybody loses. It's called the "cannibalizing effect."

Instead, we need to take advantage of client/server technology to extend the boundaries of computerization. In other words, we need to move on to new frontiers like the information highway. But can we create thousands of new client/server applications *quickly* to populate these new frontiers? To do that effectively, we need a technology base, standards, and tools. The 900 pages in this book make the case that the technology base, standards, and even some products are here today. However, still missing are a set of adequate tools that can help us mine the new frontier. It's not enough to create the application; it must also be effectively packaged, deployed, and managed.

So who's going to package, deploy, and manage these applications? We can't expect everyone to read this entire book just to become client/server literate (don't get us wrong—we would love the sales). Instead, we need to simplify the packaging and distribution of our client/server products. Of all the technologies discussed in this book, distributed objects (with frameworks) offer the best hope for creating—in record time—new client/server applications that can go where no other applications have gone before. So we're excited about the long-term prospects. However, in the short term we're in for some rough times. You may have noticed that no tool yet exists for creating CORBA-compliant client/server applications. We're just starting to see some ORBs.

So we'll be in the doldrums until we can figure out how to unleash the true power of this technology. This is sad—but true. The good news is that after we get over that rough hump, those of us that are still around will be headed straight for a new gold rush. As the Chinese proverb puts it, "We're condemned to live in interesting times." ❑

Trademarks

3Com Corp—3Com

Allen Systems Group, Inc.—IMPACT

Allerion, Inc.—Allerion

American Telephone and Telegraph—AT&T

Anderson Consulting—Foundation for Cooperative Processing

Apple Computer, Inc.—Apple; AppleTalk; Macintosh; System 7

Banyan Systems, Inc.—Banyan; Banyan Vines; Vines SMP; VinesMail

BRG Systems, Inc.—Analyze for OS/2; BEST/1-Visualizer for OS/2; Performance Assurance

Borland International, Inc.—Application FrameWorks; dBase; FoxPro; Paradox

Channel Computing—Forest & Trees

Client/Server Technologies (Microcom)—LANlord

Club Med Sales, Inc.—Club Med

Compaq Computer Corp.—Compaq SystemPro

Computer Associates, Inc.—CA-UNICENTER

Cooperative Solutions—Ellipse

DataTrade, Inc.—DataTrade

Digital Equipment Corp.—Data Distributor; DECnet; Digital; OpenVMS; VMS; VAX; VAXMail

Easel Corp.—Easel; Enfin

Gpf, Inc.—GPF

Gradient Technologies, Inc.—Gradient Technologies; iFOR/LS

Gupta Technologies, Inc.—Express Windows; Gupta; Quest; SQLBase; SQLWindows

Hewlett-Packard Corp.—DOMF; Hewlett-Packard; HP; HP-UX; OpenView

High Technology Software, Corp.—HiTechSoft

HockWare, Inc.—VisPro/REXX

HyperDesk—DOMS

Informix, Inc.—Informix; INFORMIX

Ingres Corp.—INGRES

Intel Corp.—Intel; Pentium

International Standards Organization—Remote Data Access

IBM Corp.—Advanced Peer to Peer Communications; Advanced Peer-to-Peer Network; AIX; AnyNet/2; APPC; APPN; CICS; CM/2; Communications Manager; CPI-C; CUA; DAE; Database Manager; DataGuide/2; DataPropagator Relational; DataRefresher; DB2; DB2/2; DB2/6000; DDCS/2; DDCS/6000; DRDA; DSOM; High Performance File System; IBM; IMS; Information Warehouse; LAD/2; LANDP/2; LAN Gateway/2; LAN NetView; LAN NetView Agents; LAN NetView Agents Extended; LAN NetView Agents for DOS; LAN NetView Fix; LAN NetView Manage; LAN NetView Management Utilities; LAN NetView Monitor; LAN NetView Scan; LAN NetView Tie; LAN Network Manager; LAN Requester; LAN Server; LU 6.2; MPTN; Netview; NetView DM/2; NetView/6000; NetView/PC; NetFinity; NTS/2; OS/2; OS/2 Named Pipes; OS/400; PAS/2; Person-to-Person/2; PowerPC; Presentation Manager; PROFS; PS/2; Query Manager; REXX; RS/6000; SAA; SQL/400; SQL/DS; SNA; SOM; System 370; SystemView; VM; VisualAge; VSAM; VTAM; Win-OS/2; WinSNA; Workplace Shell; Workplace OS

Information Builders, Inc.—EDA/Data Drivers; EDA/Extenders; EDA/Link; EDA/SQL; EDA/SQL Server; Focus

International Institute of Electrical Engineers (IEEE)—POSIX

KASEWORKS, Inc.—KASE:VIP; KASEWORKS

Knowledgeware, Inc.—Application Development Workbench

Legat Systems, Inc.—Legato Systems; NetWorker

Lotus Development Corp.—cc:Mail; DataLens; dBASE; Lotus; Lotus Document Imaging; Lotus Link; Lotus Notes

Luxcom, Inc.—Universal Premises Network

Massachusetts Institute of Technology—Kerberos; X Window

mdbs, Inc.—mbds; Object/1

Micrcom, Inc.—LANLord; Micrcom

Microsoft Corp.—Access; Compound Object Model (COM); MS DOS; LAN Manager; LAN Manager/X; Mail; Mail Gateways; Microsoft; Object Linking and Embedding; ODBC; OLE; SQL Administrator; Windows; Windows for Workgroups; Windows NT; Windows NT Advanced; XENIX

Micro Focus Inc.—Micro Focus COBOL

Mips, Inc.—Mips

Mozart Systems Corp.—Mozart

Network General Corp.—Sniffer

Neuron Data, Inc.—Open Interface

NeXT, Inc.—NeXTStep

Novell, Inc.—IPX; NetWare; NetWare Loadable Module; NetWare Management System; NetWare for UNIX; Novell; SFT III; SPX; Systems Fault Tolerance III; UnixWare

Object Design, Inc.—Object Design; ObjectStore

Objective Solutions, Inc.—ObjectPM

Object Management Group—CORBA; Object Management Architecture

Open Software Foundation, Inc.—DCE; Motif; OSF; OSF/1

Opening Technologies, Inc.—Opening Technologies; OPENT1

Oracle, Inc.—ORACLE; SQL*NET; Oracle Card; Oracle Forms; Oracle Glue; Oracle Open Gateway; Oracle V6; Oracle*Designer; Oracle7; OracleWare; PL/SQL; SQL*NET

PeerLogic, Inc.—PIPES

Pragma Systems, Inc.—Tower

Progress Corp.—Progress

ProTools, Inc.—Cornerstone Agent; Foundation Manager; ProTools

Santa Cruz Operations, Inc.—SCO UNIX

Pragma Systems, Inc.—Tower

Shany Computers, Ltd.—AlertView

SQL Access Group—OpenSQL

Stratus, Inc.—Stratus

Sun Microsystems Inc.—DOE; RPC; SUN; SPARC

Sunsoft, Inc.—Distributed Object Mangement; Network File System; Network Information System; NFS; OpenLook; Open Network Computing; Solaris; SunNet Manager

Sybase, Inc.—Sybase; Sybase SQL Server; Transact-SQL

Taligent, Inc.—Taligent

Tandem Computers—NonStop SQL; NonStop Guardian; Pathway

Texas Instruments, Inc.—Information Engineering Facility

Tivoli Systems Inc.—Tivoli Management Environment; WizDOM

Transaction Processing Council—TPC-A

Transarc Corp—Andrew File System; Encina

University of California at Berkeley—Berkeley Software Distribution; BSD

UNIX International, Inc.—UI; UI-Atlas

UNIX Systems Laboratories, Inc.—Destiny; OpenLook; Tuxedo; UNIX; UNIX System V

VZCorp, Inc.—VZ Programmer

WATCOM, Inc.—VX REXX

XDB Systems, Inc.—XDB

Xerox Corp.—ethernet; XNS; Xerox Network Systems

XVT Software, Inc.—XVT

X/Open Corp.—X/Open

Index

Numerics

3Com 359, 857
4GL 912, 914, 916

A

A/UX 187
Abstract class 717
Abstract Syntax Notation One
    (ASN.1) 485, 845, 854, 861
Access 912
Access Control Lists (ACLs) 230–231,
    386, 391, 673
Access node 308
Access rights 229
Accumaster Integrator 832–833
ACDI
    See Asynchronous Communications
        Device Interface (ACDI)
ACID 558, 568, 576, 581, 591, 596, 602,
    720, 742, 763
    Defined 556
ACLs
    See Access Control Lists (ACLs)
Action Technologies 640, 644, 654, 662
ActionMedia II 139, 152
ActionWorkflow 640, 662
Ada 468
AdaptFile 5000 662
Adaptive Information Systems 662
Address Resolution Protocol (ARP) 315
ADSM/2
    See Adstar Distributed Storage Man-
        ager/2 (ADSM/2)
Adstar Distributed Storage Manager/2
    (ADSM/2) 873, 892–893
    Agents 893
    Defined 892–893
    Disaster recovery 893

Advanced Peer-to-Peer Internetworking
    (APPI) 271
Advanced Peer-to-Peer Network
    (APPN) 55, 271, 334, 528, 538
    Managed Agent 884
    Network Node 334
Advanced Power Management (APM) 99
AF_INET 254
AFS
    See Andrew File System (AFS)
Agent 38–39, 41–42, 413
    Communications Manager/2 883–
        884
    DB2/2 883
    Defined 834–835
    DOS 883
    LAN Requester 875, 883
    LAN Server 883–884
    NetWare 886
    OS/2 875, 882–884
    Proxy 891
    SQL 429
    Windows 883
AIX 187–189, 191, 196, 212, 402, 410,
    414, 482, 589, 680, 814, 892
Alerts 346–347, 357, 359, 363, 517
AlertVIEW 872
    Defined 895
Aliases 384
Allen Systems Group 896
Allerion Inc. 896
Almaden Research 530, 572, 619
ALMCOPY 338
Andersen Consulting 48, 913
Andreas, Bill 702
Andrew File System (AFS) 387
Anonymous Pipes 133
ANSI 428, 765
AnyNet/2 54, 273, 488
    Gateway 305
API

Index